PRIMARY TEACHING

EDITED BY

CATHERINE CARDEN

LEARNING & TEACHING IN PRIMARY SCHOOLS TODAY

Learning Matters
An imprint of SAGE Publications Ltd
1 Oliver's Yard
55 City Road
London EC1Y 1SP

SAGE Publications Inc.
2455 Teller Road
Thousand Oaks, California 91320

SAGE Publications India Pvt Ltd
B 1/I 1 Mohan Cooperative Industrial Area
Mathura Road
New Delhi 110 044

SAGE Publications Asia-Pacific Pte Ltd
3 Church Street
#10-04 Samsung Hub
Singapore 049483

Editor: Amy Thornton
Senior project editor: Chris Marke
Development editor: Tracey Cowell
Copy editor: Clare Weaver
Proofreader: Diana Chambers
Indexer: Anne Solamito
Marketing manager: Lorna Patkai
Cover design: Wendy Scott
Typeset by: C&M Digitals (P) Ltd, Chennai, India
Printed in the UK

Library of Congress number: 2018950474

British Library Cataloguing in Publication Data

A catalogue record for this book is available from the British Library

ISBN 978-1-5264-3643-6
ISBN 978-1-5264-3644-3 (pbk)

At SAGE we take sustainability seriously. Most of our products are printed in the UK using responsibly sourced papers and boards. When we print overseas we ensure sustainable papers are used as measured by the PREPS grading system. We undertake an annual audit to monitor our sustainability.

CONTENTS

Appendices 611

ABOUT THE EDITOR AND CONTRIBUTORS

THE EDITOR

Catherine Carden is Faculty Director of Primary Initial Teacher Education at Canterbury Christ Church University. She oversees the university-based undergraduate and postgraduate primary initial teacher education programmes within the Faculty of Education. Catherine has an interest in leadership theory and practice, particularly focusing on transformative and emotionally intelligent leadership.

EDITORIAL REVIEWER

Peter Flew is Director of the School of Education at the University of Roehampton, one of the largest providers of Initial Teacher Education in England. He is a former Catholic primary school head teacher. Peter's interests include the role of Church schools in education and the effective use of data inside and outside the classroom.

THE CONTRIBUTORS

Sarah Adams is a specialist in primary education, teacher training at the School of Education, University of Leicester.

Genea Alexander is a Senior Lecturer in Primary Education at the University of Worcester. Her research interests include learning and teaching, and arts and languages education.

Kate Allott is Senior Lecturer at the School of Education, York St John University. Kate teaches primary English, history and professional studies and has responsibility for Early Years in the department. Her research focuses on early years and children's literature.

Rebecca Austin is the Primary English Team Leader at Canterbury Christ Church University. She joined the university in 2001 following over a decade working in Kent primary schools. Rebecca also provides staff development for schools.

Lucy Barker is Senior Lecturer and NQT lead at Northumbria University. Her research interests are SEND and inclusive practice; trainee teachers and teaching assistants; continuous professional development (CPD).

Dr Virginia Bower is Programme Director PGCE Primary (Flexible) Canterbury Christ Church University. Her research interests are English as an additional language and teaching primary poetry.

Mark Boylan, B.Sc., Ph.D., SFHEA, is a Professor of Education at Sheffield Hallam University. His areas of expertise are mathematics education, teacher professional learning and evaluation of policy innovations. The latter includes the evaluation of the Mathematics Teacher Exchange: China–England, also known as the primary mathematics Shanghai exchange programme, which is part of the government's mastery programme.

Mary Briggs is Principal Lecturer and Programme Lead for Primary and Early Years ITE at Oxford Brookes University. Her research interests are: assessment, mathematics, mentoring and coaching.

Cara Broadhurst is Assistant Director of the BA Primary Education (QTS) at the University of Reading. She leads the placements and partnership provision for the programme and her research interests include mentoring and, as an English lecturer, the uses of home-school literacies.

Kelly Carabott is a Lecturer in the Faculty of Education, Monash University, Australia. Previous to this life, she was a primary classroom teacher for 19 years. Her research interests include reading multimodal texts in the digital age, children's literature, educational digital technology integration and digital competence. Kelly also writes a blog in her spare time called Litology and more available at: https://ictintheclassroom.edublogs.org/

Linda Cooper has worked in education as a teacher and teacher educator for the past 20 years. She currently works in the primary education team at the University of Chichester. Her research interests include humanities and technology.

Alan Cross is a Senior Fellow in Education at the Manchester Institute of Education, University of Manchester. His research interests lie in links between science and mathematics education in the primary years.

Dr Jonathan Doherty is Senior Lecturer and Primary Research Lead at the Institute of Childhood and Education, Leeds Trinity University. Jonathan teaches on PGCE and Master's programmes, and his research interests are in learning schools, pedagogy and teacher development. He is Chair of the National Primary Teacher Education Council (NaPTEC).

Jill Dunn is a Senior Lecturer at Stranmillis University College, Belfast. Her research interests include tablet devices and young children's literacy development and participatory research with children.

Lorna Earle is a Senior Lecturer in education specialising in primary mathematics at the University of Chichester. Her research interests include developing conceptual understanding for formal methods of mathematics.

Jonathan Glazzard is Professor of Teacher Education, Leeds Beckett University. His research interests include inclusion, dyslexia, mental health and early reading development.

Sway Grantham is a part-time computing teacher at Giffard Park Primary School and a digital technology consultant. She created a blog as an NQT, has organised many teachmeets, hosted Twitter chats and loves sharing her journey with her teaching network.

Michael Green is the Head of Strategic Partnerships Education at the University of Greenwich. In addition to his role at Greenwich, he is a trustee for two multi-academy trusts and a co-operative trust.

Jan Grinstead is a Senior Lecturer for Childhood Studies at the University of Sunderland. Her research interests are centred around young children's learning and development, and professionals who work with young children. She is also a Senior Fellow of the Higher Education Academy.

Louise Johns-Shepherd, Chief Executive, Centre for Literacy in Primary Education. CLPE is a charity working to improve literacy in primary schools through creative, effective, evidence-based teaching that puts quality children's literature at the heart of all learning.

Dr Khalid Karim is a Consultant Psychiatrist and specialist in working with schools for the University of Leicester School of Psychology and Leicestershire Partnership NHS Trust.

Bonnie Kerr is a Senior Lecturer in Primary Education at the University of Greenwich, specialising in teaching education and professional studies.

Karen Kilkenny is a qualified teacher. She is currently the Primary PGCE Partnership Lead, runs the School Direct primary PGCE programme and lectures at the University of Manchester. She previously worked as the North-West Teach First primary Maths lead. Her research interests are around trainee teachers' engagement with ITT and supporting autistic learners and pupils with SEND in primary classrooms.

Paul Killen is a Lecturer in primary teacher training at Liverpool John Moores University where he teaches mathematics and professional studies. Paul's research interests lie in how children develop mental mathematical skills and how such skills link to mathematical understanding.

Dr Zenna Kingdon is a Senior Lecturer at the University of Wolverhampton, with expertise in Primary Education, Pre-school Education and Pedagogic Theory. Her research interests focus on play and in particular role play and exploring the concept of flourishing in early childhood.

Deborah Langston is Principal Lecturer and the Primary Partnership Lead at the University of Worcester. Prior to her current role, she taught in a range of primary schools for 26 years and was a Head Teacher for eleven years in a small, inclusive primary school. Her research interests include Special Educational Needs and Disabilities (SEND) with a particular interest in working memory, behaviour management, the importance and value of teamwork, and teacher efficacy.

Sean MacBlain is a senior academic at Plymouth Marjon University and worked previously as a Senior Lecturer in Education and Developmental Psychology at Stranmillis University College, Queens University Belfast, and for over 20 years as an educational psychologist in private practice.

Geraldine Magennis is Senior Lecturer in Education and Literacy at St Mary's University College, Belfast. Her personal research interests relate particularly to reading acquisition in the primary years as well as comparative educational models. Geraldine is also a qualified Life Coach.

Mary McAteer is Director of Professional Learning Programmes, Edge Hill University, Ormskirk. Her research interests include teacher professional learning, and action research/participatory and emancipatory research.

Conor McAteer is a Newly Qualified Teacher.

Diane McClelland is an experienced primary school teacher who has recently joined the academic staff of Stranmillis University College, Belfast. Her main interests include literacy, play-based and outdoor learning, child psychology and education in Uganda.

Darren McKay is a Senior Lecturer at Bath Spa University on the Primary PGCE and Early Years Initial Teacher Training programmes. He is a member of the Primary Science, Professional Studies and Early Years ITT teams. He is currently undertaking research exploring the development of beginning teachers' knowledge of teacher competence and their understanding of what influences it.

Amber McLeod is a Lecturer in the Faculty of Education, Monash University, Australia. Amber was previously a microbiologist and then taught English as an additional language in Japan, Brunei and Australia. Her research focus is on increasing digital competence in the community, and as the Director of Pathway Programs at Monash, Amber is passionate about developing transferable skills in students.

Claire Morse is Senior Lecturer in primary mathematics at the University of Winchester, teaching across multiple routes into primary teaching. She also teaches on the Master's programme, developing a group of teachers who are interested in teaching primary mathematics for mastery. Prior to being a senior lecturer, Claire was an Adviser for Southampton Local Authority and a primary teacher, mathematics subject leader and leading mathematics teacher.

Susan Ogier is Senior Lecturer in Primary Education, specialising in Art and Design. She works at the University of Roehampton, on both undergraduate and postgraduate courses. Her research interests include investigating the social, emotional and well-being aspects of teaching in art and design, and the role of developing an understanding of personal identities.

Janet Oosthuysen is Course Leader for the BA in Primary Education (with QTS) at Bradford College. Her research interests include critical thinking for child and adult learners, and philosophy for children.

Dr Michelle O'Reilly is a specialist in qualitative methods and childhood studies at the School of Media, Communication and Sociology and School of Psychology, University of Leicester, and Leicestershire Partnership NHS Trust.

Dr Ioanna Palaiologou CPsychol AFBPsS, FRSA is an Academic Associate at UCL Institute of Education and a child psychologist with specialism on child development and learning theories. Her research interests focus on early childhood education, child development, play and learning and digital technologies.

Noel Purdy is Director of Research and Scholarship and Head of Education Studies at Stranmillis University College, Belfast. His main research interests include pastoral care, special educational needs and teacher education.

Avril Rowley is a Lecturer in primary teacher training at Liverpool John Moores University and is the head of year 1. Avril is a former teacher with a Ph.D. in Educational Management. Her teaching interests include mentoring, effective models of leadership and dynamic teaching and learning models in primary education.

Mark Sackville-Ford is Senior Lecturer in Education (Professional Studies) at Manchester Metropolitan University and prior to this he was a Behaviour Specialist Support Teacher for a Local Authority. His research focuses on young people's experiences of education and the complexities of school ethos and atmospheres.

Cat Scutt is Director of Education and Research at the Chartered College of Teaching and a Ph.D. student at the UCL Institute of Education, London. Cat is interested in using research to inform decision-making at a classroom, school and system level.

Elaine Skates has been the Chief Executive of the Council for Learning Outside the Classroom (the national charity for LOtC) for four years and as such is involved in the Strategic Research Group for Learning in Natural Environments and has commissioned research into the impact of residential learning experiences on behalf of the Learning Away Consortium.

Glenn Stone is Principal Lecturer in education and head of the undergraduate primary teacher training programme at the University of Chichester. His research interests include teacher education and teacher professionalism.

Julie Sutton is a Senior Lecturer in Primary Education at the University of Worcester. Her research interests include music, pedagogy and professional practice, and teaching the primary foundation subjects.

David Waugh is Associate Professor (Teaching) at the School of Education, Durham University. He has published many books supporting the teaching of primary English. His teaching interests focus on children's literature, phonics and early reading, spelling, writing and grammar. David has also written five children's novels, one – *The Wishroom* – with 45 children from 15 schools.

Deborah Wilkinson is a Senior Lecturer in education specialising in primary science at the University of Chichester. She is interested in how questions are used to develop learning during science lessons.

EDITOR'S PREFACE

The World of Initial Teacher Education (ITE) is constantly changing and, as such, it felt timely to develop a new core text for primary student teachers. In doing so we spoke to a large number of ITE lecturers and students to gain perspectives on what was needed and wanted from such a text. We found that students want to be able to engage with a core text that offers a combination of practical, pragmatic ideas, which link directly to the classroom, and makes links to quality research and evidence. However, we did not want to simply provide information, facts and case studies, but we also wanted to get students to think about and challenge aspects of primary education. The route to becoming a great teacher is littered with a multitude of conversations and questions that shape our practice and invite us to reflect. We hope that this text provides the answers.

Learning to teach, and about teaching, involves engaging with differing perspectives, voices and expertise. This engagement shapes a teacher's philosophy and approach to teaching and learning. To get you started, we wanted to capture voices from across the world of ITE in this book and have been fortunate to have worked with a large number of chapter authors from a wide variety of ITE institutions across the UK and beyond, who all have significant expertise. I would like to thank all the chapter authors for their contributions.

From concept through to final draft of the content, we have engaged with a range of reviewers, including many current student teachers, in the production of this book and we thank them for the time they gave to this process and, more importantly, for their opinions.

I would like to thank my co-author of Chapter One, Virginia Bower, for her time and inspiring conversations, and my sons, Oliver and Toby, who put up with my constant critical commentary of their own education. I apologise for not having a 'normal job like other mums'!

We hope that this book provides you with information, guidance, relevant examples and ideas for your own classroom, which aids your pathway through your initial teacher education programme. We also hope that we have been able to introduce you to a wide range of educational research, evidence, policy and frameworks, as well as questions that get you thinking and rethinking primary education, but, most importantly, we hope that we have given you the inspiration to be the best teacher you can be.

Catherine Carden

FOREWORD

Welcome to the best, most challenging, rewarding and important profession in the world.

You have already made two excellent choices. You have chosen to become a teacher and you have chosen to pick up this book. As someone who has worked in education since the late eighties and in teacher training since the late nineties, I still believe that both teachers and teacher trainers are laying the foundations for everything that matters most in society. This is particularly so for those working in the primary phase. Whatever the children they teach go on to achieve, all educators are in it for the same reason: to make the maximum positive difference – either for the children or for the teachers who are working with them.

Teacher training has changed and evolved in many ways during the period I have been involved in it. As with most things in education, it has been buffeted about by different ideologies as different policy makers have been in charge. Everyone is an 'expert' in education as everyone has been to school. I often wonder: if a brain surgeon was told by patients that they know how to do the job as they have been on the operating table, how would the surgeon respond? In teacher training there have been arguments over the years about who should lead – schools, universities, private organisations. These arguments can be an enormous distraction from what really matters.

In truth, the most important thing is that, however teachers are trained, the experience must expose them to the best practice, the best research, the most important thinking and give them carefully crafted opportunities to develop their own practice to maximise this. In order to achieve this many different kinds of expertise and experiences must be involved. Most importantly though, student teachers must have the opportunity to constantly reflect on the relationship between all of this and the 'big picture', the reason they came into the profession, which is to make a difference to children's lives.

Despite all the ideological changes throughout the years, the things that teachers in training need the most have stayed the same. They need to work alongside people who can help them make sense of the complexity of classrooms and show them how to manage behaviour, support learning and develop understandings, attitudes and values in a way that has the most positive impact.

As well as the things you need to know and be able to do to be a good teacher, there are also quite a lot of qualities and support systems that you need to develop. Resilience, empathy, patience and, above all, a sense of humour, which you share with your children and your colleagues, are all essential. Your peer, friend and family network is also really important. Make sure that this includes time with people who have nothing to do with teaching, as well as those that do. Sharing ideas and worries about school with people who know about it is good, but you also need to completely switch off at times.

There are also some more 'literal' resources you are likely to find useful. As well as the obvious things like pens, highlighters, post its, labels, files, organisers etc., some great story and poetry books for all ages are a must when you suddenly need to fill five minutes for a class of restless children. Obviously you also need books for your own reading – in addition to this one, which you should keep near you at all times! Good teachers read widely, look at research, become familiar with educational debates and constantly think about how it all relates to their own practice. Social media can also be good for this, though opinions can sometimes be heated and skewed on Twitter and Facebook, so treat them with caution.

This book is a rich source of research, ideas and advice to get you started. It will hopefully get you excited by some of the big ideas that will bring education to life for you and your children, but it is also pragmatic and 'grounded' in the reality of primary schools today. Importantly, it also gives you insights into international comparisons and methods of educating that are very different to those used the UK. This is so important in helping you to develop your own 'big picture' ideas about the kind of teacher you want to be and why you think education is so important.

I believe this book will set you on your way to an exciting, varied, challenging and, ultimately, supremely worthwhile career. Over the years that come you will have an impact on so many young lives and make a real difference to the communities you work in.

Enjoy and thrive in this wonderful role.

Samantha Twiselton, OBE, Professor of Education and Director of Sheffield Institute of Education at Sheffield Hallam University; Vice President (external), Chartered College of Teaching

ACKNOWLEDGEMENTS

We would like to thank all of the students, teachers and Initial Teacher Education (ITE) staff who have worked with us to develop this book. Your comments and feedback have shaped the content, style and focus throughout. From the start of this project, we wanted to work on a text that was truly reflective of primary teacher education today. Without your help, advice and thoughtful review comments, this would not have been possible.

Thanks go to the ITE staff at the following institutions for their support, contributions, reviews and feedback:

Bath Spa University
Birmingham City University
Bradford College
Canterbury Christ Church University
Durham University
Edge Hill University
Leeds Beckett University
Leeds Trinity University
Liverpool John Moores University
Manchester Metropolitan University
Monash University
Newman University
Northumbria University
Nottingham Trent University
Oxford Brookes University
Plymouth Marjon University
Sheffield Hallam University
Stranmillis University College
UCL Institute of Education
University of Birmingham
University of Brighton
University of Chester
University of Chichester
University of Cumbria
University of Derby
University of East London
University of Gloucestershire
University of Greenwich
University of Hertfordshire
University of Huddersfield
University of Leicester
University of Manchester
University of Northampton
University of Plymouth
University of Reading
University of Sunderland
University of Sussex
University of the West of England
University of Warwick
University of Winchester
University of Wolverhampton
University of Worcester
York St John University

Thanks also to:

College of Teaching
Centre for Literacy in Primary Education (CLPE)
The Council for Learning Outside the Classroom

GUIDE TO YOUR BOOK

"We are the Student Panel. We have road tested the chapter features for this book to make sure that they work for you. We hope you enjoy this book and that it helps you succeed in your teacher training and future career!"

The Student Panel

Dani,
BA Primary Education

Laura-Louise,
PGCE Primary Education

Mitchell,
BA Primary Education

Harriet,
BA Primary Education

"WHAT DOES THIS BOOK OFFER FOR TRAINEE TEACHERS?

This easy yet informative read cleverly pulls the theory behind primary education and teaching together, with all the information you may need in a good balance of theory and practical ideas, allowing trainee teachers to develop their teaching and writing skills at the same time. Giving you a wider perspective on the world of teaching, this book will support your course studies, inform your philosophy of education and improve your teaching practice."

THE LEARNING FEATURES IN THE BOOK

KEY WORDS

'Enable you to quickly assess prior knowledge of the subject before reading a chapter and to reflect back on what you have read afterwards, to see if your understanding has changed. I also used them for a handy essay checklist.'

CRITICAL QUESTIONS

'Help you to engage with the text and directs reflection on your reading, encouraging more critical responses. I used them to critique my own practice, reminding me of areas pushed to the back of my own practice.'

KEY THEORY

'A quick and easy summary that breaks down key teaching theories, with relevant page references in a table of information. I found the thought-provoking questions helped to develop my criticality.'

KEY READING

'The supporting statements and alternative reading materials, e.g. policy papers, really helped develop my knowledge and deepen my understanding. They will help to broaden your perspectives and provide short and sweet practical ideas for the classroom.'

CLASSROOM LINK

'Building upon the key reading I found the extra details about how to practically implement ideas in the classroom and encouraging good practice invaluable. The key questions will encourage you to think deeper and will highlight good practice.'

CASE STUDY

'Applying the learning to real-life school contexts, the case studies detail real practical situations and highlight the relevance of your learning. Drawing upon your own experiences will help you to make connections with these real-life examples. They also highlight the sort of help that a student teacher can expect.'

CHAPTER SUMMARY

'These comprehensive yet concise summaries, involving theory and opposing ideas, will leave you with points for thought. I found them useful as a guide to content or to help clarify my learning.'

ASSIGNMENTS

'The advice on assignments is clear, facilitates you to still be independent, but gives you guidance to help you get started. I used it as a useful checklist of key points and to help form my opinions on newly-discussed subjects.'

REFERENCES

'I found the wealth of resources for further reading here really supported my assignments and broadened my knowledge.'

PART 1

UNDERSTANDING PRIMARY TEACHING

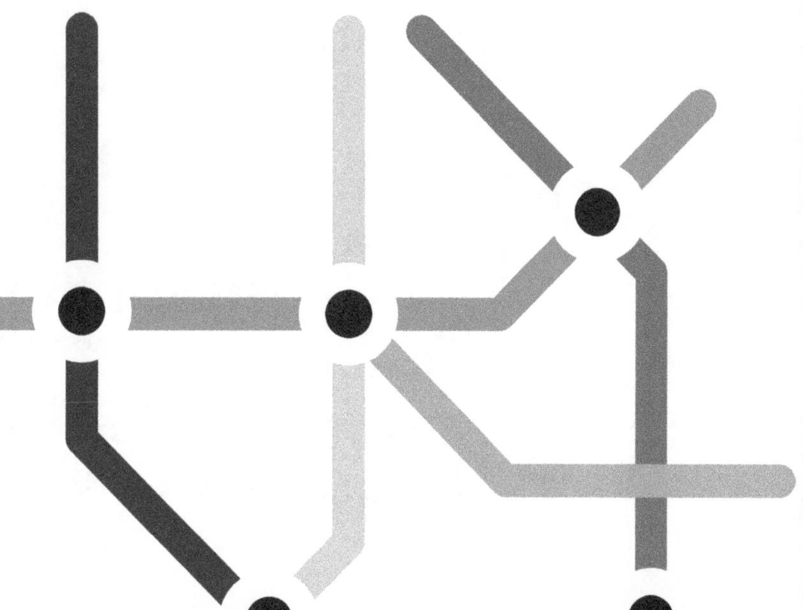

LEARNING *WITH* AND *FROM* CHILDREN

- ☐ INVOLVE PARENTS where possible
- ☐ FIND OUT what children do in their spare time and plan activities which include reference to these
- ☐ USE WRITING JOURNALS where children can record anything they wish
- ☐ START ALL NEW TOPICS by FINDING OUT what CHILDREN KNOW
- ☐ DESIGN HOME CORNERS role play areas book corners to relate to CHILDREN'S LIVES
- ☐ CREATE BILINGUAL RESOURCES and displays recognising and celebrating difference
- ☐ PLAN FOR PLENTY OF DISCUSSION and INTERACTION in EVERY LESSON.

1

WHAT IS TEACHING?

Catherine Carden is Faculty Director of Primary Initial Teacher Education, Canterbury Christ Church University. Her research interest is leadership in education.

Dr Virginia Bower is Programme Director PGCE Primary (Flexible) Canterbury Christ Church University. Her research interests are English as an additional language and teaching primary poetry.

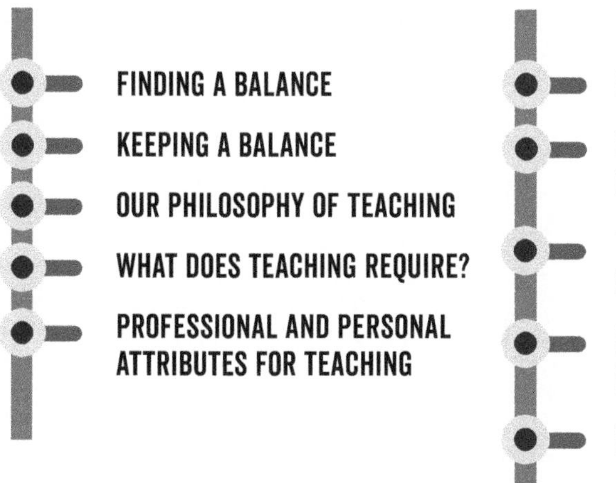

KEY WORDS

- Brave
- Creative
- Collaboration
- Empower
- Innovative
- Learning
- Mindset
- Principles
- Risk
- Teaching

INTRODUCTION

This chapter seeks to answer the question 'What is teaching?', while at the same time addressing the opposing question, 'What is teaching *not*?'. It is likely that, should you pose these questions to a group of children or parents, teachers or university tutors, you would get a whole range of different responses, dependent on personal experience, attitudes, beliefs and so forth. It is inevitable, therefore, that some of what is contained in this chapter you will challenge, question and contend, and this is welcomed. In order to enjoy a long and successful career in teaching, you *need* to challenge, question and contend, but this approach needs to build on principles and beliefs underpinned by knowledge and experience. These principles and beliefs will empower you to be creative, innovative and brave, and at the same time will prop you up when times are tough.

Picture an old-fashioned set of weighing scales. On one side are the exciting ideas, resources, plans and innovations you are determined to use to motivate and inspire the children in your class. On the other side are the nationally prescribed and school initiatives/policies with which you must comply. A successful balance between these demands leads to a more manageable teaching life, where compromises are made but enough of 'yourself' is able to emerge.

Figure 1.1 Finding a balance

If the balance gravitates more towards compliance, accountability and a lack of autonomy and trust, then you may feel your principles are being eroded; your foundations underpinning who you are as a teacher begin to crumble.

Figure 1.2 A lack of balance

Ball (2004: 147) describes how teachers might feel that they cannot be true to themselves – an 'alienation of self' leading to 'inauthentic practice and relationships'. There is then the danger of teachers becoming technicians rather than professionals (Alexander, 2004).

CRITICAL QUESTION

How can the balance be maintained and who can control this?

The ideas presented in this chapter, and throughout the book, will set you thinking about the type of teacher you want to be and how you will find a balance to achieve this. What should also emerge is a vision of the *learning* that emanates from excellent teaching – children learning with and alongside other children and adults, within a culture and environment that celebrates diversity, promotes innovation and recognises that, through collaboration, communication and cooperation, learning will flourish. Within this, we need to ask the question why some children 'struggle' and 'fail' at school while others 'flourish' and 'succeed'. Consider your own interpretation of the terms 'succeed' and 'fail', while focusing on how you can ensure that there are opportunities for all to 'flourish and succeed'.

CRITICAL QUESTION

Can, and should, all children 'flourish and succeed' at school?

This chapter begins with an examination of the philosophy underpinning our own ideas about teaching and learning, followed by a section entitled 'What does teaching require?' which suggests some traits which, if developed, should support you throughout your teaching career. The chapter then goes on to explore the following areas, which have been chosen because of what we perceive as their importance to successful teaching and learning:

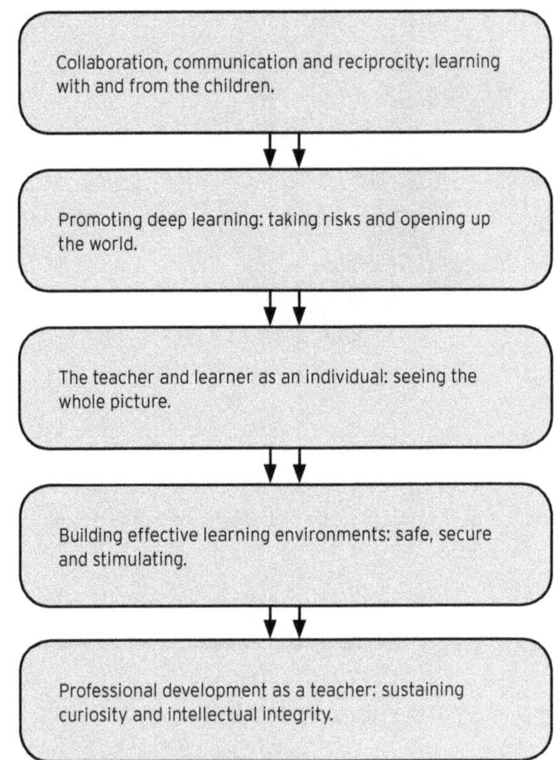

WHAT IS TEACHING? OUR PHILOSOPHY

Our approach to teaching is underpinned by a socio-cultural perspective, wherein learning and teaching are viewed as collaborative and reciprocal, non-hierarchical, dynamic and social (Johnson, 2006), 'rooted in society and culture' (Vygotsky, 1978: 7). Within this approach, thinking, communicating, interacting, re-evaluating and reflecting lead to more complex thinking and deep learning, promoted through 'meaningful activities and self-directed learning' (Lueg *et al.*, 2016: 1674). This is a long way from the traditional image of a teacher standing at the front of the classroom delivering information to waiting ears and adopting the all-knowing persona. Instead, this approach views effective, sustainable and successful teaching and learning as dependent on underpinning foundations built on respect, rapport and relationships. This reciprocal model of teaching and learning is described most aptly by Freire:

> *to teach is not to transfer knowledge but to create the possibilities for the production or construction of knowledge*
>
> (Freire, 2001: 30)

To create these 'possibilities', the focus needs to be on the children actively involved in, if not leading, the learning, carefully orchestrated by our planning, resourcing and facilitation. Analogously, this might be described as the teacher writing the music and then conducting the performance, with the children as the 'stars of the show'.

KEY THEORY

In his seminal text, *The Culture of Education*, Bruner (1999: 53) presents what he describes as 'models of mind and models of pedagogy': a synthesis of ideas that have emerged from educationalists, researchers, teachers and learners over time, relating to how teachers teach and learners learn. These models may help you to develop your own thinking in terms of how we perceive children's minds and how this affects our approach to teaching. Have a look at Table 1.1 below which summarises these ideas.

Table 1.1 Bruner's models

Learning through imitation	**Learning through didactic exposure**	**Learning through collaboration and discussion**	**Learning through building on existing knowledge and understanding**
Children perceived as not knowing but wanting to know	Children perceived as empty vessels, waiting to be filled	Children perceived as having ideas to be shared and, through sharing, come to understand the views of others	Children perceived as ready to recognise their existing knowledge, and relate and compare this to new findings
Adults as models who encourage the development of talents and skills through practice	Adults present pupils with 'facts, principles and rules of action' (p. 55)	Adults collaborate and mediate in an attempt to 'build an exchange of understanding' (p. 57)	Adults help the child 'reach beyond his own impressions to join a past world that would otherwise be remote and beyond him as knower' (p. 63)
Knowledge grows in an habitual way Apprenticeship model **Question:** Is 'simply demonstrating "how to" and providing practice at doing so' enough? (p. 54)	Knowledge is obtained by listening and absorbing Poor performance is the fault of the child **Question:** Are children 'blank slates' or 'empty vessels'?	The child is the centre of the learning **Question:** 'How are beliefs turned into hypotheses that hold not because of the faith we place in them but because they stand up in the public marketplace of evidence, interpretation, and agreement with extant knowledge?' (p. 60)	The child is empowered **Question:** How will you enable a child to 'reach beyond his own impressions'?

Hopefully, the table above, referencing some of Bruner's ideas, has started you thinking about the sort of teacher you want to be. Developing a personal philosophy and set of beliefs for teaching is essential, and ideas for this will be further developed later in the chapter. As important, however, is a realisation of what it means to be a teacher and the qualities you might need to develop. The next section explores these.

WHAT DOES TEACHING REQUIRE? AN EXAMINATION OF PROFESSIONAL AND PERSONAL ATTRIBUTES

Richards (2014: 10) writes that teaching requires 'intellect, emotional intelligence, imagination and sensitivity'. We would add to this, flexibility, energy, enthusiasm, integrity and resilience. Alongside this, there is a need for high levels of personal and professional organisation, to enable your working life to be manageable and sustainable. This section will examine each of these attributes.

INTELLECT

We sometimes have students saying to us that they are 'not clever enough to teach older children' or they refer to themselves as 'not as intelligent as others'. Teaching is not about being clever or having a high IQ. Instead, focus needs to be on the willingness to read, research, investigate and see yourself as a learner among other learners and enjoy the process.

EMOTIONAL INTELLIGENCE

Vital attributes are empathy and understanding in relation to the children and adults we work alongside. A recognition is needed that colleagues and pupils will come from diverse backgrounds, and this should both be celebrated and explicitly recognised in our approaches to teaching, learning and developing relationships.

IMAGINATION

The ability to imagine what might be, not what is. This enables you to work with what cannot be changed, while developing strategies and pedagogies that go beyond the prescribed requirements.

SENSITIVITY

This should be shown towards the lives of others and with attention to your own well-being. Schools can be highly pressurised workplaces, and developing support networks for children, parents, colleagues and yourself can ensure sensitivity towards the needs of others.

FLEXIBILITY

This refers to so many aspects of becoming a teacher. Schools are dynamic, ever-changing environments where even the best-laid plans change. The day's timetable might suddenly alter because a member of staff is ill; or because of the weather; or an expected visitor does not turn up. The ability groups you have spent so long organising are suddenly no longer appropriate because the mathematics topic has changed promoting unexpected clarity for some and confusion for others. New children arrive in your class mid-term, perhaps from traumatic backgrounds speaking a language other than English. Developing a flexible and responsive learning environment will enable you to manage this unpredictability. After all,

> *The reality is that classroom life is complex. Learning is not a linear process that can be tracked neatly on a graph, no matter how much we try to make it appear so.*
>
> (Kidd, 2014: 103)

ENERGY AND ENTHUSIASM

Energy levels can be difficult to maintain, day in, day out and it is important to manage your workload effectively. The government have recently published documents to support schools and teachers with this.

KEY READING

www.gov.uk/government/publications/reducing-teachers-workload/reducing-teachers-workload

Effective time management will allow you to stay enthusiastic, teaching across the curriculum. Even if it is not your 'favourite' subject to teach, it is important to remember that for some children, it *is* their favourite. Use their knowledge and enthusiasm to ignite your own.

INTEGRITY

It could be argued that teaching is a profession that has a moral purpose (Fullan, 2001). Teachers are certainly an influential factor towards children developing into purposeful citizens who positively contribute to society. Teachers are role models for those they teach, some of the parents they interact with and colleagues with whom they work. To act with integrity at all times can be challenging but must be the aim. A good reference point is to remember why it was that you decided to enter this profession in the first place.

RESILIENCE

Teaching is challenging. The demands put on teachers can at times be intense and the unpredictability of working with children reduces levels of control for the teacher. The term 'resilience' is used a great deal in the world of education, but rarely explored in terms of what 'being resilient' actually means. Going beyond the commonly held view that resilience is bouncing back from adverse situations, Pemberton defines the notion of resilience as 'the capacity to remain flexible in thoughts, behaviours and emotions when under stress' (no date). This resonates with later discussion in this chapter relating to developing a growth mindset.

KEY READING

http://carolepemberton.co.uk/resilience-coaching/

PERSONAL ORGANISATION

The daily life of a teacher is not only busy but also requires several mindset shifts. For example, a teacher's day may include the following foci: finalising resources for the day's learning; discussions with a teaching assistant about the day ahead and the role they are required to play within this; discussion with parents about their child; teaching and learning; pastoral care and intervention; assessment; data collection and analysis; attending and/or leading staff meetings; reflecting on the learning achieved that day to feed in to tomorrow's planned learning ... and sometimes more. To achieve all of this in a professional manner, high levels of personal organisation are required. Being organised is not simply about doing things in the right order by the right time, but it is about prioritising activities, knowing what is most important and what will have to wait.

CRITICAL QUESTION

Which of these attributes are already strengths and which might cause you the most angst?

COLLABORATION AND RECIPROCITY: LEARNING WITH AND FROM THE CHILDREN

To develop effective collaborative learning experiences, we need first to develop strong relationships with children, based on an excellent knowledge of the local contexts of their lives. An awareness of the 'ecological, social, and economic context of the place in which they live' (Freire, 2001: 122) is vital if we are to 'become acquainted with their way of being in the world, if not become intimately acquainted then at least become less of a stranger to it' (ibid.). This enables us to plan, resource and teach in a way that is relevant and meaningful to the children. It requires us always to discover what the children already know and build on this. One way of doing this might be to start a new topic on a Friday, rather than a Monday. In this way, you can introduce the concepts, find out what children already know, set them some homework to explore the topic over the weekend and then adjust your plans before the following week.

Learning needs to be perceived as a shared experience, where openness and a willingness to accept that we all have different knowledge, underpin the classroom ethos. A group of pupils and teachers will know things as individuals; as a collaborative group they will know more and begin to realise that they can extend their knowledge through listening and sharing. Vygotsky (1978: 88) wrote that 'human learning presupposes a specific social nature and a process by which children grow into the intellectual life of those around them', and we need to develop ways to capitalise on this inherent sociability.

INFO 1.1

Learning with and from children

- Involve parents where possible
- Find out what children do in their spare time and plan activities which include reference to these
- Use writing journals where children can record anything they wish
- Start all new topics by finding out what children know
- Design home corners/role-play areas/book corners to relate to children's lives
- Create bilingual resources and displays, recognising and celebrating difference
- Plan for plenty of discussion and interaction in every lesson.

CLASSROOM LINK

What does this mean for classroom practice?

Some practical ideas:

- Involve parents where possible - reading with children, encouraging parents from other cultures/who speak other languages to share experiences/literature/artefacts.
- Find out what children do in their spare time and plan activities that include reference to these - resources/books/websites/television programmes. You could encourage children to bring in texts or objects from home that link with the topic. Remember though that some sensitivity is needed here - there may be things children do not want to share and would rather keep for home only.
- Use writing journals where children can record anything they wish - words and phrases, song lyrics, poems, drawings/notes.
- Start all new topics by finding out what children know - using KWL grids/online collaborative spaces, e.g. padlet/working walls.
- Design home corners/role-play areas/book corners to relate to children's lives, or where possible, encourage the children to design them.
- With the children, create bilingual resources and displays, recognising and celebrating difference within and beyond the classroom (Bower, 2017).
- Plan for plenty of discussion and interaction in every lesson. Alexander (2004: 21) fears that interaction between teachers and children is often based on questions that only require brief answers with 'an emphasis on recalling information rather than on speculating and problem-solving'. Try to ensure that there is time for extended interactions, using talk partners, group discussion, debates, for example.

Within a teaching model centred on collaboration and reciprocity, children challenge and develop teachers' learning, and there is the potential for a 'transformation of participation' (Rogoff, 1994: 209) to occur. Read the case study below to see an example of this.

CASE STUDY

The incident occurred in a Year 6 class (10 and 11 year olds), with a Bulgarian boy - Petr. This child had limited spoken and written English at this stage, as he had only been in England for a few months. The learning focus was on identifying the oceans of the world and there was a map on the interactive whiteboard, with all the ocean names erased. I asked if anybody would like to write in one of the ocean names. Petr's hand shot up and he approached the board confidently, rapidly writing in each of the oceans (correctly). He then pointed to Bulgaria on the map and proceeded to talk about his home country, his family and where they lived, and the places he had visited. The other children were fascinated and asked him questions and listened attentively. I abandoned my own lesson plan and passed the lesson over to him, and I am sure that the children and I benefited far more than they would have if I had stuck to my plan! An all-round positive learning experience. It was also extremely good for Petr's self-esteem and spoken English practice.

Collaboration and reciprocity are closely aligned with effective communication, and excellent teaching promotes this through planning for interaction, discussion, activity, questioning and reflection. Sustained opportunities are vital, in order that children can immerse themselves in the learning; it cannot be rushed. It is important to pause at key moments and take time to investigate and explore further when children make interesting points, have incredible ideas, say something a little 'left field', have a misconception or wish to share their own personal experiences. We must not be quick to move on; instead, we need to relish these moments and promote reflection and discussion whenever possible.

CRITICAL QUESTION

How might the curriculum and planned schemes of work prevent teachers from 'slowing down' and provide time for collaboration and communication?

PROMOTING DEEP LEARNING: TAKING RISKS AND OPENING UP THE WORLD

To learn effectively children need to be inspired, enthused and curious. They need to develop in a way that will ensure that they are prepared to function in, and positively contribute to, the modern world. For this to happen, both teachers and children need to take risks with their teaching and learning, and be prepared to be challenged along the way. The following example describes how a student teacher was prepared to take these risks and, through a creative and innovative approach, promote enjoyment and deep learning.

What does this mean for classroom practice?

The student contacted me (VB) to ask advice about the English lessons she was preparing for her Year 3 class for the following week. She was unsure as to the progression the children should be making towards writing their own haiku poems. I wrote her a 'skeleton' set of plans for the week, which she could then adapt and create more detailed plans to support all the children's needs. This was the planning sheet I provided:

Day 1 - Does anybody know what a haiku is? Discuss haikus. Read lots of examples. Discuss the history of haikus. Children to explore some examples in their groups. Discuss syllables - what they are and how many in haikus.

Day 2 - Recap what haikus are and what they are trying to portray (tend to be focused on nature/senses, etc.). Read some more. Children to read some aloud. Choose a topic and ask children to mind map vocabulary for that topic. Collect vocabulary on board and discuss. Begin to model how a haiku might come together - asking children to contribute ideas. Explain that tomorrow you are all going to write one as a class and then they are going to work on their own haikus.

Day 3 - Read more haikus. Shared writing - create a haiku as a class. Children to choose their topic and start gathering vocabulary. They could begin writing their haiku in rough. Share some ideas.

Day 4 - Read some haikus. Read one that you have made up. Ask children to share some of their vocabulary. Children to work on their own haiku and then share with others.

I arrived the following week to observe her haiku lesson on day 3 of the sequence, and was delighted to witness some really significant learning, where adults and children worked and learned seamlessly together. The children had all named their groups, using the names of famous haiku poets. They had an excellent understanding of the origins of this poetic form and they had learnt some Japanese vocabulary. They used a 'back and forth' activity to elicit words relating to the topic upon which they were to write their haiku poems - you say a word, I say a word, etc. - and this was first modelled by the student teacher and her assistant. The student had invented what she described as a 'naiku' - a model which was *not* a haiku - and the children explored *why* it was not a haiku and subsequently what features made up a haiku. They then began structuring their own haikus. All this in just in one lesson, possible because the student had examined the skeleton plan she had been sent and had been flexible enough to expand on the ideas, plan for exciting activities using a range of excellent pedagogies and had, by her own enthusiasm and flexibility, promoted a deeper level of learning.

Biesta (2013: 1) believes that education, by its very nature 'always involves a risk'; that the children we teach are not simply objects to be moulded and disciplined but are subjects of action and responsibility. Thus, children must not simply be the recipients of education but the co-constructors of it. This is risky, as when co-construction exists the teacher relinquishes control. Some teachers find this challenging; they like to be in control. In the example above, the student teacher was not afraid to use 'risky' pedagogies, relinquish some control, and put the learning in the hands of the children.

The notion of risk-taking depends on what you consider to be a risk. The decision to take a risk, instead of 'playing safe', is sometimes rejected for fear of it negatively affecting outcomes. This is more likely to reflect the current culture of accountability than be a reflection on a teacher's philosophy of education. As Dadds

(2001) argues, because of the increased accountability and expectations for linear progression, coverage of the curriculum – safe teaching – becomes the focus rather than learning. The focus comes away from responding to the needs of the children, and merely reacts to the prescribed requirements of imposed curricula. Ironically, taking risks that open up the world to children in an engaging, exciting and different way will positively affect learning and progress, resulting in more positive outcomes. The tension here tends to be between curriculum coverage and the desire to take risks.

We would suggest that one way to avoid this tension is to focus on *learning* rather than content. Think back to the earlier example of the haiku lessons. Here, the focus was on the children's learning. Yes, the outcome was to write their own haiku poems, but along the way they learned so much more. W.B. Yeats is attributed as saying 'education is not the filling of a pail, but the lighting of a fire', and the student teacher certainly lit the children's fire with regard to this genre. Biesta (2013: 44) suggests that a teacher is 'someone who, in the most general sense brings something new to the educational situation, something not already there' and this was reflected in the haiku lessons. The student teacher brought expertise to the educational situation in the form of scaffolding learning through exciting activities, in order for the children to become independent and curious learners.

'The lighting of a fire'? Something, perhaps, to grapple with when getting to grips with 'What is teaching?' Whenever you hesitate about taking a risk with your teaching, consider these words: 'we are kings of our own classroom and most of the time no one else is looking' (Kidd, 2014: 119) and go for it. The results will be career-changing for you and life-changing for those you teach.

What are the benefits of focusing on learning rather than focusing on delivering the required content?

THE TEACHER AND LEARNER AS AN INDIVIDUAL: SEEING THE WHOLE PICTURE

Effective teaching comes about through the choices you make. If you gave ten teachers the same learning objective for a lesson, they would be likely to come up with ten different plans, using a range of pedagogies and practices, resources, activities and assessment methods. The most successful of these would build on the children's prior knowledge, relate to the world in which they live, use resources to stimulate discussion and motivate learning, and would encourage the children to lead the learning where possible. Kidd (2014: 104) recognises that 'each child will respond to different approaches and we build a repertoire of techniques to help them. This takes time, experience and judgement. It is not easy and it relies very much on building positive relationships and trust in classrooms'. This goes a long way beyond the once-popular notion of categorising children as either visual, auditory or kinaesthetic learners (VAK) and focuses on knowing the individuals you teach – and knowing yourself as a teacher – and designing the learning to suit their needs. We are not suggesting that each child in a class should be taught differently utilising individual lesson plans, but, rather, that acknowledgement and celebration of the diversity within your class will lead to a much more imaginative and flexible approach to the curriculum. Kidd (ibid.: 102), agrees that 'we cannot cope with teaching each [child] differently ... we need to find patterns in order to survive', while also arguing that we must 'reject suggestions of simple solutions'.

Meeting individual needs and preferences for learning may seem like a truly daunting task, but it is something that we all gradually get better at, if we are prepared to be creative and open-minded.

CLASSROOM LINK

What does this mean for classroom practice?

Consider your use of resources: Use a variety of resources and manipulatives to support learning. Do not think that all children need to be using the same resources; instead, offer options and choice. Use resources as a method of differentiation.

Consider the availability of resources: Consider where your resources are stored. Are they put away in a cupboard where the children cannot access them? Consider making resources available on tables or different areas of the classroom and ensure children are aware of how and when to access these.

Consider the learning activity: Do all children need to be doing the same activity? Vary the activity to support, challenge and to meet individual needs. This may be using different tasks, through scaffolding or through enabling children to access very different activities that still enable them to achieve the learning.

Consider how technology can support learning: There are many opportunities to support learning through technology in very different ways. Explore different options, offer choice for the children to engage with these and enjoy learning from the children.

Consider the way you use your body: Goldin-Meadow and Singer (2005) suggest that teachers who gesture alongside their verbal instructions have a greater impact on children's learning and understanding of concepts and that children are highly attuned to the movements of the teacher. They suggest that this is even more powerful when what is spoken is conveying a differing message to what is being gestured. Therefore, always consider where you are and what you are doing in order to support learning.

Prioritise learning and process over outcomes and product: Outcomes are the end product of learning. A poem is not the learning but the product of learning. Avoid putting all your focus on the outcome and focus on the learning. Is it important that all the outcomes are the same? Could the children choose how to present the outcomes of their learning? Could this choice motivate and inspire learners?

When considering teachers and children as individuals, it is essential to think holistically about the cognitive, social and emotional development and learning that takes place. As teachers, we often feel that we are being judged upon the outcomes of the children we teach: under pressure to focus on academic development and attainment rather than on social and emotional development and achievement. That is understandable but, in fact, a better awareness of the child – and ourselves – as a whole will lead to better teaching and learning and, in turn, to better results. This will include a good understanding of the stages of cognition that impact on 'what we can expect [children] to learn or hope to teach' (Wood, 1998: 49). It will also involve finding out as much as possible about the backgrounds of the children and their life experiences. This may vary greatly from child to child, and it should be remembered that children will process and understand their learning differently from one another according to these differing experiences or opportunities.

There are several approaches to ensure that the whole child is being educated. The ASCD's Whole Child Initiative is just one example. Launched in 2007, this initiative aims to ensure that each child is healthy, safe, engaged, supported and challenged.

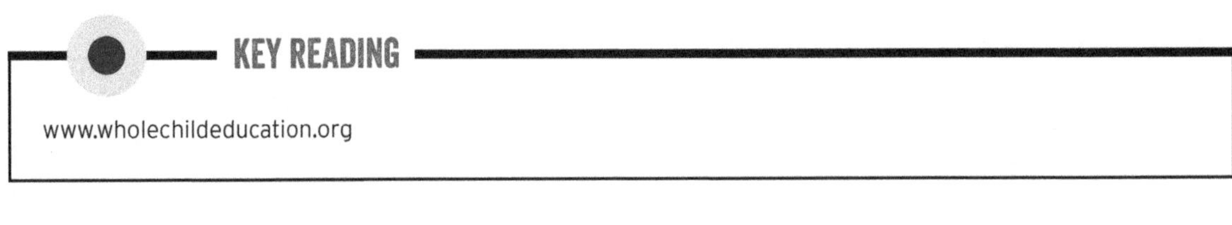

KEY READING

www.wholechildeducation.org

CRITICAL QUESTION

How would teaching differ if teachers were measured on how happy and healthy the class were?

The question above may raise a smile, but it is a serious question. In their blog piece for *The Conversation* (2015) Lauren Schiller and Christina Hinton claim that there is a 'significant correlation between happiness and academic success'. So, perhaps if teachers gave more time to ensuring happiness, the academic outcomes might naturally follow.

BUILDING EFFECTIVE LEARNING ENVIRONMENTS: SAFE, SECURE AND STIMULATING

Children spend a lot of their time in school – in fact, a minimum of 190 days per year (Long, 2016), and during term time children spend more time in school each week than they do in waking hours at home. Positive and effective learning environments are, therefore, vital (see Chapter 24 for an exploration of inclusive learning environments). It is useful to look at the learning environment through Maslow's Hierarchy of Needs (1943) (see Figure 1.3).

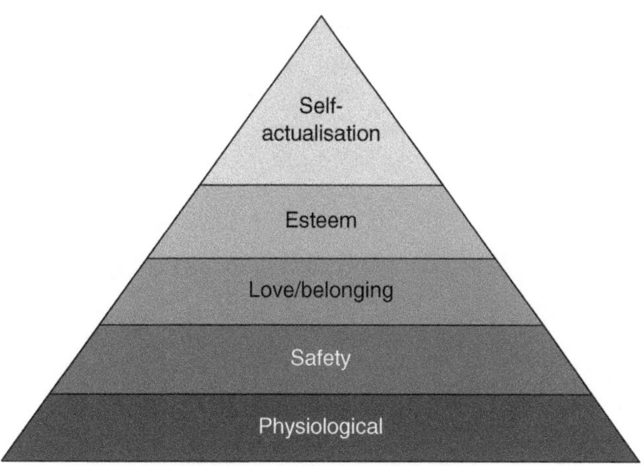

Figure 1.3 Maslow's Hierarchy of Needs

BASIC NEEDS: PHYSIOLOGICAL AND SAFETY NEEDS (FOOD, WATER, WARMTH, REST, SECURITY, SAFETY)

To meet children's basic needs it is vital that the learning environment provided is inviting and comfortable. This is not always easy when squeezing a large number of children into a fairly small space. Most teachers dream of larger, airier classrooms, but you have to work with what you have. Consider the temperature of the room and use the windows to let in air – classrooms can become quite stuffy and smelly on a summer afternoon. Carefully use the lighting and consider the use of additional (always safe) lighting such as lamps in a reading corner, for example.

Figure 1.4 The reading corners in a Year 3 classroom at Blenheim Primary School, Essex

Consider your approach to access to water in the classroom. Do children have bottles on their desk? Ensure your learning environment is physically safe and secure, but also send messages of being an emotionally safe and secure space where children feel that they belong. Consider here, how the children can co-create the learning environment with you, making suggestions and choices around layout and content. The learning environment belongs, after all, to the children, not the teacher.

PSYCHOLOGICAL NEEDS: BELONGINGNESS, LOVE AND ESTEEM NEEDS (RELATIONSHIPS, FRIENDS, ACCOMPLISHMENT AND PRESTIGE)

When considering psychological needs in the context of a learning environment, a good place to start is to consider the layout of the room. How are the tables laid out? Who is sitting with whom and why? Is there a balance between suitable learning groups and allowing children to learn alongside their friends?

Figure 1.5 A class slogan co-created by all the children in the class at Blenheim Primary School, Essex

These may seem challenging questions to answer with the issue of not being able to please each and every child. However, it is important to see the learning environment as a flexible rather than a fixed space. The layout should not remain the same day in, day out. Instead, see your classroom as a stage requiring scene changes for each differing learning episode with the actors moving to work in differing areas of the stage among different cast members depending on the scene. Share and display work, successes and triumphs; celebrate success. Use the classroom walls to add a vibrant, welcoming, purposeful and celebratory nature to the environment, ensuring that all cultures and languages are promoted, so that children can 'recognise and identify with their surroundings' (Bower, 2017: 50).

SELF-FULFILMENT NEEDS: SELF-ACTUALISATION (ACHIEVING FULL POTENTIAL, CREATIVE ACTIVITIES)

A learning environment needs to have purpose and communicate high expectations. As mentioned above, it is important to share work, and successes yet purposeful environments are also environments that are clearly set up for learning to take place. Consider access and availability of resources and aim to create an atmosphere of creation rather than chaos. Think outside the box. Can children collate thoughts and responses through writing on desks or windows? Can a display evolve over a term of work rather than being a final piece? Use the space to inspire, set a challenge and motivate through taking some risks and experimenting.

CLASSROOM LINK

What does this mean for classroom practice?

A student teacher's lesson was recently observed, where the children were exploring and creating their own newspaper headlines. The student encouraged the children to write their headlines on post-it notes and they then stuck these to the flipchart. As children added their own, they were also reading their peers', learning from each other. The flipchart remained there as the children went on to do their newspaper reports during the week - not just a useful reminder but also a valuable source of vocabulary for them.

Building effective learning environments is also about creating an ethos whereby errors are not only accepted but welcomed. In fact, they are not errors at all but merely steps to success. Making mistakes is a fundamental part of learning, yet many of us feel ashamed to make mistakes, get things wrong or fail at anything. This mindset limits learning. Dweck refers to this as having a fixed mindset (Dweck, 2006). In brief, a fixed mindset characterises itself through a need to be perfect, be the best and always correct, leading to a fear of failure. Children and adults may avoid entering situations where there is the potential to get things wrong; they put a lot of pressure on themselves while at the same time may avoid challenging themselves, and not achieve their full potential. We need to ensure that our classrooms do not promote a fixed mindset, but aim for what is instead termed a 'growth mindset'. The promotion of a growth mindset will embed an expectation that learning takes effort (Dweck, 2006) and will support learners with embracing challenge, taking risks, learning from mistakes and developing tenacity – the perfect mindset to enable learning to flourish.

CRITICAL QUESTION

Is your classroom a growth mindset classroom? And if not how can you develop this?

PROFESSIONAL DEVELOPMENT AS A TEACHER: SUSTAINING CURIOSITY AND INTELLECTUAL INTEGRITY

An essential aspect of being a teacher is recognising that we are also learners and always will be. Part of this is the need for a proactive approach to professional development. The current prevalence of school-based teacher education, where student teachers are learning 'on the job', potentially without access to research findings or theoretical underpinning of ideas, coupled with a lack of funded professional development for teachers, means that opportunities for teachers to keep up to date with the latest research – beyond practical ideas or policy implementation – appear limited.

If, however, we are prepared to consider the concept of professional development as more than attending a course or training, the possibilities are boundless. Arguably, professional development in terms of opportunities for extended discussion between colleagues is more useful than traditional forms of professional development where knowledge is transmitted from an 'expert' or where awareness is raised about new policies and how they should be implemented. Leung (2004: 38) writes that 'there is no neat one-to-one correspondence between external stimulus or provision of new knowledge and the desired teacher uptake (and subsequent change in practice) intended by sponsoring authorities and policymakers'. Perhaps it is more likely that change will be enacted as a result of extended discussions and a sharing of theory, practice and experiences, and that professional development is most useful when it is 'self-directed, collaborative, inquiry-based learning' (Johnson, 2006: 243).

A valuable way to ensure this self-direction is always to be questioning and reflecting on your own practice and thinking (the importance of reflection during placement is explored in Chapter 18). Skilled reflection is the foundation of highly effective teaching. It can, however, be painful and uncomfortable, for a number of reasons.

Inevitably, where teaching and learning are concerned, there are issues about which we hold strong beliefs, and learners may well need to be supported through what Meyer *et al.* (2010) refer to as 'threshold concepts'. The idea of threshold concepts 'builds on the notion that there are certain concepts, or certain learning experiences, which resemble passing through a portal, from which a new perspective opens up, allowing things formerly not perceived to come into view' (ibid.: ix). Learners have to go through the process of knowing something in a particular way, gaining some new knowledge – through reading or experience or discussing with others, for example – then revising and challenging – even completely changing – the way they think about something. This process is rarely easy; it can be disturbing, distressing, frustrating and can challenge our sense of who we are, as it entails 'a letting go of earlier, comfortable positions and encountering less familiar and sometimes disconcerting new territory' (Rust, 2005: 54) as new knowledge is assimilated.

This 'troublesome' knowledge (Timmerman, 2010: 4) is gained at different rates by different individuals, influenced as the process is by, among other things, a person's openness to change; the timing of the approach to a threshold concept; the distance between their existing knowledge and beliefs and the new concepts; and the ability to accept that a change in the way we look at the world might be painful both cognitively and emotionally. For us as teachers, it is worth keeping in mind these threshold concepts and this troublesome knowledge, not only when we think about our own learning, but when we imagine how the children we teach are feeling when we introduce them to new concepts and knowledge. An openness to the challenge is a powerful and significant factor in our professional development as teachers.

CHAPTER SUMMARY

Training to be a teacher is fundamentally about discovering the kind of teacher you want to be. This can include a realisation that you might not 'fit' into every setting and that the process of becoming a qualified teacher needs to involve gaining experience in different settings so that you start to recognise where you feel most comfortable.

It is hoped that this chapter has in some way begun to answer the question 'What is teaching?' In summary, teaching is about creating a safe, supportive and trusting environment that fosters learning. Yet always aim to go way beyond this towards what Faltis and Abedi (2013: viii) describe as 'extraordinary pedagogies' wherein they believe that 'schools and educators must learn and do more than the ordinary'.

Dadds (2001: 43) writes that current pedagogy 'is silencing enquiry and diverse critical perspectives of both teachers and children' and the repercussions of this are potentially wider than merely in relation to learning. As teachers, educators and researchers, we cannot ignore the political climate in which we work, but we have to believe that it is possible to work creatively within it. This relies on professional judgement, challenging our own assumptions and attitudes, and a realisation that commitment to our own continuing professional development is essential. Thus, we can develop opportunities to share ideas and experiences; stay open to the challenge of learning, broadening and deepening our own knowledge and understanding; go beyond the normal and expected in order to engage and motivate children; and recognise, utilise and celebrate what children bring to the classroom.

That, for us, is teaching.

ASSIGNMENTS

If you are writing an assignment discussing 'what is teaching?' you may wish to:

- consider your own philosophy of education;
- explore how good teaching supports children's learning;
- consider the challenges and barriers to innovative teaching and learning, and why these challenges exist;
- consider the importance of safe, secure and stimulating learning environments as an important factor in high quality teaching.

REFERENCES

Alexander, R. (2004) Still no pedagogy? Principle, pragmatism and compliance in primary education. *Cambridge Journal of Education*, 34(1): 7–33.

Ball, S.J. (ed.) (2004) *The RoutledgeFalmer Reader in Sociology of Education*. London and New York: RoutledgeFalmer.

Biesta, G. (2013) *The Beautiful Risk of Education*. Boulder, CO: Paradigm Publishers.

Bower, V. (2017) *Supporting Pupils with EAL in the Primary Classroom*. Buckingham: Open University Press.

Bruner, J. (1999) *The Culture of Education*. London: Harvard University Press.

Dadds, M. (2001) The politics of pedagogy. *Teachers and Teaching*, 7(1): 4358.

Dweck. C. (2006) *Mindset: How you can fulfil your potential*. London: Constable Robinson.

Faltis, C. and Abedi, J. (2013) Extraordinary pedagogies for working within school settings serving non-dominant students. *Review of Research in Education*. March, 37: vii–xi.

Freire, P. (2001) *Pedagogy of Freedom*. Oxford: Rowman & Littlefield.

Fullan, M. (2001) *Leading in a Culture of Change*. San Fransisco, CA: Jossey-Bass.

Goldin-Meadow, S. and Singer, M. (2005) Children learn when their teacher's gestures and speech differ. *Psychological Science*, 16(2): 85–9.

Johnson, K.E. (2006) The sociocultural turn and its challenges for second language teacher education. *TESOL Quarterly*, 40(1): 235–57.

Kidd, D. (2014) *Teaching: Notes from the front line*. Carmarthen: Independent Thinking Press.

Leung, C. (2004) Developing formative teacher assessment: Knowledge, practice, and change. *Language Assessment Quarterly*, 1(1): 19–41.

Long, R. (2016) The school day and year (England). *House of Commons Briefing Paper*. Available at: http://research-briefings.files.parliament.uk/documents/SN07148/SN07148.pdf (accessed 25/06/18).

Lueg, R., Lueg, K. and Lauridsen, O. (2016) Aligning seminars with Bologna requirements: Reciprocal peer tutoring, the solo taxonomy and deep learning. *Studies in Higher Education*, 41(9): 1674–691.

Maslow, A.H. (1943). A theory of human motivation. *Psychological Review*, 50(4): 370–96.

Meyer, J.H.F., Land, R. and Baillie, C. (eds) (2010) *Threshold Concepts and Transformational Learning*. Rotterdam: Sense.

Pemberton. C. (no date) *Resilience Coaching*. Available at: http://carolepemberton.co.uk/resilience-coaching/ (accessed 30/04/18).

Richards, C. (2014) Primary teaching: A personal perspective, in Cremin, T. and Arthur, J. (2014) *Learning to Teach in the Primary School* (3rd edn). London: Routledge.

Rogoff, B. 1994, Developing understanding of the idea of communities of learners, *Mind, Culture and Activity*, 1(4). Available at: www.tandfonline.com/doi/abs/10.1080/10749039409524673 (accessed 25/06/18).

Rust, C. (ed.) (2005) *Improving Student Learning Diversity and Inclusivity*. Oxford: Oxford Centre for Staff and Learning Development.

Schiller, L. and Hinton, C. (2015) It's True: Happier students get higher grades. *The Conversation*, 30 July. Available at: http://theconversation.com/its-true-happier-students-get-higher-grades-41488 (accessed 30/04/18).

Timmerman, J.A. (2010) Changing our minds: The developmental potential of threshold concepts, in Meyer, J.H.F., Land, R. and Baillie, C. (eds) (2010) *Threshold Concepts and Transformational Learning*, pp. 3–19. Rotterdam: Sense.

Vygosky, L.S. (1978) *Mind in Society. The Development of Higher Psychological Processes*. London: Harvard University Press.

Whole Child Education. Available at: www.wholechildeducation.org/about (accessed 30/04/18).

Wood, D. (1998) *How Children Think and Learn* (2nd edn) Oxford: Blackwell Publishing.

2

WHAT IS TEACHER TRAINING?

Karen Kilkenny is a qualified teacher. She is currently the primary PGCE partnership lead, runs the School Direct primary PGCE programme and lectures at the University of Manchester. She previously worked as the North-West Teach First primary Maths lead. Her research interests are around trainee teachers' engagement with ITT and supporting autistic learners and pupils with SEND in primary classrooms.

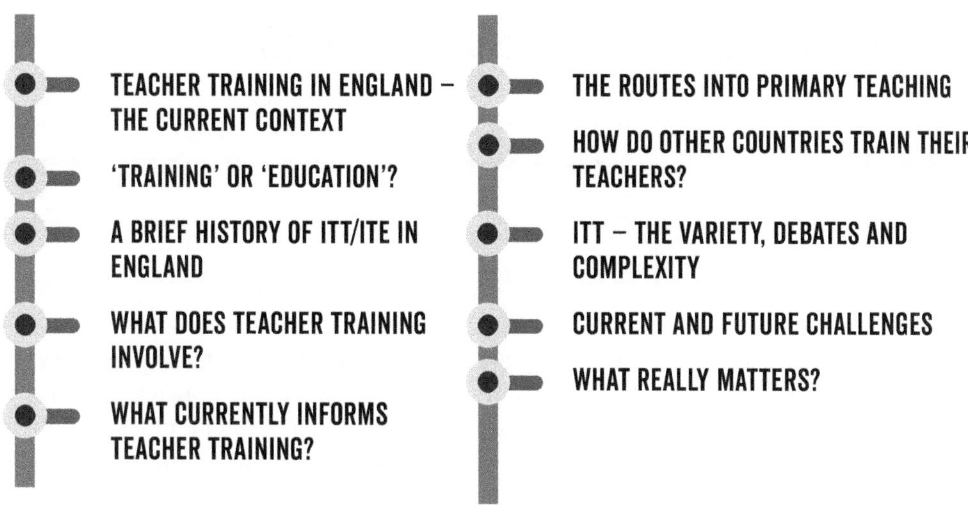

KEY WORDS

- Continued Professional Development (CPD)
- Department for Education (DfE)
- Employment-based route (EBR)
- Higher Education Institution (HEI)
- Initial Teacher Education (ITE)
- Initial Teacher Training (ITT)
- Newly Qualified Teacher (NQT)
- School-led training (SLT)

INTRODUCTION

This chapter explores our understanding of the term 'teacher training'. It begins with a brief history of the development of professional teaching qualifications in England. It then focuses on current provision for ITT, including a brief overview of the various 'routes' into primary teaching. This chapter predominantly focuses on the English ITT system, although other home nation systems and international ITT examples are explored for comparison. Political interests and policies that influence teacher training will be considered alongside the ITT curriculum. The chapter explores some of the tensions between different stakeholders and policy makers to allow a broad consideration of currently contrasting dynamics in ITT. Additionally, data from a small-scale case study exploring primary trainee experiences in one school-led ITT route is used to exemplify aspects of school-led and university-led ITT routes. The chapter supports you to increase your awareness of the diversity, debates and complexities within primary teacher training.

TEACHER TRAINING IN ENGLAND – THE CURRENT CONTEXT

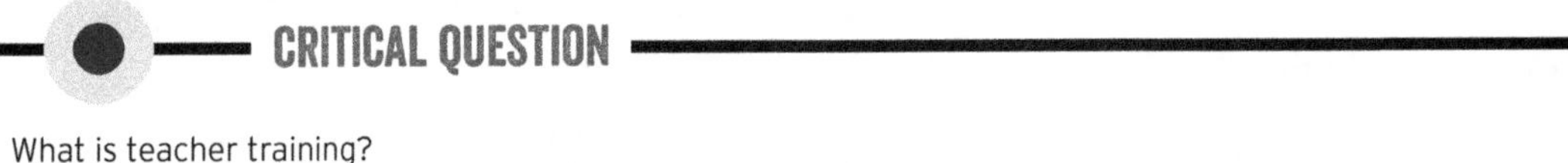

What is teacher training?

The question 'What is teacher training?' may have, in previous decades, been a relatively simple question. It can now lead to considerable complexity and uncertainty. In essence, teacher training refers to the process by which teachers gain the knowledge, skills, attitudes and behaviours they require to perform their role effectively. However, what this may entail goes far beyond this generalised definition and beyond the initial training required for basic qualification. However, it is the 'initial' aspect of teacher training that will be the main focus in this chapter.

The last ten years has arguably seen the most significant period of change in ITT in England, with the introduction of a range of different ITT routes (McNamara *et al.*, 2017). The key political driver of reform is the aim to improve the national educational profile compared to other international systems, through enhanced results in teacher effectiveness measures.

> *No education system can be better than the quality of its teachers.*
>
> (DfE, 2010: 3)

Human capital, demonstrated through a highly educated population, is widely accepted as a key determinant of economic success (Donaldson, 2010). Consequently, persistent political spotlight on the education system has resulted in a highly charged and fluid landscape of educational policy. As a result, elements of this chapter, although accurate at the point of writing, may be superseded by the time it has gone to print.

'TRAINING' OR 'EDUCATION'?

In this chapter the terms 'initial teacher training' (ITT) and 'trainees' (referring to those being trained within the ITT routes) are used. However, it is important to acknowledge that other terms have and continue to be used. In particular, the change of one word – 'education' to 'training' – can be interpreted as a significant transformation in ideology. Historically, the term 'initial teacher education' (ITE) was used by the Higher Education Institutions (HEIs) who planned and delivered the curriculum for pre-service teachers in faculties of education. However, as Stephens *et al.* (2004) discuss, the increased centralisation and prescription of ITT content since the 1990s has led to a significant shift around the notion of what teacher education and/or training is. McNamara *et al.* (2017) suggest that a clear shift in focus of the learning culture took place with the formal redesignation in 1994 of 'teacher education' as 'teacher training'. While initial teacher *education* indicates a 'learning' approach, initial teacher *training* implies a model that is practical in nature. The apparent move towards a practice-based approach, with a seemingly reduced focus on academic understanding, continues to be a source of tension for teacher educators (TE) and policy makers, many of whom see training as a predominantly craft-process. The expansion of school-led, employment-based and assessment-only ITT routes can be seen to support this latter perspective. The shift and diversification of ITT models has also resulted in the term 'pre-service' teachers or 'students' becoming outdated as many newer ITT routes include significant school-based time, sometimes associated with a salary and school contract (McNamara et al., 2017).

A BRIEF HISTORY OF THE DEVELOPMENT OF PROFESSIONAL TEACHING QUALIFICATIONS IN ENGLAND

The 1838, an 'on the job' training schools model was established as a solution that bridged the gap for school leavers prior to accessing 'proper' college teacher training, alongside alleviating the teacher recruitment shortage (Hagger *et al.*, 1995). However, the dangers of training in this 'mechanical' approach, in which 'pupil teachers' only learned the same skills, approaches and breadth of ideas as those demonstrated by the staff that they worked with, was seen as a limitation (Hagger *et al.*, 1995). It came to be acknowledged that, following the 'copying and replicating' phase, the college training phase provided opportunities for a broader and more effective professional engagement of future teachers. Interestingly, as recent political policy change has brought an increase in school-based training, which arguably thrusts classroom trainees quickly into teacher shadowing, the limitations seen in the 19th century are once again being raised.

Between the late 1960s and 2010, the university-led 1-year Post Graduate Certificate in Education (PGCE) and 3-/4-year Bachelor of Education (B.Ed) courses were the predominant ITT routes, largely delivered in university or college (HEI) settings with a significant focus upon the 'theory' of education, intermittently supported by short teaching placements in schools. The course content was decided by the HEI with schools having limited input. This 'complementary' partnership (see Figure 2.1) arguably failed to maximise the experience of teachers in practice as valuable contributors to the ITT process and practical application (Hagger *et al.*, 2015). HEIs were criticised for their 'ivory tower' approach to theory (Shaw, 1992) and were considered as somewhat detached from the daily reality of the classroom (Furlong *et al.*, 2000).

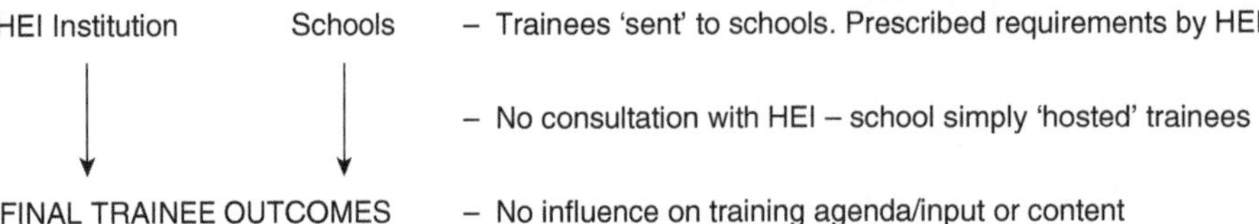

Figure 2.1 Complementary partnership historical model

The 1992 DES circular indicated a political commitment towards increasing the influence of schools and 'practical experience' in ITT. This came, in part, from feedback from new teachers (DES, HMI 81/87, 1992), indicating their perception of overly high levels of theoretical training and insufficient practical preparation for the role. The new 'collaborative' partnership models (see Figure 2.2) emerged and this was seen as a positive collaboration of both partner strengths. Taking this further, Kenneth Clarke, Secretary of State at the time, suggested that 80 per cent of ITT should be school-based (as cited in Furlong and Smith, 1996). This initiated a movement to greater roles for schools in ITT which has gained considerable momentum in the last 10 years.

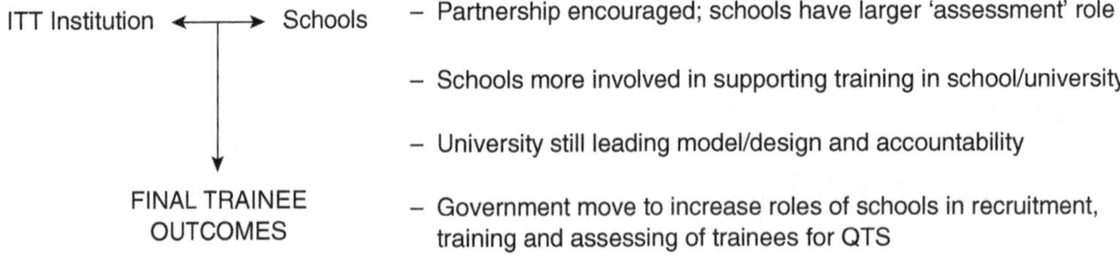

Figure 2.2 Collaborative partnership model

TEACHER TRAINING – WHAT DOES IT INVOLVE?

Teacher training is not a one-off process completed within a defined time frame, but rather a continuum of professional growth and development that spans an entire teaching career. An expectation that ITT will cover all that new teachers need to know and do is unrealistic.

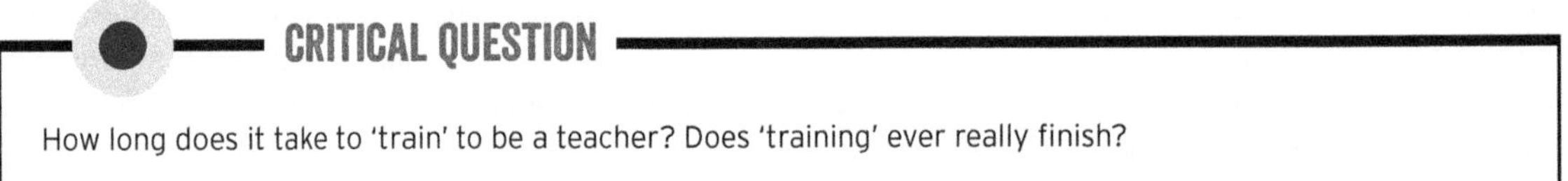

CRITICAL QUESTION

How long does it take to 'train' to be a teacher? Does 'training' ever really finish?

The Newly Qualified Teacher (NQT) period directly after the initial teacher training period is a key time to consolidate newly acquired skills, embed good practice and develop understanding of pedagogical approaches, and its importance is often overlooked. Teacher training is a career-long process involving three key stages: initial, induction (NQT) and continuing professional development (see Table 2.1). In today's climate of continual change and innovation, lifelong learning is a critical educational goal (Dunlop and Grabinger, 2008). The view that teachers are eternal learners is a useful principle to take into practice. Without the willingness to maintain an active level of professional reflection on new ideas and a regular evaluation of the effectiveness of one's own practice, there is a high risk that teachers will stagnate and miss opportunities to develop practice and enhance pupil learning. A continued engagement with learning should be part of professional development at all stages of a teaching career (Kramer, 2018). In 2007, the OCED concluded:

> *Initial education cannot provide teachers with the knowledge and skills necessary for a life-time of teaching ...*
>
> (OECD, as cited in Donaldson, 2010: 34)

This idea was later supported by the Carter Review (DfE, 2015), which suggested that structures were needed to ensure that NQTs were better supported in their induction year and beyond.

Table 2.1 The three general stages of teacher training

Stage of teacher training	Who provides this training/support?	What might this include?	Key issues
Initial	HEI; SD provider; SCITT; Teach First and employing school; employing school (post-grad apprenticeship) *See more detail in Table 2.2	• Evidence of trainee meeting Teachers' Standards (2013) • Delivery of ITT core content (2016) • Placements in at least two different settings • Minimum 120 days in school (except assessment only) • Access to a taught course • Academic assignments (for PGCE/PGDE awards)	• Variation in the interpretation and delivery of the core content for ITT document • Balancing practice in schools with opportunities to discuss/learn pedagogy and subject knowledge, particularly within SBR/employment-based routes • Salaried routes - no requirement for the trainee to be supernumerary - therefore, balancing the contractual expectations of being a staff member and needs as a training teacher can be challenging

(Continued)

Table 2.1 (Continued)

Stage of teacher training	Who provides this training/support?	What might this include?	Key issues
Induction or NQT period	Employing school along with the registered appropriate body (e.g. local authority)	• Induction/NQT period equivalent to 189 school days or 3 terms • No set time limit for starting/completing an induction period (England) • An induction mentor/ tutor should be assigned • A monitoring and support programme should be in place including guidance from a designated induction tutor; observation and feedback of teaching; regular professional reviews of progress and observations of effective practice • A 10% reduction in teaching timetable should be arranged, in addition to teacher planning, preparation and assessment (PPA) time • Formal assessment reports should be written by the mentor at the end of each assessment period • The final report supports the decision to recommendation of the successful completion of the induction period • CPD opportunities and training should be a feature of the NQT year	• Part-time teaching posts will take longer to complete the induction period • Variability in support and mentoring provided by employing schools • Short-term supply placements of less than one term, or equivalent, cannot count towards induction

Stage of teacher training	Who provides this training/support?	What might this include?	Key issues
Continuing professional development (CPD)	Employing school The individual teacher External agencies - local authorities, HEIs, schools and/ or private training companies	• Teacher performance management/ appraisal identifies areas of strength and development points (against Teachers' Standards) • Access to internal and external training courses • Development of additional responsibilities within school, e.g. subject coordinator, phase lead • Engagement with further educational or academic research and study, e.g. becoming an ITT mentor/ subject coordinator, further academic qualifications, research as a practitioner, developing specialisms	• School budgets can affect access • Workload and time can affect engagement • Funding can challenge longer term CPD opportunities

KEY READING

DfE (2016b) Induction for Newly Qualified Teachers:

www.gov.uk/government/uploads/system/uploads/attachment_data/file/580039/Statutory_Induction_Guidance_December_2016.pdf

WHAT CURRENTLY INFORMS ITT?

As mentioned earlier, HEIs historically assumed responsibility for the organisation and content of ITT programmes as the 'experts' in the field of teacher education. However, this autonomy could lead to a discrepancy between what was needed in schools and what HEIs were providing (Furlong *et al.*, 2010). In the late 1980s the political drive to create 'world-class schools' gained momentum, as did the prominence of centralised decisions about what to teach and how to teach it. This led, in 1992, to the introduction of a national framework of trainee teacher competences required for qualified teacher status. These are currently known as the Teachers' Standards (2013) and now present a series of competences for all teachers, irrespective of the length or stage of career. This is currently the key evidence base in the assessment of trainees prior to the recommendation of qualified teacher status (QTS), irrespective of the ITT route followed.

In 1998 the first National ITT Curriculum was introduced with a view to provide a consistent approach to ITT content, along with a mandatory NQT year induction period to confirm QTS. The most recent review of ITT provision was the Carter Review (DfE, 2015), which led to a revised core curriculum content document (DfE, 2016a). This current ITT framework includes government recommendations about the specific experiences, skills and knowledge that trainees should have, attached to each of eight Teachers' Standards, plus Part Two of the Standards relating to professional attributes and attitudes. This framework is to be interpreted and delivered by an ever-increasing number of ITT providers. The statutory school-based experience requirement for primary trainees, with the exception of QTS-only routes, was again increased in 2013, having seen a rise from 75 to 90 to a current minimum of 120 school-based days within 1-year courses, resulting in significant change in course structure and content. As the time in school has increased, so then the dynamics between teacher educations and school partners has had to adapt (Brown *et al.*, 2016). The requirement to pass the 'skills test' in literacy and numeracy prior to trainees embarking upon ITT courses remains in place for all routes.

KEY READING

The framework of core content for initial teacher training (ITT) (2016):

www.gov.uk/government/uploads/system/uploads/attachment_data/file/536890/Framework_Report_11_July_2016_Final.pdf

More details on the structure and content of the skills tests and changes from February 2018: http://sta.education.gov.uk/

CRITICAL QUESTION

What are the merits and limitations of having a defined core content for ITT?

THE ROUTES INTO PRIMARY TEACHING

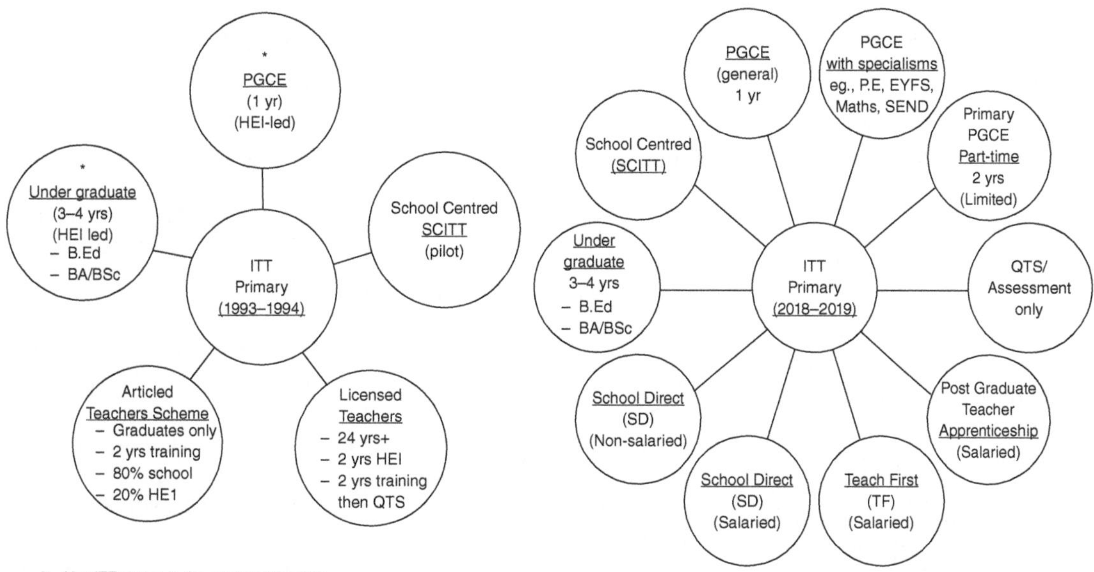

Figure 2.3 ITT routes into primary teaching (England)

KEY FEATURES OF EACH ITT ROUTE (ENGLAND)

Table 2.2 Overview of routes into primary teaching

Overview of Routes into Primary Teaching **(Based upon 2018-19 routes)**
General entry requirements for Primary ITT (based upon criteria for 2018-19 intake)
• All trainees must hold GSCE (or equivalent) in English, Maths and Science at grade C (grade 4) or higher • All entrants must pass the professional skills tests • PGCE trainees must have a degree in order to enrol on a PGCE/PGDE course • Individual ITT providers will set their own entry requirements for their programme. Provider websites will provide more details for applicants
General information regarding ITT routes (based upon criteria for 2018-19 intake)
• All completed routes result in the recommendation of Qualified Teacher Status (QTS) • A minimum of 120 days is spent in school for all routes (with the exception of Assessment Only) • All routes have to include experience in at least two schools, in contrasting key stages • Some routes result in a PGCE or PGDE award (this should be checked as some routes provide Master's-level credits, some do not)

(Continued)

Table 2.2 (Continued)

HEI/University-led PGCE	Primary PGCE with specialism (e.g. Maths, P.E., Early Years, Modern Languages)	School Centred Initial Teacher Training (SCITT)
• 1 year • Fees paid by trainee • Undergraduate degree required • Non-salaried • University-led training when not in school • Apply to HEI via UCAS • Taught course is organised by the university, utilising staff and school partner expertise • Academic assignments are completed as part of the PGCE qualification (some with/without Master credits attached)	• 1 year • Fees paid by trainee • Undergraduate degree required • Non-salaried • Can be university-led or SCITT-led course (Apply to relevant provider through UCAS) • Academic assignments are completed as part of the PGCE qualification • Additional time and expectations set for the specialist subject - teaching and assignments	• 1 year • Fees paid by trainee • Some SCITTs offer PGCE qualification (through an accrediting HEI), some offer assessment only qualification • Candidate applies directly to the SCITT via UCAS • Taught course and placement organisation is led by the SCITT • HEI provider supports and validates the academic aspects of the PGCE qualification (if offered)
School Direct (SD) (non-salaried)	**School Direct (salaried)**	**Teach First**
• 1 year • Fees paid by candidate • Undergraduate degree required • Non-salaried • Apply to the SD lead school via UCAS • SD lead school must have an accrediting provider (HEI/SCITT) • SD lead school organise all/some of the taught course (depending upon accrediting provider) • Academic assignments are completed as part of the PGCE qualification	• 1 year • Undergraduate degree required • Usually required to have 3 years' professional work experience • Employed during training and salary paid • Not required to be supernumerary • Apply to the SD lead school via UCAS • SD lead school must have an accrediting provider (HEI/SCITT) • SD lead school organise all/some of the taught course (depending upon accrediting provider) • Academic assignments are completed as part of the PGCE qualification	• 2 year • PGDE (Professional Graduate Diploma in Education) awarded after the 2nd year • Undergraduate degree required • Employed during training and salary paid • Not required to be supernumerary • Apply to Teach First • HEI provider supports and validates the academic aspect of the qualification • Teach First source main employing school • Second additional placement has to be organised by the trainee and school mentor (1st year) • Build up to an 80% teaching commitment • 2nd year - leadership development programme and NQT year

Postgraduate teacher apprenticeship	Undergraduate course with QTS (B.Ed, BA, BSc)	Assessment (QTS) only
• 1 year (new for 2018-19) • Employed during training and salary paid • Not required to be supernumerary • School-based training • Can be offered as assessment only or be accredited with a PGCE by an HEI partner • Apply to the apprenticeship provider directly via UCAS • ITT provider and school decide the structure of the apprenticeship • 20% off-the-job training to be delivered by an accredited ITT provider • Trainee is required to undertake an 'End point assessment' (EPA) in the final term • Transferral of this qualification to other countries is as yet unexplored	• 3 or 4 years • Fees paid by trainee • No previous degree required • Non-salaried • Apply to HEI provider via UCAS • HEI providers, with school partner input, deliver the taught course content • Combination of learning the principles of teaching and learning alongside regular practical school experience	• Variable time scale • Available to unqualified teachers, with a degree, who have taught in at least 2 schools/early years or further education settings and have experienced two consecutive age ranges • Can be offered by HEIs or SCITTs • Detailed evidence of Teachers' Standards being met is required • Assessed and accredited by an assessment-only provider • Transferral of this qualification to other countries may be required checking, due to lack of PGCE/academic award
Part-time course (limited)		
• 2 years • Can be offered by HEI-led or school-led courses • Can be offered in some cases as a salaried SD route • Applications to the HEI/SCITT provider via UCAS • Exact course structure and expectations should be checked with each provider		

CLASSROOM LINK

What does this mean for classroom practice?

What ITT will you need to prepare for:

- your first day in the classroom?
- your first placement?
- your first year in teaching?
- the years beyond your first year?

Consider what you need in terms of:

- subject knowledge;
- pedagogical knowledge (the theory, method and practice of teaching).

CRITICAL QUESTION

How will your professional training and education needs change over time?

HOW DO OTHER COUNTRIES TRAIN THEIR TEACHERS?

The Institute of Education (as cited by House of Commons Education Committee, 2012) highlighted that no other country in the world has training that is as school-based as England, making it worthwhile considering the rationale for this and to what extent this impacts upon teacher quality. To understand where ITT methodology in England sits in a broader sense, it is useful to consider the ITT structures in other countries.

While Singapore and Finland utilise a significant amount of practical classroom application, both ITT methodologies are firmly built upon highly academic and pedagogical knowledge foundations (Barber and Mourshed, 2007; Zuljan and Vogrinc, 2011). Singapore's only ITT provider advocates a *teach less, learn more* approach based on quality of experience rather than quantity (Lee, 2004 as cited in Low *et al.*, 2012: 65). In contrast, the ITT routes in England have moved in the opposite direction in recent years. The Education White Paper (2010) cited the teaching schools of Finnish ITT and outlined its commitment to develop 'training' or 'teaching schools' in line with this. This, however, lacked awareness of the distinctive approach used and the place of research in Finnish professional education (Hulse and Hulme, 2012).

The 'Bologna Process' refers to a process that continental European countries have been subject to since 1999. This was established to facilitate and improve the transparency and mobility of students and teachers, and for their qualifications across Europe to become less complex, more transparent and more 'readable' (Vogrnic and Krek, 2014). The process aimed to consider the qualifications, competences and skills that different European teacher education training offered and to generate an 'agreed' list of fundamental elements for effective ITT.

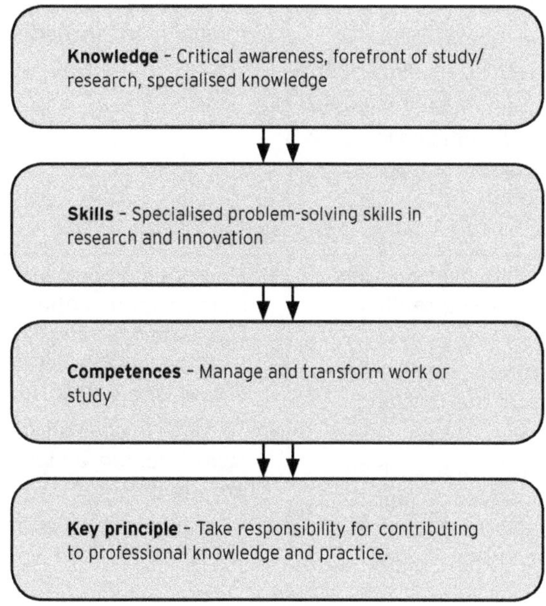

The key principles agreed included:

These widely agreed principles prompted change to balance these elements within ITT across Europe.

Table 2.3 Some features of ITT in the UK and beyond

Scotland	Republic of Ireland (RoI)
• All ITT is provided by 9 Scottish universities; there are currently no school-led training routes. • To teach in any Scottish state school, you must have a degree, and gain a Teaching Qualification (TQ), since 1984, by following a programme of Initial Teacher Education (ITE). • Teachers must register with the General Teaching Council for Scotland (GTCS). Routes: • Dominated by the 4-year B.Ed. degree and the 1-year PGDE.	• All ITT is provided by 6 Colleges of Education; there are currently no school-led training routes. • Applicants must satisfy the Irish Language requirement and a high standard of fluency is required in the Oral Irish test. • Teachers must register with the Teaching Council. Routes: • B.Ed degree OR

(Continued)

Table 2.3 (Continued)

Scotland	**Republic of Ireland (RoI)**
• Some development of the concurrent BA and BSc programmes in recent years. • Some limited expansion into the MA with Education and MSc with teaching qualification. • A move to phase out the traditional B.Ed degree and replace with degrees that combine in-depth academic study with professional studies and development is being explored.	• A minimum of a level 8 degree plus a Postgraduate Diploma in Education (Primary) - to qualify for second-level teaching.
Northern Ireland	**Wales**
• All ITT courses are provided by 4 universities or university colleges; there are currently no school-led training routes. • All HEI initial teacher education programmes must have accreditation from the Teaching Council. • All teachers must register with the Teaching Council and must have completed an induction period or completed the requirements of 'Droichead' – The Integrated Professional Induction Framework. Routes: • 4-year B.Ed undergraduate course • 1-year PGCE	• Most training programmes are university- or college-based, although there is the Welsh Graduate Teaching Programme (GTP), led by three regional training centres, and Teach First (TF) as alternative ITT routes. • To teach in a Welsh state school, you must have a degree, and gain QTS by following a programme of ITT. • All teachers in Wales are also required to register with the Education Workforce Council (EWC). Routes: • University-led PGCE or PGDE. • Undergraduate B.Ed offered alongside BA/BSc (more commonly for secondary) • The GTP (1 yr) – similar to School Direct (salaried) programmes in England, but managed and delivered by the three regional teacher training centres. • Teach First Leadership Development Programme – 2-year salaried 'on the job' programme leading to a (PGDE) qualification.
Finland	**Singapore**
• All ITT organised by 8 university providers; there are currently no school-led training routes. • In-service training each year is undertaken by all qualified teachers.	The National Institute of Education (NIE) is the sole teacher education institute. There are no school-led training routes at present. Before they enrol at NIE for their initial teacher education training, all successful candidates are required to complete a teaching period in schools as untrained teachers. The NIE provides all levels of teacher education, ranging from initial teacher preparation, to graduate and in-service programmes.

Scotland	Republic of Ireland (RoI)
Routes: • Every teacher is required to hold a Master's degree (except in vocational education - Master's or Bachelor's) • Concurrent Master's with pedagogical training built into the Master's OR • Consecutive - pedagogical training built in after the Master's • Every student teacher participates in a teaching practice at a 'university teacher training school'. The teacher training schools, which belong to the universities' faculties of education, are central in the training of prospective teachers.	Routes: • Bachelor of Arts (Education)/Bachelor of Science (Education)/Bachelor of Education • Diploma programmes • Postgraduate Diploma in Education programmes BA (Education) • BSc (Education)

How does teacher training in England compare to the training of teachers in other countries?

ITT – THE VARIETY, DEBATES AND COMPLEXITY

The move to expand school-led, school-based routes has significantly altered the landscape of ITT over the last decade. Most HEIs valued the cautious yet valid moves to explicitly link theory with more quality practical application (Furlong *et al.*, 1988) in addressing the limitations of previous didactic ITT models (Pollard, 2014). However, the rapid growth of school-led training routes has led to much discussion about the priorities within ITT and concern about the variation in the quality of this provision that naturally occurs with an expanding field of providers (Brown *et al.*, 2016). Teacher educators argue that in addition to this, the increasingly centralised influences on education generally has already led to schools expecting trainees to be able to apply national frameworks, policies and strategies, leaving little room for innovation and development of professional autonomy (Hulse and Hulme, 2012). Many HEI teacher educators question how opportunities for developing an intellectual rigour of pedagogy can fit in to the practically intense daily classroom experience of some approaches (Furlong *et al.*, 2000; Brown *et al.*, 2016). Furthermore, in meeting a range of Ofsted and quality assurance measures, HEIs work with the clear tension between their retained responsibilities for the accountability of ITT effectiveness and delegated delivery of school-based training. Moss (as cited in House of Commons Education Committee, 2012) highlights the significant difference between 'increased involvement' of schools and 'taking over responsibility' for professional training, suggesting that the latter may not always represent the aspiration or capacity of school partners who themselves have very demanding daily roles.

SCHOOL DIRECT AND SCITT

School Direct (SD) was introduced in 2012 as a new school-based, school-led training route with the recommendation of QTS to be accredited by HEIs. An internal report from the House of Commons Education Committee (2012: 3) concluded 'a partnership between school and university is likely to provide the highest quality ITE ... including significant school experience, but also theoretical and research elements'.

In launching the SD programme, the government were emulating the already established Teach First (TF) programme, which has claimed to train teachers who have the greatest impact in deprived urban areas (Teach First, 2018). However, with figures suggesting that only approximately 50 per cent of TF participants remain in classrooms by their 5th year, the long-term investment of costs, effectiveness and impact of this ITT model remains unclear (Nuffield Foundation, 2016).

Professionals in schools delivering ITT, through SCITT or SD routes, are dedicated to supporting and developing the profession and improving educational outcomes. Nonetheless, the nature of local market conditions has created a competitive rather than collaborative ITT landscape. As the number of ITT providers grows, then so arguably does the variability in quality delivered (McNamara *et al.*, 2017). Teacher educators acknowledge the need to continually update ITT practice through improved partnerships with aspiring, forward-thinking schools, many of which have made a successful transition towards being teacher educators. However, as this number grows, so does the concern that the 'practical' insight of practitioners and the influence of local pedagogies of 'what works here' may not be sufficiently rigorous to underpin practice with the theoretical knowledge deemed necessary for teachers to become skilled lifelong, reflective practitioners (Furlong and Smith, 1996; Walker Tileston, 2004).

A REVIEW OF TEACHER TRAINING IN SCOTLAND

A review of the Scottish Education System was published around the time of the DfE White Paper (2010), but with rather different conclusions.

www.gov.scot/Resource/Doc/337626/0110852.pdf

The Donaldson Report (2010) findings suggested that within the most successful international systems there is not a focus on 'prescription', but on investing time in developing reflective, enquiring professionals who can engage with the complexities of education and lead change. There is a requirement for SD programmes to engage with elements of academic enquiry and reflection, and many SD-led schools provide comprehensive provision around this, but it routinely goes unmentioned in the 'on the job' promotion profile. This has led to many misinformed philosophies of what is important and expected in ITT in comparison to the reality.

Donaldson (2010) acknowledged the potential of an, as yet unestablished, school-based route in Scotland to strengthen the practical application element of ITT, but cautioned that 'simply advocating more time in the classroom ... is not the answer to creating better teachers' (p. 4). Additionally, Donaldson (2010) stressed the need for sufficient academic rigour as a prerequisite for the development of such routes, echoing Hoyle and John's (1995) summary of reflection, autonomy, knowledge and responsibility for development as essentials of being in a profession.

CASE STUDY

Trainee perceptions of a SD route

End-of-course evaluations from a cohort of SD trainees indicated that their expectations of the PGCE training had shifted during the course. This study aimed to understand pre-course influences on perceptions and expectations in order to improve the course awareness of future SD trainees.

The focus group - 44 SD PGCE trainees.

Research question

'Do the initial expectations of primary SD trainees meet the reality of their experiences?'

Methodology

1. Initial survey - to gather trainee expectations and perceived advantages of this route (all trainees).
2. Mid-point survey - to ascertain the extent to which initial expectations had/had not been realised (all trainees).
3. Focus group interview - to discuss in detail any changes in expectations over the programme (8 trainees).

Initial questionnaire

Five main categories emerged from the initial survey investigating expectations and perceived positives of this training route (see Table 2.4), the most prominent response being around 'practice-based' learning. Trainees used terms such as 'on the job', 'practical' and 'hands on', phrases in line with the 'Get into Teaching' website (available at: https://getintoteaching.education.gov.uk) and media terminology. Most SD trainees expected a 'less academic, more practical' training, deeming this a key advantage. Other advantages included the close proximity to placement schools, being able to teach from day one and potential job prospects, again mirroring promotional materials. Trainees' perception of the university role was to support 'academic' elements such as assignments, general support and troubleshooting. There was very little mention of influencing classroom practice, approaches and pedagogy, again mirroring the recent portrayal of HEIs.

(Continued)

(Continued)

Table 2.4

Responses to questionnaire 1 were grouped according to the following categories Following axial coding process, (Glaser and Strauss, 1967)
Practice-based learning
Employability
Mentoring and support
Manageability and personal
Academic and course content

Key outcomes emerging over the course of the study:

- Trainees concluded that spending more time in the group of schools was advantageous and a very positive outcome of this route, although the amount of classroom-based time was more comparable to HEI-led PGCE trainees than anticipated.
- 'Teaching from day one' had not been the reality that some trainees expected as they had viewed themselves as 'covering' classes. Interestingly, latter comments suggested that they would have not felt prepared or skilled to do this in reality.
- Most trainees agreed that the relationships with schools and staff were developed and seeing practitioners in daily practice was helpful.
- Most trainees had not yet gained teaching posts from their partner schools.
- Trainees' initial expectations of learning by 'hands on' and practical replication was no longer deemed adequate sole preparation for teaching. Trainees reported gaining a lot from observing theory in practice regularly, but were clear that without theory input, they would have felt less confident in their practice. *It is hard to judge whether I've got more from the hands on approach as university tutors are excellent and provide great subject and pedagogical knowledge that has been invaluable* (trainee comment).
- All trainees reported unexpected benefit in their learning from the university input, reporting that working with experts in the field provided opportunities to implement/share up-to-date research and approaches with current school practitioners.
- Variability in the quality and experience of SD school-led training was identified by several groups as a key issue.
- When school-led training was rated as outstanding by trainees, it was due to the balance of pedagogy, research, subject knowledge and practical application.
- When school-led training was rated as poor by trainees, it was when it involved classroom observation alone.
- Trainees suggested the value of both quality school-led sessions and the expertise from the university as an effective, rounded collaboration for their ITT.

Conclusions

- The marketing of school-led ITT routes and terminology is misleading and gives trainees a narrow view of the skills and knowledge required to become an effective teacher.
- The quality of school-led training directly influences trainee confidence and readiness for the profession. This was inconsistent.
- Trainee understanding of what they need from ITT in order to make them an effective practitioner broadens over time as they gain a balance of good training and experiences across pedagogy, subject knowledge and practical application areas.

Actions

- The university invested significant time in working with all SD partners to train and share expertise to support them to move into the role of teacher educators.
- Information materials about the course structure, evidence-informed features of effective ITT and partnership roles were distributed to all SD applicants at interview stage.
- SD trainee induction days supported the transition to professional learner and reflective practitioner.

CRITICAL QUESTION

Reflecting upon the case study, did any of the findings surprise you?

CURRENT AND FUTURE CHALLENGES FOR ITT

Despite policy makers expressing the need to improve teacher quality and international standing through 'learning lessons of other countries' success' (DfE, 2010: 3), research findings, established good practice and evidence from countries that outperform England do not appear to inform policy change within ITT (Vogrinc and Krek, 2014). International training perspectives promote teacher education as a lifelong experience, not a 'quick fix' solution to get classrooms staffed (Vogrinc and Krek, 2014), nor a process that simply generates a 'technicians' toolkit' to get through the first two years (Moss, as cited in House of Commons Education Committee, 2012). However, media promotion of newer ITT routes does not seem to promote a mixed academic/practical approach, even if that is what SD providers actually deliver, leading to a narrow understanding of the complex role of teachers by many entering the profession. Irrespective of the teacher training route, the seeming continued government reduction of the value of educational theory, research and reflection is regarded by Pollard (2014) and many ITT providers to be putting the critical understanding of the teaching and learning process in danger (Hanushek and Woessmann, 2015). Thiessen (2000) agrees, suggesting that the increase of employment-based routes risks presenting the profession as a simple 'paint by numbers' approach based upon gathering classroom tips rather than skilling new teachers to go well beyond re-creating the best of current or past practice (Donaldson, 2010). Hulse and Hulme (2012: 315) summarise the challenged face by all current ITT providers:

> *The challenge for initial teacher education programmes, then, is to prepare beginning teachers for a working environment dominated by centralised initiatives, whilst encouraging critical reflection and nurturing a positive professional identity.*

WHAT REALLY MATTERS?

What should perhaps be at the centre of teacher training agendas is impact on teacher quality. A collective partnership of shared expertise across all routes to ensure the training and retention of highly skilled, adaptable practitioners who can impact positively upon future generations will support the acquisition of the aim of creating world-class schools.

> *the foundations of successful education lie in the quality of teachers and their leadership. High quality people achieve high quality outcomes for children.*
>
> (Donaldson, 2010: 2)

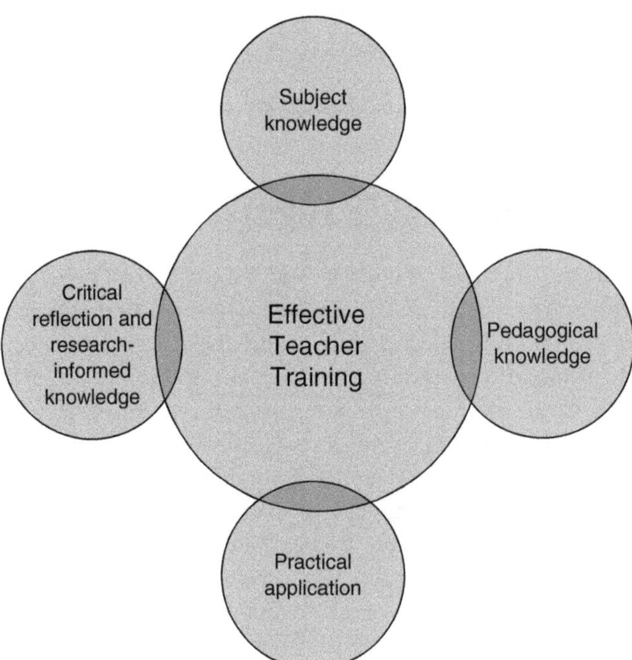

Figure 2.4 Effective teacher training

CRITICAL QUESTION

What do you think you need from your ITT? How have your thoughts and perceptions altered after reading this chapter?

CHAPTER SUMMARY

It is clear that there is no one single response to the debate about what effective teacher training looks like. The pendulum of methodology has swung considerably from HEI dominant to school based and school led. The agendas and rationale behind ITT reform continue to divide opinion and generate much discussion. While most would agree that there is highly effective ITT practice being delivered through newer ITT routes, the emerging variability as a result of growing numbers of providers remains a challenge.

ASSIGNMENTS

If you are writing an ITT assignment on initial teacher training or the issues around teaching as a profession today, it will be useful for you to think through the following:

1. What are the key issues affecting the success of the teaching profession currently? What are the current areas of debate specifically around ITT? What are the influences in this area?
2. What are the merits and challenges around each different ITT route in England? What is your position on this and why?
3. How do ITT routes in other countries compare to ITT routes in England? What can we learn from looking at other ITT routes around the world? Can you find examples that can support your argument?
4. What do you consider are the key features and priorities for ITT for trainee teachers? What evidence is there to support or challenge your priorities?

Below are some useful texts to read and reference if writing an assignment on initial teacher training or factors influencing the teaching profession. These offer some contrasting opinions and views from which to consider the key arguments, evidence and debates.

1. Policy and research evidence in the 'reform' of primary initial teacher education in England

   Olwen McNamara, Jean Murray and Rebecca Phillips

   A report for the Cambridge Primary Review Trust

   February 2017

   ISBN: 978-0-9931033-2-2

(Continued)

(Continued)

2. The beginnings of school led teacher training: New challenges for university teacher education

   Professor Tony Brown, Dr Harriet Rowley and Kim Smith

   Manchester Metropolitan University

   2015

   www.esri.mmu.ac.uk/resgroups/schooldirect.pdf

3. Carter Review of Initial Teacher Training (ITT)

   Sir Andrew Carter OBE

   The Department for Education

   January 2015

   www.gov.uk/government/uploads/system/uploads/attachment_data/file/399957/Carter_Review.pdf

4. Educational Excellence Everywhere; Government White Paper

   The Department for Education

   2016

   www.gov.uk/government/uploads/system/uploads/attachment_data/file/508447/Educational_Excellence_Everywhere.pdf

REFERENCES

Barber, M. and Mourshed, M. (2007) *How the World's Best-performing Schools Systems Come out on Top*. USA: McKinsey & Company.

Brown, T., Rowley, H. and Kim, S. (2016) *The Beginnings of School-Led Teacher Training: New challenges for university teacher education*. Manchester: Manchester Metropolitan University e-space.

DES (1992) *Curriculum Organisation and Classroom Practice in Primary Schools: A discussion paper* London: HMSO.

Department for Education/Welsh Office (1992) *Circular 9/92 Initial Teacher Training (Secondary Phase)*. London: Crown Copyright.

Department for Education (DfE) (2010) *The Importance of Teaching – The Schools White Paper*. London: Stationery Office.

DfE (2011) *Teachers' Standards Guidance for School Leaders, School Staff and Governing Bodies*. London: Crown Copyright.

DfE (2015) *Carter Review of Initial Teacher Training (ITT)*. London: Crown Copyright.

DfE (2016a) A *Framework of Core Content for Initial Teacher Training (ITT)*. London: Crown Copyright.

DfE (2016b) *Induction for Newly Qualified Teachers (England). Statutory guidance for appropriate bodies, headteachers, school staff and governing bodies*. London: Crown Copyright.

DfE (2018) *Initial Teacher Training Allocations: Academic year 2017 to 2018*. Available at: www.gov.uk/government/statistics/initial-teacher-training-allocations-academic-year-2017-to-2018 (accessed 26/03/18).

Donaldson, G. (2010) *Teaching Scotland's Future – A report of a review of teacher education in Scotland*. Scotland: Crown Copyright.

Dunlop, J. and Grabinger, S. (2008) Preparing students for lifelong learning: A review of instructional features and teaching methodologies. *Performance Improvement Quarterly*, 16(2): 6–25.

Furlong, V. (1988) *Initial Teacher Training and the Role of the School*. Virginia: Open University Press.

Furlong, J. and Smith, R. (1996) *The Role of Higher Education in Initial Teacher Training*. London: Kogan Page.

Furlong, J., Whitty, G., Whiting, C., Miles, S. and Barton, L. (2000) *Teacher education in transition: Re-forming professionalism*. Maidenhead: McGraw Hill.

Getintoteaching.education.gov.uk. (2018) *Get Into Teaching – Your future, their future*. Available at: https://getintoteaching.education.gov.uk/ (accessed 22/03/18).

Glaser, B. and Strauss, A. (1967) *The Discovery of Grounded Theory: Strategies for qualitative research*. Chicago: Aldine Publishing Company.

Hagger, H., Burn, K. and McIntyre, D. (1995) *The School Mentor Handbook: Essential skills and strategies for working with student teachers*. London: Routledge

Hagger, H., Burn K., Mutton T. and Menter, I. (2015) *Beginning Teachers' Learning: Making experience count*. St Albans: Critical Publishing.

Hanushek, E., Schwerdt G., Wiederhold, S. and Woessmann, L. (2015) Returns to skills around the world: Evidence from PIAAC, *European Economic Review*, 73: 103–30.

House of Commons Education Committee (2012) *Great Teachers: Attracting, training and retaining the best: Government response to the Committee's Ninth Report of Session 2010–12*. London: Stationery Office. Available at: https://publications.parliament.uk/pa/cm201213/cmselect/cmeduc/524/524.pdf (accessed 02/03/18).

House of Commons Library Briefing Paper (2016) Roberts, N. and Foster, D. *Initial Teacher Training in England*. London: Parliament Press.

Hoyle, E. and John, P. (1995) *Professional knowledge and professional practice*. London: Cassell.

Hulse, B. and Hulme, R. (2012) Engaging with research through practitioner enquiry: The perceptions of beginning teachers on a postgraduate initial teacher education programme. *Educational Action Research*, 20(2): 313–29.

Kramer, M. (2018) Promoting teachers' agency: Reflective practice as transformative disposition. *Reflective Practice*, 1–14.

Low, E., Taylor, P. and Ng, P. (2012) Towards evidence-based initial teacher education in Singapore: A review of current literature. *Australian Journal of Teacher Education*, 37(5): 65–77.

McNamara, O., Murray, J. and Phillips, R. (2017) *Policy and Research Evidence in the 'Reform' of Primary Initial Teacher Education in England*. York: Cambridge Primary Review Trust.

Nuffield Foundation (2016) *The Longer-Term Costs and Benefits of Different Initial Teacher Training Routes. IFS Report 118*. (online). London: The Institute for Fiscal Studies. Available at: www.ifs.org.uk/uploads/publications/comms/R118.pdf (accessed 27/03/18).

Pollard, A. (2014) *Reflective Teaching in Schools*. London: Bloomsbury.

Shaw, R. (1992) School-based training: the view from the schools. *Cambridge Journal of Education* 22(3): 363–75.

Stephens, P., Egil Tønnessen, F. and Kyriacou, C. (2004) Teacher training and teacher education in England and Norway: A comparative study of policy goals. *Comparative Education*, 40(1): 109–30.

Teachfirst.org.uk. (2018) *Teach First Impact Report – Our work and its impact*. Available at: www.teachfirst.org.uk/sites/default/files/2017-09/teach_first_impact_report.pdf (accessed 22/03/18).

Thiessen, D. (2000) A skillful start to a teaching career: A matter of developing impactful behaviors, reflective practices, or professional knowledge? *International Journal of Educational Research*, 33(5): 515–37.

Vogrnic, J. and Krek, J. (2014). *Overview of EU Practices in Pre-service Teacher Education – International comparison modernising teacher education*. Ljubljana: University of Ljubljana.

Walker Tileston, D. (2004) *What Every Teacher Should Know*. London: SAGE Publishing.

Zuljan, M. and Vogrinc, M. (eds) (2011) *European Dimensions of Teacher Education: Similarities and difference*. Ljubljana: University of Ljubljana.

3

WHAT ARE THE REALITIES OF BEING A TEACHER IN THE UK TODAY?

Janet Oosthuysen is Course Leader for the BA in Primary Education (with QTS) at Bradford College. Her research interests include critical thinking for child and adult learners, and philosophy for children.

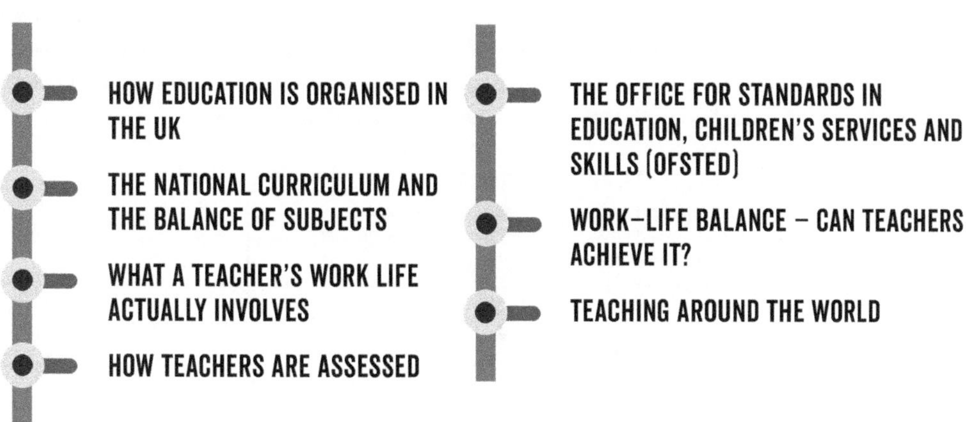

KEY WORDS

- Academies
- Accountability
- Assessment
- Faith schools
- Local education authorities (LEA)
- National Curriculum
- Ofsted
- Standardised Assessment tests (SATs)
- Teaching unions
- Work-life balance

INTRODUCTION

In this chapter, we will explore the different aspects of being a teacher in the UK today. We begin by looking at different school systems currently prevailing in England and Wales, and move on to looking at the National Curriculum, a teacher's roles and responsibilities, and how they are assessed. We will also look at other people a teacher has to work with, and briefly, at safeguarding responsibilities. We examine support for teachers, including unions, and how to maintain a good work–life balance. Finally, we compare a selection of countries' teacher training requirements to see how different they are from England and Wales.

HOW IS EDUCATION ORGANISED IN THE UK?

The education system in England and Wales has undergone several periods of transformational change. The 1944 Education Act introduced the tripartite system of *grammar schools, technical colleges* and *secondary moderns*, parts of which system are still in operation in some areas of the UK today. It was based around the 11+ examination, so-called as it was taken at the age of 11 in the final year of primary school, and it determined which secondary school you would go to. Some educationalists want to return to this system.

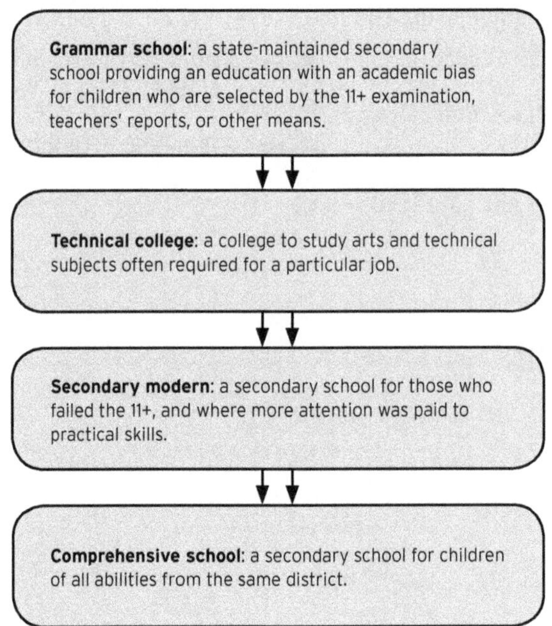

The next big change in the organisation of educational establishments was the introduction of *comprehensive schools* in 1965. This system was not based on selection, but on geographical area. Often it meant that grammar and secondary moderns were put together. Margaret Thatcher stopped this amalgamation being compulsory in 1970, but most schools had changed by then. This does, however, explain the continued existence of the two conflicting and apparently incompatible systems, side by side, in some areas of the country.

CRITICAL QUESTION

What has been the effect of parental choice on primary schools in the UK? Do you agree with it?

In all the cases above, primary schools functioned as what were called 'feeder schools'. A cluster of primary schools would 'feed' the local secondary school. Going to a particular primary school then would mean you knew which secondary school you would go to. Thatcher changed this by allowing 'parental choice' in the 1988 Education Act, meaning that parents could now choose a primary school from outside their area. This continues to the present day.

The next big change began in 2000, with the introduction of *academies*. Up till then, the country had been divided into local education authorities (LEAs) based on local government areas, and the LEAs had been run by local councils. The academy structure took control of these schools away from the LEAs and made them directly responsible to government, from where they received some of their funding.

Academies: state-maintained but independently run schools in England set up with the help of outside sponsors.

Free schools: are part of the academisation process, and can be set up by faith groups, parents and education charities by an application to the Department of Education.

CRITICAL QUESTION

How has the academisation of primary schools affected the education system?

Academies are self-governing and may get extra support from private or corporate sponsors. Some academies are part of academy chains or multi-academy trusts (MATs) where numbers of academies are run by the same trust. At present, the academisation of the education system at both primary and secondary level is continuing, although forced academisation only happens currently if a school is graded 4, or fail.

None of the systems that have been tried, and continue to be tried by central government, are wholly supported across a wide range of thinking, and all have flaws. Different political viewpoints are worth investigating to see the variety of opinions about them.

WHAT IS THE NATIONAL CURRICULUM?

We are establishing a national curriculum for basic subjects. It is vital that children master essential skills: reading, writing, spelling, grammar, arithmetic; and that they understand basic science and technology. And for good teachers this will provide a foundation on which they can build with their own creative skill and professionalism.

(Margaret Thatcher, 1987)

CRITICAL QUESTION

'Instead of a national curriculum for education, what is really needed is an individual curriculum for every child.' Do you agree?

Until the introduction of the National Curriculum in 1988, teachers in England and Wales had a great deal of autonomy over which subjects they taught, and how they taught them. The National Curriculum changed that. For the first time, teachers in England and Wales had to follow a set of prescribed subjects, detailed down to individual targets and levels. It saw the introduction of core and foundation subjects – core being English, maths and science, and foundation being everything else – history, geography, music, art, design technology, PE and modern foreign languages with Religious Education still an anomaly, as it is not on the National Curriculum but still a legal obligation. All state schools are expected to follow the National Curriculum, although academies, faith schools and free schools are exempt. They are, however, expected to follow a broad and balanced curriculum.

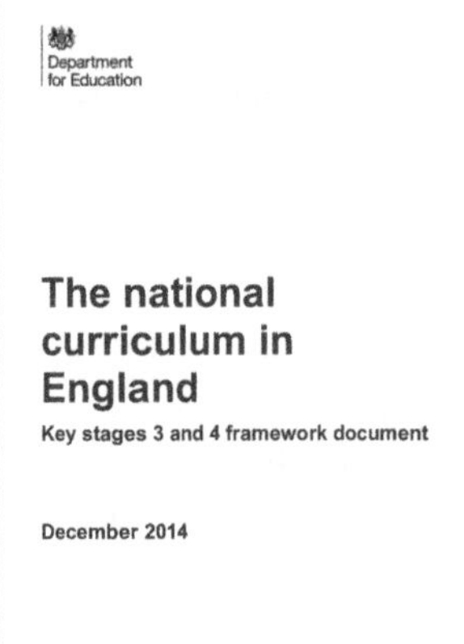

Department for Education

The national curriculum in England

Key stages 3 and 4 framework document

December 2014

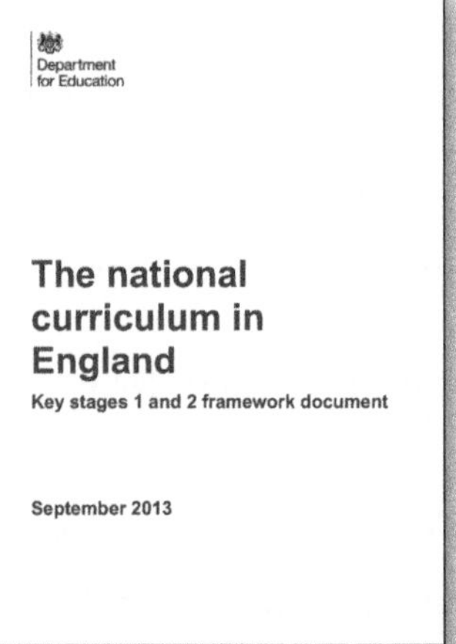

Department for Education

The national curriculum in England

Key stages 1 and 2 framework document

September 2013

Figure 3.1 Department for Education documents

The beginning of the National Curriculum document states:

> *Every state-funded school must offer a curriculum which is balanced and broadly based, and which promotes the spiritual, moral, cultural, mental and physical development of pupils at the school and of society, and prepares pupils at the school for the opportunities, responsibilities and experiences of later life.*
>
> (DfE, Statutory guidance, 2014)

This is a clear statement of intent for the National Curriculum's implementation. The breadth of the curriculum is meant to prepare students for their life and work after school, but also to make them into model citizens. Student teachers today are trained to be aware of spiritual, moral, social and cultural aspects of learning (SMSC), and to make sure that their teaching reflects this.

KEY READING

Statutory guidance: National Curriculum in England: primary curriculum. DfE, updated 2015.

This is the full National Curriculum in detail.

www.gov.uk/government/collections/national-curriculum

Independent Review of the Primary Curriculum: Final Report – Jim Rose, 2008 (often called the Rose Report).

Now 10 years old, the Rose Report is a good background to all the different aspects of a primary school.

www.educationengland.org.uk/documents/pdfs/2009-IRPC-final-report.pdf

The National Curriculum divides the primary school into 3 stages: Early Years and Foundation Stage (EYFS), which is nursery and Reception classes, Key Stage 1 (KS1), which is Year 1 and Year 2, and Key Stage 2 (KS2), which is Years 3-6. KS2 is often divided into upper and lower. Originally, at the end of every key stage there were standardised assessment tests, or SATs, that were nationally administered. These aimed to give a national picture of attainment. At the same time, the introduction of a league table of schools, based on their SATs results, allowed for the comparison of schools in the same area, and indeed nationwide. These league tables have now been abolished. Currently, the government, responding to parental pressure, has promised to remove KS1 SATs by 2022, but other SATs remain.

CRITICAL QUESTION

Do you agree that English, maths and science are more important than other subjects on the curriculum?

THE BALANCE OF SUBJECTS IN THE NATIONAL CURRICULUM

There is no doubt that the primary school curriculum is usually skewed towards the core subjects, with even science sometimes taking a back seat. As a result, most teacher training will give a good grounding in these subjects. It must be said, though, that the National Curriculum states, as does most research on the subject, that a broad and balanced curriculum is necessary for children to become fully rounded individuals, and that it also is the most effective way to raise standards.

As a result, the foundation subjects play a crucial role in the education of the child. The Chief Inspector of the Office for Standards in Education, Children's Services and Skills (Ofsted), has recently complained about the constricted curriculum, something that she says schools are offering to children. By this, she means that schools are failing to deliver the foundation subjects in full, and this is being looked at increasingly during an Ofsted inspection.

Two subjects that are not included in the National Curriculum are Religious Education (RE) and Personal, Social, Health and Economic education (PSHE). RE is a legal requirement in schools, and the syllabus is worked out locally, so that it can be responsive to the religions represented in an individual area. PSHE is fitted into the curriculum as and when there is time – different schools will prioritise it differently. There are moves to make both part of the National Curriculum, to give them the same status as other subjects, but at present only Relationship and Sex Education (RSE), a part of PSHE, is.

WHAT DOES A TEACHER'S WORK LIFE ACTUALLY INVOLVE?

Almost all primary schools have teaching hours from 9 a.m. to 3 p.m., although individual schools vary. This variation is allowable so long as they are open for 190 days over the school year. Academies and free schools can set their own hours. There is, however, an obvious expectation that teachers are in before 9 a.m. and stay after 3 p.m. Student teachers are usually asked to be in school between 8 a.m. and 5 p.m.

Most teachers will divide their work between pupil-facing work and paperwork. The two are obviously linked, the paperwork generally informing the teaching. The National Curriculum documents inform the content of the planning, with each year and subject having its own objective. Usually in a school, planning is done in teams, and broad themes are set for the individual class teacher to follow. If the school has two or more classes in every year (two form entry), the teachers usually work together in planning and other support. This is the first of many sets of relationships for a teacher to negotiate.

THE PEOPLE IN A TEACHER'S DAY

> *Behind every great teacher, is a great teaching assistant.*
>
> (Anon.)

It can seem sometimes that a teacher is autonomous, in sole charge of their classroom, but in reality there are many different sets of people involved in their working life. First, with them in the classroom, there are teaching assistants (TAs) who support the learning in class. Sometimes these are employed to look after particular children with special needs, but often they are general support staff that a teacher must include in any planning. While schools vary in the way in which they use TAs, the class teacher usually determines their daily tasks.

KEY READING

Making the best use of teaching assistants - Education Endowment Foundation, 2016.

Part of the teachers' toolkit series, the EEF document explains how best to use TAs, though it is a website worth browsing thoroughly.

https://educationendowmentfoundation.org.uk/public/files/Publications/Campaigns/TA_Guidance_Report_MakingBestUseOfTeachingAssisstants-Printable.pdf

Each school will also have staff responsible for different areas of the curriculum – subject leads and special educational needs coordinators (SENCOs). These staff members are responsible for the work in their specialist areas and will inform the class teacher of school policy, new developments and sometimes of new ways of working. Some schools have leads for different areas – creative curriculum leads, for example, who inform the class teacher among other things, of different school-wide events. Some schools still have home–school liaison teachers, part of whose job is to involve parents in the school life of their children.

At the top of the school hierarchy is the head teacher and, depending on the size of the school, deputy heads too. These form the senior management team (SMT), and determine the ethos and policies of the school, alongside the governing body. In a normal day, an ordinary class teacher will not be involved with the governors, but the head teacher is usually in school every day. Academies' and free schools' daily management will be broadly similar but will also have the involvement of sponsors, faith groups or special interest groups depending on the make-up of the academy.

Alongside these school-based staff, the individual class teacher has a role with the parents of the children in their class. It is a cliché to say that parents are the child's first teacher, but it is also very true, and research shows that involving parents in school work of all different kinds, not just in the home, improves learning outcomes. Meeting and greeting, sending regular communications home and building relationships is, therefore, a crucial part of a teacher's role. Parents can also play an important role within the class, listening to children read or helping on school trips, for example. It is worthwhile mentioning too that this liaison also may include any foster parents, social workers working with families and other support workers.

SAFEGUARDING

This brings the discussion on to safeguarding. A crucial part of a teacher's role is safeguarding the children in their care. This is discussed more fully in the following chapters, but it is a vitally important part of the teacher's core tasks. Usually, the teacher will refer any children seemingly at risk to the safeguarding lead in school – the Designated Safeguarding Lead (DSL) – so the initial job a teacher has to do is to make sure they know who that is, and also what the safeguarding policy in the school is.

BEHAVIOUR MANAGEMENT

INTRINSIC VS. EXTRINSIC MOTIVATION

Primary schools are very good at extrinsic motivation – external rewards such as points or stars that add up to bigger rewards and attempt to modify behaviour. Intrinsic motivation, which is, for example, one of the teaching standards – 4b. a love of learning – is more difficult, but research shows, longer lasting.

CRITICAL QUESTION

Do you think intrinsic or extrinsic motivation is best for behaviour management?

Aside from any teaching and planning, one of the aspects of teaching that often causes concern, particularly for the new teacher, is behaviour management. This can be part of the pressure that builds on teachers on top of paperwork and teaching. Class sizes are usually no more than 30 pupils, although budgetary constraints mean that this can be increased. A total of 30:1 seems like a daunting ratio for the new teacher and something like a con trick that the children will rumble. There has been a lot of research into behaviour management, and several reports, particularly in recent years the Bennett Report (2017), explaining how best to achieve it. It may be some comfort to know that every teacher has gone through this, and most manage. All teacher training will include behaviour management and there are many sources of advice – see the end of the chapter for some pointers.

KEY READING

Creating a Culture: How school leaders can optimise behaviour - Tom Bennett, DfE, 2017.

This is the most up-to-date report on behaviour in British schools. It also offers a lot of advice.

https://assets.publishing.service.gov.uk/government/uploads/system/uploads/attachment_data/file/602487/Tom_Bennett_Independent_Review_of_Behaviour_in_Schools.pdf

Above all, the teams that you work in will be more than willing to offer advice. Children are not, however much they may seem to be, all-knowing monsters, and always respond to humour and clear boundaries. Individual schools usually have policies to follow on praise and rewards, which also help, and will also have policies for punishment too. All these will help with your behaviour management. The main thing to remember is to ask for help and guidance. Never allow it to become a huge problem before you approach others.

HOW ARE TEACHERS ASSESSED?

Student teachers are assessed by both their training institution and the school they train in, and are assessed against the Teachers' Standards, which are in two parts, the first about teaching in the classroom, the second about personal and professional conduct. There are eight standards in Part One, all subdivided into micro standards, and they address every aspect of life inside the classroom. *You can see the full set of standards in the Appendices at the end of this book.* Remember that these are what you will be able to do when you are trained – they can look daunting, but the purpose of your training is to get you to this standard.

Part Two of the standards make interesting reading. It is the part of a teacher's job that all teachers understand is necessary, but one that those outside the teaching profession rarely acknowledge, unless the standards are broken for any reason. A recent introduction is the standard on British values, a present government initiative. British values consist of democracy, the rule of law, individual liberty and mutual respect, and tolerance of those with different faiths and beliefs. These need to be implicitly and explicitly taught in lessons and will form a part of your planning.

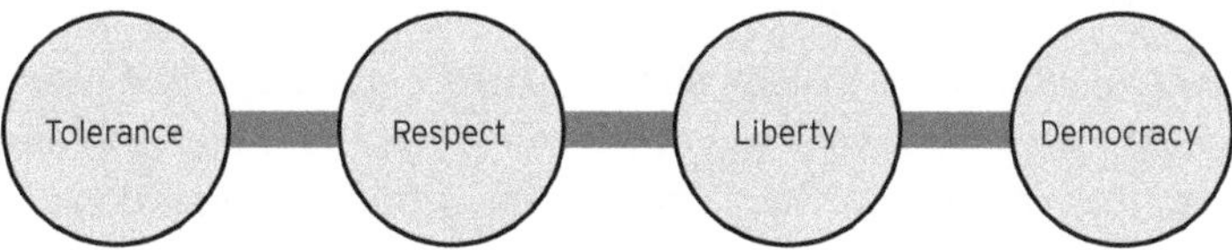

Contentious in some communities, Ofsted incorporates an analysis of how the children are being taught the values in their inspection.

CRITICAL QUESTION

What do you see as British values? Are they the same as Ofsted's list? Can you see any issues with the term?

Once employed in a school, the Teachers' Standards are still used as a benchmark to assess teachers. Most teachers will be observed regularly by the SMT in their school, though the frequency of these observations are usually dictated by school policy often negotiated with the various teaching unions. Many of these observations are not necessarily someone sitting in your classroom and watching you teach, as many schools now use different methods to reach conclusions about a teacher's performance. Some schools look at or video pupils in your lesson to see how your teaching is having effect; some schools favour book scrutiny where children's workbooks are examined to see if policies are being followed and if the children are making enough progression; still others favour learning walks where, usually, a predetermined set of questions are evidenced. Sometimes the focus is a particular teaching strategy; sometimes the focus is staff development.

SATs results, and the SATs subjects, are often crucial to the assessment of teachers' performance. Many in the teaching profession find these to be an unfair marker, as results can be dependent on the cohort, not the teaching, and one set of students in one year may perform much better than another simply due to their backgrounds.

Done in a supportive manner, these observations and assessments can help teachers reflect on their performance and improve, which is clearly the intention. There is no doubt that at first they can be very stressful, but once they can be seen simply as a means to get even better, and sometimes to show how well different aspects of your class are working, they become part of the teacher's daily life. The teaching unions have policies on observation that it is always good to have read.

THE OFFICE FOR STANDARDS IN EDUCATION, CHILDREN'S SERVICES AND SKILLS (OFSTED)

An Ofsted inspection is usually by a team of inspectors. They look primarily at a selection of teaching, at data around learning, and at the management of the school. The schools are graded in different areas, and overall, after what is usually a three-day inspection. They are graded on a 4-point scale: 1 (Outstanding), 2 (Good), 3 (Requires improvement, or RI) and 4 (Inadequate). You will have seen the Ofsted banners outside schools, displaying their judgements – if they are good.

The inspection reports are published on Ofsted's and the school's website so that interested parties can read them in detail. Any school judged inadequate will be put into 'special measures' and until recently was forced into academisation. Now, they are given special support and more frequent inspections.

Ofsted has recently moved to reduce the fear and burden of inspections on schools. Their recent workload document makes it clear that schools should not make special efforts in advance of an inspection, something that made many teachers laugh hollowly. Until the consequences of a bad inspection are reduced, it is unlikely that many schools will obey Ofsted's suggestions.

HOW DO TEACHERS ACHIEVE A GOOD WORK–LIFE BALANCE? IS IT EVEN POSSIBLE?

> *Work life balance is about adjusting working patterns and policies so that everyone - regardless of age, race or gender, can find a rhythm that enables them more easily to combine work with their other responsibilities or aspirations.*
>
> (Work-life balance toolkit for education professionals, ATL, 2017)

So, how do teachers manage their workload? You will have heard of many teachers leaving the profession and of the stress that those who remain are under. At the time of writing, the government has been putting extra money into schools for schemes to protect children's mental health – but what about teachers?

A good analogy to make clear the importance of looking after your mental health is being on an aeroplane listening to the safety talk. They always tell you to put an oxygen mask on yourself before any children in your care, because the children will need you to be strong and able to look after them. The same applies in a classroom. It is pointless wearing yourself out looking after children if you then have to give up.

The teaching unions are aware of the pressures and the new National Education Union is at the time of writing running a workload campaign, with the hashtag #make1change. There is a workload tracker, to manage a work–life balance, and advice on how to deal with this within an increasingly stretched and burdened system. It has seen workplace meetings set up well-being committees, and marking policies changed to lighten the load, among many different ideas.

#make1change is a good place to look for tips to manage your workload. Some people have a never work past 8 p.m. rule, others never work on a Friday, others that at least one day of the weekend is free from work. Some use the famous 5-minute lesson plan from @teachertoolkit. Another increasingly popular idea is to learn mindfulness or meditation.

KEY READING

Government response to the Workload Challenge, February 2015.

www.gov.uk/government/publications/workload-challenge-for-schools-government-response

Teacher Workload Survey 2016 Research Report, February 2017.

www.gov.uk/government/publications/teacher-workload-survey-2016

Policy paper: Reducing teacher workload, (DfE). Updated 10 March 2018.

www.gov.uk/government/publications/reducing-teachers-workload/reducing-teachers-workload

Work-life balance toolkit for education professionals (ATL).

www.atl.org.uk/Images/Worklife balance toolkit maintained.pdf

Above are four different documents regarding workload: three from the government and the last from the Association of Teachers and Lecturers Union (ATL). All are interesting background reading, with the ATL document being practical advice.

Schools manage workload best when they work together as a whole. John Tomsett (2015) says:

> *Ultimately, the DfE can do very little to reduce workload - it is up to school leaders to set a culture where staff are cared for, well-trained and valued and policies are based on common sense and the principle that we shouldn't be doing things unless they clearly help improve student outcomes.*

The best head teachers will do this. Perhaps one of the best ways to ensure your work–life balance is to choose your first school carefully. Ask questions, talk to teachers who work there. Find out if this is a stressed or a supportive school.

The fact remains that teacher workload is an issue that has been at the forefront of professional dissatisfaction for a long time. Many teachers are leaving the profession because of it, and others are sure that it is impossible to achieve. The recent publications by the DfE show that they have begun to take this seriously, and the campaigns by teachers' unions are adding to the pressure. It is difficult to fight a system as an individual teacher, but the profession now has a real chance to make a real difference to a teacher's working life if they work together.

TEACHING AROUND THE WORLD

While the situation varies greatly from country to country, around the world teaching is seen as a degree-based profession. There has to be a recognition of different circumstances – in rural India, for example, many teachers are not qualified; in Nigeria, there is a three-year A-level route into teaching, but these are the exceptions. Finland is rare in that it only allows Master's-level teachers, as does France, but the most common route is at least a three-year bachelor's degree. In India, where there are many rural schools with teachers who have no qualifications, the government have introduced a minimum requirement of a B.Ed to be a teacher and allowed unqualified teachers a five-year period to gain the degree or lose their jobs.

CRITICAL QUESTION

Is it right that in many countries, teaching early years requires lower qualifications?

In the USA, the situation is complicated by a number of factors, such as state mandates, years of experience, the age of students, and school subject. Most states require a bachelor's degree, and often part of the degree is a teacher training programme, with an internship of 8–12 weeks following in a local school. Each teacher then needs a licence and state certification, unless they work in a private school where this is not required.

CHAPTER SUMMARY

- There are different types of school in the UK, including state schools and academies. All provide different experiences for the teacher.
- A teacher has many different roles to negotiate during their work day - planning the delivery of the appropriate level of the National Curriculum, differentiated where necessary, managing the behaviour of their students, and ensuring that safeguarding procedures are known and used.
- A teacher also has to liaise with many different groups of people over a working day: TAs, parents, other members of staff, the SMT, and many others.
- Teachers are assessed against the Teachers' Standards.
- Ofsted is the inspecting body for UK educational institutions and can grade a school between 1 and 4, 1 being excellent, 4 being a fail.
- Balancing this and a life outside work is a challenge. This is now being addressed by the profession, as the number of teachers leaving due to unrealistic expectations is at critical levels.

ASSIGNMENTS

If you are writing an assignment on the realities of being a teacher today, you may want to:

- consider what makes children learn - what motivates them?

- consider the different approaches to inclusion in a classroom.

What steps would you take to manage your workload?

How do you look after children's mental health while also looking after yourself?

REFERENCES

ATL (2017) Work–life balance toolkit for education professionals. Available at: www.atl.org.uk/Images/Worklife balance toolkit maintained.pdf (accessed 29/06/18).

Bennett, T. (2017) *Creating a Culture: How school leaders can optimise behaviour.* DfE. Available at: https://assets.publishing.service.gov.uk/government/uploads/system/uploads/attachment_data/file/602487/Tom_Bennett_Independent_Review_of_Behaviour_in_Schools.pdf (accessed 18/2/18).

DfE (2014) *Statutory Guidance: National curriculum in England: framework for key stages 1 to 4.* Available at: www.gov.uk/government/publications/national-curriculum-in-england-framework-for-key-stages-1-to-4 (accessed 25/6/18)

DfE (2018) Policy paper: Reducing teacher workload Updated 17 January 2018. Available at: www.gov.uk/government/publications/reducing-teachers-workload/reducing-teachers-workload (accessed 18/2/18).

Rose, J. (2008) *Independent Review of the Primary Curriculum: Final report.* London: DfE.

Tomsett, J. (2015) *This Much I Know About Love Over Fear.* Carmarthen: Crown House Publishing.

USEFUL WEBSITES

https://educationinspection.blog.gov.uk/2016/02/08/inspection-timescales/ (accessed 18/2/18).

http://news.bbc.co.uk/1/hi/6564933.stm (accessed 18/2/18).

https://educationendowmentfoundation.org.uk/evidence-summaries/teaching-learning-toolkit/ (accessed 18/2/18).

https://educationinspection.blog.gov.uk/2016/01/20/busting-myths-on-ofsted-inspections/ (accessed 17/2/18).

http://peterpappas.com/2011/09/learning-walks-power-teacher-to-teacher-pd.html (accessed 17/2/18).

www.atl.org.uk/policy-and-campaigns/make1change (accessed 18/2/18).

www.theguardian.com/teacher-network/2017/jul/19/tips-to-help-schools-reduce-teacher-workload (accessed 18/2/18).

www.theguardian.com/education/2009/nov/20/parents-school-choice-social-divide (accessed 18/2/18).

www.margaretthatcher.org/document/106941 (accessed 18/2/18).

www.teachertoolkit.co.uk/ (accessed 18/2/18).

www.theguardian.com/teacher-network/2018/jan/05/lessons-from-2017-more-relaxed-career-lesson-planning-marking-behaviour-management-work-life-balance (accessed 17/2/18).

www.atl.org.uk/latest/new-union/ministers-wont-tackle-workload-we-need-neu-make-difference (accessed 17/2/18).

www.teachers.org.uk/learning-walks-model-policy (accessed 17/2/18).

www.verywellmind.com/differences-between-extrinsic-and-intrinsic-motivation-2795384 (accessed 17/2/18).

TIMELINE OF CHILDHOOD

LINKED TO THEORY

DURING THE MIDDLE AGES

Aries (1962) claims during this period of history childhood was not an important life stage and society did not have images clearly depicting children. However, much of the art work depicts children as versions of small adults in society at a slightly older age rather than babies or toddlers. Children were portrayed with others, not alone and perhaps because of their very low life expectancy not something to get attached to. Cunningham (1995) suggests that during this period mothers not only recognised the first seven years of life but were encouraged to bring up their children with kindness and they mourned their loss.

DURING THE EIGHTEENTH CENTURY

Rousseau cited in Hendrick (1997) argued that childhood was a valued stage of life and emphasised the natural goodness and virtuousness of children. This ideology was lost during the industrial revolution but then revived by social reformers who debated that children should be protected from adult realities of the world.

DURING THE NINETEENTH CENTURY

Mass education influenced society's perception as it was used to shape and mould pupils' behaviour whose attendance was compulsory (Hendrick,1997).

DURING THE TWENTIETH CENTURY

Successive governments regarded children as society's most valuable assets, placed them top of their agenda and passed laws to secure their proper development by the provision and monitoring of services. Children still viewed as dependent on adults and the state (Hendrick, 1997).

PREVIOUS GENERATIONS HAD THEIR CONCEPT OF BEING 'A CHILD' WHICH DIFFERS FROM THAT WHICH WE HOLD TODAY (ARCHARD, 1993)

4

WHO ARE OUR 21ST-CENTURY CHILDREN?

Jan Grinstead is a Senior Lecturer for Childhood Studies at University of Sunderland. Her research interests are centred around young children's learning and development, and professionals who work with young children. She is also a Senior Fellow of the Higher Education Academy. Acknowledgements are given to Dr Wendy Thorley (Jan's colleague at University of Sunderland) for her assistance with writing this chapter.

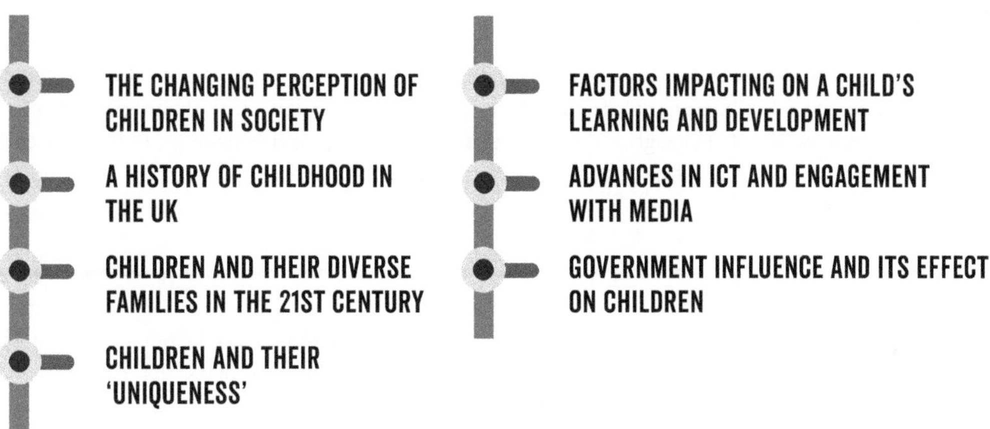

KEY WORDS

- Adverse Childhood Experiences
- Childhood Theory
- Factors
- Family
- Government
- Learning
- Society
- Teaching

INTRODUCTION

This chapter will explore ideas about what it means to be a child in the 21st century. There has been significant research and publicity around the changing worlds of children over the past 50 years, leading to increased recognition of children's rights. These include the United Nations Convention of the Rights of the Child (UNCRC) and building up to recent legislation changes across the United Kingdom, informing the Children and Family Act 2014 and the Special Educational Needs Code of Practice 0–25 years (2014). This chapter asks how perceptions have changed and examines some of the reasoning behind these changes. This will involve exploring the factors that influence society's notion of childhood and the experiences that children have during childhood, which impact on their learning and development, alongside the developing research into how children are portrayed within society.

THE CHILD IN SOCIETY

Our society's perception and notion of being 'a child' changes and evolves over time; different generations of people experience and socially construct their values and principles based on their interactions across the environment and those within it. Throughout the generations the notion and perception of 'being a child' has been and will continue to be debated due to the complex nature of the subject.

KEY THEORY

Cooley's (1998) theory claims children see themselves how others see them as a reflection of these perceptions; such notions support debate about the importance of how professionals within children's lives behave, as well as family members and those of the wider society, including other children the child may meet.

Vygotsky's (1978) social constructivist learning theory suggests that the 'more knowledgeable others' tend to be parents, teachers and peers. Rapid, evolutionary changes in the way that society communicates using information communication technology (ICT) has extended the range of the 'more knowledgeable others' and who they may be. Conversely, this has also led to much higher levels of feelings of loneliness, stress and anxiety for many young people due to cyber bullying.

Research-based informed teaching and learning has evolved since the publication of the Plowden Report (1967). Today, the majority of education professionals know more about how learners learn, what impacts on learners learning and how teachers should teach.

ADVERSE CHILDHOOD EXPERIENCES

The 21st century has seen the rapid development of understanding of children's learning and has raised awareness of the impact of Adverse Childhood Experiences (ACEs) on children and young people's life chances. Alongside developing understanding of ACEs, the rapid development of neurosciences has led to greater appreciation of why some children and young people struggle to succeed in academic settings. This knowledge has become available due to growing technological advances. While such developments are imperative for professionals working with and supporting children and young people to enable them to provide appropriate and timely support, interventions and understanding, technology has also expanded the world for children and young people themselves.

The growth in cyber bullying, online grooming and child sexual exploitation has reflected the negative possibilities of technological advances and social media usage. Such concerns have led to children and young people within the UK now experiencing much higher levels of emotional and mental ill health, anxiety and self-harm to such an extent that Child and Adolescent Mental Health services cannot support these children and young people when they require support, and schools are now becoming the central focus for enriching children's lives and addressing a far greater holistic approach to 'education'.

Teachers cannot be responsible for all factors that impact on children's learning and development, such as poverty, basic needs not being met, lack of sleep, poor nutrition and violence. However, good teachers use research-based knowledge to make good decisions to enhance their students' learning in context (Good and Lavigne, 2018). An important facet of the role of teaching is to get to know the children and to continue developing professional knowledge and skills to meet children's needs in an ever-changing world. More responsibility has been placed on professionals for children's learning, development and well-being, and to keep their knowledge and skills current, particularly from government and society as a whole.

INFO 4.1

Timeline of childhood - linked to theory

During the Middle Ages

Aries (1962) claims during this period of history that childhood was not an important life stage and society did not have images clearly depicting children however much of the art work depicts children as versions of small adults in society at a slightly older age rather than babies or toddlers. Children were portrayed with others, not alone and perhaps because of their very low life expectancy not something to get attached to.

Cunningham (1995) suggests that during this period mothers not only recognised the first seven years of life, but were encouraged to bring up their children with kindness and they mourned their loss.

During the eighteenth century

Rousseau cited in Hendrick (1997) argued that childhood was a valued stage of life and emphasised the natural goodness and virtuousness of children. This ideology was lost during the industrial revolution but then revived by social reformers who debated that children should be protected from adult realities of the world.

During the nineteenth century

Mass education influenced society's perception as it was used to shape and mould pupils' behaviour whose attendance was compulsory (Hendrick, 1997).

(Continued)

(Continued)

During the twentieth century

Successive governments regarded children as society's most valuable assets, placed them top of their agenda and passed laws to secure their proper development by the provision and monitoring of services. Children still viewed as dependent on adults and the state (Hendrick, 1997).

Previous generations had their concept of being 'a child' which differs from that which we hold today (Archard, 1993).

A HISTORY OF CHILDHOOD IN THE UK

KEY READING

Watch *The Children Who Built Victorian Britain Part 1* produced by BBC Four; this gives insight to childhood during Victorian time. Professor Jane Humphries uses the actual words of these child workers (recorded in diaries, interviews and letters) to let them tell their own story.

You can find the video at: www.youtube.com/watch?v=87eVOpbcoVo

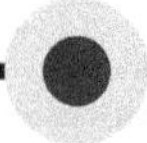

CRITICAL QUESTION

How different would your childhood experiences have been if you had been a child in a different era?

CHILDHOOD THEORISTS OF THE 20TH CENTURY

KEY THEORY

Bronfrenbrenner's ecological theory (1979) suggests that each facet of the ecological system influences the child and thus by internalising and applying these experiences the child influences each facet of the system.

Edwards (2015) summarised Bronfenbrenner's (1979) theory as the:

- micro system being the most influential to the child and the people having the closest relationships to the child within the family, school, places of worship and local community;
- meso system being the people who interact with each other across institutions and influence the child's experiences, such as parent/teacher relationships;

- exo system which the child will not directly experience but decisions that are made will affect the child, such as government elected and funding of education opportunities;
- macro system being the broader social, cultural, economic and political structures that influence each other, such as legislation, valuing equality of opportunity, individual achievement based on merit and global economic fluctuations;
- chrono system based on historical influences, such as the generation of the child and family life.

CRITICAL QUESTION

How may your own childhood experiences influence your values and principles regarding teaching and children learning?

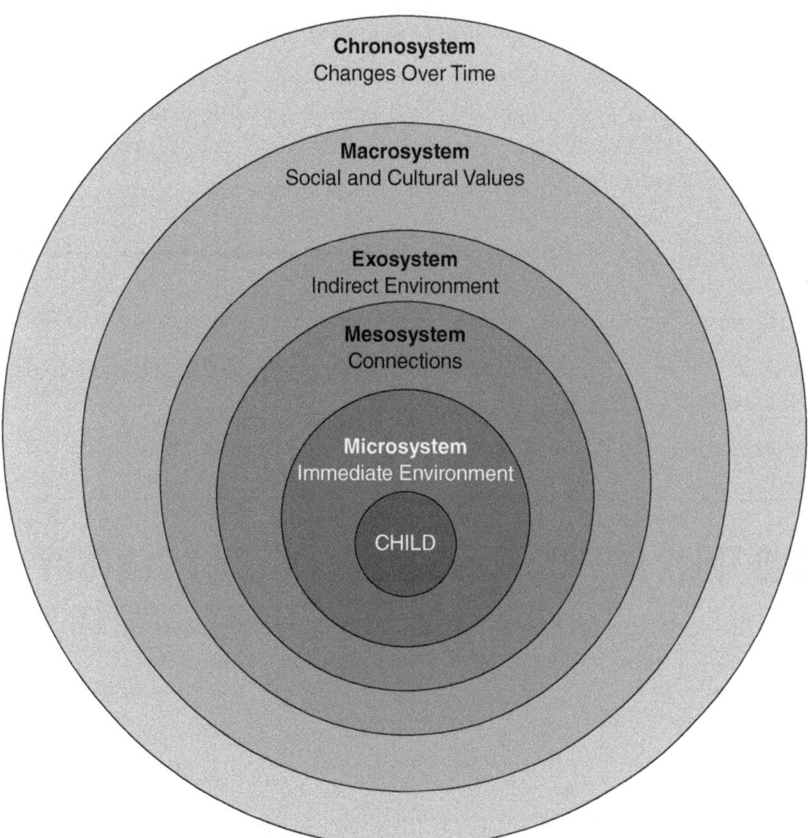

Figure 4.1 Bronfenbrenner's Ecological Systems Theory

KEY THEORY

Bourdieu's theory about capital and habitus can be linked to family function and culture. Bourdieu's theory (1977) cited in Sullivan (2002: 145) states that 'cultural capital consists of familiarity with the dominant culture in a society, and especially the ability to understand and use "educated" language. The possession of cultural capital varies with social class, yet the education system assumes the possession of cultural capital'.

He further suggested in 1990 that 'habitus' is a framework of dispositions moulded within the home environment that create regular modes of behaviour exhibited in certain circumstances in particular ways. Within the school, therefore, it can be difficult to break the cycle of this agency. This can make it difficult for those pupils at the lower end of the social gradient (Marmott, 2016) to succeed in the education system, because Bourdieu (1977) cited in Sullivan (2002: 149) also states that 'like cultural capital, habitus is transmitted within the home'.

What this means for schools and their staff is recognising how children perceive their experiences within the school and within classrooms, and how their experience is informed by their interactions established in the home and with everyone else in the school and classroom, both pupils and adults.

Bourdieu's concept suggests that teachers should be more readily able to consider individual pupil action and reaction within educational settings by recognising pupil experience (habitus from early years and any previous school experience). Perry's (2006) evidence also endorses this theory that it is relationships in schools that matter most for children and young people.

CRITICAL QUESTION

What language used across the education system do children in the 21st century need to understand?

How may attitudes and values differ in habitus between those at the top end of the social gradient and those lower down on the gradient?

How may family habitus and cultural capital impact on children's learning and attainment?

CHILDREN AND THEIR DIVERSE FAMILIES IN THE 21ST CENTURY

Children still tend to live with both parents, although Jenkins *et al.* (2009) found that attitudes across society towards marriage was more relaxed and other family structures were accepted as more common as two-parent families were on the decline.

> *Families are now a mix of cohabiting parents, stepfamilies, single parent families, those living apart together and civil partnerships, as well as the traditional nuclear family.*
>
> (ibid.: 5)

Child Trends Databank (2015) states:

> *the proportion of children living with both parents, following a marked decline between 1970 and 1990, has fallen more slowly over the most recent two decades, dropping from 69 percent in 2000 to 64 percent in 2012. By 2015, the proportion had increased, to 65 percent.*

Within the UK, every 10 years the government conducts a census of the population, the last one being in 2011. This enables the government to predict the needs of the population alongside the ability to reflect upon changing households and families. In November 2017, the Office for National Statistics (ONS) produced *Families and Households* to highlight changes across society. They noted that there were 19 million families within the UK, of which 12.9 million were married or civil partnership couples, and that cohabiting partners were the largest growth family typology overall. This means that for those working with children, there is a diverse range of 'parents' in contact with the school, including those living with same-sex couples, those with step-parents and those with birth parents. In addition, there were also 3.9 million people living alone, some with whom were single parents. The overall number of families within the UK is illustrated in Figure 4.2 below.

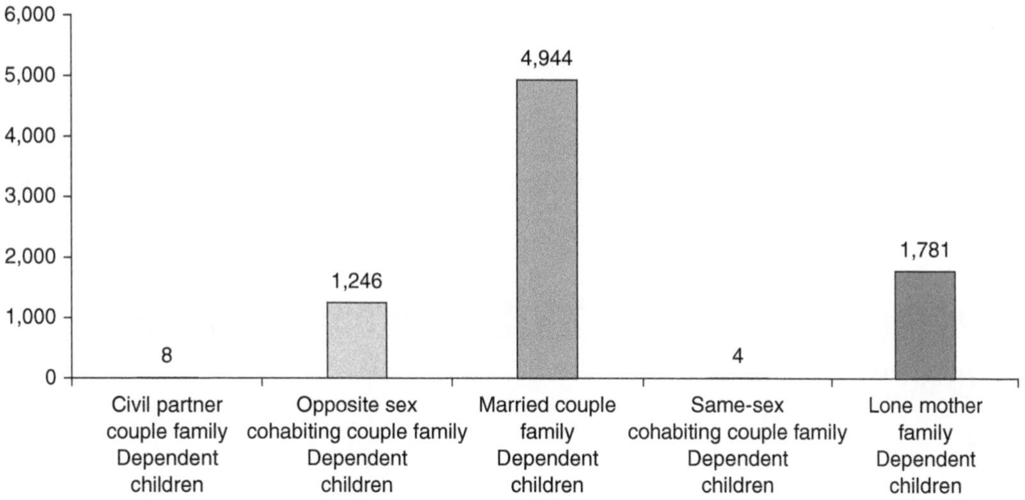

Figure 4.2 Family typologies with children in the household (counted by 1,000s)

It is important that professionals working with children and young people recognise that pupils in schools, irrespective of age, live in a diverse range of family typologies, in order to develop cultural understanding and identify the needs of those children and young people they work with. This enables positive parent partnerships to develop. Within these diverse households there will be child carers, children living in multi-generational households, children who are asylum seekers or refugees, alongside children who are looked after by kinship carers, foster carers, reside in children's homes or have been adopted from care.

CRITICAL QUESTION

How may preconceptions of family typologies influence the teaching and learning of children in school?

UNIQUE CHILDREN OF THE 21ST CENTURY

The ideology of children's 'uniqueness' (*Early Years Foundation Stage*, DfE, 2017) has permeated into society's construction of the concept of child development. This can also be linked to recent research data gathered and analysed by neuroscientists from brain scans. Jensen (1998) suggests that it can be atypical for a child to be adrift from normative stages of development by 6 months to 2 years. The idea of uniqueness can be linked to new knowledge of genetics and everyone owning their individual DNA. Differentiation of individual learning and developmental needs can be challenging when teaching groups of over 25 children (Gardner, 1993; Florian *et al.*, 2006; Landrum and McDuffie, 2010).

CRITICAL QUESTION

What is your understanding of differentiation of teaching and learning practice in school?

One of the biggest challenges that schools may face is ensuring that those pupils with Specific Educational Needs and Disabilities (SEND) are fully supported and able to achieve alongside their peers. For more on this, see Chapter 17.

FACTORS IMPACTING ON A 21ST-CENTURY CHILD'S LEARNING AND DEVELOPMENT

POVERTY

Children's learning and development in the 21st century is influenced by every experience they engage with and respond to. Living in poverty in the 21st century continues to have a negative impact on children's learning and development. Statistics collated by Save the Children (date accessed 16.04.2018) show that a child who lives in poverty is 50 per cent less likely to achieve five GCSEs at 16 years of age. Oakley and Tinsley (2013: 5) stated, 'Today, 17.5% of all children live in households below the relative income poverty threshold, compared to over 25% in 1999 based on a headline measure that defined child poverty as living in a household with less than 60% of median equivalised household'. These percentages do not apply to all Local Authorities and so it is useful to find out the percentages that have been collated about the area where a school is placed. Goodman and Gregg (2010: 4) suggested 'that the gap in attainment between children from the poorest and richest backgrounds, already large at age five, grew particularly fast during the primary school years. By age eleven, only around three-quarters of children from the poorest fifth of families reached the expected level at Key Stage 2, compared with 97 per cent of children from the richest fifth'.

ADVERSE CHILDHOOD EXPERIENCES

KEY READING

The Adverse Childhood Experiences Study (ACE Study) is a research study conducted by the American health maintenance organisation Kaiser Permanente and the Centers for Disease Control and Prevention (1995-1997), leading to a wide range of publications that are listed at: www.theannainstitute.org/ACE%20STUDY%20FINDINGS.html

This study has been replicated internationally and is widely recognised for predicting future indicators for children as they progress to adulthood; for example, see The Public Health Wales NHS Report (2015) at:

www.cph.org.uk/wp-content/uploads/2016/01/ACE-Report-FINAL-E.pdf

Also see Liverpool Johns Moore University (2016) study from Hertfordshire, Luton and Northamptonshire available at:

www.cph.org.uk/wp-content/uploads/2016/05/Adverse-Childhood-Experiences-in-Hertfordshire-Luton-and-Northamptonshire-FINAL_compressed.pdf

The Adverse Childhood Experiences Study (ACE Study) is a research study conducted by the American health maintenance organisation Kaiser Permanente and the Centers for Disease Control and Prevention (1995–1997) that evidenced a range of factors influencing children's learning and development. The outcomes have led to far more understanding of how children's experiences have a lifelong lasting impact on the child through to adulthood – for example, children who experience four or more ACEs have reduced life expectancy of twenty years.

The following diagram (Figure 4.3) highlights how ACEs impact upon the child; of particular note is the impact upon neurological development that in turn influences the child's behaviour and decision-making processes with regard to risk-taking behaviours.

What is significant about understanding ACEs is that this helps to identify those children who may be overlooked as vulnerable children. There are three main areas of ACEs: abuse, household challenges and neglect. While neglect (emotional and physical) along with abuse (emotional, physical or sexual, or a combination of these) can feature highly within recognition of vulnerable children in the 21st century, many more live in households that present challenges but are not accommodated as vulnerable. These children include those who live with domestic violence, a parent dependent on alcohol or drug use, parent/carers with mental health indicators, parents who have separated or divorced, parents or a close relative who has died, in poverty where 'being hungry' is not uncommon and those with parents in prison.

Data indicators are well documented for those who are subject to abuse or neglect, once they are known to children's services; however, there is no official record of how many children have a parent in prison, a parent

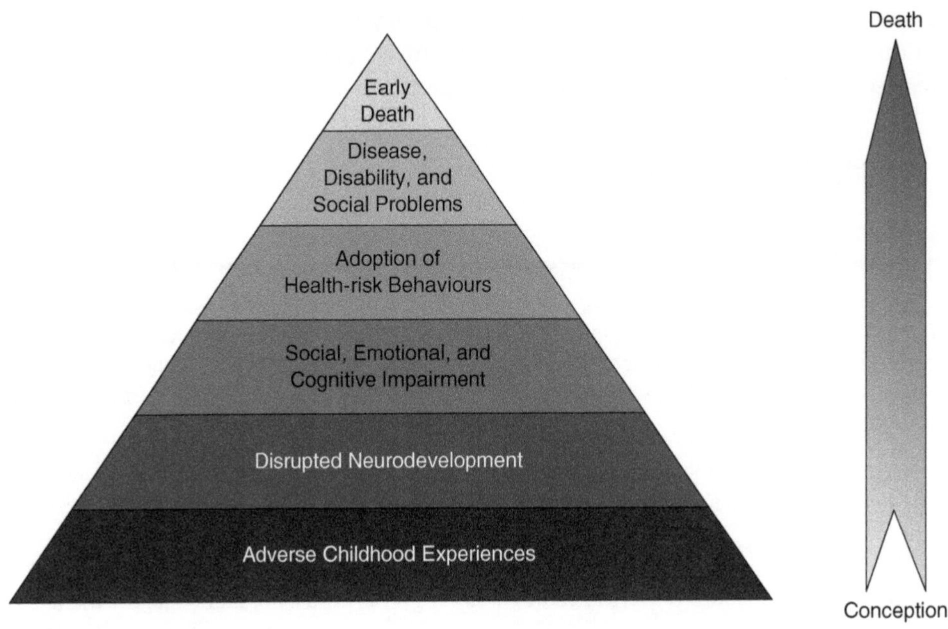

Figure 4.3 Mechanism by which adverse childhood experiences influence health and well-being throughout the lifespan

who has died or parents who were co-habiting and have separated. For this reason, it is essential that teachers appreciate the impact of ACEs, as more than 50 per cent of their class cohort could be experiencing adversity. These children and young people are three times more likely to engage in under-age drinking of alcohol, cigarette smoking and drug taking, which in turn impacts upon their health and well-being, and reduces their life expectancy and life chances. Furthermore, they are also fourteen times more likely to attempt suicide as young people at a time when suicide in young people is increasing to over 300 suicides per year in the UK (Young Minds, 2016) alongside four to five times more likely to experience depression, anxiety or self-harm, which is also increasing every year, with children in the early years diagnosed with depression, anxiety or attempting self-harm. These children and young people are also more likely to become teenage parents themselves (four to five times more likely than their peers with lower ACEs scores) and, as a consequence, leave their education as academic 'failures' who do not gain the GCSE outcomes they will need to progress into career pathways as adults.

While some of these children may display their feelings as 'unacceptable' behaviour traits, many more withdraw. Those who do 'communicate' through behaviour are often then excluded, either temporarily or permanently, from schools. School exclusion rates are increasing at a concerning level across the UK, so much so that the Education Select Committee began investigations in February 2018 to determine how and why so many more children, some as young as three years of age, were being excluded from schools and nurseries across the UK. The main aspect is a combination of 'zero' behaviour policies implemented in schools and general 'behaviour' of children in schools.

On 5 February 2018, Barnardo's produced findings from their latest survey that

> *Almost half of children aged from 12 to 16 in England feel sad or anxious at least once a week with worries about their future and school their biggest concerns* (n.p.).

More concerningly, by the age of 16 in their GCSE year, 83 per cent pointed to school as a stress they experienced and 80 per cent were concerned about their future. While there have been suggestions that social media is the main cause of stress and anxiety for children and young people, this survey dispels this as a myth in that only 12 per cent were concerned about social media bullying and 15 per cent indicated they had seen something that troubled them on social media.

Under current review and reform is the role of teachers in supporting children and young people with mental health well-being, part of which is the identification of Mental Health First Aiders within school as a nominated teacher. However, Barnardo's (2018, n.p.) evidenced that this is not the choice of young people themselves, who indicated that teachers would be their last preference as someone to talk to, not their first, as noted: '*When asked who they would talk to if they felt sad or anxious 38% said teachers, 71% said family members, 63% said friends*'. This highlights the importance of friends and family for children and young people, and emphasises the importance of partnership working in schools with parents.

KEY READING

Barnardo's (2018) survey shows that half of all schoolchildren feel sad or anxious every week, to which Barnardo's Chief Executive, Javed Khan, said:

- Although these can be normal emotions experienced while growing up, children need support to deal with the pressures of everyday life.
- We need to create a culture where everyone has a greater understanding of what keeps children mentally well and when professional help is needed.
- We want parents and carers to be confident in recognising if their children are unhappy, and teachers and that other professionals should be sufficiently trained, adequately resourced and available to support them.

Press release, 5 February 2018: www.barnardos.org.uk/news/New-survey-shows-half-of-all-schoolchildren-feel-sad-or-anxious-every-week/press_releases.htm?ref=128176

ADVANCES IN ICT AND ENGAGEMENT WITH MEDIA

Munro (2011) identified that 99 per cent of children aged 12–15 years had used the internet along with 93 per cent of 8–11 years and 75 per cent of 5–7 years, numbers that increase each year as technology advances. With many schools now adopting a technological approach to learning and teaching, children are encouraged from an early age to engage with technology via apps, tablets, computers and mobile phones. This has increased concerns by the UK Council for Child Internet Safety (UKCCIS). The majority of concerns raised about children and young people engaging online, particularly with social media, relate to cyberbullying. It is estimated that between 8 and 11 years, 34 per cent of children have been bullied online, but this may be much higher due to children not reporting instances of cyberbullying. Cyberbullying has also led to some teens committing suicide within the UK, although full statistics for child suicide are difficult to determine due to how these are reported and recorded. However, what was also evident was that there are susceptible groups targeted within cyberbullying, including children with SEND, children in receipt of free school meals (FSM), children from Black and minority ethnic (BME) groups, children of Gypsy-Roma, Traveller of Irish Heritage, European and East European groups, children from Chinese groups and children of mixed ethnicity (Barnardo's, 2018).

This is concerning due to the increased use of media and social networks by children from 2011 to 2017, when Ofcom (2017) produced its report into children's and parents' media use and attitudes. Ofcom indicated that as many as 1:4 aged 8–11 years and 3:4 aged 12–15 years had a social media presence, particularly within social platforms that had age restrictions. While technology offers far more creative learning possibilities encouraging children and young people to engage with the internet or social media, it does not come without risk. It is these risks that schools and professionals, including teachers, are asked to ensure that all pupils are informed about.

GOVERNMENT TO INFLUENCE OR NOT TO INFLUENCE THAT IS THE QUESTION

Successive governments have passed a series of legislation from which subsequent documentation of policy and procedures have been disseminated to schools that have impacted on the teaching and learning of children within schools. In the documents published for schools, a child is aged between 0 and 19 years of age if non-disabled and up to 25 years of age if statemented with a specific educational learning disability. Yet, a child aged 16 years can marry with their parents' consent and engage in consenting sexual activity with any adult of their choice. A child aged 16 years can smoke but cannot purchase tobacco products from shops until 18 years of age; is charged full adult price for holidays usually over age 10 and when over 14 years is charged adult price for bus travel. A child can create and engage in Facebook, Instagram, Snapchat, etc. and while there are restrictions in place with a suggested age at which a young person should be allowed to have these accounts, many parents will set up their account on the child's behalf or the child fabricates their date of birth (Munro, 2011; UKCCIS, n.d).

The Education Act 1988 and the introduction of the National Curriculum changed children's learning experiences both positively and negatively, and government intervention continues to be greatly debated within the education sector and across society. The Department for Education's website (date accessed 15.02.2018) has 13 Contents sections, such as Administration and Finance, Curriculum, Early Years Foundation Stage, Looked after children and Safeguarding children and young people, which contain approximately 49 statutory documents for primary schools. Changes to the content of curriculum subjects have been constant, and the methods of assessment to monitor children's attainment of knowledge and skills continue to be part of each government's agenda.

CRITICAL QUESTION

What are the key factors that may affect teaching and learning in the classroom linked to current understanding of childhood?

CHAPTER SUMMARY

- Society's perception of being a 'child' changes, constantly evolves and, due to the complex nature of the subject, continues to be debated.
- Children live in a diverse range of family typologies, such as married couple, civil partnership couples, lone parents, step-parent family, etc.
- Research theories about social capital, ACEs, poverty, advances in ICT and engagement with media shows positive and negative impact on children's learning attainment.
- An important part of a teacher's role is to get to know the children, and to continue developing professional knowledge and skills to meet children's needs in an ever-changing world.

ASSIGNMENTS

If you are writing an assignment discussing 'Childhood in the 21st century' you may wish to:

- consider how childhood has changed over time from the experiences of Victorian children to your own childhood and childhood today;
- explore developments in neuroscience and how this has changed understanding of the impact of attachment issues and adverse childhood experiences;
- consider the challenges and barriers that are present across education when supporting children who have experienced loss, trauma or have an ACEs score over 5;
- consider the importance of safe, secure and stimulating learning environments as an important factor in providing 'safe' places for children's learning and development;
- reflect upon children's mental well-being and how this can be incorporated into the school ethos for all children individually and collectively.

When completing assignments, this structure may be useful: Introduction, Main part of assignment - Point, Evidence, Explanation, Discussion, Defend and Debate, Conclusion.

REFERENCES

Barnardo's (2018) Press release, 5 February. Available at: www.barnardos.org.uk/news/New-survey-shows-half-of-all-schoolchildren-feel-sad-or-anxious-every-week/press_releases.htm?ref=128176 (accessed 01/03/18).

Bronfenbrenner, U. (1979) *The Ecology of Human Development*. Cambridge, MA: Harvard University Press.

Child Trends Databank (2015). *Family Structure*. Available at: www.childtrends.org/?indicators=family-structure (accessed 01/03/18)

Cooley, C.H. (1998) *On Self and Social Organization*. Chicago: University of Chicago Press.

Department for Education (2017) *Statutory Framework for the Early Years Foundation Stage: Setting the standards for learning, development and care for children from birth to five*. Crown Copyright.

Edwards, M. (2015) *Global Childhoods*. Critical Publishing: St Albans.

Florian, L., Hollenweger, J., Simeonsson, R., Wedell, K., Riddell, S., Terzi, L. and Holland, A. (2006) Cross-cultural perspectives on the classification of children with disabilities: Issues in the classification of children with disabilities. *The Journal of Special Education*, 40(1): 36–45.

Gardner, H. (1993) *Multiple Intelligences: The theory in practice*. New York: Basic Books.

Good, T.L. and Lavigne, A.L. (2018) *Looking at Classrooms* (11th edn). Oxford: Routledge.

Goodman, A. and Gregg, P. (2010) *Poorer Children's Educational Attainment: How important are attitudes and behaviour? York:* Joseph Rowntree Foundation.

Jenkins, S., Pereria, I. and Evans, N. (2009) *Families in Britain*. IPSOS Mori London: Policy Exchange.

Jensen, E. (1998) *Teaching with the Brain in Mind*. Alexandria, VA: Association of Supervision and Curriculum Development.

Landrum, T. J. and McDuffie, K. A. (2010) Learning styles in the age of differentiated instruction. *Exceptionality*, 18: 6–17.

Marmott, M. (2016) *The Health Gap*. London: Bloomsbury Publishing.

Munro, E. (2011) *The Protection of Children Online: A brief scoping review to identify vulnerable groups*. London: Childhood Wellbeing Research Centre.

Oakley, M. and Tinsley, M. (2013) *Outcomes, Not Just Incomes Improving Britain's Understanding and Measurement of Child Poverty*. London: Policy Exchange.

OfCom (Office for Communications) (2017) *Children and Parents: Media use and attitudes report 2017*. Office for Communications. Available at: www.ofcom.org.uk/research-and-data/media-literacy-research/childrens/children-parents-2017 (accessed 27/11/17).

Office for National Statistics (2017) *Families and Households 2017*. Office for National Statistics. Released November 2017.

Perry, B. (2006) Applying principles of neurodevelopment to clinical work with maltreated and traumatised children: The Neuro Sequential Model of Therapeutics, in Boyd, N. (ed.) *Working with Traumatized Youth in Child Welfare*. New York: The Guildford Press.

Plowden, B. (1967) *Children and their Primary Schools*. The Plowden Report: A Report of the Central Advisory Council for Education (England). London: Her Majesty's Stationery Office.

Save the Children (2018) *What we do/Education*. Available at: www.savethechildren.org.uk/what-we-do/education (accessed 16/04/18).

Sullivan, A. (2002) Bourdieu and Education: How useful is Bourdieu's theory for researchers? *Netherlands Journal of Social Sciences*, 38: 144–66.

UK Council for Child Internet Safety (UKCCIS) (n.d) *Advice on Child Internet Safety 1.0: Universal guidelines for providers*. Her Majesty's Government. Available at: https://assets.publishing.service.gov.uk/government/uploads/system/uploads/attachment_data/file/251455/advice_on_child_internet_safety.pdf (accessed 16/04/18).

Vygotsky, L. S. (1978) *Mind in Society: The development of higher psychological processes*. Cambridge, MA: Harvard University Press.

Young Minds (2016) *Our Strategic Plan*. Available at: https://youngminds.org.uk/about-us/reports/our-strategic-plan-2016-20/ (accessed 04/10/18).

5

WHAT MATTERS IN EARLY CHILDHOOD?

Dr Zenna Kingdon is a Senior Lecturer at the University of Wolverhampton, with expertise in Primary Education, Pre-school Education and Pedagogic Theory. Her research interests focus on play and in particular role play and exploring the concept of flourishing in early childhood.

Dr Ioanna Palaiologou CPsychol AFBPsS, FRSA is an Academic Associate at UCL Institute of Education and a child psychologist with specialism on child development and learning theories. Her research interests focus on early childhood education, child development, play and learning and digital technologies.

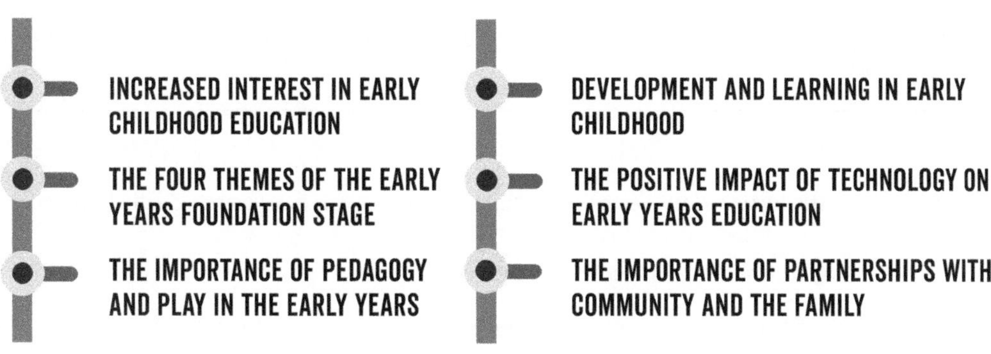

KEY WORDS

- Policy
- Pedagogy
- Curriculum
- Play
- Qualifications
- Partnerships with parents

INTRODUCTION

Early childhood (from birth to eight years of age) is a very important stage in children's lives in terms of their development and growth. Overwhelming evidence from research and especially neuropsychological research (Goswami, 2015) suggests that early childhood is a critical period for children's physical, social emotional and cognitive development and supports the importance of an enriched, stimulating, play-based early childhood learning environments. In this chapter we explore key issues that matter in early childhood and discuss the importance of policy, research, pedagogy, curriculum and play, as well as development and learning and partnerships with parents.

POLICY AND CURRICULUM MATTER

From the late 1990s there has been an increase in policy governing the provision of early childhood education. Governments in countries from England to Australia and New Zealand, including many European countries, have developed curriculum frameworks and regulated at national level what is to happen in the early childhood sector (Cohen *et al*, 2004; Oberhuemer, 2005; Papatheodorou and Moyles, 2012).

KEY READING

The early years learning framework for Australia: Belonging, being and becoming:

www.acecqa.gov.au/sites/default/files/2018-02/belonging_being_and_becoming_the_early_years_learning_framework_for_australia.pdf

A number of reasons for the increased interest in early childhood education have emerged which include:

- recognition of the status of education in a knowledge economy,
- recognition that what happens in the early childhood has repercussions for the rest of a child's life as it can prevent social exclusion and support children in finding ways out of poverty as adults (Siraj-Blatchford, *et al* 2008, Taggart, 2015),
- recent developments in neuroscience research demonstrating the impact of high-quality early childhood provision and providing a framework in which there can be clear communication between parents and settings (Oberhuemer, 2005).

In the 21st century, shaping of education policy by both the media and politicians is considered the norm in England, but this was not always the case. In 1976 Prime Minister Jim Callaghan indicated a desire for education to be more closely aligned to the economic needs of the nation. This was a significant turning point in the direction and politicisation of education in England and Wales (Phillips and Harper-Jones, 2002) and steadily from that point we have seen increased governmental intervention which impacts on both pedagogy and curriculum.

Internationally, the introduction of early childhood curricula took many shapes; from overarching guidance through to prescriptions of what should be taught and assessed. Whilst the nature of curriculum is a contested principle much of the literature suggests that it should be focussed on children's interests and their needs (Hedges *et al* 2011). In almost every early childhood curriculum in the Western World there is recognition demonstrated that the best way young children learn is through a play-based curriculum in which they have choice and control.

In England, a series of curricular were developed for the early years from 1996. In 2008, The Early Years Foundation Stage (EYFS) (DCSF, 2008) largely amalgamated what went before. The EYFS created a distinctive phase for children from birth to five and has been considered to be developmentally appropriate, advocating a play-based curriculum that also merged notions of education and care (Roberts-Holmes, 2012). The EYFS (DCSF, 2008) was referred to as a principled approach and was arranged around four broad themes:

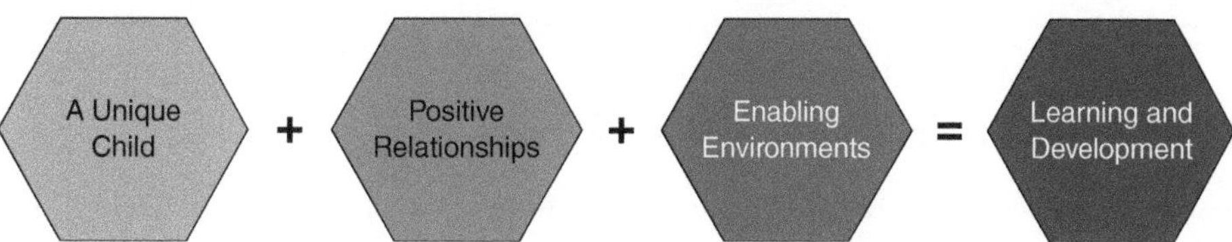

Fig 5.1 The four themes of the EYFS

There was a clear expectation that the curriculum would be delivered through a play-based experiential approach. The EYFS (DCSF, 2008) had been delivered for less than two years when Dame Clare Tickell was appointed to carry out an independent review of the EYFS to consider how this could be less bureaucratic and more focused on supporting children's early learning. The review was to cover four main areas: scope of regulation, learning and development, assessment and welfare (DfE, 2010). In total, Tickell (2011) made 46 recommendations about changes that should be made to the EYFS, recommending that personal, social and emotional development, communication and language, and physical development are identified as prime areas of learning. Alongside the prime areas she proposed four specific areas in which the prime skills would be applied: literacy, mathematics, expressive arts and design, and understanding the world. She commented that:

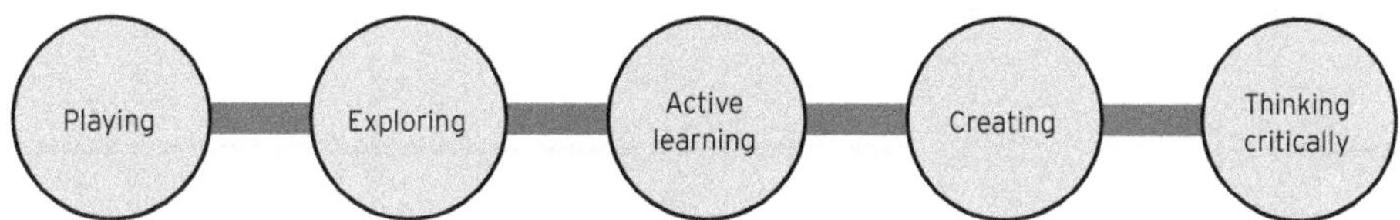

should be highlighted in the EYFS as key characteristics of effective teaching and learning (Tickell, 2011).

The revised EYFS (DFE, 2012) was published in 2012 and since then a number of minor changes have occurred, but these have been focused on safeguarding and care, rather than the content of the curriculum.

CRITICAL QUESTION

What should matter as key priorities in the early years?

KEY READING

In June 2018, the government announced the new Early Learning Goals that will be piloted in 25 schools from September 2018. View at:

www.tes.com/news/proposed-new-early-learning-goals-full-details

It has proposed 17 early learning goals focusing on pupil development across language and communication, reading and writing, numbers, art and design, physical development, self-confidence and relationships, and understanding of the world (DfE, 2018).

RESEARCH AND THEORY INFORMING PRACTICE MATTER

Over the last two decades successive governments have developed what has been referred to as research informed policy. A number of national organisations within the early childhood sector in the UK have engaged in writing reviews, undertaking research and developing policy (Fitzgerald and Kay, 2016). These include:

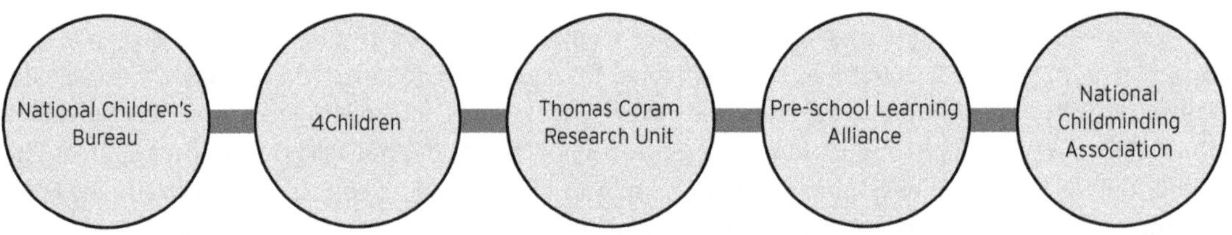

Research has successfully informed many aspects of policy. The most influential research was The Effective Provision of Pre-School Education (EPPE) Project (Sylva *et al*, 2004) that has led to an up-skilling of the early years workforce that has been funded by successive governments.

RESEARCH FOCUS

The EPPE Project - findings from pre-school to end of Key Stage One. This key document explores the image of pre-school education. It includes some case studies of good practice and gives useful context for trainee teachers.

http://dera.ioe.ac.uk/8543/7/SSU-SF-2004-01.pdf

Early childhood education has moved from a position in which there was little political intervention to the current position in which ministers are central in determining policy direction and curriculum content. Within the early childhood sector, education has moved from a position of relative inconsequence, prior to the Rumbold Report (1990), to one in which successive governments have framed it as providing the long-term solution to a number of societal ills (Osgood, 2009; McGillivray, 2008).

CRITICAL QUESTION

How important is early childhood education? Can a focus on quality provision here solve some of society's long-standing problems?

PEDAGOGY MATTERS

Pedagogy is a term that was initially defined by the ancient Greeks. The term did not mean teachers who were people who delivered education on a specific subject. Instead, the term comes from a combination of two words – lead (ἄγω) and child (παῖς) – so it was used to refer to the training of the child that was led by an adult who normally was educated. Contemporary views on pedagogy (Male and Palaiologou, 2015; Pascal and Bertram, 2012; Oliviera-Formoshino and Formoshino, 2012) suggest that the term goes beyond the simplistic approaches. Pedagogy is instead a complex term that encompass the process of learning and teaching as well as the nature and quality of learning, techniques and strategies, and the relationships between learners, teachers, families and the community. Consequently, in early childhood education pedagogy should be underpinned by an in-depth understanding of:

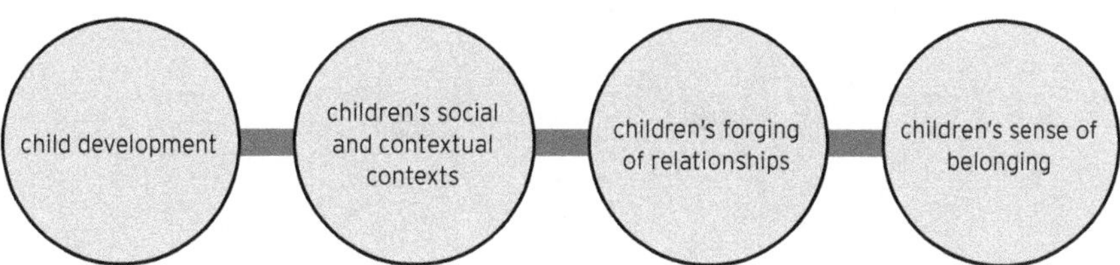

and offer rewarding, positive and meaningful experiences to children. In that sense, pedagogy in early childhood from holistic lenses is defined as the organisation of the educational environment for playful learning (spaces, times, materials, learning groups, adult–child interactions, assessment and planning with the child activities and/or projects that interest them), considering parental involvement and respecting all (professionals, parents, children, community) values, beliefs and identities.

PLAY MATTERS

There is a clear commitment to play within early childhood. Research into play has been studied from a variety of disciplines including: biology, psychology, anthropology, education and cultural studies (Wood, 2007). There is evidence that the neuro-physiological development of the brain supports the importance of children making connections between learning and experiences through play (Gopnik *et al*, 2001).

Concepts of play have usually been constructed from an adult perspective (Pyle and Alaca, 2016). Children's and adults' perceptions of play vary greatly and what constitutes play for one child might not be so for another. An activity such as singing may be considered work in the classroom but play when in the playground, which further complicates the discussion (Pyle and Alaca, 2016). Little prominence has been placed on discussing children's perceptions of play; instead much of the focus is on adult definitions (Colliver and Fleer, 2016). This absence of the child's perspective on play is concerning many researchers and practitioners (Pyle and Alaca, 2016).

Not only is most of the literature concerned with adult constructs (Howard *et al*, 2006), but it seems that,

> *Increasingly, play is viewed through an educational lens that privileges policy imperatives to boost adult-determined outcomes through play.*
>
> (Colliver and Fleer, 2016, p. 1560)

This again undermines the child's perspective and their experiences of play. Much of the developmental potential of play comes from children recognising it as a play activity, rather than perceiving it as adult directed and, therefore, learning (Howard *et al* 2006).

Observations suggest that children define play using three different factors: behavioural, environmental and social contexts (ibid., 2006). For children to define an activity as play it is likely to include the following:

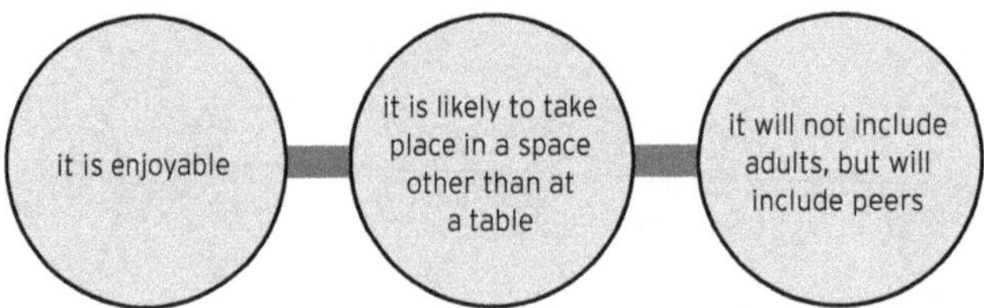

Children were more likely to perceive parallel and co-operative activities as play, whilst they were less likely to categorise solitary activities as play (Howard *et al*, 2006).

Considering children's perceptions of work and learning is also important (Pyle and Alaca, 2016). They demonstrate that children often acknowledge that learning can occur through work and through play. In other classrooms where the children did not acknowledge that play and learning are connected, the children were noted as describing their teachers in terms of providing instruction, demonstrating a more didactic approach. It is apparent, therefore, that the pedagogical approach of the practitioner is essential in enabling children to recognise the connections between play and learning (Theobald *et al*, 2015).

CLASSROOM LINK

What does this mean for classroom practice?

The environment should create **opportunities for encouraging children to play.** It should offer a number of areas where children can engage in all of the above types of play and explore such things as:

- a water area
- a library where children can go and take books to read
- a symbolic play area
- a science and experiments area
- a games and construction area
- easy access to the outside.

The organisation of the space should not be permanent and should be evaluated frequently and change, dependent on the activities and projects that take place in the classroom. It should also incorporate materials produced by children, such as displays that change frequently, or materials that children bring from home.

A variety of materials should be available for children to access. Materials should include miniatures or replicas of real objects (such as dolls, stuffed animals) or real objects (such as plants, wooden sticks). It is important to have pre-structured materials (such as educational toys) and open object materials (such as clay, wooden blocks, cooker) that are revised frequently. Such materials are very important for symbolic play. Other materials such as paintings, story books and picture books are essential features. It also needs to be evaluated frequently so children do not get used to them and lose interest.

Children's experiences influence their attitudes and it is important that from an early age they become *used to adult involvement in their play and view adults as co-operative play partners* (Howard *et al*, 2006: p. 392). When children reject adults in play situations (i.e. where children only see adult involvement as a task), this has implications for the ability of practitioners to enrich and extend learning opportunities (Howard *et al*, 2006). Adults thus need to consider how they engage with children in order to recognise play constructs. Play should not be something that only occurs away from adults, unadulterated by their participation. Adults need to ensure their participation is supportive, values children as equal play partners and does not dominate the play so that it becomes 'work' rather than 'play'.

CRITICAL QUESTION

How can adults participate in play without dominating it?

Learning is a process of engagement rather than attainment. For some children the relationship between play and learning is inextricably intertwined, but for others, with fewer opportunities to engage with adult-initiated play activities, they do not recognise the relationship. For adults to fully understand the child's perspective of play, further research needs to be conducted (Theobald *et al*, 2015; Pyle and Alaca, 2016). What remains clear at this stage is that play is central to children's learning in early childhood education.

TYPES OF PLAY

Types of play	Description	Examples
Symbolic play	When a child uses objects to symbolise for something else	A wooden spoon become a guitar or a big paper box becomes a castle where the child gets inside
Rough and tumble play	When children during their play become physical towards each other but with no intention to be violent	Children tickle each other
Socio dramatic play	The enactment of real-life situations or experiences	Children pretend they cook a meal or pretend they are fireworks
Social play	Children engage in play with rules of social interaction	Children have created a shop and they are buying and selling things using pieces of paper for money
Creative play	Children explore, try out new ideas and or making, changing things	A child takes a box of cereals and makes it into an armour
Communication play	Children engage in the use of words, songs, rhymes	Children pretend they talk on the phone or they present the news like the TV presenters
Dramatic play	Children dramatise events that were not directly participants	Children dramatise a popular show from the TV or a wedding
Locomotor play	Children play through movement	Children play musical chairs, chase, climbing
Deep play	Children engage in risky play	Walking on the top of a brick wall, balancing on a high beam, coming down the stairs jumping
Exploration play	Children engage in manipulative behaviours	Throwing, stacking bricks
Fantasy play	Children using imagination, they engage in make believe play	Children pretend they are astronauts travelling in space or they become giants climbing magic trees
Imaginative play	Children engage in play creating situations where the conventional rules do not apply	Running scared and shouting 'help' as they are 'chased' by a dragon
Mastery play	Children try to control the physical environment	Children dig a hole and carry water in it to make a lake
Object play	Children through their sense explore objects	Smelling flowers, touching fabrics and sense how they feel
Role play	Children take a role that is not associated with their normal domestic experiences	Children become taxi drivers, doctors, pilots
Recapitulative play	Children engage in play that allows them to explore ancestry, history, rituals, stories, rhymes	Children create a cave or an ancient temple

Adapted by Hughes, B. (2002) *A Playworker's Taxonomy of Play Types* (2nd edition). London: PlayLink.

DEVELOPMENT AND LEARNING MATTER

As will be explored in Chapters 6 and 7, development and learning have a crucial role in early childhood education. Development refers to how children grow:

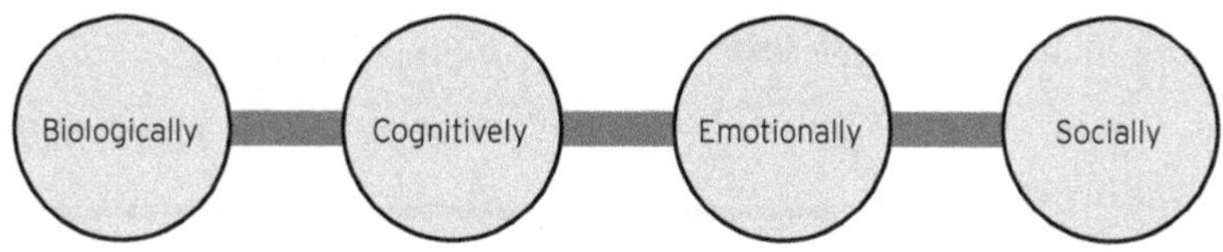

The term is used to describe the maturational progression in early childhood. Learning refers to children's acquisition of knowledge, skills and dispositions resulting from interactions and influences from the environment in which they live. Children from birth have the capacity to be competent and skilful learners, shaped by the family, culture and community they grow in (Bertram and Pascal, 2010). Central to children's development and learning is their own experiences that are mainly acquired with exploring different materials, activities and experiment through play.

CRITICAL QUESTION

How can adults (and teachers) support children's development?

CHILDREN'S MULTIMODAL COMMUNICATIVE PRACTICES IN A DIGITAL AGE MATTER

With digital technologies (i.e. touch screen devices, Internet Connected Toys) permeating children's everyday lives at home, early childhood education should create opportunities to integrate technologies in playful explorations for children. Technologies not only offer entertainment for children, but they have potential for knowledge building and can facilitate children's learning and explorations by engaging in playful co-participation which allows them to create meanings and communicate. Thus, Yelland (2015, p. 235) urged for the provision of *contexts so that young children can experience different modes of representations which in turn afford them the opportunity to formulate new understandings about their world.*

PARTNERSHIPS WITH FAMILIES AND THE COMMUNITY MATTER

Partnership and parental engagement are important aspects of early childhood education. The governments of Australia, New Zealand and Sweden, for example, have all endorsed the importance of home-education connections and the impact for children's well-being and achievements in their pre-school curriculum documents (Australian Government Department of Education, Employment and Workplace, 2009; New Zealand Ministry of Education, 1996; Swedish Government, 2010). Similarly, academic research outcomes stress that parental engagement is essential for a successful learning community and learners' academic achievements (Wolfe, 2014; Miller *et al.*, 2014). Palaiologou and Male (2018, p. 76) propose that:

> *the discussion on partnerships should start from the premise that families, learners, community and school should all be involved in the creation of learning environments and collaborate in meaningful ways to create educational experiences that will be beneficial to all involved in the process.*

CLASSROOM LINK

What does this mean for classroom practice?

What do good links with families and the community look like in the classroom?

There are many ways that you can work to involve parents in their children's learning in an early years classroom. Some examples of good practice include:

- Parents visiting to talk about their careers, faiths or communities
- Opening up your learning space so parents and carers feel free to observe the setting
- Sharing news and suggestions for activities through emails and other communications
- Holding events to showcase your practice and to support learning at home
- Your setting should be reflective of its community. Learn about the community through the children and parents

CRITICAL QUESTION

Can good links with parents and the local community enhance the effectiveness of educational settings? Will children in these settings learn more?

CHAPTER SUMMARY

This chapter has discussed the key issues that matter in early childhood. You must remember:

- Policy in early childhood has rapidly changed the last two decades especially since the introduction of the EYFS as statutory curriculum framework for children from birth to five.
- Although there is overwhelming evidence on what constitutes effective practice in early childhood, the EYFS places emphasis on school readiness and *classification of children, teachers and schools* (Roberts-Holmes, 2015, p. 3).
- Play, development, learning and partnerships with parents and the community should be central to the pedagogy in early childhood.

ASSIGNMENTS

If you are writing an ITE assignment on what matters in early childhood, it will be useful for you to think through the following:

1. What are the key priorities of the Early Years Foundation Stage? What are your views for the developmental areas?
2. When organising your learning environment critically engage with the following three questions:
   - What should be learned? (outcomes of the educational programme)
   - When should it be learned? (the development of the learner and when should something be introduced)
   - How is it best learned? (programme design, teaching techniques and strategies - the role of play)
3. As children are now using digital technology from a very young age, what are your views? How can digital technology can be integrated in early childhood curriculum?

These two books are comprehensive guides on issues of play and learning that matter in early childhood:

Brooker, L., Blaise M. and Edwards, S. (2014) *The SAGE Handbook of Play and Learning in Early Childhood.* London: SAGE.

Bruce, T., Hakkarainen, P. and Bredikyte, M. (2018) *The Routledge International Handbook of Early Childhood Play*. London: Routledge.

This book provides a comprehensive guide of the EYFS:

Palaiologou, I. (2016) *Early Years Foundation Stage: Theory and practice*. London: SAGE.

REFERENCES

Alexander, R. (2008) Pedagogy, Curriculum and Culture, in Murphy, P., Hall, K. and Soler, J. *Pedagogy and Practice: Culture and Identities*. London: Sage.

Ang, L. (2014). Preschool or Prep School? Rethinking the Role of Early Years Education. *Contemporary Issues in Early Childhood*, 15(2): 185–99. Available at: http://doi.org/10.2304/ciec.2014.15.2.185 (accessed 04/06/12).

Australian Government Department of Education, Employment and Workplace (2009) *The Early Years Learning Framework for Australia: Belonging, being and becoming*. Barton: Commonwealth of Australia.

Bertram, T. and Pascal, C. (2010) Understanding child development, in T. Bruce (ed.) Early *Childhood: A guide for students* (2nd edn), London: SAGE, pp. 71–86.

Brooker, L. (2011) Taking children seriously: An alternative agenda for research. *Journal of Early Childhood Research*, 9(2) pp. 137–49.

Brooker, L., Blaise M. and Edwards, S. (2014) *The SAGE Handbook of Play and Learning in Early Childhood*. London: SAGE.

Bruce, T., Hakkarainen, P. and Bredikyte, M. (2018) *The Routledge International Handbook of Early Childhood Play*. London: Routledge.

Cohen, B., Moss, P., Petrie, P. and Wallace, J. (2004) *A New Deal for Children? Re-forming Education and Care in England, Scotland and Sweden*. Bristol: The Policy Press.

Colliver, Y. and Fleer, M. (2016) 'I already know what I learned: Young children's perspectives on learning through play, *Early Child Development and Care*, 186(10): 1559–70.

DCSF (2008) *Statutory Framework for the Early Years Foundation Stage*. London: DCSF.

DfE (2012) *Statutory Framework for the Early Years Foundation Stage*. Runcorn: DfE.

DfE (2018) *Proposed New Early Learning Goals*. London: DFE.

DfEE (1996) *Desirable Outcomes for Children's Learning on Entering Compulsory Education*. London: DfEE.

DfEE (2000) *Curriculum Guidance for the Foundation Stage*. London: DfEE.

DfES (2001) *National Standards for Under 8s Day Care and Childminding*. Nottingham: DfES.

DfES (2002) *Birth to Three Matters*. London: DfES.

DfES (2004) *Every Child Matters Agenda*. London: DfES.

Ellis, S. and Moss, G. (2014) Ethics, education policy and research: The Iphonics question reconsidered. *British Educational Research Journal*, April: 40(2): 241–60.

Fitzgerald, D. and Kay, J. (2016) *Understanding Early Years Policy (*4th edn). London: Sage.

Gopnik, A., Meltzoff, A. and Kuhl, P. (2001) *How Babies Think the Science of Childhood*. London: Phoenix.

Goswami, U. (2015) *Children's Cognitive Development and Learning* (CPRT Research Survey 3). York: Cambridge Primary Review Trust.

Hamilton, D. (1999) The pedagogic paradox (or why no didactics in England?), *Pedagogy, Culture and Society*, 7(1): 135–52.

Hedges, H. Cullen, J. and Jordan, B. (2011) Early years curriculum: funds of knowledge as a conceptual framework for children's interests. *Journal of Curriculum Studies*, 43(2): 185–05.

HMIE (2006) Pilot inspection of the education functions of Clackmannanshire Council in October 2005. Edinburgh: SEED.

Howard, J. (2010) Early years practitioners' perceptions of play: An exploration of theoretical understanding, planning and involvement, confidence and barriers to practice. *Educational & Child Psychology*, 27(4): 91–102.

Howard, J., Jenwey, V. and Hill, C. (2006) Children's categorisation of play and learning based on social context. *Early Child Development and Care*, 176(3&4): 379–93.

Langston A. (2011) A guide to the revised EYFS: Part 1 an overview. *Nursery World*, 111(4277): 15–18.

Leach, J. and Moon, B. (2008) *The Power of Pedagogy*. London: Sage.

Male, T. and Palaiologou, I. (2015) Pedagogical leadership in the 21st century: Evidence from the field, *Educational Management Administration and Leadership*, 43(2): 214–31.

McGillivray, G. (2008) Nannies, nursery nurses and early years professionals: Constructions of professional identity in the early years workforce in England. *European Early Childhood Research Journal*, 16(2): 242–54.

Miller, K., Hilhendore, A. and Dilworth-Bart, J. (2014) Cultural capital and home-school connections in early childhood. *Contemporary Issues in Early Childhood*, 15(4): 329–45.

Morton, K. (2014) Ofsted chief writes to inspectors to outline reporting priorities, *Nursery World*, 24 March, London: MA Education.

New Zealand Ministry of Education (1996) *Te whariki: He whariki matauranga mo nga mokopuna o Aotearoa: Early childhood curriculum*. Wellington, New Zealand: Learning Media.

Oberhuemer, P. (2005) International perspectives on early childhood curricula. *International Journal of Early Childhood*, 7(1): 27–37.

Ofsted (2017) Bold beginnings: The Reception curriculum in a sample of good and outstanding primary schools. Manchester: Ofsted.

Oliviera-Formoshino, J. and Formoshino, J. (2012) *Pedagogy-in-Participation: Childhood association educational perspective*. Porto: Porto Editora.

Osgood, J. (2006) Editorial: Rethinking professionalism in the early years: English perspectives. *Contemporary Issues in Early Childhood*, 7(1): 1–4.

Osgood, J. (2009) Childcare workforce reform in England and 'the early years professional': A critical discourse analysis. *Journal of Education Policy*, 24(6): 733–51.

Osgood, J., Elwick, A., Robertson, L., Sakr, M. and Wilson, D. (2017) Early years teacher and early years educator: A scoping study of the impact, experiences and associated issues of recent early years qualifications and training in England. Available at: http://tactyc.org.uk/research/ (accessed 04/06/12).

Palaiologou, I. (2012) *Child Observation for the Early Years* (2nd edn). London: SAGE.

Palaiologou, I. and Male, T. (2018) Formation of partnerships: An ecological paradigm. In Z. Brown and S. Ward (eds) *Contemporary Issues in Childhood: A bio-ecological approach*. Abingdon: Routledge, pp. 83–97.

Papatheordorou, T., and Moyles, J., (eds) (2012) *Cross-Cultural Perspectives on Early Childhood*. London: SAGE.

Phillips, R. and Harper-Jones, G. (2002) Whatever next? Education policy and New Labour: The first four years, 1997–2001. *British Education Research Journal*, 29(1): 125–32.

Pascal, C. and Bertram, T. (2012) Praxis, ethics and power: Developing praxeology as a participatory paradigm for early childhood research. *European Early Childhood Education Research Journal*, 20(4): 471–92.

Peers, C. (2006) What does a pedagogue look like? Masculinity and the repression of sexual difference in ancient education, in *Discourse: Studies in the Cultural Politics of Education.* 27(2): 189–208.

Pellegrini, A.D. (2009). *The Role of Play in Human Development.* Oxford: Oxford University Press.

Pyle, A. and Alaca, B. (2016) Kindergarten children's perspectives on play and learning, *Early Child Development and Care*, 27 October: 1–13.

Roberts-Holmes, G. (2012) "It's the bread and butter of our practice": Experiencing the Early Years Foundation Stage. *International Journal of Early Years Education*, 20(1): 30–42.

Roberts-Holmes, G. (2015) The "datafication" of early years pedagogy: "If the teaching is good, the data should be good and if there's bad teaching, there is bad data". *Journal of Education Policy*, 30(3): 302–15. Available at: http://doi.org/10.1080/02680939.2014.924561_(accessed 04/06/12).

Rose, J. (2006) *Independent Review of the Teaching of Early Reading.* Nottingham: DfES.

Rumbold, A. (1990) *Starting with Quality.* London: HMSO.

Siraj-Blatchford, I., Taggart, B., Sylva, K., Sammons, P. and Melhuish, E. (2008) Towards the transformation of practice in early childhood education: The effective provision of pre-school education (EPPE) project. *Cambridge Journal of Education*, 38(1): 23–36.

Siraj-Blatchford, I., Sylva, K., Muttock, S., Gilden, R. and Bell, D. (2002) *Researching Effective Pedagogy in the Early Years.* Research Report No. 356. Norwich: DfES.

Siraj-Blatchford, I., Taggart, B., Sylva, K., Sammons, P., and Melhuish, E. (2010) Towards the transformation of practice in early childhood education: The effective provision of pre-school education (EPPE) project. *Cambridge Journal of Education*, 38(1): 23–36.

Smith, M. (2006) *The Role of the Pedagogue in Galatians in Faculty Publications and Presentations.* Liberty University. Available at: http://digitalcommons.liberty.edu/cgi/viewcontent.cgi?article=1114&context=sor_fac_pubs (accessed 04/06/12).

Soler, J. and Miller, L. (2003) The struggle for early childhood curricula: A comparison of the English Foundation Stage Curriculum, Te Whariki and Reggio Emilia. *International Journal of Early Years Education*, 11(1): 57–68.

Swedish Government (2010) *Curriculum for the Pre-school Lpfö.* Stockholm: Government of Sweden.

Sylva, K. Melhuish, E. Sammons, P. Siraj-Blatchford, I. and Taggart, B. (2004) *The Effective Provision of Pre-school Education (EPPE) Project: Final report.* Nottingham: DfES.

Taggart, B. (2015) Effective pre-school, primary and secondary education project (EPPSE 3-16+). London: DfE.

Theobald, M., Danby, S., Einarsdóttir, J., Bourne, J., Jones, D., Ross, S. Knaggs, H. and Carter-Jones, C. (2015) Children's Perspectives of Play and Learning for Educational Practice, *Education Sciences*, 5: 345–62).

Thomson, R. (2011) EYFS review prioritises how children learn. *Nursery World*, 5 April Available at: www.nursery world.co.uk/nursery-world/news/1096034/eyfs-review-prioritises-children-learn> (accessed 04/06/12).

Tickell, C. (2011) *The Early Years: Foundations for life, health and learning*. Available at: http://media.education.gov.uk/MediaFiles/B/1/5/%7BB15EFF0D-A4DF-4294-93A1-1E1B88C13F68%7DTickell%20review.pdf (accessed 26/01/12).

Ward, H. (2018) What's wrong with Ofsted's Bold Beginning report? Available at: www.tes.com/news/ofsteds-bold-beginnings-report-flawed-and-should-be-scrapped-says-open-letter (accessed 19/04/18).

Wolfe, V. E. (2014) The voice of the parent: Perceptions of the United Kingdom resilience programme. *Educational and Child Development*, 31(4): 58–71.

Wood, E. (2007) Reconceptualising child-centred education: Contemporary directions in policy, theory and practice in early childhood. *Forum*, 49(1 & 2): 119–34.

Wood, E. (2017) Board policy issues, in BERA-TACTYC Early Childhood Research review 2003–2017. Available at: www.bera.ac.uk/project/bera-tactyc-early-childhood-research-review-2003-2017 (accessed 19/04/18).

Yelland, N. (2015) Playful explorations and new technologies. In J. Moyles (eds) *The Excellence of Play Maiden head*: Open University Press, pp. 225–360.

6

WHAT DO STUDENT TEACHERS NEED TO KNOW ABOUT CHILD DEVELOPMENT?

Dr Ioanna Palaiologou CPsychol AFBPsS, FRSA is an Academic Associate at UCL Institute of Education and a child psychologist with specialism on child development and learning theories. Her research interests focus on early childhood education, child development, play and learning and digital technologies.

KEY WORDS

- Childhood
- Constructs of development
- Development
- Emotional
- Factors impacting on development
- Learning
- Social

INTRODUCTION

Child development is linked to the process of learning. Understanding a child's development is an important aspect when teaching as it helps you to organise your learning environment, observe and understand certain behaviours, and plan activities to support children. This chapter explores child development for student teachers. It introduces some ways in which we understand child development. It summarises different views of the development process, and investigates the factors that impact on development and sees how all of that can influence learning.

A DEFINITION OF 'DEVELOPMENT'

CRITICAL QUESTION

What is development?

Development *refers to the behavioural, biological, physiological and psychological changes that occur as a child transitions from a development infant to an autonomous teenager* (Fernald *et al.*, 2017, p. 21). Development is the process of an individual's growth and maturation, *change and transformation, and it is frequently conceptualised in terms of moving through a sequence of age-approximate stages* (Vogler *et al.*, 2008, p. 5).

From a developmental psychology viewpoint, the term is used to describe patterns of change over time, which begin at conception and continue throughout life (Baltes, 1987). Baltes proposed the following principles that evolve around the study of human development.

INFO 6.1

Baltes on 'What is development?'

- Development is **lifelong**: human beings develop at all ages from childhood to old age and involve processes that might not exist from birth, but emerge during the lifespan.
- Development is **multidimensional**: meaning that development cannot be studied only by single criterion such as quantified (increase-decrease) or qualitative (attitudes - dispositions - behaviours) changes in humans.
- Development is **multidirectional**: which means that there are many abilities that take different directions in everyone; in other words, development can vary for each of us.
- Development has **gains and losses**: all development has aspects of growth (e.g. gain weight) and decline (e.g. decrease of vision) and is changeable over the lifespan.

- Development is **plastic**: meaning the flexibility and/or the capacity to modify behaviours or development. For example, a child after a car accident cannot walk anymore, the child will internally modify functions associated with walking and other functions will take over to balance the loss of physical movement.
- Development is **contextual**: as it is depending on the environment in which we live and is shaped by socio-economic, educational and political factors. For example, a child growing in a war zone and a child growing in a peaceful environment will have different factors impacting on their development.
- Development is influenced by **history**: events that take place during the early stages of life can impact on development. For example, changes of education systems (e.g. Pupil Premium) impact on children who need it and the lack of it might affect their intellectual development.
- The study of development is **multidisciplinary**: not all development can be explained only by one discipline such as psychology. Other disciplines, such as sociology or anthropology, might help us to understand the breadth and depth of development (see section below, 'Development as a Sociological Construct').

Baltes thus offers a view of development that is not limited to the study of changes that happen in human development from a biological, physiological and psychological perspective, but also as an interwoven relationship between those aspects and the environment, content and history.

Source: Baltes, P.B. (1987) Theoretical propositions of life span developmental psychology: On the dynamics between growth and decline. *Developmental Psychology*, 24: 247–53.

To develop an understanding of development, we need to take all such perspectives into consideration and seek to synthesise the disciplines that study humans.

> *In child development, ideas change, sometimes rapidly... . The theories of child development offer signposts to different routes to understanding young children ... there are so many contradictions and paradoxes that, for all signposts, you end up in a maze.*
>
> Penn (2008, pp. 37–40)

DEVELOPMENT AS A PSYCHOLOGICAL CONSTRUCT

Development is mainly studied through developmental psychology as a process of maturation and growth. Within the field of psychology there are different schools of thought, however, that have developed their own explanations on how and why development occurs (see Chapter 5). Key to all these theories is the attempt to understand *how and why change happens and why some aspects of behaviour remain the same* (Levine and Munsch, 2011, p. 30).

The main domains of development are:

Physical development: the biological and physiological changes that occur in the body and brain (i.e. change in size, weight, development of fine motor skills).

Cognitive development: the changes that occur in the way we think, understand the world, solve problems and rationalise. Key elements of cognitive development are memory, perception, attention, thinking and language.

Social-emotional development: changes that occur in the way we understand ourselves, regulate our emotions as well as connecting with others and forming relationships.

DEVELOPMENT AREAS AND KEY CHARACTERISTICS

Developmental areas	Key characteristics
Physical development	*Large motor development:* Balancing Walking
	Running Jumping Climbing *Small motor development:* Hand preference Turns with hand (pages, lids) Holds (pens, pencils, scissors) Dresses and undresses Makes puzzles Builds with small blocks
Emotional development	Shows interest Shows happiness Shows affection Shows enjoyment Shows sympathy Shows empathy Shows distress Shows fear Shows anger Shows sadness

Developmental areas	Key characteristics
Personal development	Stays in the setting without difficulty Makes eye contact Develops relationships with practitioners Makes relationships with other children Participates in role play Participates in social play Participates in symbolic play Gets involved in the daily routine of the setting
Social development	*Engaged in:* Watching others during play or activities Playing by him/herself Parallel play Play with others Making friends Having friends Following rules Taking turns Sharing with others Seeing things from another point of view Helping others during play or activities
Cognitive development	*Attention:* Concentration span during activities or play Distraction *Memory:* Recognises familiar objects and people Can name familiar objects and people Searches for hidden, favourite objects Recalls and narrates stories *Perception* (how sensory information is organised and interpreted): Identifying objects, colours Locating - is able to know distances, sizes, directions Categorising of information into meaningful patterns Reasoning *Problem solving:* Sorting objects by colour, size, weight Classification of objects (big/small, more/less) *Language:* Spoken language (uses single words, uses sentences, singing, takes part in conversations, asks questions, narrates a story) *Numeracy:* (understands meaning of numbers, understands use of numbers, counting and ordering)

(Continued)

(Continued)

Developmental areas	Key characteristics
Literacy	Holds a pen/pencil Pretends to write Pretends to read Attempts scribbles Letter-like writing 'Reads' pictures Holds books Turns pages Points at text Narrates stories from the pictures in the book Understands that print conveys messages
Creativity	Makes marks on paper Makes shapes Shows interest in drawing Shows interest in singing Shows interest in dramatic play Shows interest in telling stories/making stories Combines materials and objects together to create e.g. a drawing, story

Adapted from Palaiologou, I., (2016) Child Observation: A Guide for students of early childhood (3rd ed), London: SAGE, Learning Matters. pp. 178-182.

CRITICAL QUESTION

If children are beginning to develop an ability to reason and understand cause and effect at age 7, how should this impact your teaching of children of this age?

DOMAINS OF DEVELOPMENT

More than a series of milestones, child development is a complex process.

Psychologists have sought explanations to changes in all the three domains of development (such as physical, cognitive, social-emotional) using the following lenses:

NATURE VS. NURTURE

'Nature' refers to the genetic factors that impact on development, 'nurture' refers to the influences of the environment. For many years in the field of psychology many upheld the view that inherited genetic factors (nature) are responsible for development. Others argued that the environment is responsible for all behaviours and all behaviour can be modified by the environment. Today, we tend to accept that both nature and nurture impact on development. For example, children who are genetically able to make sounds (nature) will develop these sounds to words and sentences, and will be able to read and write and engage in interactions with others, adults and instruction (nurture).

CONTINUOUS VS. DISCONTINUOUS (OR STAGE-LIKE DEVELOPMENT)

There are many who suggest that development is a continuous process of *gradual accumulation of a behaviour, skill, or knowledge* (e.g. Keenan, 2002, p. 5). Such an approach favours the view that development is unfolding from one stage to another 'building from previous abilities' (Keenan, 2002, p. 5) to develop and master new ones.

On the other hand, there are those who support the idea that development is happening in stages and each stage is distinctly different from one another (discontinuous).

KEY THEORY

Such a view is epitomised by the *Developmental Stage Theory* proposed by Piaget (1958). His views have heavily influenced educationalists on how to create learning environments and plan curricula for children. In Piagetian theory child development is seen as a universal process whereby children progress from one stage to the next in terms of their physical, cognitive, socio-emotional and moral competencies. These progressions from one stage to the next are influenced by children's direct experiences and, as they mature with age and direct experiences, their competencies and abilities become more complex and abstract.

CLASSROOM LINK

What does this mean for classroom practice?

Creating direct experiences for children

Piaget (1958) proposed that when children acquire (accommodate) a new knowledge skill (schema), they need through practice and experience to process it and make links with other pieces of knowledge (assimilation). He proposed that as humans we need a balance between accommodation and assimilation (equilibrium). Central to Piaget's explanation of development is that it resulted from direct active exploration and experimentation from the environment.

Although his theory focused on children's growth and development, his ideas have influenced education as terms such as *active learning* or *discovery learning* captured his ideas. In such approaches the teacher is seen as a facilitator of learning, rather than offering direct instruction, and the key focus should be on the process of learning through exploration and experimentation, allowing time for children's collaboration as well as individual activities.

For example, in the classroom the teacher introduces a new mathematical concept (so children are asked to accommodate a new schema). After explaining it to the children, she divides them into small groups and provides practical activities so they can have the time to understand the new concept through active experiences (so children can assimilate the new schema).

Theorists such as Sternberg and Okagagi (1989) argue, however, that development can be studied or understood as being one or the other, and being continuous and discontinuous.

STABILITY VS. CHANGE

This debate focuses on whether certain behaviours in our development change or remain stable throughout our lives. For example:

CRITICAL QUESTION

Is aggression or anxiety something that stays stable throughout our lives?

We see young children in the playground kick or push others when they want something and cannot have it. Such behaviour stays stable or changes with maturation and interactions with the environment (nurture). Longitudinal studies on children's behaviour (e.g. Weems, 2008; Nagin and Tremblay, 1999) have concluded that some behaviours remain stable throughout our lives (e.g. being shy) and some can be modified, moderated or changed (e.g. a phobia towards swimming). Such a view has implications for interventions that can change behaviours considered to be preventing children from achieving their full potential in life.

CRITICAL QUESTION

How can teachers support children to change certain behaviours?

CLASSROOM LINK

What does this mean for classroom practice?

Reception class tasks such as sitting on the carpet for story time can be challenging for some children. Children may avoid doing this by asking to go to the toilet or doing something else. If a teacher simply insists, the child may respond by disrupting the 'carpet time', moving around or disturbing children nearby.

In some cases, children simply need support to adjust or change their behaviours. Some suggestions:

- Give the child a way to quantify the time that they need to stay still (water-clock or egg timer).
- Allow the child to choose the text for story time - to engage them more in the event.
- Ensure the child has visited the toilet before carpet time.

DEVELOPMENT AS A SOCIOLOGICAL CONSTRUCT

Conceptualisations of learning are mainly underpinned by psychological theories of development, especially as informed by developmental psychology. Development is an important aspect for childhood, policy and education. This is central to the United Nations Convention on the Rights of the Child (UNCRC) that defines that the term 'development' should be interpreted in a broad sense, adding a qualitative dimension so that not only physical health is intended, but also:

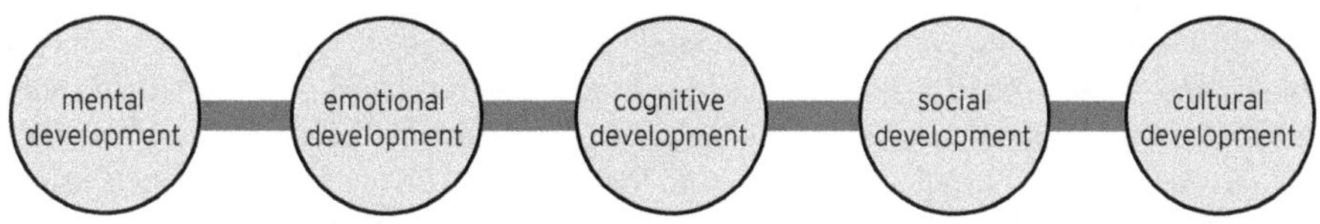

Since the introduction of the UNCRC researchers have tried to create synergy between developmental psychology and sociological discourses in the study of development in young children:

> *Developmental psychology can be seen as a discourse which not only contributes to the construction of our images of children and our understanding of children's needs, but also to the construction and constitution of the whole childhood landscape.*
>
> (Dahlberg *et al.*, 1999, p. 36)

The most influential theory in the discourse of development comes from the sociology of childhood which urged for a new way of thinking (paradigm) that goes beyond the developmental child (e.g. Qvortrup *et al.*, 1994; James and Prout, 1997; Jones, 2009). Opposed to just viewing the child through the developmental lens, the sociology of childhood proposes a view of the child as 'beings', and as competent and active participants in society from an early age, rather than 'becoming' so (Olsson, 2009; Uprichard, 2008).

> *Research in the last decades has impressively confirmed that children from an early age are explorers with boundless curiosity and that they are judicious decision makers and social actors each with their own unique goals, interests and ways to communicate feelings and intentions.*
>
> (Doek *et al.*, 2006, p. 32)

Thus, in any discussion or study of development it is important to take on board the view that *children are living here and now; relationships and solidarities between children; creating relationships between adults and children; democratic and ethical ideas and ways of working together with children* (Jones, 2009, p. 32). Moreover, it is important in any conceptualisation of development to examine the *dynamic interplay between biological and environmental facts* (Fernald *et al.*, 2017, p. 21) as emerging ideas of the sociology of childhood shape attitudes and affect development. Finally, our understanding of children as 'beings' and active participants in all aspects of their lives calls for the discourse on development that considers *the plurality of developmental pathways and children's roles in influencing their own development* (Estep, 2002, p. 143).

CLASSROOM LINK

What does this mean for classroom practice?

As mentioned in Chapter 5, in the Early Years Foundation Stage there is an emphasis on 'school readiness'. Developmental scales, stages and milestones are used to assess children's readiness for learning and/or readiness for school. Readiness for learning means the individual's capacity to process and learn specific subjects based on the average rates of a group of children from the same age. Readiness for school is referred to as the academic capacities of an individual based on physical, intellectual and social developmental areas that are essential to exist for children to be able to fulfil school requirements (Scott-Little *et al.*, 2006). However, as has been explored in this chapter, *child development is malleable and can be enhanced by interventions affecting the child, the environment or both* (Fernald *et al.*, 2017, p. 21).

Thus, any assessment of a child's readiness to learning and/or school should be underpinned by sensitivity, a nurturing care of the child's experiences, environment and culture, and be accompanied by an assessment narrative that is not limited only on an interpretation of tests and developmental scores, but rather from a breadth and depth of behaviours, attitudes, aptitudes and positions, and other skills that provide a holistic narrative of the child considering the situations children live in.

WHAT FACTORS IMPACT ON DEVELOPMENT?

Many social and cultural factors affect children's learning and development. Neaum (2016) notes that there are patterns of underachievement for children from certain identifiable groups. Undoubtedly, social and cultural factors have an impact on children's learning and development both positively and negatively.

KEY THEORY

Nutbrown and Clough (2006) identify a range of areas that are known to have an impact on issues of inclusion and exclusion within education and society:

- Challenging behaviour
- Disability
- Emotional and behavioural difficulty
- Employment status
- Gender
- Housing
- Language
- Mental health
- Physical impairment
- Poverty
- Race/ethnicity
- Religion
- Sexual orientation
- Social class
- Special educational needs.

Black *et al.* (2017), based on extensive research of factors that impact on the development, of children, offer a framework that conceptualise the life course of childhood development. Black *et al.* (ibid., p. 79) suggest:

> *Children reach developmental potential when they acquire competencies for academic, behavioural, socio-emotional and economic accomplishments. Multiple factors influence the acquisition of competencies, including health, nutrition, security and safety, responsive caregiving and early learning; these domains interact with each other and can be mutually reinforcing through the process of development. All are necessary for nurturing care and occur through bi-directional interactions, initiated by both children and caregivers and sustained by their environments.*

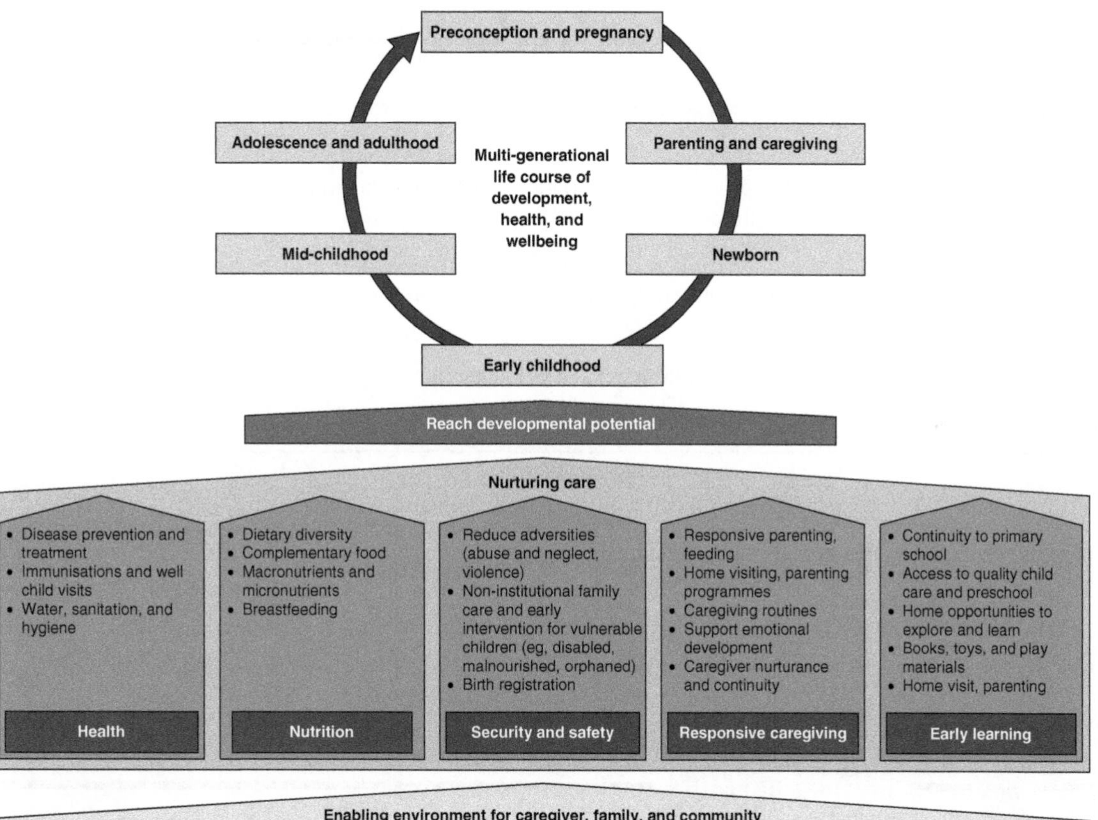

Figure 6.1 The effects of contexts, environments and nurturing care through the multigenerational life

(Source: Black *et al.*, 2017, p. 79)

Thus, it is perhaps true to summarise that multiple factors impact children's development and these factors are unique to each individual child. So, what does this mean for your classroom practice?

CRITICAL QUESTION

Can a teacher plan activities and create a learning environment that supports the development of all children in their class?

CLASSROOM LINK

What does this mean for classroom practice?

When planning activities and organising your learning environment, you should consider the nurturing factors that impact on children's learning as well as their background contextual development of the children (socio-economic, political and cultural context).

For example, planning for transitions from home to school or from one year to another will need to consider not only the educational continuation, but also the economic, cultural and psycho-social factors that might impact on the child and the family.

Questions need to be included on how the transition will impact on children's ability to learn, and to interact with other children and adults.

HOW DOES DEVELOPMENT IMPACT ON LEARNING?

Development is strongly linked with children's ability to learn. To create effective learning environments teachers need to have a good understanding of their children's development, abilities, skills and interests.

CRITICAL QUESTION

Should the design of your learning environment be informed by the children in it?

It is also important to have a good understanding of developmental theories as they help you to create strategies and techniques in your teaching. See Chapter 7 on 'How do children learn?'

Doherty and Hughes (2014, p. 11) illustrated the importance of development as central to learning with the following image:

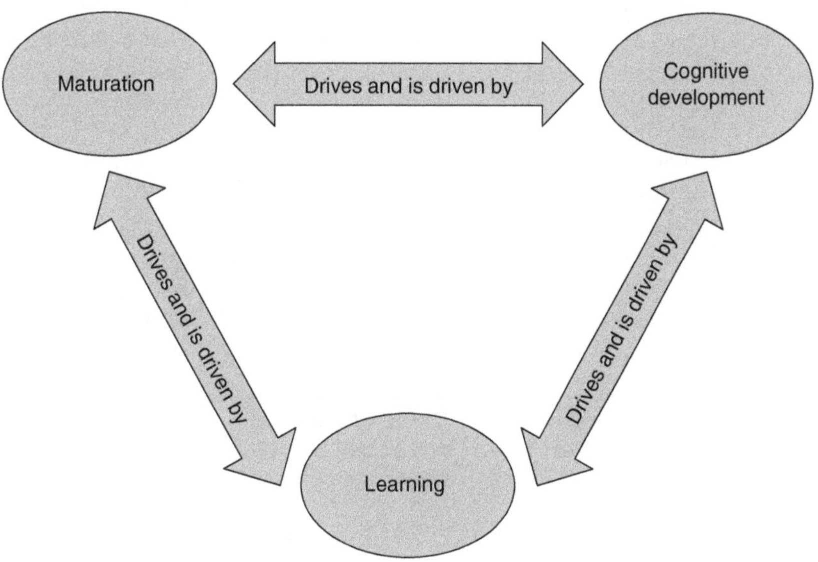

Figure 6.2 Development and learning

However, as research (i.e Nutbrown and Clough, 2006 and more recently Black *et al.*, 2017) has shown us, development is influenced by many factors such as the environment, poverty, deprivation and culture. For example, poverty is associated with deficits in language and children's cognitive abilities and functioning at three years that can become more pronounced by the age of five (Fernald *et al.*, 2011), consequently impacting on learning.

The importance of development in the learning process is mostly obvious when there is a developmental delay, which is either biological or psychological.

How can development be disrupted?

Kevin Crowley, in his text *Child Development: A Practical Introduction* (Crowley, 2014, p. 100) summarises the ways in which development can be disrupted:

Disruption	Description	Examples	Implications for learning
Developmental delay	Development proceeds at a slower pace than normal	A 4-year-old child who has not learned to talk	The child cannot start reading and writing

(Continued)

(Continued)

Disruption	Description	Examples	Implications for learning
Regression	Child falls off course of normal development or demonstrates a loss of development achievements	A child was talking normal and now has started to stutter	The child loses confidence and refuses to do any reading in the class
Asynchrony	Different aspects of development proceed out of step with one another	A child whose language development follows the same course as peers, but is behind in social development	A child cannot work with others or does not wait for his /her turn subsequently fights with others and creates disturbance in the class
Precocity	An accelerated rate of development that may be linked to psychopathology	A child who worries excessively about 'grown-up matters'	The child might lack concentration as the worries take over and they cannot focus on any of the activities of the classroom. Cannot sit down and runs around the class
Developmental deviation	Behaviours that are qualitatively different from normal behaviour	Echolalia in children with autism (tendency to repeat back people's speech with no purpose)	The child cannot listen to simple instructions and follow them

CHAPTER SUMMARY

This chapter discussed how we understand child development and its impact on learning. You must remember:

- development includes all the changes in an individual over their lifespan. It is studied in domains: physical, cognitive, social and emotional. Development, however, is a holistic process and the domains are interlinked with each other;
- environmental and social, political and economic factors do impact on the child's development which is an interplay between biological and environmental factors;
- it is important to have a good understanding of children's development and theories that explain development as it will help you to develop teaching and learning strategies in your classroom.

ASSIGNMENTS

If you are writing an ITT assignment on key theorists of development, it will be useful for you to think through the following:

1. What are the common characteristics and the differences among them?
2. Which theory explains development in a way that can support you in your teaching?
3. To what extent do you think a single theory answers all our questions about development?

The following books are very useful reading to guide you in your understanding of key issues and theories of development with examples of their applicability into practice:

Bates, B. (2016) *Learning Theories Simplified ... and how to apply them to teaching*. London: SAGE.

Doherty, J. and Hughes, M. (2014) *Child Development: From theory to practice 0–11* (2nd edition). Edinburgh: Pearson.

Crowley, K. (2014) *Child Development: A practical introduction*. London: SAGE.

To further your understanding on brain development and its impact on human development and learning:

Blakemore, S.J. and Firt, U. (2005) *The Learning Brain*. Oxford: Blackwell Publishing.

These three books are comprehensive guides on the applicability of psychology in education with examples from practice:

Buckler, S. and Castle, P. (2014) *Psychology for Teachers*. London: SAGE.

Long, M., Wood, C., Litleton, K., Pasenger, T. and Shehy, K. (2011) *The Psychology of Education* (2nd edition). London: Routledge.

Wolfolk, A., Hughes, M. and Walkup, V. (2013) *Psychology in Education* (2nd edition). Edinburgh: Pearson.

REFERENCES

Baltes, P.B. (1987) Theoretical propositions of life span developmental psychology: On the dynamics between growth and decline. *Developmental Psychology*, 24: 247–53.

Black, Maureen M., Susan P. Walker, Lia C.H. Fernald, Christopher T. Andersen, Ann M. DiGirolamo, Chunling Lu, Dana C. McCoy, Günther Fink, Yusra R. Shawar, Jeremy Shiffman, Amanda E. Devercelli, Quentin T. Wodon,

Emily Vargas-Baron and Sally Grantham-McGregor (2017) Early childhood development coming of age: Science through the life course. *The Lancet*, 389(10064): 77–90.

Crowley, K. (2014) *Child Development: A Practical Introduction*. London: SAGE.

Dahlberg, G., Moss, P. and Pence. A.R. (1999) *Beyond Quality in Early Childhood Education and Care: Postmodern Perspectives*. London: Falmer Press.

Doek, J.E., Krappmann, L.F. and Lee, Y. (2006) Introduction to the general comment, in *Implementing Child Rights in Early Childhood*. The Hague: Bernard Van Leer Foundation/UNICEF/UN Committee on the Rights of the Child, pp. 31–4.

Doherty, J. and Hughes, M. (2014) *Child Development: From Theory to Practice 0–11* (2nd edn). Edinburgh: Pearson.

Estep Jr, J.R. (2002) Spiritual formation as social: Toward a Vygotskyan developmental perspective. *Religious Education*, 97(2): 141–64.

Fernald, L.C., Weber, A., Galasso, E. and Ratsifandrihamanana, L. (2011) Socioeconomic gradients and child development in a very low income population: Evidence from Madagascar. *Development Science*, 14: 832–47.

Fernald, L.C.H., Prado, E., Kariger, P. and Raikes, A. (2017) *A Toolkit for Measuring Early Childhood Development in Low- and Middle-Income Countries*. Washington, DC: World Bank Publications.

James, A. and Prout, A. (eds) (1997) *Constructing and Reconstructing Childhood: Contemporary issues in the sociological study of childhood*. London and Washington, DC: Falmer Press.

Jones, F., (2009) *Rethinking Childhood: Attitudes in contemporary society*. London: Continuum.

Keenan, T. (2002) *An Introduction to Child Development*. London: SAGE.

Levine, L.E. and Munsch, J. (2011) *Child Development: An active learning approach*. London: SAGE.

Nagin, D. and Tremblay, R.E (1999) Trajectories of boys' physical aggression, opposition and hyperactivity on the path to physically violent and non violent juvenile delinquency. *Child Development*, 70(5): 1181–96.

Neaum, S. (2016) *Child Development for Early Years Students and Practitioners* (3rd Edn). London: SAGE.

Nutbrown, K. and Clough, P. (2006) *Inclusion in the Early Years*. London: SAGE.

Olsson, L.M. (2009) *Movement and Experimentation in Young Children's Learning: Delouze and Guattari in early childhood education*. London: Routledge.

Penn, H, (2008) *Understanding Early Childhood: Issues and controversies* (2nd edn). Maidenhead: Open University Press.

Piaget, J. (1958) The growth of logical thinking from childhood to adolescence. AMC, 10, 12.

Qvortrup, J., Bardy, M., Sgritta, G. and Winterberger, H. (eds) (1994) *Childhood Matters: Social theory, practice and politics*. Aldershot: Avebury Press.

Scott-Little, C., Kagan, S. and Frelow, V. (2006) Conceptualization of readiness and the content of early learning standards: The intersection of policy and research? *Early Childhood Research Quarterly*, 21(2): 153–73.

Sternberg, R. and Okagaki, L. (1989) Continuity and discontinuity in intellectual development are not a matter of 'either-or'. *Human Development*, 3: 158–66.

United Nations (1989) *Convention on the Rights of the Child*. Defense International and the United Nations Children's Fund. Geneva: United Nations.

Uprichard, E. (2008) Children as 'being and becomings': Children, childhood and temporality. *Children & Society*, 22: 4.

Vogler, P., Crivello, G. and Woodhead, M. (2008) *Early Childhood Transitions Research: A review of concepts, theory, and practice*. Working Paper No. 48. The Hague, The Netherlands: Bernard van Leer Foundation.

Weems, C.F. (2008) Developmental trajectories of childhood anxiety: Identifying continuity and change in anxious emotions. *Developmental Review*, 28(4): 488–502.

WHY THEORIES MATTER FOR TRAINEE TEACHERS

No single theory can fully explain how children learn

Each theory adds significantly to how we make sense of what is a highly complex and challenging aspect of children's development

Theories provide a means by which teachers can critically discuss their pupils' learning

Critical discussion of theories avoids simplistic interpretations of behaviours in the classroom that may be overly subjective and lacking in real evidence

In their simplest form, theories are a means of explaining those complex phenomena that we do not fully understand

7

HOW DO CHILDREN LEARN?

Sean MacBlain is a senior academic at Plymouth Marjon University and worked previously as a Senior Lecturer in Education and Developmental Psychology at Stranmillis University College, Queens University Belfast, and for over 20 years as an educational psychologist in private practice.

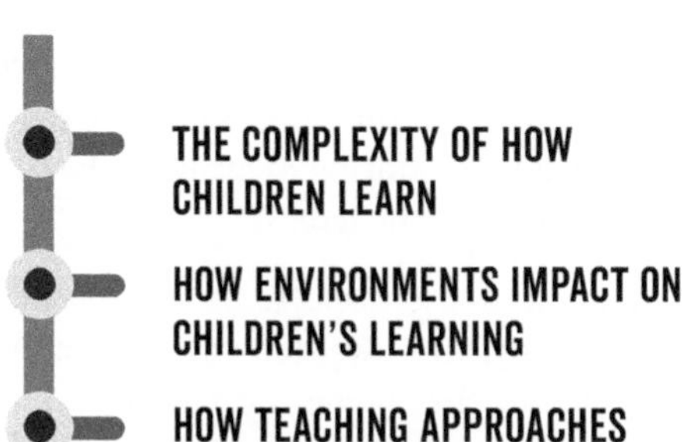

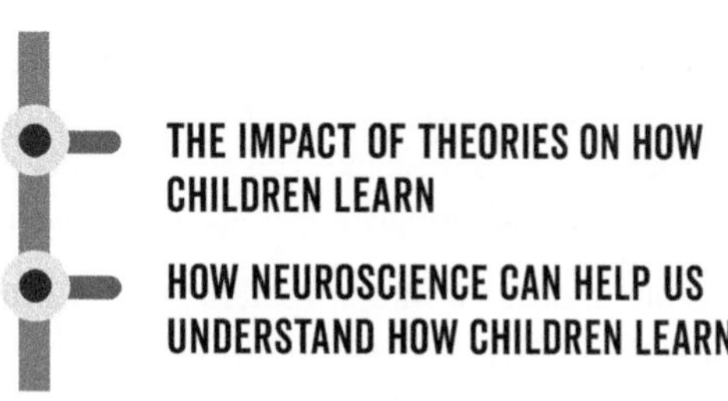

KEY WORDS

- Childhood
- Cognition
- Early Years
- Emotional literacy
- Learning
- Teaching
- Theory

INTRODUCTION

How children learn is a question that has exercised the minds of academics and practitioners for generations and one that remains at the centre of much debate and even controversy about how children should be taught. This chapter will support teachers in developing their understanding of how children learn and key principles that underpin effective teaching in the modern classroom. The chapter will begin by examining what is meant by the term 'learning' and will then explore the relevance of 'environment' and what makes for 'effective' teaching, before examining how key theorists have endeavoured to explain learning. Finally, the role that emerging research in neuroscience can play in our understanding of children's learning will be explored.

WHAT DO WE UNDERSTAND BY LEARNING?

Learning is a complex term and one that is so often used in a way that belies its complexity and fails to acknowledge the sophisticated nature of children's thinking as they grow and develop. Jarvis (2005, pp. 2–3), for example, highlighted this complexity when he challenged us to consider if we understand learning, *as a set of cognitive mechanisms or rather as an emotional, social and motivational experience?* What, he concluded, should be the focus of learning in children – 'facts or skills?' This is a dilemma that challenges the thinking of many teachers in the UK today as they become increasingly accountable for meeting targets and achieving results.

While it is possible to observe similar patterns of learning in children, it also needs to be appreciated that each child learns differently; this assertion lies at the very heart of why, after over ten years of education, significant numbers of children leave school with poor levels of literacy and numeracy, and often present as demotivated and turned off to the very idea of formal learning and enquiry. It cannot be overstated that every child brings to each learning situation a unique set of preconditions, genetic coding and environmental experiences, which are present, even before birth (Bronfenbrenner, 1979; Bronfenbrenner and Ceci, 1994; Gray and MacBlain, 2018).

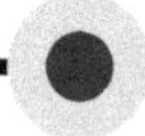

CRITICAL QUESTION

Each child learns differently, so how can we begin to understand the learning that takes place in a classroom of 30 children?

Given this complexity, how can we begin to understand this process that occurs daily for each child in every classroom? Marzano (2007) and Marzano and Kendall (2006) have offered a very useful framework, as follows:

KEY THEORY

Marzano and Kendall offered a useful taxonomy of learning defined by three systems: *Self-System*, *Metacognitive System* and *Cognitive System*, in addition to a *Knowledge Domain*, which are key to effective learning (see below). Marzano further identified three sub-sets of knowledge, which he saw as *Information*, *Mental Procedures* and *Physical Procedures* (see Figure 7.1).

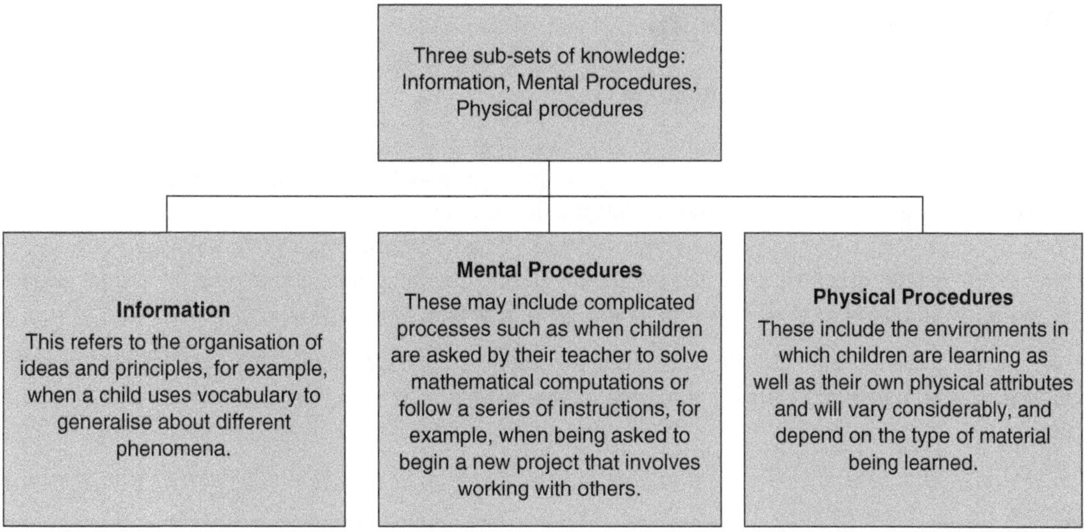

Three sub-sets of knowledge: Information, Mental Procedures, Physical procedures

Information
This refers to the organisation of ideas and principles, for example, when a child uses vocabulary to generalise about different phenomena.

Mental Procedures
These may include complicated processes such as when children are asked by their teacher to solve mathematical computations or follow a series of instructions, for example, when being asked to begin a new project that involves working with others.

Physical Procedures
These include the environments in which children are learning as well as their own physical attributes and will vary considerably, and depend on the type of material being learned.

Figure 7.1 Marzano's sub-sets of knowledge

CLASSROOM LINK

What does this mean for classroom practice?

When children are asked by their teacher to commence a new task:

- their *Self-System* begins a process whereby they make a decision to actively engage with the new task or carry on with what they are already doing;
- their *Metacognitive System* then sets goals if the task is engaged with and monitors the progress of these goals;
- finally, the *Cognitive System* processes the child's already existing information with the new information, while
- the *Knowledge Domain* furnishes the content.

CRITICAL QUESTION

Why is it important for teachers to encourage children to set themselves goals when asked to engage in new learning tasks?

FACTORS AFFECTING LEARNING

DOES A CHILD'S ENVIRONMENT REALLY MATTER?

Each child's learning is shaped by the environments in which they grow and learn, and by the adults who manage their learning. Though curricula are generally similar in schools, the ethos of every school is different, as is the catchment area of the school, managerial structure and levels of resourcing. Wider factors also impact significantly on children's learning; for example, the use of digital technology, which, today, typically begins for most children following birth (MacBlain *et al.*, 2017). A further and quite concerning factor that impacts greatly on many children's learning is poverty (Field, 2010; MacBlain *et al.*, 2017).

In a recent report, *Unsure Start: HMCI's Early Years Annual Report 2012/13 Speech 2014,* Sir Michael Wilshaw (previously, Her Majesty's Chief Inspector, Ofsted) emphasised how poverty can be detrimental to children's learning.

KEY READING

Ofsted's Annual Report 2013/14:

www.gov.uk/government/news/ofsted-annual-report-201314-published

Sir Michael emphasised how young children from the poorest backgrounds 'are less likely to follow instructions, make themselves understood, manage their own basic hygiene or play well together'. By the time children begin formal education most, he stressed, can read simple words, talk in sentences and perform simple numerical operations; Sir Michael emphasised how far fewer children from the poorest families 'can do these things well'. Children from poor families, he proposed, are much more likely to 'lag behind at age three' than their better-off peers, with many underperforming by the time they finish primary school and maintaining poor levels of performance while at secondary school (Wilshaw, 2014: 3).

Elsewhere, it has been recognised (Sharma, 2007) that by the age of six years many children growing up in wealthy families and who are intellectually less able are more likely to have done better than intellectually able children growing up in poor families. While most children now use tablet computers almost as second nature and begin school having had daily access to a range of digital technology in their homes, many children from poorer homes do not and may, therefore, be at a significant disadvantage. This is important, as when used properly, digital technology offers children many opportunities for extending their learning and developing much-needed skills for the future.

CRITICAL QUESTION

How can schools support children from the poorest families in confronting issues around social mobility and what might be the hidden costs to society if they do not?

DOES THE NATURE OF A CHILD'S TEACHING REALLY MATTER?

In an attempt to better understand what makes for effective teaching in schools, Hattie (2008) synthesised the findings of educational research that involved many thousands of students; his work is now recognised as one of the largest collections of evidence-based outputs undertaken in the field of education.

KEY READING

A web search of the research of John Hattie will reveal many pieces for you to access to learn more about his data and findings. A useful list of '250 influences of student achievement' can be found here:

www.visiblelearningplus.com/sites/default/files/250%20Influences.pdf

Hattie focused on six primary areas that he saw as central to children's learning in schools: the children themselves; their homes; the teachers; the schools; curricula; and teaching and learning approaches that occur in schools. Hattie then proposed that the key to making real differences in children's learning lay in the need to make teaching and learning 'visible', i.e. where teachers actively evaluate their own teaching and view the learning taking place in their classrooms through the eyes of the pupils they are teaching (Hattie, 2008; Hattie, 2012; Hattie and Yates, 2014). Importantly, Hattie also proposed that a significant factor in pupils' experience is the competence of their teachers; he drew particular attention to how it is, 'tempting for teachers to re-do the successes of the previous year, to judge students in terms of last year's cohort, and to insist on orderly progression through that which has worked before' (2008:1).

CLASSROOM LINK

What does this mean for classroom practice?

Making their teaching visible is a key feature that leads teachers to have a better understanding of how their pupils learn and encourages them to critically self-appraise how they will teach each new cohort of children. In confronting the issue of how teachers can engage in such a process, MacBlain and Bowman (2016) drew upon the work of Marzano (2005; 2007; Marzano and Kendall, 2006) (referred to earlier), to emphasise how 'good' teachers:

- set goals and offer feedback;
- provide their pupils with simulations and competition that are 'low stake' in nature;
- provide support for their pupils when faced with the acquisition of new knowledge;
- are consistent in maintaining classroom rules that are clear, ensuring that these are followed;
- establish and sustain positive relationships with their pupils and communicate high expectations of them.

KEY READING

For further insights into the ideas of Hattie and Marzano, view the following two YouTube videos:

'Why are so many of our teachers and schools so successful?' John Hattie at: TEDxNorrkoping,

www.youtube.com/watch?v=rzwJXUieDOU

'The Art & Science of Teaching' - Dr Robert Marzano:

www.youtube.com/watch?v=YhB_R_FT9y4

CRITICAL QUESTION

What teaching qualities did your own teachers model to you when you were at school and how did these impact positively on your own learning?

DO THEORIES REALLY MATTER?

To help us further in our understanding of how children learn, we can look at how notable theorists have sought to explain the principles that underpin learning and how these might be observed in practice.

INFO 7.1

Key theorists

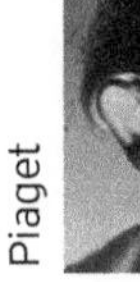

Piaget

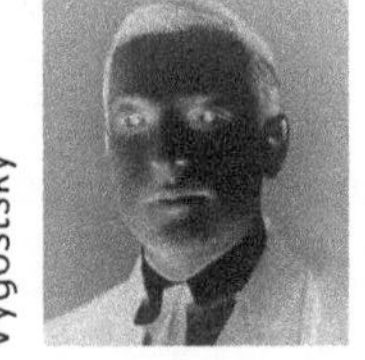
Vygostsky

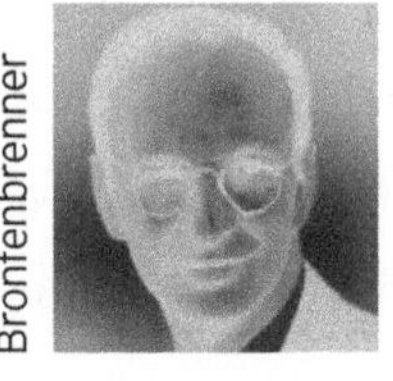
Bronfenbrenner

Bruner

Feuerstein

Recently, Walsh (2018), cited in MacBlain (2018: 8) commented:

> *As a teacher educator, I am often confronted with a response of apathy when I introduce students, particularly those in the initial years of their degree programme, to any form of theoretical issue or philosophical debate. Familiar comments include: ... 'it is only when I am in the classroom that I really learn - all this theoretical stuff is just a waste of time'. These students appear only interested in the everyday practices of the classroom context and fail to appreciate [how] ... we need to look at notable philosophies and theorists to help us unravel and deconstruct our own understandings ...*

Walsh goes further, citing McMillan (2009: 8) who proposed that:

> *an ability to reflect on appropriate theories is essential to equip students to become competent professionals ... Failing to embrace these theoretical issues may result in what could be described as narrow and shallow perceptions of what constitutes high quality practice ..., which Walsh (2017) suggests will do little to address the real learning needs and interests of the young child.*

No single theory, of course, can fully explain how children learn; while different, each theory does, however, add significantly to how we make sense of what is a highly complex and challenging aspect of children's development. More importantly, perhaps, theories provide a means by which teachers can critically discuss their pupils' learning, as opposed to exchanging simplistic interpretations of behaviours in the classroom that may be overly subjective and lacking in real evidence to support them. In their simplest form, theories are a means of explaining those complex phenomena that we do not fully understand (Gray and MacBlain, 2018; MacBlain, 2014). The first theory we will explore, though developed some decades ago, does, nevertheless, provide a very helpful framework for understanding and managing the types of learning behaviours teachers observe every day in their classrooms.

INFO 7.2

Why theories matter for student teachers

- No single theory can fully explain how children learn.
- Each theory adds significantly to how we make sense of what is a highly complex and challenging aspect of children's development.
- Theories provide a means by which teachers can critically discuss their pupils' learning.
- Critical discussion of theories avoids simplistic interpretations of behaviours in the classroom that may be overly subjective and lacking in real evidence.
- In their simplest form, theories are a means of explaining those complex phenomena that we do not fully understand.

THE BEHAVIOURISTS: DO BEHAVIOURS REALLY SHAPE CHILDREN'S LEARNING?

Behaviourism is premised on the view that associations develop between stimuli and responses and that these account for learning. Gray and MacBlain (2018: 47) have commented thus:

> *you may have worked in settings that regularly employ a range of strategies to shape and maintain appropriate behaviour ... verbal praise, positive body language (smiling, nodding, thumbs up) ... class behaviour charts and/or smiley-face stickers. You may also have heard practitioners ... [talk] about the need for children to learn that actions have consequences and will certainly have been alerted to the setting's behaviour management policy and your role in implementing it in a consistent way. The notion that actions have consequences is directly informed by behaviourism.*

IVAN PAVLOV (1849–1936)

Any exploration of *Behaviourism* needs to start with the Russian physiologist Ivan Pavlov who conducted experiments on dogs and observed how they formed associations. His ideas formed the very basis of how later behaviourists came to view and research learning not only in animals but in people.

EDWARD THORNDIKE (1874–1949)

Thorndike developed Pavlov's ideas, which he applied to children. He argued that children's learning occurred mostly through trial and error and suggested that when outcomes of learning are positive, connections are then formed that lead to the repetition of behaviours.

JOHN WATSON (1874–1954)

Watson also applied the principles of *Classical Conditioning* to children and, in 1913, established the school of *Behaviourism*. Watson extended Pavlov's original ideas as well as those of Thorndike, making the following assertion:

> *Give me a dozen healthy infants, well-formed, and my own specified world to bring them up in and I'll guarantee to take any one at random and train him to become any type of specialist I might select ... regardless of his talents, penchants, tendencies, abilities, vocations and the race of his ancestors.*
>
> (Watson, 1928: 82)

BURRHUS SKINNER (1904–1990)

Skinner then took these ideas even further; he recognised, for example, that reinforcement that is positive strengthens behaviours while reinforcement that is negative, lessens behaviours. Examples of positive reinforcement between a teacher and a child might include the teacher smiling at the child or giving verbal praise when the child has successfully completed a task or demonstrated behaviours desired by the teacher. Examples of negative reinforcement can also be observed in classrooms where teachers use 'time out' when a pupil is presenting with unacceptable behaviours. Importantly, Skinner observed how the frequency with which reinforcement followed behavioural responses was an important factor in increasing behaviours; in doing so, he developed what is an extremely useful concept for understanding children's learning, *Operant Conditioning*, which is based on the idea that learning is not wholly a passive process as was thought by the early Behaviourists but rather, an active process. In contrast to *Classical Conditioning, Operant Conditioning* asserts that it is the learner and not the object that triggers changes in behaviour. With *Operant Conditioning*, also referred to as *Instrumental Conditioning*, learning takes place when behaviours initiated by the child are either rewarded or punished, and when associations are formed between behaviours and the consequences of those behaviours.

Some years ago, Bigge and Shermis (2004: 113) indicated how Skinner had suggested that 'the first task of teachers is to shape proper responses, to get children to pronounce and write responses properly' and their principal task, 'as consisting of bringing proper behavior under many sorts of stimulus control'. Importantly, Skinner also viewed computers as offering one of the most effective ways of learning in that children can follow carefully designed programmes where every stage of learning was reinforced through rewards and where small steps in learning could be built in to instructional programmes so that children would not experience failure and have their motivation to succeed constantly reinforced.

CLASSROOM LINK

What does this mean for classroom practice?

The principles underlying *Behaviourism* can be seen daily in classrooms where teachers positively reinforce the behaviours they desire in their pupils and negatively reinforce those behaviours they want to extinguish. Teachers also put much effort into shaping their pupils' learning by offering praise, providing verbal and written feedback to aspects of their pupils' work and by using such instruments as 'star charts' and 'ticks' for doing well. Though this often takes place at a subconscious level, teachers who understand the principles behind *Operant Conditioning* may actively work to modify children's behaviour (often referred to as *behaviour modification*); for example, when a child is presenting with behaviours that are disruptive to others, such as calling or shouting out when they want to be heard.

PIAGET: HOW IMPORTANT IS ENVIRONMENT?

Piaget believed that young children, when presented with new information, may not immediately understand it if they have not already constructed knowledge and understanding that is relevant to the new information and that has been gained through interacting with their environments. Through interacting with their environments, even from their first years, children, he believed, build internal mental representations within their brains, which he referred to as *schema*. Nutbrown (2006: 7) has explained *schema* as 'a way of labelling children's consistent patterns of action' and suggested that it is possible for teachers to actually observe *schema* or patterns of children's learning behaviours in action. Piaget also placed much emphasis on how children act on their environments (Hayes, 1994: 143–4), which he proposed is at the very centre of children's thinking. Through acting on their environments, children 'assimilate' and then 'accommodate' new information, which guides their behaviours, and their learning. *Assimilation* can be understood in terms of new information being absorbed by the child within their *schema* without any real manipulation of that information, while *Accommodation* is where *schema* then develop in order to facilitate the acquisition of the new information.

KEY READING

To learn more about these concepts, view the following YouTube video: 'Schemas, assimilation, and accommodation' www.youtube.com/watch?v=BMc9TPwoVxQ (Miller, B., 2014), which explores 'schemas', 'assimilation' and 'accommodation'.

CRITICAL QUESTION

What type of environments and activities might teachers create in their classrooms that allow them to observe 'assimilation' and 'accommodation' in action?

Further to his notion of *schema*, Piaget suggested that cognitive development follows a number of stages that are 'invariant'; in other words, children pass through one stage before progressing through to the next. The first of these is the *Sensorimotor Stage* (0–2 years) when children learn through their senses, followed by the *Preoperational Stage* (2–7 years) when language becomes a key feature, extending and facilitating rapid growth of schema through two processes, *Assimilation* and *Accommodation*. This stage involves two further sub-stages, the *Preconceptual* (2–4 years) and the Intuitive (4–7 years). It is during the former that children can be observed to engage increasingly in imaginative and symbolic play, which involves increasing usage of words and symbols to represent objects or people (Gray and MacBlain, 2018; MacBlain, 2018). Piaget proposed that during the later *Intuitive Stage* (4–7 years) children develop their thinking to levels where they can remove themselves from learning situations to view the whole, as opposed to being able only to view the details; he referred to this as *decentring*. He also proposed that children's thinking remains limited at this stage; a child at this stage, for example, when observing an adult pouring a fixed amount of water from a short fat glass into a long slim glass, will typically believe that there is more water in the long slim glass. Piaget referred to this type of thinking as *conservation* and argued that children's capacity to conserve marks the end of the *Preoperational Stage* and the commencement of the *Concrete Operational Stage* (7–11 years). Development during these stages is important as this provides the basis for much of the learning that teachers see in later years.

A fundamental difference between the *Preoperational Stage* and the *Concrete Operational Stage* is that in the latter, children now have capacity to apply logic as a means of problem solving; thinking is becoming more flexible, though it remains constrained by a need to also have concrete objects present and visible (Gray and MacBlain, 2018). This stage is followed by the *Formal Operational Stage* (11–15 years) when cognitive development is at its highest level. Thinking is much more flexible and symbolic and, importantly, is not limited by the actual and personal experiences of children or their immediate realities. Children engage in more sophisticated thinking and can transcend themselves from their immediate environments through language. Thinking is more logical, and children can be observed to engage in deductive reasoning when they test hypotheses and become much more reflective.

VYGOTSKY: DO SOCIAL CONTEXTS AND CHILDREN'S CULTURES REALLY IMPACT ON THEIR LEARNING?

Vygotsky saw learning as, essentially, experiential in nature, with much of children's learning occurring even before they commence formal education. Whitebread (2012: 127) has articulated this very well:

> *all learning begins in the social context, which supports children in the processes whereby they construct their own understandings ... all learning exists first at the 'inter-mental' level in the form of spoken language, and then at the 'intramental' level (i.e. within the child's mind, in the form of internal language, or thought) ... This has been termed the 'social constructivist' approach to learning.*

Students, when first introduced to Vygotsky's theory soon come across references to the 'Zone of Proximal Development' (ZPD), which Vygotsky (1978: 86), cited in Gray and MacBlain (2012: 77), defined as:

> *those functions which have yet to mature but are in the process of maturing ... 'buds' or 'flowers' of development rather than 'fruits' of development. The actual development level characterizes the cognitive development retrospectively while the ZPD characterizes it prospectively.*

Vygotsky placed enormous emphasis on the cultures that children are born into and the social environments in which they grow up. He viewed culture as those social patterns of behaviour and beliefs that are passed on between generations through such 'tools' as art, nursery rhymes and stories. Cultural tools today are, of course, much more sophisticated and include, for example, television, social media and digital technology. These cultural tools play a major role in children's learning; the importance of these to children's learning was recognised some years ago by Pea (1993: 52):

> *these tools literally carry intelligence in them, in that they represent some individual's or some community's decision that the means thus offered would be reified, made stable as quasi permanent, for the use of others.*

For Vygotsky, the most important cultural tool was language; the importance he gave to language was highlighted some years ago, as follows (Vygotsky, 1987, cited in Holzman, 2006: 115):

> *Speech does not merely serve as the expression of developed thought. Thought is restructured as it is transformed into speech.*

Through language, children become active members of the communities in which they live and it is the reciprocal nature of this social engagement that lies at the heart of 'Social Constructivism'. Vygotsky suggested that every function in the cultural development of children, 'appears twice: first, on the social level, and later, the individual level; first, between people ... and then inside the child' (Vygotsky, 1978: 57).

Vygotsky believed that infants are born already with the foundations for thinking; for example, memory and visual recognition (Rose and Wood, 2003). He also emphasised how infants are born with the ability to learn through guidance from others, which allows for the passing on of those cultural norms inherent to the communities they are born into and the wider societies in which they live. At the core of his theory lie four stages, which, unlike those in Piaget's theory, are not unidirectional, but instead, develop progressively and follow an incremental pathway – i.e. children can move backwards or forwards between stages as their thinking matures and as a result of their experiences. Gray and MacBlain (2015: 97) have described Vygotsky's notion of stages, as follows.

PRIMITIVE STAGE

Children under 2 years of age use vocal activity as a means of emotional expression and for social engagement ... behaviour becomes increasingly purposeful and goal-directed ... thought and language are separate ...

PRACTICAL INTELLIGENCE

... the child's language uses syntactic (rules of speech) and logical forms. These forms of speech are linked to the child's practical problem solving activities ...

EXTERNAL SYMBOLIC STAGE

Thinking aloud is common ... enables the child to self-regulate and plan their activities

INTERNALISATION OF SYMBOLIC TOOLS

Between 7 and 8 years of age ... Problem solving continues to be guided by speech ... leads to greater cognitive independence, flexibility and freedom ...

Like Bruner, Vygotsky saw cognitive development in children as developing through their social interactions and through the support they received with learning from others. In contrast, Piaget believed that children's cognitive development arose from their explorations of the environments in which they live.

CRITICAL QUESTION

How might teachers in primary schools work with parents to support them in understanding how their children's cognitive development can be enhanced through language-based social interactions that are meaningful and have purpose?

BRONFENBRENNER: DOES BIOLOGY AND ENVIRONMENT INTERACT TO INFLUENCE LEARNING?

Bronfenbrenner is best known for his *Ecological Systems Model*, now redefined as the *Bioecological Model*. Bronfenbrenner viewed political, economic and cultural factors as having a much greater impact on children's learning than did many other theorists. His theory also has at its core the idea that a child's unique biology plays a central and distinct role in their development. His ideas on children's learning, therefore, can be viewed as the interrelationship between children and their environments, while acknowledging that every child is biologically different. Rose and Wood (2016: 86) have more recently emphasised how researchers have been increasingly choosing to adopt a more multidimensional approach to explaining how children learn:

> *genes (biology) and experiences (environment) are indivisible, interrelated and interdependent ... children's learning is a holistic and multi-layered process affected by shifting and interacting multiple layers of influence ... These 'layers of influence' are articulated in the ecological systems model of human development originated by Bronfenbrenner*

Bronfenbrenner's model envisages layers that encompass children as they develop, which impact on their uniquely individual biological maturation; these have been likened to Russian dolls, where smaller dolls are placed within much bigger ones (Linden, 2005).

Bronfenbrenner gave a name to each layer surrounding the child, the closest and most immediate being the Microsystem: immediate environments (family, school, peer group, neighbourhood and childcare environments). Next is the Mesosystem: comprising connections between immediate environments (i.e. a child's home and school) and outside of this is the Exosystem: external environmental settings which only indirectly affect development (such as a parent's workplace) and then the Macrosystem: the larger cultural context (Eastern vs. Western culture, national economy, political culture, subculture). The Chronosystem refers to the patterning of environmental events and transitions over the course of life.

CRITICAL QUESTION

How might a child's biological attributes affect their learning?

BRUNER: CAN DIFFERENT STRATEGIES IMPROVE CHILDREN'S OUTCOMES FOR LEARNING?

At the centre of Bruner's theory of learning is the idea of Instrumental Conceptualism, with the following three elements: acquiring new information or knowledge, transforming and manipulating knowledge, and the checking of knowledge. Bruner's ideas on learning were well articulated by Brown (1977: 74) as follows:

> *Bruner's thesis was that the study of children in problem-solving situations had concentrated too much on the nature of the tasks and the stimuli presented to the child, and too little on the dynamic qualities the child brought to the tasks in order to solve them.*

Bruner proposed that children represent their worlds through three modes:

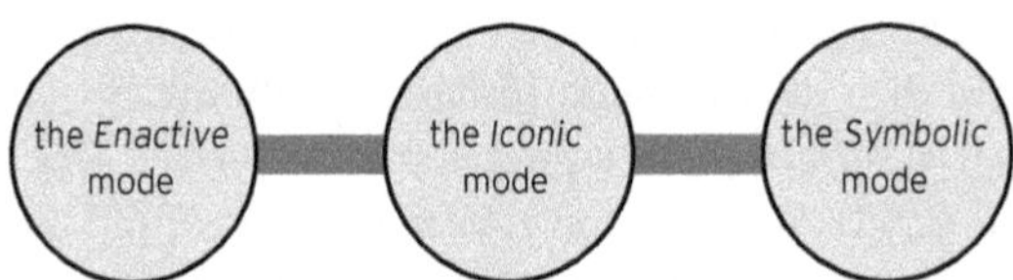

The first refers to actions, the second to images and pictures, and the third to words and symbols. The three modes do not follow in succession, as was the case with Piaget's ideas of successive stages, but instead, are integral to one another with their use being linked to the experience of the child. With the *Enactive* mode, a newly born child's view of objects, for example, becomes connected to their physical movements. With the *Iconic* mode, children internally represent objects as images, thus allowing them to progress their thinking. By storing images children extend their thinking to objects that are not present in their immediate environments. This mode, however, is limited in that images are restricted to specific observable features – for example, colour, shape and smell. The *Iconic* mode is not enough to allow children to represent internally abstract concepts, such as happiness; to do this, children require language. It is this key element that lies at the very heart of the *Symbolic* mode. Brown (1977: 75) explained the difference between images in the *Iconic* mode and symbols that are central to the *Symbolic* mode in this way:

> *A photograph or a model of a cow would be an icon in that it would represent the animal in a very real and obvious way. The symbols C-O-W have no such characteristics. They only signify the existence of the animal by consensus of those who use the word.*

As language develops, children can remove themselves physically from situations while still being able to think about them. They can communicate verbally with others in increasingly sophisticated ways about events that are elsewhere and that may take place in the future. Crucially, they can participate in problem-solving activities and in reflection, two elements that Bruner saw as the most critical features in children's learning.

Bruner was especially interested in the strategies children used when learning new tasks and when problem-solving. He suggested that the cognitive structures of children who engage a great deal in reading and writing may, for example, differ from those of children who overly absorb themselves in activities that are less language oriented such as drawing and construction activities (Brown, 1977). He also proposed that the cognitive structures of children who engage a great deal with adults and older peers using spoken language may differ from those of children who do not. Interestingly, Bruner also believed that when children actively and purposely engage in writing activities that a fundamental and transformative process occurs, whereby they come to engage in thinking that is characterised by deeper reflection and critical analysis not only of their own thinking, but also that of others. Though originally coined by Wood *et al.* (1976), cited in Gray and MacBlain (2015: 6), the term *Scaffolding* is largely associated with Bruner. *Scaffolding* refers to a process, whereby adults working alongside children support and progress their learning.

CLASSROOM LINK

What does this mean for classroom practice?

Bruner emphasises the importance of creating learning environments that offer children opportunities to actively engage in new learning and apply their own intellectual resources through exploration and discovery. The level of interest a child has in a subject is a key factor and key motivator. Bruner also stresses the importance of teachers knowing the existing knowledge of their pupils and building on this; here we acknowledge his concept of a 'Spiral' curriculum where teachers present children with choice and work alongside them to create opportunities for developing new learning through, for example, extending their vocabulary, encouraging their listening skills, modelling new and effective strategies and directing them in collaborating with other children in group activities such as creative play and problem-solving tasks.

FEUERSTEIN: CAN CHILDREN THINK DIFFERENTLY ABOUT THEIR OWN LEARNING?

Feuerstein proposed that the belief systems we hold about children's learning directly influence our perceptions of what they are capable of; we should, he believed, view human potential as having almost no limits, though at the same time acknowledging how artificial barriers can prevent desired and positive change in how children engage in learning. Feuerstein believed that every child, no matter what their degree of difficulty, can, with appropriate support, become effective learners. When teachers adopt this belief system they free themselves from constrained thinking that impedes any vision they might have of what they can achieve with their pupils; certain consequences also start to emerge within their pupils' learning, a process Feuerstein referred to as 'Structural Cognitive Modifiability' or the idea that the actual cognitive structure of children's brains become altered through an enabling process where they increasingly engage in learning how to learn (Burden, 1987). Feuerstein emphasised that the central feature in learning how to learn is 'Mediated Learning Experience', which he explained as follows:

> *stimuli emitted by the environment are transferred by a 'mediating' agent, usually a parent, sibling or other caregiver. This mediated agent, guided by his intentions, culture, and emotional investment, selects and organises the world of stimuli for the child ... Through this process of mediation, the cognitive structure of the child is affected.*
>
> (Feuerstein *et al.*,1980: 16)

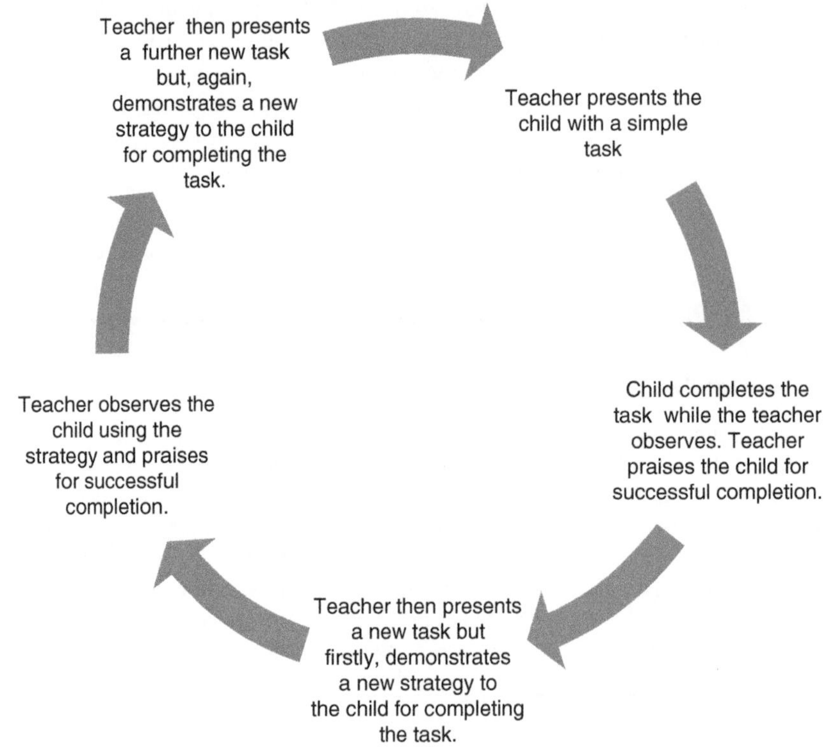

Figure 7.2 An example of spiral learning

A key element here is that the teacher (mediator) ensures pupils understand what is expected of them and takes care to explain to pupils why they are being asked to engage with learning tasks and they understand that the tasks have value beyond the immediate task.

CRITICAL QUESTION

What aspects of Feuerstein's theory might teachers adopt to support them in working with children with additional needs and/or disabilities?

KEY THEORY

For further insights into Feuerstein's ideas, view the following YouTube video: *Feuerstein Institute - Step Forward* (Guggenheim, C., 2013).

www.youtube.com/watch?v=Th9nw99Kw-4&list=PLyHTdVRj_jrpMSg0GXnXF42T2-bDHXZqH&index=2

CLASSROOM LINK

What does this mean for classroom practice?

Feuerstein made an important distinction between 'ability' and 'potential' and in doing so emphasised the difference between 'static' and 'dynamic assessment'; the former refers to assessment situations where children are tested on a particular occasion, with the results of the tests then being taken as an 'accurate' measure of a child's ability. Dynamic assessment, on the other hand, takes place over time, with much greater emphasis being afforded to what children might achieve in their learning when given the correct type of guidance and support.

NEUROSCIENCE: WHAT CAN STUDIES OF THE BRAIN TELL US ABOUT CHILDREN'S LEARNING?

It is quite astonishing how few books written about teaching and learning deal with the brain and yet it is this part of the human anatomy that regulates learning in every child. Following birth and during the first years learning develops at an accelerating pace and involves the strengthening of connections between neurons. Neurons do not contact directly with each other but instead have miniscule gaps between them known as *synapses*. Electrical impulses travel across these *synapses* and, as this happens, chemicals are released, which are understood as transmitter substances. Hardy and Heyes (1994: 262–3) have indicated that while all messages in the nervous system are carried as nerve impulses that 'their interpretation depends upon which part of the brain receives the message: in one part an impulse might be interpreted as a spot of light, in another as a sound ...'

KEY THEORY

Because *synapses* are known to develop in newly born children and during the first years at a fantastic rate (in a newly born child, that section of the brain called the cerebral cortex can create over a million synapses per second), researchers and academics have emphasised the importance of providing stimulation to children in their first months and years. While many synapses become established within children's brains, many do not and are gradually abandoned by the brain; this continues throughout life and by adolescence around half of synapses have been shed. It is recognised that our brains work on a basis of 'use it or lose it'; therefore, the more children engage in active learning such as play and communicate through language, the stronger such connections will become.

KEY READING

For further information on how the brain supports children's learning, view the following You Tube video, *The Learning Brain*:

www.youtube.com/watch?v=cgLYkV689s4

CHAPTER SUMMARY

- How children learn is a complex question that continues to exercise academics, researchers and practitioners.
- The environments and teaching approaches used by teachers are key determinants that impact on outcomes for children's learning and how they come to realise their potential.
- The nature of learning is highly sophisticated and complicated, and directly involves functioning within the brain.
- Key theorists have endeavoured to explain learning, and while no single theory can fully explain children's learning, they all provide important frameworks with which teachers can explore learning and communicate effectively with others about the nature of children's cognitive functioning.

ASSIGNMENTS

If you are tasked with writing an assignment on aspects of children's learning or being asked to prepare for a class seminar, you may wish to consider the following as preparation:

- Reflect on your own experiences of learning in the primary years and identify a number of aspects of your learning experience that you found most helpful and why.
- Talk with three or four fellow students from other courses and ask them to write down a definition of learning, then consider their definitions and/or explanations against two of the theories of learning you have read in this chapter and how they might differ.
- Look at a sample of primary school websites on the internet and determine if it is possible to identify from the information they provide what their theoretical approach to learning is, then consider if this is something primary schools need to do.
- If possible, speak with one or two teachers while you are on school placement and discuss with them any theoretical approaches they have found useful in supporting their practice; more particularly, identify their evidence for supporting their views.
- Try to identify actual examples when teachers have employed the principles of 'Behaviourist' theory to manage children's behaviours in the classroom.

The following sources provide useful further reading:

Gray, C. and MacBlain, S.F. (2018) *Learning Theories in Childhood* (3rd edn). London: SAGE. (This book offers a detailed account of the main learning theories in this chapter and is a most useful resource.)

Hattie, J. and Yates, G.C.R. (2014) *Visible Learning and the Science of How We Learn*. London: SAGE. (This book offers a clear account of what it means to make our teaching visible and how doing so supports teaching and learning in children.)

MacBlain, S.F. (2018) *Learning Theories for Early Years Practice*. London: SAGE. (This very readable book covers an enormous range of aspects relevant to young children's learning through providing the current context in which young children commence their learning, the theories that have informed practice and the challenges ahead for teachers and practitioners working with young children - a very readable and accessible text.)

REFERENCES

Bigge, M.L. and Shermis, S.S. (2004) *Learning Theories for Teachers* (6th edn). Boston, MA: Pearson.

Bronfenbrenner, U. (1979) *The Ecology of Human Development*. Cambridge, MA: Harvard University Press.

Bronfenbrenner, U. and Ceci, S.J. (1994) Nature–nurture reconceptualized in the developmental perspective: A bioecological model. *Psychological Review*, 101: 568–86.

Brown, G. (1977) *Child Development*. Shepton Mallet: Open Books.

Burden, R.L. (1987) Feuerstein's instrumental enrichment programme: Important issues in research and evaluation. *European Journal of Psychology of Education*, 2(1): 3–16.

Feuerstein, R., Rand, Y., Hoffman, M. and Miller, R. (1980) *Instrumental Enrichment*. Baltimore, MD: University. Park Press.

Field, F. (2010) *The Foundation Years: Preventing poor children becoming poor adults – Report of the independent review on poverty and life chances*. London: Cabinet Office.

Gray, C. and MacBlain, S.F. (2015) *Learning Theories in Childhood* (2nd edn). London: SAGE.

Gray, C. and MacBlain, S.F. (2018) *Learning Theories in Childhood* (3rd edn) London: SAGE.

Hardy, M. and Heyes, S. (1994) *Beginning Psychology: A comprehensive introduction to psychology* (4th edn). Oxford: Oxford University Press.

Hattie, J. (2008) *Visible Learning: A synthesis of over 800 meta-analyses relating to achievement*. London: Routledge.

Hattie, J. (2012) *Visible Learning for Teachers: Maximising impact on learning*. London: Routledge.

Hattie, J. and Yates, G.C.R. (2014) *Visible learning and the science of how we learn*. London: SAGE.

Hayes, N. (1994) *Foundations of Psychology*. London: Routledge.

Holzman, L. (2006) Activating postmodernism. *Theory and Psychology*, 16(1): 109–23.

Jarvis, M. (2005) *The Psychology of Effective Learning and Teaching*. Cheltenham: Nelson Thornes.

Linden, J. (2005) *Understanding Child Development: Linking theory to practice*. London: Hodder Education.

MacBlain, S.F. (2014) *How Children Learn*. London: SAGE.

MacBlain, S.F. (2018) *Learning Theories for Early Years Practice*. London: SAGE.

MacBlain, S.F. and Bowman, H. (2016) Teaching and learning, in D. Wyse and S. Rogers (eds) *A Guide to Early Years & Primary Teaching*. London: SAGE.

MacBlain, S.F., Dunn, J. and Luke, I. (2017) *Contemporary Childhood*. London: SAGE.

Marzano, R. (2005) *School Leadership that Works: From research to results*. Alexandria, VA: ASCD.

Marzano, R. (2007) *The Art and Science of Teaching: A comprehensive framework for effective instruction*. Alexandria, VA: ASCD.

Marzano, R. and Kendall, J.S. (2006) *The New Taxonomy of Educational Objectives* (2nd edn). Thousand Oaks, CA/ London: SAGE.

McMillan, D. (2009) Preparing for educare: Student perspectives on early years training in Northern Ireland. *International Journal of Early Years Education*, 17(3): 219–35.

Nutbrown, C. (2006) *Threads of Thinking: Young children learning and the role of early education*. London: SAGE.

Pea, R.D. (1993) Practices of distributed intelligence and designs for education, in G. Salomon (ed.) *Distributed Cognitions* (pp. 47–87). New York: Cambridge University Press.

Rose, J. and Wood, F. (2016) Child development, in D. Wyse and S. Rogers (eds) *A Guide to Early Years & Primary Teaching*. London: SAGE.

Sharma, N. (2007) *"It Doesn't Happen Here" – The Reality of Child Poverty in the UK*. Ilford: Barnardo Press.

Vygotsky, L.S. (1978) *Mind in Society: The Development of Higher Psychological Processes*. Cambridge, MA: Harvard University Press.

Walsh, G. (2017) Why playful teaching and learning?, in G. Walsh, D. McMillan and C. McGuinness (eds) *Playful Teaching and Learning* (pp. 7–20). London: SAGE.

Walsh, G. (2018) 'Foreword' to MacBlain, S.F. (2018) *Learning Theories for Early Years Practice*. London: SAGE.

Watson, J.B. (1928) *Psychological Care of Infant and Child*. New York: Norton.

Whitebread, D. (2012) *Developmental Psychology & Early Childhood Education*. London: SAGE.

Wilshaw, W. (2014) *Unsure Start: HMCI's Early Years Annual Report 2012/13, Speech 2014*. London: Ofsted.

Wood, D., Bruner, J.S. and Ross, G. (1976) The role of tutoring in problem solving. *Journal of Child Psychology and Psychiatry*, 17(2): 81–100.

KEY THEORISTS

PIAGET
1896 - 1980

VYGOSTSKY
1896 - 1934

BRONFENBRENNER
1917 - 2005

BRUNER
1915 - 2016

FEUERSTEIN
1921 - 2014

WILL IT WORK FOR ME... AND OUR CHILDREN

THIS SET OF QUESTIONS CAN HELP YOU TO THINK ABOUT WHETHER OR NOT A GLOBAL STRATEGY OR ANY OTHER NEW IDEA IS WORTH CONSIDERING

Do people promoting the idea have a commercial interest in it? Are they selling books or training?

Do the people promoting the idea have a particular view on education or teaching that they are trying to push?

What is the evidence that this idea or approach will work? What types of evidence are there for this? How convincing is this evidence?

If there is evidence that the approach works abroad, are there other explanations such as culture or the type of society that might be important, but that are not easy to reproduce here?

Has anyone tried the new idea in a situation like yours? What happened?

What might be the long-term consequences or unintended outcomes of these ways of working?

Is it possible to begin to experiment with the new ideas or do you need to buy into the whole package?

Do the potential benefits outweigh the potential negative consequences?

8

HOW CAN I BRING EVIDENCE-BASED PRACTICE INTO MY CLASSROOM?

Mark Boylan, B.Sc., Ph.D., SFHEA, is a Professor of Education at Sheffield Hallam University. His areas of expertise are mathematics education, teacher professional learning and evaluation of policy innovations. The latter includes the evaluation of the Mathematics Teacher Exchange: China-England, also known as the primary mathematics Shanghai exchange programme, which is part of the government's mastery programme.

KEY WORDS

- Academies
- Direct instruction
- Evidence-informed teaching
- Free schools
- Mastery
- Mathematics
- Policy globalisation

INTRODUCTION

This chapter enables you to critically reflect on choices about what practices to adopt or not in classrooms, particularly strategies that originate overseas, thus supporting you to bring evidence-based practice into your classroom. Increasingly, governments and teachers look abroad for ideas to improve schools and teaching. In this chapter, the term 'global strategies' is used to refer to these types of ideas or practices from other countries. Underlying the belief that global strategies will make education better is the idea that it is possible to identify 'what works' in education. This raises important questions about educational evidence in general and how things work in education.

As background, we will look at the global 'what works' movement and different types of evidence. This leads to discussing why teachers and schools should be wary of claims that techniques or approaches will work for everyone and everywhere. Four examples are then considered that have transnational origins and have influenced educational policy, schools and teachers in England. These are a focus on teaching as instructional techniques, the academies and free schools programme, forest schools and global influences on English mathematics education.

The chapter ends by providing a set of question for teachers to use to answer the question 'will "what works" there, work for me here?'. These can also be used to critically review any new practice, whatever its origins.

GLOBAL INFLUENCES IN EDUCATION

In many countries, a prominent feature of educational policy and practice is increasing globalisation. Globalisation in education refers to the adoption of similar strategies in different countries, often due to governments, and sometimes schools and teachers, importing or copying them from ones found overseas. This is not new: even before the start of modern education systems, teachers and governments have been interested in how teaching happens or schools are organised in other countries. Universities are a good example. The first university that still exists today was established in Morocco. The first in Europe was in Italy. Then they spread across Europe and later the world.

A common process for global strategies spreading is that governments or teachers identify something they think is a problem. Then they look abroad for answers. New practices are adopted but they are usually changed or translated in some way when implemented in the new setting. Then, once they have become integrated, the

KEY THEORY

Comparative education is the name given to the study of differences between educational systems. This includes comparing policy, curricula and teaching practices. Increasingly, teachers are able to access outcomes of comparative education research published by The Organisation for Economic Co-operation and Development (OECD) and others, and also access video material that gives a window into practice in classrooms overseas. Looking at how teachers in other countries teach can be a powerful way to reflect on practices that are taken for granted in England.

global origins of the new ideas are often forgotten. An example of this process of forgetting where ideas come from is that in England most people would think of Oxford and Cambridge and not Morocco or Italy as the sites of the first universities.

Looking overseas for educational ideas has increased in recent years. Partly this is because we increasingly live in a globalised world. But over the last 10 years the emphasis on looking abroad has also increased as international comparative tests have become more important to governments (see Chapter 11 for more on the *Programme for International Student Assessment* or PISA tests). In addition, the OECD that runs PISA also does other studies of education systems that influence policy makers. These studies try to link outcomes with the organisation of schooling, such as school-type, and ways that teaching and learning happen.

CRITICAL QUESTION

Why do Shanghai, China, Singapore, Finland and Ontario in Canada often do well at international comparative tests?

How different are these jurisdictions to England in terms of size, population and culture?

In what ways do these factors influence children's outcomes?

'WHAT WORKS' AND 'EVIDENCE-BASED EDUCATION'

The influence of the OECD and PISA has been strengthened by another recent global tendency in education. There is a wider movement to promote the use of research and other evidence in education. Sometimes this is referred to by the terms 'what works' and 'evidence-based education'. In England, the Education Endowment Foundation (EEF) is a 'What Works Centre'. The EEF funds trials of education programmes as well encouraging schools to inform what they do with research evidence. At a school and teacher level, an international 'ResearchED' movement has emerged consisting of events and publications that aim to connect the teaching profession with research.

Advocates for evidence-based education often claim that education needs to be more like medicine. In medicine, different treatments are tested. These studies are compared and summarised in reviews and then recommendations are made to doctors and other medical professionals about best treatments. However, others argue that education is not like medicine and so this way of thinking is not appropriate. Regardless of the view you take on this, it is important to know that increasingly discussion of research and evidence is important in teaching. People who put forward ideas for what teachers and schools should do will often refer to evidence. This chapter ends with guidelines to help you identify whether or not their claims are justified.

TYPES OF EVIDENCE

Schools and teachers need to assess evidence in order to decide whether a new approach might work for them. The table below summarises a selection of different forms of educational evidence that are important for teachers and the meanings of these terms are explained. The table is organised in terms of the size and scale of the evidence collected. It is important to remember that big does not necessarily mean better. The quality of evidence relies on how evidence has been collected and not only to the amount of evidence there is or the amount of data collected.

INFO 8.1

Types of educational evidence

Type	Notes/examples
Global comparative studies	These include studies that involve testing pupils. But this also includes comparative studies using other methods such as analysis of video of teaching in different countries.
Meta-analyses and synthesis	Researchers look at evidence from many studies and combine this into recommendations. Examples are the *Sutton Trust Toolkit and* John Hattie's *Visible Learning for Teachers.* Recommendations derived from reviews of international research can also be considered global strategies and open to questions about whether practices will transfer from one place to another.
National studies of differences in outcomes	Researchers study patterns in differences in outcomes in countries. For example, outcomes from different types of schools or for pupils with different characteristics are analysed.
Randomised Controlled Trials	A practice or programme is studied by comparing two samples of schools, teachers or pupils. One group experience or use the practice and programme and one group do not. Once schools or teachers have been recruited to trials, groups are formed randomly. If the two groups being compared are large enough, it is argued that randomisation will mean that any other important differences will be split more or less evenly between the two groups. So, if one group does better than the other, it can be concluded that it is likely this is to do with the practice or programme.
Quantitative and qualitative research on groups of schools, individual schools, classrooms and teachers	Most educational research fits into this type and there is a great variety in terms of the number of schools, teachers and pupils involved, as well as how the research is conducted. Quantitative research involves the collection and/or analysis of numerical data. Qualitative research involves other sorts of data. Studying groups of schools or even individual schools or teachers can help provide evidence on why particular approaches seem to be better than others.

Type	Notes/examples
Local school and teacher evidence	Schools and teachers generate a lot of evidence. Arguably, most educational evidence is of this form but it is not usually formally summarised. More formal examples of local evidence production are approaches such as teacher action research. More informal examples are teachers trying out different practices and seeing what happens in their classrooms. So, every teacher can be considered an evidence producer, but this is not often recognised or this evidence base drawn on in any systematic way.

CLASSROOM LINK

What does this mean for classroom practice?

The Education Endowment foundation publishes a summary of evidence known as the *Sutton Trust - EEF Teaching and Learning Toolkit* (https://educationendowmentfoundation.org.uk/evidencesummaries/teachinglearningtoolkit). The Sutton Trust is an education charity interested in promoting social mobility that funded the work to develop the review. The toolkit aims to provide accessible information for teachers and school leaders when considering changes they might make.

One example of this is the *Review of evidence on written marking*, April 2016:

https://educationendowmentfoundation.org.uk/public/files/Publications/EEFMarkingReviewApril2016.pdf

The document explores some examples of good practice from schools. Can you take some of the learning here and apply it to your marking practice?

Accessible summaries of research such as the *Sutton Trust – EEF Teaching and Learning Toolkit* can be useful tools for teachers. However, it is important to recognise the complexity of education. Dylan Wiliam, who has influenced policy on assessment for learning, puts it like this:

> *Everything works somewhere and nothing works everywhere.*
>
> (Wiliam, 2013)

Similarly, John Hattie (2012) argues that if something is working in your classroom or school but does not appear to be supported by the evidence summaries, it may be better to ignore the advice. Other people have expressed concerns with the focus on 'what works' more generally. For example, Gert Biesta points out that the focus on outcomes that can be measured in numbers can miss what is important in education (Biesta, 2017).

KEY READING

One of the best ways to be critical about educational evidence generated by other people is to do your own research. If you start from your own research questions, then evidence becomes much more meaningful and you will be more motivated to find it and to reflect on it. Elaine Wilson (2017) in Chapter 1, Becoming a reflexive teacher, in *School-based Research: A guide for education students*, offers good advice on critical reading of research texts, and in Chapter 3, Reviewing the literature and writing a literature review, she gives detailed advice on how to access educational evidence.

BEWARE THOSE WHO CRY 'FAKE NEWS'

One of the implications of the arguments made so far is that evidence is complex. Also, another issue that schools and teachers have to contend with is that it is not always easy to work out who or what are reliable sources of evidence. One approach is to trust those who talk about the importance of evidence and promote teacher engagement in research. However, perhaps even more caution is needed with people who do this. In politics, we have become used to the cry of 'fake news' about stories that are demonstrably true, while the people who complain about fake news promote their own untruths and conspiracy theories. Similarly, in education, some promoters of 'evidence-informed teaching' are quick to critique evidence for practices or ideas they don't like, while declaring their own beliefs as 'proven'.

A really important idea here is the notion of 'confirmation bias'. This means being more open to hearing and believing evidence that confirms what we already believe, and ignoring or discounting evidence that our beliefs might need revising. However, it is easier to recognise other people's confirmation bias than our own. One way to overcome this is:

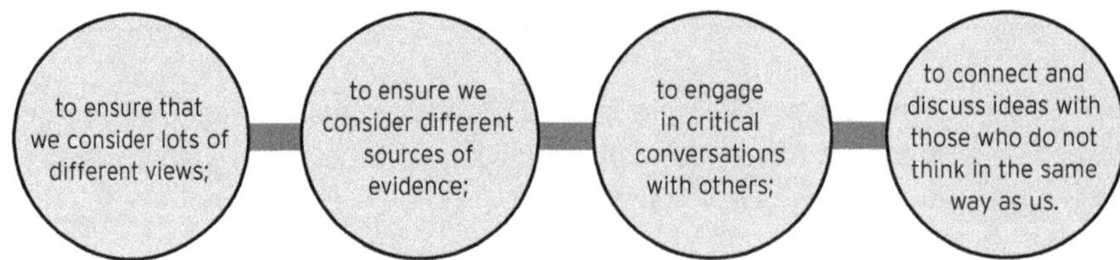

KEY READING

Phillip Adey and Justin Dillon (2012) have edited a collection of studies of educational myths *Bad Education: Debunking myths in education*. Reading any one of the chapters in this book would provide a model of how evidence can be carefully considered and some beliefs that are seen as 'common sense' may not be based on evidence.

TEACHING AS INSTRUCTIONAL TECHNIQUE

Having considered some important background ideas on global influences and evidence, four examples of different ideas that have originated outside the UK are discussed in the rest of this chapter. The first of these is the idea that teaching can be viewed as a set of instructional techniques. One popular version of this idea has been promoted by Doug Lemov and his ideas of *Teach Like a Champion* (Lemov, 2015). This consists of 62 (previously 49) techniques that he claims are effective. Lemov's work originated in the USA and has spread internationally, including to the UK.

Interestingly, Lemov's work is recommended by some educators who promote the ResearchED network and conferences aimed at promoting research evidence to teachers. However, there have been no systematic studies of this approach, although the claim is made that Lemov's techniques are 'proven'. There does not appear to be a single randomised controlled trial of either the methods – taken as a package – or of the professional development of teachers in these approaches. This does not mean that there is no research basis for any of Lemov's chosen techniques. For example, he recommends extending wait time after asking questions to give learners thinking time and to generate more responses. There is a body of research that supports this, although rigorous research on this is dated. However, it is the sort of practice that individual teachers can easily try out and find out if it works in their classroom. Another of his recommendations is to make praise 'precise'. This is supported by evidence from studies by Carol Dweck on growth mindsets (2006). A growth mindset is one in which success is seen as mainly to do with effort, and that one's ability and capacity to learn are always extendable. However, other techniques that Lemov recommends have not been researched, and more importantly, the combination of techniques has not been considered as a package or whether some of the techniques are better than others, or the circumstances in which they do or do not work.

CLASSROOM LINK

What does this mean for classroom practice?

Bringing evidence-based teaching into your classroom

How does your learning from looking at Lemov's work relate to your classroom practice? Before deciding whether or not to apply the (original) 49 principles in your practice, it is important to evaluate them - to look for evidence of studies of the technique or related practice.

To consider the approach in full, categorise the principles into the following groups:

1. There is research evidence for the technique.
2. There is no evidence for the technique.
3. There is evidence against the technique.
4. It might be difficult to generate evidence either way - perhaps because the technique is open to interpretation and could be done in lots of ways by different teachers.

Think about Dylan Wiliam's advice that nothing works everywhere - are there particular groups of pupils (for example, age, background or SEND characteristics) that some of these techniques might not work with?

It may be that Lemov's techniques are helpful for at least some teachers. With 62 techniques, it is likely that most teachers will find something in the list that will work for them. Even if they don't, reviewing the techniques can be an opportunity to reflect on their practice. However, selecting a technique is likely to be most successful if teachers experiment with the recommendations and adapt them to their own circumstances. It may be that this selection, experimentation and adaption are as important or even more important than the initial recommended technique. Without research we cannot know for sure. In addition, underlying Lemov's idea is that all teachers and all children are the same everywhere and the techniques will work for everyone. This is questionable. Further, there may be unintended consequences of some of these techniques or of viewing teaching as a set of separate techniques.

KEY READING

Advice for teachers that carefully considers evidence tends to be more cautious about recommendations or recognises the complexity of what this might mean in practice. The EEF has produced guidance for KS2/KS3 maths guidance: https://educationendowmentfoundation.org.uk/tools/guidance-reports/maths-ks-two-three/. This guidance can be used to inform your lesson planning. It does not include 'quick fixes' but advice that you will need to reflect on.

CHARTERS, ACADEMIES AND FREE SCHOOLS

One recent policy in England has been turning schools into academies and the opening of free schools. These policies have their origins in the USA and in Sweden. In England, an academy is a school funded directly by central government. They contrast with community schools that have a relationship to the local authority. Academies are run by a variety of different types of bodies, often in groups of schools called multi-academy trusts or MATs. Initially, before 2010, academies were set up as sponsored academies – these were schools that were required to convert to academy status because they were judged to not be meeting the needs of their pupils. After 2010, all successful schools were able to convert to academy status if they chose to.

Free schools are a particular type of academy. The first wave of free schools in England was approved in 2010. These schools tended to have particular features – for example, serving a particular type of student, often based on religion, or offering a specialised curriculum. More recently, any new schools have to be opened as free schools and so the difference between them and other academies is now not always clear. Before the academy and free school policy spread to England, in the USA charter schools were established. Similarly, they are schools that are government funded but independent of local educational boards. In Sweden, similar types of schools were established called free schools, and this is where the name of the English versions came from.

KEY THEORY

There are many different organisations that are responsible for promoting Charter Schools in the USA. One influential organisation is KIPP (Knowledge is Power Programme) that helped develop the 'no excuses' approach to schooling. This involves a traditional approach to behaviour management in which pupils are expected to follow adult direction exactly and without question. Some successful multi-academy chains in England have modelled themselves on the KIPP approach and, similar to US charters, are supported by a range of private financial businesses and international educational businesses.

Other successful schools in England have gone in other directions - for example, at Wroxham School an emphasis is put on pupil self-responsibility as a way of not limiting pupils' learning. This has also achieved improvement in pupil outcomes (Swann *et al.*, 2012).

Given that very different approaches can be successful in terms of test outcomes, other issues need to be considered when looking at types of school and educational philosophies. These include longer-term consequences for pupils, teachers and society. For example, it is increasingly recognised that school regimes that are overly focused on pressurising students and teachers to perform well on tests and in league tables can have negative consequences for well-being.

Academies and free schools are controversial in England. There is a lot of disagreement about whether they have been more successful, less successful or achieve more or less the same outcomes as other types of schools. Undertaking comparison of schools is complex due to the different types of academies and free schools, and the need to compare them with schools that are governed differently but have similar profiles of pupils. However, overall, the evidence appears to be that the type of school governance – that is, who is responsible for the school – does not make a difference by itself to educational attainment (Andrews and Perera, 2017).

Perhaps this finding should not be surprising. Studies in the USA had already found a similar pattern before the policy was taken up in England. Some charters do better than other local schools, but some do not. Recent studies of some of the charters that appear successful, such as the no excuses charters, suggest that these approaches may have longer-term negative outcomes. No excuses charters have been criticised for making students too compliant with teachers and so lacking independence. Students who succeed in getting to college when they leave no excuses charters have higher rates of dropping out from college than students who had other school experiences. This echoes research by Jo Boaler who found that ex-pupils of a school in which pupils were taught in more formal ways ended up in lower income jobs than pupils of a school where they had more freedom, even though results were similar (Boaler, 2005). In Sweden, after initial enthusiasm and success, support for free schools has waned (Weale, 2015).

Interestingly, in the USA similar concerns are reported, as in England, about how those schools that are not subject to local oversight behave. For example, in the USA and in England a similar pattern has been noticed of charters and academies paying some school leaders very high salaries and 'gaming' results. 'Gaming' is a term that is used to refer to a range of different ways that schools may 'play the system'. Examples are:

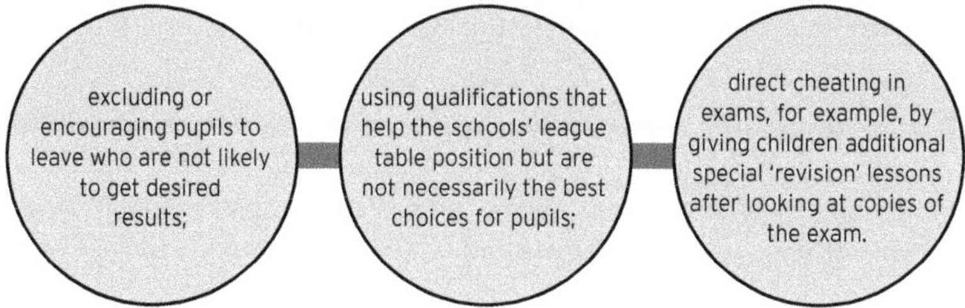

The fact that some schools 'game' the system also underlines that it is not easy to use exam results to compare types of schools in any simple way.

CRITICAL QUESTION

If there is no evidence that academies and free schools are more successful in England than other types of schools, why do they continue to be promoted?

FOREST SCHOOLS

Unlike academies and free schools, which began in England as government policy, the forest school movement has been developed by enthusiastic teachers and school leaders. In 1993, a group of early years educators from Somerset went to Denmark to look at pre-school education. The teachers from England were inspired by observing the importance of learning outdoors. On returning to England they applied what they had seen to a crèche and their ideas informed a training course for early years educators (see Cree and McCree, 2012). From these small beginnings, forest schools have spread into a national movement that not only informs early years practice, but has also spread into primary schooling. Increasingly, primary schools try to offer some sort of forest school, or similar outdoor learning experience, as part of their curriculum, at least in KS1.

In terms of evidence, forest schools are interesting because they spread from teacher to teacher and area to area, without much research evidence on outcomes, at least in terms of attainment outcomes. Early years' practitioners and teachers generated local evidence as they tried out and developed the approach. Educators became enthusiasts for outdoor learning because they saw the effect on the children they worked with. More recently, the value of forest schools and outdoor learning has begun to be more formally recognised. The Scottish government now emphasises the value of outdoor education in its curriculum. A recent study looking generally at learning in outdoor settings in the South West of England involving 160 schools found positive effects for teachers and children (Waite, 2016). However, there is still little formal research evidence as yet of the value of forest schools.

While forest schools originated abroad, it is important to recognise that the idea found fertile ground given the long history in the UK of valuing outdoor learning for young people – for example, in the Scouting movement, Steiner education, the Woodcraft Folk and in Outward Bound education. Also, in the 1960s the Plowden Report emphasised the importance of play, creativity and a focus on children's interests at the centre of the curriculum. Forest schools also help to address more recent concerns about the importance of children getting a wide range of experiences and the long-term harm of over-safe and technologically dependent play (Fairclough, 2017).

CRITICAL QUESTION

Advocates of forest schools are clear about their benefits. Outdoor play-based learning is seen as valuable for both physical and mental health. Does it matter whether or not this approach also improves attainment outcomes?

MATHEMATICS EDUCATION IN ENGLAND

Over the last 25 years, mathematics education in England has been shaped in a number of ways by international influences. Before the introduction of the National Numeracy Strategy (NNS) in 1998, there was a great deal of interest in mathematics teaching in other countries. Studies of education in, or exchange programmes with, Hungary, Switzerland, Taiwan and Japan took place. In addition, the designers of the NNS looked at research evidence on effective teaching from other countries.

The 2014 National Curriculum was written informed by looking at the mathematics curriculum in high-performing educational systems. These included Shanghai, Singapore and Massachusetts (that does much better than the rest of the USA in mathematics). The desire to learn from elsewhere is also seen in the government's promotion of East Asian mathematics education. Chapter 31 focuses on mastery and the National Centre for Teaching Mathematics (NCETM) formulation of how to achieve this, known as 'teaching for mastery'. In the current chapter, the way this is being implemented and the background to this are considered.

A variety of different projects and programmes, taken together, comprise the mastery innovation. Some of these are promoted by private businesses or educational organisations, such as various Singaporean-informed textbook schemes or curriculum development projects. However, the government is central to promoting teaching for mastery. One example of a government-funded programme is the Mathematics Teacher Exchange (MTE). The MTE involves English teachers and school leaders visiting Shanghai to observe practice and teachers from Shanghai visiting England to demonstrate teaching. Here, the global influence is direct with teachers experiencing Shanghai teaching approaches for themselves.

The example of English mathematics education is one that also shows that movement of ideas is more complex than simply transfer from one place to another. For example, Singaporean mathematics education was influenced by the Cockcroft Report (1982). This was an important report into English mathematics education. Another influence in Singapore was Bruner's (1966) theory of enactive, iconic and symbolic representation, which was translated as concrete–pictorial–abstract in Singapore. So, ideas that began in the West were further developed and refined in the East before moving back in a different form. This is an example of global entanglements in education. What Western educators have done has influenced East Asian educators whose work is now influencing Western teachers.

KEY THEORY

There have been a number of studies of East Asian-informed mathematics education approaches that have been introduced into England. One of these is the evaluation of the Mathematics Teacher Exchange: China-England. In this study, practice in Shanghai and England are compared. Various reports have been published into how this is influencing practice and outcomes in England. www.gov.uk/government/publications/evaluation-of-the-maths-teacher-exchange-china-and-england

BECOMING CRITICAL ABOUT EVIDENCE AND GLOBAL STRATEGIES

The four examples of global strategies vary in terms of the way they have been promoted and who has promoted them. Lemov's *Teach Like a Champion* is a book and a CPD programme that has been marketed to teachers directly. Doug Lemov and his organisation make money from teachers buying the book or taking their courses. As well as through effective marketing, the ideas have spread from teacher to teacher, and school to school through recommendations. Forest schools have also spread in these ways, even though it is based on a very different philosophy of education. Academies and free schools have been promoted by governments due to their fit with a more general belief that marketisation and competition will improve education. Global influences on mathematics education in England have included all these different ways that ideas spread or are promoted: private textbook businesses market their products; teachers who are enthusiasts for new ideas encourage their networks to get involved; government-funded initiatives provide money and formal support.

Another important issue is how ideas and practices are translated as they move from one place to another. English 'teaching for mastery' that the NCETM promotes is related to what happens in Shanghai and Singapore but it is the NCETM's interpretation of East Asian mathematics. These ideas are then further translated by schools and teachers when they put them into practice. One view of this process is that this is a mistake and good ideas should be replicated exactly. This view goes along with the idea that if we all adopted the 'best' teaching approaches, education would be better. However, another view is that there is not a single 'best' way and that teachers need to think deeply about teaching and learning, consider different approaches, and then adapt ideas in ways that suit them and their pupils and schools.

Education has long been a focus for political arguments. People have different views on what schools are for and how pupils should be taught and learn. More recently, education has also become, at least partly, a market where people and large organisations aim to make money from schools and education. In these circumstances, it is really important that teachers (and schools) question ideas that are promoted to them, wherever they come from. The box below has some useful questions to ask when considering the evidence for ideas, including global strategies. Teachers are not only responsible for themselves, but also for the experience of the children they teach. In business, there is a phrase called 'due diligence' – if a company is going to invest in or buy a product from another company, the directors are supposed to check out the company. Teachers have a similar responsibility towards their pupils when considering new ideas.

INFO 8.2

Will it work for me and our children?

This set of questions can help you to think about whether or not a global strategy or any other new idea is worth considering:

- Do the people promoting the idea have a commercial interest in it? Are they selling books or training?
- Do the people promoting the idea have a particular view on education or teaching that they are trying to push?

- What is the evidence that this idea or approach will work? What types of evidence are there for this? How convincing is this evidence?
- If there is evidence that the approach works abroad, are there other explanations such as culture or the type of society that might be important but that are not easy to reproduce here?
- Has anyone tried the new idea in a situation like yours? What happened?
- What might be the long-term consequences or unintended outcomes of these ways of working?
- Is it possible to begin to experiment with the new ideas or do you need to buy into the whole package?
- Do the potential benefits outweigh the potential negative consequences?

Teachers need to be careful 'consumers' of evidence and of global strategies. Savvy consumers check out different products and compare what they have to offer. But more than this, teachers not only should 'buy' others' ideas but also be active producers of evidence themselves. The example of forest schools shows that a few committed teachers can end up changing practice across a whole education system. While carefully considering evidence is important, teachers have to also consider their values and purposes.

An important question to ask is not only what works, but also 'what works for what?' (Biesta, 2017). This question points to the importance of asking about all the outcomes and effects of educational practices, and not only to focus on attainment. This includes enquiring into unintended consequences. Spending time, energy and money getting better at teaching children to take tests may miss out the bigger purposes of what schools and education should be for. This means it is important to ask not only will this work here for me, but what does 'working' mean?

CHAPTER SUMMARY

- Increasingly, education is influenced by looking at strategies from other countries.
- This is part of a movement for evidenced-based education, sometimes referred to as 'what works'.
- There are lots of types of evidence and teachers need to understand them - but more is not necessarily better.
- Sometimes, people who claim to be interested in evidence-informing education can be selective about the evidence they promote.
- Teaching techniques that are marketed as easy solutions have not necessarily been properly tested.
- Academies and free schools are policies adopted from the USA and Sweden but the evidence is mixed about their success both abroad and in England.
- Forest schools have spread because of enthusiasm of practitioners who generate local evidence of what is effective.
- Mathematics education in England has been the focus of various global influences, the latest of which is the teaching for mastery policy.

(Continued)

(Continued)

- By asking critical questions, teachers can be careful consumers of new ideas and evidence, but more important is for teachers to generate evidence for themselves.
- Teachers need to think carefully about their values and purposes when considering new ideas.

ASSIGNMENTS

The material in this chapter may be relevant to a range of different assignments that you might be asked to write. It will also be useful if you are writing an assignment on evidence-based teaching in general as well as the specific focus of the chapter - global influences. Suggested questions and texts are provided on these two areas.

Evidence-based teaching

What is your view on how far education is similar or different from medicine?

What is the value of the different types of evidence for teachers?

What are the challenges for teachers in accessing evidence?

There are different views on how educational research should be conducted. Ben Goldacre, a science journalist, was asked to write a paper for the English government on evidence in education.

Building evidence into education:

http://media.education.gov.uk/assets/files/pdf/b/ben%20goldacre%20paper.pdf

This view has been criticised. For example, Marc Smith, a teacher, argues that this approach might not be as simple as it seems when applied in education:

www.theguardian.com/teacher-network/2013/mar/26/teachers-research-evidence-based-education

Others raise more general concerns about the dangers of education being focused on measurement; for example, Terry Wrigley in 'Not So Simple: the problem with "evidence-based practice" and the EEF toolkit' in *Forum,* 58(2): 237-52.

Global strategies

When looking at a particular strategy it is important to try to get an understanding of what the practice or approach looks like in the original country before it is translated into a new place. People who are putting forward new approaches will often make their own interpretation.

If looking at a global strategy, what material and literature can you access that will provide an insight into the practices overseas? Think broadly. You may find useful web-based documents, policy documents (for example, curriculum documents), video material and multimedia, reports by organisations such as the OECD, as well as research articles. Using primary sources can be very powerful. Primary sources, in this context, are materials that directly describe what is happening in other countries.

In this report of the evaluation of Mathematics Teacher Exchange, there is comparison of English and Shanghai practices on pages 15-18, and in more detail on pages i-iv:

https://assets.publishing.service.gov.uk/government/uploads/system/uploads/attachment_data/file/536003/Mathematics_Teacher_Exchange_Interim_Report_FINAL_040716.pdf

The structure of this description may be useful to consider how to organise your comparison between two countries.

REFERENCES

Adey, P. and Dillon, J. (eds) (2012) *Bad Education: Debunking myths in education.* Maidenhead: McGraw-Hill Education (UK).

Andrews, A. and Perera, N. (2017) *The Impact of Academieso on Educational Outcomes.* London: EPU. Available at: https://epi.org.uk/wp-content/uploads/2017/07/EPI_-Impact_of_Academies_Consolidated_Report-.pdf (accessed 16/04/18).

Biesta, G. (2017) Education, measurement and the professions: Reclaiming a space for democratic professionality in education. *Educational Philosophy and Theory*, 49(4): 315–30.

Boaler, J. (2005) The 'psychological prisons' from which they never escaped: The role of ability grouping in reproducing social class inequalities. *Forum*, 47(2): 125–34.

Bruner, J.S. (1966) *Toward a Theory of Instruction*: Cambridge, MA: Harvard University Press.

Cockcroft, W.H. (1982) *Mathematics Counts: Report of the committee of inquiry into the teaching of mathem*atics *in schools.* London: Her Majesty Stationery Office.

Cree and McCree (2012) A brief history of Forest School in the UK, Part 1. *Horizons*, 60.

Dweck, C. S. (2006) *Mindset: The new psychology of success.* New York: Random House.

Fairclough, M. (2016) *Playing with Fire: Embracing risk and danger in schools.* Woodbridge: John Catt Educational.

Goldacre, B. (2013) *Building Evidence into Education.* Available at: http://media.education.gov.uk/assets/files/pdf/b/ben%20goldacre%20paper.pdf (accessed 16/04/18).

Hattie, J. (2012) *Visible Learning for Teachers: Maximizing impact on learning.* Abingdon: Routledge.

Lemov, D. (2015) *Teach Like a Champion 2.0: 62 techniques that put students on the path to college.* London: John Wiley & Sons.

Swann, M., Peacock, A., Hart, S. and Drummond, M. (2012) *Creating Learning Without Limits.* Maidenhead: McGraw-Hill Education (UK).

Waite, S. (2016) *Natural Connections Demonstration Project, 2012–2016: Final Report.* Natural England.

Weale, S. (2015) 'It's a political failure': How Sweden's celebrated schools system fell into crisis. *The Guardian.* Available at: www.theguardian.com/world/2015/jun/10/sweden-schools-crisis-political-failure-education (accessed 16/04/18).

Wiliam, D. (2013) Assessment: The bridge between teaching and learning. *Voices from the Middle*, 21(2): 15.

Wilson, E. (2017) *School-based Research: A guide for education students* (3rd edn). London: SAGE.

Wrigley, T. (2016) Not so simple: The problem with 'evidence-based practice' and the EEF toolkit. *Forum*, 58(2): 237–52.

EDUCATION IN FINLAND

AT A GLANCE

- Pre-school education at age 6 is compulsory.
- Basic education is provided within a single structure ages 7-16.
- The school year is 190 days from mid-August to June.
- A national core curriculum is set with the objectives and core content to be covered. This is reviewed every 10 years.
- Schools design their own curricula based on the national framework to allow for local or regional requirements.
- Focus on skills for life rather than test results.
- No national tests for pupils during basic education.
- Assessment is part of daily schoolwork.
- Outdoor learning is a high priority with the use of beaches, lakes and forests as learning resources throughout basic education, but especially in the pre-primary stage.
- Schooling in Finnish and Swedish dependent on pupils' Mother Tongue.
- Pupils excel in international tests.
- Teaching is child-led and focused on social and emotional development.

9

DOES CURRICULUM REALLY MATTER?

Paul Killen is a lecturer in primary teacher training at Liverpool John Moores University where he teaches mathematics and professional studies. Paul's research interests lie in how children develop mental mathematical skills and how such skills link to mathematical understanding.

Avril Rowley is a lecturer in primary teacher training at Liverpool John Moores University and is the head of year 1. Avril is a former teacher with a Ph.D. in Educational Management. Her teaching interests include mentoring, effective models of leadership and dynamic teaching and learning models in primary education.

KEY WORDS

- Aims and values
- Children
- Compulsory education
- Curriculum
- Debate
- Development
- Facts
- Global comparisons
- History
- Learning
- PISA
- Politicisation
- Progressive learning
- Rote learning
- Statutory testing
- 21st century

INTRODUCTION

This chapter will consider how the National Curriculum in England has come full circle over the last 160 years from a fact-based approach to learning, through to innovative theme-based curriculum approaches and back to fact based, once again. It summarises the history of curriculum development in England and asks you to consider what we can learn from this. We will explore the current National Curriculum and ask what a 21st-century curriculum may support in terms of teaching and learning. To explore the concept of curriculum further, we will draw on examples from education models in Singapore and Finland, and consider them alongside the English curriculum.

THE HISTORY OF CURRICULUM DEVELOPMENT IN ENGLAND

THE IMPACT OF INDUSTRIAL REVOLUTION

> *Now, what I want is Facts. Teach these boys and girls nothing but Facts. Facts alone are wanted in life. Plant nothing else, and root out everything else. You can only form the minds of reasoning animals upon Facts: nothing else will ever be of any service to them. This is the principle on which I bring up my own children, and this is the principle on which I bring up these children. Stick to Facts, sir!*
>
> (Charles Dickens, *Hard Times*)

Hard Times was published in 1854 and Dickens characterised the school in the fictitious town of Coketown as an example of how not to educate children. The novel was set against the backdrop of the rapid industrialisation of society in the mid-1800s, which saw a surge in child labour (Griffin, 2014). The widespread use of child labour in factories triggered outrage among many influential politicians. In 1833, the government allocated a grant to voluntary Sunday school providers who would offer a rudimentary education to young factory workers on a part-time basis (Griffin, 2014).

THE END OF THE 19TH CENTURY

In the latter part of the 19th century, we begin to see a common curriculum established. Schools were expected to provide a restricted curriculum with the emphasis almost exclusively on the '3Rs' (reading, writing and arithmetic).

CRITICAL QUESTION

Why did 19th-century educationalists choose to focus on reading, writing and arithmetic? What impact did this have on the further development of curriculum in this country?

In 1862, the government, concerned about the rising cost of education, announced a new policy, often referred to as the 'Revised Code'. Schools were now to be paid according to children's attendance and how much children had learned. This became known as 'payment by results'. Each year inspectors from the Board of Education visited schools to test pupils' reading, writing and arithmetic.

This was the first occasion that government monitored schools. The amount of money a school received was dependent upon what the inspectors saw. Teachers' pay commonly depended on the size of the grant the school was awarded. Many teachers thus changed how they approached teaching, concentrating exclusively on preparing the children for the yearly visit of the inspector.

CRITICAL QUESTION

How far do you think we have progressed over the past 160 years? To what extent do primary school teachers still focus on 'the visit of the inspector'?

The Elementary Education Act of 1870 was the very first piece of British legislation that addressed education on a national scale by establishing the principle of education for all children aged 5–13. New 'Board Schools' were to be set up to supplement the existing voluntary schools. The Act did not provide free education for everyone, only in proven cases of poverty. The fact that schooling was going to be available for all children did not yet mean that it was compulsory for all; this did not happen for another ten years.

POST SECOND WORLD WAR

Compulsory education for all children from 5 to 14 came about in the 1944 Education Act and the school leaving age was set at 15 from 1947. For the first time, it was proclaimed that 'public education be organised in three progressive stages to be known as primary education, secondary education and further education' (Lawson and Silver, 2007). The 1944 Act said virtually nothing about the content of the curriculum and gave governors and head teachers control of the school curriculum.

THE PLOWDEN REPORT IN THE 1960S

The next major event in developing the modern primary curriculum was the Plowden Report of 1967. Here there was a recognition that a limited focus on mathematics and English and rote learning of key facts was not the best way to serve our children for their future. Plowden sought to put the child at the centre of learning and began the debate around mixed-ability teaching.

> *Individual differences between children of the same age are so great that any class, however homogeneous it seems, must always be treated as a body of children needing individual and different attention.*
>
> (Plowden, 1967)

The work of Plowden became embroiled in the debate about so-called 'progressive teaching methods' with some voices in education suggesting that teachers must move away from 'progressive' teaching and back to more traditional pedagogy.

1988 EDUCATION REFORM ACT

It was not until 1988 that England had its first National Curriculum. It also defined, the different categories or 'key stages' in education that we still use today.

The Act outlined what subjects children would study from age 5–16. It introduced the term 'core subjects' – mathematics, English and science. There were six 'foundation subjects' (history, geography, technology, music, art, physical education) and a foreign language. By this time, education was heavily politicised. Teachers had little say in the design or construction of the 1988 National Curriculum.

Associated with the new curriculum was the new system of testing. Each Key Stage now had a corresponding age-related assessment with the introduction of Standard Assessment Tests (SATS). Results would be published in so-called 'league tables' recording children's performance in the core subjects.

EDUCATION, EDUCATION, EDUCATION

In 1997, the New Labour government came to power with the mantra 'education, education, education'. The big impact for primary schools in this period was the introduction of the 'numeracy hour' and the 'literacy hour'. Now teachers were not only told what to teach, they were given guidance on how and when to teach it. The numeracy and literacy hour were replaced in 2003 with the Primary National Strategy, although the content of each subject was not significantly changed.

In 2005, the then Education secretary Ruth Kelly announced that children should be taught reading by using 'synthetic phonics'. Many at this time denounced this as the evidence was based on a very small-scale research in a very small area of Scotland.

Is it important that the curriculum continues to change and develop? Why?

THE NATIONAL CURRICULUM TODAY

The current version of the Primary National Curriculum was introduced in 2014.

KEY READING

In 2012, educationalist Andrew Pollard commented in an IoE blog piece on the then proposed primary curriculum (which became statutory in 2014).

https://ioelondonblog.wordpress.com/2012/06/12/proposed-primary-curriculum-what-about-the-pupils/

This is an opinion piece and should be read in that knowledge. Nonetheless, it provides useful information about the development and design of today's National Curriculum and gives some insight into the ideologies that informed it.

CRITICAL QUESTION

Does the current curriculum 'open up' opportunities for creative teaching? How important is this?

The fact that we call it a 'national curriculum' is a moot point. Academies and Free Schools are not obliged to follow it and are permitted to design their own curriculum. The 2014 version of the primary curriculum essentially divides Key Stage 2 into two discrete parts: Lower Key Stage 2 (Years 3–4) and Upper Key Stage 2 (Years 5–6). It retains the concept of three core subjects, although many may say that since the Science KS2 SATS were abolished in 2009, the subject has lost some of its importance and is treated by schools as another foundation subject. In addition to the core subjects, there are eight foundation subjects (art and design, computing, design and technology, geography, history, languages, music and physical education). In relation to the subject headings, this is identical to 1988. However, the detail is much more enlightening.

CRITICAL QUESTION

In the National Curriculum programme of study for Key Stages 1 and 2, 86 pages are devoted to English, 45 for mathematics. Art and design is only given two pages.

Does this reflect the values our government gives different subjects?

KEY READING

The perceived lack of a broad and balanced curriculum in primary schools is a current theme in education. In this piece, the Ofsted Chief Inspector, Amanda Spielman, explores the narrowing of the primary curriculum:

www.wiredgov.net/wg/news.nsf/articles/DNWAAS2BJN

TODAY'S CURRICULUM

WHERE ARE WE NOW?

In 1921, Albert Einstein visited Boston where he was looking at a set of questions that Thomas Edison used to screen job applicants. One of these questions was 'what is the speed of sound?' When asked about this, Einstein reputedly responded:

> *I don't know. I don't burden my memory with such facts that I can easily find in any textbook ... the value of an education is not the learning of many facts but the training of the mind.*
>
> (cited in Calaprice, 2013)

Today, what we do in schools, and how we do it, is more than ever defined by the end of Key Stage assessments and how well students perform in them. It is important to ask:

CRITICAL QUESTION

Is the primary curriculum we deliver fitting for our 21st-century needs? What is the purpose of education in the 21st century?

The year 2018 sees a trial introduction of computer-based times tables test for children in Year 4.

CRITICAL QUESTION

In a country where most adults have a calculator on their mobile phone, is it really important for children to learn their times tables?

In February 2016, the Minister for Education, Nick Gibb, gave a speech at the University of Durham, where he made the case for schools teaching knowledge and putting the acquisition of knowledge at the centre of our education system. He said:

> *Put simply, a commitment to social justice requires us to place knowledge at the heart of our education system. And this is not a statement of opinion – it is a fact.*

CRITICAL QUESTION

Does this focus on knowledge mirror 19th-century thinking around the curriculum? Is this fitting for the 21st century?

EVALUATING THE CURRENT CURRICULUM

In 2015, the Compass Group produced a document that considered what learning could look like in the 21st century. It describes education in England today as 'narrow, top down and out of date'.

> *The Conservative led Coalition Government has also promoted a narrow, traditional, over-tested and unimaginative curriculum that cannot fully equip learners for a modern and rapidly changing world. We are educating for a world of 20th-century work, using largely 19th-century structures just when the 21st century is finally kicking in and leaving the old world fast behind.*

KEY READING

Learning for the 21st century: The Final Report of the Compass Inquiry into a New System of Education. Compass Education Group (2015)

www.compassonline.org.uk/wp-content/uploads/2015/03/Compass-BIG-Education-DIGITAL-Final.pdf

This publication is informed by a range of contributors and examines a number of the key issues that should be considered when thinking of how our 21st-century schools could look. The discussion and proposals are the result of an inquiry that lasted 20 months that considered the context and purpose of education in the 21st century.

In March 2018, the President of the Confederation of British Industry (CBI), Paul Drechsler, made a speech to the Association of School and College Leaders in Birmingham entitled 'Education is more than knowledge alone'. He noted that the key things employers are looking for are not featured in our current curriculum. Drechsler called on policy makers to make education more than results and rote learning. Rather, he believes that pedagogical approaches should encourage:

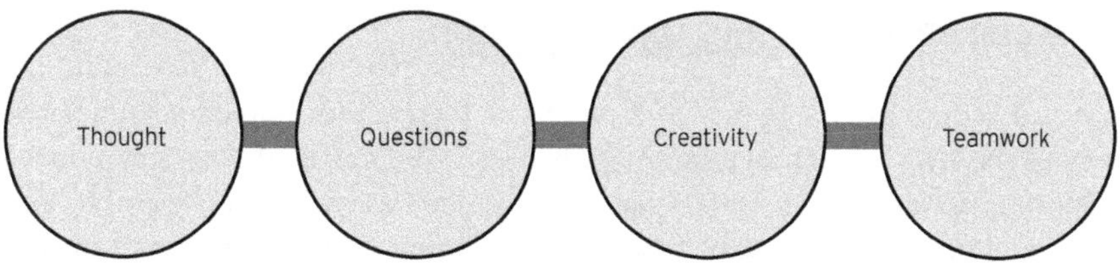

He suggested that school should be about the wider preparation for adult life.

> *The OECD are clear that we are now doing more rote learning than almost anywhere else in the world. Yes, times tables are important. But if memorising facts is all students are doing, there's much they are missing out on ... it doesn't have to be like this. Singapore, Finland and the best schools in the US all show it doesn't have to be done this way. There, education has a clear objective, with clear standards on core subjects, clear lines of appropriate accountability, and all based on developing the whole person.*
>
> (Drechsler, 2018)

INTERNATIONAL PERSPECTIVES ON THE NATIONAL CURRICULUM

Throughout the many incarnations of the National Curriculum, there have been inevitable comparisons with educational models in countries that are perceived to have similar – or often superior – educational outcomes (Waldow *et al.*, 2014). These comparisons are drawn from the triennial Programme for International Student Assessment (PISA) tests that measure the knowledge and skills of 15-year-old students across international member states (OECD, 2018). PISA was established as a testing system in 1997 through the Organisation for Economic Co-operation and Development (OECD) to record students' skills and understanding in science, mathematics, reading, collaborative problem solving and financial literacy as a means of standardising global student performance (Waldow *et al.*, 2014). This resulted in a form of global 'league tables' which impacts on national education reform agendas (Grek, 2009; Kamens, 2013; Meyer and Benavot, 2013; Sellar and Lingard, 2013; Wiseman, 2010). This has led to increased comparisons across nations. Countries, including the UK, borrow educational ideas cross-nationally with the intention that this will improve their rankings in international tests scores. International policy makers use PISA results as a normative model by which to compare their own educational programmes and argue for reforms to bring them into line with international standards (Breakspear, 2012). Indeed, in England, the 2010 White Paper (DfE, 2010) on education notes that the overriding influence for its proposed education policy change came from the results of the 2006 PISA tests.

The international influence on the standardisation of education has become more intense in recent years with many countries looking to Scandinavia and the Far East for answers to the growing gap in international educational outcomes (Waldow *et al.*, 2014; Morris, 2015). In particular, countries such as Finland and Singapore are cited as having discovered the educational panacea, which has led to many countries, including England, adopting aspects of these curricula to improve their own (Morris, 2015). Finland's progressive approaches to schooling and Singapore's success in mathematics have both been emulated here in recent years.

THE CURRICULUM AND PRIMARY SCHOOLING IN FINLAND

Finland is often hailed as an outstanding model of education. Its results in international tests are consistently higher than those of the UK. The gap in attainment between the most and least able pupils is one of the smallest internationally (Howard, 2015). The UK has sought to replicate the successes of the Finnish education system with the assumption that to take some aspects of their system and then to transplant them here would result in similar academic success for its pupils. However, Finnish teachers are given the freedom to teach the curriculum using whichever pedagogies they feel best suit their classes, which is a liberty that exceeds that available to UK teachers (Kyrö, n.d.). The UK government has defended the new curriculum as one that does not prescribe pedagogies – only content – to ensure equality of education across the country. Knowledge and skills set out in the English curriculum are deemed to be the essentials needed for every child to succeed in life and, thus, equipping them for life and the workplace.

One of the main aspects of the Finnish education system regularly held up for comparison with the UK is its late school starting age (Kyrö, n.d.). In Finland, children spend the early years of their education until the age of six in daycare centres or kindergartens where they are involved in creative play to enhance their health and well-being. Kindergartens focus on ensuring that children are happy and well balanced. In the UK, some would argue, the focus is on teaching children to read and write. Good social habits are taught at this stage as a foundation to later learning and at least 90 minutes per day is spent playing outdoors (Howard, 2015). The focus on play at this stage of education is very carefully planned to develop children's attention span, perseverance, concentration and problem-solving skills ready to start formal schooling. From the age of six, Finnish children attend compulsory pre-primary education which is play-based and creative – they have no formal education until they start school at the age of seven (Finnish National Agency for Education, n.d.). All forms of education are free and, in pre-primary and primary (basic schools), children are entitled to free school meals and textbooks as standard, and subsidised transport if they live far from the school they attend.

Once in the formal school system, Finnish children are taught that equality and working together are the keys to educational success. Schools are non-selective and formal examinations are not taken until the age of 18. Finnish children are not streamed according to ability, nor are they required to sit entrance examinations to selective secondary schools as all schools offer parity of opportunity for all. Children with special educational needs are taught in mainstream schools under the philosophy that all children are entitled to the right to educational support to suit their individual needs (Finnish National Agency for Education, 2018).

INFO 9.1

Education in Finland - at a glance

- Pre-school education at age six is compulsory.
- Basic education is provided within a single structure ages 7-16.
- The school year is 190 days from mid-August to June.
- A national core curriculum is set with the objectives and core content to be covered. This is reviewed every 10 years.
- Schools design their own curricula based on the national framework to allow for local or regional requirements.
- Focus on skills for life rather than test results.

(Continued)

(Continued)

- There are no national tests for pupils during basic education.
- Assessment is part of daily schoolwork.
- Outdoor learning is a high priority with the use of beaches, lakes and forests as learning resources throughout basic education but especially in the pre-primary stage.
- Schooling in Finnish and Swedish dependent on pupils' Mother Tongue.
- Pupils excel in international tests.
- Teaching is child-led and focused on social and emotional development.

One of the main aspects of the Finnish education system that the UK has adopted is the use of outdoor learning through Forest School pedagogies. In Finland, this is not viewed as an add-on to basic education but rather an integral part of teachers' pedagogies in subjects (Howard, 2015) and the use of outdoor spaces is embedded into the curriculum. In the UK, outdoor learning has evolved to become the Forest School approach inspired by the Finnish (and other Scandinavian countries, including Denmark and Sweden) philosophies of outdoor learning but it takes on a very different form whereby teachers must have specific Forest School Association (FSA) qualifications to teach these pedagogies. This has led to criticism of the fact that Forest School approaches, as a philosophy in the UK, are becoming a far more corporate and institutionalised version of the Scandinavian model on which they were based (Leather, 2016).

In the UK, Forest School sessions involve pupils in activities that develop the whole child through teamwork and learning to take supported risks – an element of life, which many feel, has been sanitised in modern childhood (Savery *et al.*, 2017; Connolly and Haughton, 2014). These activities take place perhaps once a week for part of the year – weather permitting. In Finland, the Forest School approach is integral to learning and in many kindergartens children spend 95 per cent of the school day outdoors exploring through play to learn about the world around them regardless of the weather or season (Knight, 2013; Howard, 2015).

EDUCATION IN SINGAPORE

Education in Singapore is based on the British model dating back to colonial days and is recognised as an international world curriculum leader in science and maths (OECD, 2018). Pedagogies are influenced by a range of traditions. Teachers rely heavily on textbooks, worksheets and plenty of drill and practice, especially in subjects such as mathematics. The main aim of the curriculum is to prepare children for school tests and national exams with a large proportion of time dedicated to increasing levels in mastery of procedures and problem solving. Hence, classroom practice is mainly focused on curriculum coverage and facts rather than teaching skills-based learning strategies to pupils. The types of pedagogies heralded in the West as the most effective means of learning, such as group work, collaborative tasks and child-led activities, are rarely utilised by teachers in the Singapore education system. Instead, they teach according to a well-defined, centralised, national curriculum with testing points at the end of both the primary and secondary phases. These exams are high stakes. Exams at the end of primary school determine which secondary school children will attend and there are high levels of competition to get into the secondary schools that are perceived to be the best.

Teachers in Singapore do not focus on pupils' prior knowledge or understanding but instead are more interested in whether or not children know the correct answer to a specific problem. This system works for the pupils in the Singaporean education system – as their PISA results show – but the government is beginning to question whether or not they are developing a workforce prepared for the challenges of the workplace in the 21st century. Since 2004, *Teach Less, Learn More* (Loong, 2004) was identified as a framework that Singaporean teachers should follow to increase the levels in innovation and creativity in their pupils. This is still taking time to become embedded into teachers' pedagogies, mainly due to the high-stakes examination programmes. Teachers still feel the need to teach facts to enable their pupils to pass the tests (Tan *et al.*, 2008).

One of the key aspects of the Singaporean curriculum success, their mathematics curriculum, has come to the attention of schools in the UK with many now opting to use similar pedagogies in their own classrooms. Gone are the days when these schools streamed their Key Stage 2 classes to allow for the differentiation required to cover an increasing range of abilities. In its place are lessons with no differentiation and a scripted lesson format aimed at improving maths mastery focused on a narrower range of topics at a deeper level of understanding. Teaching has come full circle back to the reliance on textbooks and whole-class teaching.

CLASSROOM LINK

What does this mean for classroom practice?

Singapore maths

Since its introduction to the UK in 2014, over 8,000 schools have introduced 'Singapore Maths' schemes into their curriculums with the government providing £41 million over four years to support the three-step approach to learning. The initiative is also advocated by the National Centre for Excellence in Teaching Mathematics (NCETM) and Ofsted who have highly praised the focus on deeper understanding of concepts in the mathematics curriculum.

This video from the NCETM gives some insight into the use of mastery approaches in one primary school in London:

www.youtube.com/watch?v=l3v5qfpXBal

The new approach to mathematics education is continuing to gain momentum in schools throughout the UK and it will not be for at least another ten years whether we will know if the gamble has paid off.

INFO 9.2

Education in Singapore - At a Glance

- Based on British system.
- Emphasis on testing with schools ranked based on results of standardised tests.
- Pupils excel in international tests, especially mathematics.
- Strong emphasis on maths and science.

(Continued)

(Continued)

- Pupils start school at six years old.
- Schooling in English and pupils' official Mother Tongue (Mandarin, Malay or Tamil).
- Selective examinations at the end of primary education determine secondary school allocation.
- Focus on knowledge and skills.
- Pedagogies focused on drill and practice.
- Centralised control of the curriculum.
- Differentiation is built into the school system - pupils streamed from Year 5 (UK equivalent).

INTERNATIONAL CURRICULUM INFLUENCES IN THE UK

The UK government's approach to educational policy in recent years has been heavily influenced by the international curricula that produce the highest PISA results. The factors of most interest to policy makers in the UK have been:

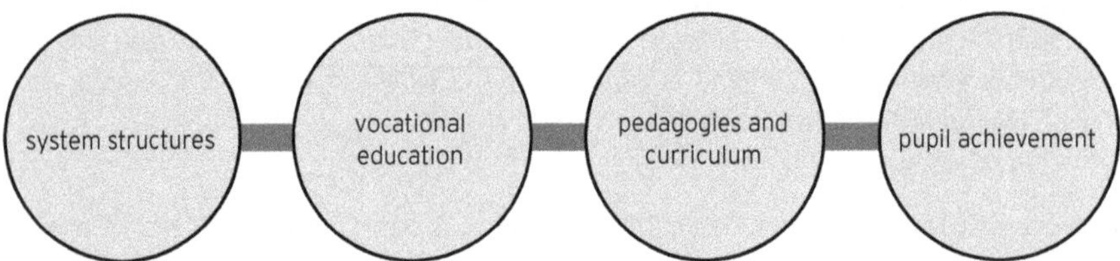

A simple replication of these systems and approaches in other countries do not take into consideration the socio-economic contexts in which educational systems are based. It is reductive to think that education can be a success just based on policy change without looking at the ethos of the schools and society from which the ideas are being 'borrowed'. As an initial start, the comparisons of the population sizes of both Finland and Singapore are dramatically smaller than that of the UK, with Singapore at 4,839,400, Finland at 5,313,399 and England at 51,460,000 (Oates, 2011). Whereas Singapore has a multiracial population with high rates of immigration and four official languages (Yang *et al.*, 2017), Finland has an almost homogeneous population with only 5 per cent of the population born outside the country. In addition, Finland has the lowest wage inequality of any country in the EU, whereas the UK has the highest (Eurofound, 2015) and Singapore has the second worst income inequality in the world (OECD, 2016; Department of Statistics Singapore, 2016). Child poverty in the UK is double that of Finland (UNICEF Office of Research, 2017). The national contexts of both Finnish and Singaporean societies are dramatically different from the UK and it will be interesting to see whether, in the next PISA tests in 2018, it will be able to make its mark in the top rankings of this international league table.

outcomes. Despite nuances in the language used, they employ broadly similar terminology to indicate levels of overall achievement by each institution, e.g. 'needs urgent improvement' to 'outstanding'. Comparable procedures are in place to follow up on schools that perform unsatisfactorily. Likewise, those institutions that are dissatisfied with the process and/or results of their inspection have recourse to air their complaints. Individual school inspection reports are then available for public consumption (see Perry, 2013).

At face value, the above-described process appears largely uniform and robust in its design. There are, however, important differences in emphasis within the four jurisdictions. In Scotland, a collaborative approach is taken. Inspectors are viewed more as coaches than examiners. Contrarily, in England, a high-stakes approach is the norm where the external examining body is regarded as the main arbitrator and the results can be potentially used for 'naming and shaming' schools. The role of the ETI is central in Northern Ireland; it is coupled with self-evaluation, which is regarded as key to driving up improvement especially for underachieving schools (ETI, 2010, 2012). Consider the implications of comparing systems where there are varying degrees of subjectivity inherent in their school evaluation models. For instance, how do you judge the reliability of results generated by countries that rely predominantly or solely on teacher autonomy, such as is the case in Singapore and Finland respectively? Equally, are the results gathered by countries that require external and self-evaluation input as demonstrated by more than 75 per cent of countries reviewed by the OECD (Organisation for Economic Co-operation and Development) any more valid in their data collection and interpretations (OECD, 2011)? (See European Commission/EACEA/Eurydice, 2015 for more on school evaluations across Europe.)

CRITICAL QUESTION

Can we really compare education systems when there is such variation in school evaluation models?

It is essential to exercise caution when viewing the school inspection process and the subsequent interpretation of any results garnered when searching for answers to these fundamental questions (Shewbridge *et al.*, 2014).

KEY READING

The websites for each region's inspection body:

Education Scotland: https://education.gov.scot/

Estyn: www.estyn.gov.wales/inspection

ETI: www.etini.gov.uk/

Ofsted: www.gov.uk/government/organisations/ofsted

MEASURES OF SITE-LEVEL PERFORMANCE

Perhaps a narrower measure of an individual school's success comes in the form of statutory examination results. These are tests in literacy and numeracy taken at key points during pupils' school careers. In England, compulsory testing occurs at the end of primary schooling (Year 6/age 10–11). Results are presented in the form of average progress scores and average 'scaled scores'. Additionally, the percentages of pupils who have achieved the expected standard as well as those who have achieved a high level of attainment are disclosed. In Northern Ireland and Wales, statutory assessments are given mid-way and at the end of primary education. In Wales, the results are reported to parents in the form of their child's standardised score, their score in comparison to others the same age in Wales, as well as a progress score. In Northern Ireland, levels of progression are used to judge pupils' attainment and this information is provided to parents.

Scottish authorities reintroduced compulsory assessments in 2017. Presently, compulsory testing is conducted at the beginning, middle and end of pupils' primary schooling. The data is expressly collected for use by teachers and parents to share. The pupils do not receive the results. Local authorities have access to school level data, while the Scottish government only has access to national trends emanating from the assessments.

CRITICAL QUESTION

Why are results shared with different parties in different assessment systems? Which of those listed above is the best system?

Although the main reason such data is collected is to inform teachers and parents of individual attainment and progress, it is also used to rank schools, thus satisfying consumer demand. In England, primary schools' results are published in the form of league tables. Up until recently, the other regions within the UK refrained from doing so. In 2001, Wales and Northern Ireland abolished this practice, followed by Scotland in 2003. However, in 2016, Scottish authorities reversed this decision by publishing reading, writing and numeracy results, showing how well Scottish pupils faired in the new Curriculum for Excellence. Wales reintroduced the publication of performance information in 2015, with schools colour-coded – green, yellow, amber or red – in a bid to raise standards. Although Northern Ireland does not publish school rankings, media outlets often take such data and arrange institutions accordingly to form league tables.

Considering the plethora of data available, indicating schools' individual and comparative performances, it is essential to remind you here of certain caveats that exist in the interpretation of this data. Naturally, league tables are often the first port of call for parents as they decide on the school to which they send their children. Yes, it is likely that satisfying consumer demand will help increase performance levels since local accountability is built into the UK system. However, some critics claim that league tables merely encourage competition over collaboration, and so wealth and status provide gateways into higher performing schools, thus creating inequalities in the school populations being compared. (Find a link to Birrell's blog below.) Is it fair to judge those schools that have greater family and community challenges (i.e. poverty, illiteracy, drug and alcohol issues, unemployment, etc.) with the same kinds of instruments as those that do not?

CRITICAL QUESTION

Given the diversity of challenges facing schools, is it fair to judge all schools using the same criteria?

It is also possible that the relentless public pressure to perform at an increasingly elevated rate will impact on curricular breadth and depth. Some suggest that in order to enhance a school's public profile, some children's educational experiences are curbed. Whatever discrepancies might exist in the process of arriving at a percentage or letter grade regarding a school's performance, it is also debatable as to how possible it is to authentically measure a school's ethos and character.

KEY READING

Birrell, G. (2015) *The disgrace of our segregated school system*. Faculty of Education blog at Canterbury Christ Church University. www.consider-ed.org.uk/the-disgrace-of-our-segregated-school-system/

Carden, C. (2013) Mum, what happens if I don't pass the test? *Teacher Primary*, 7(8).

Gardner, J. (2016) Education in Northern Ireland since the Good Friday Agreement: Kabuki theatre meets danse macabre. *Oxford Review of Education Journal*, 42(3): 346–61.

CRITICAL QUESTION

How 'fair' do you regard measures of educational quality to be in the UK?

FROM AN INTERNATIONAL PERSPECTIVE

While it is not possible to compare all aspects of international education, perhaps the most fundamental question then becomes:

CRITICAL QUESTION

What must students know and be able to do in order to function fully in life and work?

Unsurprisingly, this leads us back to the core subjects of literacy, mathematics and science. As a result, extensive databases have been compiled, some from as far back as 1959, as a means of tracking global trends in this regard. Two such databases, created by the IEA (International Association for the Evaluation of Educational Achievement) are frequently cited as evidence of developments in primary education from across the world.

These are TIMSS (Trends in International Mathematics and Science Study) and PIRLS (Progress in International Reading Literacy Study).

Since the mid 1990s, TIMSS has monitored achievement in mathematics and science every four years, at the 4th (9–10 years old) and 8th grades (13–14 years old). PIRLS, administered every five years, has since 2001 carried out the same in reading at the 4th grade level. An important addition, in the latest iteration of PIRLS is the ePIRLS, a computerised assessment of online reading comprehension. This time around, 50 and 57 countries respectively from across the globe participated in PIRLS 2016 and TIMSS 2015. Comprising some 450 pages, it is only possible to share some of the key highlights of the current PIRLS (Mullis and Martin, 2016; Mullis *et al.*, 2017) and TIMSS (Martin *et al.*, 2016; Mullis and Martin, 2013; Mullis et al., 2016) results for the 4th grade. (See Key Information below for full reports.)

PIRLS 2016 (4TH GRADE)

PIRLS focuses on three main aspects of reading literacy:

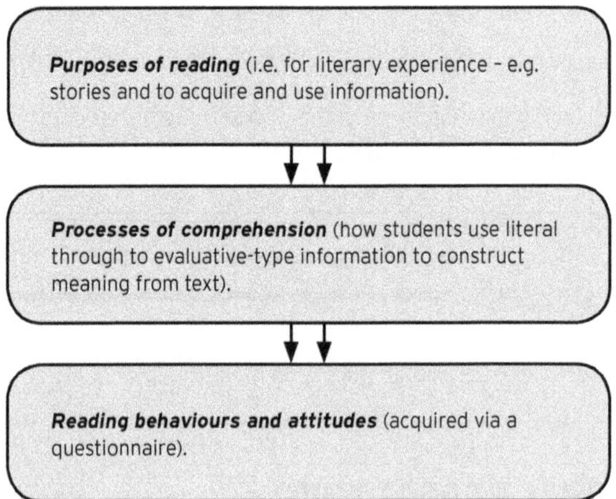

TIMSS 2015 (4TH GRADE)

TIMSS concentrates on two main aspects of mathematics:

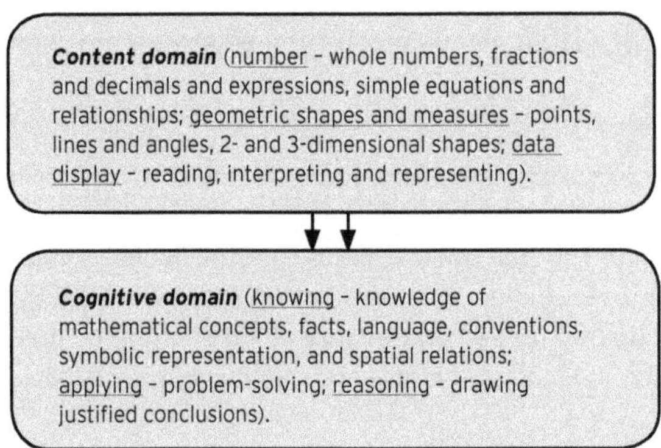

In science, it focuses on the same two main aspects as above:

Content domain (life science - life cycles, ecosystems and human health; physical science - matter, energy, forces and motion; Earth science - the Earth's structure, processes and history and the solar system).

Cognitive domain (knowing - knowledge of facts, relationships, processes, concepts, and equipment; applying - aforementioned facts, etc.: reasoning - analysing data and other information, drawing conclusions, and extending their understandings to new situations).

KEY READING

Find the full PIRLS 2016 report here:

http://pirls2016.org/wp-content/uploads/structure/CompletePDF/P16-PIRLS-International-Results-in-Reading.pdf

Find the PIRLS 2016 Assessment Framework here:

https://timssandpirls.bc.edu/pirls2016/downloads/P16_Framework_2ndEd.pdf

Find links to the full TIMSS 2015 report and Assessment Frameworks here:

http://timssandpirls.bc.edu/timss2015/international-results/#/?playlistId=0&videoId=0

HOW DO WE COMPARE ON THE INTERNATIONAL STAGE?

The UK as a whole is not represented in the latest TIMSS 2016 nor the PIRLS 2015 results, but rather only Northern Ireland and England. In terms of overall achievement in reading, Northern Ireland was placed joint 6th, with England in joint 8th. In fact, both jurisdictions have increased their scores since the previous collection of data in 2011. As depicted in Figure 10.1, they are placed among many of the countries that are often cited as the world's leading role models in education. In terms of mathematics attainment, although there is a sizeable gap between the top five achievers in the TIMMS 2016 study, it is still noteworthy that Northern Ireland (6th place) and England made it inside the top ten (10th place). (See Figure 10.2.)

Before attempting possible explanations for such impressive rankings, it might be best to begin by considering some philosophical beliefs that underpin the notion of childhood. Educational psychology has long since identified the holistic development that occurs across a number of dimensions within the first eight years of life. It is widely accepted that during this period, children experience physical growth spurts and are at an

Figure 10.1 International Reading Achievement in Reading (Mullis et al.*, 2017)*

optimal time to acquire complex and expansive language. They begin to develop emotional regulation while learning to socially interact with various people and situations. Cognitively, they begin to mature while also becoming morally aware (Boyd and Bee, 2014). Therefore, some countries regard this prolific stage of development as a time for children to learn life experiences in the home/community setting. By contrast, others favour the more formal interactions characteristic of pre-school environments. Indeed, countries such as the USA, Japan, Denmark and France allow for home schooling if desired.

MANDATORY SCHOOL AGE

Inevitably, questions arise around the maturational and formal experiential differences that exist among the various comparator school populations. This is understandable since there are quite apparent discrepancies in mandatory school entry ages within the sample group (See Info 10.1). For instance, even among the top achievers, there is considerable disparity.

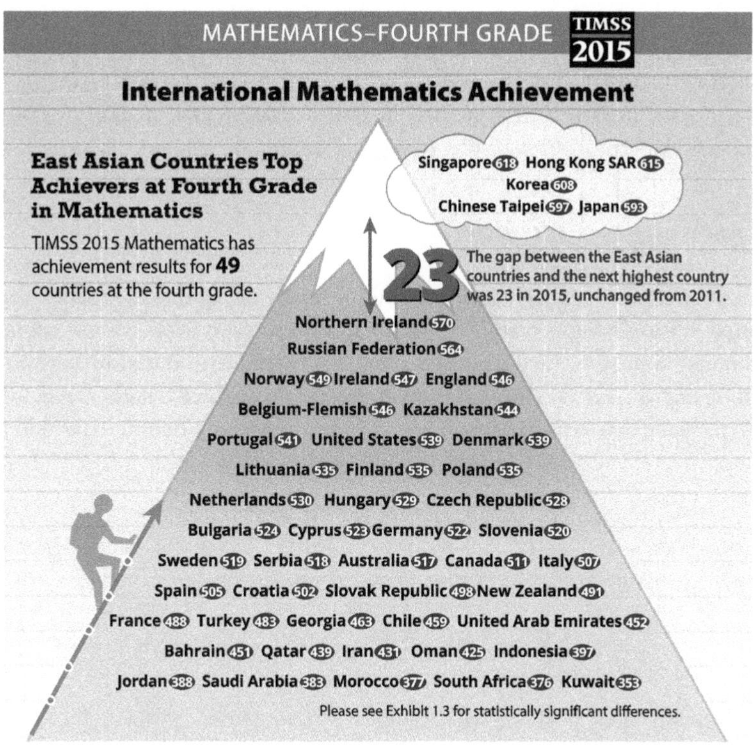

Figure 10.2 International Mathematics Achievement (Mullis et al., 2016)

INFO 10.1

Age	Country
Four	Northern Ireland
Five	Cyprus, England, Malta, Scotland, Wales
Six	Austria, Belgium, Croatia, Czech Republic, Denmark, France, Germany, Greece, Hungary, Iceland, Republic of Ireland, Italy, Liechtenstein, Luxembourg, Netherlands, Norway, Portugal, Romania, Slovakia, Slovenia, Spain, Switzerland, Turkey
Seven	Bulgaria, Estonia, Finland, Latvia, Lithuania , Poland, Serbia, Sweden

Source and further info: www.nfer.ac.uk/eurydice/compulsory-age-of-starting-school

Indeed, some countries allow for flexibility within their admissions policies while others do not. Despite these differences, both the PIRLS (Mullis *et al.*, 2017) and TIMMS (Mullis *et al.*, 2016; Martin *et al.*, 2016) studies found that two of the most influential factors of academic success involve attending high-quality, well-resourced, pre-primary education and having positive parental engagement. Therefore, it would appear that as long as one (or preferably both) of these aspects is honoured, academic success is more likely.

A FOCUS ON LITERACY AND MATHEMATICS

The notable placement of England and Northern Ireland in the literacy and mathematics rankings may also be in some part attributed to the emphasis placed on these two core subjects in the last two decades. In the former case, the National Literacy and Numeracy Strategies (DfE, 2011) were introduced in the late 1990s. They were more than stand-alone endeavours targeting only two core curricular areas. Rather, they represented 'one of the most ambitious change management programmes in education'. Consequently, they left behind,

> *a legacy of high quality training materials, teaching and learning frameworks and well-trained teaching professionals and leaders of learning in schools, settings and more widely in the education sector.*
>
> (2011, p. 2)

According to the same report, there were significant improvements across the board.

Around the same time in Northern Ireland, the government committed to a comprehensive and ambitious school improvement programme (DENI, 1998). At the heart of this lay literacy. However, a House of Commons Committee of Public Accounts report in 2006 was less than glowing in its review of such a scheme. Original targets were unmet and provision was still considered unequal. In the meantime, work was well underway for the beginning phase of implementation of the revised curriculum (Council for Curriculum, Examinations & Assessment [CCEA]) in 2007. Not only were the early years elevated in status (with the introduction of the unique Foundation Stage), but again literacy and numeracy took centre stage.

CRITICAL QUESTION

Is a focus on literacy and mathematics the right approach?

In a bid to remedy the shortcomings of the initial school improvement strategy, the Northern Ireland government produced two significant documents in the years that followed.

First came *Every School a Good School: A policy for school improvement*, published in 2009. Its aim was to galvanise strength from within schools, believing that teachers and principals are best placed to make decisions on how to move their institutions forward through structured self-evaluation procedures. Two years later, *Count, Read:*

Succeed (DENI, 2011) outlined explicitly the roles that various stakeholders had to play in order to meet a new set of targets in literacy and numeracy. As yet, there has been no formal review of both documents' impact other than individual institutions' progress. The Welsh introduced a Literacy and Numeracy Framework (Welsh Government) in 2013 to help drive up standards. However, Estyn reported 'modest' progress after two years. Reasons for this outcome related to a lack of time to allow sufficient implementation to occur.

SCIENCE

Turning to science, the picture is much less complimentary for England and Northern Ireland. The former is placed joint 15th, with Bulgaria while the latter comes in 23rd alongside the Slovak Republic (see Figure 10.3).

Figure 10.3 International Science Achievement (Martin et al.*, 2016)*

It is perhaps fair to say that, by comparison, science has been treated as 'the poor relation' within the various curricula across the UK because of the central status given to literacy and numeracy. Although included in each jurisdiction's curriculum, science has been subsumed into the 'World Around Us' area of learning in Northern Ireland, where it had previously been a stand-alone, core subject. It has received something of an uplift with the advent of STEM (Science, Technology, Engineering and Maths) subjects of late; however, England and Northern Ireland still struggle to 'make the grade' in the TIMMS rankings. Some of this may be due to a perceived lack of interest in science by some pupils in Northern Ireland and England, especially by the time they reach post-primary school.

CRITICAL QUESTION

How important is science as a subject in primary education?

Leonardi et al. (2017) in a report commissioned by the Wellcome Trust, found that science education is still beset with a lower-status image. When they asked respondents how important they think certain subjects are to their respective Senior Leadership teams, the following statistics emerged:

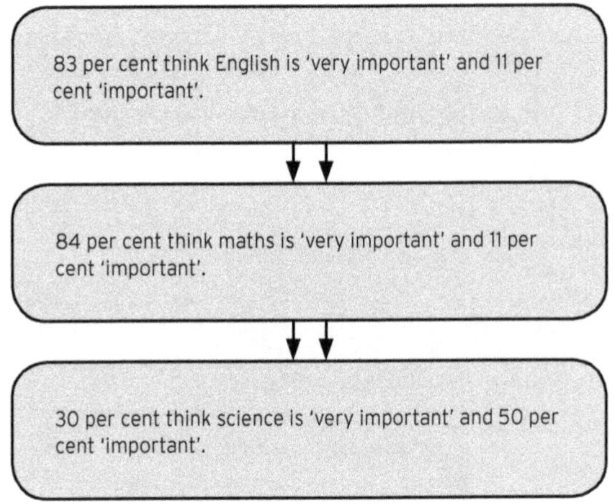

When asked how important it was for pupils to study science, 57 per cent of non-specialist teachers 'strongly agreed' and 39 per cent 'agreed'. Of the same group, only 36 per cent 'strongly agreed' while 59 per cent 'agreed' that science skills are transferable. These figures do not speak of a high regard for science education.

STEM

Why do countries such as Singapore perform outstandingly in science (and maths) in particular?

Cultural factors strongly shape a country's educational policies and practices. Despite changes in their current educational model occurring, Hogan (2014) succinctly paints a picture of how Singapore runs its schools. He comments on the presence of top-down models of leadership with emphasis placed on knowledge reproduction and didactic pedagogy. The following quote captures this cultural approach,

> *parents, students, teachers and policy makers share a highly positive but rigorously instrumentalist view of the value of education at the individual level. Students are generally compliant and classrooms orderly.*
>
> (ibid., p. 3)

Additionally, teacher selection and evaluation is rigorous, while substantial investment in capacity building and professional development at all levels helps strengthen the delivery of (science) education. It is also important to note that teacher evaluations are linked to higher salaries and bonuses (Sclafani, 2008). Finland and Singapore share similar cultural views in relation to the highly respected and intellectual status of teaching. Again, the selection of teacher candidates in Finland is very thorough and teaching programmes are academically demanding. Consensus around pupil success and teacher autonomy, driven by school self-evaluation and pupil feedback, are the hallmarks of education in this part of the world.

Pit this against the cultural wave of pupil-centred educational practices that exist in the UK while still being obliged to prepare pupils for high-stakes, standardised testing. Although some school self-evaluation occurs (e.g. Northern Ireland), schools' performances and, therefore, priorities are dictated to a large degree by adherence to national curricula and external evaluation rather than teacher-led judgements. After all, meeting consumer demand increases the pressure to perform very well due to the publication of school data and league tables.

Following the economic downturn in 2008, the public sector in the UK has suffered significantly in regards to financial support. Consequently, this has stymied funding for salaries, professional development and school resourcing. The collapse of the administrative institutions has exacerbated this situation in Northern Ireland. The consequences of Brexit on education in the UK are yet to be seen. Because of these and other stressors, teacher morale is low. In other words, when it comes to education in England and Northern Ireland, there is a much weaker sense of collective values and social cohesion.

However, there is cause to be hopeful in regards to support for science. The Wellcome Trust (Leonardi *et al.*, 2017, p. 10) recently launched their Primary Science Campaign with a vision that,

> *all pupils will experience an exciting, inspiring and relevant science education at primary school that leaves them well-prepared to progress further in science, and well-informed about science in their everyday lives.*

KEY READING

Explorify, which is a key aspect of the Primary Science Campaign, is a free resource full of engaging, creative science activities for all primary school teachers. It is designed to stimulate curiosity, discussion and debate while supporting teachers to encourage children to think like scientists.

https://explorify.wellcome.ac.uk/

This approach, alluding to a mixture of knowledge-replication and knowledge-production, might bode well when viewed alongside Hollins and Reiss's 2016 comparative paper.

KEY THEORY

Hollins and Reiss's (2016) paper, A review of the school science curricula in eleven high achieving jurisdictions (*The Curriculum Journal*, 27(1): 80–94), which outlines insights on the science curricula of 11 high-achieving jurisdictions. They conclude that there was a distinct convergence happening between East and West. TIMMS's top participants such as Japan, Hong Kong, Finland and Singapore are promoting greater pupil creativity, application and scientific literacy, while lower achievers such as Australia and the USA are becoming more knowledge focused.

CHAPTER SUMMARY

Many are familiar with the old adage, 'the grass looks greener on the other side' and indeed this is applicable to the field of comparative education. It is tempting to look to other lands for quick fixes and infallible practices as a means of driving up standards of attainment and quality of provision. This is particularly true since technological advancements and increased accessibility to institutional data has made it more difficult to conceal poor performance profiles. Consequently, it is imperative that new insights into how children learn drive any changes in curricula and assessment rather than the enticement to improve our place in the world educational rankings.

While it is healthy to venture beyond our own borders, caution is advised. Like many aspects of life, educational policies and practices are deeply rooted in their particular cultural, social, political and oftentimes religious contexts. As claimed by Mourshed *et al.* (2010, p. 24) in their very significant and in-depth analyses of 20 education systems worldwide, *it is a system thing, not a single thing*. Therefore, it is essential to keep this fact in mind if tempted to emulate the educational norms of other countries, especially if they are widely regarded as being successful. Always remember that at the heart of education is the lived experience of individuals. Subsequently, this complex and dynamic phenomenon does not translate easily or successfully across cultures (even within the UK) without careful, critical and insightful treatment. However, this should not deter educators from examining the potential of such action. It is also worth remembering that the world has many examples of good educational practice to learn from the UK.

ASSIGNMENTS

If you were writing an Initial Teacher Education assignment on comparative education, it would be useful to think through the following:

1. What is your view on the 'success' of the primary education system within your jurisdiction? Why do you think this and how can you be sure of this opinion?

2. Why is it important to explore how other places within and beyond the UK educate their young? What and how are they measuring achievement? What examples can you use to support your assumptions?

3. Having taken a broad view of primary education as practised by our closest neighbours as well as in various places around the world, what in your view might be changed or enhanced to make current provision better within your jurisdiction? Provide specific examples to support your answer, not forgetting the messiness of policy transfer.

REFERENCES

Ball, S.J. (2015) What is policy? 21 years later: Reflections on the possibilities of policy research. *Discourse: Studies in the Cultural Politics of Education*, 36(3): 306–13.

Birrell, G. (2015) The disgrace of our segregated school system. Faculty of Education blog at Canterbury Christ Church University. Available at: www.consider-ed.org.uk/the-disgrace-of-our-segregated-school-system/ (accessed 16/04/18).

Boyd, D.G. and Bee, H.L. (2014) *The Developing Child* (13th edn). Harlow: Pearson Education.

Carden, C. (2013) Mum, what happens if I don't pass the test? *Teacher Primary*, 7: 8.

Council for the Curriculum, Examinations & Assessment (CCEA) (2007) *The Northern Ireland Curriculum*. Belfast: CCEA.

Department for Education (DfE) (2011) *The National Strategies 1997–2011: A brief summary of the impact and effectiveness of the national strategies*. London: DfE.

Department of Education (DENI) (1998) *School Improvement Programme – Northern Ireland literacy strategy*. Bangor: DENI.

DENI (2009) *Every School a Good School: A policy for school improvement*. Belfast: DENI.

DENI (2011) *Count, Read, Succeed: A strategy to improve outcomes in literacy and numeracy*. Belfast: DENI.

Education and Training Inspectorate (ETi) (2010) *Together Towards Improvement: A process for self-evaluation*. Bangor: Department of Education.

ETI (2012) *Chief Inspector's Report 2010–12*. Bangor: Department of Education.

European Commission/EACEA/Eurydice (2015) *Assuring Quality in Education: Policies and approaches to school evaluation in Europe*. Eurydice report. Luxembourg: Publications Office of the European Union. Available at: www.cesifo-group.de/ifoHome/facts/DICE/Education-andInnovation/Education/Organisation/policies-approaches-school-evaluation Europe/fileBinary/policies-approaches-school-evaluation-Europe.pdf (accessed 16/04/18).

Gardner, J. (2016) Education in Northern Ireland since the Good Friday Agreement: Kabuki theatre meets danse macabre. *Oxford Review of Education Journal*, 42(3): 346–61.

Hogan, D. (2014) *Why is Singapore's school system so successful, and is it a model for the West?* Available at: https://theconversation.com/why-is-singapores-school-system-so-successful-and-is-it-a-model-for-the-west-22917 (accessed 16/04/18).

Hollins, M. and Reiss, M.J. (2016) A review of the school science curricula in eleven high achieving jurisdictions. *The Curriculum Journal*, 27(1): 80–94.

House of Commons Committee of Public Accounts (2006) *Improving Literacy and Numeracy in Schools (Northern Ireland)*. London: The Stationery Office.

Leonardi, S., Lamb, H., Howe, P. and Choudhoury, A. (2017) *'State of the nation' report of UK primary science education: Baseline research for the Wellcome Trust primary science campaign*. London: The Wellcome Trust. Available at: www.stem.org.uk/system/files/elibrary-resources/2017/09/%27State%20of%20the%20nation%27%20report%20of%20UK%20primary%20science%20education%20-%20baseline%20research%20for%20Wellcome%20Trust.pdf (accessed 16/04/18).

Maguire, M., Braun, A. and Ball, S. (2015) 'Where you stand depends on where you sit': The social construction of policy enactments in the (English) secondary school. *Discourse: Studies in the Cultural Politics of Education*, 36(4) 485–99.

Martin, M.O., Mullis, I.V.S., Foy, P. and Hooper, M. (2016) *TIMSS 2015 International results in science*. Boston, MA: TIMSS & PIRLS International Study Centre. Available at: http://timssandpirls.bc.edu/timss2015/international-results/timss-2015/science/student-achievement/ (accessed 16/04/18).

Mourshed, M., Chijioke, C. and Barber, M. (2010) *How the World's Most Improved School Systems Keep Getting Better*. USA: McKinsey & Company.

Mullis, I.V.S. and Martin, M.O. (eds) (2013) *TIMSS 2015 Assessment Frameworks*. Boston, MA: TIMSS & PIRLS International Study Centre. Available at: https://timssandpirls.bc.edu/timss2015/downloads/T15_Frameworks_Full_Book.pdf (accessed 16/04/18).

Mullis, I.V.S. & Martin, M.O. (eds) (2016) *PIRLS 2016 Assessment Framework* (2nd edn). Boston, MA: TIMSS & PIRLS International Study Centre. Available at: https://timssandpirls.bc.edu/pirls2016/downloads/P16_Framework_2ndEd.pdf (accessed 16/04/18).

Mullis, I.V.S., Martin, M.O., Foy, P. and Hooper, M. (2016) *TIMSS 2015 International Results in Mathematics*. Boston, MA: TIMSS & PIRLS International Study Centre. Available at: http://timssandpirls.bc.edu/timss2015/international-results/timss-2015/mathematics/student-achievement/ (accessed 16/04/18).

Mullis, I.V.S., Martin, M.O., Foy, P. and Hooper, M. (2017) *PIRLS 2016 International Results in Reading*. Boston, MA: TIMSS & PIRLS International Study Centre. Available at: http://pirls2016.org/wp-content/uploads/structure/CompletePDF/P16-PIRLS-International-Results-in-Reading.pdf (accessed 16/04/18).

National Foundation for Education Research (NFER) (2017) *Compulsory Age of Starting School* Available at: www.nfer.ac.uk/eurydice/compulsory-age-of-starting-school (accessed 16/04/18).

For schools to meet the challenge of a continually changing context and to develop their internal capacity to enhance pupil learning, there must be recognition and understanding of these three factors that act to influence their 'internal capacity' to meet the challenge of change (Stoll, 1999). In recognising the complexity of the interaction of these factors, we can begin to appreciate the unique and individualised nature of the challenges faced by schools and, therefore, what drives them in today's context. What follows is an exploration of the development of the external contextual forces (or context) within which all schools are situated today; this includes both political action and global change.

KEY READING

Stoll, L. (1999) Realising our potential: Understanding and developing capacity for lasting improvement. *School Effectiveness and School Improvement*, 10 (4): 503-35.

This reading will develop your understanding of the context within which schools operate and how they are able to cope with and respond effectively to the changing school context. The three key contexts include the individual teacher, the school learning context and external contextual factors; it is these factors that influence a school's internal capacity to engage in school and teacher learning in order to enhance pupil learning.

POLITICISATION AND IDEOLOGY

The politicisation of education can be seen as one of the most important and influential developments of the external context. This development needs to be explored in light of the educational ideologies that have underpinned and driven this process. An educational ideology can be defined as a 'set of ideas and beliefs held by a group of people about the formal arrangements for education' (Meighan and Harber, 2007: 218). The process of politicisation is, therefore, inherently linked to the system of beliefs or the ideology held by those who are in power and are influential as policy decision-makers: 'Policy-making does not happen in a vacuum or bubble' (Forrester and Garratt, 2016: 1). Through an exploration of key moments and policies in the development of this process, we will see an evolving picture of tensions and change in the relationship between society, the state and schools.

THE 1944 EDUCATION ACT: EDUCATION AND THE ECONOMY

Although seen as a centralising measure, the 1944 Education Act (Ministry of Education, 1944) established a balance of power between Local Education Authorities, schools and the government. Control over curriculum content and professional practice remained within the remit of schools and LEAs (Dale, 1989). The context of the education system was, therefore, a 'national system locally administered' (Barber, 1994: 119). The movement towards centralised control can be seen as resulting from the social and economic context of the time where post-war policies were that of the welfare state and equality of opportunity in order to tackle the extreme poverty of the 1930s. Perhaps, and most importantly, a strong link had been made between the quality of educational provision and the success of the economy; it can be argued that this is one of the most important ideological drivers behind the movement towards political and centralised control.

CRITICAL QUESTION

Is the strength and success of a country's economy linked to the strength and success of its education provision?

This link is still asserted today, where the new Secretary of State for Education, Damien Hinds stated:

> *it is through education, skills and training from the early years into adulthood that we will make sure no one is left behind - delivering a modern country that is globally competitive and fit for the future.*
>
> (Hinds, 2018)

The establishment of the relationship between the purpose of education, the development of a suitable workforce and a successful economy acts as a continuing and strong ideological driver behind the external context within which schools are situated today.

1988 EDUCATION REFORM ACT AND THE MARKETISATION OF EDUCATION

The 1988 Education Reform Act introduced coherency of content of curricula and new levels of visibility and accountability of schools in relation to educational attainment through league tables, Ofsted inspections and data reporting methods. This was seen to be a fully centralising measure, which placed education fully within political control (Abbott *et al.*, 2013), the legacy of which remains embedded in current educational policy and practice.

Additionally, the 1988 Education Reform Act instigated the beginnings of the marketisation of education, where Margaret Thatcher's 'free-market' philosophy, which guided conservative thinking of the time, was intended to improve institutional efficiency and allow market forces to take the place of government intervention in public services in order to raise standards (Abbott *et al.*, 2013; Ball, 2008; Thatcher, 1993). Such a shift in philosophy had significant impact, not just on schools, but also on parents, as they became 'educational consumers' (Brooker, 2002). Their role became one of exercising market forces through choice, with the expectation that standards would be raised through the process of competition. This philosophy remains today and acts as a significant driver on school policy and practice.

SCHOOL-LED SYSTEM OF DEVELOPMENT

The concern over standards has prompted, and continues to prompt, the instigation of mechanisms to raise accountability and visibility of schools through marketisation and placing power in the hands of parents as educational consumers. These are aspects that still influence the external educational context within which schools operate today.

PART 2

ESSENTIAL PRINCIPLES FOR TEACHING

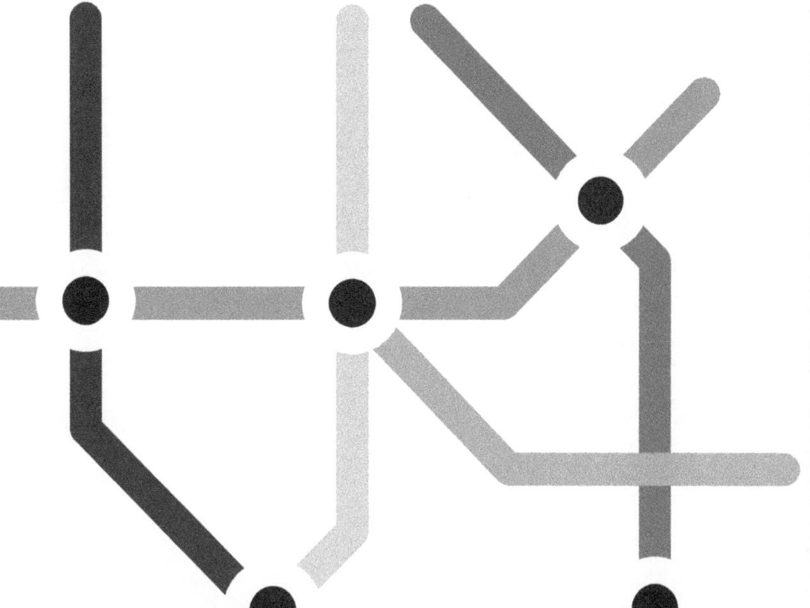

12

WHY IS TEACHER PROFESSIONALISM IMPORTANT?

Glenn Stone is principal lecturer in education and head of the undergraduate primary teacher training programme at University of Chichester. His research interests include teacher education and teacher professionalism.

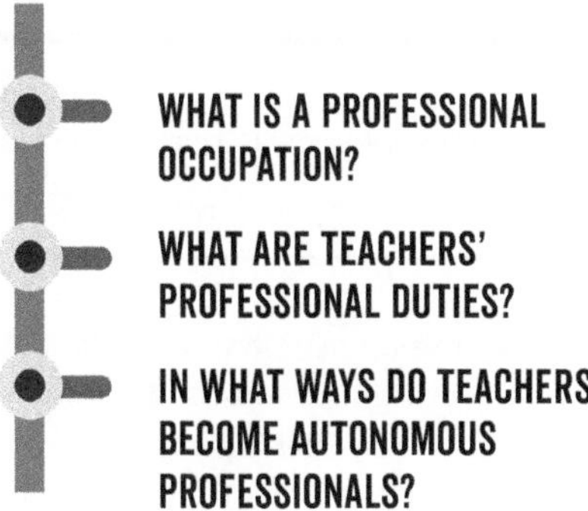

- WHAT IS A PROFESSIONAL OCCUPATION?
- WHAT ARE TEACHERS' PROFESSIONAL DUTIES?
- IN WHAT WAYS DO TEACHERS BECOME AUTONOMOUS PROFESSIONALS?

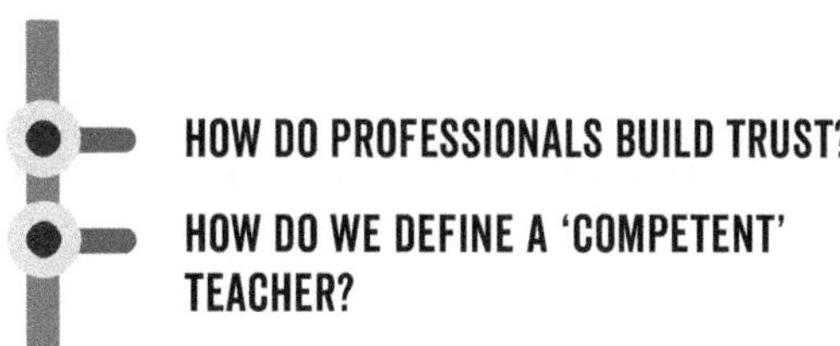

- HOW DO PROFESSIONALS BUILD TRUST?
- HOW DO WE DEFINE A 'COMPETENT' TEACHER?

KEY WORDS

- Autonomy
- Competency
- Duty
- Integrity
- Professional
- Professionalism
- Trust

INTRODUCTION

Why is teacher professionalism important? This chapter aims to answer this by setting out some of the key considerations for teachers working as professionals. This chapter explores the concept of the professional as an occupational group and provides a rationale for why teachers should be classified as professionals. It goes on to explore the teacher's professional duties and considers the importance of professional obligations. This connects to ideas of professional discretion, competence and trust that are important for professionalism, and thus the chapter concludes by bringing these ideas together and inviting student teachers to consider their own professionalism in response.

WHAT IS A PROFESSIONAL OCCUPATION?

CRITICAL QUESTION

What is the link between the status of teachers as professional and the professionalism ascribed to the teaching profession?

The term 'professional' may be seen as redundant due to its everyday use by people to describe attitudes, behaviours or work carried out by those not associated with the traditional professions. A domestic cleaner may advertise by using the phrase 'professional service' or may be described by their clients as having completed a 'professional standard' of cleaning. Their equipment could be marketed as achieving a 'professional finish'. However, does the 'professional cleaner' carry the same responsibility as the professional teacher? Both have used the term 'professional' to describe their work.

In another sense of the word, Carr (2000) illustrates how a footballer gains 'professional' status when he or she is able to earn money from playing football, as opposed to an 'amateur' footballer who may practise the sport as a hobby. Even when bank robbers and criminals are portrayed in television and film, characters can be described as 'real pros' in the way they have carried out the crime. Professional cleaning services; professional cleaning products; professional footballers; professional criminals: this list could continue and it may be possible to attach 'professional' nomenclature to any occupation, job or activity known to us. Thus, it is important to focus further on the professional attributes and values associated with teaching, and how the use of the word 'professional' in the context of education connects to wider aims of education.

Teachers may rightfully desire to be considered 'professional' because there are aspects of their work that set them aside from other occupations.

CRITICAL QUESTION

What does 'professional' mean?

KEY THEORY

The traditional professions of medicine and law are often cited as being unmatched examples of professions as, among other things, they have deeply rooted moral and ethical purposes. These professions are concerned with doing public good. Aside from any profiting that may be possible from medicine and law, the reason for medical and legal professions is so that others in society can benefit and, therefore, they have altruistic aims. Teachers too are concerned with doing public good and education is similarly viewed as being a necessity for societal progression. Consideration of the universal value of education then helps us to understand why teachers should be considered as professionals:

> *it is significant that the kind of service that professionals are in business to provide have increasingly come to be regarded as human rights... many of the services now under the control and direction of the more or less established traditional professions - health care, legal aid, arguably education, and so on - are apt to be characterised as welfare rights... there can be no doubt that talking of rights to education, health care and legal access seems to make more sense than talk of rights to good plumbing, hairdressing, car maintenance or an annual holiday abroad... the best philosophical handle we are likely to secure on the righthood of health care, education and legal redress is in terms of a notion of what is necessarily or indispensably conducive to overall human flourishing... human life per se is bound to be impoverished in circumstances where disease, injustice and ignorance are rife and their remedies in short supply.*
>
> (Carr, 2000: 27-8)

When facing challenges as a student teacher or practising teacher, it is useful to be reminded of the moral purpose of education as outlined above. Teachers aid human flourishing, and this should be no small motivation for those wanting to teach.

If we argue that education has a moral and ethical dimension that connects it to the broader aims of society, it may then be argued that all those who work in education should be classed as professional. However, a midday meals supervisor, teaching assistant, school receptionist and others working in school will also be expected to act professionally. Can they be classified as professionals in the same way as teachers? To unpack this idea, it is worth considering another aspect of professions – the licence to practise.

Consider the implications of professional misconduct for a teaching assistant and a teacher. Depending on the severity of the offence, they may both lose their jobs or be suspended from work. However, the implication for the teacher is greater than that of the teaching assistant in so far as the teacher's professional status is jeopardised. A search of 'teacher misconduct' on the UK government's education webpages can reveal a plethora of cases where teachers have been found in breach of the Teachers' Standards, their professional obligations and what would be reasonably expected of those working in the teaching profession. Teachers are, therefore, held to account for their professional conduct and expectations are high. Furthermore, the outcome reports for teacher misconduct frequently refer to wider reputational damage to the teaching profession. While cases of misconduct are rare (in the context of the overall population of teachers) and extreme, the implication is that teachers need to be aware of how their own personal behaviour and conduct not only signifies their personal professionalism, but also the status of the teaching profession as a whole. This is embedded in Part Two of the Teachers' Standards that make clear that teachers should uphold public trust by considering their professionalism within and outside of school.

WHAT ARE TEACHERS' PROFESSIONAL DUTIES?

What is the relationship between professionalism and professional frameworks?

As professionals, it is important for practising teachers to be aware of:

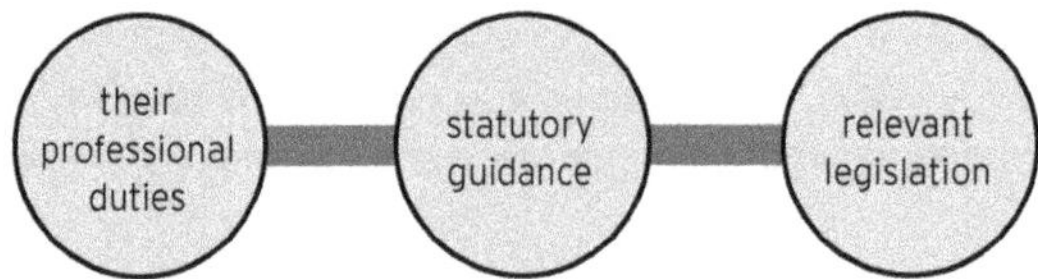

Education is also political and, therefore, professionals need to be able to adapt to changes in their duties. For example, teachers have had the statutory duty to teach the National Curriculum in state-maintained schools, but the content of this can be changed based on the view of the government. This section outlines some of the key professional duties for primary teachers.

DUTY NOT TO DISCRIMINATE

The Equalities Act (2010) lists nine protected characteristics:

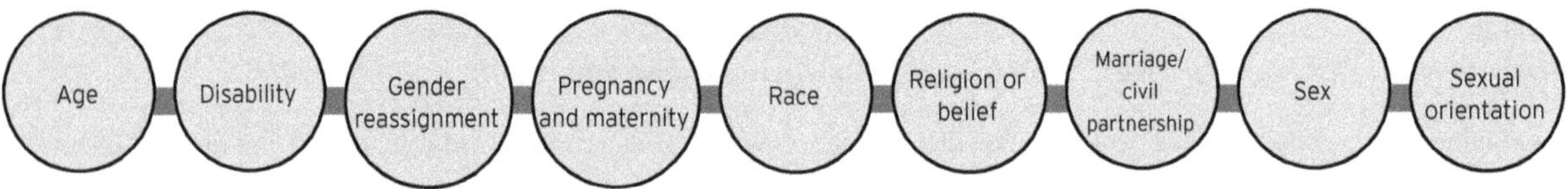

Schools need to consider the protected characteristics when making strategic decisions, such as hiring staff or setting admissions criteria. Teachers also need to be aware of the protected characteristics and ensure that they do not discriminate against children, their families or the wider community. Unfair treatment of a protected group is considered as discrimination. For example, a teacher should not prevent a child who is enabled by a wheelchair from attending a school trip.

Furthermore, teachers should work to reduce inequalities in society and can aid this by educating children in anti-discrimination. For example, primary teachers should feel confident to teach about different types of families, avoid stereotypes based on gender, respond appropriately if they hear children using homophobic or racist language, and so on.

DUTY TO PROVIDE FOR AN INCLUSIVE CURRICULUM

In addition to the Equalities Act 2010, the Special Educational Needs and Disability Code of Practice (DfE/DoH, 2015) provides further guidance for the statutory legislation from the Children and Families Act 2014 that apply to schools:

> *Those concerned with making special educational provision for the child must secure that the child engages in the activities of the school together with children who do not have special educational needs. (Children and Families Act 2014 c.6)*
>
> *Teachers should use appropriate assessment to set targets which are deliberately ambitious. Potential areas of difficulty should be identified and addressed at the outset. Lessons should be planned to address potential areas of difficulty and to remove barriers to pupil achievement.*
>
> (DfE/DoH, 2015: 94)

As professionals, teachers need to be knowledgeable about the children they teach, have the skills to identify needs and remove barriers to ensure all pupils are included in a broad and balanced curriculum.

The concept of a broad and balanced curriculum is important for all children, not just children with Special Educational Needs and Disabilities. The school curriculum and the National Curriculum are not synonymous. While teachers working in state-maintained schools are obligated to teach the National Curriculum, this is considered to be a minimum entitlement. All schools are free to teach beyond the National Curriculum and so teachers need be mindful of the breadth of opportunities for learning.

DUTY OF CARE

CRITICAL QUESTION

What would you do if you notice a child is being bullied in school?

What steps would you take to ensure children stay safe on a school trip?

What would you do if a child falls ill during the school day?

When answering those questions, it is reasonable to assume that anyone working with children will be mindful of their general well-being. Teachers take steps to ensure that children are not bullied; they carry out risk assessments before embarking on school trips; they call for a first aider when a child becomes unwell. These acts may reasonably be considered part of teachers' duty of care.

When parents and carers drop off at the school gates, they entrust teachers with keeping their children safe during the school day. The term *in loco parentis* is sometimes used to suggest that teachers make decisions about young people 'in place of the parents'. This has become common law (deriving from precedent, rather than statutes). When it comes to health and safety within schools and on extra-curricular trips, the Health and Safety at Work etc. Act 1974 states that employees are required 'to take reasonable care for the health and safety of himself and of other persons who may be affected by his acts or omissions at work.' Teachers should, therefore, take reasonable steps to keep children safe at all times.

DUTY TO PREVENT RADICALISATION OR EXTREMISM

The Prevent strategy is one aspect of counter-terrorism measures introduced in 2003 by the UK government that aims to:

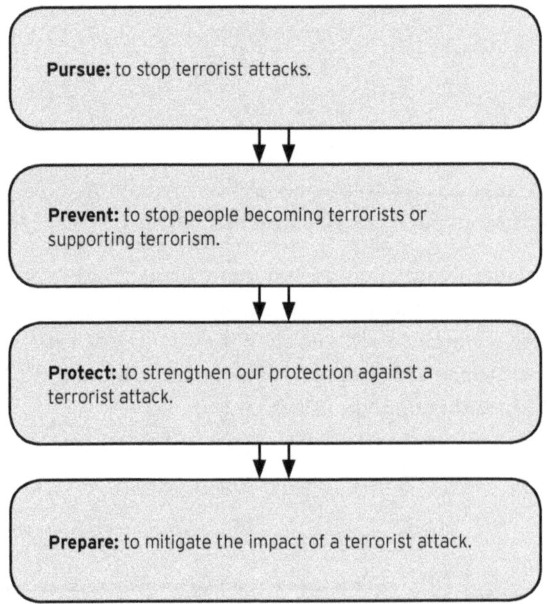

A review of the Prevent strategy (HM Government, 2015) strengthened the strategy as a response to more recent threats from extremism and radicalisation. Explicit mention is given to Islamic extremism and the way that Prevent has been reported in the media can lead people to believe that it is an initiative to deal with terrorism deriving from one branch of religion. However, teachers need to be aware that extremism in both violent and non-violent forms is not solely concerned with Islamic extremism. Furthermore, teachers should be proactive in teaching against hate in all its forms. Subsequent legislation through The Counter Terrorism and Security Act 2015 indicates schools' statutory requirement to 'have due regard to the need to prevent people from being drawn into terrorism'. Teachers should also 'build pupils' resilience to radicalisation by providing a safe environment for debating controversial issues and helping them to understand how they can influence and participate in decision-making' (Department for Education, 2015: 8). Schools are not required to have a separate Prevent policy, but teachers should access and be aware of safeguarding and refer to school guidance on this issue.

CLASSROOM LINK

What does this mean for classroom practice?

PSHE and Citizenship lessons can be a useful conduit for tackling challenging ideas in primary education. Schools should also teach a broad and balanced curriculum and provide for children's Spiritual, Moral, Social and Cultural (SMSC) development. Most of the education related to SMSC, PSHE and Citizenship will support the government's Prevent agenda. However, if teachers have concerns about offences of hate, radicalisation or extremism, they should follow their school's safeguarding procedures.

IN WHAT WAYS DO TEACHERS BECOME AUTONOMOUS PROFESSIONALS?

Decades of reforms to education have resulted in a new managerialism in schools where private sector ethos and practices executed by powerful management structures dominate. This new managerialism has also resulted in a type of professionalism that can be measured. Teachers who comply with the expectations of school leaders, meet performance management objectives and standardise their practice in line with others may be considered more professional than teachers who want to adopt their own agenda. Therefore, the rise of new public management structures has consequences for professional discretion, trust and competence (Evetts, 2009). However, these concepts do not exist in isolation. There is a relationship between professional discretion, trust and competence (see Figure 12.1) that can both support and erode teacher professionalism, as will now be explored.

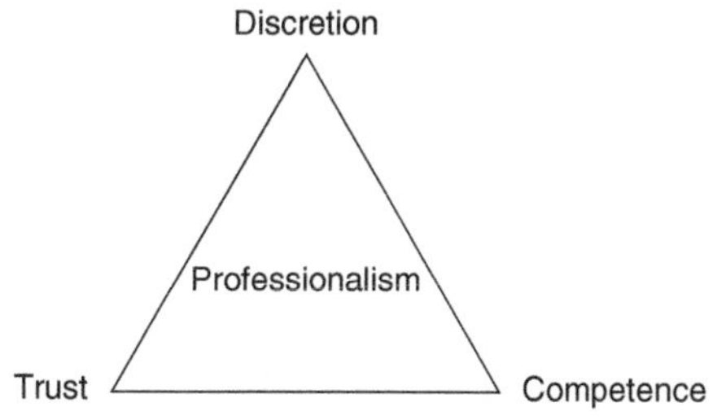

Figure 12.1 Consequences for professionalism

CRITICAL QUESTION

Should teachers teach from detailed schemes of work and textbooks or should they plan their own lessons?

Should teachers deliver a curriculum mandated by others or devise their own?

Should lessons conform to a timetable or should lesson time be flexible?

When thinking about the questions above, the common-sense response is often one that implies negotiation. Teachers can adapt commercially produced schemes of work; they can stray from the curriculum when needed; they can adapt lesson times slightly within a broader structure. Indeed, this is how many primary teachers operate. However, the questions set out above are also a way into debates about whether the teacher acts as a technician or as an autonomous professional.

When followed to the letter, textbooks and schemes of work can be criticised as restricting the creativity of the teacher. A detailed, published scheme of work, if imposed, can be seen as eroding professionalism if the implication is that teachers cannot produce effective lessons on their own. However, planning scaffolds offered by schemes of work or textbooks can also help reduce teacher workload and primary teachers may make a professional decision to subscribe to them. Therefore, polemic arguments about teacher professionalism can be unhelpful as a pragmatic response is often found in classrooms. This is not just true of pedagogic decisions, but also in response to broader changes. For example, when faced with new initiatives or structures, teachers may be compliant with expectations but will also negotiate a way forward that retains some of their autonomy (Forrester, 2000). In other words, teachers need to use their professional discretion to guide decisions in the classroom.

Questions of what to teach, how to teach and when to teach certain concepts are equally matched with questions about what to assess, how to assess and when to assess. The ability to shape these aspects can link teacher autonomy with the moral purposes of profession:

> *a concern with "doing a good job" cannot be separated out from a concern about individual and collective teacher autonomy and teacher power because 'doing a good job' involves being in a position to fully deploy one's expertise and to shape what gets done.*
>
> (Gewirtz *et al.*, 2009: 4)

Teacher autonomy remains important to teacher professionalism, even though this can be a professional challenge when external organisations and other stakeholders are seen to set the agenda. The Ofsted report, *Bold Beginnings* (Ofsted, 2017), provides a contemporary illustration of how those on the periphery of the teaching profession can shape it and, as a consequence, raise further questions about the autonomy of the profession.

KEY THEORY

Key theory: *Bold Beginnings*

Her Majesty's Inspectorate (HMI) carried out a review of 41 'good' and 'outstanding' primary schools in England that had been identified 'because they typified the findings of longitudinal research into the importance of high-quality, early education; namely, that children who do well by the age of five have a greater chance of doing well throughout school' (Ofsted, 2017: 31). Their report into the practice of these schools finds some commonality deemed to be effective and provides a number of recommendations. These include an emphasis on the direct teaching of language, reading, writing and mathematics. It also highlights where summative assessment has been useful:

> *Checks of children's phonics knowledge, standardised tests (for reading, for example) and scrutinies of children's work provided the essential information that Year 1 teachers needed.*
>
> (Ofsted, 2017: 4)

However, the report was seen by some as a catalyst for bringing further accountability into the Reception year and met with concerns about a shift away from play-based pedagogies:

> *The need for summative assessment for accountability purposes demands that children are seen as empty vessels that can be filled with knowledge: knowledge which is quantifiable and fixed. A chaotic, meaning-making, active child will not do. This kind of child does not fit the model as it cannot be measured and converted into data... Learning through play does not fit the model as it cannot be quantified and measured. It has too many outcomes which are slow to emerge and is therefore not useful for data collection.*
>
> (Olusoga and Pierlejewski, 2018)

Whether or not this Ofsted report ends up being the catalyst for change in Reception practice is somewhat connected to questions about the extent to which teachers can use their own professional judgement to decide what Reception practice should look like. It should be noted that this is a different question from what actually does constitute effective practice; it is merely a point about who has the authority to decide.

ACCOUNTABILITY

Autonomy and trust go hand in hand. Teachers gain autonomy as a result of being trusted. However, strong accountability in the school system has often been thrown into these debates. This has been the rhetoric of successive governments, following the influential McKinsey Report (Barber and Mourshed, 2007) that connects high levels of autonomy with high levels of accountability in top-performing school systems. Therefore, to be trusted and given greater autonomy, teachers need to accept their responsibility to raise standards and be accountable for outcomes. In a market-driven education system, one school's collective accountability is published in league tables so that it can be compared with the performance of other schools. National statistics are then shared with the wider society and discussed through the media. The benefit of this is that it provides transparency; the danger of this explicit accountability is that trust in the teaching profession can be eroded when standards fall. When trust is eroded, the public will often turn to politicians for answers to the problem of educational standards, relying on political answers to pedagogic problems. Consequently, there is less trust in teachers to raise standards on their own. The most successful example of this may well be the 1997 UK general election when Tony Blair pledged his three priorities – 'education, education, education'. The Labour government's landslide victory gave them the political mandate to bring in national strategies for raising attainment in English and maths, along with greater accountability in schools.

COMPETENCE

Along with autonomy and trust, competence can be perceived as integral to teacher professionalism. Internationally, there has been a trend towards the licence of teachers through the use of standards and competency statements. The Centre of Study for Policies and Practices in Education (2013) notes how high-performing education systems have professionalised the work of teachers in this way and suggests that the professional status of teachers is benefited by a clear description of competences. However, competency has become entwined with accountability. The market-driven Global Educational Reform Movement, while intending to raise standards and teachers' status as professionals, might not always align with teachers' conceptions of professionalism and competency. Kidd (2014) argues for a radical reform of education, and subsequently the conception of the professional teacher, by arguing for pedagogical activism:

> *What if every teacher took an oath to... refuse to compete... see beyond the horizon of tests... value children's happiness... understand the importance of relationships... know that children need hope... refuse to give up on a child... refuse to despair... recognise that trust is built by sharing... keep up to date with new developments... never stop questioning.*
>
> (Kidd, 2014: 114-15)

Radical thinking such as this would require alternative views of competency models, far from the current evaluation of teacher performance measured by pupil outcomes in, arguably, a narrow set of subjects. It is, therefore, important for student teachers today to think critically about their own hopes for the future shape of the profession.

CRITICAL QUESTION

What would you include in a list of competences for primary school teachers?

THE TEACHERS' STANDARDS

In England, there are currently eight standards for teachers (DfE, 2011) that envelop desired skills and knowledge. There is also a second part that relates to working with professional frameworks. When considering what

Kidd, D. (2014) *Teaching Notes from the Front Line*. Crown House Publishing: Carmarthen.

Ofsted (2017) *Bold Beginnings*. Available at: www.gov.uk/government/publications/reception-curriculum-in-good-and-outstanding-primary-schools-bold-beginnings (accessed 18/4/18).

Olusoga, Y. and Pierlejewski, M. (2018) Bold beginnings or black holes? The encroachment of summative assessment into the reception curriculum. Available at: www.bera.ac.uk/blog/bold-beginnings-or-black-holes (accessed 18/4/18).

THE ROLE OF THE TEACHER IN A LESSON

EXPLAINING *SAY IT!*

Talk through ideas and concepts

Express it verbally and add action and drama when needed

Keep explanations simple and to repeat key ideas

DEMONSTRATING *SHOW ME!*

Show children how to do a task independently

Do this step by step

Keep demonstrations short and focused

Children with EAL benefit from visual and oral explanations

MODELLING *THINK IT OUT LOUD!*

Explain your decisions and choices as you go

Ask yourself questions

Identify any patterns or problems

Make mistakes and solve them as you work through

Get it wrong and go back and correct your mistakes

CLASSROOM LINK

What does this mean for classroom practice?

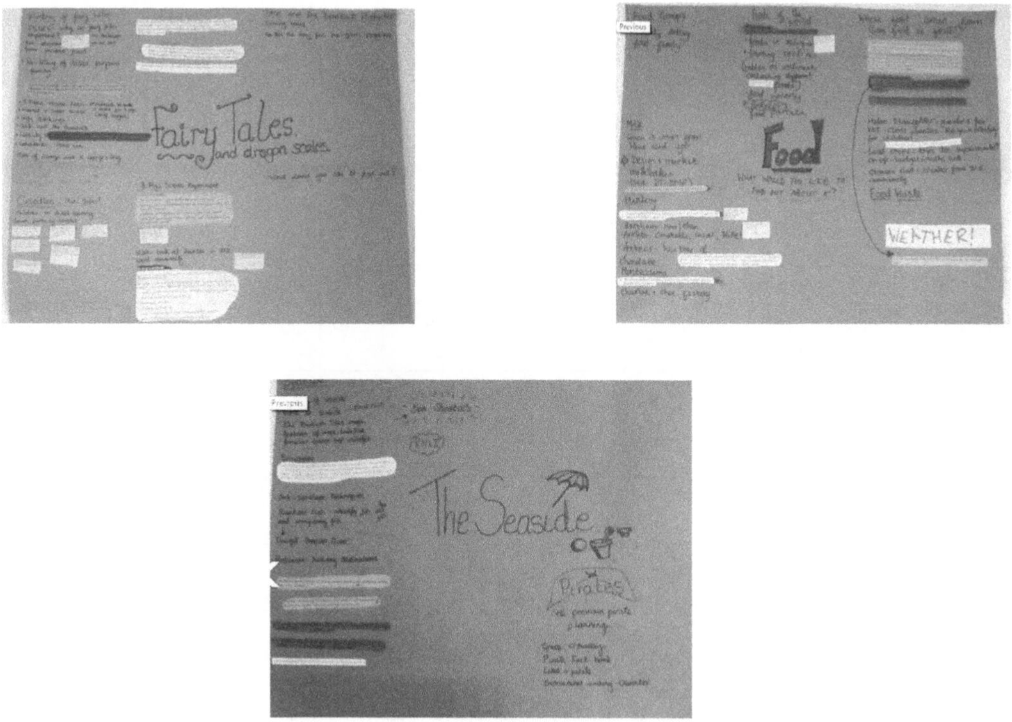

Figure 13.3 Photographs to show how the Key Stage 1 curriculum was developed at Barnham Primary School

The long-term plan may indicate the skills, attitudes and knowledge to be developed. When planning the curriculum, a school may consider three key themes:

Breadth – this will ensure that the full range of Core and Foundation subjects (and subject-specific skills) are taught.

↓

Depth – opportunities for children to study topics in detail.

↓

Coherence – meaningful links between subjects are recognised (e.g. developing numeracy and literacy skills in other subjects).

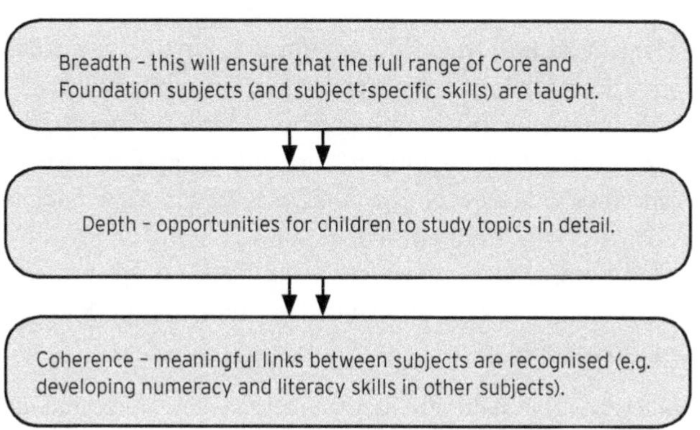

CRITICAL QUESTION

How can teachers ensure that long-term plans cover a number of curriculum areas and offer a breadth of learning?

For example, what curriculum areas do you think may be covered in the topic 'Fairy tales and dragon scales'?

CLASSROOM LINK

What does this mean for classroom practice?

	Autumn	Spring	Summer
Reception	All about Me/Seasonal Celebrations	Dinosaurs	Growing Up and Moving On!
Year 1/2	From field to feast	Fariy tales and dragon scales	Shorelines, Shanties and Secrets
Year 3/4	Chocolate	Greeks	Wonderful West Sussex
Year 5/6	Local Study linked to World War 2	The Amazon	Themes in Social History – Art and Culture

Figure 13.4 Long-term plan for Barnham Primary School

It is useful to be aware that some schools may produce a long-term plan for each subject area – e.g. a map to show genres in English or units of work (and working scientifically) in science.

MEDIUM-TERM PLANNING

The long-term plan is then organised into the medium-term plans, which are usually focused on individual year groups (however, you may find that you are on a placement with vertically grouped or mixed age groups). Some schools choose to 'block' units of work over a half term or term (so may plan for a block of history one term and geography the next, rather than teaching history and geography each week over the course of a year). The medium-term plan often indicates the proposed relationship between key questions, attitudes and attention to specific subject-based skills and knowledge. The aim should be for the school to construct the medium-term plan to provide an engaging learning experience. When on placement, you may find that your school has chosen to purchase schemes of work and will adapt these to cater for the needs of their pupils (see further reading for useful links to websites).

Regardless of whether or not a school elects to purchase a medium-term plan, Pollard (2014) believes that each scheme of work should be driven by four key questions:

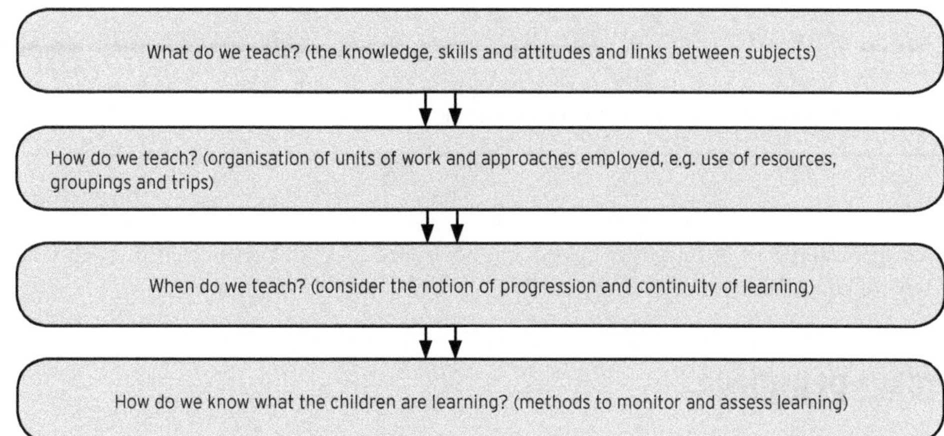

OBJECTIVE FROM NEW NATIONAL CURRICULUM 2014
OBJECTIVE FROM PERSONAL AND THINKING SKILLS DOC 2014

Jack and the Beanstalk (production)

Science
- Children to form beans, recapping on learning from 'Field to Feast' topic

Literacy
- Retell story from giant's perspective.

ICT/Art
- Children to design posters and leaflets for production.

Music
- Children to learn songs for production
- Children to learn nursery rhymes

Fairy tales and dragon scales!

History of fairy tales

PSHCE
- Why are fairy tales important?

Literacy/PSHCE
- Retelling of range of classic fairy tales

Art
- Illustrations as an art form
- Learn about the work of a range of artists, craft makers and designers, describing the differences and similarities between different practices.

History/PSHCE
- The tale of St George and St George's day

Castles (mini project)

History
- Learn parts of a castle.
- What was the purpose of a castle?

Children to lead learning
- Children recognise that time and resources need to be managed.
- Children show a willingness to complete tasks and continue until they do so.
- Children can set goals.
- Children attempt more than one approach when tackling a problem.
- Children can explain what they have learnt, presenting to a particular audience.

Estate Agents

ICT
- Produce a brochure to sell a fairy tale house.
- Use technology to create, organise, store, manipulate and retrieve digital content.

Design Technology
- Three bears house plan
- Design and plan own dream home
- Build Hansel and Gretel's house

Geography
- Visit house within the local community
- Use simple fieldwork and observations skills to study the geography of their school and its grounds, and the key humans and physical features of its surrounding environments.

Science/Design Technology
- Design a sturdy house for the three little pigs.
- Pupils should be taught to identify and name a variety of man-made materials, describing simple physical properties and make comparisons.
- See 'Working scientifically' section of Science curriculum
- Children to explain their conclusions with reasons.

Figure 13.5 An example of medium-term planning

CRITICAL QUESTION

How do teachers ensure that planning is resulting in learning?

Have a look at the example of medium-term planning (see Figure 13.5) and consider it through Pollard's key questions. How well does the plan meets these aims?

SHORT-TERM PLANNING

Short-term plans (weekly/daily/individual plans) are constructed from the medium-term plans and outline the specific teaching and learning approaches that will be employed. The short-term planning format will vary according to each school.

THE IMPORTANCE OF IDENTIFYING MISCONCEPTIONS

Before delivering a sequence of lessons, it is useful to begin the unit of work by establishing what the children already know. This can be achieved by using 'cold tasks' (short, focused assessment tasks to establish what children know prior to delivering the unit of work), including language and fact sort cards, concept cartoons, concept mapping, drawings, quizzes, or you could use KWHL grids (what I know, what I want to know, how I will find out and what I have learnt). These approaches, along with careful questioning, also afford you the opportunity to identify if children have any misconceptions that will need to be challenged.

CRITICAL QUESTION

What are 'misconceptions' and why is it important to be aware of them?

The Teachers' Standards (DfE, 2011) specify that for teachers to 'demonstrate good subject and curriculum knowledge' they must 'have a secure knowledge of the relevant subject(s) and curriculum areas, foster and maintain pupils' interest in the subject, and address misunderstandings'. Most subject-specific theory books outline common misconceptions, identifying these for different topics within the subject and for different age groups. Researching this prior to planning a specific lesson will be very beneficial; being aware of the possible misconceptions enables you to plan to assess whether children in the class have certain misconceptions and how to address these effectively. Most misconceptions are formed through a simple misunderstanding or flawed connections in thought processes, so having an understanding of what common misconceptions are and *how* and *why* they have formed may help you to explain concepts with more clarity and depth. It also ensures that you are not caught off-guard by what may be presented as a very convincing argument. There will always be new misconceptions that arise and take you by surprise, such as the child who became very upset about being asked to use a particular clock to tell the time, 'because it was wrong, it was going backwards'. Further probing revealed why the child thought that clock was wrong (the previous week the clocks were put back an hour and the child had helped change the time on that particular clock). However, the child had interpreted the 'clocks going back' as that particular clock now 'running backwards', and therefore unreliable for telling the time. Having an understanding of common misconceptions for a topic is essential, but alongside this you must also be prepared to probe a child's understanding, which may uncover new ones.

CLASSROOM LINK

What does this mean for classroom practice?

It is important that in your planning you have considered possible misconceptions so that these can be challenged. Research common misconceptions relating to the subject and content you are covering in your lesson and plan for them.

WRITING A LESSON PLAN

TERMINOLOGY AND HOW IT GUIDES LESSON PLANNING

Before unpacking the features of a lesson plan it is useful to consider some of the key terminology that is often used in school. The following terms are commonly used, so it is worthwhile taking time to consider what these mean.

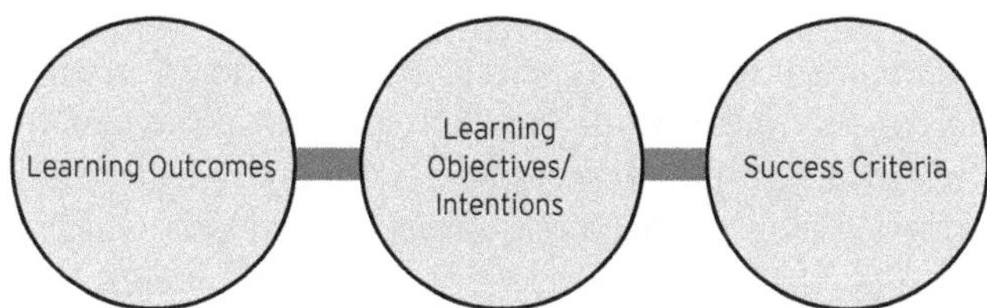

LEARNING OUTCOMES

These are specified in the Programmes of Study in the National Curriculum. It is the learning that children need to 'master' or achieve by the end of the unit of work/end of year or end of Key Stage. The Learning Outcomes often need to be broken down into smaller chunks of learning to create a Learning Objective or Learning Intention for an individual lesson. For example, the Learning Outcome in the National Curriculum states that pupils in Year 5 should be taught to:

- *Compare and group together everyday materials on the basis of their properties, including their hardness, solubility, transparency, conductivity (electrical and thermal) and response to magnets.* (DfE, 2014)

This is clearly too much to cover in a single lesson. Each of the terms solubility, transparency and electrical conductivity would be at least one lesson, so the Learning Outcome needs to be broken down.

The Learning Outcome could be chunked into the following Learning Objective:

- *To compare everyday materials based on their thermal conductivity.*

If it is a science lesson, there will often be an objective linked to working scientifically in addition to the conceptual knowledge, so the Learning Objective for the working scientifically element might be as follows:

- *To conduct a comparative fair test to find out which material is the best thermal conductor.*

THE LEARNING OBJECTIVE

This is essentially what you are aiming to teach children in terms of skills and knowledge. You need to know what you are aiming for during the lesson so that you can plan suitable activities to help children learn. Some schools use WALT (We Are Learning To) to clarify the purpose of a Learning Objective for the children. We like to think of the Learning Objective as being like a dart board, as it helps focus thinking about the outcomes of the lesson and what they are 'aiming' to achieve (like the darts aiming for the dart board). It might even be useful to have a visual prompt on display so that children understand the Learning Objective and that this is what they need to learn by the end of the lesson (see Figure 13.6).

Following on from the Learning Objective, you can then write the Success Criteria (or WILF – What I am Looking For).

THE SUCCESS CRITERIA

These describe *how* the children will meet the Learning Objective and are often presented as 'I can' statements for the children. The Success Criteria, when written well, can help you (and the children) to assess their learning easily. It can be suggested that the Success Criteria is not differentiated because it is expected that all children will be able to achieve it with varying levels of support (however, when you are on placement you may find that schools choose to differentiate the Success Criteria). We often think of the Success Criteria as being like a trophy and will use the mini-plenaries or the plenary to ask children to reflect upon how successful they have been in meeting the Learning Objective. Sometimes, you might present children with the Learning Objective and ask them what they think they need to do in order to successfully achieve it (you will, however, have planned for the Success Criteria, so will be able to guide their thinking).

It is useful to practise writing Learning Objectives and Success Criteria. You might like to have a go at using the National Curriculum (DfE, 2014) to do this. Your mentor in school will be able to provide you with feedback.

CRITICAL QUESTION

Do children always need to be told the Learning Objective and Success Criteria at the beginning of a lesson?

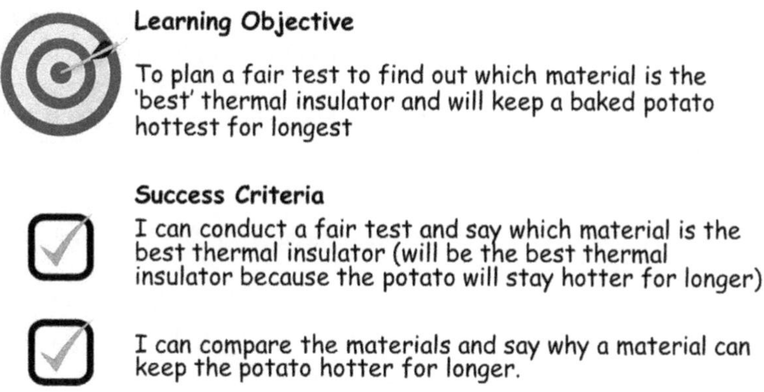

Figure 13.6 Articulating the Learning Objective and Success Criteria to children

Only after carefully considering the Learning Objective and Success Criteria should you turn your attention to considering the activities that children will engage in. The next section will consider how a lesson plan may be formulated.

WHAT DOES A GOOD LESSON PLAN ENTAIL?

A FOCUS ON THE LEARNING

The most important element of any planning is knowing what you want the children to learn. This must be carefully considered in relation to:

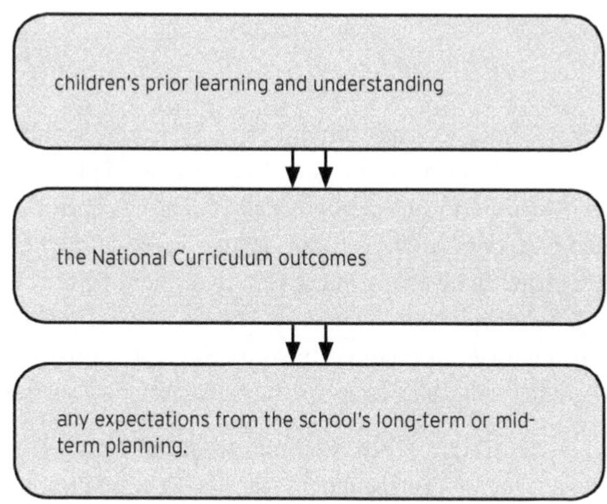

An effective teacher will first take into account these aspects, carefully defining the intended learning and then consider how they will know whether the learning has taken place. As such, the cyclical nature of planning becomes evident, with prior knowledge and attainment being used to inform the intended learning for a specific lesson. This is followed by the consideration of how the learning will be assessed; the results of the assessments then informing the intended learning of subsequent lessons. It is important when assessing a lesson that any feedback provided focuses on the Success Criteria rather than superficial aspects of presentation and should be constructive (Cremin and Arthur, 2014). The planning process could be visualised in the following way, as illustrated in Figure 13.7.

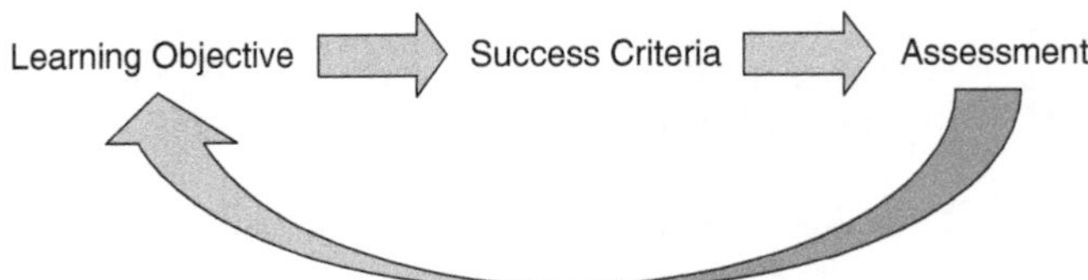

Figure 13.7 The planning cycle

A 'good lesson' can mistakenly be thought to be one where the children had fun or engaged well with an activity; however, both of these can occur with no relevant learning taking place. It can be a temptation for beginning teachers to find an activity that they think the children will really enjoy and engage with, and try to build a lesson around this, without considering what the children will specifically learn, whether it is relevant and whether they will make progress as a result.

Planning is one the most time-consuming parts of teaching, so it is often tempting to download plans from the internet. Indeed, when looking on the internet there are many lessons that look as though they would be fun and engaging to teach, and some may be a useful starting point in the planning process. However, it is important to consider the learning that is expected and how this will be realised when delivering the outcomes from the National Curriculum. It is also pertinent to think about the reason why you are choosing to deliver a lesson in a certain way.

HOOKS

A 'hook' introduces the learning to pupils in a meaningful way. Over time, you may find that one of the most essential resources you develop is a good dressing-up box! From Pirate Pete to Izzy Imperative, a characters 'hook' can help bring children's learning to life; perhaps a character has a problem they need help with or a visitor from another time period (e.g. Lord or Lady Tudor) arrives to explain what life was like from their personal experiences. The teacher in role can be a very effective way of drawing the children into the scenario, but a hook is not reliant on this. A letter or item could be left in the classroom for the children to find and explore together, the classroom could be changed or adapted in some way – a clumsy dragon may have paid a visit! These methods not only stimulate the children's curiosity, but also provide a platform for experiential learning.

Experiential learning occurs when people are given the opportunity to experience things first-hand and learn through doing. David Kolb devised a theory of experiential learning in which learners go through a cycle of concrete experience and reflection, drawing conclusions and then planning or trying out what has been learnt (for more information, see Aubrey and Riley, 2016). This cycle can be applied equally to learners in the classroom – if they are given opportunities to reflect on their learning – and also to teachers, when they take time to reflect on their lessons and critically evaluate the success of their approaches in order to influence future lessons.

method for multiplication). However, care needs to be taken to ensure that the demonstration is short and focused, otherwise children will become quickly disengaged (think about the types of YouTube clips that you might watch – they are often only 1–2 minutes in duration). If you have a recording feature connected to your interactive whiteboard, you could record your demonstration so that children can rewatch it during the lesson and be reminded of key features of the learning. Children who have English as an Additional Language (EAL) particularly benefit from the visual and oral explanations provided by demonstrations (see Nexus EAL website in the Useful Links section to understand further how to support EAL learners so that they can access the learning in the classroom more effectively).

MODELLING (*THINK IT OUT LOUD!*)

During the process of modelling an idea, the teacher 'thinks aloud', explaining their decisions and choices. During modelling, the teacher will ask themselves questions, identify any patterns or problems (e.g. if undertaking a piece of shared writing, the teacher may justify why a word has been chosen or why a grammatical feature has been used). When working on a problem, the teacher may model how children might go about solving the problem. There should be time to discuss ideas. During modelling, the teacher is the 'expert' but shows children that learning can be a messy process and that they can make changes to their work.

Careful consideration of how the input is presented is an important step when planning a lesson, because when undertaken effectively it can help to 'bridge the gap' between the teaching input and the independent work that follows (see the Gradual Release Model below). However, there may be occasions when the input is flipped and the lesson begins with a problem, and children are provided with the chance to solve a problem before teaching input is given.

KEY THEORY

Gradual Release Model

Pearson and Gallagher (1983) proposed the idea of the Gradual Release Model, which is essentially a scaffolded instruction approach for moving from whole-class input to independent work. The following table has been adapted from the work of Levy (2007) and shows how transitions can be supported.

	The teacher's role	The learner's role
I do it Teacher has the main responsibility and shows learners what to do	Shares the Learning Objectives and Success Criteria so that learners understand the aims and purpose of the lesson Demonstrates, explains and models ideas	Listens Chance to ask questions May take notes
We do it Guided Instruction	Guides Works with students Checks, prompts and questions Provides additional modelling	Asks and responds to questions Works with teacher and classmates (use of partner talk)

(Continued)

(Continued)

	The teacher's role	The learner's role
You do it together Collaborative learning	Moves among groups Clarifies confusion Provides support Questions	Works with peers in small groups Collaborates on tasks or problems Consolidates understanding
You do it Independent work	Provides feedback Assesses	Works alone Takes on full responsibility for learning

PLANNING FOR MASTERY

The mastery approach was first formally introduced in the 1960s by Benjamin Bloom. The main ideas of this approach are that children in the class move through a curriculum at the same pace and do not move on until they have grasped a concept. Children who grasp concepts quickly are challenged through depth and breadth of their understanding rather than being accelerated onto new content. The Education Endowment Foundation (2018) analysed research that indicates that a mastery approach is effective, although it can be challenging to implement. Schools need to consider how they implement this approach carefully. The Education Endowment Foundation go on to suggest that mastery is most effective when pupils work at the same pace, work collaboratively and take responsibility for each other's learning – something that needs to be considered in our planning.

CRITICAL QUESTION

Some people consider 'applying' to be a high-order thinking skill, while others consider it to be a low-order thinking skill. Why do you think this is? Can you think of any examples to justify both viewpoints?

At times you may wish to teach a topic and then apply it to a problem in context. At other times you may choose to introduce a topic through a problem context. Can you think of benefits for both approaches?

The mastery approach is at the forefront of education at present, as the 2014 National Curriculum, although not officially specified as a mastery curriculum, has strong suggestions of this approach in its aims and assessment. For example, the aims of the mathematics curriculum specify that, 'The expectation is that the majority of pupils will move through the programmes of study at broadly the same pace. .... Pupils who grasp concepts rapidly should be challenged through being offered rich and sophisticated problems before any acceleration through new content.' In terms of assessment, pupils are judged to either be meeting age-related expectations or not.

14

HOW MIGHT WE FRAME 'BEHAVIOUR' IN PRIMARY SCHOOLS?

Mark Sackville-Ford is Senior Lecturer in Education (Professional Studies) at Manchester Metropolitan University and prior to this he was a Behaviour Specialist Support Teacher for a Local Authority. His research focuses on young people's experiences of education and the complexities of school ethos and atmospheres.

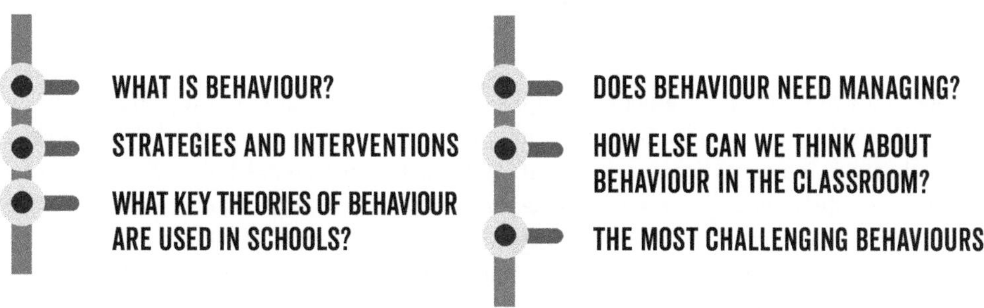

KEY WORDS

- Behaviour
- Behaviourism
- Discipline
- Humanism
- Iceberg models
- Language of behaviour
- SEND code of practice
- Stress

INTRODUCTION

This chapter explores the complexities about thinking with behaviour. Behaviour Management continues to be an area of concern for student teachers, and this chapter will examine some of the key issues. The chapter asks how we might think more deeply about behaviour in order to understand it better. We consider key theories of behaviour that influence behaviour management in schools. We then ask how we can support children and young people to manage their own emotions and behaviour and the impact that this might have on the teacher. We then explore the ways that the SEND Code of Practice can help us to think about behaviour. Finally, we consider how best to work with young people whose behaviours we find the most challenging.

WHAT IS BEHAVIOUR?

BEHAVIOUR IS COMPLEX

I start the chapter with this simple statement to emphasise that many colleagues in primary schools find behaviour something challenging to understand and work with. I have attended, and delivered, many courses around behaviour and behaviour management, and still find it a complex concept to comprehend. For the student teacher, their perceived lack of experience can mean behaviour management is a worry and it is also something that they will be assessed on against the teacher's standards. The complexities around behaviour seem to stem from the fact that there is a huge amount of information available, and there is sometimes a tension between school behaviour policies, government agendas and day-to-day classroom practices. I believe that each child is unique and their behaviour might change on a daily/hourly/minute basis. All this means that working with behaviour does not become about finding the correct secret formula. Instead, it is a tentative experiment that frequently changes. Behaviour is often treated very differently from learning, with policies such as 'behaviour for learning' attempting to bring the two concepts closer together. The chapter proposes that the student teacher should avoid attempting to find the 'correct method' and instead think more deeply about what behaviour actually is. Locating your own position about behaviour and aligning this with your personal values can be empowering. If we then fold in theories of behaviour, ideologies of education and teacher identities, we are able to work more critically with managing behaviour. Practical aspects of behaviour are important, but I believe they are secondary to developing an understanding of behaviour.

In its most simple form, behaviour can be thought of as a form of communication, like a language we do not yet understand. Any behaviour, both positive and negative, usually communicates something to another person. A yawn in the middle of your mathematics class communicates something to you. It is the job of the teacher to understand the language of behaviour and interpret the meaning. Is the child simply tired? Does it reflect complexities in the home circumstances of the child? Does it reflect something about teaching and learning? Maybe it is a combination of these, but the act of noticing behaviour is important.

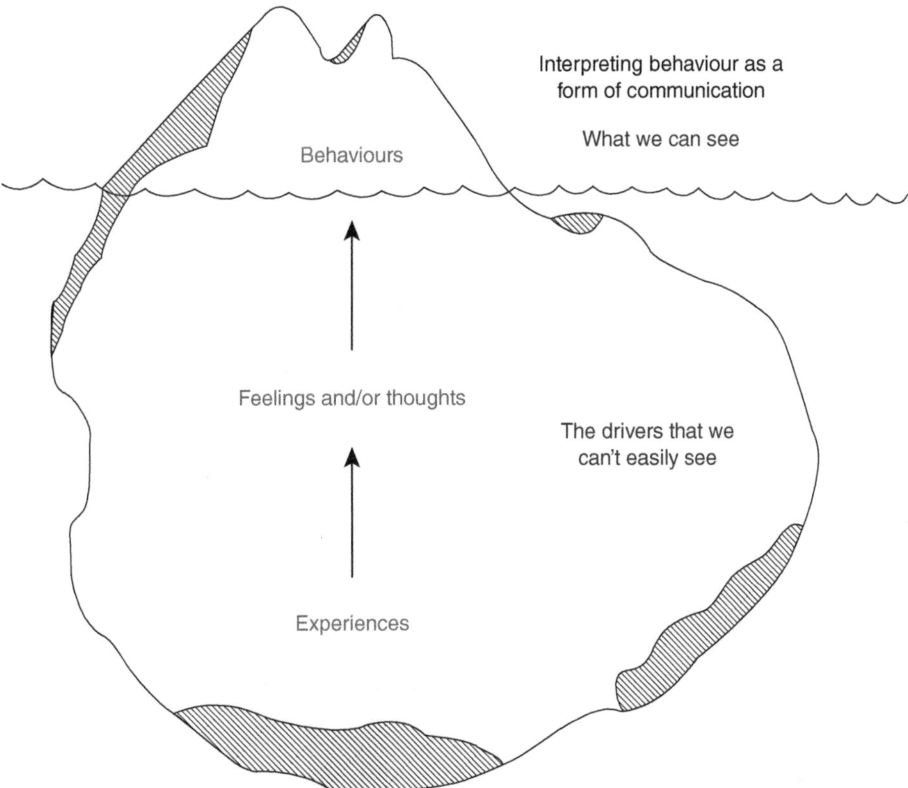

Figure 14.1 Cognitive behaviour iceberg model

This image illustrates a cognitive model for thinking with behaviour. The iceberg is a familiar metaphor for understanding the concept of the 'tip of the iceberg'. If we label behaviour at the tip, this is the outward manifestation of something. Beneath the surface of the water we find the drivers for behaviour. At the base, and most significantly, we find experiences. Experiences lead to feelings and/or thoughts, which then drive the behaviours. This model is useful for beginning to think about the behaviours that we see and to understand that they are driven by things that are often difficult to see. It has clear links with the theories underpinning Cognitive Behaviour Therapy (CBT) and uses psychological ideas of development.

CLASSROOM LINK

What does this mean for classroom practice?

In your classroom practice you may identify children in your class who are frequently shouting out. If your everyday strategies do not seem to be working, consider the cognitive behaviour iceberg model to support your understand of their behaviour.

The list below explores the reasons why this behaviour may be occurring. Listing possible reasons in this way is a useful tool to begin thinking about how your practice can be adapted.

A reflective teacher experiments with ideas until they find an approach that works for the child and the class.

Table 14.1 Behaviour = 'Shouting Out' in class

Possible ideas	Experiences	Feelings and thoughts	Possible teacher action
1. Attention-seeking behaviour	They get little attention from adults in their lives	They feel frustrated or silenced They think 'nobody ever listens to me'	*Meet the need:* Give the child specific attention. Give them jobs around the classroom that gives you an opportunity to talk to them.
			Reduce the behaviour: Reduce the dependency on getting attention. Use rewards and praise consistently. Introduce structure system to reduce shouting out (e.g. token system)
2. Impulsive behaviour	They need to live within the immediate moment	They feel scared and in survival mode (fear) They think 'I need to go at 100 miles an hour' Or 'If I don't do this now, x will happen'	*Meet the need:* Support the child to learn relaxation/ mindfulness techniques. Make them feel safe and secure in the classroom. Be a trusting and consistent adult, including with rules.
			Reduce the behaviour: Give them a whiteboard so they can non-verbally answer all the questions. Use Assessment for Learning (AfL) strategies.
	They cannot control it	This is not a 'cognitive behaviour' issue – seek different iceberg model	
3. They always know the answer	They get positive feedback from praise	They feel happy and confident They think 'my teacher likes my answers'	Reduce the attention and rewards given for answering the questions. Separate out the child from the answering of the question, so that they get approval from the teacher in other ways. Use Assessment for Learning (AfL) strategies.
	They always find the work easy	They feel bored They think 'the work is always so easy'	Increase the level of challenge of work so that the child is working at the correct level.

Table 14.1 begins to map out the thinking process that can be generated by analysing a behaviour using this iceberg model and by no means is this exhaustive. There has to be an element of uncertainty because we

cannot be sure what the drivers are, hence why it is hidden beneath the surface of the water. This is the start of trying to think more deeply about behaviour. The child is not shouting out for the sake of it, but there are factors driving the behaviour.

CRITICAL QUESTION

How can you put the cognitive iceberg model into practice to better understand a child's behaviour?

STRATEGIES AND INTERVENTIONS

The iceberg is also useful to deal with confusion with the terminology around strategies and interventions. I suggest the following definitions.

STRATEGIES

These are directed towards the behaviour at the tip of the iceberg. They tend to be short term and designed to create order and discipline in the classroom. They include things such as rule reminders, praise and sanctions, giving clear boundaries for behaviour, loss/gain of special time and visual systems (e.g. rainbow/sun/cloud), and these are often implemented by adults working within the classroom.

INTERVENTIONS

These are directed to factors below the surface of the water (experiences, thoughts and feelings). They acknowledge that behaviour is often entrenched and takes time to change. They include things such as emotional work, therapeutic interventions, forest school social and stories, and are often implemented by other adults working in schools or specialist staff (e.g. pastoral/learning mentors, behaviour specialist, therapists).

Strategies and interventions may happen at a variety of scales. Strategies may be in place without the need for interventions, depending on the individual needs of the child. Often, we will put both strategies and interventions in at the same time since they operate on different aspects. Together they seek to reduce the behaviours while supporting a child to develop.

COMFORT – CHALLENGE – STRESS

Another factor that complicates the picture is the fact that our behaviour is influenced by our own state on any particular day. This is based on the Learning Zone Model developed by Senninger (2000) and interpreted here in relation to behaviour.

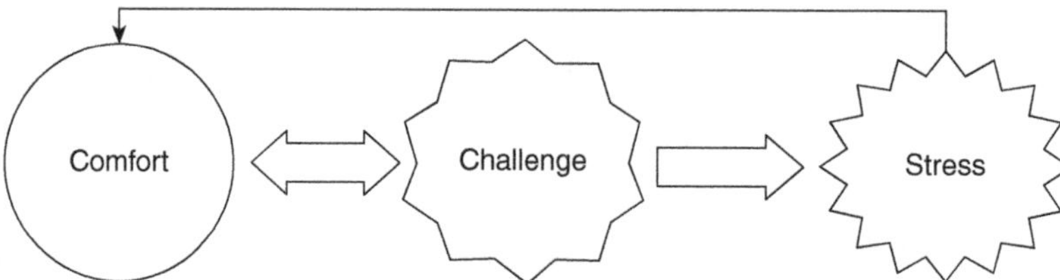

Figure 14.2 Comfort-Challenge-Stress Model

The Comfort Zone can be described as a 'safe haven', a place where one is content to be and needs can be met. The Challenge Zone is the place where we might encounter a difficulty. For Senninger, this was connected to learning, and in the Challenge Zone is the place where learning takes place. Note that you may move freely between the Comfort and Challenge Zones. For challenge related to behaviour, this may include developing new skills such as increasing self-control or concentration, so more focused on concepts rather than increased knowledge. Thinking through this model in relation to behaviour is helpful in explaining why children's behaviours and responses to the teacher may vary according to the zone they are in. When stress occurs, the child's behaviour can move into crisis. This is the place where a child may be in need of support or the child has lost the ability to regulate their emotions or anxiety. This is an overwhelming state, where the individual is unable to think beyond the immediate stressor (real or perceived). Note here that a child who has experienced the Stress Zone cannot move back to the Challenge Zone, and instead there is a need to move to the Comfort Zone.

CRITICAL QUESTION

You introduce a new strategy to help a child reduce a particular behaviour, such as continually getting out of their seat. This works on the first day, but the next day it has no impact. Should you abandon the original strategy?

This shows how our state of mind and well-being significantly influence behaviour. We can all relate to this as adults, and also see that each individual has different stressors as well as different things that offer comfort. These factors complicate behaviour and our reactions to it, meaning that it often doesn't develop in a linear way. It is helpful for us to plan for the setbacks and have realistic expectations about how we can change behaviours in the classroom.

Our relationship with young people is critical in understanding how we can help to support them.

WHICH KEY THEORIES OF BEHAVIOUR ARE USED IN SCHOOLS?

It is critically important to consider theories in order to understand behaviour. Many school behaviour policies are driven by the same subheadings and don't acknowledge that the processes within their policy are linked to theory. Indeed, I suggest that sometimes these theories do not even match the ethos and values of the particular school. This can be confusing for staff and students within the setting.

THEORY OF CONTROL (BEHAVIOURISM)

CRITICAL QUESTION

How have behaviour management theories manifested themselves in your school experience? Is your school behaviour policy underpinned by a particular theory?

Behaviourism covers a range of theories around behaviour that seek to control behaviour and maintain discipline in schools. They are based on experiments by psychologists on animals such as Pavlov's dogs and Thorndike's cats, which revealed that through conditioning, the behaviour of the animals could be changed. In simplistic terms, then, positive behaviour is reinforced through rewards, while negative behaviour is reinforced through punishments. In schools we see significant evidence of behaviour management built on theories of behaviourism. Most behaviour policies begin with a section on rewards and sanctions. These include rewards such as stickers, verbal praise, golden time and house points, while sanctions include loss of playtime, loss of golden time, time out, name moved to a 'sad cloud'. Some schools also incorporate these approaches into the whole school through systems such as Canter's (2010) *assertive discipline*. What these have in common is the belief that children will respond to control and clear boundaries when consistency of rule application is applied.

CRITIQUE

We are so used to this approach to behaviour that it is very easy to accept this as the norm. The simplicity of rewards and sanctions, and the consistent application of these make it very desirable to teachers. However, it is a highly contentious and complex system. Take praise, for example: there is some evidence to suggest that too much praise can be demotivating for children (Kohn, 1999).

Here there is a sense that children become motivated to learn or behave well only for the praise, or what Kohn refers to as 'bribes', rather than on any intrinsic values.

Relating behaviourism to Figure 14.1, we also see that it only operates at the tip of the iceberg. There is generally no interest in understanding the drivers to the behaviour, and rather a need to put the correct strategies in place to control that behaviour. It can, therefore, be suggested that controlling the behaviour does not support a person to learn a better response, and thus there is little impact on long-term behaviour. In terms of learning, it views behaviour as a barrier, rather than explaining that there may be behaviours most suited to learning.

Porter (2014) gives a good summary of the limitations bought about by praise and rewards. The lack of a holistic approach, which takes into account human thinking, means that factors such as the difference between internal and external motivation are reduced. Aspects such as self-esteem are not considered relevant in approaches that rely on behaviourism.

THEORY OF GUIDANCE (HUMANISM)

KEY THEORY

Behaviourism

- Based on notions of discipline and control.
- Based on psychological theories, including conditioning and reinforcement.
- Dominant within school behaviour policies.
- Doesn't attempt to understand behaviour or what might be causing it.
- Views children as different from adults and frames relationships in a different way.

Theories of guidance offer an alternative approach to behaviourism and are built on a fundamentally different set of values and assumptions around humans. Here, students and teachers are seen to be equally invested in learning, which results in a distributed sense of power and responsibility. Guidance approaches build on Carl Rogers' (e.g. 1980) humanist theory, which asserts that human behaviour is related to needs rather than consequences, where children and adults have equal rights to have their needs met. Within this approach there is an ethics of caring, where the social and emotional needs are important. There is a shift away from how to teach, to an emphasis on how children learn.

This approach to behaviour fits well with Maslow's 'hierarchy of needs' (1970), which shows that once individual basic needs are met, there are more complex needs that require attention (see Figure 1.3 on page 17). Concepts such as belonging, autonomy and happiness become critical parts of child development. Behavioural difficulties within the guidance approach are seen as a manifestation of unmet need. Returning to Figure 14.1, there is a move from focusing on the behaviour itself, to attempting to understand the drivers for the behaviour, which lie beneath the surface of the water. Behavioural interventions focus on supporting children to develop self-awareness, self-regulation, empathy, cooperation and agency. Schools that advocate this approach will work hard to develop the emotional well-being of their students, with frequent opportunities for participation and voice. The strong values underpinning this approach will pervade all aspects of school life, including approaches to learning and the ideological foundations for this.

CRITIQUE

Porter (2014) discusses how the research over the past 50 years indicates that, compared with guidance approaches, controlling approaches are less effective and more harmful to children.

Some argue that the controlling behaviours are so embedded in society and culture that it is difficult to move away from them. It appears true that we are influenced by our own parenting and schooling styles, which took more controlling approaches. Some see the guidance approach as 'soft' and means that children are less likely to learn 'right from wrong'.

What appears to happen in many schools that move forward with guidance approaches, such as Restorative Approaches, is that they believe in the philosophy and practices underpinning them, but they seem unable to leave behind the strong foundations of previous behaviour policies. So we end up with strange hybrid policies, which retain aspects of behaviourism. This does not work and leads to confusion for staff when confronted with new situations. Guidance approaches require a complete rewrite of behaviour policies, resulting in a different way to value people and think with behaviour.

KEY THEORY

Humanism

- Based on ideas of shared power and trust
- Based on Humanist theories where behaviour is related to need
- Virtually absent from school behaviour policies (or seen in hybrid version)
- Holistic approach to behaviour which links with learning
- Believes children and adults are equals and have similar rights
- Values the individual

DOES BEHAVIOUR NEED MANAGING?

CRITICAL QUESTION

What is your personal philosophy of behaviour? How does this relate to the type of teacher you aspire to be? How does your own approach to behaviour relate to your philosophy and what are tensions?

In this section, the question is raised on whether behaviour needs managing at all. First, we consider the way that politics influences the language and practices of behaviour, through words such as discipline. The use of words such as discipline gives a sense that behaviour needs managing. Next, we consider how supporting children to develop an inner locus of control means that we need to support rather than manage behaviour. Where we manage, this can lead to problems of self-control later in the child's life. Finally, we consider the importance of the mood or climate in the individual classroom. It is this mood that determines whether the individual teacher believes in managing behaviour or not.

IS BEHAVIOUR POLITICAL?

As well as the theoretical aspects of behaviour that are often overlooked in favour of approaches of 'what works', a further complication is that behaviour is politically influenced. One way that new governments show that they are serious about education is for them to assert that they are serious about 'discipline'. The use of the word discipline reveals a sense of how behaviour is framed around enforcing a certain set of rules. It clearly aligns with behavioural approaches that seek to control behaviour. The word also implies that there is a 'problem' with behaviour in schools and this suggests that it is the fault of the teacher. The political agenda is filled with assumptions that influence everyday practice in schools.

Two documents have fairly recently asserted the current political positioning in relation to behaviour. One is from the Department for Education (DfE, 2016) titled *Behaviour and Discipline in Schools: Advice for headteachers and school staff*. The language of this document is very strong and it makes suggestions to what should be included in behaviour policies as well as using phrases such as 'power of discipline'. Furthermore, there is a focus on the negative applications of discipline, including punishments, teachers' powers, confiscation and detention. While it is not explicit, there is a clear ideological position taken by this document. Such an approach is also compounded by documentation from Ofsted (2014), including *Below the Radar: Low-level disruption in the country's classroom*. This document suggests that teachers have a problem with disruptive behaviour, which results in the loss of learning. It suggests that familiarity and friendliness of teachers leads to a lack of respect towards the teachers from students. The suggested behaviours are no longer seen as normal behaviours (e.g. talking to your friend) and instead are signs of weakness. There are strong implications around pedagogy and again a blurring between learning and behaviour. To hear the phrase 'low-level disruption' enter the vocabulary of teachers makes this into something real, whereas actually it can be viewed as a social construction. Teachers now talk of low-level disruption and cement its position in their vocabulary. Similarly, my concerns around behaviour policies in the UK are also driven by these policies, which actually state what should be included in the policy. This does not acknowledge any theory and despite much of the content being non-statutory, its presence in official documentation means it is widely adopted without question.

INNER LOCUS OF CONTROL

The inner locus of control is a term from psychology used to define the intrinsic ability for the individual to regulate their own behaviours. The inner locus of control is developed when children are able to explore behaviours and learn about the impact of them on others. Linking this with the theories of behaviour mentioned earlier, controlling methods of behaviour management do not allow the inner locus of control. Children here do not learn the complex interchange between humans and instead learn a set of rules. There does not necessarily need to be an understanding of these rules, but rather the rules should be consistently followed by the individual. Where the inner locus of control is underdeveloped we see children unable to manage their own behaviours. I have observed this happening at the transition between primary and secondary education. Children have had their behaviours managed by the primary school at the expense of the inner locus of control. When the child moves to a different setting where this style of management is not replicable, and the high school is unable to micro-manage behaviour, we find that the child can struggle to manage themselves.

A positive aspect of the guidance approach is that it is able to support a child to develop their inner locus of control. Children are able to make mistakes with their behaviour and rather than being punished, these are seen as opportunities for learning. Through support and discussion to understand behaviour and its impact, the child develops a broad range of skills, and develops their inner locus of control. The child develops empathy and can then apply this learning to a wide range of contexts. This is a much more sophisticated approach than learning a narrow set of rules that is specific to one school. The child no longer behaves well to avoid punishment and to please the adult, but instead the behaviour is intrinsically motivated because it is preferable. Positive behaviours actually produce positive emotions, thoughts and feelings for the individual. This links directly with the ethics of care discussed already and associated with guidance approaches.

CLASSROOM CLIMATE

The final aspect that I would like to briefly explore here is the climate in the individual classroom. Often, teachers can feel powerless within some of the structures around behaviour management that I have already described. I want to put it to you that you have significantly more influence than you might actually think.

Classroom climate or ethos is something that is difficult to define or grasp in your classroom since it is almost intangible and indeterminate. I conceptualise classroom climate as the everyday lived experiences of that classroom and, importantly, the way that children feel welcomed, safe, able to express themselves and able to learn. Despite the politics and policy around behaviour, the individual teacher determines what their classroom is like. Linked to behaviour, then, it is about the values that underpin your philosophy of education.

Specifically, in relation to behaviour, classroom climate is about having a broad understanding of the theories underpinning behaviour. Knowing yourself and the kind of teacher you want to be is also important since you have to reconcile these two things. Often, when we have challenging times with behaviour, we can allow our own values to slip and teachers can fall into authoritarian styles of leadership, which defaults to a style of behaviour management that is controlling (behaviourism).

CRITICAL QUESTION

What have your own previous teachers done that have resulted in you demonstrating positive behaviours?

What do you do as a teacher to ensure positive learning behaviours in your classroom?

HOW ELSE CAN WE THINK ABOUT BEHAVIOUR IN CLASSROOMS?

One complexity around the work of behaviour is that there are differing ideas depending on whether the behaviour is framed as something within the child or something that exists due to the context. The iceberg model described earlier makes the assumption that the behaviour is within the child and it is our response to this behaviour that ultimately leads to changes in behaviour. In my work as a specialist behaviour teacher, I was often asked to observe a child in a classroom setting, and the assumption was that I would be better able to understand their behaviours. However, often it was the other aspects of the classroom that were of interest rather than the child in question. Therefore, there are other faces of the iceberg that warrant thought.

STATUTORY FRAMEWORKS

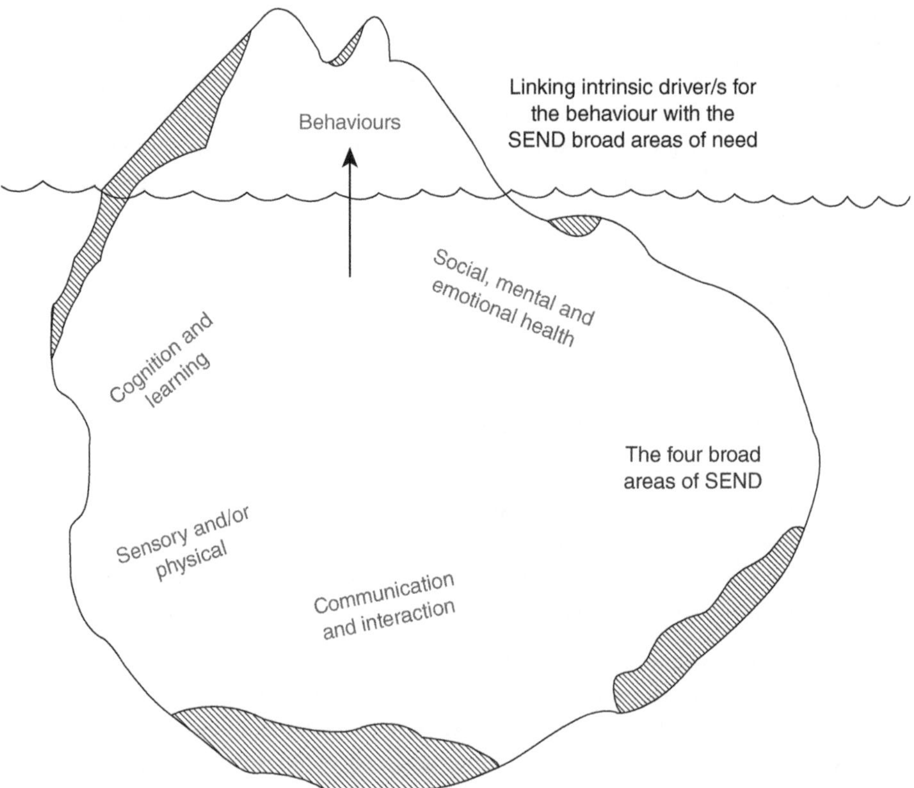

Figure 14.3 SEND Code of Practice and Behaviour

Figure 14.3 shows the way that we can link the broad areas of need from the revised *SEND Code of Practice* (2015). One feature of this code was that the category that previously included behaviour, 'emotional and behavioural difficulties', was abolished. Many teachers have assumed that this category was replaced by 'Social, mental and emotional health' (SMEH), but I believe that this is a mistake. SMEH is not the same as 'emotional and behavioural difficulties', since it describes factors influencing behaviour rather than naming behaviour itself.

This iceberg again places behaviour at the tip of the iceberg rather than it being an intrinsic need. Behaviour is, therefore, framed as a symptom of an unmet need, which covers all the areas of the code of practice. The broad areas of need are purposefully written in a haphazard way to illustrate that this is a messy business. The iceberg supports the teacher in considering if the presenting behaviour could be driven by something other than 'behaviour'. I have worked with many young people who have struggled with aspects of cognition, such as having a poor working memory or limited receptive language skills. These barriers have become so difficult for the individual that often it is easier to mask these with behaviours that could be considered disruptive. These young people have an unmet need and require support to overcome them.

Some young people will have needs that mean that their presentation fits across more than one broad area of need. Young people with autistic spectrum conditions, for example, might have deficits with sensory processing as well communication and interaction difficulties. It is, therefore, important to remember that the four broad areas of need are not discrete but merely offer guidance. Behaviour, therefore, transcends a particular need from the code of practice. SMEH may be a strong predicator for challenging behaviours within a school context, but it is important to view this alongside the other iceberg models. In critiquing this model there is clearly a link with labelling and medicalising behaviour, which are both highly problematic. There is not space here to explore these arguments in detail, but both the SEND and Cognitive models place the 'problem' of behaviour within the child. In many cases it is much more complex and the context around these behaviours are critical, which is partly fulfilled by the final iceberg model.

TEACHING AND LEARNING

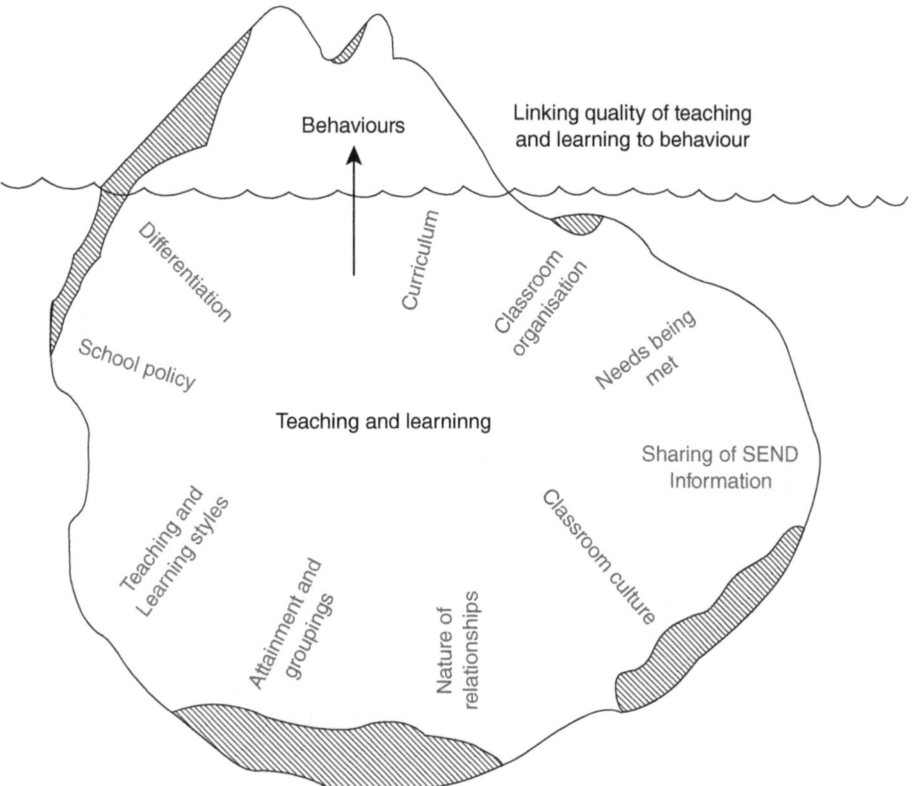

Figure 14.4 Teaching, learning and behaviour

Figure 14.4 is an illustration that shows the importance of teaching and learning in relation to behaviour. This is the third and final iceberg model used here and shows how the complex decisions and responses of the classroom teacher will influence behaviour. You will probably be able to add even more ideas below the surface of the water to show how teaching and learning influences behaviour. We could probably add even more environmental factors such as the temperature of the room or the comfort of the furniture, for example.

Interestingly, some of these factors may be beyond the control of the individual teacher. For example, school policy, sharing of information and curriculum factors may already be in place and the individual teacher may feel disempowered to affect these. Other factors are clearly influenced by the teacher, such as classroom climate, seating plans, culture of the classroom, differentiation and varied learning styles evidenced in planning.

This final iceberg is important as it reminds us that behaviour is not always the responsibility of the child. One weakness of the other iceberg models is that they are built upon the assumption that behaviour is intrinsic, that there is something within the child that determines the way that they behave. The teaching and learning iceberg reminds us that there are many factors beyond the child, external ones that have a significant impact on behaviour.

This is not about blame and I do not want this model to become another way to criticise teachers. This could easily be linked to the documents that I have discussed around the politics of behaviour. I hope instead that it encourages teachers to step back and attempt to view the practices and habits in their classrooms again. It is easy to forget the influences that the teacher has on behaviour and particularly, when struggling with a difficult class we can feel a sense of helplessness. Attempting to change some of these factors may result in positive changes for behaviour. Ask colleagues for support and advice as this is a sign of strength rather than weakness.

Taken together, the three iceberg models presented in this chapter should be viewed as three faces of the same floating piece of ice. By combing these into one three-dimensional structure, we can merge the thinking and theories behind each to show that the manifesting behaviour is driven by a variety of things. The role of the teacher is to attempt to think with the models in order to support the behaviour, and understand and address the hidden drivers rather than simply the behaviour that is seen.

THE MOST CHALLENGING BEHAVIOURS

I firmly believe that no child enjoys it when their behaviours become challenging for the teacher, and while habits and patterns may develop, they do not really choose to do this. I hope this chapter has communicated that there are many factors and drivers for behaviour, and while it is complex, there is always more we can do to support the child.

For some children, the everyday strategies and interventions that take place in schools will not be enough. This does not mean that these strategies and interventions are poor; it just means that reasonable adjustments are needed for specific children.

PLAN FOR BEHAVIOURS

When things are challenging, it is easy for the staff in school to be lost with how to deal with these. A good written plan for behaviour can be extremely powerful. This is likely to be more detailed than an Individual Education Plan, and might be called a 'behaviour management plan' or 'positive handling plan'.

A sound plan will describe the zones of behaviours for the child and give the response to each of these stages. You will describe the reminders and support you give to the child at these different stages. You will also need to consider at what point your priority shifts from supporting the child with their learning to supporting them and stopping them from entering the crisis point. Thinking about the Comfort–Challenge–Stress Zone might be useful here. Levels of stress as described in Figure 14.5 are only normally experienced for children with complex behaviours.

Zone	**Comfort**	**Challenge**	**Stress**	**Recovery**	**Learning**
Behaviours	Child is comfortable in school. They are able to learn and listen well and respond to adults.	Child may be agitated. They may start to refuse to work. They may be louder and begin to exhibit disruptive behaviours.	Child in distress. May be at risk from harming themselves and others. Destructive behaviours (throwing, destroying).	Child withdrawn. Child upset and crying.	Child is ready to talk about the incident (this may be some time later).
Response	Support and encourage with learning.	Distraction techniques (e.g. jobs). Monitor and support. Give rule reminders. Support to move back to comfort zone through interests. Avoid challenging work.	Make environment safe; Use voice and script. Seek support from colleagues. Meet duty of care to keep the child safe; use of restrictive physical intervention (as a last resort).	Support to return to comfort zone. Provide nurturing and therapeutic responses (play-based opportunities). Meet basic needs – offer a drink, remove layer of clothing if hot. Observe and monitor.	Use structured approach based on zones of cognitive iceberg model *Experiences*: What happened? *Feelings*: How were you feeling? *New behaviour response*: What can we do the next time you feel like this?

Figure 14.5 Zones of behaviour

For some children, scripting responses at each stage might be useful. A script is a key phrase that you say in response to the different ranges of behaviour. By scripting it, you allow all the adults working with the child to use the scripted phrase, thus allowing a more consistent response. This consistency can sometimes be enough to break negative cycles of behaviour.

SEEK SUPPORT

It is easy for the class teacher to feel isolated and lost in response to behaviours. Remember that many of your colleagues may have experienced similar things in the past. Seek support and advice from them as well as from the SENCO of your school. This is a sign of professional strength rather than a particular weakness.

There may be external support also available to support you with the child. The Behaviour Support Service may be able to offer additional support, including observations of your classroom and the behaviours. This fresh pair of eyes can be helpful in giving you new ideas. They may also be able to offer intervention support. Additional external professions are well placed to offer support and advice, including Educational Psychology, professionals from CAMHS and teams to support families.

CASE STUDY

What does this mean for classroom practice?

James is a Year 5 class teacher in his third year of teaching. There is one child in his class who presents with challenging behaviour. Typically, this involves hiding under the table, which is unusual for a child of this age, and/or running out of the classroom. At the same time there is a girl in the same classroom who seemingly copies the behaviours of the boy. When he hides under the table, so does the girl.

James tries his everyday strategies for the first term. He builds good relationships with the children and attempts to understand the complexities of their lives that seem to drive these behaviours. Using the iceberg models seems to indicate that the behaviours are mainly around getting attention, although this is more complex for the boy. James gets increasingly frustrated since he has prided himself on good behaviour management. These challenging behaviours seem to increase around Christmas when he is feeling overwhelmed.

In the spring term, James gets support from the SENCO who makes a referral to the Behaviour Support Service and a specialist teacher comes to support him. In conjunction with this teacher, a detailed plan is put in place to respond to the 'hiding under the table' behaviour. This includes a script to respond and incorporates take-up time and tactical ignoring. It is agreed with all staff working in this part of the school, so that everybody can follow the plan. The senior leadership team are fully supportive of this and the final step in the plan is for the headteacher to become involved. This is not done in a way to undermine James but to communicate to the children the seriousness of their behaviours.

Gradually, through time this plan starts to become effective. After only a few cycles the child understands the consistent approach to running off or hiding under tables. He actually mutters, 'I know where this is going', climbs out from under the table and gets on with his work. There is a point reached where the behaviours flip and disappear completely. Relationships are maintained in the classroom. Importantly, the copying behaviour from the girl also disappears since there is nothing to copy any more. James feels positive and empowered by the experience, and the collaboration of working with other professionals.

Now consider what aspects of this chapter are drawn upon within the Good Practice example. This does not directly name the theories of behaviour that underpin the approach taken, so attempt to consider how theory influenced things. What kind of teacher do you think James is or hopes to be?

CRITICAL QUESTION

How do we decide when a behaviour is beyond our everyday practice as a teacher, and become something we could classify as 'most challenging'?

CHAPTER SUMMARY

In this chapter we have considered how we might frame behaviour, in the primary classroom. The following main features have been covered:

- Behaviour has been framed as something highly complex since there is an overlap between practice, theories and policies.
- Behaviour is a form of communication that we must learn to understand.
- Teachers should locate their own theories and values around behaviour and consider how this might manifest in their classroom. They should continuously work to understand what behaviour is and how we interpret it.
- The iceberg models of behaviour are useful tools for showing how multiple factors, including psychological, medical and contextual, lead to the presenting behaviours.
- Complex and challenging behaviours require support beyond the individual teacher.

ASSIGNMENTS

If writing an ITE assignment around behaviour, it will be useful to think through the following:

1. As behaviour is so complex you will need to focus on one particular aspect. Where possible, draw on an experience you had while on school placement and structure your assignment around this specific incident. What happened in the classroom? Or how did the adults respond?
2. Next, draw on theories of behaviour. What assumptions and theories were relevant to the incident? How does this position the adults and their responses? Maybe consider the behaviour policy in relation to this.
3. Analyse the incident from a variety of angles. Avoid being too critical of staff responses and attempt to understand their approach, framing it within the context within which they are working. How does the particular school, classroom, year group impact on behaviour?
4. Based on your developing thinking, how would you now negotiate the same incident if it occurred again? What is your anticipation of future practice? How does your new position relate to your values and the teacher you aspire to be?

Useful readings

Nash, P., Schlösser, A. and Scarr, T. (2016) Teachers' perceptions of disruptive behaviour in schools: A psychological perspective. *Emotional and Behavioural Difficulties*, 21(2): 167–80.

Frederickson, N. and Cline, T. (2015) *Special Educational Needs, Inclusion and Diversity* (3rd edition). London: McGraw-Hill Education (Behaviour in schools, Ch. 15, p. 428).

(Continued)

(Continued)

The following sources provide useful further reading:

Kohn, A. (2011) Feel-Bad Education: Contrarian essays on children and schooling. Boston, MA: Beacon Press.

This is a good book in helping you to think differently about education. It is useful for professional studies aspects of teacher education since it asks specific questions about small but significant aspects of practice.

Porter, L. (2014) Behaviour in Schools. London: McGraw-Hill Education.

This is a powerful book about behaviour in schools, which successfully combines theory and practice. In this edition there is a clear argument in relation to behaviourism and guidance approach and it gives more detail than is possible in this chapter. I strongly recommend this book.

Rogers, B. (2015) Classroom Behaviour: A practical guide to effective teaching, behaviour management and colleague support (4th edn). London: SAGE.

Rogers offers very practical advice around classroom management. Although it is perhaps rooted in theories of behaviourism, this is a useful book for a student teacher to consider holistic aspects of behaviour, including language.

REFERENCES

Canter, L. (2010) *Assertive Discipline: Positive behavior management for today's classroom*. Bloomington, In: Solution Tree Press.

Department for Education and Department of Health (2015) *Special Educational Needs and Disability Code of Practice: 0 to 25 years*. Available at: www.gov.uk/government/publications/send-code-of-practice-0-to-25 (accessed 25/06/18).

Department for Education (DfE) (2016) *Behaviour and Discipline in Schools: Advice for headteachers and school staff.* Available at: https://assets.publishing.service.gov.uk (accessed 25/06/18).

Kohn, A. (1999) *Punished by Rewards: The trouble with gold stars, incentive plans, A's, praise and other bribes*. Houton Miffin: Dublin.

Maslow, A.H. (1970) *Motivation and Personality*. New York: Harper & Row.

Ofsted (2014) Below the radar: Low-level disruption in the country's classroom. Available at: https://assets.publishing.service.gov.uk

Porter, L. (2014) *Behaviour in Schools*. London: McGraw-Hill Education.

Rogers, Carl (1980) *A Way of Being*. Boston, MA: Houghton Mifflin.

Senninger, T. (2000) *Abenteuer leiten – in Abenteuern lernen*. Münster: Ökotopia.

DEVELOPING RULES FOR SPEAKING AND LISTENING

Making EYE CONTACT with the speaker

EVERYBODY having A TURN at SPEAKING

ONE PERSON speaking at A TIME

SPEAKING in a CLEAR VOICE

Using APPROPRIATE VOCABULARY

Being CLEAR about what you mean and supporting what you say with evidence

Using the LANGUAGE OF REASONING, e.g. I think, because, therefore

RESPONDING to the OTHER SPEAKER

Using QUESTIONS to CLARIFY UNDERSTANDING

Making EXTENDED CONTRIBUTIONS

Using FACIAL EXPRESSIONS and GESTURES.

(Source: Glazzard, J (2016) *How to be a Primary Teacher*. Northwich: Critical Publishing)

15

TALK AND COMMUNICATION: COULDN'T THEY JUST SIT DOWN AND SHUT UP?

Kate Allott is Senior Lecturer at the School of Education, York St John University. Kate teaches primary English, history and professional studies and has responsibility for Early Years in the department. Her research focuses on early years and children's literature.

David Waugh is Associate Professor (Teaching) at the School of Education, Durham University. He has published many books supporting the teaching of primary English. His teaching interests focus on children's literature, phonics and early reading, spelling, writing and grammar. David has also written five children's novels, one - *The Wishroom*, with 45 children from 15 schools.

KEY WORDS

- Accent
- Communication
- Dialect
- Discussion
- Language
- Questioning
- Talk

INTRODUCTION

This chapter focuses on the importance of talk and communication in the primary classroom. It begins by exploring why talk and communication are central to children's learning and development, and presents key theories supporting this. It goes on to cover how you can create a classroom climate conducive to speaking and listening. It outlines the challenges that teachers face when developing talk in the classroom and offers support for planning and assessment. The chapter considers the importance of questioning for learning and offers case studies and classroom examples to support you to link theory to practice.

WHY IS IT IMPORTANT TO DEVELOP TALK AND COMMUNICATION?

Children who have good language skills at the age of five are much more likely to achieve well and to develop good social skills. Yet children from poorer families are, on average, almost a year behind children from higher income families in terms of vocabulary development, and more than 50 per cent of teenagers in some disadvantaged areas have poor communication skills – those very skills that are the most important factor in succeeding in the jobs market (I CAN, 2017). It is impossible to overestimate the importance of helping children to develop their language and communication skills. Talk has several very important functions:

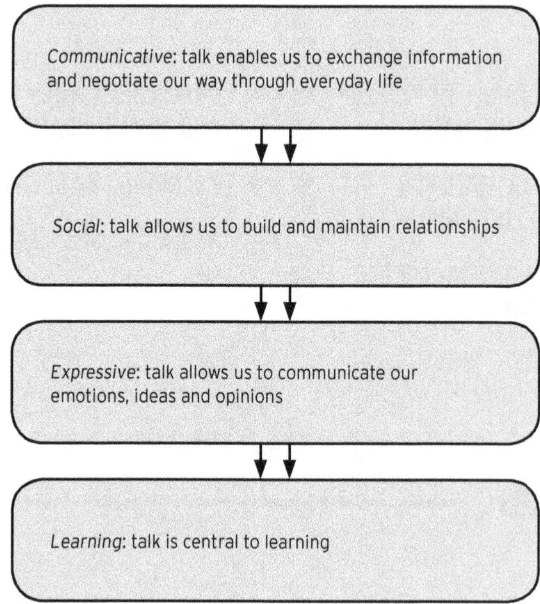

To understand the communicative function, imagine a child newly arrived in this country and attending school, not as yet knowing any English. There is talk all around him, but he can make no sense of any of it. He can sense that some of what adults say are instructions, but he can only follow them by observing the other pupils. He cannot make even the simplest request – for example, to go to the toilet. He may not be able to join in any playtime games, apart perhaps from a game of football. The school day is baffling and tedious. As his English develops, the world opens up.

The importance of the social function can be seen as children's language skills develop. Children make friends (and fall out with them), tell each other stories and jokes, and chat with adults. Play often involves much talk – to plan, make rules and create narratives in socio-dramatic play. A school is a community, and communities depend on good relationships. Children with poor language skills may become isolated and lonely, and this can colour their whole attitude to school. The Bercow Report (DCSF, 2008) even points out that children with speech, language and communication difficulties are more likely to be bullied than other children. The National Curriculum programme of study for years 1 to 6 (DfE, 2013: 17) emphasises the social aspects of talk, through statutory requirements such as:

- maintain attention and participate actively in collaborative conversations, staying on topic and initiating and responding to comments;
- gain, maintain and monitor the interest of the listener(s);
- select and use appropriate registers for effective communication.

The expressive function also has wide implications. A baby is only able to express its needs in the simplest way – by crying. Toddlers may express anger by hitting people or throwing things. Children cry, expressing emotions, but without adequate language to explain their feelings, adults are quite often unable to help them. So children who do not have good language skills to express their emotions can become frustrated and may resort to inappropriate expressions such as aggressive behaviour, or may become withdrawn. Expressing feelings and thoughts has a value beyond the emotional benefit: children are also learning to understand themselves better and to manage their own emotional responses. There is far less emphasis on this function of talk in the programme of study, with only this mention:

> *Give well-structured descriptions, explanations and narratives for different purposes, including for expressing feelings.*
>
> (DfE, 2013: 17)

However, the central purpose of the school is children's learning, and language is essential to learning. At a basic level, teachers use language to inform and to explain. But language for learning means more than this transmission mode in which teachers talk and children listen. Language is a tool for thinking, individually and with others; it allows children to solve problems, reflect, reason, share ideas, challenge each other and learn from each other.

KEY THEORY

The work of the Russian psychologist Vygotsky helps us understand the relationship between thought and language. Vygotsky considered that language is not simply how we express our thinking. He suggested that thoughts are actually structured and restructured by their expression in words, and so using language to communicate helps children to develop ways of thinking. His view was that language development begins with social interaction, but then moves to egocentric speech (speech for oneself) and eventually inner speech, as children begin to use language to guide themselves, and that this is a sign of increasing cognitive maturity. But Vygotsky also emphasised the importance of the support of more knowledgeable 'others' in developing children's language and thought.

(Vygotsky, 1978)

Vygotsky's theories are supported by research evidence. Children use language, either alone or in pairs or groups, as a thinking tool. Mercer *et al.* (1999) showed that planned, adult-led activities improved children's language skills and also helped their independent problem-solving, while Brown and Palincsar (1989) showed that teachers' language use provides a model for children of skills such as questioning, reasoning and explaining, which guides children in their own language use when solving problems. Language and thinking are interdependent, and together they are central to learning. Goodwin (2001) describes the 'articulate classroom' as one where all children's voices are heard and valued, talk underpins the curriculum, and language is a focus of study as well as a medium for learning. Children, in other words, become conscious of the language they use and can discuss it, just as they become conscious of their own thought processes and can discuss and control them – and in the process become both more effective language users and better learners.

CREATING THE CLIMATE FOR SPEAKING AND LISTENING

In this section, we will examine some of the factors that can enable teachers to foster successful speaking and listening. There will be a focus on three key elements: ground rules, physical organisation and organisation of children and other adults.

INFO 15.1

Developing rules for speaking and listening

- making eye contact with the speaker
- everybody having a turn at speaking
- one person speaking at a time
- speaking in a clear voice
- using appropriate vocabulary
- being clear about what you mean and supporting what you say with evidence
- using the language of reasoning, e.g. *I think, because, therefore*
- responding to the other speaker
- using questions to clarify understanding
- making extended contributions
- using facial expressions and gestures.

Source: Glazzard, J (2016) How to be a Primary Teacher. Northwich: Critical Publishing

These seem eminently sensible rules, but it is worth considering how many of them might be devised by a class working in groups and sharing their ideas, based on their experiences of discussion, both positive and negative. If that approach were taken, children would acquire 'ownership' of the rules and might be more likely to adhere to them as a result. Of course, they could be prompted by suggestions from the teacher or be shown examples from previous classes, but ultimately the children's rules will provide a reference point for everyone, including the teacher, when problems arise.

PHYSICAL ORGANISATION OF THE CLASSROOM

Classrooms can be organised in a variety of ways. Some teachers create tables for four to six children so that group discussion can take place easily, while others create horseshoes of desks so that everyone can see everyone else during class discussions. Yet others arrange desks in rows so that discussion will be limited to near neighbours, and class discussions will focus on the teacher with anyone contributing remaining almost unseen by most of the class. In Russian classrooms, this difficulty is overcome by having children come to the front of the room to answer questions or explain their work (Alexander, 2000). Many teachers adopt a flexible approach, arranging furniture in different ways according to the level of discussion they wish to encourage in different lessons. This is a key factor in successful speaking and listening: the physical environment needs to match the kind of talk and communication required.

Should the layout of a classroom be adjusted depending on the learning activity planned?

MANAGING PEOPLE

Alongside organising the physical environment, it is important to consider how children should be grouped for different speaking and listening activities, and what the functions of those groups will be. For example, groups of six might include one person to act as Chair, another to record discussion and another to 'envoy' the key points to other groups. Children might talk in pairs, with one being A and the other B. All As might then move on and share ideas with different Bs so that a larger pool of knowledge is developed. Alternatively, children might begin by discussing a topic in pairs before joining another pair to share ideas and then fours becoming eights to broaden things still further before a class discussion takes place. As with physical organisation, flexibility is important, as is understanding the stage a class has reached in its ability to engage in productive discussions. Teaching assistants can be invaluable in helping to manage groups, especially when problems are anticipated, but it should be stressed that they should avoid dominating discussions and try instead to prompt and encourage.

Managing speaking and listening can, then, involve developing structures and procedures, as well as changing the physical environment. However, we also need to take into account some very basic factors that can affect the success of our talking classrooms, as the classroom link below illustrates.

CLASSROOM LINK

What does this mean for classroom practice?

Other adults in the classroom

Many teachers work with teaching assistants. It is important to plan for them and with them so that speaking and listening activities are focused and productive. Be clear about what you expect from other adults in the classroom and ensure that they facilitate rather than dominate discussions. It is important that a good balance is achieved between adult and child talk, as well as between speaking and listening in the classroom.

CRITICAL QUESTION

How would you manage a classroom assistant who tended to dominate discussions with groups of children?

SUPPORTING LISTENING ACROSS THE CURRICULUM

Books and articles on speaking and listening tend to focus on speaking more than on listening, yet the National Curriculum (DfE, 2013) mentions *speaking* on six occasions compared with nineteen for *listening*. The repetition at different stages of 'taking turns and listening to what others say' is important: if children are to develop their ability to articulate their ideas, they will need to have a receptive audience, which includes people who will test and discuss their ideas.

Woolley (2014) maintains that listening activities need to have clear goals, which might include making notes and sharing information. It is important to consider strategies for developing listening skills. These might include the following:

- Developing with the children class rules for listening and emphasising the importance of attentiveness and good manners.
- Providing prompts for listening, so that children listen carefully to find answers to questions or information. For example, before reading a text to children, the teacher might give out cards with key words from the text and then pause occasionally to ask whose words have been mentioned and in what context. This not only encourages listening but also enhances reading comprehension.
- Organising groups to discuss and feed back on what they have heard so that children can share their understanding of what they have heard.
- Inviting a physical response such as raising a hand whenever a particular aspect of the lesson is heard. For example, in a phonics session, Y1 might stand up when they hear a word in a passage that includes the phoneme they are focusing upon, while Y4 could do the same in a shared reading session when they hear an adjective.

- Reading texts that include true and untrue statements, and asking children to note when they hear something false.
- Asking children to retell what they have just heard in, say, six words. These might not form a sentence, but could be simple prompts to aid subsequent writing.
- Encouraging recording of information in chart or diagram formats so that they can make notes quickly and concisely, and teaching note-taking skills.

CLASSROOM LINK

What does this mean for classroom practice?

Encourage children to listen to each other in class discussions

A key challenge in class discussions is getting children to speak so that others can hear them and getting children to listen to each other. Work on developing rules for discussions, involving children in deciding what they should be, so that you have a reference point when problems arise. Be a role model by showing that you are listening to children's contributions and are interested in them. Some children are reluctant to speak in front of the whole class, so prefacing whole-class discussions with paired talk will enable them to share their ideas with more confidence. Remember that children tend to respond to the person who asks them a question, so if you are very close to them, they may speak more quietly than if you are further away.

WHAT CHALLENGES DO WE FACE WHEN DEVELOPING TALK AND COMMUNICATION?

Probably the biggest challenge in terms of developing talk and communication in the classroom is giving it sufficient weight. The history of speaking and listening in education has been one of reports and initiatives emphasising its importance, followed by very little action. Ofsted's report *Moving English Forward* (2012) confirmed that the issue of a lack of attention to speaking and listening, which it identified in its first report on English in 2005, remained relevant, and even suggested that a focus by schools on test results had led to this situation. Inspectors suggested that pupils needed to be given time to think, plan and discuss, as well as to write. But this is not the only challenge.

THE NATURE OF TALK IN THE CLASSROOM

However important teachers consider talk to be, there are a number of classroom management issues that need to be addressed if it is to be given the focus it needs. These include the following:

- *Group size*: it is difficult to manage talk, with a group of 30, and teachers need effective strategies for managing turn-taking, deciding who is to speak, monitoring paired talk, and so on.

- *Relationships:* talk is affected by unequal power relationships in schools, between adult professionals and children. Children may be inhibited by the imbalance; teachers may not listen carefully to the 'junior partners' in talk.
- *Didactic purpose:* teachers need to teach children, and they may feel that the need to show that children are making progress reduces opportunities for extended talk.

Beyond this, there is a significant challenge in the traditional nature of communication in classrooms. This features extensive use of what is known as the IRF exchange, which consists of an *initiation* or question from the teacher, a *response* from a pupil, and *feedback* from the teacher. It was first identified in research by Sinclair and Coulthard (1975). An example would be:

Teacher: What is the name of the river that runs through London?

Pupil: The Thames.

Teacher: Good, well done.

Typically, the question is one to which the teacher already knows the answer – a display question or pseudo-question. Teachers need to reflect on why they ask so many questions as part of their teaching, and to be clear about what the purpose of each question is. Children's responses are often very brief: teachers need to consider the quality of the responses they are given, and whether a different strategy would ensure more thoughtful and extended responses. There are also questions about the feedback: what is its purpose, and what is its impact? Does it suggest that everything a child says must be judged by the teacher? Do children need continual reassurance that what they say is right? The challenge for teachers is to consider the educational value of such exchanges.

CLASSROOM LINK

What does this mean for classroom practice?

Developing questioning

Questions, particularly recall questions, are sometimes used as a behaviour management technique rather than as an effective way of developing children's thinking and learning. A small pool of children may always be keen to answer, while others do not put their hands up, and if asked to contribute will remain silent or say they do not know the answer. The dialogic teaching approach (Alexander, 2008) suggests a different way of managing questions. Careful planning can help: for example, a key question, focused on the main learning objective, with supplementary questions which lead up to the key question or develop responses to it. A 'no hands up' policy can ensure that all children know that they can be expected to answer any question. This can be combined with thinking time, or use of talk partners, for questions that need a more considered response. Rather than giving undifferentiated praise, such as 'Well done' or 'Fantastic', for responses, a follow-up question, or response such as 'Thank you' or 'Could you say more about that?' can make children less dependent on teacher approval. Questioning can be used strategically for assessment purposes.

SPEECH, LANGUAGE AND COMMUNICATION NEEDS

There are general challenges in relation to speaking and listening in the classroom, but there are also challenges in relation to individual pupils. Speech, language and communication needs (SLCN) are very common but often undiagnosed, so teachers need to be constantly aware of the language skills of each child in the class (The Communication Trust, 2014). They include a range of very different needs, and teachers must learn to be aware of these and knowledgeable about them. Children may have difficulties with producing some sounds, making their language hard to understand, or have very limited vocabularies, or have difficulty putting words together to express their ideas, or find it hard to use language appropriately in different social situations. Some of these issues may be temporary, but they could also be long term, and children may have more than one speech, language and communication need.

Many teachers also have the challenge of managing a class that includes children learning English as an additional language.

KEY THEORY

The Canadian Jim Cummins, a leading expert on bilingual education and second language learning, considered that learners of additional languages needed to develop both everyday language for social and communicative purposes, which he called *Basic Interpersonal Communication Skills* (BICS), and also language for thinking and learning, which he called *Cognitive Academic Language Proficiency* (CALP). He suggested that children could develop BICS quite quickly, probably within 18–24 months, while mastering CALP took much longer - up to seven years.

Cummins' theory suggests that there is a danger that once children have developed BICS, schools assume that their learning of English as an additional language is complete. However, children do not progress automatically from BICS to CALP, and language support and teaching continues to be needed. A further danger is that because their continuing language needs are not recognised, they are placed inappropriately in low-attaining groups. Conteh (2012) identified other challenges for schools in providing appropriately for learners of English as an additional language because of what she described as myths about language learning: that children become confused if languages are not kept separate; that when exposed to English speakers, they will absorb the language without explicit teaching; that language diversity is a problem and only English should be spoken in the classroom; and that it is very difficult for older learners to acquire a new language. These myths can have a damaging effect on schools' capacity to make good provision for EAL learners.

CRITICAL QUESTION

How can we plan for and for assess pupils' language and communication?

PLANNING FOR SPEAKING AND LISTENING

There are two basic approaches to planning for speaking and listening – to start with the learning outcomes and plan activities to address them, or to trawl through planning for different subjects, looking for opportunities to build in speaking and listening. If the second approach is adopted, it is important that a broad range of activities is included, but if this can be done, it has the advantage of providing meaningful contexts for talk. An enhanced focus on speaking and listening is also likely to enrich the learning in different subjects. It is important, though, that teaching goes beyond simply providing an opportunity to talk; children need explicit teaching in, for example, how to share and develop ideas and views in group discussion, or how to speak in a formal debate, or how to ask questions in a hot-seating activity. Planning, therefore, needs to include learning outcomes specifically for speaking and listening, matched to the type of talk involved. Success criteria can often be developed with the children themselves, which is likely to mean they understand them better and will think more carefully about their language use.

Because the programme of study includes only a page on speaking and listening, to cover all year groups from 1 to 6, schools need to map out expectations for children at different ages. This is a useful exercise as it means that teachers have ownership of the expectations, rather than having them imposed from outside. It also means that they need to be agreed through staff working together, and this provides everyone with a clear overview and understanding of progression. Assessment is then based on the school's own descriptors, and there can be agreement as to how and when it takes place.

ASSESSING SPEAKING AND LISTENING

It is relatively easy to assess pupils' learning in mathematics. Their answers are written on the page, often with 'working out' to show their thinking. It is probably harder to assess writing because there is an element of subjectivity: while we may be able to tick the 'has used similes' box, it presumably matters whether the simile is a good one. But assessing pupils' talk is probably the most difficult assessment task a teacher faces. It is ephemeral, unless we actually record it – often a problematic process in schools because of the levels of background noise and children's reaction to being recorded. Then there are the questions of focus. Are we assessing use of Standard English, or how fluent the pupil is, or how effectively they use talk to explain, describe, reason and so on, or how wide their vocabulary is? The National Curriculum programme of study (DfE, 2013) suggests that all of these and much more need to be taught; is it possible to assess everything that is taught in any meaningful way? But without assessment, how can we plan purposeful and relevant teaching? How can we demonstrate that children have made progress – that the child who is reluctant to speak in front of the whole class, and who does so haltingly and inaudibly in Year 1, is not doing exactly the same in Year 6?

It is more realistic to focus for assessment purposes on a limited number of aspects of speaking and listening in any one activity, rather than trying to cover a range of diverse objectives. In a group discussion, for example, assessment might focus on skills of discussion – staying on topic, attending to and building on the contributions of others – or on children articulating opinions and arguments; it would probably be difficult to do both in a meaningful way for a group of five or six children.

Any assessment of speaking and listening needs to be sensitive to issues such as children's accents and dialects, which, as they grow older, become a significant part of their identity, linking them to the community they are

What does this mean for classroom practice?

Self- and peer-assessment of speaking and listening

Self- and peer-assessment of speaking and listening can empower children and make them more aware of their own communication skills. Video-recording allows pupils to observe themselves engaged in presentations, discussions and debates. Children may need some pointers as to what to look for, but may also be able to develop their own criteria for assessment. Although such activity is time-consuming, the impact on speaking and listening is likely to be significant. Self-assessment is important because how we communicate is linked to our self-image, and it can be difficult, and even painful, to see and hear ourselves as others see and hear us; it is helpful, therefore, for children to have ownership of this assessment. Peer-assessment is important because communicating opinions of other children's speaking and listening needs to be done honestly but sensitively, and learning to do this develops communication skills.

growing up in. It is important to note that the National Curriculum programme of study (DfE, 2013) states that children should be developing mastery of Standard English (if, of course, they are not already Standard English speakers) but that there is no reference at all to accent. The reference to 'appropriate registers' suggests that there are contexts in which dialects other than Standard English would be appropriate.

Accents and dialect

There is often confusion about accents and dialects. Crystal and Crystal explain the distinction succinctly:

> *An accent is a person's distinctive pronunciation. A dialect is a much broader notion: it refers to the distinctive vocabulary and grammar of someone's use of language. If you say eether and I say iyther, that's accent. We use the same word but pronounce it differently. But if you say I've got a new dustbin and I say I've gotten a new garbage can, that's dialect. We're using different words and sentence patterns to talk about the same thing.*

(Crystal and Crystal, 2014: 15)

While Browne emphasises the importance of discussing language with children and stresses 'the need to respect one's own language and that of others':

> *Perhaps the role of the school in relation to accents should be to counter negative attitudes to them, since these can affect self-esteem and identity. A distinctive regional accent may identify a new entrant to school as coming from a different place or as being an outsider and impede the child's acceptance as a member of the new local community.*

(Browne, 2009: 23)

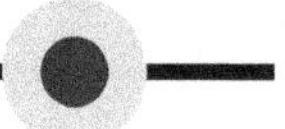

CASE STUDY

Promoting talk in the primary school

Molly, an experienced early years teacher, found that her approach, which had been very successful with previous classes, was not working for her new class which was boy-heavy and had a high proportion of summer-born pupils. The children were finding it difficult to settle and to develop relationships, and attainment levels were low, particularly in language and communication and personal, social and emotional development. A new approach was needed. As an early years practitioner, Molly saw the environment as the 'third teacher', and decided to begin her changes there. The room had been a typical primary classroom, full of bright colours, walls covered in displays, and a wealth of resources for play available and visible in the room. Molly began with a major clear-out, and developed a calmer, simpler, more home-like environment with a reliance on natural materials, quiet colours, interesting textures, and fewer resources carefully selected for their learning potential. She constructed small dens and corners where children could play and talk together. The outdoor area was also redeveloped, with an emphasis on provision to support talk and imaginative play - for example, an outdoor home area where lampshades hung from tree branches, and a miniature log cabin with small wooden figures for small world play.

The impact on the class was clear. Children became more deeply involved in their play, and that play was increasingly focused on talk. Relationships improved and they began to make friends. Children who would not speak to adults were observed talking to other children in the dens and comfortable corners. The staff could interact with children more effectively, and the impact on language was marked.

Molly's initiative was taken up by the other Reception teacher and the nursery teacher, with the same very positive outcomes. Key Stage 1 teachers were the next to review and change the classroom environment to support development of communication skills. Throughout the school homely and attractive touches were seen - 'real' furniture, windows kept clear to enhance natural light in the rooms, thoughtful use of colour, much less display but often on a much bigger scale and much more thoughtfully considered. The aim was to create a calm atmosphere where children felt at home and were confident to talk, but also where the environment stimulated imagination and discussion.

Staff then began to consider how they could build in opportunities for talk in the daily routine. Classes established a 'talking time' after lunch, for 15 minutes or so. The time might be used for circle time activities, or activities from the *Philosophy for Children* approach (Lipman *et al*., 2010); what was important was that all children participated and that they saw that talk was valued by their teachers.

The most important step was still to come, though. The changes made so far had ensured that talk had a higher profile in the school, that all children had regular opportunities to talk and that language development in the early years had improved. But staff felt unsure about the quality of the talk and its impact on learning. They felt that they needed professional development to help them assess talk and develop high-quality talk that supported children's learning effectively. This became the last phase of the initiative.

DISCUSSION

The case study demonstrates that there is no quick and easy solution to improving language and communication in schools. Focusing first on the physical environment can be a good start, as changes are relatively straightforward to implement, and can win over staff who are less committed. However, there is a danger that it becomes more of an interior design strategy than a pedagogic one. The purpose must be kept in mind. Beyond the physical environment, changing practice in meaningful ways requires considerable commitment and a willingness to reflect honestly on classroom practice. Even when teachers have identified the problems with their own approach – talking too much, asking too many questions and so on – it can be very difficult to move away from what has become the normal form of interaction in schools.

CHAPTER SUMMARY

This chapter has identified some key elements in the development of successful speaking and listening in schools. These include:

- recognising that there are different functions for speaking and listening, and enabling children to experience talk in different situations and for different purposes;
- understanding the nature of talk and the effect that group size, relationships and the type of learning involved can have upon what we might expect from children and from ourselves as teachers;
- creating an environment in which speaking and listening are not only valued and encouraged, but are also facilitated through the physical environment;
- remembering the importance of developing listening skills as well as speaking skills;
- recognising that there are developmental stages in children's development as speakers and listeners, and that basic language proficiency can be acquired much more quickly than academic language proficiency, particularly for those who are learning English as an additional language;
- the importance of planning opportunities for talk;
- the importance of and challenges associated with assessing speaking and listening;
- recognising the important place of accents and dialects as well as of Standard English in children's lives.

ASSIGNMENTS

If you are writing an ITE assignment discussing the importance of talk and communication you may wish to:

1. consider your own philosophy on talk and communication;
2. consider the relationship between language and thinking, referring to key theorists such as Vygotsky and Mercer;
3. explore some of the challenges teachers face in developing children's communication skills;

(Continued)

(Continued)

4. examine the requirements of the curriculum;
5. consider variations in language use for different purposes and by different people, for example, formal and informal language, accent and dialect, bilingualism.

If you are writing an assignment on developing talk and communication in the classroom, it will be useful for you to think through the following:

1. What are the key functions of talk and how can these be developed? (Look at communication, expression, social relationships and learning.)
2. How can children's listening skills be developed?
3. What is the role of the teacher in modelling talk and communication?
4. How can classrooms be organised to promote successful speaking and listening?
5. How can talk and communication be planned for and assessed?

Below are some useful texts to read and reference if writing an assignment on talk and communication. These offer some contrasting opinions and views from which to consider the key arguments, evidence and debates.

The following sources provide useful further reading:

Alexander, R. (2008) *Towards Dialogic Teaching: Rethinking classroom talk* (4th edn). York: Dialogos.

Allott, K. and Waugh, D. (2016) *Language and Communication in Primary Schools*. London: SAGE.

Conteh, J. (2012) *Teaching Bilingual and EAL Learners in Primary Schools*. London: SAGE.

The Communication Trust *Initial Teacher Education Resources*. Available at: *www.thecommunicationtrust.org.uk/resources/resources/resources-for-practitioners/initial-teacher-education/* (accessed 25/06/18).

Gross, J. (2011) *Two Years On: Final report of the communication champion for children*. London: Office of the Communication Champion. . Available at: www.aacknowledge.org.uk/page/communication-champion-final-report (accessed 25/06/18).

Vygotsky, L.S. (1978) *Mind in Society: The development of higher psychological processes*. Cambridge, MA: Harvard University Press.

Waugh, D. (2017) Talk, reading comprehension and writing, in Jones, D. and Hodson, P. (eds) *Unlocking Speaking and Listening: Developing spoken language in the primary classroom* (3rd edn). London: David Fulton.

Allott, K. and Waugh, D. (2016) *Language and Communication in Primary Schools*. London: SAGE.

Jones, D. and Hodson, P. (eds) (2017) *Unlocking Speaking and Listening: Developing spoken language in the primary classroom* (3rd edn). London: David Fulton.

Saxton, M. (2017) *Child Language: Acquisition and development* (2nd edn). London: SAGE.

REFERENCES

Alexander, R. (2000) *Culture and Pedagogy: International comparisons in primary education*. Oxford: Blackwell.

Alexander, R. (2008) *Towards Dialogic Teaching: Rethinking classroom talk* (4th edn). York: Dialogos.

Brown, A. and Palincsar, A.S. (1989) Guided, co-operative learning and individual knowledge acquisition, in L. Resnick (ed.) *Knowing, Learning and Instruction*. New York: Lawrence Erlbaum.

Browne, A. (2009) *Developing Language and Literacy 3–8* (3rd edn). London: SAGE.

Conteh, J. (2012) *Teaching Bilingual and EAL Learners in Primary Schools*. London: SAGE.

Crystal, B. and Crystal, D. (2014) *You Say Potato: A book about accents*. London: Macmillan.

DCSF (2008) *The Bercow Report: A review of services for children and young people (0–19) with speech, language and communication needs*. Nottingham: DCSF.

Department for Education (DfE) (2013) *The 2014 Primary National Curriculum in England*. London: DfE.

Glazzard, J. (2016) *How to be a Primary Teacher*. Northwich: Critical Publishing.

Goodwin, P. (2001) *The Articulate Classroom: Talking and learning in the primary school (early years and primary)*. London: Routledge.

I CAN (2017) *Reaching Out: Impact report 2016/17*. London: I CAN.

Lipman, M., Sharp, A. and Oscanyon, F. (2010) *Philosophy in the Classroom*. Philadelphia, PA: Temple University Press.

Mercer, N., Wegerif, R. and Dawes, L. (1999) Children's talk and the development of reasoning in the classroom. *British Educational Research Journal*, 25(1): 95–111.

Ofsted (2012) *Moving English Forward*. Manchester: Ofsted.

Sinclair, J. and Coulthard, M. (1975) *Towards an Analysis of Discourse: The English used by teachers and pupils*. Oxford: Oxford University Press.

The Communication Trust (2014) *Talk of the Town Evaluation Report*. London: The Communication Trust.

Vygotsky, L.S. (1978) *Mind in Society: The development of higher psychological processes*. Cambridge, MA: Harvard University Press.

Woolley, G. (2014) *Developing Literacy in the Primary School*. London: SAGE.

CHARACTERISTICS OF EFFECTIVE LEARNING

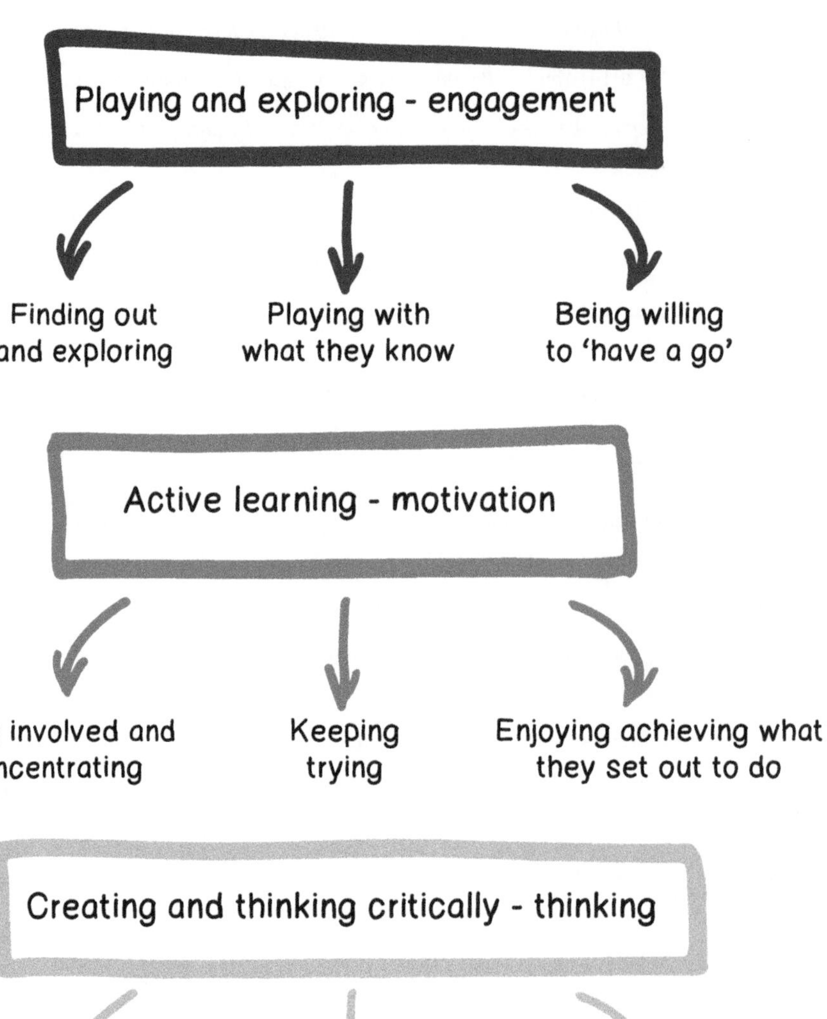

16

WHAT IS ASSESSMENT?

Mary Briggs is Principal lecturer and Programme Lead for Primary and Early Years ITE at Oxford Brookes University. Her research interests are: assessment, mathematics, mentoring and coaching.

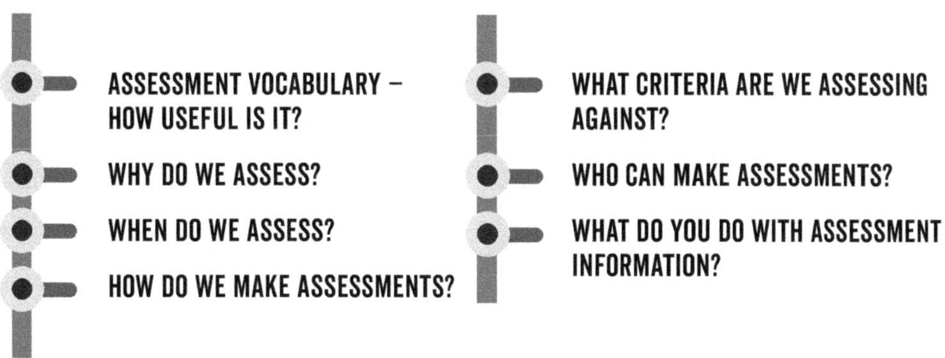

KEY WORDS

- AfI
- Assessment
- Differentiation
- DIRT
- Formative
- Summative

INTRODUCTION

This chapter explores aspects of assessment within learning and teaching. Assessment is one of the most challenging areas for those entering the profession and is, therefore, an aspect of learning and teaching that is addressed often after initial training in professional development. It is difficult because it really needs to come first in order to know about pupils' prior knowledge so that effective planning can take place, as Figure 16.1 shows, but what usually occurs is that students teach and then assessment is placed at the end of the cycle, thus only informing the next lesson.

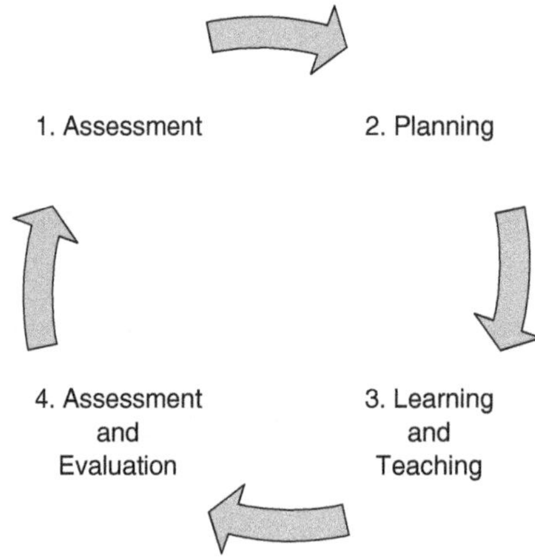

Figure 16.1 The planning and assessment cycle

Assessment is a key skill to develop from the beginning of your training because of the accountability associated with formal assessment. However, it is the day-to-day assessment build-up from knowledge of the learners you will teach that is crucial for progression in learning and developing quality teaching approaches.

We will begin by asking what is assessment and what are the terms teachers need to know about when reading or discussing assessment and will then go on to find out more about why and how assessments are made. The chapter will end with an evaluation of your understanding of the processes involved in assessment, and its importance in the learning and teaching cycle. Before you start reading you will find it helpful to read the assessment and marking policy from any current placement school alongside this chapter which focuses on overarching principles.

A VOCABULARY FOR ASSESSMENT

Assessment is any judgement you make as a teacher about children's learning.

> *There are three main forms of assessment: in-school formative assessment, which is used by teachers to evaluate pupils' knowledge and understanding on a day-today basis and to tailor teaching accordingly; in-school summative assessment, which enables schools to evaluate how much a pupil has learned at the end of a teaching period; and nationally standardised summative assessment, which is used by the Government to hold schools to account.*
>
> (McIntosh, 2015: 5)

CRITICAL QUESTION

Are the terms used in assessment helpful in developing knowledge and skills in this area?

It is important as part of your professional knowledge that you are aware of the terms used when discussing assessment. Review the following list and decide which are helpful in developing your understanding of assessment theory and practice. You will see that there is a wide range of activities associated with assessment in schools.

INFO 16.1

Foundation stage profile	The EYFS profile summarises and describes pupils' attainment at the end of the EYFS
Norm referenced	is a type of test, assessment, or evaluation that yields an estimate of the position of the tested individual in a predefined population, with respect to the trait being measured.
Target setting	is the process of identifying something that you want to accomplish and establishing measurable goals and time frames.
Summative assessments	are used to evaluate student learning, skill acquisition and academic achievement at the conclusion of a defined instructional period - typically, at the end of a project, unit, course, term, programme, or school year.
Ipsative	is an assessment based on a learner's previous work rather than based on performance assessments against external criteria and standards.
Criterion referenced	is a style of assessment that uses scores to generate a statement about the behaviour that can be expected of a person with that score.
Evaluation	a judgement about the amount, number, or value of something; assessment.
SATS	a test taken by school students as part of the national curriculum.
Teacher assessment	is the process of gathering and discussing information from multiple and diverse sources in order to develop a deep understanding of what students know, understand, and can do with their knowledge as a result of their educational experiences.
Self-assessment	assessment or evaluation of oneself or one's actions, attitudes or performance.
Diagnostic	is a type of assessment that examines what a student knows and can do prior to a learning programme being implemented.
Formative	including diagnostic testing, is a range of formal and informal assessment procedures conducted by teachers during the learning process to modify teaching and learning activities to improve student attainment.

(Continued)

(Continued)

Assessment for learning	is the process of seeking and interpreting evidence for use by learners and their teachers to decide where the learners are in their learning, where they need to go and how best to get there.
Assessment of learning	refers to strategies designed to confirm what students know, demonstrate if they have met curriculum outcomes or the goals of their individualised programs, or to certify proficiency and make decisions about students' future programs or placements.
Assessment as learning	is the use of ongoing self-assessment by students in order to monitor their own learning, which is characterized by students reflecting on their own learning and making adjustments so that they achieve deeper understanding.
Continuous assessment	the evaluation of a pupil's progress throughout a course of study, as distinct from by examination.
Floor targets	are the minimum standards set by central government for specific areas of its responsibility to the public.
Performance measures	is the process of collecting, analysing and/or reporting information regarding the performance of an individual, group, organisation, system or component.
Needs assessment	Enquiry into the current state of knowledge, resources or practice with the intent of taking action, making a decision or providing a service with the results.
Standardised test	Test with fixed content, equivalent parallel forms, standard administration and scoring, field-tested, valid and reliable.
AWL	Assessment without levels.
Testing	Valid and reliable practice of language measurement for context-specific purposes.
Validity	is a judgement about whether a test is appropriate for a specific group and purpose, and includes considerations such as whether the test really measures what you think it is measuring, whether the results are similar to examinees' performance on other tests or in class or real-world activities, and whether the use of test results have the intended effects.
Reliability	Consistency of scores/results.
Multiple choice test	Test in which examinees demonstrate knowledge, skill or ability by selecting a response from a list of possible answers.
Authenticity	How well a test reflects real-life situations.
Construct	What a test measures.
Accountability	Responsibility for educational outcomes; these outcomes are often measured through standardised testing.
Progress	Movement towards a goal. Progress is defined in terms of 'how well' and 'how much', as well as learners' rate of progress.
Tracking	Evidence that progress has been completed showing where individuals and classes are in relation to national expectations.
Differentiation	Differentiation means tailoring learning and teaching to meet individual needs.

WHY DO WE ASSESS?

Assessment should be the starting point for any planning of a scheme of learning as it identifies prior learning, avoiding repetition and targeting where children are now in relation to the topics being taught regardless of subject. Without initial assessment a teacher could make assumptions about previous learning and this could result in a mismatch between the content and the learners. Good record keeping, possibly using a tracker, can help a teacher identify this starting point. The alternative is to plan a recap as part of the first lesson of a sequence where information about existing learning can be obtained.

Assessment judgements made are the information used to track progress and to inform future planning for learning across the primary curriculum. Assessment information also enables teachers to give feedback to learners about how well they are doing, guiding them towards the next steps in their learning. There are two levels of information that the assessment gives teachers: first about individuals and then about the class. If we focus on the latter, the information about assessment across the class can assist groupings for the next lesson or plans for specific teaching interventions if there are common misconceptions or errors occurring across many learners.

Another key aspect of assessment and the information it generates is its use in relation to accountability. The assessment information allows subject leads to review the progress and attainment of all learners across a school. Schools will make comparisons between the progress of most pupils in the school, and then regionally and nationally against those who are in receipt of a Pupil Premium grant (PPG), those who speak English as an additional language (EAL) and looked-after children (LAC). The SENCO will also monitor the progress of learners with additional needs which may include some pupils from the previous groups. The teacher responsible for assessment will also make comparisons between gender – for example, an ongoing issue is boys and literacy skills nationally and so schools are likely to analyse the data to see what is happening in specific curriculum subjects.

WHEN DO WE ASSESS?

Teachers and other adults make judgements about children all the time – this is assessment. When children are learning, the focus is on the following:

- Their answers to questions asked during lessons.
- The questions they ask, as this can give you insights into their thinking during lessons.
- The explanations they give about how they have arrived at a solution or answers to questions posed – this may be during whole-class time.
- Practical evidence of responses to task – e.g. sorting magnetic items from non-magnetic items at the end of a task during lessons.

- Recording – e.g. writing – which is generally after the lesson.
- Responses to previous feedback either during or after lessons.

HOW DO WE MAKE ASSESSMENTS?

- Sharing criteria and learning intentions
- Planned questions
- Key pieces of work
- Marking
- Test/quizzes
- Observations
- Concept mapping

SHARING CRITERIA AND LEARNING INTENTIONS

It has become part of the expectations at the start of any lesson that it is good practice to share success criteria along with learning intentions, thus allowing learners to 'see what success looks like'. With the support of their teacher, success criteria can often be devised by the learners themselves (Department for Children, Schools and Families (DCSF), 2008). However, to allow for some variety in teaching approaches, some lessons may lend themselves to the pupils discovering what the learning intention is from planned activities. It is important that the teacher has a clear intention in mind, shared or otherwise, to direct the learning and ensure progression. Pupils will also learn additional skills and knowledge in any good lesson, but it is essential that core skills are acquired so that these can be built upon in future lessons.

QUESTIONING FOR ASSESSMENT

When you plan questions to use during teaching, part of the rationale for the questions is to assess learning. Questions starting with 'what' or 'who' or 'when' or 'which' will allow you to assess knowledge. For example: What is the capital of England? Who wrote *His Dark Materials*? What is 4x8? When did the Second World War end? Which of these materials are magnetic? These are closed questions that allow you to assess if a pupil has this factual knowledge or not. There can be a place for this type of question when assessing knowledge acquisition and they can be used in fast-paced starters or lesson introductions. More open questions – which often begin with 'how' and 'why' and sometimes with 'which' or 'what' – allow you to probe learners' understanding in greater depth. You are looking for the source of decisions or choices made or methods used: How did you get that answer? Why do you think that? Can you tell me how you did that?

MARKING

Schools should have clear policies on marking, which include guidance in relation to the style of marking, and you should ask any placement school for a copy to read. The following list focuses on some general issues about marking for you to consider alongside school-specific guidance.

a. Before pupils are asked to hand in work, they should know that you will be marking this specific task rather than it being self-marked or peer marked.

b. Pupils should know what you will be focusing on when marking and it should relate to individual targets set where appropriate. Some schools use the WILF acronym of What I Look For in each piece of work so all pupils know what is expected of them or WAGOLL – What A Good One Looks Like.

c. Pupils should have been reminded about any layout or presentation issues; does the school expect a date and objective, or intention or title, and should these be underlined?

d. When receiving the work, you will want to look for successes as well as aspects that will need to be developed, and these will form some future targets for the individual.

e. Indicate which answers are correct and those that are not (where appropriate and make sure you get it right). Do not mark a whole page of work wrong; see this pupil separately. Make sure that you indicate if there are any corrections to be completed and why (this will be linked to the school policy).

f. Think about younger pupils who are beginner readers. Are written comments the most appropriate for this age group? Who is the marking for – the pupils or parents/carers, or other teachers, including senior leadership team (SLT)?

g. Try to write comments that inform the pupil and that are in legible handwriting; try to avoid writing 'good' or 'well done' on its own – say why a piece of work is good.

h. Set pupils between one and three targets as part of the marking of this piece of work.

i. Choose a colour pen that is a contrast to the pupil's work; there may be a school policy about not using red. Some schools have specific colours – for example, purple for progress or praise, or pink for think (that means you are highlighting an error or misconception). However, this kind of system has been criticised as increasing teachers' workload, including from government minister Nick Gibb (2016): 'It was never a requirement by the government, never a requirement of Ofsted, and so we have to send out the message that it is not required. It's not required for there to be this dialogue on paper in different-coloured pens, this to and fro between the child and the teacher.'

j. If you are not sure what is going on when you look at a pupil's work, do not mark it; set aside time to talk to the pupil individually. We can make assumptions about difficulties based upon the recording that we see and that can lead us to plan intervention that is not appropriate.

k. Marking can assist you as a teacher in collecting evidence of pupils' progress and attainment. You can use this as formative assessment, which will inform the next stage of planning. It will give you and others an indication of the amount of help needed to complete a task, if this information is added to your comments on the work. For example, Robert worked with James on this problem in science, or Amy used a calculator for this work in mathematics. You can use it as the basis of pupil conferences and to assist you in compiling summative reports for parents.

KEY THEORY

Research on marking

In 2016, the Education Endowment Foundation (EEF) and University of Oxford published a report, *A marked improvement? A review of the evidence on written marking* (Elliott *et al.*, 2016). It was partly prompted by a concern about teachers' workloads, which were cited in a survey about people leaving the profession as a key rationale for choosing other work. The key findings from their review focused on three areas.

1. **The quality of existing evidence focused specifically on written marking is low.** The team of researchers found few large-scale, robust studies, such as randomised controlled trials, looked at marking with most studies small in scale and/or based in the fields of higher education or English as a foreign language (EFL), meaning that it is often challenging to translate findings into a primary school context or to other subjects. Most studies consider impact over a short period, with very few identifying evidence on long-term outcomes.
2. **Some findings do, however, emerge from the evidence that could aid school leaders and teachers aiming to create an effective, sustainable and time-efficient marking policy.**

   These include:

   - marking careless mistakes differently to errors resulting from misunderstanding;
   - grading every piece of work may reduce the impact of marking as pupils may focus on the grades at the expense of a consideration of teachers' formative comments;
   - the use of targets to make marking as specific and actionable as possible is likely to increase pupil progress;
   - pupils are unlikely to benefit from marking unless some time is set aside to enable pupils to consider and respond to marking;
   - some forms of marking, including acknowledgement marking (this is sometimes referred to as the 'tick and flick'), are unlikely to enhance pupil progress. Schools should mark less in terms of the number of pieces of work marked, but mark better.
3. **There is an urgent need for more studies so that teachers have better information about the most effective marking approaches.**

THE FREQUENCY OF MARKING

The impact on classroom practices has been to question how marking is conducted, the expectations of teachers in relation to the frequency of marking, and encouraging teachers to include space for pupils to respond to feedback from marking. The latter is explored in more detail under the DIRT heading later in this chapter (see pp. 293–5). It also raises the issue of teacher workloads.

In March 2018, the DfE commissioned research into workloads by CooperGibson Research (2018) and found teachers citing the areas below as those that had the greatest impact on their workloads:

- administration;
- behaviour monitoring and safeguarding;
- changing GCSE and A-Level specifications;
- data tracking;
- marking and assessment;
- planning and meetings.

What is significant about these is the number that are associated with assessment practices. Their recommendations were to reduce the amount of time spent planning and marking. Marking in class while the pupils are working can be one way of continuing to assess but not increase their workload outside the classroom. An alternative might be that teachers mark specific pieces of work in greater depth than others, which again links to the use of an appropriate DIRT lesson.

TESTS/QUIZZES

Tests and quizzes tend to be thought of in the same category as exams, but they can offer a challenge for pupils to see what they remember about a topic – for example, at the end of a unit of work in history, either individually or in groups, pupils could be asked questions to assess what they have taken from the topic. One of the disadvantages of this form of assessment is that it tests knowledge in isolation. It is possible to offer pupils a test where they should use the knowledge and skills acquired in a new situation – for example, the class may have carried out an investigation in science, following a specific process, and then be asked how to test a material through setting up another investigation and possibly a set of experiments.

OBSERVATIONS

Observation for assessment is an aspect that early years practitioners are more familiar with than those who work with older learners. One main reason for this is that the work that the younger children do is more practical in its nature with a focus on learning through play and limited recording. The only way to really assess what the children are learning is through observations. There are two kinds of observation: first, the planned observations where there is a clear focus on individuals, groups and/or specific activities; and second, there are the unplanned observations where you see significant shifts in learning that need to be recorded by the adult to add to an individual's record of achievement, but also to use to inform the future planning. Many early years settings have boards where post-it notes can be placed either under individuals' names or any areas of learning as a record of ad hoc observations. Some teachers carry small notebooks or tape recorders to note significant learning events. In some settings, one adult is floating to pick up on learning across the environment, particularly when children are involved in free-flow play activities. This can be a good time to observe children using knowledge in play situations. For example, using one-to-one correspondence and/or counting to lay the table in a role-play environment or their use of vocabulary as they engage in collaborative play. Observation can also be used as a technique in Key Stage 1 or 2 when pupils are working in a group; part of observation is not just watching the interactions, but also listening carefully to what the pupils say, which can give you insights into their thinking. This can be a useful task for a Teaching Assistant (TA) to undertake if they are given guidance about what to record during the observations.

CONCEPT MAPPING

An alternative way of finding out about pupils' understanding is to use a technique more often associated with science teaching and that is to ask pupils to construct a concept map. These can range from simple labelled diagrams and drawings to more complex maps, which involve asking pupils how they connect a wide range of words. Arrows can be added to show the direction of the relationship between items. You would need to know the context and prior experience of the pupil to know if they are making connections from what they have been taught or new connections by themselves. These can be without structure but can be supported and focused if children are given some support to guide their initial thinking. For a Year 6 class reviewing knowledge about light, the following might be used to support developing a concept map (see Figure 16.2).

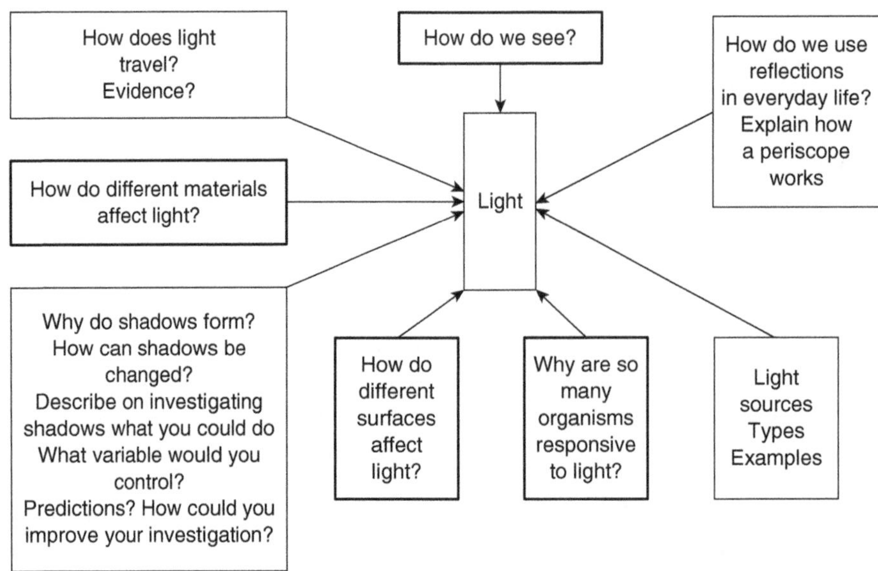

Figure 16.2 An example of a concept map

And this is an example of an outcome:

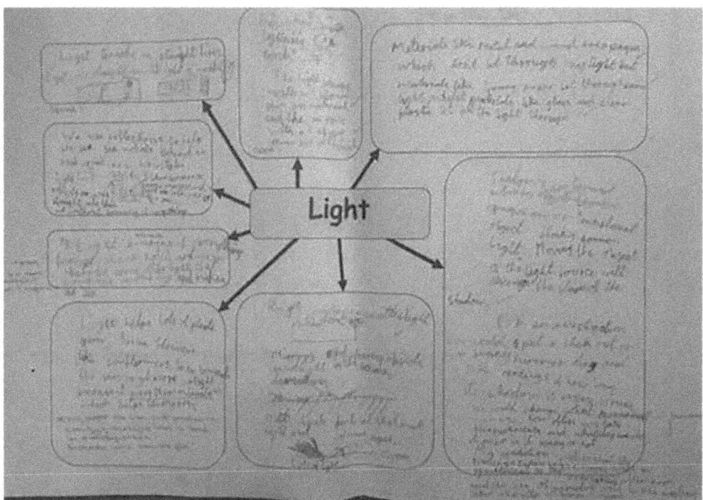

Figure 16.3 Outcome from concept map

This is an example of an outcome from a Year 4 topic:

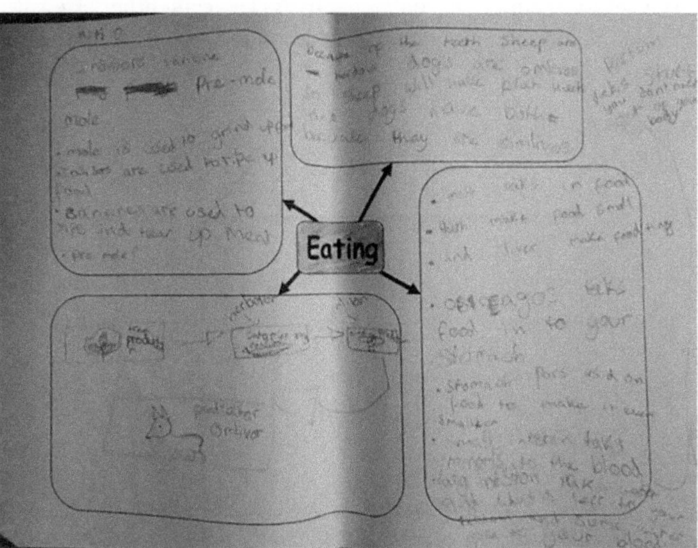

Figure 16.4 Outcome from concept map on Eating

This is an interesting example to discuss as there is evidence of scientific understanding but some SPaG issues with the recording. It is important to remember what is being assessed with any task.

CRITICAL QUESTION

What is the relationship between differentiation and assessment?

The criteria against which assessment judgements are made can be differentiation to match pupils' starting points or prior learning and achievement. However, one argument against regularly differentiating the learning intentions according to ability is that this can lower expectations of specific groups and place limits on their achievement outcomes. Another way to look at differentiation that doesn't place limits on the pupils is to consider stretching and challenging criteria for all pupils to aim for in each lesson.

CRITICAL QUESTION

Does differentiating learning according to ability lower expectations of specific groups?

WHAT CRITERIA ARE WE ASSESSING AGAINST?

All academic judgements are made against the current National Curriculum year expectations for any subject from Year 1 to Year 6. For those working below expectation in the National Curriculum, the focus is on progress made against targets set for them on an individual basis. There are other assessments made of pupils in school about their behaviour, musical talents and empathy towards other children, which all go towards building up a picture of the whole individual.

For pupils in Reception, there are the early learning goals (ELGs) and the profile. There is also an assessment of the effective characteristics of learning.

INFO 16.2

Characteristics of effective learning

- Playing and exploring-engagement - Finding out and exploring - Playing with what they know - Being willing to 'have a go'

Active learning - motivation

- Being involved and concentrating
- Keeping trying
- Enjoying achieving what they set out to do

Creating and thinking critically - thinking

- Having their own ideas
- Making links
- Choosing ways to do things

Although this is focused on the early years, engagement and motivation for learning are key elements for all age groups.

HOW ARE ASSESSMENTS RECORDED?

Many schools now have electronic tracking programmes that are used to record the data against year group expectations of the National Curriculum. These allow assessments to be recorded against expectations, sometimes using the following three categories, though some of the software breaks these three down into a total of six categories.

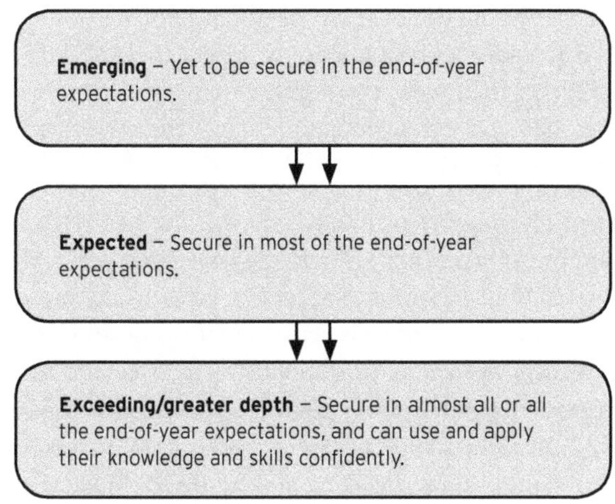

As schools use different ways to track, monitor and judge assessment data, how can we compare schools using assessment data?

WHO CAN MAKE ASSESSMENTS?

ADULTS IN SCHOOL

Everyone who meets pupils in school is making judgements about them and their behaviour, as well as their achievements across the curriculum. In the classroom, teachers, teaching assistants, nursery nurses and volunteers all have a role to play in feeding information into assessments about the learners in the class. As a teacher, you might ask someone to read with an individual and want them to comment on how the pupil completed this task; you might ask about words they struggled with or about their engagement with the task. All this information will assist you in planning the next steps in their learning, which may in this case be suggesting they try a different book or recap specific phonetic strategies to support their reading development.

THE ROLE OF PARENTS

Parents can tell teachers about their child in a different setting, the home, which is helpful to give a holistic picture of the learners in your class. Life outside the school will have an impact on how pupils behave and how they engage with learning, and parents/carers are a key source of that information. It will help you adapt your approaches to learning and teaching, and assessment to meet individual needs.

PEER ASSESSMENT AND SELF-ASSESSMENT

Pupils can assess their own and others' work, but they do require some guidance about what to look for. Pupils build up what is valued in assessment from their earliest days in school, as Bourke (2016) describes in an article exploring pupils' understanding of assessment processes. As part of the study she talked to five year olds who had not been in school very long. 'In their view, the purpose of assessment was either to tell them what they had learned, or how much they had learned. Even at this stage, these children measured progress through stars, stamps and stickers' (Bourke, 2016: 103).

To make peer and self-assessment meaningful for pupils, you will need to be clear about what the criteria are they will use to judge their own or others' work. This can be developed with the children so that the criteria are not written in 'education speak' but in words that will be clear to them as assessors. Use work from an unnamed pupil, either from another class or previous year, to model assessing as a whole-class activity to demonstrate what is expected. Pupils also need time to respond to feedback and this can be incorporated into a DIRT lesson. It is also a good idea to vary whose work pupils peer assess as well as varying what is either peer or self-assessed – i.e. it is not always the same subjects or on a regular basis. Assessments can be shared across the class or within groups to support current understanding and future learning. These activities assist in creating opportunities for pupils to take control and responsibility for their learning and build resilience. Boon (2016: 216) suggested the following in his paper about peer feedback on writing in a primary classroom, 'that children's uptake of peer feedback increased because:

- it was more useful for assessments;
- they had time to use it to improve the quality of work;
- they were allowed to discuss feedback with one another to clarify any misunderstandings about its content;
- pupils had become more thoughtful about how the feedback could be used through the reflection sheet provided.'

WHAT DO YOU DO WITH ASSESSMENT INFORMATION?

There are various uses of the information gained from the assessments you make as a teacher, but all information should feed forward into future planning of learning and teaching. One way is to assign a lesson or part of the lesson to a specific review of the feedback already given for a subject/lesson.

DIRT LESSONS

One area of recent development is planned DIRT lessons. DIRT stands for:

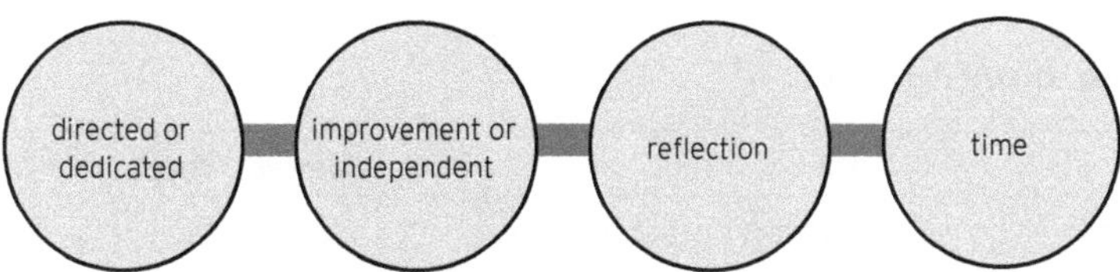

The idea behind these lessons is to give pupils feedback on an assessed piece of work and to guide them through aspects that could be improved because of the feedback from the assessment. The process starts with marking a piece of work and, as the teacher is marking, they record the following information across the class of work. The teacher is looking for which pupils have done well against the learning objective or intention of the lesson. They are also looking for common errors or misconceptions and identifying any patterns of under-achievement. You might record these areas for a whole class on a sheet like the one below as you are marking.

Marking crib sheet	**Date**	**Subject**
Praise (who has met or exceeded the expectations)	DIRT actions (these will form the activities planned to address errors/misconceptions identified from marking; initially, they might be notes prior to planning the DIRT lesson)	SPaG (Spelling, Punctuation and Grammar for any written work across the curriculum)
Concerns (who has struggled or not met the expected outcomes)		Numeracy focus (this includes the use of mathematics across the curriculum)

Essentially, from the marking you will be able to find out where difficulties have arisen in the learning and teaching, and plan activities to remediate the problems before the pupils move on to the next topic.

After marking, you will plan to address the aspects identified in the actions section of the crib sheet with all learners in the class, though there may be a need to differentiate the activities. These activities will not seek to address everything picked up in the process of marking, but focus on specific key skills and knowledge required to ensure progress in the subject. Planning a whole lesson or part of a lesson for this purpose allows the pupils time to consider the feedback and the actions they need to take in future work. It focuses their attention on the marking process rather than handing work back and assuming the pupils will read the comments and feed those forward into their next piece of work. For you, this process ensures that assessment and feedback inform future planning and teaching.

As part of this process you might also ask the pupils to complete their own evaluation, either before or after marking, using a prompt sheet like the one below which encourages pupils not just to focus on their own work, but to take responsibility for their learning and progress.

Pupil self-assessment sheet for DIRT

<table>
<tr><td colspan="2">Name</td><td>Date</td><td colspan="2">Subject/topic</td></tr>
<tr><td colspan="2">WWW (what went well)</td><td>EBI (even better if) or next steps</td><td>Working at</td><td>Target</td></tr>
<tr><td colspan="2">SPaG (where appropriate)</td><td rowspan="4">My strengths are:</td><td colspan="2" rowspan="4">It would be even better if ...</td></tr>
<tr><td>Excellent</td><td></td></tr>
<tr><td>Good</td><td></td></tr>
<tr><td>Needs improving</td><td></td></tr>
<tr><td colspan="2">Numeracy (where appropriate)</td><td rowspan="4">To make improvements I need to ...</td><td colspan="2" rowspan="4">Improvement task to be completed ...</td></tr>
<tr><td>Excellent</td><td></td></tr>
<tr><td>Good</td><td></td></tr>
<tr><td>Needs improving</td><td></td></tr>
</table>

CLASSROOM LINK

What does this mean for classroom practice?

For planning a good DIRT lesson, you will need to consider the following:

- Keep it focused - specifically keep to the areas identified from marking.
- Model and scaffold - make sure that you model the expectations and then scaffold the completion of the activities so that the pupils can succeed in meeting the expectations.
- Targeted feedback - start with what the class have completed well. Think about the use of a 'praise sandwich' - i.e. praise, focus on an area to develop and then praise again. Identify pupils who have done well. Here it is crucial that although you acknowledge those who are usually able to meet the expectations and often exceed them, you also identify effort and small successes. This helps motivate pupils to engage with future lessons and to hear what they need to do as their next steps rather than always hear that they have missed the expectations.
- Make oral feedback matter - written feedback is only one aspect of feedback that was explored as part of a review of marking in a project by EEF (Elliott *et al.*, 2016) and although written feedback provides an evidence trail for marking, it is not always the most effective form of feedback. Planning a DIRT lesson

provides you with an opportunity to give very specific class and individual feedback to pupils. Think carefully about how you phrase the feedback to motivate your learners.

- Exploit the power of peers/group - some of the activities planned for a DIRT lesson can allow pupils time to discuss how they met the expectations of previous tasks. Plan in time for members of the class to demonstrate their thinking to others, so it is not just adults modelling good practice.

The benefits of a DIRT lesson for you, as a teacher, are that it allows time to consider actions, ask questions, clarify understandings on both sides – e.g. why did errors or misconceptions arise – and clarify feedback – what does it mean? It also allows a direct link between assessment and feedback to inform future planning and teaching.

For the pupils, it allows them time to read any written feedback and to respond to this within class time. It allows the practice of skills required to move forward through teacher and peer modelling followed by completion of specific activities in the lesson. In addition, it could allow time for peer assessment response and/or opportunities to talk to a 'talk partner' or 'shoulder partner' about marked work and the associated feedback.

CLASSROOM LINK

What does this mean for classroom practice?

Plan to mark work from a specific lesson using the template for marking previously given above. Review the errors/misconceptions emerging and plan a DIRT lesson for the following day as the immediacy of feedback is important to impact on learning.

ASSESSMENT CONFERENCE WITH AN INDIVIDUAL PUPIL

An alternative to a whole-class DIRT lesson could be an individual conference with a pupil. The main purpose of this conferencing and target setting is to give pupils some goals to aim for, against which they can measure their own success. It may be possible for some pupils to conference in small groups, but there will be pupils for whom it is better to work on an individual basis.

Ahead of the discussion you will need to review all the work that a pupil has completed in the subject looking at their responses to previous feedback to evaluate the impact on their progress. Plan to spend 10 minutes with a pupil to talk about their learning in a curriculum subject (it is probably going to be most useful to concentrate on English or mathematics), review their progress and together set targets for the next few weeks' work. In setting targets, you need to choose ones that are achievable both in quality and in content. Concentrate on one area at a time so the pupil doesn't feel swamped. Always pick out things the pupil has achieved as well so the conference doesn't dwell on negative issues alone – praise success. Remember, this process is not just for SEND pupils but for all, and target setting can be a good way of raising expectations for the higher attaining pupils. Set a time by which you will review these targets.

You will need to keep a record of targets set, for example:

Pupil name:	Year:
Term:	Class:
Date of assessment:	Date of review:
Targets set:	Comment on achievement:
1. 2. 3.	

FEEDBACK TO PARENTS AND CARERS

Another use of the assessment information is to provide parents/carers with feedback about their child's learning and socialisation. Parents/carers are keen to not only find out how well they are doing in relation to academic learning, but they want to know about behaviour in the class and if their child has any friends that they play with at playtime. In short, they are interested in the whole child. This may be communicated during a parents' evening or in a written report. Discussing a child's progress in relation to national expectations can be a challenge for teachers. Parents don't always understand the expectations of assessment without levels. Making sure you are prepared with factual information for parents will aid the discussion and demonstrate your knowledge of their child.

This chapter has not provided an exhaustive list of assessment strategies, but demonstrated a few well-chosen examples of things you might consider including in your own practice. You must remember that although assessment appears hard, it is the crucial information on which a teacher plans lessons, ensuring that the match between the pupils and the content is appropriate for all learners. Here we have introduced you to some of the key issues in relation to assessment for teachers.

CHAPTER SUMMARY

In this chapter you will have learnt:

- the place of assessment in the learning and teaching cycle;
- assessment terminology;
- the role of marking;
- how to plan a DIRT lesson;
- a range of different strategies that can be employed to gather assessment information in the classroom.

ASSIGNMENTS

If you are writing an ITE assignment on assessment, it will be useful for you to think through the following:

1. What do you consider is the purpose of marking pupils' work? Why do you think this? Is this view shared by others?
2. What is the relationship between assessment and differentiation? What is the impact on learning and how would you demonstrate this was the case? What evidence would you draw upon?
3. What can we learn from our own experiences of assessment about learners' responses to feedback? How will this change your approach to pupils in school?

Also take a look at school marking policies. Find out about what is expected in practice from any training placement, setting or school.

Suggested reading as a starting point to support assignments:

Assessment in Education: Principles, Policy & Practice – journal to access research articles from international perspectives on assessment.

Elliott, V., Baird, J.A., Hopfenbeck, T.N., Ingram, J., Thompson, I., Usher, N., Zantout, M., Richardson, J. and Coleman, R. (2016) *A Marked Improvement? A review of the evidence on written marking.* London: Education Endowment Foundation. Available at: https://educationendowmentfoundation.org.uk/public/files/Publications/EEF_Marking_Review_April_2016.pdf (accessed 25/06/18).

The following sources provide useful further reading:

Peacock, A. (2016) *Assessment for Learning without Limits.* Buckingham: Open University Press.

REFERENCES

Boon, S.I. (2016) Increasing the uptake of peer feedback in primary school writing: Findings from an action research enquiry. *Education 3–13*, 44(2): 212–25, DOI: 10.1080/03004279.2014.901984

Bourke, R. (2016) Liberating the learner through self-assessment. *Cambridge Journal of Education*, 46(1): 97–111. Available at: http://dx.doi.org/10.1080/0305764X.2015.1015963 (accessed 25/06/18).

CooperGibson Research (2018) *Exploring Teacher Workload: Qualitative research.* Research brief. London: DfE.

Department for Children, Schools and Families (DCSF) (2008) *Assessment for Learning: Strategies for self- and peer-assessment.* London: DCSF. Available at: http://nationalstrategies.standards.dcsf.gov.uk/node/64499 (accessed 25/06/18).

Elliott, V., Baird, J.A., Hopfenbeck, T.N., Ingram, J., Thompson, I., Usher, N., Zantout, M., Richardson, J. and Coleman, R. (2016) *A marked improvement? A review of the evidence on written marking.* London: Education Endowment Foundation. Available at: https://educationendowmentfoundation.org.uk/public/files/Publications/EEF_Marking_Review_April_2016.pdf (accessed 25/06/18).

Gibb, N. (2016) Teachers 'wasting time on marking in coloured pens'. BBC News. Available at: www.bbc.co.uk/news/education-37705385 (accessed 25/06/18).

McIntosh, J. (2015) *Final Report of the Commission on Assessment without Levels, September 2015.* London: Crown.

ASSESS

Identify the child's current stage of development and identify their next steps in learning.

PLAN

Plan strategies and intervention(s) to support the child to make further progress in the identified area of need.

DO

Implement the intervention(s) for a specific period.

REVIEW

Review the effectiveness of the intervention(s). Decide whether to continue the intervention(s) or whether to change the intervention(s).

17

WHAT CAN TEACHERS DO TO RAISE OUTCOMES FOR CHILDREN WITH SPECIAL EDUCATIONAL NEEDS AND DISABILITIES?

Jonathan Glazzard is Professor of Teacher Education, Leeds Beckett University. His research interests include inclusion, dyslexia, mental health, early reading development.

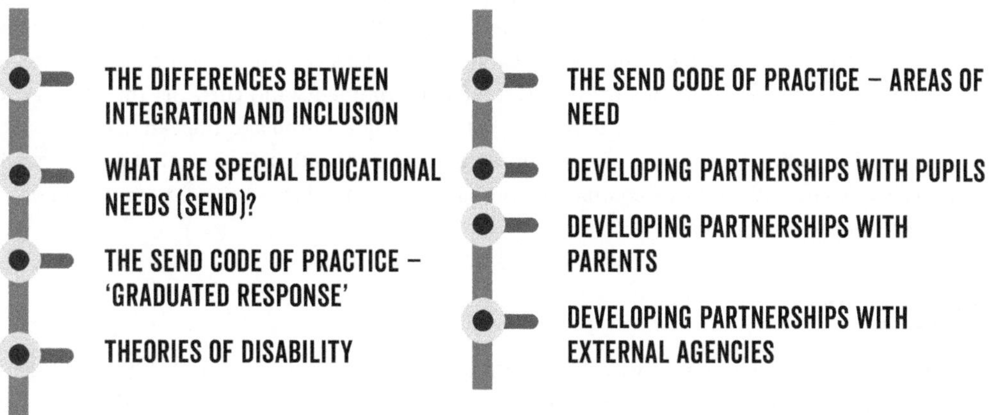

KEY WORDS

- Code of Practice
- Disability
- Inclusion
- Inclusive education
- Parent partnership
- Pupil partnership
- Special educational needs

INTRODUCTION

In this chapter we will explore the key principles of the Code of Practice for Special Educational Needs and abilities (DfE, 2015). We will begin by asking what is meant by inclusion, special educational needs and disability and we will go on to find out more about different categories of need. The chapter will end with advice to support you with writing an assignment on this topic.

WHAT ARE THE DIFFERENCES BETWEEN INTEGRATION AND INCLUSION?

THE INTEGRATION OF PUPILS WITH SPECIAL EDUCATIONAL NEEDS

The trend towards the integration of pupils with special educational needs and/or disabilities into mainstream schools arose out of increasing dissatisfaction with segregated educational provision (Black-Hawkins *et al.*, 2007). Integration as a policy drive emerged following the publication of the Warnock Report (DES, 1978), a seminal report that removed the term 'handicap' and replaced it with the term 'special educational needs'. Warnock recommended that, where possible, children with special educational needs should be integrated into mainstream schools and that those with the most severe needs could be financially supported through the introduction of local authority statements of special educational needs. These recommendations were legislated in the 1981 Education Act. During the 1980s and early 1990s, increasing numbers of children with special educational needs were integrated into mainstream schools. However, integration focused on assimilating children with diverse needs into mainstream educational environments and curricula that were generally not adapted to meet those needs. As a policy imperative, it was largely a 'dump and hope' model; it focused on children being 'present' within a mainstream educational environment rather than on the overall quality of their educational experience. Warnock's recommendations laid the foundations of the current system of special educational needs provision in England.

THE MOVE TO INCLUSION

During the mid-1990s, increasing interest was being given to the concept of inclusion. In 1994, the Salamanca Agreement (UNESCO, 1994) marked the introduction of a global commitment to inclusive education. Ninety-two governments and 25 international organisations agreed to adopt the guiding principle that all children, regardless of their physical, intellectual, social, emotional, linguistic or other conditions, should be educated in their local mainstream (or 'ordinary') school that would be attended if the child did not have a disability. The World Conference called upon all governments to 'adopt as a matter of law or policy the principle of inclusive education'. This required schools to be responsive to the diverse needs of their learners and to provide a continuum of support to match these needs. Thus, inclusion represented a proactive response on the part of schools to meet the needs of all learners, thus ensuring high-quality education.

CRITICAL QUESTION

What do you understand and believe to be the differences between integration and inclusion?

However, Avramidis *et al.* (2002: 158) have argued that inclusion 'is a bewildering concept which can have a variety of interpretations and applications'. Azzopardi (2009, 2010) has similarly argued that the term 'inclusive education' is little more than a cliché: 'a politically correct term that is used for speeches and policy-makers to silence all woes' (2009: 21). It is defined in various ways by different groups with different interests, leading to its exploitation (Sikes *et al.*, 2007). It has been argued that understandings of inclusion are not 'shared between, within and across individuals, groups ... and larger collectives' (Sikes *et al.*, 2007: 357). Parents of children with special educational needs might interpret inclusion to represent a sense of belonging and acceptance (Cole, 2005), while politicians and inspectors might focus on the capacity of schools to close the achievement gaps between those students with and without special educational needs.

CRITICAL QUESTION

Can inclusive education be offered in a special school?

EVALUATING INCLUSION

It has been argued that, as a concept, inclusion has continued to focus on notions of *assimilation* and *presence* rather than representing a struggle for equality and social justice (Hodkinson, 2012). Nearly three decades after the publication of the Warnock Report, Baroness Warnock argued that the quality of a child's educational experience was more important than the location in which it takes place (Warnock, 2005). It is deeply worrying that children with special educational needs and disabilities can experience exclusion despite being included in a mainstream environment. In these circumstances they remain a 'permanent outsider' (Warnock, 2005).

CRITICAL QUESTION

In what ways might learners with special educational needs and disabilities experience exclusion, despite being included in a mainstream school?

WHAT ARE SPECIAL EDUCATIONAL NEEDS (SEND)?

The SEND Code of Practice (DfE, 2015: 15–16) defines special educational needs in the following way:

> *A child or young person has SEN if they have a learning difficulty or disability which calls for special educational provision to be made for him or her. A child of compulsory school age or a young person has a learning difficulty or disability if he or she: has a significantly greater difficulty in learning than the majority of others of the same age, or has a disability which prevents or hinders him or her from making use of facilities of a kind generally provided for others of the same age in mainstream schools or mainstream post-16 institutions.*

Thus, it is important to remember that the term 'special educational needs' is wide-ranging and includes children who have a disability or special education need but also have high cognitive ability. These children require adaptations to enable them to achieve their full potential. The term 'special educational needs' is often used to describe children who are functioning with lower levels of cognition in comparison with their peers, but children operating across the full spectrum of ability may require special educational provision.

CRITICAL QUESTION

What are the advantages and disadvantages of labelling children as having special educational needs?

THE SEND CODE OF PRACTICE

The special educational needs and disability Code of Practice differs from previous versions of the Code. It covers the 0–25 age range and includes guidance relating to disabled children and young people as well as those with SEN.

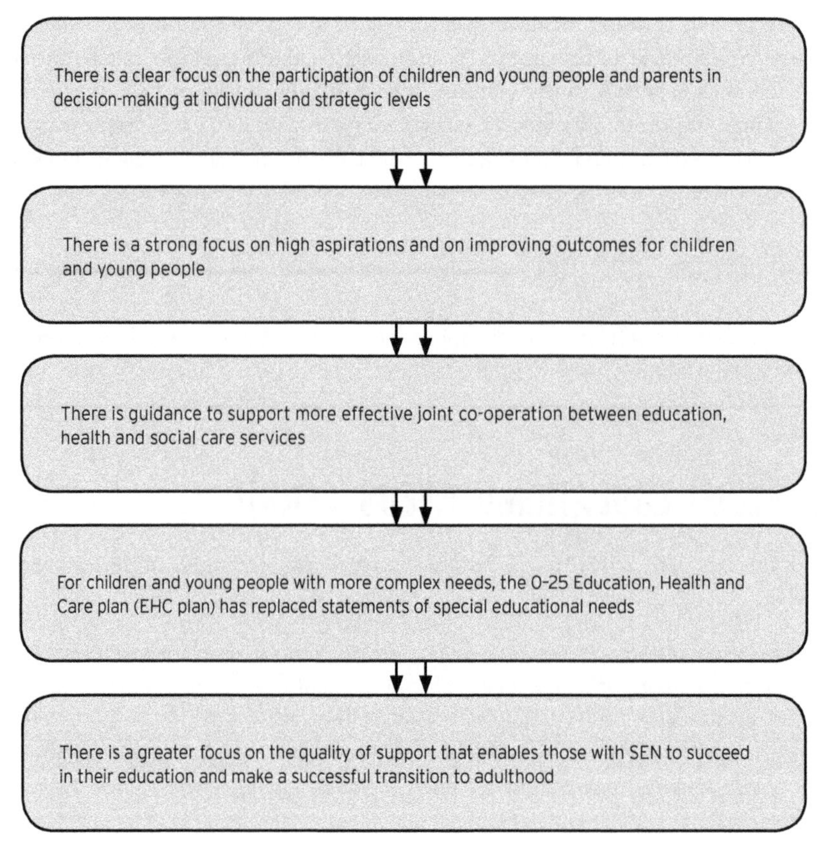

(DfE, 2015: 14)

While it is not appropriate to cover the full breadth of the Code of Practice in a chapter that is primarily targeted at student teachers, there are some key messages in the Code that are particularly relevant to students.

A BROAD AND BALANCED CURRICULUM

The Code emphasises that all pupils should have access to a broad and balanced curriculum. A child may have a specific learning difficulty in one aspect of the curriculum, but this should not prevent them from experiencing a sense of success in other curriculum areas. It is important that all pupils can experience a broad and rich curriculum so that they can explore where their talent lies. You should ensure that planned interventions in specific curriculum areas do not impede children's entitlement to a broad and balanced curriculum.

IDENTIFYING NEEDS AT THE EARLIEST POINT

The Code of Practice highlights the importance of identifying need at the earliest point. You should not wait for a formal diagnosis of special educational needs before you implement planned interventions. You should address areas of need through planned interventions as soon as you suspect that a child may have a special educational need and/or disability. If you have any concerns about a child, discuss these with the special educational needs coordinator and the child's parents to seek advice, but do not delay providing intervention. The first response should be high-quality teaching targeted at their areas of weakness. This will help to improve outcomes for the child. Regular assessments of all pupils will help you to identify pupils making less than expected progress given their age and individual circumstances.

QUALITY FIRST TEACHING

According to the Code of Practice, high-quality teaching, differentiated for individual pupils, is the first step in responding to pupils who have or may have SEN. Additional intervention and support cannot compensate for a lack of good quality teaching (DfE, 2015). Consistent high-quality teaching for all pupils will reduce the number of children who require special educational provision. Consistently poor-quality teaching can result in pupils not making expected progress and these pupils are sometimes incorrectly identified as having special educational needs.

Outcomes for children with special educational needs and disabilities compared to those without have been consistently low over several years. This includes academic attainment, access to further and higher education, access to employment and independent living. Low teacher expectations and lack of challenge in lessons result in poor outcomes. As a student teacher

IT IS YOUR RESPONSIBILITY TO ENSURE THAT ALL PUPILS MAKE PROGRESS

Your expectations, of children with special educational needs and disabilities should be high and the level of challenge you expose them to should equally be high. The practice of grouping students with SEND together can result in a culture of low expectations, which can in turn lead to poor outcomes. Flexible grouping systems, which are responsive to the needs of individual learners, are more effective. In addition, you should ensure that all learners can access higher level curriculum content in lessons. You should then consider what support specific pupils might need to enable them to master this content. For example, some pupils might be able to access higher level content if the task is broken down more into a series of smaller steps or if additional adult support is provided within lessons or in the form of a pre-teach prior to lessons. Some learners can access higher level content through peer tutoring or through high-quality feedback after each stage of a task.

THE USE OF TEACHING ASSISTANTS

Teachers are responsible and accountable for the progress and development of the pupils in their class, including where pupils access support from teaching assistants or specialist staff. The Code of Practice states that although teaching assistants are part of a package of support for a child, they must never replace the teacher. As a student teacher, you are therefore responsible for planning the child's learning and for monitoring their progress. You should also ensure that you teach the child so that you get to know them, establish a relationship and understand their next steps in learning.

AVOIDING ASSUMPTIONS

The Code of Practice emphasises that persistent disruptive or withdrawn behaviours do not necessarily indicate that a child or young person has SEN. In addition, slow progress and low attainment do not necessarily suggest that a child has SEN and should not automatically lead to a pupil being recorded as having SEN. Equally, it should not be assumed that attainment in line with chronological age means that there is no learning difficulty or disability.

CHILDREN WITH ENGLISH AS AN ADDITIONAL LANGUAGE

Identifying and assessing SEN for children or young people whose first language is not English requires careful consideration. Assessment should determine whether lack of progress is due to limitations in their command of English or if it arises from SEN or a disability. Difficulties related solely to limitations in English as an additional language are not SEN.

CRITICAL QUESTION

How might you balance your responsibilities for pupils with SEND against your responsibilities to all children?

CLASSROOM LINK

What does this mean for classroom practice?

As a teacher, you will need to consider how you might involve pupils with SEND more in decisions. You should involve pupils with SEND in setting their own goals and they should be involved in reviewing their own progress. Parents should also be involved in setting goals and reviewing their child's progress.

CRITICAL QUESTION

What strategies might you employ to develop partnerships with parents who are reluctant to engage with their child's education?

What strategies might you use to provide voice to pupils who lack the skill of verbal communication?

GRADUATED RESPONSE

The Code of Practice (DfE, 2015) provides a model for supporting pupils with SEND, which it refers to as the 'graduated response' to supporting a child's needs. This is a four-step response:

INFO 17.1

Assess: Identify the child's current stage of development and identify their next steps in learning.

Plan: Plan strategies and intervention(s) to support the child to make further progress in the identified area of need.

Do: Implement the intervention(s) for a specific period.

Review: Review the effectiveness of the intervention(s). Decide whether to continue the intervention(s) or whether to change the intervention(s).

The starting point for planning for all children should be a firm understanding of the child's current level of achievement followed by an understanding of what the next steps in development are. The objectives in the curriculum frameworks will be a useful source of reference. For those children operating below the level of the National Curriculum, teachers should plan to meet their needs through setting challenging but appropriate objectives, which support their development towards the National Curriculum standards in reading, writing and mathematics. Schools may also have their own progression frameworks that they require you to follow. Excellent teaching is teaching that is inclusive of the needs of all children. If you teach excellent lessons, you will be meeting the needs of children with special educational needs.

KEY THEORY

The Education Endowment Foundation on *Making the Best use of Teaching Assistants* (Sharples *et al.*, 2015, Webster and Blatchford, 2015).

The research drew on previous published research studies that examined the impact of teaching assistants on pupils. The research found that teaching assistants (TAs) tended to be more concerned with task completion, and less concerned with developing pupils' understanding. It also found that pupils who received the most support from TAs made less progress than similar pupils who received little or no support. The negative impact was most marked for pupils with the highest levels of special educational needs and/or disabilities (SEND). It was also found that deployment arrangements could result in a dependency effect. Children with SEND need the most skilled person working with them. Many interventions result in children spending less time with peers and therefore not developing socially, which all children need.

As a student and beginning teacher, you should consider carefully how to deploy additional adults to create maximum impact on children's learning.

THEORIES OF DISABILITY

MEDICAL MODEL

The medical model of disability 'conceptualizes difficulties in learning as arising from deficits in the neurological or psychological make-up of the child' (Skidmore, 2004: 2). In the medical model, the disability is located within an aspect of the child's biology which is impaired. The model emphasises the need to diagnose, treat and cure the disability. Until the 1980s, it was the dominant model that influenced the way people thought about disability. The model influenced the language of disability. Terms such as *syndrome*, *symptoms* and *disorder* are often associated with the medical model. It has been argued that biological perspectives on impairment and disability place insufficient emphasis on the wider environment, which influences one's ability to learn (Thomas and Loxley, 2001, 2007).

CRITICAL QUESTION

In what ways might the medical model of disability be evident in educational practices?

SOCIAL MODEL

The growth of disabled activism in the 1980s led to the development of the social model of disability (Barnes, 1991; Oliver, 1990). Unlike the medical model, the social model locates the problem of disability within society (Oliver, 1996). The model assumes that disability 'is an artificial and exclusionary social construction that penalises those people with impairments who do not conform to mainstream expectations of appearance, behaviour and/or economic performance' (Tregaskis, 2002: 457). Crucially, the model separates *impairment* from *disability*. Impairment is a biological construct within a person. However, the fundamental principle of the social model is that impairment does not need to become disabling. Disability is defined as access to goods and services. The assumption of the social model is that with the correct societal adaptations, people with impairments are still able to access goods and services. Examples of services include education, housing and employment. Adaptations can be physical (such as lifts or ramps), attitudinal or financial, but are not restricted to these categories.

CRITICAL QUESTION

What are the implications of the social model for educational practice?

AFFIRMATIVE MODEL

The affirmative model is essentially a non-tragic view of disability and impairment that encompasses positive social identities, both individual and collective, for disabled people grounded in the benefits of lifestyle and life experiences of being impaired and disabled (Swain *et al.*, 2013). While the model recognises disability as a social construct, it calls for a positive affirmation of disability so that people with disabilities are able to reclaim their disabled identities by proudly owning their disability and celebrating it. The model resists the use of 'within-person' interventions, which seek to eradicate disability from people's lives. It views disability as a positive and energising force that brings diversity into the world.

CRITICAL QUESTION

What are the implications of the affirmative model for educational practice?

BIO-PSYCHO-SOCIAL MODEL

The World Health Organization released the bio-psycho-social model for disability, the International Classification of Functioning, Disability and Health (ICF) (WHO, 2001), which aims to provide a holistic definition of health by essentially merging the medical and social models. The model recognises the complex interrelationships between biological and contextual factors that influence how disability is experienced by the individual. These are identified below:

> *Body functions and structures:* the body functions and structures of people; problems with the integrity of structures or their functions are termed impairments (functioning at the level of the body).
>
> *Activity:* the activities/tasks people undertake; difficulties undertaking those are termed activity limitations (functioning at the level of the individual).
>
> *Participation:* the participation/involvement of people in life situations; difficulties are termed participation restrictions (functioning of a person as a member of society).
>
> *Environmental factors:* the external factors (physical, social and attitudinal) which affect people's experiences (and whether these factors are facilitators or barriers).
>
> *Personal factors:* these are the internal factors which affect people's experiences (and whether these factors are facilitators or barriers).
>
> (WHO, 2001)

The model recognises that a breakdown/problem with any of the components can affect health experiences. For instance, an impairment of a body function may exist, but the impact of that is only seen when we consider how it affects an individual's ability to perform a task or participate in a life situation, and that the degree to which that participation is affected is moderated by contextual factors (personal and environmental) that act as barriers or facilitators.

CRITICAL QUESTION

What are the implications of the bio-psycho-social model for educational practice?

CLASSROOM LINK

What does this mean for classroom practice?

The medical model of disability focuses on 'expert' diagnosis and intervention/treatment. The role of the Educational Psychologist can be aligned with aspects of the medical model, especially in relation to carrying out assessments of need. The social model can be seen in practice through adaptations to the physical environment of schools (for example, the provision of ramps and lifts) so that students with physical disabilities can access education. Additionally, adaptations to the curriculum or the assessment processes are examples of the social model in action. Diversity events, which promote the celebration of diversity, are a good example of the affirmative model in action.

AREAS OF NEED

In the following sections we will explore the four categories of need that are identified in the SEND Code of Practice. We will explore the barriers to learning under each category of need and the strategies that you might use to raise outcomes for learners with specific needs. It is important to emphasise that some children have needs that cut across the various categories. For example, a student may have a mental health need that has a detrimental impact both on their ability to learn and their behaviour. In these cases, it is important to know what the primary need is so that this can be addressed, particularly in cases where the primary need is the root cause of other needs.

SUPPORTING PUPILS WITH COMMUNICATION AND INTERACTION NEEDS

Children with communication and interaction needs have varying needs and thus, their profile is varied. The difficulties may be specific to one area – i.e. speech, language or communication – or they may cut across all aspects. Some children may have difficulties with speech, including pronunciation and speech production difficulties (for example, those who stammer). Difficulties with language may relate to difficulties in not understanding words, word-finding difficulties or difficulties with sequencing grammatically correct units of language into phrases or sentences so that they make sense. Some children (for example, those with autistic spectrum conditions) may have well-developed vocabulary but may struggle to understand the rules of social communication (for example, when to take pauses in conversation, turn-taking in conversation, not jumping in, gesture). Some children with autistic spectrum conditions may have both language and communication difficulties.

Interventions for children with communication and interaction needs are dependent on the need itself – i.e. whether the need relates to speech, language, communication or a combination of these. They will benefit from being given clear instructions. It is more effective to provide one instruction at a time rather than multiple instructions. You will need to demonstrate patience towards children with speech difficulties by giving them time to plan their responses, not finishing sentences on their behalf and praising them regularly. Children with language difficulties may benefit from an explicit language intervention programme that teaches them vocabulary and how to sequence it. Children with communication difficulties may benefit from a structured communication intervention programme that teaches them the rules of communication. Many children with speech, language and communication difficulties benefit from a highly visual approach to teaching that includes the use of pictures, signs and symbols to aid communication. Written or pictorial instructions may also be helpful. Some schools use techniques such as Makaton, as a whole-school approach, where speech and language are a key barrier to learning.

What are the differences between speech, language and communication?

SUPPORTING PUPILS WITH COGNITION AND LEARNING NEEDS

Children with cognition and learning difficulties form a broad group, which includes those with moderate learning difficulties, those with specific learning difficulties (SpLD) such as dyslexia, dyscalculia and dyspraxia, and those with profound and multiple learning difficulties (PMLD). You will more likely come across children with moderate learning difficulties in mainstream classrooms. The range of difficulties in this group varies, but generally children in this group will be working below age-related expectations in one or more areas of the curriculum. These children will benefit greatly from lots of praise and additional support to enable them to complete learning challenges. This might take the form of additional adult support or additional resources or technological aids to help them complete tasks. Children with specific learning difficulties may need specific interventions that target the area of need. For example, children with dyslexia may benefit from a highly structured multisensory phonological intervention to support their reading development. They may also benefit from coloured overlays to lay over text or text printed on coloured backgrounds and additional scaffolding to complete tasks. Children with dyspraxia may benefit from a motor skills intervention programme. Children who fall into the category of PMLD tend to be taught in special schools due to the complex nature of their needs.

CRITICAL QUESTION

What factors might result in children developing cognition and learning needs?

SUPPORTING PUPILS WITH SOCIAL, EMOTIONAL AND MENTAL HEALTH NEEDS

Again, this is a broad group and includes children with attention deficit disorder, attention deficit hyperactive disorder or attachment disorder. These children may benefit from clear rules and expectations, and an individual reward and sanctions system. Behavioural problems can arise from issues such as low self-concept and self-esteem and, therefore, it is important that children can experience success in their education. It is your responsibility as a teacher to support them to recognise their strengths. Sanctions only address the consequences of behaviour, not the causes of it. If you seek to change behaviour, you need to understand what the underlying problem is and then try to address that. Some behaviour problems stem from problems at home, but others stem from children not forming positive relationships with teachers. It is, therefore, critical that you establish an effective, supportive and respectful relationship with the child and involve the child in goal setting. This is a solutions-focused approach to behaviour management.

INFO 17.2

It is estimated that one in ten children have a mental health need (DfE, 2017) and this is another broad group ranging from children who experience stress, anxiety and depression, to more serious conditions such as those who display eating disorders.

Useful resources to support your understanding of children's mental health are listed below:

www.cwmt.org.uk/

www.mentallyhealthyschools.org.uk/

www.annafreud.org/what-we-do/schools-in-mind/resources-for-schools/

KEY THEORY

Research suggests that excessive internet use can have a detrimental impact on children's mental health (OECD, 2016). The Office for National Statistics has also found an association between longer time spent on social media and mental health problems; 27 per cent of young people who engage with social networking sites for three or more hours per day experience symptoms of mental ill health compared to 12 per cent of children who spend no time on social networking sites (ONS, 2015). Research suggests that young people who are heavy users of social media are more likely to report poor mental health, including psychological distress (cited in RSPH, 2017).

CLASSROOM LINK

What does this mean for classroom practice?

According to Public Health England (2015: 14):

> *Involving students in decisions that impact on them can benefit their emotional health and wellbeing by helping them to feel part of the school and wider community and to have some control over their lives.*

Schools should ensure that children and young people have appropriate channels for expressing their views. They should be consulted about curriculum, learning and teaching, behaviour and assessment policies so that they are able to influence developments that may impact on their well-being.

CRITICAL QUESTION

To what extent is inappropriate behaviour simply a desire for children to communicate a need?

SUPPORTING PUPILS WITH SENSORY AND PHYSICAL NEEDS

Many children and young people with vision impairment (VI), hearing impairment (HI) or a multisensory impairment, (MSI) will require specialist external support. If you teach children with vision impairment you might need to provide enlarged versions of text and you may be required to use specific colours for text. It is important that they are seated in a place where they can see the teacher and maintaining a predictable, physical environment will help them to feel more secure. This will also benefit children with physical needs. Depending on the severity of the vision impairment, they might need support with moving around and they might require advance warnings – for example if they are turning a corner or going up or down steps. Children with hearing impairment will benefit from clear staged instructions, and sitting them closer to the teacher may be a useful strategy. They may use technological aids to support their hearing. Children with multisensory impairments, may have a combination of vision and hearing impairments and specialist advice may be needed to support them in their education.

How might you include children with sensory or physical needs in physical education lessons?

DEVELOPING PARTNERSHIPS WITH PUPILS

To support you in developing effective partnerships with children with special educational needs you should:

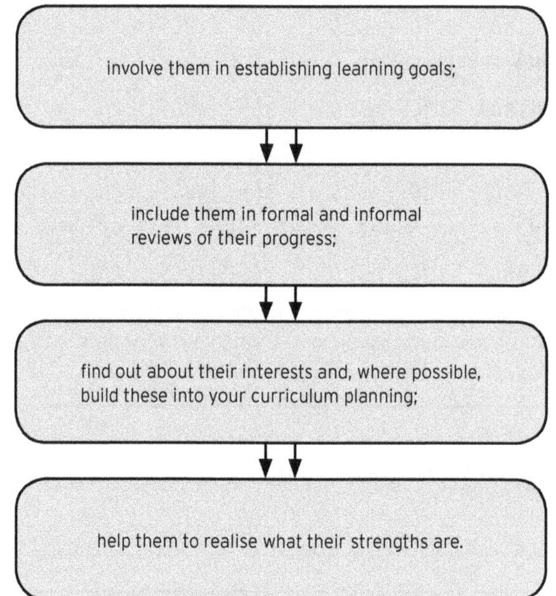

CRITICAL QUESTION

How have perspectives on children's voice changed over time?

Roger Hart's ladder of participation is a useful model for schools to progressively develop participation (Hart, 1997). The model is represented on a ladder, which moves from no participation (rung 1) to full participation (rung 8).

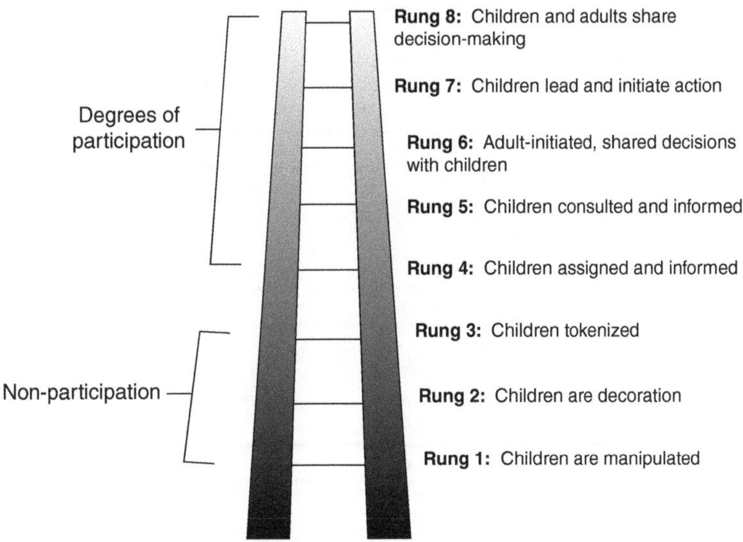

Adapted from Hart, R. (1992). Children's Participation: from Tokenism to Citizenship. Florence: UNICEF Innocenti Research Center.

Figure 17.1 Hart's ladder of participation

CLASSROOM LINK

What does this mean for classroom practice?

In the context of children with special educational needs, involving them in decisions about goal setting and giving them opportunities to identify what they want to learn would result in higher levels of participation. Involving them in negotiating a system for the management of their behaviour would demonstrate a more equal distribution of power than a teacher-imposed system.

DEVELOPING PARTNERSHIPS WITH PARENTS

To support you in developing effective partnerships with parents of children with special educational needs, you should:

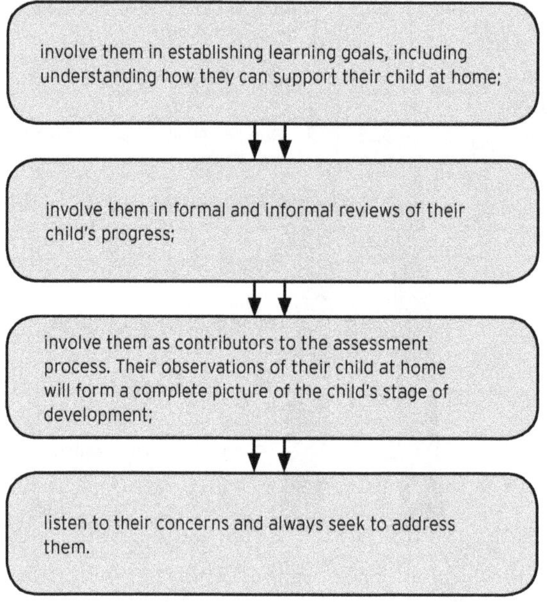

CRITICAL QUESTION

What are the advantages and disadvantages of identifying that a child has special educational needs from a parental perspective?

Parents, carers and the wider family play an important role in influencing children and young people's emotional health and well-being (Stewart-Brown, 2006; NICE, 2013). Thus, parents who form positive relationships and interactions with their child have a positive impact on the child's development.

CLASSROOM LINK

What does this mean for classroom practice?

Many children who have special educational needs also have parents who have special educational needs. Schools can introduce parent support workshops to support parents in developing positive relationships and interactions with their child. These workshops can focus on relationship building, behaviour management, the impact of internet use and social media on their child's mental health and healthy lifestyles.

DEVELOPING PARTNERSHIPS WITH EXTERNAL AGENCIES

Children with the most serious or prolonged needs may be supported by external agencies. These include but are not restricted to: educational psychologists; learning support teachers; child and adolescent mental health services (CAMHS); social care; speech and language therapists; physiotherapists and occupational therapists.

CRITICAL QUESTION

In some cases, multi-agency collaboration has not been effective. What factors might be responsible for this?

KEY THEORY

The concept of Communities of Practice was first proposed by Jean Lave and Etienne Wenger in their book *Situated Learning* (Lave and Wenger, 1991). In a respectful Community of Practice, through the process of sharing information, members learn from each other, and have an opportunity to develop professionally. (Lave and Wenger, 1991)

CLASSROOM LINK

What does this mean for classroom practice?

It is important to understand the roles of external colleagues who may be assigned to support children with special educational needs. Take the opportunity to talk to external professionals when they next visit your school to find out more about their roles and responsibilities.

CRITICAL QUESTION

To what extent might children with special educational needs become objects of surveillance and what are the likely effects of this?

CHAPTER SUMMARY

- Inclusion is a proactive response on the part of schools to meet the needs of all pupils.
- Schools must develop approaches that enable children with special educational needs and their parents to participate fully in all decisions.
- Schools must create a culture of high expectations for children with special educational needs. When expectations are high and there is a suitable level of challenge, children with special educational needs achieve better outcomes.
- Teachers must take responsibility for the education of children with special educational needs. They are accountable for their progress and must provide high-quality education to enable them to make progress.
- Teachers should plan to expose children with special educational needs to the same challenges that their peers are presented with and then consider what support they might need to meet these challenges.

ASSIGNMENTS

If you are writing an ITE assignment on special educational needs or inclusion, it will be useful for you to think through the following:

1. What are your interpretations of inclusion and how have these been shaped by your experiences and your reading?
2. What contributions can each of the models of disability make to educational practice?
3. How might commonly accepted practices in school (such as withdrawing children from classes for interventions or the use of behaviour plans) lead to exclusion rather than inclusion?

Useful texts to support you in writing an assignment are listed below:

Frederickson, N. and Cline, T. (2015) *Special Educational Needs, Inclusion and Diversity*. Buckingham: Open University Press.

Hodkinson, A. (2015) *Key Issues in Special Educational Needs and Inclusion*. London: SAGE.

This chapter has explored what is meant by the terms integration and inclusion. It has outlined the key aspects of the Code of Practice that you need to know as a student teacher. It has identified four categories of need and provided helpful suggestions for supporting these needs in the classroom.

The following sources provide useful further reading:

Glazzard, J., Stokoe, J., Hughes, A., Netherwood, A. and Neve, L. (2015) *Teaching and Supporting Children with Special Educational Needs and Disabilities in Primary Schools*. London: SAGE.

This book explores the key principles of the special educational needs and disabilities Code of Practice. It includes a full chapter on theories of disability. This will be particularly useful if you are completing an assignment on the models of disability and their application to educational practice.

Thomas, G. and Loxley, A. (2007) *Deconstructing Special Education and Constructing Inclusion*. Buckingham: Open University Press.

This book critically interrogates the concept of 'special educational needs' and contrasts this with inclusion. It will be useful if you are completing an assignment that requires you to demonstrate critical analysis of these terms.

REFERENCES

Avramidis, E., Bayliss, P. and Burden, R. (2002) Inclusion in action: An in-depth case study of an effective inclusive secondary school in the south-west of England. *International Journal of Inclusive Education*, 6(2): 143–63.

Azzopardi, A. (2009) *Reading Stories of Inclusion: Engaging with different perspectives towards an agenda for inclusion*. Saarbruken: VDM.

Azzopardi, A. (2010) *Making Sense of Inclusive Education: Where everyone belongs.* Saarbrucken: VDM.

Barnes, C. (1991) *Disabled People in Britain and Discrimination: A case for anti-discrimination legislation.* London: Hurst and Co.

Black-Hawkins, K., Florian, L., and Rouse, M. (2007) *Achievement and Inclusion in Schools.* London: Routledge.

Cole, B. (2005) Mission impossible? Special educational needs, inclusion and the re-conceptualization of the role of the SENCO in England and Wales. *European Journal of Special Needs Education*, 20(3): 287–307.

Department for Education (DfE) (2015) *Special Educational Needs and Disability Code of Practice: 0 to 25 years: Statutory guidance for organisations who work with and support children and young people with special educational needs and disabilities.* London: DfE.

Department for Education and Science (DES) (1978) Special Educational Needs: Report of the committee of enquiry into the education of handicapped children and young people (The Warnock Report). London: HMSO.

Hart, R. (1997) *Children's Participation: The theory and practice of involving young citizens in community development and environmental care.* New York: UNICEF and London: Earthscan.

Hodkinson, A. (2012) 'All present and correct?' Exclusionary inclusion within the English education system. *Disability and Society*, 27(5): 675–88.

Lave, J. and Wenger, E. (1991) *Situated Learning: Legitimate peripheral participation.* Cambridge: Cambridge University Press.

NICE (2013) *Social and Emotional Wellbeing for Children and Young People.* London: National Institute for Health and Care Excellence.

OECD (2016) PISA 2015 Results students' well-being, Volume 111. Available at: www.oecd.org/edu/pisa-2015-results-volume-iii9789264273856-en.htm (Accessed 25/06/18)

Office for National Statistics (ONS) (2015) Measuring national well-being: Insights into children's mental health and well-being. Available at: www.ons.gov.uk/peoplepopulationandcommunity/wellbeing/articles/measuring-nationalwellbeing/2015-10-20

Oliver, M. (1990) *The Politics of Disablement.* Basingstoke: Macmillan.

Oliver, M. (1996) *The social model in context in Understanding Disability.* London: Palgrave.

Public Health England (2015) Promoting children and young people's emotional health and wellbeing: A whole school and college approach. London: PHE.

Royal Society for Public Health (RSPH) (2017) #StatusOfMind Social media and young people's mental health and wellbeing. London: Royal Society for Public Health.

Sharples, J., Webster, R. and Blatchford, P. (2015) Making Best Use of Teaching Assistants Guidance Report. London: Education Endowment Foundation.

Sikes, P., Lawson, H. and Parker, M. (2007) Voices on: Teachers and teaching assistants talk about inclusion. *International Journal of Inclusive Education*, 11(3): 355–70.

Skidmore, D. (2004) *Inclusion: The dynamic of school development.* Open University Press: Maidenhead.

Stewart-Brown, S. (2006) What is the evidence on school health promotion in improving health or preventing disease and, specifically, what is the effectiveness of the health promoting schools approach? Copenhagen: WHO Regional Office for Europe.

Swain, J., French, S., Barnes, C. and Thomas, C. (2013) *Disabling Barriers – Enabling Environments.* SAGE: London.

Thomas, G. and Loxley, A. (2001) *Deconstructing Special Education and Constructing Inclusion.* Berkshire: Open University Press.

Thomas, G., and Loxley, A., (2007) *Deconstructing Special Education and Constructing Inclusion.* Berkshire: Open University Press.

Tregaskis, C. (2002) Social model theory: The story so far ... *Disability & Society,* 17(4): 457–70.

UNESCO (1994) The Salamanca statement and framework for action on special needs education. World Conference on Special Needs Education: Access and Quality. Available at: www.unesco.org/education/pdf/SALAMA_E.PDF (accessed 01/04/18).

Warnock, M. (2005) Special educational needs: A new look. *Impact,* 11. Salisbury: Philosophy of Education Society of Great Britain.

World Health Organization (2001) *Towards a Common Language for Functioning, Disability and Health.* Geneva: The International Classification of Functioning, Disability and Health. World Health Organization.

PART 3

DEVELOPING SKILLS FOR TEACHING

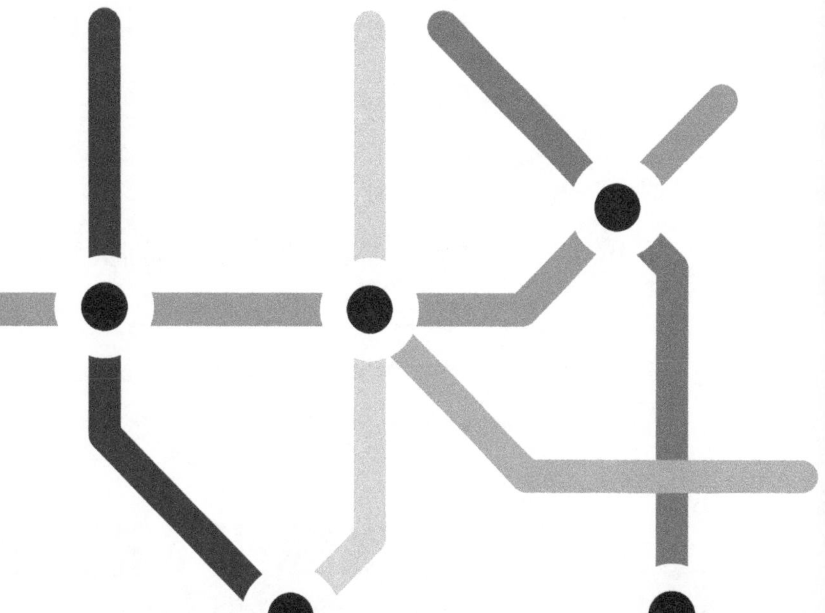

THE CHALLENGES FOR PLACEMENT

1 **YOU AREN'T AS GOOD AS YOU THOUGHT YOU'D BE**

New contexts will affect your practice

Learning doesn't happen in a straight line

Develop your resilience

2 **YOU CAN'T DO THINGS YOUR 'OWN WAY'**

Remember you are the learner in the school

Follow instructions with a questioning stance, keep an open mind

3 **YOUR MENTOR SEEMS TO BE TOO BUSY**

Mentors are teachers and teachers are busy

Your professional relationship with your mentor is important
Be mindful of this

IT'S OK; IT'S NOT MEANT TO BE EASY!

18

HOW CAN I WORK TO ENSURE A POSITIVE PRIMARY SCHOOL PLACEMENT?

Cara Broadhurst is Assistant Director of the BA Primary Education (QTS) at the University of Reading. She leads the placements and partnership provision for the programme and her research interests include mentoring and, as an English lecturer, the uses of home-school literacies.

KEY WORDS

- Feedback
- Identity
- Learning
- Mentor
- Practice
- Professional
- Reflection
- Resilience
- Tutor

INTRODUCTION

Whatever your training route, a considerable amount of time in the primary classroom will be an essential component. On some routes, this time will be called 'placement' whereas on other routes, where the majority of your time is spent in a school setting, it may have a different name. Within this chapter, placement is defined as any time in the primary classroom where you are assuming (or preparing to assume) some level of responsibility for the education of children. The terms 'mentor' and 'tutor' will be used. The former refers to the person in the school assigned to support and manage your growth as a teacher; that person may or may not be the actual class teacher you are working with. The latter refers to the link staff member from your ITE provider whose responsibilities might range from coordinating, visiting or assessing your placement. This chapter introduces the most significant ideas about how placements work and some matters that affect placement success, but for a more detailed insight, the further reading suggestions will be beneficial.

WHY AM I BEING SENT ON PLACEMENT?

I have a saying that I use with the students on my ITE programme: 'We don't send you on placement to get a good grade; we send you on placement to *learn*.' Of course we all know (students and tutors alike) that passing well is both pleasant and desirable, but it is not the core purpose of a placement experience. During your training sessions you will learn much in the way of useful knowledge and approaches, but practical application of these things is needed to support your development as a teacher. To use a lesson analogy, placement is the independent 'application' activity that follows a lesson input.

Burn *et al.* (2015) point to the value of experiential learning, explaining that participating in the process of educating children allows a student teacher to draw together knowledge gained from all sources so that it acquires newer and fuller meaning. This is called linking theory and practice, and it ensures new situational understandings which can lead to more nuanced practice. In their own research, Burn *et al.* (2015) found that 72 per cent of learning instances could be attributed to experience, although they are keen to point out that how much individual students reap from experience in school is highly dependent on their individual dispositions towards various aspects of their own learning (ibid.: 39).

It is also the case that placements are a valuable tool in helping you to find your own professional identity. You will work with many colleagues when in school, not just your mentor, and you will become aware of differing viewpoints, principles and approaches. It is a wonderful feeling to work alongside these people and realise that through listening and participating, you are developing your own distinctive and valid teacher characteristics.

WHAT APPROACHES MAKE PLACEMENT SUCCESSFUL?

BE PREPARED

In their opening chapter, Burn *et al.* (2015) offer a delightfully clear pen portrait of the ideal student teacher. This includes many qualities, but of particular note are the requirements that the student should show commitment, take responsibility for their journey and plan thoroughly. One of the best ways to do these things is to advance-prepare yourself and, although some of your preparation will be context-dependent, some main ideas are summed up in Figure 18.1.

Organise yourself	Do your research	Make a good impression
• Review the overall placement expectations • Make checklists • Use planners, etc. for deadlines • Download necessary paperwork in advance • Purchase stationery items that you might need	• Browse the school website/ policies • Read the most recent Ofsted report • Research what the school locality is like • Review school data on the DfE Performance Webpage • Use the above sources to deduce what priorities the school may have	• Contact the school to ask what they would like you to do on arrival • Do a test run of your journey • Dress smartly on your first day • Ask questions if you don't understand something that is explained to you • Show willing to be involved

Figure 18.1 Be prepared for placements

Think about the following:

- **Organise yourself:** these things may seem simple, but they can make a big difference. A mentor of a first-year student teacher that I once visited told me that she was frustrated that the student didn't always include elements in her lessons that had been agreed in planning meetings. It turned out that the student didn't use a notebook in meetings, because she didn't have one. It was no wonder that things were being missed.
- **Do your research:** having an understanding of what the school's main areas for improvement are shows that you are willing to be a team member and have already committed your time to your placement.
- **Make a good impression:** remember that you are doing more than meeting your mentor. How you do the things on the list above (see Figure 18.1) might be noticed by any staff member – for example, Robinson *et al.* (2015) note that if you telephone to make first contact, you will speak to the receptionist, who may convey their thoughts to the head teacher, and thus a good impression is vital.

BE PROFESSIONAL

CRITICAL QUESTION

What does it mean to 'be professional' in teaching?

For a detailed consideration of what this means, you will need to look back at Chapter 12, but as part of placement preparation, it is worth thinking about. The term will be used a lot during your training, but it is actually one of the hardest concepts to grasp hold of because the 'rules', such as they are, are often 'unspoken and not written down' (Glazzard, 2016: 306). Therefore, the starting point for you must be anywhere that such rules *are* written down. It is likely that your ITE provider will have a Partnership Agreement or Code of Conduct that is expected of all student teachers, so read that. Your school is likely to also have certain policies that relate to professional behaviours (e.g. dress, communications, social media), so ensure that you ask to see those too.

Professionalism, of course, extends beyond the tangible elements like punctuality and what to wear. Part of being a professional is learning to mirror the conduct around you, responding to different contexts and exercising judgement based on your increasingly accurate intuition. This is challenging but a good example, of it in action came from a student I knew who witnessed an incident with a child one afternoon where a teaching assistant seemed unhelpfully compliant to a child with additional needs. The Plowden Report of 1967 famously stated, 'At the heart of the educational process lies the child' (p. 7). While few would question that principle, the student was aware that the well-being of the teaching assistant was also at stake, alongside the mentor's overall accountability for the child. Recognising the need to preserve the teaching assistant's autonomy and also the school's ethos, the student opted to visit his tutor to discuss the matter and they devised a way he could communicate what was needed without compromising relationships. Professionalism is linked to the things you say and do, but most importantly it is about mindset. Thinking like a professional leads to behaving like a professional.

BE REFLECTIVE

Reflection can be seen as a process of appraising your practice as a teacher and delving down to analyse *why* certain things turned out the way they did. Its purpose is to recognise what needs to be jettisoned or retained in future practice – and the latter is important because there can sometimes be a tendency to focus on what needs changing, and you actually need to remember to repeat and build on the positive too.

Why is reflection important in teaching?

Being reflective is widely seen as one of the core attributes of a teacher, but why is this so? Day *et al.* (2006) note that teachers do not automatically become more effective over time – i.e. experience alone is not enough to ensure that a teacher develops. Experience must be intertwined with a cycle of reflection. There are multiple models of teacher reflection available, including Ghaye's (2010) four foci model, but one that I find particularly accessible is Brookfield's (2002) lenses of critical reflection (see Figure 18.2). This really highlights the role that different perspectives play in reflection and how, in addition to your own way of experiencing something, you need to be open-minded to your pupils' potential views; your colleagues' observations and impacts on them; and what insights and ideas literature or research can offer you.

Many have written about the need for reflection to happen *in* practice (during a lesson) as well as *on* practice (after a lesson), including Hayes (2015), but Hayes also continues to offer some additional pertinent advice.

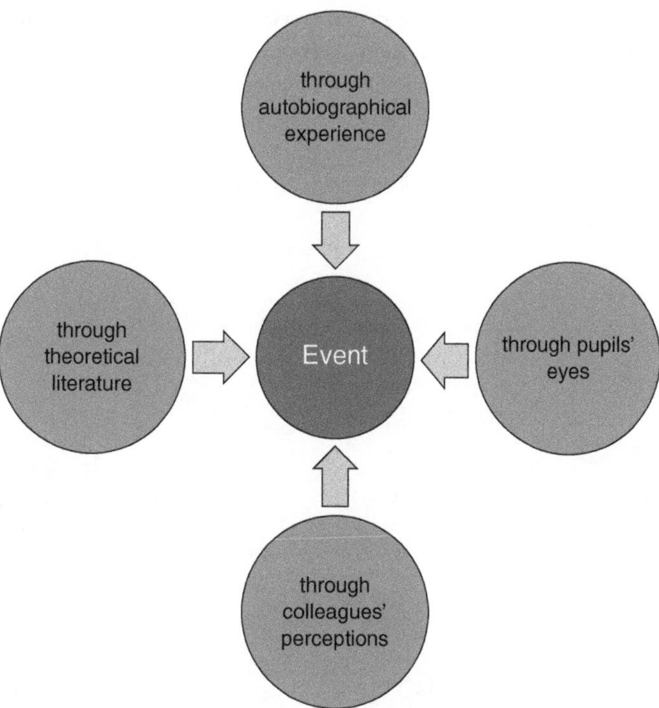

Figure 18.2 Brookfield's model of teacher reflection

He suggests that there are two key questions, the first about how well you acted as a teacher and the second about how well the children learned. It is a truism that all student teachers will start by tending to ask the first question, but you will show yourself to be a well-developed student if you can get into the habit of asking yourself the second question. In Figure 18.2 above there is no emphasis given to one lens more than any other, but if a slant was to be given, it is more responsible to show concern for what your pupils gained from your lesson – the impact it had on *them* – as your primary means of evaluation.

KEY READING

In his chapter 'Establishing your own teacher identity', Hayes explores the development of your teacher identity. This is a useful chapter for your training. It helps you to consider your own views of your teaching practice and of the role of the teacher.

Hayes's chapter can be found in Hansen, A. (ed.) (2015) *Primary Professional Studies*. London: Learning Matters, pp. 170–86.

Robinson *et al.* (2015) highlight the importance of not relying on others to reflect for you; their view is that you will develop more rapidly when *you* take responsibility for seeking out reflective angles. One way that you can try to do this is to explore the way that reflective conclusions can change, depending on what you set up as your success criteria. This is what makes reflection so interesting and is why you should try and truly see any reflective exercise or conversation with others as exploratory rather than judgemental. Figure 18.3 gives some examples of different criteria you might reflect against, but there are many more, and you can discuss how their importance can shift and be relative.

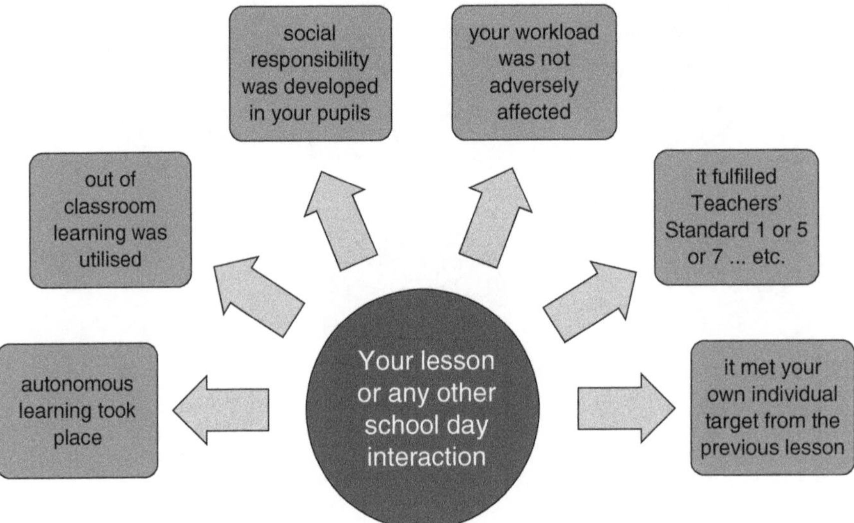

Figure 18.3 Criteria for reflection

RESPOND TO FEEDBACK

The Teachers' Standards (DfE, 2011) identify the need for teachers to take responsibility for improving their teaching and to respond to advice (Standard 8).

KEY READING

The Teachers' Standards (2011) are the framework by which you will be assessed for Qualified Teacher Status. The standards are included in full at the end of this book.

The acceptance of responsibility for developing your own teaching practice is what all mentors and tutors are looking for, as it goes hand in hand with reflection as the hallmark of a good teacher. Showing that you are *trying* in this regard is important.

After you have received feedback, it is important to be proactive in using it. You may be able to do this straight away, during the conversation, or it may be that you need some space to reflect, perhaps overnight. This is fine and in some ways may lead to richer ideas or plans. These are the sorts of things you should aim to do.

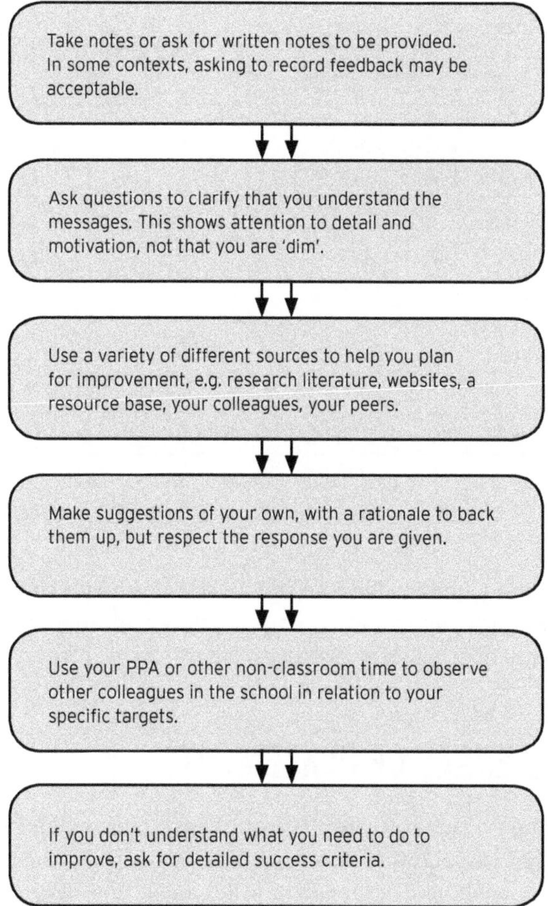

USE THE WHOLE SCHOOL AS A RESOURCE

You may have heard the proverb 'It takes a village to raise a child'. Well, it seems to me that it takes a school to train a teacher – i.e. to become a well-rounded and self-sufficient teacher, you will need advice and support from many staff members. Sometimes, this support will simply be practical in nature, i.e. when you need to find out about a particular policy or a particular set of resources, it will make sense to have a brief meeting with the relevant subject-leader or senior teacher. At other times, you will use your community of colleagues more for informal discussions to support your reflective journey, something that Lave and Wenger (1998) highly advocate. Whatever it is that you do, remember that reaching out and saying 'hello' and forming positive relationships with *everyone* in the school could be incredibly beneficial.

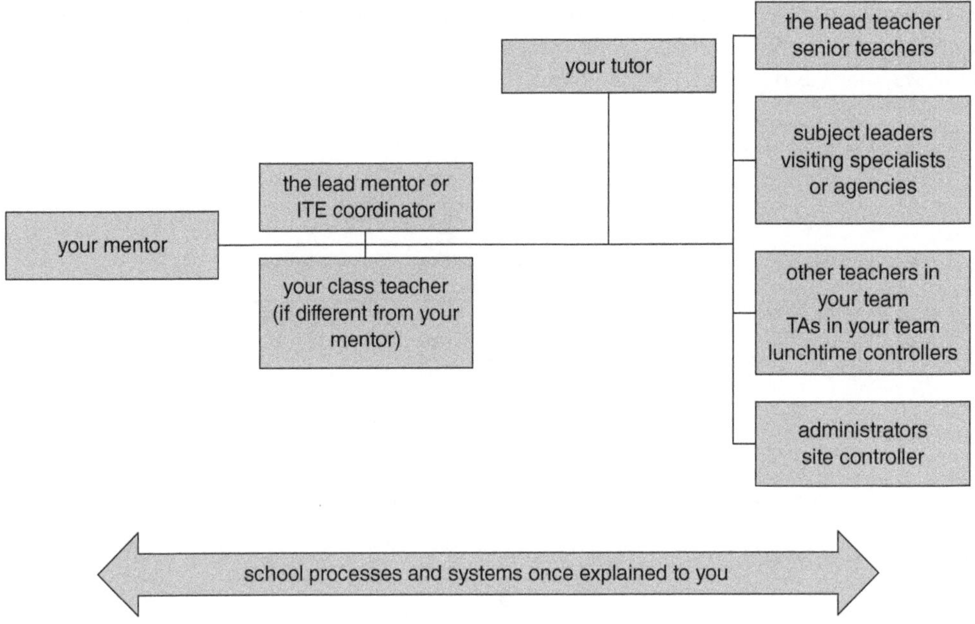

Figure 18.4 A model of possible sources of support

You will note that the model is underpinned by the various school systems that operate in your school. Use these and explore how they will help you: for example, it might be daunting to find out you have to plan for another year group teacher, but it may reduce workload overall when s/he plans something else in return.

WHAT ARE THE CHALLENGES OF PLACEMENT?

The challenges can be many and various; placement is about human interaction, after all. Gravells and Wallace (2012: 128) make the very insightful point that 'Any attempt to ensure perfection in an activity which relies on the way people behave when responding to each other's words and actions is doomed to failure'. They are not being discouraging when they write that, rather they are saying that it is important for students to recognise that, although positive groundwork can be laid, it's impossible to plan for human interactions and you must not expect one particular type of journey. The following sections discuss some challenges you might meet.

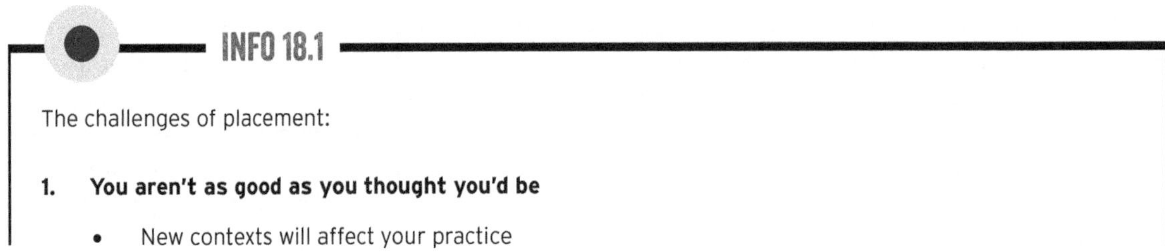

INFO 18.1

The challenges of placement:

1. **You aren't as good as you thought you'd be**
    - New contexts will affect your practice

- Learning doesn't happen in a straight line
- Develop your resilience

2. **You can't do things your 'own way'**
   - Remember you are the learner in the school
   - Follow instructions with a questioning stance, keep an open mind

3. **Your mentor seems to be too busy**
   - Mentors are teachers and teachers are busy
   - Your professional relationship with your mentor is important. Be mindful of this

It's ok, it's not meant to be easy!

YOU AREN'T AS GOOD AS YOU THOUGHT YOU'D BE OR WERE BEFORE

When this happens, it can be challenging or demoralising. It can affect confidence and also lead to frustration. I refer you back to the points made already under the heading 'respond to feedback' as practical starting points for recovering from a disappointing experience, but you may find these thoughts useful too:

- Context can be very influential in determining success. This means that obvious context shifts such as a new setting or new mentor can make a difference while you get used to new expectations and find out what is effective. Encountering difficulties at such times is normal. You will be building up a repertoire of teaching skills (a 'box of tricks'), but a key capability that only develops through time and practice is 'to understand when and how to deploy such capabilities' (Pollard, 2014: 444).
- Learning very rarely happens in linear fashion. For example, a toddler might begin to recognise what a dog is and because part of that recognition is that a dog has four legs, they may over-extend that idea and start shouting 'Dog!' when they next see a cow. Similarly, you might be pleased to notice that a behaviour management strategy has been very effective in your maths lesson and so you use it in your PE lesson – only to find it doesn't work at all. On the surface this may feel like you have 'slipped backwards' but in reality this is just an instance of the sideways nature of learning where progress was made but needs reassessing in a new context.
- Developing resilience to instances like this will be key to your development as a teacher. The overall message is don't dwell on mistakes and negative feedback. Learn from them, explain and apologise if necessary – and move on.

CRITICAL QUESTION

How much does resilience matter?

YOU CAN'T DO THINGS YOUR 'OWN WAY'

This can be frustrating because you will have been exposed to certain experiences and research that lead you to feel strongly that a particular approach is best (or sometimes, that an alternative approach is unproductive).

CRITICAL QUESTION

How much are student teachers in control of their achievements on placement?

Implementing the instructions of your school and the feedback from your mentor may clash with your ideas and lead you to feel discouraged or inclined to ignore advice. Think about the following things:

- The school has extended an offer to train you, which, in itself, is an act of openness but actually implies much more. The school has taken on the role of that which has experience and expertise to share and you are positioned first and foremost as a learner within their setting. That is not to say that mentors do not learn from their students – indeed, the best ones usually do – but what does it say about you as a learner if your actions imply that you have nothing further to learn from your setting?
- If you are set on doing things your way, are you being truly reflective? As identified above, reflection is about recognising other perspectives and every part of your practice can be examined in that light. For example, if you start a placement having read that 'house points' are unhelpful in supporting long-term behavioural changes but you have no experience of them in action, then you hold a *preconception*. Preconceptions are a very good place to start practising your reflective thinking on.
- It is the case that when you fit in with others' methods you could end up concluding that something is poor practice. In terms of your development, is this automatically a negative thing? Analysing the impact of others' practice should allow you to learn much that will help in the future, especially if your thinking can be coached, tempered or supplemented by an external source, e.g. a tutor or a literature source. Figure 18.5 suggests how the type of teacher we become is moulded by several ingredients (and these are just the ones that relate to your professional training)!

You are training yourself to become a reflective and enquiring teacher. Glazzard (2016: 29) goes so far as to say that utilising an educational approach because you have been instructed to do so is 'not sound educational practice' and, while this may be true, as a student teacher there will certainly be times when you *do* just have to follow instructions; you can do this as long as your thinking maintains a questioning stance.

YOUR MENTOR SEEMS TO BE TOO BUSY

Teachers are usually busy people and if your mentor has additional responsibilities within the school (such as deputy headship), she or he may be especially busy. If you begin to feel that your mentor is *too* busy to work with you properly, ask yourself these questions:

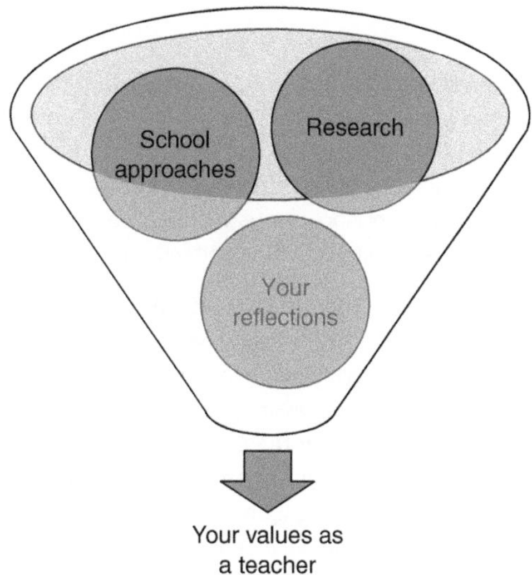

Figure 18.5 The ingredients of a teacher

- Are your expectations of your mentor reasonable?
- Is the busy-ness having an impact on your development and ability to meet expectations?
- Who else in the school could you draw on for support?

If answers to these questions don't help, then consider the options available to you. Talking directly to your mentor could be the best thing to do, but make sure you pre-arrange a slot when you can talk; people rarely respond well if they only have a moment to spare because they weren't expecting a conversation.

CRITICAL QUESTION

Why are positive relationships so important to placement success?

Being open and empathetic to how your mentor might see things will also be necessary, so use of diplomatic openers such as 'I know it's not intentional but...' will be necessary. If you are unable to raise the issue with your mentor, seek the support of your ITE provider or another staff member.

CASE STUDY

The following example of good practice exemplifies some of the messages in this chapter. The critical questions can be considered during and after reading.

(Continued)

(Continued)

Andrea settled well into her placement school. She built good relationships with all staff, offering to make cups of tea and, on one occasion, bringing in chocolates. It was noted that she worked hard. Her management of behaviour was often intuitive and initially her lesson pedagogy was thought to be sound. By the mid-point, concerns were raised over whether her lessons were having the required impact on learning. 'Teacher-talk' was extensive, teaching points were rarely rooted in context and learning experiences were transmissive. The tutor, mentor and a senior teacher all had input into feeding this back to Andrea and she admitted she felt upset and annoyed with herself.

An extra support programme began, which Andrea engaged with in many different ways. The programme included targets, which Andrea asked her mentor for examples of, so she had a clear idea of expectations. She also changed her approach in planning meetings, making sure that she asked for clarification of all terms used instead of assuming her question was just delaying everyone. Andrea felt able to visit the maths subject leader for advice on her maths provision and also the other teacher in the team for drama advice. In so doing, she discovered the maths leader had only qualified three years ago and they had an enlightening conversation about how he dealt with setbacks in training. She also changed her approach when observing her mentor, using her targets to really focus her attention on how those particular aspects varied across subjects.

Andrea showed steady progress, completing the placement at the expected standard. Her mentor praised the improvement, saying that Andrea was 'actually a really amazing colleague to work with', because she was so willing to collaborate and reflect. Looking back, Andrea said that once she knew her assessment was in doubt, she tried to really consider the impact of her lessons more, as she knew that was the perspective that would matter most to others.

HOW DO YOU EVALUATE YOUR PLACEMENT SUCCESS?

The following two questions should be part of your dialogue with yourself throughout placement:

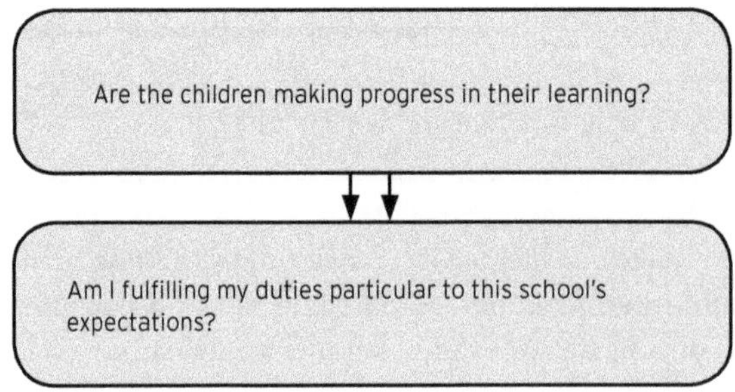

Doing these things successfully (always accounting for the stage of training) is likely to be non-negotiable when overall success is the goal. Additionally, as discussed earlier in the 'Reflection' section (see Figure 18.3), you can decide on a variety of other, more specific criteria to evaluate against. Indeed, the very nature of placement – the fact it involves frequent feedback and reflection – means that evaluation is fairly continual. This means that you should have continual awareness of how you are doing and, therefore, will have a voice in evaluations made about your practice.

The formal evaluations will relate to the Teachers' Standards and may involve you being graded. Your checking of the Teachers' Standards (or your provider's related statements) throughout placement will be an important tool in helping you review how successfully you are meeting them, but you should be aware that viewing them, particularly the 'part-standards', as a 'checklist' is unhelpful. Each Standard summarises a core attribute of a teacher, but there are many different ways to achieve these and so you should focus on deciding how you can meet/have met these broader summaries. Aim to show consistency in your practice, remembering that your evidence might link to multiple Standards.

CONCLUDING THOUGHTS

In order to conclude, it is necessary to go back to the beginning. At the start of this chapter I said that the purpose of placement is to ensure your learning. The subsequent sections have explored how complex this particular learning journey can be; indeed, the largest review of ITE in recent years, the Carter *Review of Initial Teacher Training* (2015: 21), states that 'the complexity of this process cannot be overestimated'. Bear this is mind at all times: when you meet a new approach; when the old approaches don't seem to be working; and when you're just not sure what to try. Nobody thinks what you're doing is easy – and that is one of the things that will make your sense of satisfaction stronger as you progress.

There are many other things, of course. Teachers derive satisfaction from all kinds of sources: interactions with the 'little humans' in their care; working with like-minded colleagues; and being able to make decisions that help others. I will leave the last word to an anonymous student of mine. The group, who had just completed final placement, were asked to write down the single most important thing they felt they had learned. One student wrote: 'Although you might sometimes be having a rubbish day, you might be positively impacting on someone else'.

CHAPTER SUMMARY

The importance of placement:

- It's all about your learning.
- A chance to put theory into practice.
- It helps shape your teacher identity.

What approaches make placement successful?

- **Being prepared**
    - Be organised.
    - Do research prior to starting.
    - Make a good impression.
- **Being professional**
    - Follow Codes of Conduct or policies.

(Continued)

(Continued)

- Learn to exercise judgement in context.

- **Being reflective**
  - A form of appraisal leading to improvement.
  - Reflection utilises many perspectives.
  - Reflection *on* practice and reflection *in* practice.
  - Take responsibility for it yourself.
- **Responding to feedback**
  - Be proactive.
  - Ask questions.
- **Using the whole school**
  - Seek advice from different staff members.
  - Invest in positive relationships with *all*.

What are the challenges of placement?

- **Not being as good as you thought**
  - New contexts will affect your practice.
  - Learning doesn't happen in a straight line.
  - Develop your resilience.
- **Not being able to do things your own way**
  - Remember you are the learner.
  - Follow instructions with a questioning stance.
- **Your mentor being too busy**
  - Ask yourself if you are being fair.
  - Plan a professional conversation about the issue.
- **Evaluating placement success**
  - Did children learn? Did you fulfil school expectations?

Remember what we said before: It's OK, it's not meant to be easy!

The rewards are far-reaching: you can make a difference.

ASSIGNMENTS

If you are writing an ITE assignment about your placement, there will be a number of very specific areas (covered elsewhere in this book) that you might be asked to focus on. However, it may be useful for you to think through the following general questions:

- Are there classroom approaches that have advantages and disadvantages? Can you think of any examples? How would you justify using or rejecting that approach?
- How has your placement contributed to your learning as a teacher? How can you evidence this? What other sources back up your current views?
- How far does the role of teacher expand? Why do you think this? Does policy support your thinking?

The following texts may be particularly useful if writing about and reflecting on placement:

Cremin, T. and Burnett, C. (2018) *Learning to Teach in the Primary School* (4th edn). London: Routledge.

This is a great general text for developing your understanding of the key skills and issues within primary practice.

Boyd, P., Hymer, B. and Lockney, K. (2015) *Learning Teaching: Becoming an inspirational teacher*. Northwich: Critical Publishing.

This text takes on the role of a 'critical friend' as it explores the dilemmas beginner teachers face in deciding how to make learning happen.

The following sources provide useful further reading:

Carroll, J. and Alexander, G.N. (2016) *The Teachers' Standards in Primary Schools: Understanding and evidencing effective practice*. London: SAGE.

This text is structured around The Teachers' Standards and offers advice on how to evidence your practice in each Standard.

From good to outstanding, in Robinson, C., Bingle, B. and Howard, C. (2015) *Your Primary School-based Experience*: A guide to outstanding placements (2nd edn). Northwich: Critical Publishing.

This chapter does what it says on the tin. It explores what 'outstanding' means and gives practical advice on how to elevate your practice to a consistently effective level.

REFERENCES

Brookfield, S.D. (2002) Using lenses of critically reflective teaching in the community college classroom. *New Directions for Community Colleges*, 118: 31–8.

Burn, K., Hagger, H. and Mutton, T. (2015) *Beginning Teachers' Learning: Making experience count.* Northwich: Critical Publishing.

Carter, A (2015) *Review of Initial Teacher Training.* London: DfE.

Day, C., Stobart, G., Sammons, P., Kington, A., Gu, Q., Smees, R. and Mujtaba, T. (2006) *Variations in Teachers' Work, Lives and Effectiveness.* Research Report 743. London: DfE.

DfE (2011) *Teacher's Standards.* Available at: www.gov.uk/government/publications/teachers-standards (accessed 05/07/18).

Ghaye, T. (2010) *Teaching and Learning through Reflective Practice.* London: Routledge.

Glazzard, J. (2016) *Learning to be a Primary Teacher.* Northwich: Critical Publishing.

Gravells, J. and Wallace, S. (2012). *Dial M for Mentor. Critical reflections on mentoring for coaches, educators and trainers.* Northwich: Critical Publishing.

Hayes, D. (2015) Establishing your own teacher identity, in Hansen, A. (ed.) *Primary Professional Studies.* London: Learning Matters, pp. 170–86.

Lave, J. and Wenger, E. (1998) *Communities of Practice: Learning, meaning, and identity.* Cambridge: Cambridge University Press.

The Plowden Report (1967) *Children and their Primary Schools.* London: Her Majesty's Stationery Office. Available at: www.educationengland.org.uk/documents/plowden/plowden1967-1.html#02 (accessed 05/07/18).

Pollard, A. (2014) *Reflective Teaching in Schools* (4th edn). London: Bloomsbury.

Robinson, C., Bingle, B. and Howard, C. (2015) *Your Primary School-based Experience: A guide to outstanding placements* (2nd edn). Northwich: Critical Publishing.

19

THINKING OUTSIDE THE BOX: HOW CAN YOU MAXIMISE THE POTENTIAL OF THE LEARNING AND TEACHING ENVIRONMENT?

Genea Alexander is a Senior Lecturer in Primary Education at the University of Worcester. Her research interests include learning and teaching, and arts and languages education.

Julie Sutton is a Senior Lecturer in Primary Education at the University of Worcester. Her research interests include music, pedagogy and professional practice, and teaching the primary foundation subjects.

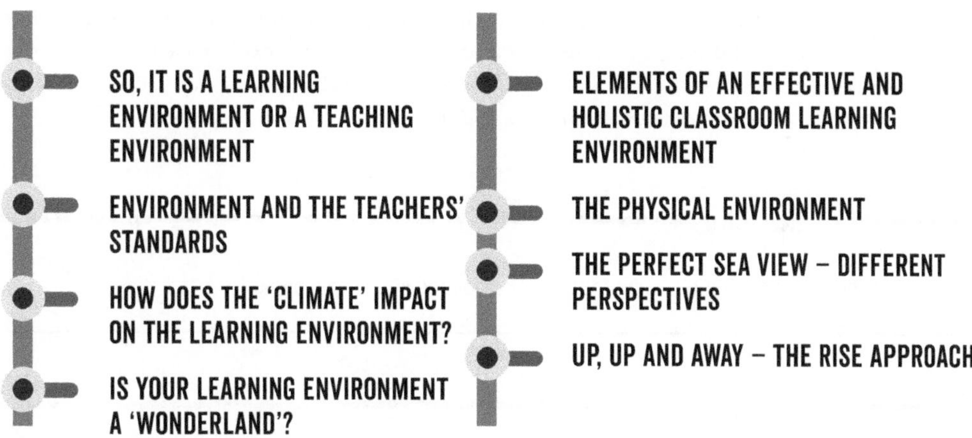

KEY WORDS

- Challenge
- Collaborative
- Enabling
- Engaging
- Environment
- Flexible
- Holistic
- Impact
- Inside
- Inspire
- Learning
- Management
- Motivate
- Outside
- Safe

SO, IS IT A LEARNING ENVIRONMENT OR A TEACHING ENVIRONMENT?

> *"Contrariwise," continued Tweedledee, if it was so, it might be; and if it were so, it would be; but as it isn't, it ain't. That's logic.*
>
> (Carroll, 1865)

It's all a question of perspective. When imagining the environment in which you will teach, it seems illogical to separate it from the environment in which children learn, thrive and progress. The Teachers' Standards (DfE, 2013) state that a teacher must: 'Set high expectations which inspire, motivate and challenge pupils: establish a safe and stimulating environment for pupils, rooted in mutual respect.'

As a teacher, you must consider the environment from both a *learning* and *teaching* perspective; that is, having high expectations, maximising the potential for it to be safe, inspiring, motivating and challenging for all, with mutual respect at the heart and an excellent and suitable resource to facilitate effective teaching and learning. While we recognise that there are dual perspectives, we choose to refer to the *learning environment*, as this truly captures the essence of what we, as teachers, are seeking to achieve – we are an integral part of the environment in which learning takes place. In this chapter, we adopt the perspective of the creation of a holistic learning environment (Barrett et al., 2017), as an intrinsic component of effective learning environment design, conducive to learning and progress. Building on learning theory, we explore each aspect, providing a rationale and practice examples in order to support you in maximising the potential of your learning environment, wherever it may be and encourage you to *think outside the box*.

KEY READING

The Teachers' Standards (DfE, 2013) can be found in the appendices of this book.

CRITICAL QUESTION

What is a holistic learning environment?

In the context of an effective learning environment, we define *holistic* as consideration of the elements that constitute the whole. Rather than an independent element, it is an *ethos,* which we believe is vital when considering the impact of a responsive learning environment and is embedded in our approach.

Miller (2000) asserts that holistic education is based on the premise that each person finds identity, meaning, and purpose in life through connections to the community, to the natural world and to spiritual values such as compassion and peace. On experiential learning theory, Kolb and Kolb (2011) state that learning is a holistic process of adaptation. It is not just the result of cognition but involves the integrated functioning of the total person – thinking, feeling, perceiving and behaving.

BUT, ENVIRONMENT IS ONLY MENTIONED ONCE IN THE TEACHERS' STANDARDS ISN'T IT?

Establishing a safe and stimulating environment for children permeates a range of Teachers' Standards and we would argue features in all of them in one way or another. This provides opportunities for teachers to ensure that they are creating an effective learning environment and maximising the potential for it to be used effectively in its widest, most holistic sense.

CRITICAL QUESTION

Review the Teachers' Standards (DfE, 2013). Identify those Teachers' Standards in which the learning and teaching environment plays a significant part of excellent professional practice. **Critically reflect**: What impact will this have on your future practice?

Creating a holistic learning environment entails providing the tools that are essential for every child to 'grow'. As teachers, it is important that we maximise every opportunity for children to actively take part in the learning process. We need to construct an environment whereby children can develop skills of independence and resilience; where they become resourceful, adaptable and flexible utilising creative and imaginative processes to overcome problems and move forward on their learning journey.

A constructivist classroom (Paige *et al.*, 2017) is an enabling one. Children experience hands-on activities, they question, discuss and think critically, making informed links with prior learning to construct new knowledge. It is learner-centred, with children working together to overcome problems, share and discuss. In such an environment, the teacher's role is that of facilitator, interacting with children to support, challenge, question and so provide opportunities to further deepen knowledge and understanding.

The cognitivist, Piaget (in Keenan et al., 2016) believed that children were actively involved in finding out about the world around them through exploration and discovery. His theory of cognitive development focused on the child as `self' and how, through trial and error, they construct new knowledge about their surroundings, which can then be applied in a similar situation.

However, this world of discovery through the eyes of the child as 'self' has been criticised by social constructivists for not acknowledging the importance of others in the acquisition of new knowledge. Vygotsky and Bruner (in Paige et al., 2017) both believed that new information was learnt through social interactions and by working interactively with 'a more experienced other', children were able to develop and progress.

If we are to follow the principle of constructivism where children are actively engaged in the construction of their learning, it is therefore important that we, as teachers, provide an environment that allows this to happen.

However, it is important for the teacher to recognise that a conducive learning environment extends far beyond what you can see. It is not just about the immediate environment; how the furniture is arranged in a classroom, the displays on the wall or how the resources are organised – it is so much more. A vibrant learning environment encompasses the physical environment of the *whole school*, together with its ethos and values.

Eaude (2008) believes a conducive learning environment is one that incorporates the formal, informal and hidden curriculum; what we can and cannot see. This brings us back to developing a 'holistic' environment as described earlier. It is important that the 'climate' within an environment is agreeable to all; it needs to be inviting and enabling, safe, supportive and nurturing with a shared ethos permeating throughout.

SO, HOW DOES THIS IMPACT ON THE LEARNING ENVIRONMENT?

When describing a school environment, you might choose words such as 'vibrant', 'calm', 'orderly', 'engaging', 'busy', having a 'buzz' ... all these words describe the atmosphere; what we feel (Eaude, 2008). If this is how we remember an environment, then surely great emphasis must be placed on getting it right for the children in our care?

The role of the teacher is significant in creating this ethos. All schools have shared values, but it is initially the teacher who establishes the ethos. Teachers need to be creative, engaging and enthusiastic if they are to have creative, enthusiastic and engaging children (NACCCE, 1999). You might have a new, bright, spacious, colourful space which is well resourced, but the atmosphere within it could be sedentary. Conversely, you might be in an old, tired, cramped space, but have a stimulating, inspiring learning environment. We will return to this later in the chapter.

> *Then she began looking about, and noticed that what could be seen from the old room was quite common and uninteresting, but that all the rest was as different as possible.*
>
> (Carroll, 1865)

A learning environment can be anywhere in which learning is taking place. Figure19.1 presents our vision of the learning environment.

All aspects of the learning environment have the potential to impact on the child and enhance or inhibit learning.

IS YOUR LEARNING ENVIRONMENT A 'WONDERLAND'?

> *Why, sometimes I've believed as many as six impossible things before breakfast.*
>
> (Carroll, 1865)

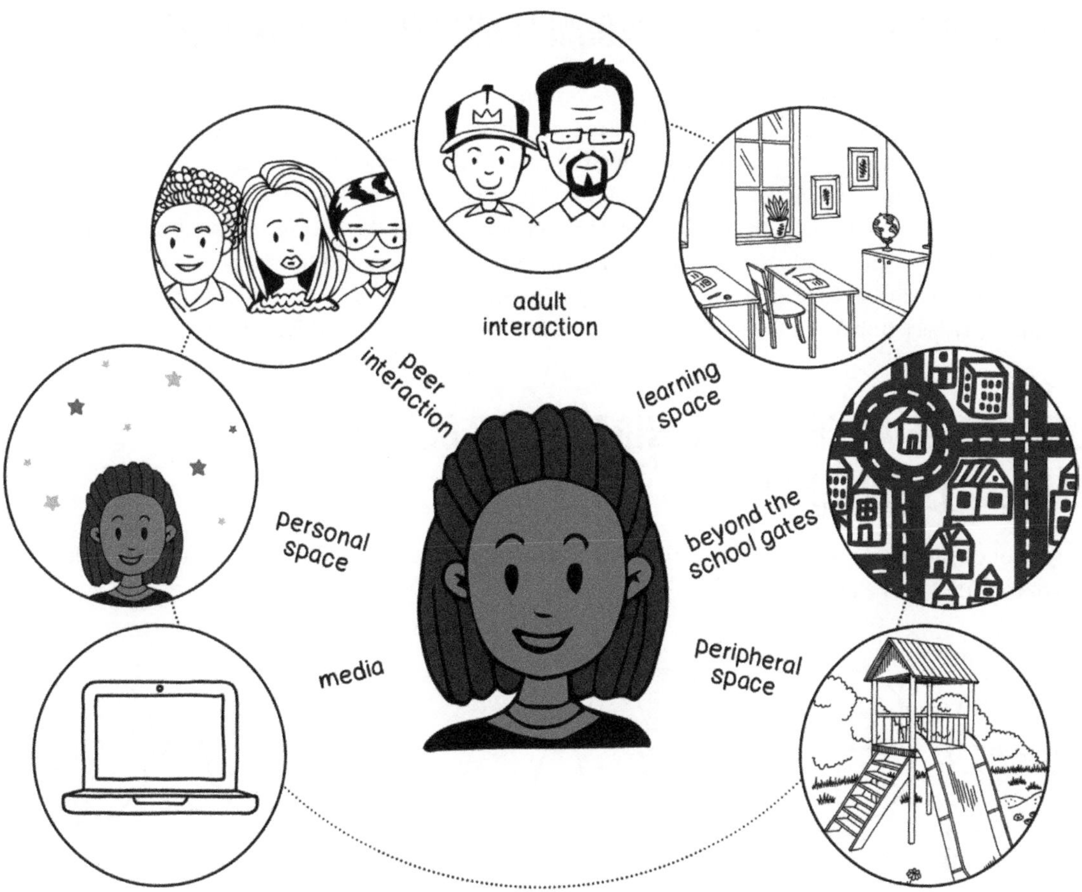

Figure 19.1 Vision of the interconnecting components of a learning environment

Figure 19.1 presents our vision of the interconnecting components of a learning environment. These components all have the potential to impact on the child and either enhance or inhibit learning. When working in harmony, a conducive learning environment is created.

Miller (2000) proposes that holistic education nurtures a sense of wonder. The learning environment is not an inanimate object. It is a myriad of fluid components which engage all of the senses; relates to personal preference and perception; a muse which sparks creativity and learning and includes non-visible aspects that are omnipresent; an invisible cloak of radiant colours to protect, nurture and motivate.

We assert that learning environments should be magical places, powerful places, places where children find themselves and it is teachers and children who are the architects of this potential 'wonderland'.

AN EXPLORATION OF THE CLASSROOM LEARNING ENVIRONMENT

In a report entitled *A Place to Learn: Lessons from Research on Learning Environments* (UNESCO, 2012) it was stated that, over the past decade, educational researchers have gravitated towards conceptualising the learning environment as an integrated whole that consists of closely interconnected elements that can be studied in multiple ways; that each individual learning environment is made up of a complex web of interacting factors and that the role of positive learning environments in promoting both the overall wellbeing and achievement of learners has drawn increased attention from researchers, policy-makers and international organisations concerned with the quality of education (UNESCO, 2012). The environment is a powerful driver; as it sets the tone and is the visual backdrop for all the learning that is undertaken in the class (Rutherford, 2016).

ELEMENTS OF AN EFFECTIVE AND HOLISTIC CLASSROOM LEARNING ENVIRONMENT

The type of classroom climate generally considered to best facilitate children's learning is one that is described by Kyriacou (1991) as being:

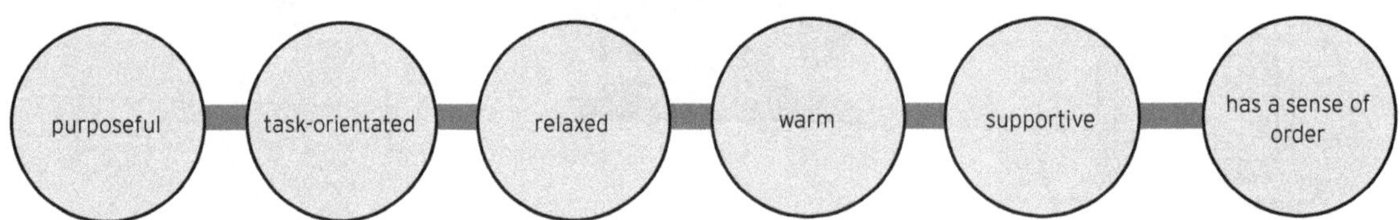

While a learning environment will be shaped by a teacher's personal educational philosophy (Ashbridge and Josephidou, 2018), as we have identified, there are a wide range of factors to consider that can be supportive in helping you to create 'An Aladdin's cave of learning' (Beadle, 2010).

A teacher's educational philosophy is an important consideration when designing an effective learning environment and moves beyond the physical constraints a teacher may face. Castle and Buckler (2018) argue that there is no best layout and that classroom layout is an ingredient in the way that a teacher wishes to interact with his or her environment.

Carroll and Alexander (2016) describe a positive classroom ethos as being key to success. Kyriacou (1991) considers the skills involved in setting up a positive classroom climate and suggests that the climate largely derives from the values that are implicit and pervade the lesson. Classrooms are inherently social spaces in which pupils can learn and thrive as individuals. On social learning theory, Thompson and Wolstencroft (2018) argue that this theory can be extended to the classroom and as a result show how the learning environment will affect how we think and what we think about. This has significant implications for our design of learning spaces and ways in which we encourage our pupils to interact with them. Kelly (in Cremin and Burnett, 2018) proposes that before engaging in social learning approaches, a number of ground rules need to be established with children. This collaboration with pupils and encouragement of pupil independence and freedom to explore for themselves all that the learning environment has to offer, has the potential to impact positively on learning. Kelly (in Cremin and Burnett, 2018) accurately depicts such independent and self-directed learners as *autonomous*.

Thompson and Wolstencroft (2018) state that effective classroom management is key to a successful lesson – putting in place all of the elements means that you can focus on the lesson and not have to worry about the behaviour of the students. Later in this chapter, we propose that there are five key elements (see Figure 19.2) that should be considered when planning for an effective, holistic learning environment.

As a teacher, you have the opportunity to become an artist. Your classroom could be described as a blank canvas and much like the artist's palette and brushes, you require certain tools in order to ensure that you have provided maximum opportunity for the learning environment to be inspiring and impact on learners who, in an environment which supports a collaborative ethos, can become contributing artists. Alongside the children feeling comfortable with each other and confident in their abilities it is important that there is an atmosphere that will help promote creative thought (Desailly, 2015). As such, moving beyond the minimum expectations as outlined in the Teachers' Standards (DfE, 2013), we believe that the learning environment should be non-threatening and embrace creativity.

THE PHYSICAL ENVIRONMENT

'The Physical Environment has a significant influence on learning. It gives children clear messages about how we value them and how we value learning' (DfES, 2004).

Furthermore, Rutherford (2016) believes that 'attention to the environment is the foundation block for establishing a clear learning culture that everything else builds upon'.

CRITICAL QUESTION

Consider different learning environments with which you have engaged. What might be the advantages and disadvantages of each in relation to potential impact on different learners?

It is important that teachers shape the physical environment to match learning intentions and so make learning purposeful. It should be, therefore, an integral part of our planning which is flexible enough to meet the needs of all learners. This highlights an interesting question about the layout of the classroom. Do classrooms remain static or are they adapted regularly? Given that the physical environment is so integral to the learning process, surely part of our planning should give due consideration to the design of the physical space? The positive impact of changing the physical appearance of a learning environment to reflect the learning intentions can be quite dramatic. You might like to consider this when planning future lessons in the classroom.

For full discussion of learning outside the classroom, see Chapter 23.

THE PERFECT SEA VIEW ON A GLORIOUS SUMMER'S DAY

Does that sound appealing? What imagery do you picture? Now consider it from the perspective of the child. Would the view be the same? Again, it's a question of perspective. *Thinking outside the box* means being confident enough in your own abilities as a teacher and in the pupils with whom you work, in order to ensure that the learning environment status quo is flexible. Relationships are key, as the classroom is far more than one interpretation of 'the box', it is a place where emotional and social, as well as physical, influences how we act, encouraging or discouraging particular ways of acting or thinking (Eaude, 2012). As Rutherford (2016) captures: *Why is it that the sea view rooms in hotels can command a premium price if environment has no impact?* That said, the learning environment is a complex and ever-changing place (Ashbridge and Josephidou, 2014).

As a teacher, you are responsible for establishing a positive *classroom climate* – a glorious summer's day. Classroom climate can be defined as the mood or atmosphere created by teachers in their classrooms, the way teachers interact with pupils, and the way the physical environment is set out (Muijis and Reynolds, 2018) and it can be argued that these crucial considerations both have the potential to facilitate learning (Kyriacou, 1991) and a major positive influence on behaviour, if set out carefully (Adams, 2011). The quality of these interactions depends not only on how well the environmental elements support learning, but also on the skill of the teacher in motivating, managing, building self-efficacy and scaffolding the learning sequences (UNESCO, 2012).

How you organise your classroom says a great deal about how you view your children's learning (Kelly, in Cremin and Arthur, 2014) and shows that pupils and their learning are of immense importance (Kyriacou, 1991). As such, it is essential to consider it from all perspectives.

OUTSIDE THE BOX: AN EXPLORATION OF THE LEARNING ENVIRONMENT BEYOND THE CLASSROOM

Key Source: The Council for Learning Outside the Classroom: www.lotc.org.uk/

Engaging learners beyond the classroom can mean maximising the potential for outdoor learning opportunities or off site learning. Catling (in Cremin and Arthur, 2014) reminds us, however, that if you plan to undertake fieldwork or study off site, you must make a *reconnaissance* visit to the location first and goes on to suggest that there are two prime reasons for doing this. One is to check for any risk factors associated with the site. The other is to identify and review the potential for and opportunities at, the site.

Pickering (2018) identifies that, when deciding which learning space is best, you must consider the learning outcomes and describes this as all that you wish the children to gain academically, socially and in terms of developing further skills for learning, can best be served by activities outside or inside. Catling (in Cremin and Arthur, 2014) suggests that, with all activities, this is about what you want the children to learn and why using the school grounds or going off site will enhance and extend the children's learning. Pickering (2018) asks us to consider how a lesson outside would contribute to more than just the lesson itself, but as part of a whole programme of holistic education. He goes on to state that learning outside can help with a child's holistic development, aiding cognitive development, health and wellbeing, their learning skills such as problem solving and teamwork and their personal development, through providing the means to work with motivating lesson activities.

These are important considerations when designing learning opportunities and should be embedded in the planning process. Know your children, identify their needs, what motivates them and those things that will enhance a personalised learning experience for them. Ask yourself: how can learning beyond the classroom contribute to this?

Pickering (2018) states that the values of learning and teaching outdoors operate on a number of levels, identifying the following areas as crucial components: cognition, health and wellbeing, motivation and aspiration, responsibility and independence and finally, collaboration and communication. In a report by Ofsted (2008), findings indicated that when planned and implemented well, learning outside the classroom contributed significantly to raising standards and improving pupils' personal, social and emotional development (Available at: www.lotc.org.uk/wp-content/uploads/2010/12/Ofsted-Report-Oct-2008.pdf - Accessed 26/04/18).

The Council for Learning Outside the Classroom (Available at: www.lotc.org.uk/ - Accessed 26/04/18) identify that learning outside the classroom is about raising young people's achievement through an organised, powerful approach to learning, in which direct experience is of prime importance and that real-world learning brings the benefits of formal and informal education together and reinforces what good educationalists have always known: that the most meaningful learning occurs through acquiring knowledge and skills through real-life, practical or hands-on activities (Available at: www.lotc.org.uk/ - Accessed 26/04/18). Forest Schools in particular have grown in popularity and a study centred on the impacts of long term Forest School programmes on children's resilience, confidence and wellbeing (Blackwell, 2015) stated that Forest School programmes are child centred and are deliberately designed to promote the holistic development of the child. The research showed that long-term Forest School programmes have a positive impact on children's resilience, confidence and wellbeing (Available at: https://getchildrenoutdoors.files.wordpress.com/2015/06/impacts-of-long-term-forest-schools-programmes-on-childrens-resilience-confidence-and-wellbeing.pdf- Accessed 26/04/18). Returning to Pickering (2018), this has the potential to impact positively on the holistic development of the child.

Knight (in Pickering, 2017) proposes that Forest School provides space and time for participants to explore both their spirituality and their creativity through nature, connecting with their inner selves through connecting with the outer wilder world and Pickering (2017) argues that the key to creative teaching outdoors is for us to be able to provide the opportunities for the children to develop critical thinking and purposeful learning outdoors and then to enable and encourage the application of these skills and values in other situations, including back in the classroom.

The case for provision of outdoor learning opportunities as part of a broad, balanced and well-planned curriculum is strong and as Pickering (2017) reminds us: if children are afforded space to explore then the creative possibilities become richer. We would argue that, through careful planning, resulting from an extensive knowledge of your children, you have the toolkit to allow you to create exciting spaces beyond the classroom, fostering creativity, autonomy and learning. Key considerations, then, can be summarised by the following questions:

- What outcomes do you wish for children?
- How can use of the outdoor learning environment meet the learning outcomes?
- Where is best: indoor or outdoor?
- Who will risk assess the learning environment?

UP, UP AND AWAY

In order to enhance your practice, we have created a supportive RISE Approach to enable you to move beyond the minimum expectations and strive for excellence in your professional practice. The key elements of the RISE Approach are outlined in Figure 19.2:

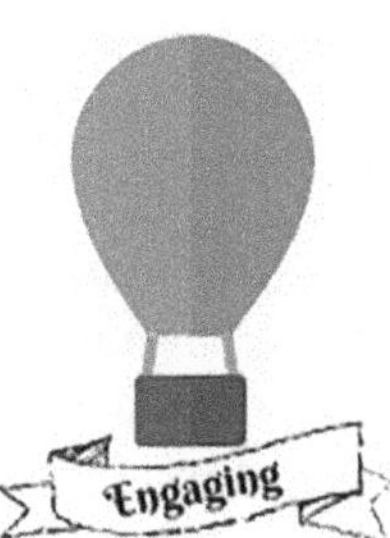

Figure 19.2

The RISE Approach is underpinned by the following key principles:

Reflection: Critically reflect on theory and practice in order to impact on your own professional practice.

Innovation: Creative spaces, happy faces! Design stimulating learning environments, alongside your pupils, to allow them to thrive.

Standards: Maintain high expectations.

Excellence: Display a commitment to professional development and improved experiences and outcomes for your pupils.

> *It sounded an excellent plan, no doubt, and very simply and neatly arranged; the only difficulty was, that she had not the smallest idea how to set about it.*
>
> (Carroll, 1865)

In the section that follows, we will offer practical guidance to help ensure that the potential for your learning environment is maximised to equip you with the tools to create the perfect sea view, wherever the learning happens to be taking place.

THE RISE APPROACH: EMBEDDING EXCELLENT PRACTICE

Earlier we asked the reader to identify the Teachers' Standards (DfE, 2013) in which the teaching and learning environment plays a significant part of excellent professional practice. The astute reader will probably have noted that a thriving learning environment encompasses all the Teacher's Standards (DfE, 2013), not surprisingly, because, if we get it right, it is the cog that makes the wheels go around. This is the philosophy behind the creation of the RISE Approach.

A LEARNING ENVIRONMENT NEEDS TO BE SAFE

It should be a non-threatening space where children feel nurtured, have a sense of belonging, can be themselves and, most importantly, are 'happy'. Children should want to come to school – it should be an extension of their home, where they form relationships, acquire life skills, develop their self-efficacy and learn new knowledge and skills. We can refer to Maslow's Hierarchy of Needs (in Eaude, 2008) here and the importance placed upon feeling safe and secure before being motivated to move onto their next stage of learning.

> *Creating safe classrooms is about creating an environment which encourages learning, where pupils are safe to interact with the teacher, without fear of ridicule or failure.*
>
> (Barnes, 2015)

A teacher needs to know their children well. They need to understand individual needs, how children learn, what motivates them and inspires them to learn. They should be caring, friendly and approachable, making time to talk to the children ... getting to know them. It is also important to develop a strong home/school link where there is an interconnectedness between the two environments as opposed to isolation.

A LEARNING ENVIRONMENT SHOULD BE ENABLING

Quite simply, the environment we create should *allow* the children to learn. The layout, availability of resources, ethos and culture should also empower the children to *want* to learn.

Children need to have a sense of ownership within their environment; it is, therefore, important that we create a space where they can develop their independence and resourcefulness. This latter point is important to remember.

Consider the following:

> *An ordered classroom is not only a pleasant environment for all to work in, including the teacher, but facilitates efficiency through its structure. In practical terms, this means that everything has a place and everything is generally in its place.*
>
> (Castle and Buckler, 2018)

What picture is created in your mind about the learning environment here? Maybe you see the learning environment as a space where the furniture is in a structured layout, everything is clearly labelled, pencil pots and books are laid out ready on the table, supportive resources have been purposefully selected and are readily available for the children? Or maybe you see more of a blank canvas? There are a few empty tables, resources are clearly labelled and accessible but not pre-selected for the pending activity.

CRITICAL QUESTION

Which environment promotes independence, requires children to be resourceful and have a sense of ownership?

As teachers, we must ensure that our ethos does not inadvertently have a negative impact on learning potential. Are the children in your class rigidly adhered to their chair for a length of time with everything laid out before them? If our ethos is to promote independence, children need to learn to become resourceful and develop problem-solving skills. They should be encouraged to *select* the resources they require to complete a task. This may mean a process of trial and error before they succeed, but the voyage of discovery along the way has been a valuable learning experience.

Of course, such a fluid environment can only be achieved where good behaviour management is in place: where rules have been agreed between the pupils and the adults and there is a clear sense of community.

It is also important to ensure that the enabling environment is *inclusive* and created with the learners in mind. This involves having consideration for all learners, creating opportunities for challenge and support. It means understanding the different learning styles within the classroom and ensuring that we craft learning opportunities that are multi-sensory and user-friendly for all.

A LEARNING ENVIRONMENT NEEDS TO BE FLEXIBLE

The environment we create should be dynamic and responsive to the needs of all children. This could be a matter of simply making the children feel comfortable by considering the impact of stimulation, individualisation and naturalness, such as light, sound and temperature (Barrett et al., 2017) or it could involve reconstructing the layout of the classroom.

If learning is purposeful, then the learning environment should also be flexible enough to meet that purpose. Being flexible and responsive supports inclusivity. Reflecting on and adapting our teaching styles in response to the learner, providing appropriate support and challenge, ensures the opportunities we provide are rich, immersive and engaging.

A LEARNING ENVIRONMENT SHOULD BE COLLABORATIVE

A holistic learning space is one that has been constructed by all those within it, as discussed previously and as such, should not be dominated by any one person. Creating a learning environment can be a matter of compromise. As a teacher, you might have particular views on what you envisage the environment to look like, but this may have to be moulded when taking all other perspectives into consideration (children, other adults, school ethos, policies and practices). By involving children in the creation of their learning environment, we are promoting independence and ownership.

It is interesting here to note the findings of a study by O'Brien (2012) which revealed that children were 'capable of critically analysing their learning environment and if offered the opportunity, can suggest and justify ideas about how to improve it'.

Remember: the pupil voice can be very powerful!

A LEARNING ENVIRONMENT NEEDS TO BE ENGAGING

> *Each child has a spark in him/her. It is the responsibility of the people and institutions around each child to find what would ignite that spark.*
>
> (Gardner, 1993)

Essentially, a learning environment should be inspiring and stimulating, providing rich and varied opportunities to enthuse and engage children. It should be a space that captures the children's interest, is exciting and motivating.

Think back to the analogy of the bright, colourful space versus the old, tired space. How influential is the ethos of the school, staff and children in creating an *engaging* learning environment?

CRITICAL QUESTION

'If you are to evidence how you establish a stimulating environment, you need to consider how you know whether the children do actually find it stimulating' (Abrahamson, 2015). **Critically reflect**: How might this be achieved? What might you be looking for?

A learning environment should be a busy, interactive place. It should be reflective of an active workshop where children are immersed in learning.

TAKE FLIGHT: CONCLUSION

A learning environment is only as effective as the people in it. As we have demonstrated, learning environments have the potential to impact significantly on learners and as such, should be considered thoroughly as part of a broad, balanced, creative and engaging curriculum in which learners are enabled to make excellent progress.

The learning environment is a very powerful tool that should be at the heart of every effective teacher's toolkit. So, take flight and transport your children with you on an exciting journey. Aim high; the sky is most certainly not the limit.

> *Which way you ought to go depends on where you want to get to...*
>
> (Carroll, 1865)

CHAPTER SUMMARY

How can you maximise the potential of the learning and teaching environment?

- Conducive to effective learning and progress
- An effective and holistic learning environment that is safe, enabling, flexible, collaborative and engaging
- Positive impact
- Educational philosophy
- Wonderland
- Indoor learning
- Beyond the classroom
- Critically reflect
- Personal space
- Peer and adult interaction
- Learning and peripheral spaces
- Beyond the school gates
- Media impact
- **RISE:**
    - **R**eflection: Critically reflect on theory and practice in order to impact on your own professional practice.
    - **I**nnovation: Creative spaces, happy faces! Design stimulating learning environments, alongside your pupils, to allow them to thrive.
    - **S**tandards: Maintain high expectations.
    - **E**xcellence: Display a commitment to professional development and improved experiences and outcomes for your pupils.

ASSIGNMENTS

If you are writing an ITT assignment on learning environment, it may be useful for you to consider the following:

Critical Reflection 1:

Consider your current educational philosophy and how this is informed by your values.

Critically reflect:

How might your educational philosophy impact on the design of an effective learning environment?

Critical Reflection 2:

Consider the two scenarios below, both in an Early Years setting.

Scenario 1:

At the start of the school day, the children are collected from the school playground and once in the classroom, are expected to go to a designated place at a table and practise forming their letters (handwriting), which has been pre-prepared for them. The teacher immediately sets to work supporting individual children and a sense of calm quickly pervades - the school day has started.

Scenario 2:

At 8.45 a.m. the school gate is opened with the expectation that all children will be in school by 8.55 a.m. A teaching assistant is waiting by the outside door to welcome the children. Most children walk into school by themselves, but some prefer the comfort of a parent coming with them. Once inside the classroom, there are a range of activities to choose from: art and craft, construction, drawing, writing, role-play. The teacher uses this time to settle the children, talking to them and supporting them with their activities. Children are expected to come together as a group ready to start the first lesson at 9.00 a.m.

Critically reflect:

- What type of learning environment has been created in each scenario?
- What is the impact for both the teacher and learner?
- Has a sense of ownership been achieved on behalf of the children?
- Has the teacher created opportunities to foster relationships and create an environment conducive to learning?

Supportive signposts

Cremin, T. and Burnett, C. (2018) *Learning to Teach in the Primary School.* Abingdon: Routledge.

Muijis, D. and Reynolds, D. (2018) *Effective Teaching Evidence and Practice.* London: SAGE.

Paige, R., Lambert, S. and Geeson, R. (2017) *Building Skills for Effective Primary Teaching.* London: Learning Matters.

REFERENCES

Adams, K. (2011) Managing behaviour for learning, in Hansen, A. (ed.) *Primary Professional Studies.* Exeter: Learning Matters.

Ashbridge, J. and Josephidou, J. (2018) in Cooper, H. and Elton-Chalcraft, S. (eds) *Professional Studies in Primary Education*. London: SAGE.

Barnes, J. (2015) in Denby, N. (ed.) *Training to Teach: A guide for students*. London: SAGE.

Barrett, P., Zhang, Y., Davies, F. and Barrett, L. (2015) Available at: www.salford.ac.uk/cleverclassrooms/1503-Salford-Uni-Report-DIGITAL.pdf (accessed 17/05/18).

Beadle, P. (2010) *How to Teach*. Carmarthen: Crown House Publishing.

Carroll, J. and Alexander, G.N. (2016) *The Teachers' Standards in Primary School: Understanding and evidencing effective practice*. London: SAGE.

Carroll, L. (1865) in *The Complete Illustrated Works of Lewis Carroll* (1982). London: Chancellor Press.

Castle, P. and Buckler, S. (2018) *Psychology for Teachers*. London: SAGE.

Department for Education (DfE) (2013) *Teachers' Standards*. London: Crown.

Department for Education and Skills (DfES) (2004) *Excellence and Enjoyment: A strategy for primary schools*. Available at: www.dfes.gov.uk/primarydocument (accessed 17/05/18).

Desailly, J. (2015) *Creativity in the Primary Classroom*. London: SAGE.

Eaude, T. (ed.) (2008) *Children's Spiritual, Moral, Social and Cultural Development*. Exeter: Learning Matters.

Eaude, T. (2012) *How do Expert Primary Classteachers Really Work? A Critical Guide for Teachers, Headteachers and Teacher Educators*. St Albans: Critical Publishing.

Gardner, H. (1993) *Frames of Mind: The theory of multiple intelligences* (2nd edn). London: Fontana Press.

Keenan, T., Evans, E. and Crowley, K. (2016) *An Introduction to Child Development*. London: SAGE.

Kelly, P. (2014) in Cremin, T. and Arthur, J. (eds) *Learning to Teach in the Primary School*. Abingdon: Routledge.

Kelly, P. (2018) in Cremin, T. and Arthur, J. (eds) *Learning to Teach in the Primary School* (4th edn). Abingdon: Routledge.

Kolb, A.Y. and Kolb, D.A. (2011) Available at: www.researchgate.net/profile/David_Kolb/publication/267974468_Experiential_Learning_Theory_A_Dynamic_Holistic_Approach_to_Management_Learning_Education_and_Development/links/5559122408ae6fd2d826eb12.pdf (accessed 17/05/18).

Kyriacou, C. (1991) *Essential Teaching Skills*. Hemel Hempstead: Simon & Schuster Education.

Maslow, A., in Eaude, T. (ed.) (2008) *Children's Spiritual, Moral, Social and Cultural Development*. Exeter: Learning Matters.

Miller, R. (2000) Available at: http://infed.org/mobi/a-brief-introduction-to-holistic-education/ (accessed 17/05/18).

Muijis, D. and Reynolds, D. (2018) *Effective Teaching Evidence and Practice*. London. SAGE.

NACCCE (1999) *All our Futures: Creativity, culture and education*. London. DFEE.

O'Brien, D. (2012) Available at: http://jotter.educ.cam.ac.uk/volume4/033-070-obriend/033-70-obriend.pdf (accessed 17/05/18).

Paige, R. Lambert, S. and Geeson, R. (2017) *Building Skills for Effective Primary Teaching*. London: Learning Matters.

Rutherford, G. (2016) *Wyche Way to Teach* (n.p.). Author.

Thompson, C. and Wolstencroft, P. (2018) *The Trainee Teacher's Handbook: A companion for initial teacher training*. London: Learning Matters.

UNESCO (2012) *A Place to Learn: Lessons from research on learning environments*. Available at: http://unesdoc.unesco.org/images/0021/002154/215468e.pdf (accessed 17/05/18).

USING TRIGGER WORDS IN BLOOM'S TAXONOMY

Knowledge	Comprehension	Application
what, who, when, name, list, define, show, identify.	compare, distinguish, illustrate, tell, predict, explain.	apply, select, solve, choose, consider, connect, plan.
Analysis	**Synthesis**	**Evaluation**
analyse, classify, relate, support, compare/contrast.	propose, formulate, draw together, invent.	judge, measure, defend, evaluate, decide, assess.

(Doherty, 2017)

20

HOW CAN QUESTIONS, PACE AND DELIVERY PROMOTE DEEP LEARNING AND THINKING?

Dr Jonathan Doherty is Senior Lecturer and Primary Research Lead at the Institute of Childhood and Education, Leeds Trinity University. Jonathan teaches on PGCE and Master's programmes, and his research interests are in learning schools, pedagogy and teacher development. He is Chair of the National Primary Teacher Education Council (NaPTEC).

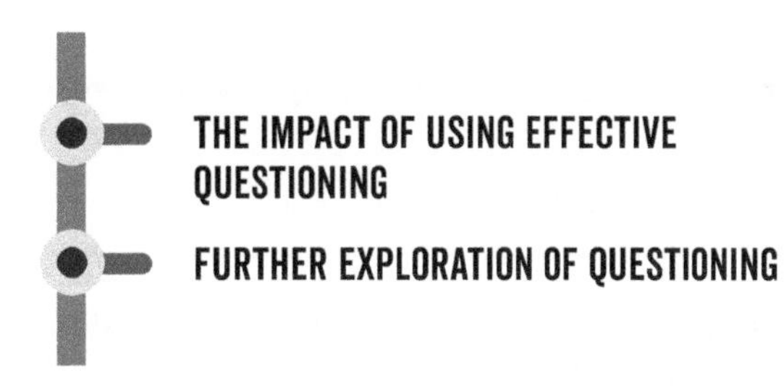

KEY WORDS

- Cognition
- Dialogic teaching
- Higher-order thinking
- Pace
- Questioning
- Questions

INTRODUCTION

Questioning and pace are two essentials for dynamic, interactive teaching. Both are key skills in an effective teacher's toolkit. High-quality teaching involves teachers in thinking about their teaching, and being flexible in *how* they teach as well as *what* they teach. They take into account how their classrooms are set up to encourage talk, how their lessons are planned, feedback they receive from pupils, their own personal awareness of their spoken and body language, their tone of voice and gestures they use as part of their teaching repertoire. These have been called 'interactive cognitions' (Meijer *et al.*, 2002) and they describe a picture of a self-aware and 'thinking teacher'. Asking good questions and being able to control lesson pace or flow are essential ingredients in setting the cognitive tone of a lesson (Kerry and Wilding, 2004), as they help to establish the intellectual climate and the levels of cognition to which pupils will aspire, opening up ideas for exploration and debates for discussion. In this chapter I will explore why asking questions is so important, the types of questions to ask for maximum effect, as well as avoiding the pitfalls of bad questions. I discuss the pace or flow of lessons and suggest a number of practical ideas for you to introduce into your teaching. The chapter will end with an evaluation of questioning tactics that you can trial in your own classroom.

WHY QUESTIONS MATTER

CRITICAL QUESTION

Which are the best types of questions to ask?

Questioning is a widely researched area in teaching and learning because of its importance in the teaching and learning process. It is an essential strategy to encourage and extend pupil thinking (Marzano *et al.*, 2001). Effective questions encourage the kinds of flexible learners and critical thinkers of the 21st century (Doherty, 2017). They are key to good teacher assessment (Hargreaves *et al.*, 2014) and deeper learning. In relation to how teachers' questions can be a powerful way to deepen learning, Kerry (2002) writes that deep learning goes beyond mere trotting out answers when required, or giving what is seen as the 'right answer' that the teacher is looking for. Effective questions should extend and challenge pupils' thinking, delving deeper and going beyond what is already known.

Questioning is a powerful pedagogical tool which can promote a thinking culture in any classroom, provided the questions are of the right type. Woolfolk *et al.* (2008) estimated that teachers ask between 30 and 120 questions every hour! That is about half of total classroom time. While teachers' questions are abundant in every classroom, not all questions have the same impact. You will no doubt already use a mix of open and closed questions in your teaching.

CLOSED QUESTIONS

Closed questions, designed to have a Yes or No response tend to dominate classrooms. They are frequently used to find out what pupils know or confirm their understanding; for example, 'If I multiply 6 and 10

Here are ten reasons why questions do matter.

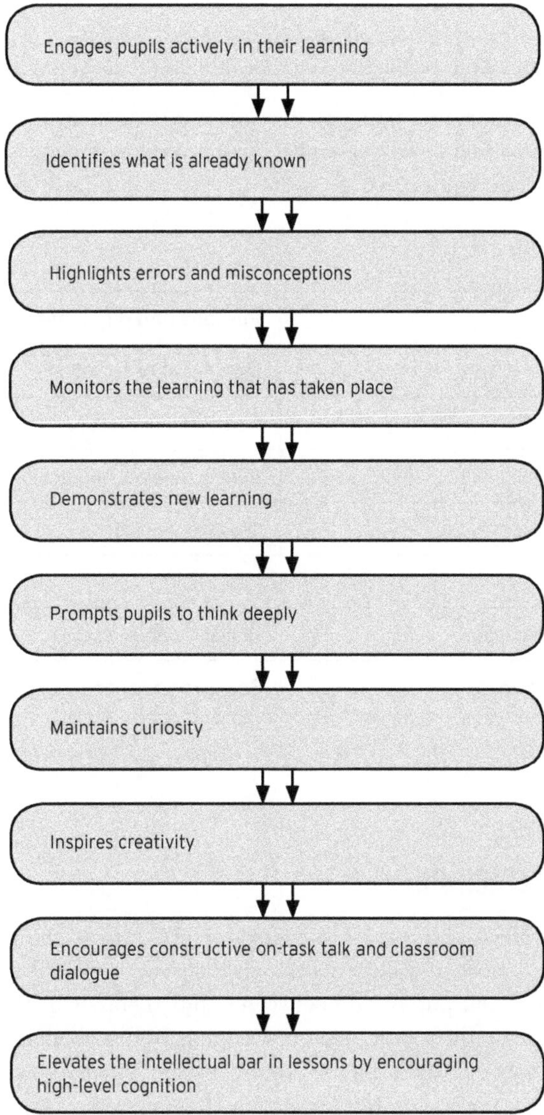

together do I get the answer 56. Yes or No?' Questions like these have a use and teachers often ask them at the start of lessons to try and involve as much of the class as possible, rather than launch into complex or open questions.

OPEN QUESTIONS

Open questions invite a variety of responses and are either general or speculative. An example of a general open question might be, 'What do you know about the main character in this story?' A speculative question could be, 'What do you think is going to happen next in the story?' Both these types of open questions require more than one word answers and tap into the higher-order thinking skills of prediction and creative thinking.

Open questioning is vital in encouraging pupils to develop and offer their own opinions (Hargreaves *et al.*, 2014). King (2002) neatly summarised how open-ended questions develop pupils' thinking abilities and examples from this are given below (see Figure 20.1).

Question type	Purpose and pupil response
What do you notice about ...?	Descriptive observations
What can you tell me about ...?	Recall of information
What does it remind you of?	Seeing patterns and analogies
What do you think will happen next?	Creative predictions
What happened after that?	Reasoning
Do you think you could do it differently?	Reflective analysis
I wonder what made you think of that?	Self-awareness and metacognition

Figure 20.1 Purpose and responses to open questions

QUESTIONS AND DIALOGIC TEACHING

Questions also matter because they are integral to a dialogic approach to teaching (see Alexander, 2015, 2017) that aims to engage pupils and promote thinking through the power of talk. This type of teaching incorporates dialogue between teachers and pupils, and between pupils themselves. It is through such interaction using language that pupils develop their ideas, explore the limits of their understanding, and learn to discuss and explain. In dialogic teaching, questions are used to provoke reasoned answers and are building blocks of further dialogue, rather than the end point. Monologic talk, the opposite of dialogic teaching, takes place in classrooms where teacher talk dominates. This is concerned with transmitting information and controlling talk. Questions reflect 'Initiation-Response-Feedback' (IRF) patterns. The IRF patterns can be seen in classrooms when a teacher asks a closed question (initiation) of a particular pupil who provides an answer (response), and finally the teacher gives feedback for that answer (feedback). In contrast, dialogic teaching is concerned with promoting supportive and purposeful classroom talk and authentic exchanges that use language as a tool for constructing knowledge.

CLASSROOM LINK

What does this mean for classroom practice?

This example of good practice is taken from the Education Endowment Foundation evaluation report (Jay et al., 2017). It describes a maths lesson on fractions with a Year 5 class. Prior to the extract below, the teacher could be seen asking a full range of question types, inviting children to clarify their answers. What you will notice is the respectful language the pupils use with each other and how the teacher allows them to discuss among themselves across the classroom:

Girl 1: *I agree with P1 but I have reason to not agree with him because you need more pieces to share it out equally.*

Boy 1: *I agree with P2.*

Boy 2: *I disagree with P3 because the smaller the number, the bigger the fraction and in pair work ...*

Girl 2: *I agree with him ... so both of them you up to 2 which is an even number ... yeah but as well ...*

Boy 3: *Basically if you halve them all you get ones.*

Girl 3: *Yeah but that's a theory. But you are saying you get an odd number but you don't ... and in the use of reasoning: in fractions the bigger the denominator the less it is, you need two 1/8ths to make a quarter.*

APPROACHES IN QUESTIONING

CRITICAL QUESTION

How do I get off to a good start with my questioning?

Student teachers are usually encouraged to consider three to four key questions as part of their planning ahead of teaching, just as they should consider lesson timings (linked to pace), assessment opportunities and classroom resources. Such practice is certainly recommended. Questions in tests and SATs are also pre-planned in advance with the same questions for everyone. Many questions, however, are personal from individuals and arise from pupil responses in lessons. These might be called 'questions in context'. A teacher's use of assessment for learning (AfL) often illuminates knowledge misconceptions for a class or an individual. Pupils can also ask questions that to the teacher may be outside of what was intended at the planning stage, but for the pupil the question is necessary to fill a gap in knowledge. At other times, pupils will ask questions because the teacher has not explained something clearly enough or it needs rephrasing differently. The 'thinking teacher' is able to respond to these by thinking on his or her feet in a way that is a powerful illustration of interactive teaching.

CRITICAL QUESTION

What skills are needed to ask good questions?

ASKING GOOD QUESTIONS

Four skills that underlie asking good questions were identified in early work by Kyriacou (1997) and are still very relevant today.

QUALITY

First, the *quality* of your questions. Phrase your questions carefully and have clarity. Be specific. There is no value in throwing out a question randomly to a class such as, 'I don't suppose we need to go over this again, do we? So let's move on'. Avoid!

TARGETING

The second thing to consider is your *targeting* of questions. This means giving consideration to which pupils the questions are intended for and even what their responses are likely to be. The advice is to distribute questions widely across the class and not focus on a few volunteers. Later in the chapter I provide a simple practical technique called *no hands up* to avoid this pitfall where the same few pupils answer the teacher's questions.

INTERACTING

Third, *interacting* refers to techniques used in questioning. Be aware of your own body language: eye contact, your tone of voice and the way you might prompt an answer from someone who is struggling to give a full or accurate response. Teachers' questions commonly involve strings of questions in a sequence. While sequencing is a useful strategy, it has the hidden danger of restricting lesson flow by staying rigidly to the planned sequence of questions. It can disrupt the natural flow and pace of the lesson. Added to this is the danger of ignoring pupil responses because their answers are outside the teacher's intended sequence.

FEEDBACK

The fourth aspect is *feedback*. As a teacher, your use of feedback in questioning can have a direct effect on the success of a lesson. Answering questions has an emotional component, and the sensitive teacher responds to a pupil's answer in ways that are affirming and protect pupils' self-esteem. This typically involves using praise and encouragement, and conveys the message that everyone's contributions are welcome and valued. It also does not involve (over-zealously) correcting a pupil's use of language, because as an unintended consequence, that pupil may feel deflated by the teacher's response and therefore reluctant to answer future questions in class.

What types of questions do you mostly use in your teaching? As a way of extending thinking and promoting learning, a typology produced by Hayes (2006) is a helpful way to think about the range of questions you can ask (see Figure 20.2).

Type of question	Use and application
Recall	Requires pupils to draw on their existing knowledge, e.g. 'What year was the Great Fire of London?'
Inciting	Invites expansion and elaboration, e.g. 'Can you explain this further?'
Critical	Questions that open up critical issues, e.g. 'Is it better for boys and girls to be taught in this school in separate classes?'
Inductive	Questions that require a summary of related facts and then to widen the enquiry, e.g. 'What do we mean when we say someone is a hero?'
Evaluating	Questions that invite critical reflection, e.g. 'Look at your work carefully. Where can you use better adjectives in it?'
Branching	These questions offer alternatives, e.g. 'In our paintings, shall we use the thick brushes or the thin brushes first?'
Overt	Direct and similar to closed questions, e.g. 'Which of these shapes covers the bigger area?'
Heuristic	Guide for self-discovery, e.g. 'If we added weight to this truck, what do you think will happen when we roll it down the slope?'
Divergent	Invite both concrete and abstract answers, e.g. 'What might happen if aliens from Mars appeared in the playground on Monday morning?'
Rhetorical	These do not need answers, e.g. 'How would we feel if we all behaved as badly to others as the character in our story?'
Reviewing	Retracing steps in learning, e.g. 'Where did you start this calculation from?'
Liberating	There is no single correct answer, e.g. 'What if the sky fell down on us now? What would you do?'

Figure 20.2 A question typology (based on Hayes, 2006)

CONTROLLING LESSON PACE

Questions form part of the pace of a lesson too. A helpful way for you to understand lesson pace is to see it as flow. It is much more than the speed at which you move through a lesson and, interestingly, your view of the pace of a lesson as a teacher may be different from the view of the pupils in your class. You might spend very little time explaining the learning objectives for the lesson and then appear to go too fast in the lesson, but at the same time that lesson could seem over-long and slow by pupils in the class.

KEY READING

Lemov, D. (2012) *Teach Like a Champion: 49 Techniques that put students on the path to college*. San Francisco, CA: Jossey-Bass.

Pace, according to Lemov (2012: 225), is the 'illusion of speed'. Effective teachers use a range of tempos in their lessons: at times it is slow to emphasise a point or pick up on understanding, and at other times they teach with high energy that seems to be at breakneck speed. In creating the illusion of speed, Lemov recommends changes in pace, such as changing the format every 10-20 minutes to achieve mastery of a topic.

This is not the same as introducing new materials and changing tack every few minutes, which leaves pupils feeling exhausted and confused. You should emphasise reference points in lessons, because when these appear to pass quickly, it gives the impression that things are moving fast and confidently forward. Lesson beginnings and plenaries are examples of good reference points to inject some pace in, before you change the tempo.

I use time limits a lot in my own teaching – for example, 'I will give you three minutes to answer the questions in front of you. Go!' Setting time limits gives the impression that you are moving ahead with this lesson and three minutes does not allow the lesson to dip in pace. I have seen many teachers use a visual clock on their interactive whiteboards to set the time allocated for an activity. The clock visually counts down the time and injects some focused pace for the work to follow. Another technique is to project forward in a lesson. This gives pupils the idea of something that will be covered later. You can even introduce an element of anticipation here by calling this the Mystery Ingredient to heighten the suspense. As a teacher, you control the pace of every lesson and its flow. By giving consideration to the pace of a lesson and using the techniques just described, pupils will perceive your lessons to be energetic and dynamic.

PITFALLS AND CHALLENGES OF ASKING QUESTIONS

CRITICAL QUESTION

How do I avoid the pitfalls and asking the wrong type of questions?

QUESTIONS TO AVOID

Powerful questions foster a deep-thinking classroom culture, provided the questions are of the right type. Let me start with what poor questions are and the type of questions to avoid asking. Hayes (2006) characterises these as falling into one or more of the following categories:

- *Superficial questions that make only limited demands on pupils.* These offer only superficial challenge.
- *Asking too few questions that provide cognitive challenge.* This can create low expectations from pupils.

- *Inappropriate vocabulary*. This can be either vocabulary that is too advanced or indeed too vague.
- *Using poor expression*. This only confuses pupils. An example here of a double negative is, 'Can you see a place in this passage where it is unsuitable not to use paragraphs?'
- *Delivery that alarms pupils*. Pupils may feel that if they answer wrongly they will get into trouble.
- *Mind-reading questions*. These are questions of the 'Guess what is in the teacher's mind?'
- *Endless lists of questions*. Overloading with questions that go nowhere and are unrelated to the work being done.

Regardless of how confidently or enthusiastically a teacher asks questions in these ways, they are barriers to learning and progress. Effective questions stimulate thinking. Effective questions actively involve teachers and pupil learners together. Effective questions make thinking visible. They extend learning and encourage reflection. Good questions are part of a dialogue between the teacher and the class, and good questions result in changes to pupils' understanding and knowledge.

LESSON PACE IS NOT ABOUT SPEED

Lesson pace drives lessons forward, but it must do so appropriately to match the needs of the class. It does not accelerate at warp speed to leave learners behind, nor does it dawdle at a snail pace where pupils become disinterested and switch off from learning. The most skilful teachers create this interactive flow between teachers and pupils, and it is a joy to witness. A question may be deemed to be good if it meets the goal and answers its intended purpose. A teacher may set a question (refer back to the ten purposes of questions at the start of the chapter) to find out what a class knows or to remove misconceptions. Here, mistakes should be seen as further learning opportunities. Questions can be intended to spark off a class debate and encourage more creative thinking, or develop skills of argument and critical thinking, and so on. Pupil responses do not have to be limited to verbal answers. Not all questions require a verbal answer. In your repertoire, include questions that require pupils to write a response (e.g. on whiteboards); to draw a response (e.g. individual or group drawing); build a response (perfect for DT lessons) or physically show a response (e.g. creating a dance motif in PE). Good questions create an exciting environment in which pupils learn, so you should devote time to consider the range of questions and how you use them in lessons across the subjects in the curriculum.

STRATEGIC QUESTIONING

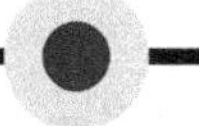

CRITICAL QUESTION

How do I adopt a more strategic approach to my questioning?

There are a number of useful questioning frameworks that allow teachers to develop a more strategic approach to asking questions.

KEY READING

De Bono, E. (1985) *Six Thinking Hats.* Boston, MA: Little, Brown and Company.

A classic text that goes through the rationale for this approach to thinking clearly, and offers very practical ways to introduce the hats into every classroom. It is a powerful thinking and questioning strategy that is well proven and used predominately in the early years of primary schools. There are six hats that equate to six ways of thinking. Yellow Hat thinking explores values and benefits. Red Hat thinking considers feelings. Green Hat looks for alternatives. The White Hat focuses on data and facts. The Black Hat plays devil's advocate and the Blue Hat manages the thinking process.

Each of De Bono's hats generates different questions that can be used with pupils to brainstorm ideas or help them solve an issue. This is an excellent thinking approach to use with primary-aged children. It is advisable to begin and end with the Blue Hat, and hats can be used in any order at any point. A useful starter is to plan your questions for each of the hats in advance, asking one question for each hat initially and building up from there. Here are some examples of possible questions with each hat.

INFO 20.1

TYPE OF HAT	POSSIBLE QUESTIONS
YELLOW	What is the benefit of doing it this way?
RED	Describe how you would feel if ...?
GREEN	Is there an alternative we haven't considered so far?
WHITE	What information do we have already?
BLACK	Should we not assess the risk involved in this?
BLUE	What do we need to change how we look at all of this?

Bloom's taxonomy (1956) provides many opportunities to scale up your questions to promote high levels of thinking. In this six-level hierarchy, lower-order questions assess knowledge and comprehension; medium-level gauge application of knowledge; and higher-order questions elicit synthesis, analysis and evaluation. Bloom related his hierarchy to a ladder where the higher the rung, the deeper the learning. Examples are:

1. **Knowledge** (Remembering) *'Can you remember ...?'*
2. **Comprehension** (Understanding) *'Explain the author's ideas about...?'*
3. **Application** (Applying) *'Where else have you seen this pattern?*

4. Analysis	(Analysing)	*'Explain to me what is happening here?'*
5. Synthesis	(Evaluating)	*'Can you see a possible solution to...?'*
6. Evaluation	(Creating)	*'Are you able to judge the value of...?'*

Using trigger words in your teaching can help your questioning considerably and has possibilities for use across the curriculum.

INFO 20.2

Using trigger words in Bloom's taxonomy:

Level	Trigger words
Knowledge	what, who, when, name, list, define, show, identify
Comprehension	compare, distinguish, illustrate, tell, predict, explain
Application	apply, select, solve, choose, consider, connect, plan
Analysis	analyse, classify, relate, support, compare/contrast
Synthesis	propose, formulate, draw together, invent
Evaluation	judge, measure, defend, evaluate, decide, assess

(Doherty, 2017)

EXPLORING IMPACT

CRITICAL QUESTION

How can I know if my questions are making an impact on pupil learning?

The impact of using effective questioning in your teaching is likely to be immediate and significant. There are many questioning tactics to choose from to promote learning and stimulate classroom dialogue, and in this section I provide eight examples.

QUESTIONING TACTICS

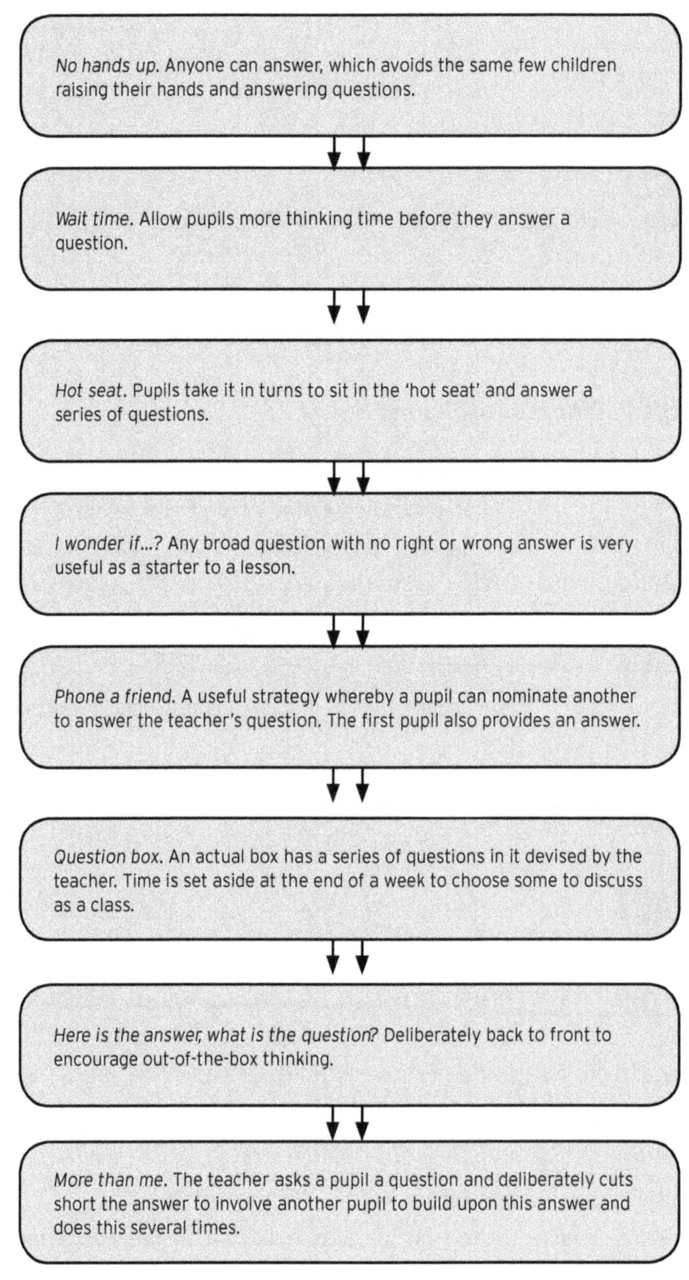

FURTHER EXPLORATION OF QUESTIONING

Research by Wragg and Brown (2001) highlight a number of characteristics of effective questioning and these provide a useful way to approach questions further with your class. These are:

- link questions to lesson learning objectives;
- visually display questions;
- provide guided practice to give pupils opportunities to consolidate their learning and for you to check their understanding;
- use closed questions to check understanding and recall, but ask more open questions than closed questions;
- encourage pupils to answer questions that demand increasingly higher-order thinking;
- create a classroom climate where pupils feel secure in taking risks and are not afraid of making mistakes.

SOME USEFUL RESOURCES

Clarke, S. Available at: www.shirleyclarke-education.org/

Excellent website from Shirley Clarke with many resources to embed assessment for learning and effective questioning in classrooms.

West Lothian Council Educational Psychology Service. *Questioning*. Raising Attainment sheet 1. Available at: www.westlothian.gov.uk/education/.

A simple three-page document but very practical and gives a very clear overview of Bloom's taxonomy. Recommended.

Wiliam, D. Content then process. Teacher Learning Communities in the Service of Formative Assessment. Available at: www.youtube.com/watch?v=029fSeOaGio

A must go-to YouTube video featuring the expert in the field.

CHAPTER SUMMARY

- Questioning and pace are essential for dynamic, interactive teaching.
- They form part of a thinking teacher's repertoire.
- They encourage and extend pupil thinking.
- Questions are a powerful pedagogical tool that can promote a thinking culture.
- Questions are integral to a dialogic approach to teaching.

(Continued)

(Continued)

- Monologic talk, reflect 'Initiation-Response-Feedback' (IRF) patterns.
- Use open and closed questions.
- A typology is a way to think about the range of questions you can ask.
- Questions form part of the pace of a lesson.
- Another way to think of pace is flow.
- Effective questions actively involve teachers and pupil learners together.
- Effective questions make thinking visible.
- They extend learning and encourage reflection.
- De Bono's Thinking Hats (1985) is a powerful thinking and questioning strategy.
- Bloom's taxonomy (1956) provides opportunities to scale up your questions to promote high levels of thinking.

ASSIGNMENTS

If you are writing an ITE assignment on questioning and lesson pace, it will be useful for you to think through the following:

1. Why do you think that teachers' questions are so important for delivery of high-quality lessons? Would everyone share this view? What is the relationship between good questions and pace in lessons?
2. Why is questioning such an important way to stimulate dialogue in class? How is this related to 'dialogic teaching'? How can pupil talk become a central feature of your classroom teaching?
3. Bloom's taxonomy is an example of one approach to promote higher-order thinking. Can you see how this might be applied to subjects across the primary curriculum? Which subjects would lend themselves more easily to this and which would be more difficult? Why?

Useful texts to support an assignment on classroom questioning are:

Clarke, S. (2005) *Formative Assessment in Action: Weaving the elements together*. London: Hodder Murray.

Dawes, L. (2014) Organising effective classroom talk, in T. Cremin and J. Arthur (eds) *Learning to Teach in the Primary School*. London: Routledge.

Doherty, J. (2017) Skilful questioning: The beating heart of good pedagogy. *Impact*. London: Chartered College of Teaching.

Paramore, J. (2017) Questioning to stimulate dialogue, in R. Paige, S. Lambert and R. Geeson (eds) *Building Skills for Effective Primary Teaching*. London: Learning Matters.

The following sources provide useful further reading:

De Bono, E. (1985) *Six Thinking Hats*. Boston, MA: Little, Brown and Company.

A classic text that goes through the rationale for this approach to thinking clearly and offers very practical ways to introduce the hats into every classroom.

Fisher, R. (2005) *Teaching Children to Learn*. Cheltenham: Nelson Thornes.

Chapter 2 is called Questioning to learn and is very readable. Accessible style with lots of advice from a guru in this field.

Hayes, D. (2006) *Inspiring Primary Teaching: Insights into excellent primary practice*. Exeter: Learning Matters.

Wisdom alongside practical ideas. Chapter 4 is great on questioning.

Paramore, J. (2017) Questioning to stimulate dialogue, in R. Paige, S. Lambert and R. Geeson (eds) *Building Skills for Effective Primary Teaching*. London: Learning Matters.

It has much to say on dialogic teaching and questioning.

Wragg, E.C. (1993) *Questioning in the Primary Classroom*. London: Routledge.

An older book now, but still packed full of great ideas and steeped in primary practice.

REFERENCES

Alexander, R.J. (2015) *Towards Dialogic Teaching: Rethinking classroom talk* (4th edn). York: Dialogos.

Alexander, R.J. (2017) *Dialogic Teaching in Brief*. Available at: www.robinalexander.org.uk/dialogic-teaching/ (Accessed 5/07/18)

Bloom, B.S. (ed.) (1956) *Taxonomy of Educational Objectives: The classification of educational goals. Handbook I: Cognitive domain*. New York: David McKay.

De Bono, E. (1985) *Six Thinking Hats*. Boston, MA: Little, Brown and Company.

Doherty, J. (2017) Skilful questioning: The beating heart of good pedagogy. *Impact*. London: Chartered College of Teaching.

Hargreaves, E., Gipps, C. and Pickering, A. (2014) Assessment for learning, in T. Cremin and J. Arthur (eds) *Learning to Teach in the Primary School*. Abingdon: Routledge.

Hayes, D. (2006) *Inspiring Primary Teaching: Insights into excellent primary practice*. Exeter: Learning Matters.

Jay, T., Willis, B., Thomas, P., Taylor, R., Moore, N., Burnett, C., Merchant, G. and Stevens, A. (2017) *Dialogic Teaching Evaluation: Report and executive summary*. London: Education Endowment Foundation.

Kerry, T. (2002) *Explaining and Questioning*. Chelthenham: Nelson Thornes.

Kerry, T. and Wilding, M. (2004) *Effective Classroom Teacher: Developing the skills you need in the classroom*. London: Pearson Longman.

King, A. (2002) Structuring peer interaction to promote high-level cognitive processing. *Theory into Practice,* 41(1): 33–9.

Kyriacou, C. (1997) *Effective Teaching in School: Theory and practice* (2nd edn). Cheltenham: Stanley Thornes.

Lemov, D. (2012) *Teach Like a Champion: 49 Techniques that put students on the path to college.* San Francisco, CA: Jossey-Bass.

Marzano, R., Pickering, D. and Pollock, J. (2001) *Classroom Instruction that Works: Research-based strategies for increasing student achievement.* Alexandria, VA: Association for Supervision and Curriculum Development.

Meijer, P. Douwe, B. and Verloop, N. (2002) Examining teachers' interactive cognitions using insights from research on teachers' practical knowledge, in C. Sugrue and C. Day (eds) *Developing Teachers and Teaching Practice.* London: Routledge Falmer.

Woolfolk, A., Hughes, M. and Walkup, V. (2008) *Psychology in Education.* Harlow: Pearson.

Wragg, E.C. and Brown, G. (2001) *Questioning in the Primary School.* London: Routledge.

21

DOES AN ENQUIRY-BASED APPROACH TO LEARNING STILL MATTER?

Deborah Wilkinson is a senior lecturer in education specialising in primary science at the University of Chichester. She is interested in how questions are used to develop learning during science lessons.

Linda Cooper has worked in education as a teacher and teacher educator for the past 20 years. She currently works in the primary education team at the University of Chichester. Her research interests include humanities and technology.

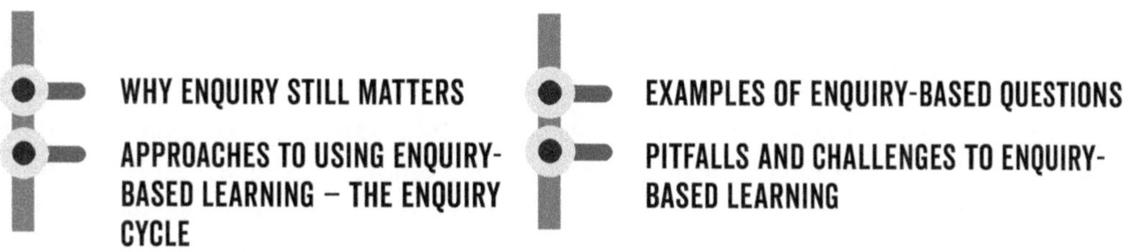

KEY WORDS

- Applied learning
- Communication
- Curiosity
- Exploration
- Problem solving

INTRODUCTION

This chapter explores the relevance and important of enquiry-based learning approaches in primary schools today. It begins by asking why enquiry still matters and discusses the ways in which the approach can support the development of learning skills. It goes on to provide some practical strategies bringing enquiry-based learning into the classroom. It illustrates how coverage of multiple curriculum subjects can be achieved through carefully planned teaching sessions, and how it is the enquiry aspect itself that supports children's expanded learning. The chapter goes on to note the pitfalls and challenges of the approach, and to address teachers' common concerns.

WHY ENQUIRY STILL MATTERS

For children to learn well they need to be engaged, curious and motivated by their learning. They need to be able to conduct meaningful investigations across the curriculum where they can ask and answer their own questions; this is why an appreciation and understanding of the benefits of enquiry-based learning is paramount to the development of good practitioners.

To define enquiry further it is perhaps useful to consider Hutchings' (2007: 10) explanation of this process; he states that, 'Enquiry, is the "action of seeking" – a process of seeking'. Importantly, the learning process is driven by an investigation owned by the students who work collaboratively to make meaning through the social construction of knowledge.

Enquiry-based learning is not a new strategy. Indeed, Dewey (1859–1952) was a great proponent of what is termed 'child-centred' education and experiences formed through educational enquiry. Fairfield (2011) commenting extensively on Dewey's writing, notes the motivational effects and the central importance of children learning through their own enquiry over and above more passive approaches to knowledge discovery. While there is not space to analyse Dewey's thoughts in depth, when discussing enquiry it is always useful to be reminded of his philosophy,

> *The only guarantee of attention is when students see for themselves the relevance of the subject matter to life and to that in which they take an unforced interest. Without this condition in place, we fashion not the virile character so prized by the conservative philosophy but "a character dull, mechanical, unalert, because the vital juice of spontaneous interest has been squeezed out."*
>
> (Fairfield, 2011: 69)

Enquiry, then, is a useful teaching approach to understand. However, while not doubting the importance of enquiry, its place in today's classroom does need to be examined. It could be easy to question if this approach is still useful or indeed realistic in the current educational environment. Time constraints and pressure to cover an extensive curriculum (DfE, 2013), as well as an emphasis on showing how your children make progress, might make fluid, open-ended investigations appear less attractive to the current practitioner.

More structured teaching approaches might better ensure the development of curriculum-prescribed subject knowledge. However, Alexander (2010) laments the test-induced regression to a valuing of memorisation and recall over understanding and enquiry. Hayes (2012) notes the numerous advantages of enquiry-based approaches that include active student engagement, responsibility and independence, developing creativity and problem solving, and greater ownership over the learning task.

Pickford *et al.* (2013) link the benefits of enquiry to higher-order thinking skills as identified by Bloom *et al.* (1956). As such, an enquiry-based approach not only aids knowledge acquisition but also helps children to apply and analyse information and to evaluate this process. These skills are often equated with high levels of achievement. Here, then, is the crux of the matter:

> *Children need not only to obtain knowledge but they need to be able to apply and investigate subject content in a way that deepens and embeds learning and this can be achieved through good enquiry.*
>
> (Pickford *et al.*, 2013)

When children learn through enquiry, they acquire a whole raft of transferable skills that can be employed in many areas of the curriculum and this empowers them to become successful learners.

APPROACHES TO EMPLOYING ENQUIRY-BASED LEARNING: THE ENQUIRY CYCLE

The process of enquiry begins by providing a safe learning environment so that children are confident to share their thinking. Children may then be guided through the process of enquiry by following the framework below (see Figure 21.1). Working through the stages may ensure that the learning is more authentic as children have more control over their learning.

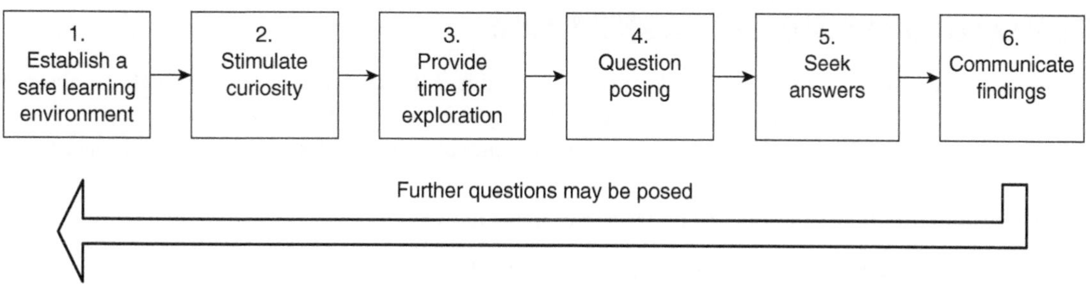

Figure 21.1 Framework to support the process of enquiry

Enquiry-based learning approaches are not identical in nature but, will usually contain similar characteristics. They commence with a clear starting point. This might be the presentation of a picture, problem, scenario, video clip, artefact, poem, piece of music or a question to be solved (Step 2 of the framework above). It is usually open-ended; students do not necessarily have to resolve the problem or question with one answer. Indeed, the problem might have several equally valid solutions. What it must do is stimulate the curiosity and interest of the learner. For instance, the starting point might be a real-world situation from which an initial question is formed for the students to investigate.

Composing good enquiry-based questions is the basis to good enquiries and can establish the structure of the future work. For instance, questions might require students to investigate one curriculum area or they might stimulate a cross-curricular enquiry. The teacher needs to select a topic that has enough substance to allow for an in-depth enquiry; it should also require children to think critically or perhaps encourage them to view topics in a different way when seeking answers. There is also merit in considering how children will communicate their findings. It is when communicating that children are able to use their reasoning skills to draw conclusions based upon the evidence they have collated (be aware that more questions may be generated).

Below are some exemplar questions that situate enquiries in the curriculum areas of history and science in Key Stages 1 and 2.

EXEMPLAR ENQUIRY-BASED QUESTIONS FOR HISTORY

- What can we learn about society in the Bronze Age from a study of the grave of the Amesbury Archer?
- What can you find out about Neolithic life from a study of Skara Brae?
- What are the similarities and differences between homes in the life of Queen Victoria and homes today?
- Why is it important to remember the life of Mary Anning?
- Who or what was buried at Sutton Hoo?
- Can the Anglo-Saxon period be considered the start of the Dark Ages?
- How and why did Boudicca upset the Romans?

EXEMPLAR ENQUIRY-BASED QUESTIONS FOR SCIENCE

The National Curriculum (DfE, 2013) for science refers to five different types of enquiry such as: observing over time; pattern seeking; identifying, classifying and grouping; comparative and fair testing and research to answer questions and solve problems. Below are some examples of enquiries that children could engage in:

- Observation over time: How does water travel through a flower?
- Pattern seeking: Where do daisies grow on the school field?
- Identifying, classifying and grouping: How can we name trees in the local park?

- Comparative and fair testing: What material would make the best parachute for our superhero?
- Research: What do the intestines do?

CRITICAL QUESTION

Can enquiry-based learning be used effectively to teach all areas of the primary curriculum?

CASE STUDY

A Year 6 class in West Sussex had recently visited the SeaCity Museum in Southampton as part of their *Titanic* project. During the visit children had the opportunity to discover what life was like for the passengers and crew through dressing up, artefact handling, and a variety of 'hands-on' learning activities. This served as the 'set starting' point for an enquiry and led naturally to the children investigating concepts linked to the unit of work.

Many questions were posed by the children during the visit and the teacher made a note of these so that they could be explored in more depth when back at school. One of the key areas that the children wanted to know more about was 'who survived and why?' This served as a good enquiry-based question as there are many ways in which children could answer this including looking at newspaper reports, eye-witness accounts and findings from the British and American Enquiries into the sinking, along with a consideration of conditions at sea.

In order to reinforce learning that had been undertaken in science (thermal insulators), it was decided to use a cross-curricular approach so that the children could apply their learning in science to a historical context. Therefore, when back in the classroom, the children were shown pictures of the passengers and crew who were on the *Titanic*. These included:

- Wally Hartley (a violinist dressed in evening attire);
- Arthur Lewis (a steward);
- a child from the Goodwin family (travelling in steerage);
- Mrs Kirtley (who wore a waterproof coat);
- Mrs Astor (a first-class passenger who only wore her thin blue dress).

The children were asked to look carefully at the type of clothing worn by each person and to predict who was most likely to survive the sinking. The children hypothesised that having more layers of clothing would help the individual stay warmer for longer and that factors such as falling into the sea would make a person cold quickly. To test the hypothesis, groups of children were given five plastic screw-top bottles (so that a thermometer could be attached) and were asked to apply fabric samples, using elastic bands, to represent the clothing worn by each person. Each bottle was filled with warm water (38 degrees Celsius). They explored what happened to body temperature when passengers were dry (in a lifeboat) and when they got wet. They also recorded what happened when the bottles were submerged into ice-cold water; this represented the sea. The children concluded that more layers were more effective at maintaining body temperature. If the 'character' was submerged in cold water, the children observed that heat was lost more quickly.

(Continued)

(Continued)

After exploring thermal insulators, the children wanted to find out more about the characters, so there was a discussion about how they might find answers using historical sources. Through the process described, the children gradually moved from investigation (conditions at sea and survival) to piecing information together to make new knowledge (using books and historical sources to find out about the characters and why they did or did not survive).

They communicated their ideas to each other and, finally, reflected on if they had satisfactorily answered the question (Who survived and why?). They considered further questions linked to hypothermia, so this iterative cycle started again.

This example illustrates that enquiry-based learning can be used to teach more than one curriculum subject in the same teaching sequence. Through enquiry, the children developed skills to support them to think like scientists and historians. The visit to the museum and the 'hands-on' exploration of artefacts enabled the children to 'explore and play' in an open-ended fashion, which encouraged them to become active participants in the learning process.

KEY READING

Black and Harrison, in their paper 'Strategies for Assessment of Inquiry Learning in Science' note that 'exploration is essential and includes playing with the equipment to understand how it works'. Furthermore, this is the phase where ideas and different lines of enquiry are formed and children are given the freedom the express these.

This paper is key reading for further understanding of strategies for enquiry learning in science.

Available at: www.kcl.ac.uk/sspp/departments/education/research/Research-Centres/crestem/Research/Current-Projects/SAILS/KCL,-SAILS-and-EU.aspx

CRITICAL QUESTION

How might learning through investigation develop children's skills?

PITFALLS AND CHALLENGES OF ENQUIRY-BASED LEARNING

Byrne *et al.* (2016) in a recent study on enquiry-based learning in science note that one of the obstacles to pursuing this strategy is lack of confidence in subject knowledge, which causes teachers to return to the security of more didactic teaching methods like teacher talk and use of textbooks. Indeed, good enquiry-based teaching makes many demands on the practitioner. Children may not only raise challenging questions that test teachers' knowledge, but also test teachers' understanding of their pedagogic knowledge. Teachers need to know how to allow children to investigate and to learn that, in doing so, they can meet the requirement of formal assessments. Hayes (2012) lists other possible barriers, such as the creation of overload (learning needs to be incremental and enquiry could present too much material for a student to consider at one time), as well as the development of misconceptions in a curriculum that makes demands on accurate subject knowledge, with teachers failing to spot or correct mistakes. Finally, enquiry-led learning is simply time-consuming, and difficult to schedule in a school day.

THE ROLE OF THE TEACHER

Many of the challenges listed above can be overcome by the careful consideration of the role of the teacher. It would be easy to think that the role of the teacher is minimal in this type of approach. Indeed, the opposite is true. As Hutchings (2007: 13) explains, 'enquiry-based learning does not, it is important to stress, leave the students entirely to themselves'. Young children will not necessarily make connections or enquire on their own – the role of the teacher is crucial.

THE ROLE OF THE TEACHER IN THE ENQUIRY CYCLE

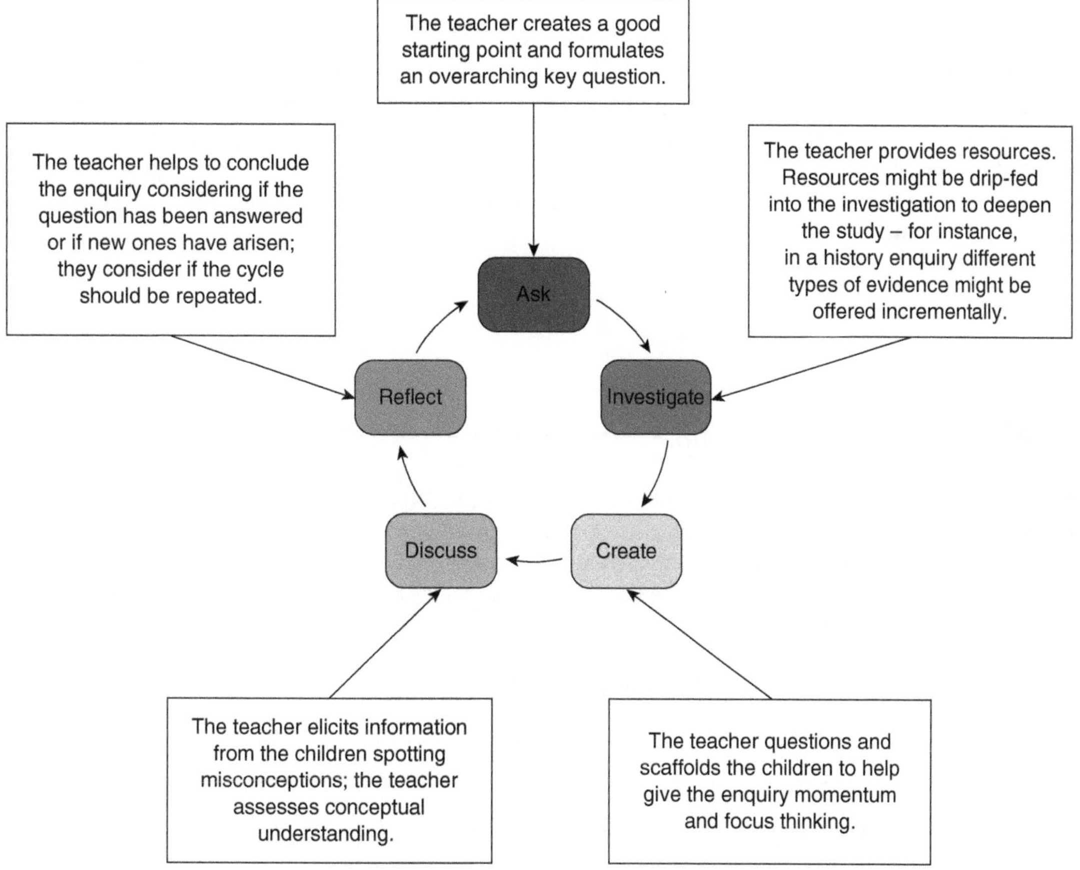

Figure 21.2 Bruner's (1965) Cycle of Enquiry – with the role of the teacher added

The challenge for the teacher is to ensure that they guide and scaffold children's learning, checking that they are actively engaged so that they not only participate, but also that they make progress and achieve their potential (Byrne *et al.*, 2016). When conducting group work during an enquiry, children may show conceptual understanding, but it is likely that during the excitement and pace of the talk, the children will discuss their findings using informal language choices. Good open-ended questioning, or indeed the establishment of a reciprocal dialogue between the teacher and the children, can enable the practitioner to find out what the children have discovered; importantly, then, the practitioner avoids telling the children what they need to know.

Thinking carefully about the different level of questions can ensure that children who are exceeding age-related expectations are challenged in their offered responses. Targeting different levels of questions according to the classification of the taxonomy provided by Bloom *et al.* (1956) can trigger different levels of responses from different individuals and, therefore, help the teacher more accurately assess the progress made within a class. They can also use this as an opportunity to respond to and repeat answers given to them using replies that model the correct subject-specific vocabulary.

ADDRESSING TEACHERS' CONCERNS ABOUT ENQUIRY-BASED LEARNING

Teachers worry that an investigation can leave children with misconceptions or that open-ended tasks do not consolidate subject knowledge. There is also the fear that in an enquiry where the students lead their own learning and make their own decisions, they could waste time pursuing an irrelevant line of thinking or leave the enquiry unanswered. However, researchers argue that learning from mistakes is an important part of the process (Black and Harrison, 2016; Hutchings, 2007). Moreover, it is the teacher's active engagement in the process that will help them to spot any misconceptions and pose questions that enable children to carefully reconsider their answers.

CHAPTER SUMMARY

Enquiry is recognised as an effective way of engaging and motivating children. As well as providing a vehicle by which children can apply their conceptual knowledge, enquiries also develop a raft of important transferable skills. It is recognised that employing open-ended enquiries can be a challenge in today's classroom; however, as a teacher there is merit in understanding how these may be overcome. To achieve this you might consider the following questions:

- Have I considered my role during the enquiry process?
- Have I considered how I might plan for good enquiry-based questions?
- Have I established a 'safe' learning environment so that children can pose questions and take risks?
- Have I considered the resources that are needed to support exploration and curiosity?

ASSIGNMENTS

If you are writing an ITE assignment linked to enquiry, it will be useful for you to justify whether you believe that an enquiry-based approach leads to better learning. It would be useful for you to think through the following ideas:

1. What are the benefits and barriers to employing an enquiry-based approach?
2. Why should teachers consider using enquiries?
3. What are the transferable skills that enquiry-based approaches to learning develop?

To develop critical analysis, you might consider the difference between enquiry and didactic methods, and the impact of both on learners.

REFERENCES

Alexander, R. (2010) *Children, Their World, Their Education: Final report and recommendations of the Cambridge Primary Review*. London: Routledge.

Black, P. and Harrison, C. (2016) *Strategies for Assessment of Inquiry Learning in Science*. Kings' College London. Available at: www.kcl.ac.uk/sspp/departments/education/research/Research-Centres/crestem/Research/Current-Projects/SAILS/KCL,-SAILS-and-EU.aspx (accessed 27/02/18).

Bloom, B., Englehart, M., Furst, E., Hill, W. and Krathwohl, D. (1956) *Taxonomy of Educational Objectives: The classification of educational goals. Handbook I: Cognitive domain*. New York, Toronto: Longmans, Green.

Bruner, J.S. (1965) *The Process of Education*. Cambridge, MA: Harvard University Press.

Byrne. J., Rietdijka. W. and Cheek, S. (2016) Enquiry-based science in the infant classroom: 'letting go'. *International Journal of Early Years Education*, 24 (2): 206–23. Available at: http://dx.doi.org/10.1080/09669760.2015.1135105 (accessed 26/02/18).

DfE (2013) *The National Curriculum in England*. Available at: www.gov.uk/government/publications/national-curriculum-in-england-primary-curriculum (accessed 27/02/18).

Fairfield, P. (2011) *Education after Dewey*. London: Continuum.

Hayes, D. (2012) *Foundations of Primary Teaching*. London: Routledge.

Hutchings, W. (2007) Enquiry-based learning: Definitions and rationale. Manchester: Centre for Excellence in Enquiry-Based Learning, University of Manchester. Available at: www.campus.manchester.ac.uk/ceebl/resources/essays/hutchings2007_definingebl.pdf (accessed 27/02/18).

Pickford, T., Garner, W. and Jackson, E. (2013) *Primary Humanities: Learning through enquiry*. London: SAGE.

22

HOW CAN WE BUILD POSITIVE RELATIONSHIPS WITH CHILDREN AND PARENTS?

Noel Purdy is Director of Research and Scholarship and Head of Education Studies at Stranmillis University College, Belfast. His main research interests include pastoral care, special educational needs and teacher education.

Jill Dunn is a Senior Lecturer at Stranmillis University College, Belfast. Her research interests include tablet devices and young children's literacy development and participatory research with children.

Diane McClelland is an experienced primary school teacher who has recently joined the academic staff of Stranmillis University College, Belfast. Her main interests include literacy, play-based and outdoor learning, child psychology and education in Uganda.

- WHY BUILDING RELATIONSHIPS WITH CHILDREN AND PARENTS MATTERS
- HOW TO BUILD POSITIVE RELATIONSHIPS WITH CHILDREN
- HOW TO BUILD POSITIVE RELATIONSHIPS WITH PARENTS
- BUILDING RELATIONSHIPS WITH CHILDREN – PITFALLS AND CHALLENGES
- BUILDING RELATIONSHIPS WITH PARENTS – PITFALLS AND CHALLENGES
- THE POSITIVE IMPACT OF BUILDING RELATIONSHIPS WITH CHILDREN AND PARENTS

KEY WORDS

- Communication
- Family
- Parents
- Partnership
- Relationships

INTRODUCTION

The focus of this chapter is on relationships, and how it is essential for you as a student teacher to build appropriate, positive, respectful and effective relationships with the children in your class, but also with their parents. (N.B. In this chapter we use the term 'parents' to refer to parents, guardians and carers.) The chapter begins by explaining the importance of relationship building before offering practical approaches supported by two illustrative case studies. Finally, a number of key challenges and pitfalls are highlighted.

WHY DOES BUILDING RELATIONSHIPS WITH CHILDREN AND PARENTS MATTER?

Relationship building is central to all effective teaching and learning, and the most fundamental relationship in teaching and learning is between the classroom teacher and the child. It is important for you as a student teacher to foster caring, respectful and professional relationships with the children in your class as the foundation upon which positive learning outcomes can be built.

Maintaining good relationships with children is often highlighted as one of the key strategies to help create a good and safe learning environment, and it has been recommended that all teachers should also maintain high standards of ethics and behaviour within and outside school by 'treating pupils with dignity, building relationships rooted in mutual respect, and at all times observing proper boundaries appropriate to a teacher's professional position' (DfE, 2011: 14).

The relationship between the individual child and their teacher thus underpins effective education, where the teacher is committed to facilitating the child's learning, but also where the teacher is committed to meeting the pastoral needs of the child: knowing and valuing the child as an individual, irrespective of background, age, gender or ability.

CRITICAL QUESTION

Can a positive relationship with children in the classroom support them beyond the classroom?

Furthermore, caring, approachable teachers who provide opportunities for children to discuss their emotions can have a significant impact on children's mental health (Hornby and Atkinson, 2003; DENI, 2016). One head teacher expressed it in these terms: 'It all comes down to relationships; if you get those right, all else follows. If you don't, then you won't achieve very much of anything' (Best, 1995: 5).

Outside the school environment few relationships in life are as significant and enduring as the relationship between children and their parents, or the adults who raised them. Indeed, families are the first social unit in which children learn and develop (OECD, 2017a). Parents' involvement in children's learning begins at birth by providing guidance, developing habits, imparting values, supporting learning experiences and sharing expectations (OECD, 2017b). As teachers, we have a strong identity as educators; however, it is crucial that we recognise that 'parents are children's first and most enduring educators' (QCA, 2000: 9).

KEY READING

The *Effective Pre-School, Primary and Secondary Education* (EPPSE) study highlighted the importance of the Home Learning Environment (HLE) for pre-school children's academic environment and it also reported at age 14 the early years HLE still predicted academic outcomes (DfE, 2012).

RESEARCHING THE CASE FOR ENGAGING PARENTS IN THEIR CHILDREN'S LEARNING

The case for engaging parents in their children's learning is widely reported in the literature. In a review of the research evidence, Desforges and Abouchaar (DfES, 2003) stated that parental involvement in the form of at-home good parenting has a significant effect on children's achievement and, more recently, Goodall et al. (2011) declared that the more engaged parents are in the education of their children, the more likely their children are to succeed in the education system.

Bronfenbrenner's Ecological Systems Theory (1979) illustrates the value of parents and teachers working together. Bronfenbrenner presented the child's environment on five different levels with the microsystem representing the environment with which the child has direct contact, such as home and school. The next level, the mesosytem, represents how well the different parts of the microsystem interact with each other – for example, the relationship between parents and teachers, and how these interactions have a direct impact on a child's development. Therefore, both research and theory signpost us very clearly towards working in partnerships with parents, as the following case study illustrates.

CASE STUDY

Daniel and his younger brother lived on a farm and came from a very caring home with supportive parents. Daniel struggled with reading and had an aversion to books. On advice from his class teacher, Mrs Steenson, Daniel's mum brought the boys to the library regularly and encouraged them to borrow books about farming and other topics of interest. As the weeks went on and Mrs Steenson got to know the family, it became clear that both boys idolised their father, a successful farmer who had clearly no time for school and education. This attitude began to impact significantly on Daniel's learning outcomes in school. The mother met regularly with Mrs Steenson who outlined a variety of strategies to encourage home engagement with Daniel's learning.

It was during these times that the teacher discovered that Daniel's dad could not read very well, had struggled greatly with literacy at school and had never felt supported. This lack of a male support at home had clearly impacted on Daniel and his brother. In response, Mrs Steenson organised a 'Parents as Partners' information and support evening to outline parental strategies for encouraging children's literacy at home.

(Continued)

(Continued)

Daniel's mum attended and found the evening very worthwhile. She then reported back to her husband on the importance of parental support, especially in relation to reading. Daniel's dad realised how his attitude had impacted negatively on his sons and endeavoured with the support of his wife and the class teacher to be a more effective role model in the area of literacy. Daniel's dad also began to attend other parents' evenings and parental interviews. As a result, his sons could see the value their dad now placed upon learning and reading in particular and how interested he was in finding out about his children's experiences at school. The change in attitude to reading of Daniel and his brother was truly transformational in terms of their subsequent achievements and future aspirations.

In evaluating the example of good practice presented here, consider the following questions:

- How did the class teacher, Mrs Steenson, build positive relationships with Daniel and his family?
- What impact did this have on Daniel?
- What else might the class teacher have done?

CRITICAL QUESTION

How might this case study inform your practice as a student teacher?

HOW CAN WE BUILD POSITIVE RELATIONSHIPS WITH CHILDREN?

At the outset of your teaching career, there is an obvious and incontrovertible need for all student teachers to become familiar with the curriculum and to develop a high level of subject knowledge. However, the old adage also still rings true that teachers don't just teach *subjects*, they teach *children*. It is, therefore, crucial at the very outset that you look beyond the *pupil* (as a learner, a score or a grade) and see the unique, individual personality and abilities of the *child* who has grown up in a particular set of personal and community circumstances. This appreciation of the individuality of the child in your class is a first step in relationship building, but also in planning effectively differentiated learning experiences for children in your class.

It is also clear that children must have their most basic needs met first before they will be ready to learn. American psychologist Abraham Maslow represented this as a *hierarchy of needs* in which our *deficiency needs* (for survival, safety, belonging and self-esteem) must be met first before our *growth needs* can be met or *self-actualisation* (the realisation of individual potential) can become possible. In terms of teaching, this means that a child who does not feel safe, included or valued by their teacher will have little interest, for instance, in learning about fractions, irrespective of the extent of your subject knowledge. Similarly, a child who does not feel that you care about them is very unlikely to come forward to report any difficulty, whether academic or pastoral.

Once seen as quite unrelated and even mutually exclusive, there has been a growing realisation of the complementary relationship between the *academic* and the *pastoral* elements within teaching. In his seminal text on pastoral care, head teacher Michael Marland wrote that:

> *All pastoral care has a teaching element, and the converse is equally true: you cannot "teach" at all effectively without establishing some form of relationship. The pedagogic concern inevitably has a personal element.*
>
> (Marland, 1974: 8)

Relationship building is, therefore, closely linked to the quality of teaching and learning within class. Purdy (2013) quotes one head teacher in an inner-city school where over 50 per cent of the pupils receive free school meals and over 70 per cent are on the SEN register, who places a high value on developing and maintaining positive relationships throughout the school:

> *Relationships need to be right at all levels: that's the starting point. Pastoral care is central to everything we do but it can't be separated from the curriculum. It has to be symbiotic. For us, pastoral care is based on achievement ... [it] means having and instilling high expectations; giving our pupils a second and a third and a fourth chance; encouraging them to learn from their mistakes; and helping them achieve their full potential.*
>
> (Jordan, cited in Purdy, 2013: 16)

In the following example of good practice, we read of one newly qualified teacher whose personal engagement and creative relationship building were key to addressing anxiety-based school refusal:

CASE STUDY

Mr Best was in his first year of teaching and had Harry, a 10-year-old boy, in his class. Harry had complex social, emotional and behavioural difficulties, and had a classroom assistant for two hours each day. He came from a loving home where his parents cared for him and his three siblings, all of whom had ASD. His dad had recently lost his job.

One morning quite out of character, Harry refused to get out of his dad's car to come in to school, so in the end his dad took him home. This continued to happen over the next few days despite encouragements from his dad, headteacher and Mr Best.

Finally, Mr Best found an opportunity to chat with Harry to find out why he disliked coming to school and what sort of activities he would like to do. Harry divulged that he was worried about his dad being lonely at home on his own when the children all went to school and his mum went to work. Harry also revealed that he really liked to play with Lego.

(Continued)

(Continued)

Next morning Harry's dad brought him to school, but this time Mr Best met them in the car park. He showed Harry his own giant box of Lego he had specially brought from home, and described all of the things he had built with it as a child. Mr Best and dad assured Harry that his dad would not be lonely and the headteacher brought Harry's dad into her office for a cup of tea while Harry went in to class and really enjoyed playing with the Lego.

This strategy worked. After twenty minutes Harry settled and was able to join in all of the class activities without exhibiting any anxiety. Following this Mr Best encouraged Harry to build Lego structures for ten minutes each morning and then present what he had made to the other children. Harry continued to come in to school without any fuss, and soon it was possible to reduce further the Lego time until Harry was able to come in to school unaccompanied. Harry's anxiety decreased as he felt safe and valued in an atmosphere of encouragement where his needs were being met. His dad was also full of praise for the school's efforts to support his son within a caring environment. Notably too, at the outset of his teaching career Mr Best had learnt the importance of creatively tuning in to children's individual needs.

In evaluating the example of good practice presented here, consider the following questions:

- How did the class teacher, Mr Best, build a positive relationship with Harry?
- What impact did this have on Harry?
- What skills are involved in building positive teacher/child relationships?

CRITICAL QUESTION

How might this case study inform your practice as a student teacher?

THE IMPORTANCE OF PROFESSIONALISM IN YOUR RELATIONSHIPS WITH CHILDREN

As student teachers, it is also important that relationships developed with children are appropriate, professional and observe 'proper boundaries' (DfE, 2011: 14). Sometimes, student teachers can struggle to make the transition from their identity as a student to a new role or identity as a teacher, and you may even find that you are closer in age to the children in your class than to some or all of the other teachers in the school. Being an effective teacher means adopting a caring, approachable manner in class, but care must also be taken not to overstep the boundaries in terms of excessive informality, trying to become the children's 'friend', or engaging with children through social media.

HOW CAN WE BUILD POSITIVE RELATIONSHIPS WITH PARENTS?

There is no simple, common way to describe a modern family. Families are composed of a myriad of structures and individuals who are constantly evolving (Church *et al.*, 2018). Indeed, family structures throughout the world have changed faster between 1960 and the modern day than any other period of history (Christensen and Aldridge, 2013). If we are going to work with families, then we need to know a little about the child's family structures.

For example, does the child live with both parents or does he or she spend time moving between two households? Does the child live with, or have contact with, extended family such as grandparents and half/step siblings? Do parents work full-time and who do children go home to after school? While all families have a right to privacy, the more understanding and empathy we have for families, the more likely we will be able to encourage all parents to get involved in their children's learning. Here are some ways for you to develop your understanding of the children in your class.

BE PRESENT IN THE PLAYGROUND

One way of finding out more about a child's family is to be present in the playground at the start and end of the school day. This is a valuable approach as it allows parents to see you as approachable, and is also an opportunity for brief communication about practical daily issues, but as a student teacher you must follow your school's stance on this.

KNOW THE SCHOOL POLICY FOR MORE FORMAL DISCUSSIONS WITH PARENTS

While we have already acknowledged the importance of brief informal discussions, it is also important to know the procedures the school has set in place when parents want to have a longer or more formal discussion about their child. The playground or the classroom with children present is not the place for this, so it is important to find out what the expected opportunities are for both informal and formal discussions with parents. As a student teacher, you will not normally be involved in these, but it is valuable information as you move into the profession.

PARENT–TEACHER MEETINGS

Schools will arrange parent–teacher meetings at least once a year. These are formal meetings where children's progress is discussed and information is shared. It would be very useful to ask your teacher if you could sit in on a parent–teacher meeting as a trainee to allow you to see how this meeting is conducted. It is an opportunity to see how the teacher opens and closes the consultation, the setting and layout of the meeting, what information is shared, how the teacher delivers more difficult messages and negotiates more challenging conversations, and how the meeting is documented.

SCHOOL-LEVEL COMMUNICATION WITH PARENTS

As a student teacher, you should make yourself aware of how your school communicates with parents. This can be through the school website, printed notes and newsletters, social media and specific apps such as Seesaw.

This is a worthwhile exercise to see not only how the school presents itself to the wider community, but also to see what type of information is shared with parents.

GET PARENTS INVOLVED

Many schools actively encourage parents to become more involved in their children's learning by running sessions for parents – for example, to help them understand the use of phonics, or show them specific approaches for teaching aspects of numeracy. These can be face-to-face or even through videos posted on the school's website. Every school is different, so no one single approach will meet every school's needs. Therefore, it is pertinent for you as a student teacher to consider the variety of opportunities provided by different schools and reflect on their effectiveness.

WHAT ARE THE PITFALLS AND CHALLENGES IN BUILDING RELATIONSHIPS WITH CHILDREN?

- Many student teachers can feel under pressure to focus solely on test scores at the expense of the child's holistic development, and can struggle to find the time to build relationships with children and/or to find out about their interests and background.
- It can be easy to feel overwhelmed by the pastoral challenges faced by some children, and out of your depth as an inexperienced teacher. In such circumstances it is important to know the pastoral care or safeguarding policy and the formal reporting procedures in the school, but also to take advantage of informal advice from more experienced colleagues.
- It is important yet challenging to maintain high behavioural expectations in class as a means of creating a safe, stable and predictable classroom environment where children can feel able and motivated to learn and to progress towards self-fulfilment (Maslow, 1970).
- Inevitably, there will be some children with whom you will struggle to develop positive relationships. While you should make every effort to prepare appropriately differentiated and well-resourced lessons, the child's behaviour may be due to circumstances outside school (remember to report any safeguarding concerns immediately) and beyond your control. Consult with more experienced colleagues to develop proactive in-class strategies, respond to inappropriate behaviours fairly and consistently in line with the school's behaviour policy, and strive at all times to maintain a positive relationship with the child.

WHAT ARE THE PITFALLS AND CHALLENGES IN BUILDING RELATIONSHIPS WITH PARENTS?

- It is important to maintain a professional relationship with parents, which includes avoiding the use of first names and keeping your social media accounts private.

- Try to develop an attitude to parental partnerships as an equal partnership, recognising parents' knowledge about their children, and actively encouraging a two-way flow of information.
- Avoid educational jargon as the language and policies within education can be very confusing and can contribute to parents feeling they lack competence and knowledge.
- Don't make assumptions about groups of parents. This can be challenging when we do not share the same experiences or social capital as some parents.
- It is important to realise that a 'one size fits all' approach to working with parents is neither realistic nor effective.
- Effective parenting is a very difficult task and it is essential to understand that just because a parent finds parenting hard, this does not mean they do not love their child.
- Remember that parental engagement is never complete, as each new school year brings a new cohort of parents.

EXPLORING IMPACT

CRITICAL QUESTION

How do you know if your work to involve parents is having an impact?

Measuring the direct impact of building positive relationships with children and parents can at first glance seem more difficult than, for instance, measuring the impact of a new teaching strategy. However, the research cited (e.g. DfES, 2003; Goodall *et al.*, 2011), the approaches proposed and the case studies outlined in this chapter have all demonstrated how approaches and interventions based on good communication and positive relationships can have a significant and measurable impact on pupil well-being, engagement and, ultimately, on learning outcomes. Both case studies in particular highlight how teachers (even in their first year of teaching) can be creative and proactive in addressing the needs of individual children in their class, enlisting the support of parents, and leading to measurable impact in terms of learning outcomes in the classroom.

FURTHER EXPLORATION OF BUILDING RELATIONSHIPS WITH CHILDREN AND PARENTS

As a student teacher, remember that there is lots to be learned from more experienced colleagues about building positive relationships with children and parents, and these colleagues will also often be able to share experiences and learning which will help you to avoid the most common pitfalls. Take every opportunity to listen, ask and learn at this stage in your career.

CHAPTER SUMMARY

- Building positive relationships with children and parents is an integral part of being a primary teacher.
- Building relationships with children is predicated on an understanding of their most basic need to feel safe, valued and included in the classroom before being ready or able to learn. It also assumes an understanding of the uniqueness, not only of the children themselves, but of their family backgrounds.
- Relationship building can be challenging and takes time and effort.
- Relationship building can be seen as an invaluable learning partnership established on the basis of mutual respect and two-way communication.
- Engaging meaningfully with parents can be facilitated *formally* through parent-teacher meetings, but can also be maintained and developed quite *informally* by simply being available and approachable to parents for a 'quick word' in the playground at the beginning or end of the school day.
- Positive relationships lead to happier children, happier classrooms and in turn better learning outcomes.

ASSIGNMENTS

If you are writing an ITE assignment on building positive relationships with children and parents, it will be useful for you to consider the following questions:

1. To what extent do you think that building positive relationships with children is linked to raising their academic attainment?
2. What strategies would you adopt to help ensure positive relationships with parents, and how important are these relationships to children's learning?
3. How can building positive relationships with children have an impact on relationships with parents?
4. How would you work to encourage greater involvement by disengaged or disaffected parents?

The following sources provide useful further reading:

MacBlain, S., Dunn, J. and Luke, I. (2017) The changing nature of families, in MacBlain, S., Dunn, J. and Luke, I. (eds) *Contemporary Childhood*. London: SAGE, pp. 85–107.

This chapter will help you develop an understanding of the increasing diversity of families that you will work with as a teacher.

Evans, S. (2017) Dealing with parents. Times Educational Supplement. Available at: www.tes.com/teaching-resources/blog/dealing-parents (accessed 06/07/18).

This article provides lots of practical advice for teachers to help ensure that communication with parents is effective.

Hiltz, J. (2015) Helicopter parents can be a good thing. *Phi Delta Kappan*, 96(7): 26-9.

Although overprotective parents are often criticised, this article argues that they can actually be a valuable asset for teachers.

Purdy, N. (2013) Pastoral care: Origins, definitions and roles, in *Pastoral Care 11-16: A critical introduction*. London: Bloomsbury.

This chapter provides a useful overview of what we mean by pastoral care, and the importance of building relationships with children.

REFERENCES

Best, R. (1995) Concepts in pastoral care and RSE, in R. Best, P. Lang, C. Lodge and C. Watkins (eds) *Pastoral Care and Personal–Social Education – Entitlement and Provision*. London: Cassell.

Bronfenbrenner, U. (1979) *The Ecology of Human Development*. Cambridge, MA: Harvard University Press.

Christensen, L. and Aldridge, J. (2013) *Critical Pedagogy for Early Childhood and Elementary Educators*. New York: Springer.

Church, J., Hegde, A., Averett, P. and Ballard, S. (2018) Early childhood administrators' attitudes and experiences in working with gay and lesbian parented families. *Early Child Development and Care*, 188(3): 264–80.

Department for Education (DfE) (2011) *Teachers' Standards: Guidance for school leaders, school staff and governing bodies*. Available at: www.gov.uk/government/uploads/system/uploads/attachment_data/file/665520/Teachers__Standards.pdf (accessed 06/07/18).

Department for Education (DfE) (2012) *Effective Pre-school, Primary and Secondary Education 3-14 Project: Final report from the Key Stage 3 phase: Influences on students' development from age 3–14*. London: Institute of Education.

Department for Education and Skills (DfES) (2003) *The Impact of Parental Involvement, Parental Support and Family Education on Pupil Achievement and Adjustment: A literature review*. London: DfES.

Department of Education Northern Ireland (DENI) (2016) *Protecting Life in Schools: Helping protect against suicide by supporting pupils' emotional health and wellbeing*. Available at: http://dera.ioe.ac.uk/25931/1/ENGLISH%20Protecting%20Life%20in%20Schools.pdf (accessed 06/07/18).

Goodall, J., Vorhaus, J., Carpentieri, J., Brooks, G., Akerman, R. and Harris, A. (2011) *Review of Best Practice in Parental Engagement: Research Report DFE-RR156*. London: DfE.

Hornby, G. and Atkinson, M. (2003) A framework for promoting mental health in school. *Pastoral Care in Education*, 21(2): 3–9.

Marland, M. (1974) *Pastoral Care*. London: Heinemann Educational Books.

Maslow, A. (1970) *Motivation and Personality* (2nd edn). New York: Harper & Row.

OECD (2017a) Parental involvement, student performance and satisfaction with life, in *PISA 2015 Results (Volume III): Students' well-being*. Paris: OECD Publishing, pp. 155–71.

OECD (2017b) *Starting Strong V: Transitions from early education childhood and care to primary education*. Available at: http://dx.doi.org/10.1787/9789264276253-en (accessed 06/07/18).

Purdy, N. (2013) Pastoral care: Origins, definitions and roles, in *Pastoral Care 11–16: A critical introduction*. London: Bloomsbury.

QCA (2000) *Curriculum Guidance for the Foundation Stage*. London: QCA/DfEE.

23

HOW CAN OPPORTUNITIES BEYOND THE CLASSROOM MAXIMISE LEARNING OUTCOMES?

Elaine Skates has been the Chief Executive of the Council for Learning Outside the Classroom (the national charity for LOtC) for four years and as such is involved in the Strategic Research Group for Learning in Natural Environments and has commissioned research into the impact of residential learning experiences on behalf of the Learning Away Consortium.

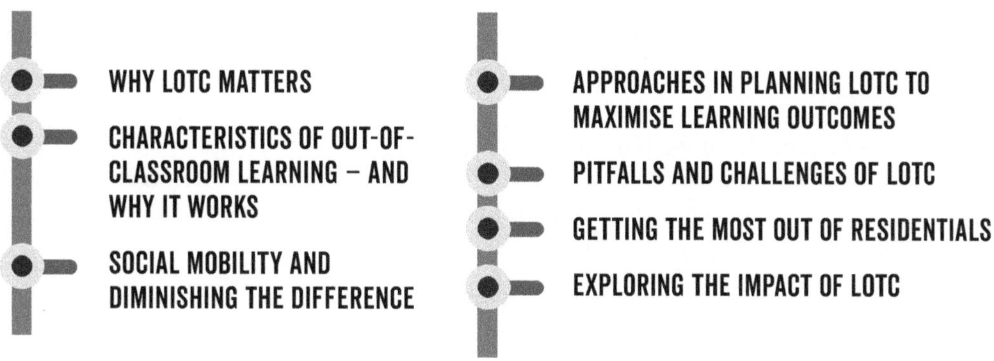

KEY WORDS

- Cultural learning
- Learning in natural environments
- Learning outside the classroom
- Outdoor learning
- Residentials

INTRODUCTION

All schools offer some learning outside the classroom (LOtC) opportunities – including learning in the school grounds, educational visits and residentials. This chapter will help you to consider what schools are trying to achieve by offering pupils these experiences, and which experiences will be most effective in achieving which outcomes, This chapter will also help you to consider how we can plan and evaluate learning outside the classroom to maximise the benefits for pupils.

In this chapter we will explore the short-term benefits that can be achieved when learning is taken beyond the classroom walls and how taking a strategic approach to planning these experiences can lead to medium- and long-term impacts for pupils' academic achievement and personal development. Drawing on evidence, we will learn about how to plan to maximise learning outcomes and will go on to consider the practical considerations of planning and leading an LOtC activity. Finally, we will consider tools for evaluating LOtC experiences.

WHY LEARNING OUTSIDE THE CLASSROOM MATTERS

THE EVIDENCE BASE

Learning outside the classroom (LOtC) is the use of any space beyond the classroom for teaching and learning. LOtC experiences can be close to home or further afield, indoors or outdoors, and can be short or long in duration (see Figure 23.1).

There is a wealth of evidence in support of the benefits of LOtC, but the evidence base is broad in that it focuses on a very varied range of activities, from Forest School to museum visits to overseas expeditions. Some of these activities may be sub-categorised as 'outdoor learning', and others more as 'cultural learning' and much of the evidence can also be categorised into these areas.

An important piece of evidence in the outdoor learning space is the 2015 evidence review from the Blagrave Trust and the Institute of Outdoor Learning (Fiennes *et al.*, 2015), which goes into depth about the difficulties of drawing conclusions from a review of a varied range of interventions.

However, despite the broad range of LOtC activities and learning locations, there are a few studies that evaluate the impact of LOtC across the full range of provision and identify a number of shared benefits of these activities.

CRITICAL THINKING

Is it possible to evaluate the impact of LOtC given the range of learning experiences that this term can cover?

The first of these is the 2008 research from Ofsted, which concluded that when planned and implemented well, learning outside the classroom contributed significantly to raising standards and improving pupils' personal, social and emotional development.

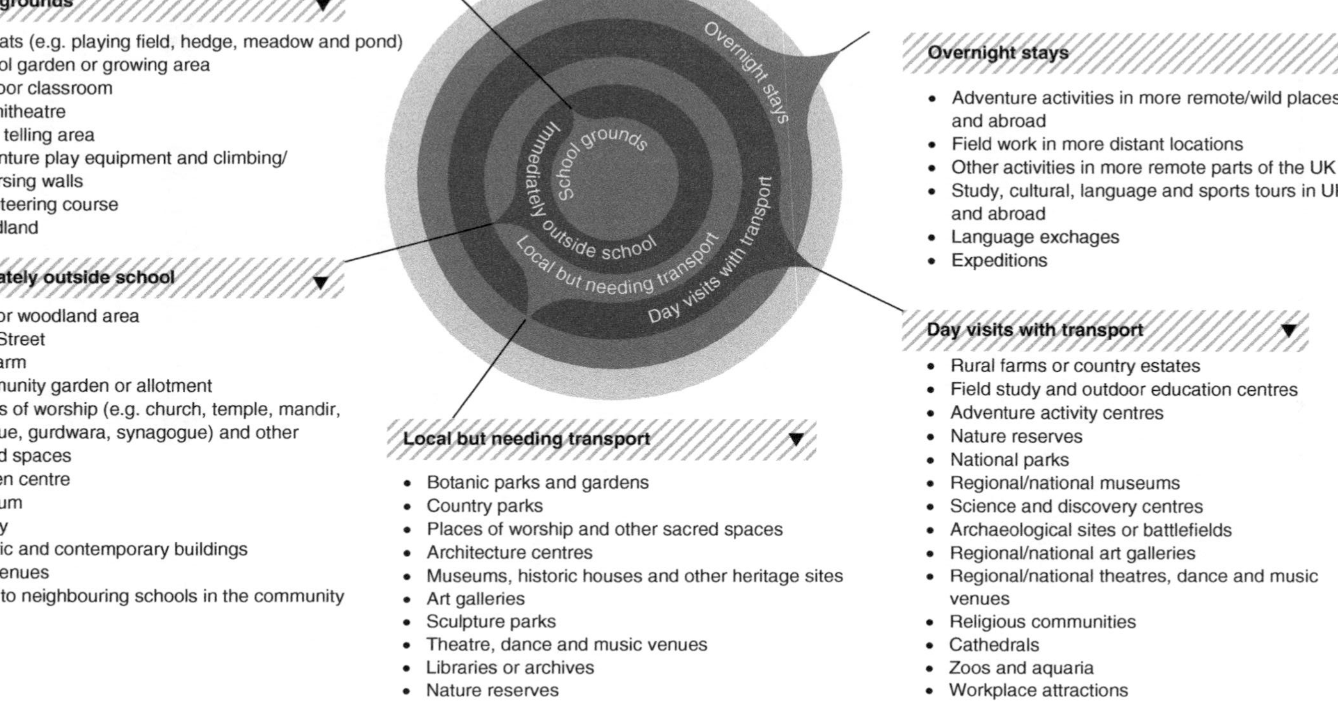

Figure 23.1 LOtC opportunities can be close to home or further afield and take place in various locations indoors and outdoors

KEY READING

In 2008, the *Every Experience Matters* review (Malone, 2008) drew on evidence around the globe and concluded that by experiencing the world beyond the classroom children:

- achieve higher results in knowledge and skill acquisition;
- increase their physical health and motor skills;
- socialise and interact in new and different ways with their peers and adults;
- show improved attention, enhanced self-concept, self-esteem and mental health;
- change their environmental behaviours, values and attitudes for the positive, and their resilience to be able to respond to changing conditions in their environment.

The full report can be found here:

http://attitudematters.org/documents/Every%20Experience%20Matters.pdf

When thinking about priorities in schools today – whether we are thinking about pupil progress, supporting pupils to develop their attitude to learning, SMCS, or considering how a school responds to rising obesity and concerns about young people's mental health – it is clear that a progressive programme of learning outside the classroom experiences can make a significant contribution to meeting these priorities. However, we hear so often that LOtC can be overlooked due to pressures on teacher workloads and school budgets. LOtC is all too often seen as an add-on or extra-curricula activity, which is why it is sometimes not at the top of the list of school improvement priorities. In comparison, schools that see LOtC as being integral to curriculum delivery and supporting achievement find LOtC much easier to justify.

We can take this one more step to consider the potential long-term impacts of a sustained programme of learning outside the classroom. Thinking about natural environment interventions as an example, this model of the life-time trajectory of an individual illustrates the impact that investment in learning outside the classroom in early life might have across a person's lifetime (see Figure 23.2).

CHARACTERISTICS OF OUT-OF-CLASSROOM LEARNING AND WHY IT WORKS

Taking the evidence back to the potential short-term impacts of an isolated experience, the evidence from the *Every Experience Matters* review (Malone, 2008)) suggests that whether the learning takes place in woodland or in an art gallery, there are a number of shared benefits of LOtC experiences, which make them such valuable tools for teaching and learning.

Learning outside the classroom interventions share a number of characteristics that are intrinsically linked to the impact of the experiences. These can be seen as the magic ingredients that make LOtC work.

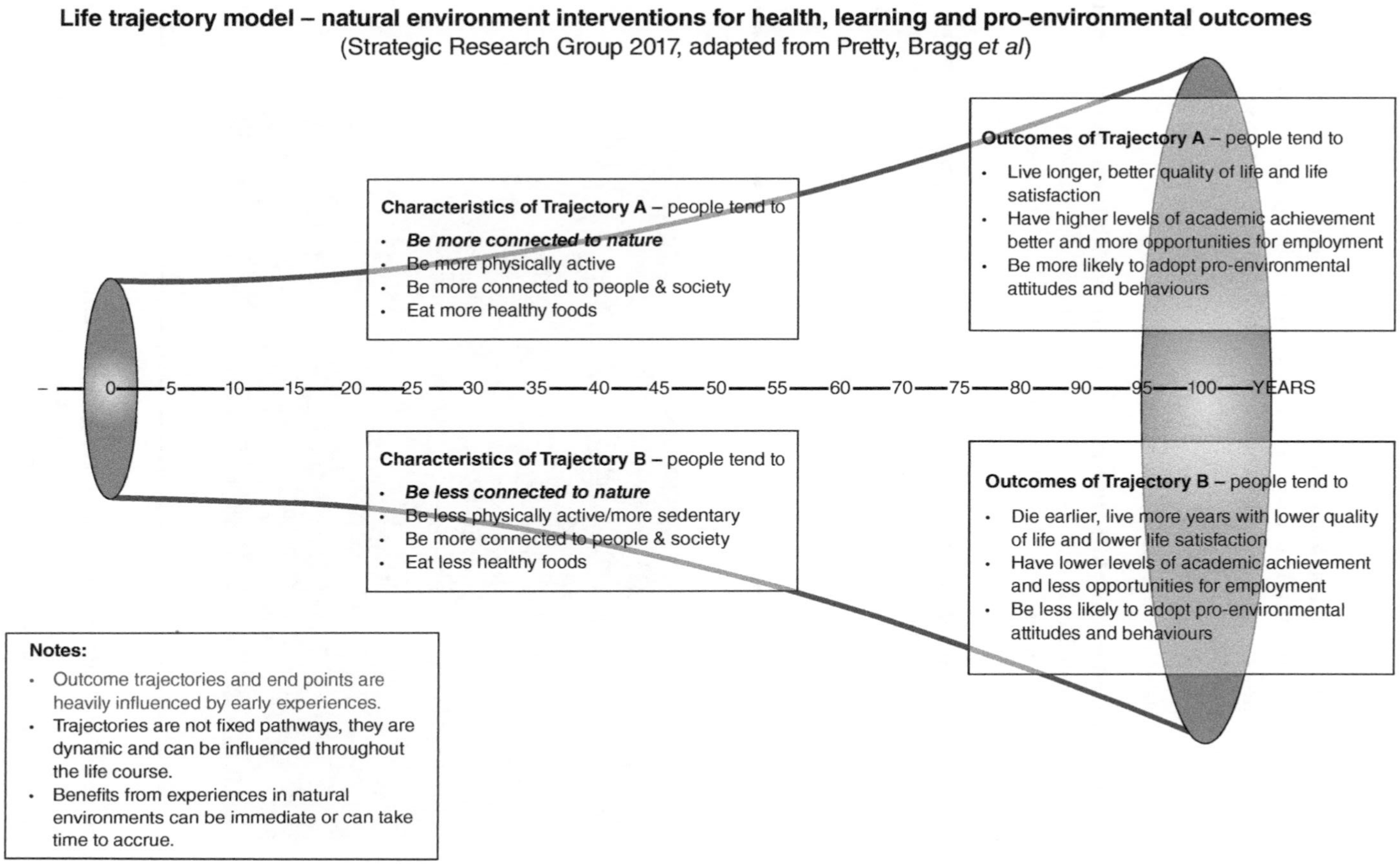

Life trajectory model – natural environment interventions for health, learning and pro-environmental outcomes
(Strategic Research Group 2017, adapted from Pretty, Bragg *et al*)

Characteristics of Trajectory A – people tend to

- ***Be more connected to nature***
- Be more physically active
- Be more connected to people & society
- Eat more healthy foods

Outcomes of Trajectory A – people tend to

- Live longer, better quality of life and life satisfaction
- Have higher levels of academic achievement better and more opportunities for employment
- Be more likely to adopt pro-environmental attitudes and behaviours

– 0—5—10—15—20—25—30—35—40—45—50—55—60—70—75—80—90—95—100—YEARS

Characteristics of Trajectory B – people tend to

- ***Be less connected to nature***
- Be less physically active/more sedentary
- Be more connected to people & society
- Eat less healthy foods

Outcomes of Trajectory B – people tend to

- Die earlier, live more years with lower quality of life and lower life satisfaction
- Have lower levels of academic achievement and less opportunities for employment
- Be less likely to adopt pro-environmental attitudes and behaviours

Notes:

- Outcome trajectories and end points are heavily influenced by early experiences.
- Trajectories are not fixed pathways, they are dynamic and can be influenced throughout the life course.
- Benefits from experiences in natural environments can be immediate or can take time to accrue.

Figure 23.2 Early contact with nature has been linked with long-term positive life outcomes

These magic ingredients are as follows:

- **The wow factor that makes the learning memorable and engaging (resulting in affective benefits and reinforcing academic learning).** As Malone explains in *Every Experience Matters* (2008), 'Experiential learning is a process that develops knowledge, skills and attitudes based on consciously thinking about an experience. Thus, it involves direct and active personal experience combined with reflection and feedback. Experiential learning is therefore personal and effective in nature influencing both feelings and emotions as well as enhancing knowledge and skills.'
- **The application of knowledge and skills to the real world, which increases the quality and depth of learning (cognitive benefits).** As Nundy (2001) concluded, fieldwork has the capacity to allow pupils to operate at levels of learning higher than those attainable within the classroom alone, thus significantly enhancing achievement.
- **The opportunity to learn (and teach!) in new ways (benefiting pupil learning behaviours and teacher CPD).** Benefits to teacher CPD were reported in both the 2015 evaluation from the Learning Away project (York Consulting, 2015) and the 2016 final report from the Natural Connections project (Waite *et al.*, 2016) – both large-scale evaluated programmes in the field of LOtC.

INFO 23.1

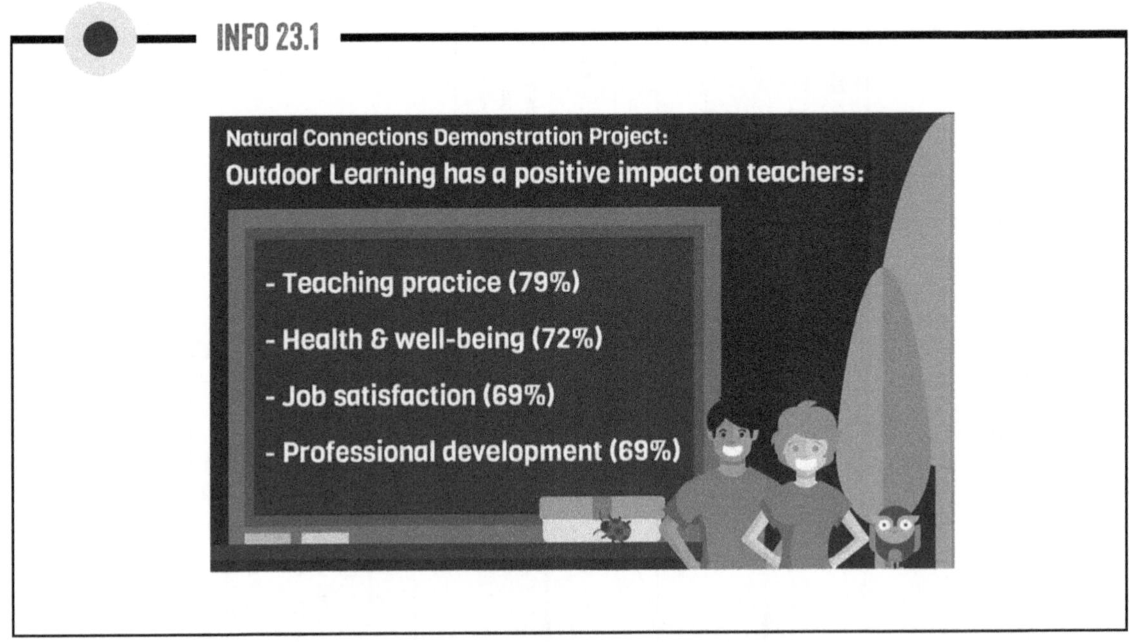

- **The impact on relationships, which has a long-term benefit back inside the classroom.** In 2015 the Learning Away final evaluation report (York Consulting, 2015) cited evidence from long-term follow-up surveys, that 79 per cent of KS2 pupils said, because of the trip, they knew teachers better; 65 per cent of secondary students said their teachers had a better understanding of how they liked to learn.

SOCIAL MOBILITY AND DIMINISHING THE DIFFERENCE

Intuitively, we understand that disadvantaged young people who do not have access to the same breadth of experiences at home – those who have never visited a farm, zoo, art gallery or seen the sea – stand to benefit the most from accessing LOtC experiences through their schools. Research from the Education Endowment Foundation in 2014 (Torgerson *et al.*, 2014) demonstrated how memorable LOtC experiences could be effectively utilised as part of a programme to improve achievement in writing. The project used memorable experiences, such as trips to local landmarks or visits from Second World War veterans as a focus for writing lessons along with an approach called 'Self-Regulated Strategy Development' (SRSD) to help struggling writers in Years 6 and 7.

CRITICAL QUESTION

Why are LOtC experiences so memorable for some children?

The effect size was statistically significant, meaning that it is unlikely to have occurred by chance, and can be envisaged as saying that participating pupils made approximately nine months' additional progress compared to similar pupils who did not participate in the intervention. The effect was larger for pupils receiving free school meals, with pupils in that group showing 18 months' additional progress as a result of the project.

APPROACHES IN PLANNING LOTC TO MAXIMISE LEARNING OUTCOMES

The 2008 Ofsted report *Learning Outside the Classroom – how far should you go?* found that learning outside the classroom was most successful when it was an integral element of long-term curriculum planning and closely linked to classroom activities.

KEY THEORY

The *Learning Outside the Classroom – how far should you go?* report can be found here:

http://lotc.org.uk/wp-content/uploads/2010/12/Ofsted-Report-Oct-2008.pdf

This was echoed in the 2016 evaluation of the Natural Connections large-scale demonstration project (Waite et al., 2016) which recommended that schools should match outdoor learning with other school priorities and the findings of the Learning Away final evaluation report in 2015 (York Consulting, 2015), which recommended that residentials are fully integrated with the curriculum and ethos of the school.

Recommendations from these pieces of research have informed the development of the LOtC mark accreditation, which recognises and supports the development of LOtC across all subject areas, and these pieces of research also inform the approaches advocated in this chapter.

There are a number of recommendations around the importance of support for staff CPD and senior leadership support which, as a newly qualified teacher, you may not have much influence over. However, you can certainly think strategically about how LOtC can help you address the needs of your class/individual students and plan the experiences as part of your curriculum planning.

CRITICAL QUESTION

How can you ensure that LOtC experiences are integrated into your long- and medium-term planning?

ASK YOURSELF – WHAT DO YOU WANT TO ACHIEVE?

This is the fundamental question when planning any LOtC experience or programme. The needs of every group of children is different, so consider the needs of your class – what are the barriers to their learning or are there any particular outcomes you or the school would like to achieve? Are pupils in your class lacking any particular type of experience? For example, urban children may have very little experience of natural places, whereas children from rural schools may have little experience of visiting busy urban venues, using public transport or visiting cultural venues.

FOCUS ON LEARNING OUTCOMES AND LINKS TO CLASSROOM TEACHING

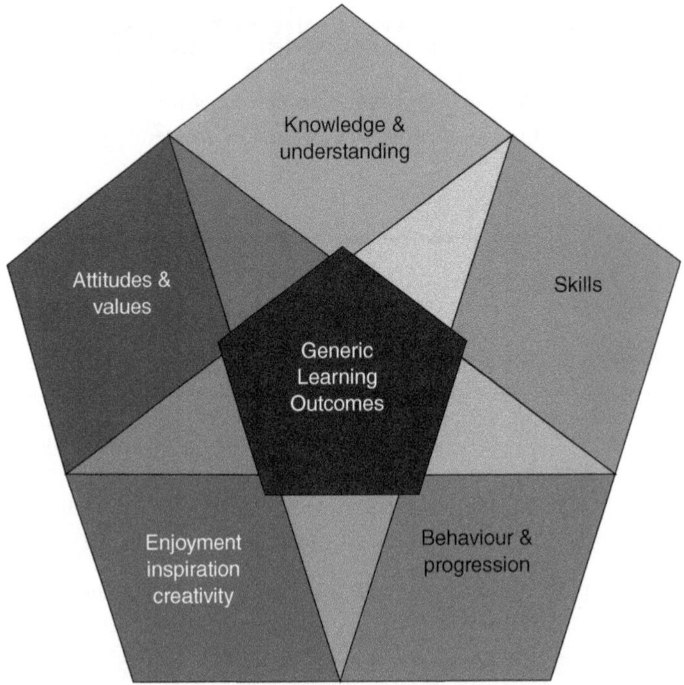

Figure 23.3 Learning outcomes include a broad range of outcomes – including those needed to support people's health and well-being and a healthy natural environment

Think about curriculum aims and topics, and then consider how LOtC experiences can be used to enhance learning and the delivery of the curriculum. Consider how the experience can be linked to classroom teaching in different subject areas; for example, to achieve SMCS outcomes or enthuse writing.

DURATION AND PROGRESSION

The regularity and duration of LOtC activities is an important consideration. The outdoor learning evidence review from the Blagrave Trust (Fiennes *et al.*, 2015) found that overnight and multi-day activities had a stronger effect than shorter ones. For this reason, LOtC activities should never be planned in isolation as one-off 'trips'. They should always be planned as part of a progressive programme of experiences in order to maximise the impact. The more frequent the experiences, the more impactful your LOtC programme will have been. Using the school grounds and local area for learning will make regular LOtC experiences realistic on a limited budget.

KEY READING

Free guidance on planning, running and evaluating effective LOtC experiences is available on the Council for Learning Outside the Classroom's website: www.lotc.org.uk. You can also sign up to the free termly newsletter through the website.

PITFALLS AND CHALLENGES OF LEARNING OUTSIDE THE CLASSROOM

We hear a lot about the barriers to learning outside the classroom: funding; health and safety; pressure on staff time; a narrowing curriculum; and focus on academic results being the top five.

CRITICAL QUESTION

What might make teachers reticent to plan residential trips?

However, evidence (Dillon and Dickie, 2012) shows that the underlying cause of schools not doing more LOtC is more closely tied to teacher confidence than demographic factors. If teachers have the right support and CPD, then a can-do attitude will help to overcome the other barriers.

TEACHER CONFIDENCE AND COMPETENCE

The best piece of advice is to secure a mentor to support you the first couple of times you plan an LOtC activity. Build your confidence and experience by starting with shorter activities in the school grounds or local area, building up slowly to activities further afield. This will also help you build your confidence in managing behaviour beyond the classroom. A gradual approach will also ensure that other stakeholders, including your pupils, parents and TAs, have time to build up their own confidence. I once worked with an infant school that did very little LOtC and then suddenly embarked on a whole-school visit to the seaside, a three-hour coach journey away. It was a fantastic experience, but very challenging for staff, anxious parents and some of the children who had no experience of environments such as motorway service stations. A more gradual build-up with trips closer to home would have meant this was not such a leap forward for everyone involved.

RISK MANAGEMENT

Managing risk is a major source of anxiety around planning educational visits. The risk management process should be sensible and proportionate to the level of risk associated with the activity. That means it should not take you hours to plan a simple activity in the school grounds! However, it is vital that you follow your employer's guidance and that you are adequately supported as you plan your first educational visit so find out who the educational visit, coordinator is at your school and ask them to support you through the process.

KEY READING

Choosing LOtC venues and providers who hold the LOtC Quality Badge will help you identify good quality and safe provision, and help you reduce red tape when planning the visit. Search for LOtC Quality Badge holders at www.lotcqualitybadge.org.uk

The Outdoor Education Advisers' Panel website will help you access guidance. Find your local adviser and Educational Visit Coordinator, or Visit Leader training in your area at http://oeap.info/

GETTING THE MOST OUT OF RESIDENTIALS

Schools taking part in the Learning Away action research developed strategic planning methods to maximise learning outcomes for their pupils taking part in residentials. This case study, written by a teacher at the school, is an example of how teachers can plan progressive LOtC activities as an integral element of long-term curriculum planning and closely linked to classroom activities.

CASE STUDY

The Christ Church Learning Away partnership aims to provide a high-quality, annual residential experience as an integral part of our creative curriculum for all pupils from Year 2 to Year 6. These are not presented to parents or children as 'extras' or 'holidays', but rather as an important part of the term's area of research.

As most of our residential experiences take place at Crosby Hall Educational Trust (CHET), which provides a safe, contrasting environment in a rural setting close to our schools, we feel it is important to ensure that pupils do not repeat the same sorts of activities year after year. Our experiences are therefore very carefully planned to extend and enhance the areas of research (termly themes) being explored in class.

Parents and children are involved at the planning stage and are asked to share their ideas for events and activities. This puts pupil voice at the core of our residentials as well as helping to allay some of the anxieties of the parents. Following these initial consultations, dedicated planning days prior to the residential visits then take place at the centre, working closely with the CHET staff. Our model of developing bespoke residentials is new not only to us, but also to the centre, which had previously tended to offer a menu of activities from which schools could choose.

We spend a lot of time referring to the skills they build while they are away. Upon return to class we continue to reiterate these skills daily, to allow the children to be more independent. The skills are displayed as 'Thinking Caps' as a constant reminder.

Back in class, we plan activities to build on the skills and experiences the children have had on residential.

- **Literacy** lessons draw on pupils' memories of the residential, such as soundscapes of things pupils had heard during a night time walk, and descriptive poetry.
- In **art**, pupils make photo collages of the residential learning activities, and in ICT they produce photo stories of their visit, highlighting what they enjoyed and learned.
- One group of children became a **marketing team** for the venue of a Year 6 residential, producing persuasive leaflets and advertisements to boost visits.
- Another group of children used skills they learned during an **orienteering** activity on residential to produce their own trail round school. The pupils then **led sessions with some of our younger children** and taught them the orienteering skills that they had learned.

Pupil voice plays an important part in this process, with children discussing the objectives covered during the residential, highlighting those still to be addressed and with the opportunity to include additional strands of enquiry which might have emerged at the residential.

Staff have seen a real benefit to holding residentials at different times of the year and the positive impact that this has had on staff/pupil relationships. Similarly, they have seen a marked impact on pupil engagement and motivation.

KEY READING

Free case studies and resources to help you plan residential experiences and online training modules are available on the Learning Away website at www.learningaway.org.uk

EXPLORING THE IMPACT OF LEARNING OUTSIDE OF THE CLASSROOM

It is perhaps strange, given the resources needed in terms of staff time and funding for learning outside the classroom experiences, that senior leaders and governing bodies do not require evidence of the impact of learning outside the classroom practice as a matter of course. However, evidence from the 2017 report from

Learning Away, *The State of School Residentials in England* (LKMCo, 2017) demonstrates that the evaluation of residentials is a real weakness in schools. Learning outside the classroom is sometimes seen as the only space in education in some schools where it is acceptable to do something simply because it is 'fun', with no need to measure the impact. However, in light of the pressures on school funding and teacher time, fun is extremely hard to justify, and is certainly the first thing to be cut.

It is as important to measure the impact of learning outside the classroom as any other intervention, both from the point of view of understanding what works in order that practitioners can learn from past experiences, evidence the value of LOtC and also to make the case to senior leaders and governors for future learning outside the classroom activities.

It is true that there are challenges with evaluating LOtC. For example, how do you evidence that improvement in pupils' attainment in English in SATs this year is as a result of your experiential writing residential or as a result of any number of classroom-based strategies that may have impacted in this area? However, this is the case with evaluating the impact of any intervention – LOtC evaluation is certainly not unique in this regard. Other challenges arise when looking at the evaluation of non-academic outcomes – such as personal development or character traits.

SUMMATIVE ASSESSMENT

Summative assessment takes place at the end of a topic, subject or term to assess performance. It can involve formal tests or exams, structured projects, or formal observations. It produces a discrete result that can easily be quantified.

The usual sources of quantitative data used for monitoring in schools is valuable data with regard to evaluating LOtC too – attainment and progress data, number of red cards, attendance, etc. Teacher observations can be very valuable here, too, and applying widely used evaluation practice from the Early Years Foundation Stage can be very illuminating.

Triangulating the quantitative data with observations recorded during the activity and pupil/teacher views collected after the event is a good way of strengthening the evidence of the impact of LOtC because if three sources of data are pointing to a particular intervention having a measurable result, the more reliable that conclusion will be judged to be (see Figure 23.4).

FORMATIVE ASSESSMENT

Formative assessment is assessment *for* learning and is part of the learning process, allowing teachers and pupils to constantly review progress and adjust teaching accordingly.

Formative assessment is ongoing and is a process of constantly monitoring pupil understanding, and adjusting teaching and practice to suit the pupils and maximise their learning. It is usually very informal, and although conclusions and activities can be recorded, there won't necessarily be any readily quantifiable data produced.

Formative assessment works very well with learning outside the classroom. The key to using formative assessment as part of your evaluation strategy is allowing the learners to tell you what they've got from the session, and what they'd still like to know/achieve. A major goal of this kind of continuous assessment is the encouragement of reflective learning among the participants.

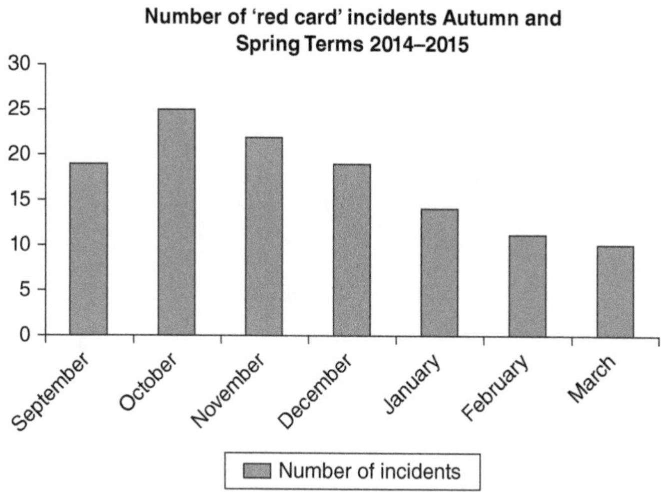

Figure 23.4 One school used red card incident data to monitor the impact of their new outdoor learning programme introduced in September 2014

3–2–1

3	things I learned today ...
2	things I found interesting ...
1	question I have ...

Figure 23.5 A summative assessment tool for an LOtC activity

REFLECTIVE LEARNING

Modern teaching places an emphasis much more firmly on reflective learning, meaning teaching in a way that allows space for learners to analyse their own learning experience and integrate it into their lives. This allows for a deeper understanding of the topic in hand, but also for greater personal development as a result of educational activities. As with formative assessment, this makes it very compatible with LOtC.

My outdoor learning self-assessment for summer 2015

By Alexandra

☺ Super self-assessment!

At Thorpe Woodlands I learned	I found this tricky
I learned to work as a team I leard to hold on to a sip wire. I leared to put the stick right.	I found this tricky becaus on the train for it skil's I fell off the sit wire.
My favourite part was	**My best moment was**
My favourite part was the big fold because it was fun.	My best moment was finding the sticks **because** miss BB hided my sticks. He he! I did!
I got better at	**I prefer learning ~~inside~~ / outside because**
I got better at doowing the big folled because I dint look at the flour. Well done ☺	I prefer learning outside because I like playing in the snown. ✓
Something I would like to try next half term	
I would like to go to the forist beause it ~~was~~ will be fun. ✓	

Figure 23.6 An example of an outdoor learning self-assessment tool

METHODOLOGY FOR EVALUATING LOTC

Your evaluation strategy is very much part of the process of planning an LOtC experience. Think about the methods you will use to evaluate the residential at an early stage. Before the LOtC experience you might:

- collect baseline data: gender, Pupil Premium, additional needs, attendance, attainment;
- write a pen portrait about one or two children you will follow in detail during the residential: background information; interaction with peers and adults; attitude to learning and school; personality traits;
- identify the focus group;

- use circle time to visualise the venue, discuss concerns, involve children in conversations around risk management.

During the experience you might:

- record observations/write notes;
- take and annotate photographs;
- take video and sound recordings;
- give children cameras to record their experiences;
- use reflective discussion.

After the experience you might:

- use circle time to revisit and reflect on the experience;
- talk to focus group pupils to gain evidence of impact;
- update pen portraits with observations;
- compare baseline data;
- compare progress of the focus group against the aims of the experience.

FURTHER INFORMATION

High Quality Outdoor Learning is a publication from the Outdoor Council and available from the Institute of Outdoor Learning. It is a valuable tool in training teachers and youth workers, as well as promoting the use of outdoor learning. www.outdoor-learning.org/Good-Practice/Good-Practice/High-Quality-Outdoor-Learning

Countryside Classroom is a single destination web resource where teachers can find and access the resources, places to visit and people to ask that will support their teaching about food, farming and the natural environment. www.countrysideclassroom.org.uk/

Children Learning Outside the Classroom from Birth to 11 (Sue Waite). This textbook helps students and professionals understand the importance of getting children learning outside the traditional classroom, and is packed full of creative information and ideas for teachers and practitioners to incorporate outdoor activities throughout the school curriculum.

Dirty Teaching – a beginners guide to learning outdoors (Juliet Robertson) offers tips and tricks to help any primary school teacher to kick-start or further develop their outdoor practice.

Learning Outside the Classroom – a CLOtC Member's Handbook is a practical guide to LOtC sent to all new members of the Council for Learning Outside the Classroom. Students can sign up to membership at www.lotc.org.uk/membership/

CHAPTER SUMMARY

Learning outside the classroom benefits:

- Knowledge and skills
- Well-being
- Personal, social and emotional development
- Relationships
- Attitudes and values

Characteristics of LOtC activities - magic ingredients:

- Memorable learning
- Real-world application
- New ways of learning and teaching
- Improved relationships = long-term impacts in the classroom and in later life

Maximising impact on learning outcomes:

- What do you want to achieve?
- Focus on learning outcomes
- Plan as a progressive programme
- Build confidence
- Manage risk

Evaluation:

- Triangulate data
- Formative assessment
- Reflective learning

ASSIGNMENTS

If you are writing an ITE assignment on LOtC, it will be useful for you to think through the following:

- Do you believe that LOtC has more impact than traditional classroom teaching? If so, when and how should it be best utilised and for what objectives (achievement, mental health, personal development, etc.)?

- What LOtC interventions are most effective in your opinion? Compare the methodologies and characteristics of different approaches/projects (forest school/curriculum-focused LOtC such as advocated by LOtC; Natural Connections/Learning Away). Can you find evidence that certain approaches are more impactful in delivering some outcomes than others?
- What are the benefits of LOtC to teachers? Can you find any evidence that shows LOtC has a positive impact on teaching practice?

Useful texts

Knight, S. (2017) *Forest Schools in Practice*. London: SAGE.

Long, K. (2018) *Awe in Action: Delivering high impact learning*. Stoke-on-Trent: K. Long Publishing.

MacFarlane, C. (2013) *Write Out of the Classroom*. London: Routledge.

Waite, S (2011) *Children Learning Outside the Classroom from Birth to 11*. London: SAGE.

Useful research

York Consulting (2015) *Evaluation of Learning Away: Final Report*. Available at: http://learningaway.org.uk

Waite, S., Passy, R., Gilchrist, M., Hunt, A. and Blackwell, I. (2016) *Natural Connections Demonstration Project, 2012-2016: Final report*. Natural England Commissioned Reports, NECR215.

REFERENCES

Bragg, R. (2014) Nature-based interventions for mental wellbeing and sustainable behaviour: The potential for green care in the UK. A thesis submitted for the degree of Doctor of Philosophy in Environmental Sciences.

Dillon, J. and Dickie, I. (2012) *Learning in the Natural Environment: Review of social and economic benefits and barriers*. Natural England Commissioned Reports, Number 092.

Fiennes et al. (2015) The existing evidence-base about the effectiveness of outdoor learning. Available at: www.outdoor-learning.org (accessed 09/07/18).

LKMCo (2017) *The State of School Residentials in England*. Commissioned by the Learning Away Consortium.

Malone, K. (2008) *Every Experience Matters: An evidence based research report on the role of learning outside the classroom for children's whole development from birth to eighteen years*.

Nundy, S. (2001) *Raising Achievement through the Environment: The case for field work and field centres*. NAFSO Publications.

Ofsted (2008) *Learning Outside the Classroom. How far should you go?* Available at: http://lotc.org.uk/wp-content/uploads/2010/12/Ofsted-Report-Oct-2008.pdf_(accessed 09/07/18).

Pretty, J., Angus, C., Bain, M., Barton, J., Gladwell, V., Hine, R., Pilgrim, S., Sandercock, S. and Sellens, M. (2009) Nature, childhood, health and life pathways. Interdisciplinary Centre for Environment and Society Occasional Paper 2009–02. University of Essex.

Torgerson, D., Torgerson, C. *et al.* (2014) *Improving Writing Quality.* Durham University and the University of York. Commissioned by the Education Endowment Foundation.

Waite, S., Passy, R., Gilchrist, M., Hunt, A. and Blackwell, I. (2016) *Natural Connections Demonstration Project, 2012–2016: Final report.* Natural England Commissioned Reports, Number 215.

York Consulting (2015) *Evaluation of Learning Away: Final report.* Available at: http://learningaway.org.uk (accessed 09/07/18).

24

HOW DO WE ENSURE THAT OUR CLASSROOMS ARE TRULY INCLUSIVE?

Deborah Langston is Principal Lecturer and the Primary Partnership Lead at the University of Worcester. Prior to her current role, she taught in a range of primary schools for 26 years and was a Head Teacher for eleven years in a small, inclusive primary school. Her research interests include Special Educational Needs and Disabilities (SEND) with a particular interest in working memory, behaviour management, the importance and value of teamwork, and teacher efficacy.

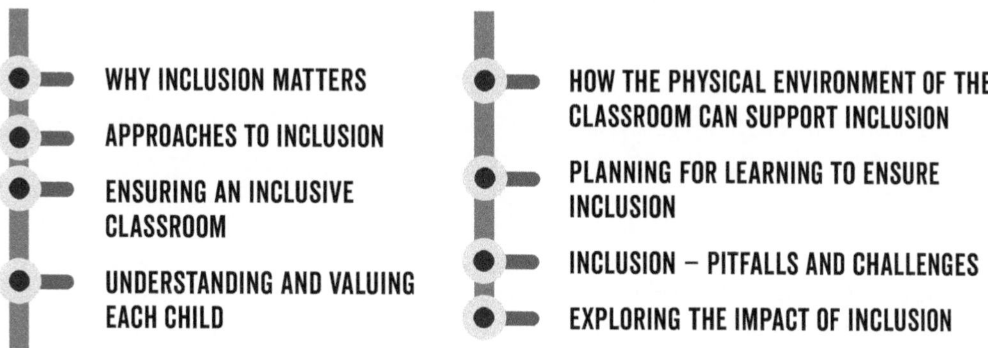

KEY WORDS

- Acceptance
- Barriers to learning
- Choice
- Diversity
- Equal access
- Exclusion
- Personalisation
- Participation
- Stereotype
- Values

INTRODUCTION

In this chapter we shall explore the rich diversity that is brought into the primary classroom by its pupils and school community. What might be the range of social and academic needs exhibited by pupils within primary school classrooms and how do teachers gauge the needs of their pupils? Next, we shall consider some examples of how classrooms might be enhanced and developed to enable true inclusivity by promoting the voices of children and the communities in which they live. To conclude, we will reflect upon how teaching professionals are able to gauge whether their classroom really is an inclusive space for all.

KEY READING

National Center On Universal Design For Learning (2018). Available at: www.udlcenter.org/aboutudl/whatisudl

WHY INCLUSION MATTERS

> *every child has unique characteristics, interests, abilities and learning needs ...*
>
> *education systems should be designed and educational programmes implemented to take into account the wide diversity of these characteristics and needs ...*
>
> (UNESCO, 1994: viii)

As an island nation, the United Kingdom has always been a diverse society; however, in recent years since the promotion of terms in education such as 'British values' (DfE, 2014) and 'social cohesion' and increased press coverage of acts of terrorism, inclusion appears to be a topic which is becoming increasingly high on everyone's agenda.

CRITICAL QUESTION

What are 'British values'?

No one would argue that for a society to function effectively, its schools need to be places of educational excitement where all children can aspire, flourish and achieve, but the challenge for governments and educators alike appears to be how to ensure that there is equality for all.

Education can be a powerful force for change. Within the UK, the government regularly refers to the pupil performance gap in schools, and inspectorate from the Office for Standards in Education (Ofsted) (DfE, 2017: 40) considers, during inspection, how this achievement gap is being narrowed. On a broader scale, and one could argue that this is more important, consideration is also given by Ofsted to how schools are enabling pupils to develop and utilise social skills within a variety of contexts. The expectation is that they learn alongside pupils from a range of diverse backgrounds. Consequently, not only because Ofsted inspect *and* expect achievement and success from inclusion, but because our society thrives on equal opportunity, most educational professionals ensure that all children, whatever their learning needs and family background, have outstanding opportunities at school and beyond to enable them to succeed. Unicef (1989: 9), in Article 29 of the The United Nations Convention on the Rights of the Child, considers that the development of the child's personality, talents and mental and physical abilities are paramount and that schools should facilitate this, enabling children to reach their fullest potential.

This is why inclusion matters and why all teaching professionals must do their utmost to ensure that their classrooms are places where all children thrive.

KEY READING

Unicef (1989) The United Nations Convention on the Rights of the Child. Available at: https://downloads.unicef.org.uk/wp-content/uploads/2010/05/UNCRC_united_nations_convention_on_the_rights_of_the_child.pdf?_ga=2.125781698.910888668.1522330915-2007425667.1522330915

APPROACHES TO INCLUSION

Historically, there has been a range of theoretical and practical models that have explored the notion of how we partly or fully include (or indeed do not) all children within the educational system in the UK. The word 'inclusion' became widely recognised within educational quarters internationally after *The Salamanca Statement* was published (UNESCO, 1994) and was first used in the UK in the SEN green paper *Excellence for All Children* (DfEE, 1997: 4) in 1997. Nowadays, we are all aware of the terminology 'inclusion' in relation to schools and some of the tensions and dilemmas that surround it.

Educational professionals must clarify in their own mind what inclusion truly means to them and their school if they are to create an inclusive educational environment. Within this chapter, the definition I shall consider is broad and does not merely refer to children with SEND in a mainstream setting. I shall reflect upon how learning opportunities can be available to all rather than simply categorising learners and making generalisations.

ENSURING AN INCLUSIVE CLASSROOM

CRITICAL QUESTION

What might be the range of social and learning needs that student teachers encounter during their school placements and beyond?

HOW LONG IS A PIECE OF STRING?

One of the most satisfying aspects of the varied role of the primary school teacher is that each day is different. No matter how carefully teachers try to predict the learning responses of their pupils, they will regularly be surprised by their reactions. A primary school classroom should be a hub of motivating learning opportunities and if the student teacher sees themselves as a lead learner, an active listener and a facilitator, then they will start to become acutely aware of the importance of an environment that supports personalisation. This is not to say that classrooms should be a 'pick and mix' of structures and strategies, or that consistency should be banned; however, to ensure that pupils collectively thrive within the learning environment, it must be carefully and sensitively planned. Daily reflections should also be part of the shared ownership between pupils and teaching colleagues.

The Teachers' Standards (DfE, 2011: 12) state that educational professionals must have

> *a clear understanding of the needs of all pupils, including those with special educational needs; those of high ability; those with English as an additional language; those with disabilities; and be able to use and evaluate distinctive teaching approaches to engage and support them.*

This expectation is one of, if not *the* most challenging of the Teachers' Standards to achieve, and excellent teachers spend their whole career reflecting on and refining their pedagogical approaches in order to hone their skills accordingly. Be it terminology such as, 'More Able Pupil', 'SEND', 'EAL' or 'Pupil Premium' (the list goes on), it is important that the student teacher gets to know each child as an individual. This allows a mutually beneficial relationship in which the child is able to find a safe and secure classroom space whereby they can take risks and enjoy learning.

UNDERSTANDING AND VALUING EACH CHILD

What is the best way to get a true understanding of the social and learning needs of all your pupils?

For teachers and student teachers to create a learning environment in which their pupils will thrive and feel included, they need to have a detailed knowledge of each and every child in their care. We know that learning is a complex process, so the more knowledge that teaching professionals possess, the easier will be the task of crafting a learning opportunity, which will ultimately be successful. Children bring a diverse range of experiences, so the starting point for a successful social and learning journey is to ensure there are a myriad of opportunities available for pupils to share their life experiences and feel that these are valued. This is particularly important for children who join a cohort outside the normal school intake year, and it is a wise teacher who takes special care to support and encourage the 'newbie'.

Valuing everyone as an equal member of the class team can be achieved both directly by the teacher modelling their own expectations and values, but also more subtly by the way in which the classroom environment and learning opportunities are structured. Thought also needs to be given to the policies of the school, which, alongside clear leadership from the headteacher and senior leadership team, give a 'steer' to teachers and student teachers. This can sometimes become challenging if the individual values of the teaching professional do not totally align with the whole-school values in evidence in policy and whole-school practice.

CRITICAL QUESTION

How can a student teacher directly model inclusive practice?

By taking an interest in the day-to-day experience of all their pupils and indeed their families, the teaching professional is able to show children that they value them as human beings, not merely as learners or pupils. For example, a professional, yet informal, conversation at the classroom door before school, or indeed on the playground, goes a long way towards removing any unspoken barriers that might occur between home and school, and begins to build a partnership where the child is at the centre of everything.

CRAFTING THE PHYSICAL ENVIRONMENT OF THE CLASSROOM TO SUPPORT INCLUSION FOR ALL

Taking time to ensure that the physical environment of the classroom itself is inclusive is always time well spent. Children need to take ownership of their classroom as partners with the teacher and, if they have a hand in its organisation, structure and development, they are also more likely to care for it and show it respect. Even the very youngest of children are able to help and sometimes their 'child's-eye view' sees anomalies or issues that the adult teacher may well not be aware of. Ensuring that the classroom space is inclusive for all is often the first challenge a newly qualified teacher (NQT) faces, and the student teacher would be using time wisely if they were to consider the following aspects of the physical environment and its impact on the learning of their pupils.

- Lighting
  - Does the classroom make the most of opportunities for the use of natural light?
  - Do blinds need pulling back so children can see properly, or indeed does the sun shine into a particular pupil's eyes so they are unable to see the interactive whiteboard?
- Seating arrangements
  - Can everyone travel around the classroom comfortably with space to move effectively?

  - Is everyone able to see and hear adequately when they are seated?
  - Are chairs at a comfortable height for all pupils when writing?
  - Might more specialised seating be needed for some children?
  - Would a sensory cushion support increase focus for a particular child?
- Display
  - Are resources such as visual timetables large enough and are they displayed at an appropriate height?
  - Can everyone clearly see number lines and alphabet strips, and are they written in an appropriate font?
  - Do all children have equal opportunities to have their work displayed or is 'only the best' on show?
  - Are there signs and labels written in the range of languages spoken by all the pupils in the class?
  - Are children asked whether there are certain types of display that support their learning?
  - Is the interactive whiteboard background managed effectively to ensure that all children – e.g. those with dyslexic tendencies can read text to the best of their ability?
- Use of the outdoors
  - Are all children given opportunities to learn outside of the classroom?
  - Is there easy access for everyone to exit and enter?
- Access to resourcing
  - Are resources easily accessible to all? For example, are resources labelled appropriately? Are they at child height?
  - Are recording devices utilised if children have weak working memory?
  - Can all children have access to concrete resources should they need them, e.g. use of bead strings, place value cards in maths sessions?

HOW MIGHT TEACHER PROFESSIONALS AND STUDENT TEACHERS PLAN FOR LEARNING IN AS INCLUSIVE A WAY AS POSSIBLE?

Considering the physical environment of the classroom and the 'beyond-school' environment of the pupils in one's care is only part of the picture when it comes to ensuring equal access to learning for all. Possibly the most challenging aspect to overcome is how to design each learning opportunity appropriately. Much has been written about 'Quality First Teaching' since the terminology was first used by the Department for Children, Schools and Families (DCSF) in its *Personalised Learning: A practical guide* (DCSF, 2008: 9) and also about the 'Waves of intervention model' (DfES, 2006) promulgated by The National Strategies (see Figure 24.1), but the fact remains that at the heart of excellent learning and teaching for all lies:

accurate assessment of need, regular reflection by teacher and pupil, and professional reflexivity.

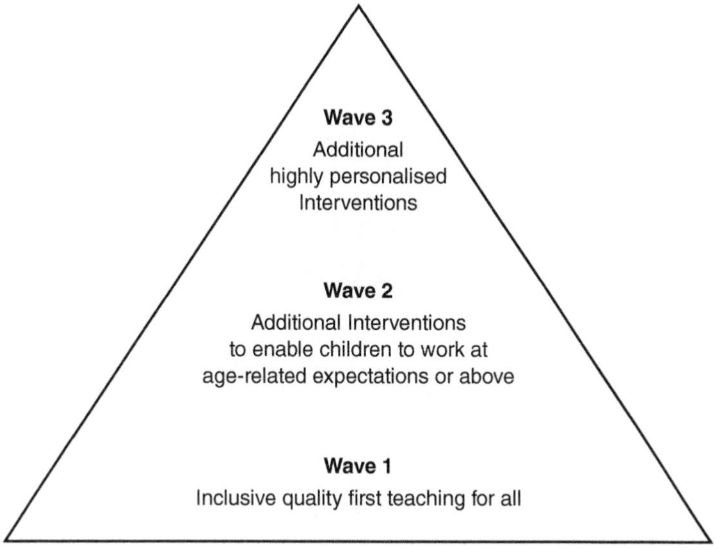

Figure 24.1 The waves of intervention model

One way of student teachers crafting appropriate learning opportunities is to consider the principles and guidelines of 'Universal Design for Learning' (Meyer *et al.*, 2010: 111). The majority of primary teacher colleagues now make learning opportunities increasingly relevant for their pupils by starting to plan for foundation subjects collaboratively with the children, considering their interests and expertise before a medium-term plan or scheme of work has been developed. In my view, this builds the very fundamentals of inclusive practice as every child's voice has an opportunity to be heard. Enabling the children to then have a choice in developing their learning opportunity and time to reflect upon how they might evidence their progress is a powerful way to develop metacognition. The Education Endowment Foundation (EEF) considers the development of metacognitive approaches to have a high potential impact on pupil progress (EEF, 2018).

PITFALLS AND CHALLENGES OF INCLUSION IN PRIMARY SCHOOLS

As aforementioned, one of the challenges (but also the pleasures) of developing a totally inclusive learning environment within the classroom is that, by their very nature, all children are different and have different strengths and needs. Add to this the constraints placed on teachers and students from limited funding of resources, access to appropriate physical spaces and changing statutory government expectations, and it is no wonder that Standard 5 of the Teachers' Standards is probably the area that students find most challenging to confidently achieve. Florian *et al.* (2017: 2) acknowledge that 'commitment to high levels of inclusion and achievement makes high demands on those who work in classrooms and schools'.

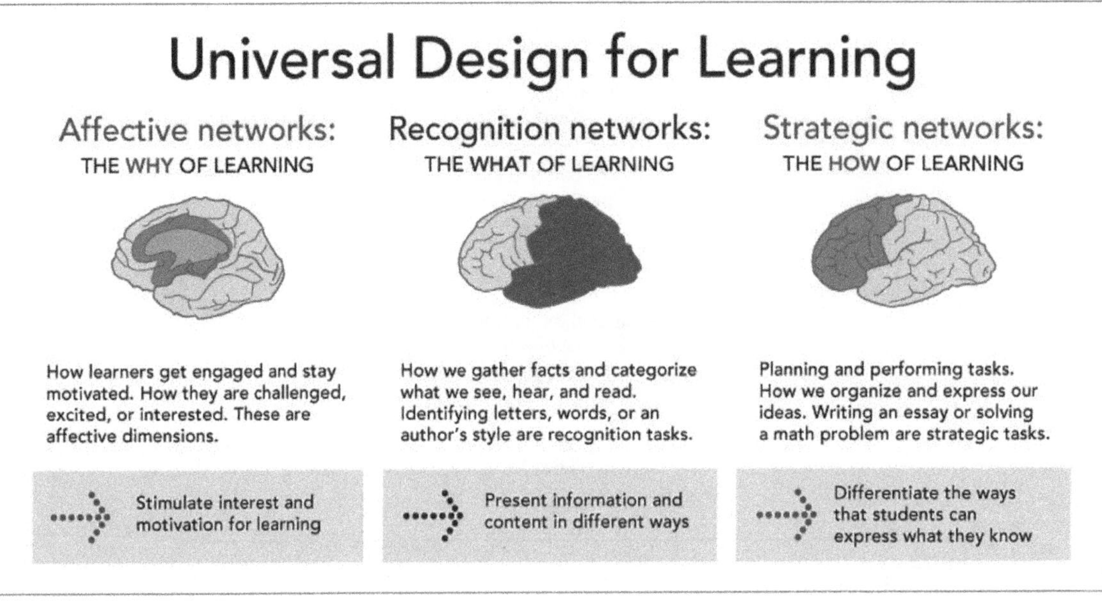

Figure 24.2 Metacognitive approaches and pupil progress (Meyer et al., 2010: 111)

CRITICAL QUESTION

Why might a commitment to high levels of inclusion make a 'high demand' on teachers?

It is vital, therefore, that the student teacher realises the challenge that they face and embraces it. They need to be proactive in accessing the support they require from school colleagues such as their mentor and the SENDCo in order for them to reflect effectively and consider the most appropriate way to structure the learning environment for their pupils. Staying abreast of current educational developments is vital and there are so many excellent online resources and communities of practice that the student teacher need never feel isolated or inadequate if they take control of their own professional development.

Perhaps the best way to explore inclusion in practice is to focus on the work of one school.

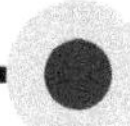

CASE STUDY

Ledbury Primary School (LPS) is a large, dynamic primary school nestled within the market town of Ledbury and its community. Visitors to school comment positively on the values-based education and facilities, the stimulating environment and inclusive, caring, family ethos. They describe the atmosphere as friendly, respectful and nurturing. School colleagues care about the individual and pride themselves on the warmth of a community in which all the pupils feel valued. Ofsted visited in 2018 and commented:

'The highly inclusive nature of the school, based on its core values, ensures that pupils who have special educational needs (SEN) and/or disabilities are integrated fully into school life.'

This inclusive ethos grew as the school embraced the principles of values-based education led by a headteacher who is passionate about making a positive difference to children's lives (Duckworth, 2009).

Inclusion in the school is as much about how the pupils are towards each other, as it is about the SEN inclusion provision by the staff in school. Pupils learn the language of, and demonstrate in their actions, an understanding of kindness and quality relationships. Pupils with additional needs immediately feel a part of the LPS family as no child is ever turned away.

The vision statement at LPS is 'Determined to Succeed'. Whatever a child's abilities are, every child experiences success. School colleagues feel it is important to work with a child's strengths and look for opportunities for every child to engage with learning that develops those areas. For example, some of the children with a diagnosis of autism have excellent mathematical understanding and can support their peers by explaining methodology. They may find communicating to their peers challenging, but with the support of an adult, these pupils relish the task of teaching others.

Sometimes children join the school who require additional support in self-regulation so they can function in a mainstream classroom. These pupils may have experienced early trauma and their emotional resilience is underdeveloped. The school invested in training programmes that help staff to understand theories in attachment, PTSD, mental health first aid, functional reflex therapy and emotion coaching. Alongside the values-based universal approach, expertise in specific areas enables staff to confidently work with both with pupils and their parents. School colleagues are fully aware that they must use a flexible approach in their teaching and behaviour strategies with some pupils. Until these pupils are able to self-regulate and have a stable emotional state, they find learning challenging. Staff understand this process and are patient. Their expectations are high but realistic for these pupils, and they do not pressurise them and cause further stress.

Having specialist roles in a primary school enables an inclusive ethos to operate without overburdening staff. The school has planned over time to have a permanent SENCO, a Well-being Co-ordinator, Nurture Group provision and a colleague who works with small groups of pupils developing emotional resilience. While the teachers are trained in the programmes, much of the specific work is delivered outside the mainstream classroom where pupils can relax and have the time to engage openly and with support from specific adults. The pupils gain confidence and the ability to rejoin their mainstream class with a positive attitude towards learning and relationships.

(Continued)

(Continued)

One of the fundamental rules is 'no shouting' at LPS. Indeed, this is their only rule. This works; if the adults in school are calm and consistent, and have the ability to communicate clearly, pupils have a secure environment in which they can flourish, be confident and learn.

The school feels proud to be recognised for its inclusive work. The headteacher believes that true inclusion takes 'a team effort' but that there are 'excellent rewards when children who have struggled in previous placements experience success and thank you for the support and understanding you have given them - you watch their future grow with pride'.

CRITICAL QUESTION

What can we learn from this school? How can student teachers adapt and develop these ideas for their classrooms?

The flexible approach to teaching and the development of strategies to support behaviour for learning at Ledbury Primary School might well be considered by students when adapting to their teaching role both on placement and during their NQT year. It is all too easy to over-plan and cling to the security of a lesson crafted the previous day without 'reading the room' and carefully considering mid-session the needs of the children. The very best lessons (and indeed, the very best teachers) take account of the children's needs as they change and develop during the course of the lesson. Like colleagues at LPS, a student teacher should have high expectations of the pupils in their care, and yet a patient and realistic approach too. Taking time to develop quality relationships and consider core values is never time wasted.

EXPLORING THE IMPACT OF INCLUSION

The impact of an inclusive classroom is not difficult to measure. Observations of children:

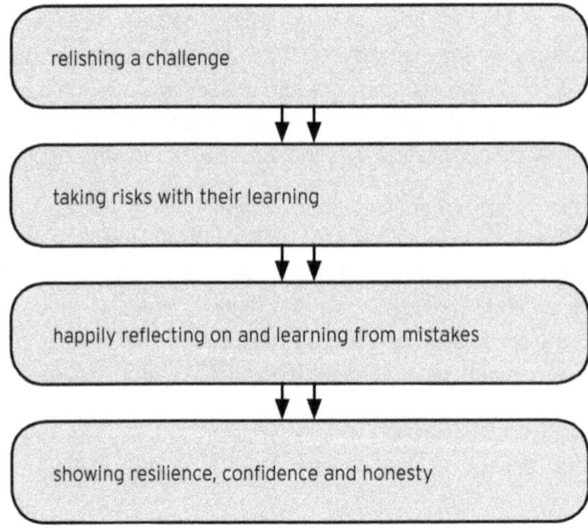

are all evidence of a classroom environment that promotes inclusion. Sometimes, however, it is too easy as a teaching professional to get so engaged in driving the learning within the classroom that the power of observation gets forgotten. Student teachers should regularly give themselves time to stand back and observe the children in their care. So much can be gleaned by careful observation of pupil learning behaviours. Colleagues within the early years have become adept at utilising observation as a finely tuned assessment tool, but I would argue that observation is a skill that should be exploited by all primary practitioners whatever the age of the pupils that they teach.

Another measure of the success of inclusive strategies is the evidence of appropriate learning progress for all children. The inclusive classroom ensures that all children, no matter their starting point, make the progress they deserve. This 'hard' evidence would be expected to be shared with senior colleagues within school in order for them to monitor standards of learning and teaching across the school, and this is when our aforementioned attainment gap between groups of children will be considered.

CRITICAL QUESTION

How can you ensure that you can 'evidence' progress for all children in your class?

Careful analysis of children's starting points and then periodic checks on their understanding and skill development on a daily, weekly and half-termly/termly basis are the ways in which the very best teacher colleagues ensure that no child 'slips through the net'. Planning for how and when this assessment should take place would support the student teacher to carefully track the progress of the children in their care and give them a greater understanding of how to plan for misconceptions and further development.

CHAPTER SUMMARY

- Classrooms are becoming increasingly diverse.
- Teaching professionals can facilitate social mobility.
- It is vital to engage positively with the community in which the school is placed geographically.
- Teacher professionals must have an in-depth knowledge of their pupils both socially and academically.
- School policies have a vital role to play in promoting equal opportunity for all.
- The physical environment of the classroom requires careful planning.
- Lesson planning should create opportunities for pupil voice and choice.
- It is vital to ensure that one's own professional development is prioritised.
- Observation is a powerful tool for gauging whether the classroom is inclusive.

ASSIGNMENTS

If you are writing an ITE assignment on inclusion it will be useful for you to think through the following:

- What is your definition of inclusion? Why do you define it as such? Is this a view shared by others?
- How important is inclusion to the primary classroom? To what extent does it impact upon outcomes for children? Support your reflections with appropriate evidence and data.
- What can we learn from looking at educational inclusion around the world? Can you find examples of outstanding practice that might be easily embedded within a primary classroom in the UK?

Useful texts

Woolley, R. (2018) *Understanding Inclusion: Core concepts, policy and practice*. London: Routledge.

REFERENCES

Department for Children, Schools and Families (DCSF)(2008) *Personalised Learning: A practical guide*. Available at: http://webarchive.nationalarchives.gov.uk/20130323074445/https://www.education.gov.uk/publications/eOrderingDownload/00844-2008DOM-EN.pdf (accessed 29/03/18).

Department for Education (DfE) (2011) *Teachers' Standards: Guidance for school leaders, school staff and governing bodies*. Available at: www.gov.uk/government/uploads/system/uploads/attachment_data/file/665522/Teachers_standard_information.pdf (accessed 29/03/18).

Department for Education (DfE) (2014) *Promoting Fundamental British Values as Part of SMSC in schools*. Available at: www.gov.uk/government/uploads/system/uploads/attachment_data/file/380595/SMSC_Guidance_Maintained_Schools.pdf (accessed 29/03/18).

Department for Education (DfE) (2017) *Ofsted School Inspection Handbook*. Available at: www.gov.uk/government/publications/school-inspection-handbook-from-september-2015 (accessed 29/03/18).

Department for Education and Employment DfEE (1997). *Excellence for All Children*. Available at: http://www.educationengland.org.uk/documents/pdfs/1997-green-paper.pdf (accessed 29/03/18).

Department for Education and Skills (DfES) (2006) *Primary National Strategy: The waves model*. Available at: http://webarchive.nationalarchives.gov.uk/20090109015452/http://www.standards.dfes.gov.uk/local/ePDs/leading_on_intervention/site/u2/s4/ss2/sss1/index.htm (accessed 29/03/18).

Duckworth, J. (2009) *The Little Book of Values*. Carmarthen: Crown House Publishing.

Education Endowment Foundation (EEF) (2018) *Evidence Summaries*. Available at: https://educationendowmentfoundation.org.uk (accessed 29/03/18).

Florian, L., Black-Hawkins, K. and Rouse, M. (2017) *Achievement and Inclusion in Schools* (2nd edn). London: Routledge.

Meyer, A., Rose, D.H. and Gordon, D. (2010) *Universal Design for Learning: Theory and practice.* Wakefield, MA: CAST Professional Publishing.

UNESCO (1994) The Salamanca statement and framework for action on special needs education. Available at: http://unesdoc.unesco.org/images/0009/000984/098427eo.pdf (accessed 29/03/18).

Unicef (1989) *The United Nations Convention on the Rights of the Child.* Available at: https://downloads.unicef.org.uk/wp-content/uploads/2010/05/UNCRC_united_nations_convention_on_the_rights_of_the_child.pdf?_ga=2.125781698.910888668.1522330915-2007425667.1522330915 (accessed 29/03/18).

25

IS DATA THE WHOLE STORY? THE DATA-LED ACCOUNTABILITY OF TEACHERS

Darren McKay is a Senior Lecturer at Bath Spa University on the Primary PGCE and Early Years Initial Teacher Training programmes. He is a member of the Primary Science, Professional Studies and Early Years ITT teams. He is currently undertaking research exploring the development of beginning teachers' knowledge of teacher competence and their understanding of what influences it.

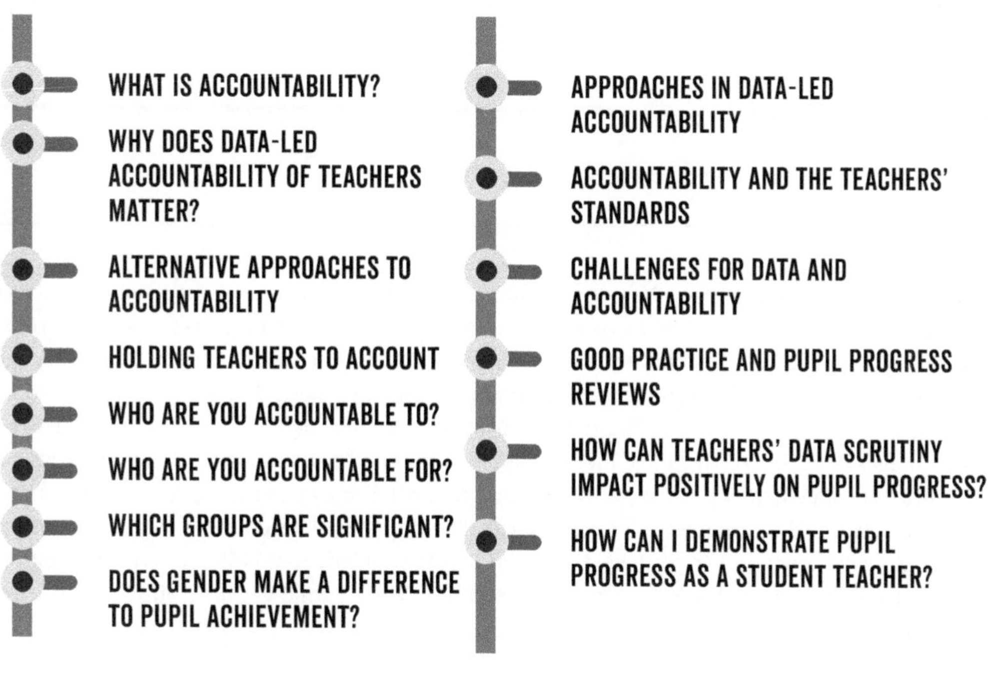

KEY WORDS

- Accountability
- Formative assessment
- Impact
- Pupil progress
- Summative assessment
- Tracking

INTRODUCTION

This chapter explores what accountability is and who teachers are accountable to. We will review the range of data that is generated by schools at a variety of levels and how it can be used to support pupil progress. We will look at two examples of how schools use data to hold teachers to account and, more importantly, support pupil progress in the classroom. We will discuss the notion of data overload and drill down to what data teachers need to support pupil progress. Finally, we will discuss how teachers can ensure that they keep sight of the individual learner.

WHAT IS ACCOUNTABILITY?

Being accountable requires us to justify our actions or decisions, to explain what we have done or are going to do, and why we have decided to take this course of action. There is a sense that actions are planned and have been thought through. There is no sense of reacting to the situation on instinct, using your tacit knowledge.

CRITICAL QUESTION

Why does data-led accountability of teachers matter?

Accountability can come from within the organisation, often referred to as internal accountability (West *et. al*, 2011) or from interested parties beyond the organisation, referred to as external accountability (West et al., 2011). Smith (2016) describes educational accountability in terms of external targets and expectations which schools are required to meet. This external accountability necessitates school leaders to justify and explain their performance to Ofsted, Multi Academy Trust (MAT) leaders or the Local Authority (LA) in terms of percentages of children who have met or exceeded imposed benchmarks. The children who have not reached these prescribed criteria require a robust and often detailed explanation as to why they have not made the progress expected or attained the grade allocated to their age. This data-driven accountability can lead to organisations narrowing their curriculum (Harlen, 2014) to ensure that children have the best opportunity they can to meet or exceed these external expectations. The internal accountability of the school is driven by external accountability.

ALTERNATIVE APPROACHES TO ACCOUNTABILITY

Crooks (2011) and Hutchinson and Young (2011) present the New Zealand and Scottish educational systems as alternative views of internal accountability. In these countries, self-evaluation drives the internal accountability whereby schools set their own targets and evaluate progress towards their achievement. In New Zealand, there is no compulsory nationally standardised testing, instead schools focus on the use of formative assessment to adapt the curriculum, with an emphasis on quality rather than breadth (Crooks, 2011). School leaders complete a rigorous self-evaluation process that takes into account progress towards targets agreed at school level. The New Zealand equivalent of Ofsted, the Education Review Office (ERO), uses the school self-evaluation process as one way to hold schools to account. In Scotland, there has been a similar focus on internal accountability.

The Scottish government published six drivers of improvement:

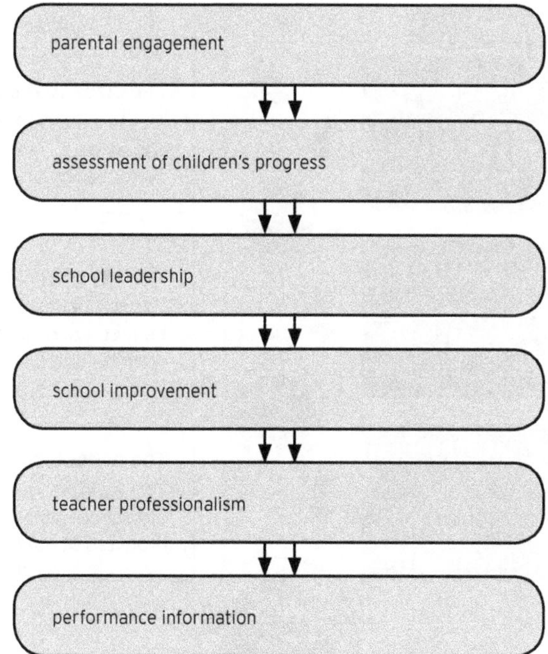

(Scottish Government, 2016).

Schools and local authorities use these drivers as the key indicators for improvement planning. ERO uses the self-evaluation of the improvement plans as a way to hold the schools (and LAs) to account. The internal accountability mechanisms of the schools inform the external judgements made by ERO.

West *et al.* (2011) suggest that the predominant forms of school accountability in England can be thought of as hierarchical and market driven, hierarchical because schools are held to account for their outcomes by governing bodies, MATs, LA and Ofsted; market accountable due to parents having a choice where to send their child by using freely available information to make comparisons such as published league tables and Ofsted reports.

HOLDING TEACHERS TO ACCOUNT

There is a considerable amount of data generated about each child. Some will be statutory, such as phonics screening scores or end of Key Stage statutory attainment, and some will be non-statutory, such as scores on a weekly spelling test or feedback comments on work. This data will be used to give an overall picture of a child's performance in school and will often be used to populate tracking records held on a school centralised system. Senior leaders will use the collated data so that judgements can be made about a class's performance, thus holding teachers to account. This internal accountability is distributed across the school and flows from the whole school to the individual child.

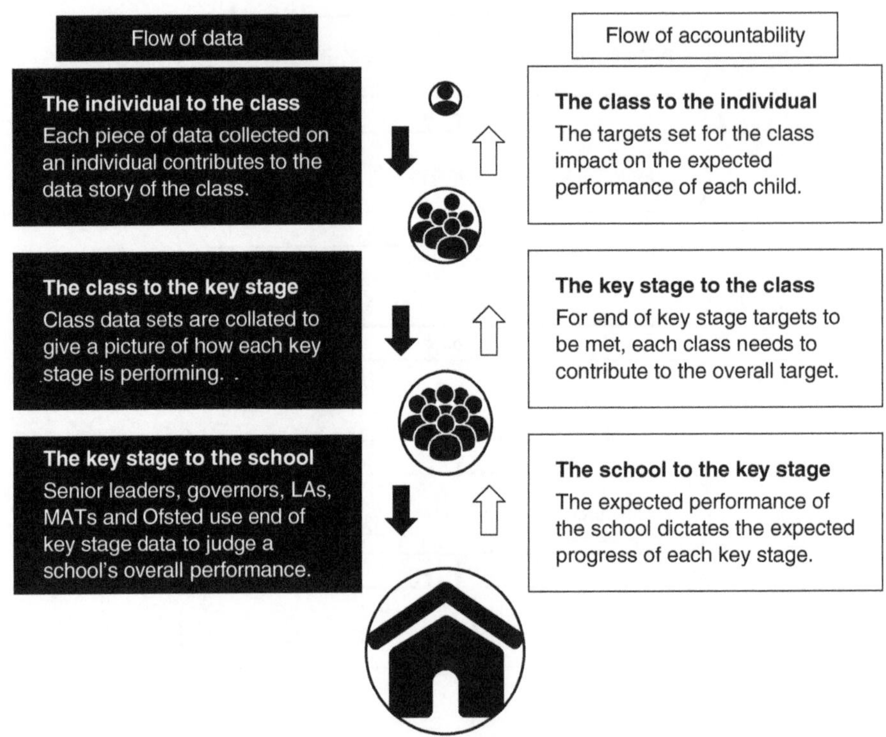

Figure 25.1 Data generated by schools showing the flow of accountability between each level

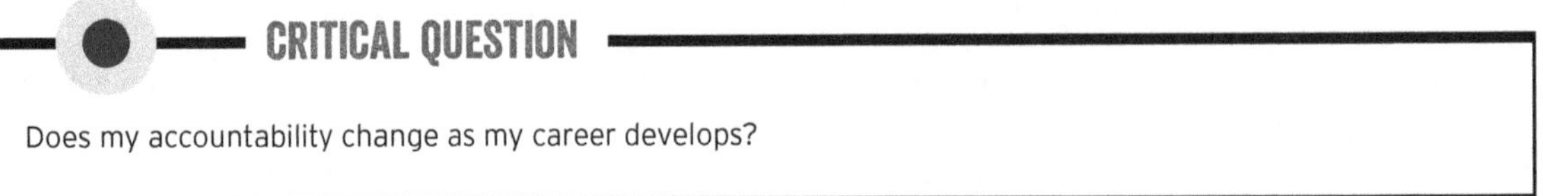

WHO ARE YOU ACCOUNTABLE TO? WHO ARE YOU ACCOUNTABLE FOR?

The table below illustrates how, as teachers, we are accountable to numerous individuals and bodies, from the very beginning of our teaching careers (see Table 25.1). This can seem overwhelming when broken down in this way, but I believe it is useful to illustrate what teachers are accountable for and to whom. We can see that at the top of each list of individuals a teacher will be accountable to is you – the teacher. By putting yourself first and focusing on how you can improve, through grasping each and every training opportunity offered, you can help to ensure that you are the most effective teacher you can be. In my opinion, children must come a very close second. Surely one of the main reasons we decided to become teachers was to impact in a positive way on the lives of children. I strongly believe that by keeping yourself and the children at the very centre of your accountability, you will be able to justify your impact on the children's learning more readily. This is because you have initially held yourself to account to become the best teacher you can possibly be. I am not dismissing the accountability from others. I am instead suggesting that by holding yourself to account, keeping the learning experiences of the children you teach exciting, relevant and engaging, you will be in control.

Table 25.1 A hierarchy of accountability from student teacher to teacher with a leadership role

Accountable to	Role	Accountable for
Yourself **Children** Parents Class teacher/mentor Training institution	Student teacher	**Teaching:** Personal development as a teacher in training **Learning:** Progress and attainment of the children you teach
Yourself **Children** Parents Induction tutor/mentor middle leaders Senior leaders Headteacher Governors	Newly Qualified Teacher	**Teaching:** Personal development as a Newly Qualified Teacher **Learning:** Progress and attainment of the children you teach
Yourself **Children** Parents Other Middle leaders Senior leaders Headteacher Governors Multi-Academy Trust/local authority HMI/Ofsted	Early career teacher & Middle/senior leader	**Teaching:** Personal development as a teacher **Learning:** Progress and attainment of the children you teach **Teaching:** Professional development of other colleagues **Leading:** Progress and attainment of the children others teach

WHICH GROUPS ARE 'SIGNIFICANT'?

In terms of accountability and data, a significant group is a group of children who are not performing as expected. Their performance is either higher or lower. Children identified as having a special educational need (SEN), looked after children (LAC) and children eligible for the Pupil Premium grant are all significant groups whose progress and attainment are closely monitored nationally and consequently at school level. Children from ethnic minorities are also considered as significant groups.

CRITICAL QUESTION

Why do schools track progress of significant groups?

Currently, the government in England has identified disadvantaged children as the significant group who do not perform as well as all other children. Disadvantaged pupils are defined as

> *those who were registered as eligible for free school meals at any point in the last six years, children looked after by a local authority and children who left care in England and Wales through adoption or via a Special Guardianship or Child Arrangements Order.*
>
> (DfE, 2017: 16)

These children are among those who are targeted to gain from the Pupil Premium grant, introduced by the coalition government in 2011. The 2016 and 2017 end of Key Stage 2 (KS2) data identifies that the largest gap in attainment is between disadvantaged and all other children: 21 percentage points in 2016 and 20 in 2017. The progress measures for these two groups remain at less than 1.0 scaled point difference (DfE, 2017). It has been government policy for several years to narrow the attainment gap between disadvantaged and all other children. As the curriculum and form of statutory assessment for the end of KS2 were changed in 2014, it is not possible to make reliable comparisons to gaps in previous years. However, in 2013 Ofsted published a report about the group of children and young people who were not achieving academically as well as expected for their age.

KEY READING

Ofsted (2013) Unseen Children: Access and achievement 20 years on. Evidence report. Available at: www.gov.uk/government/publications/unseen-children-access-and-achievement-20-years-on

In the report, the term 'unseen children' was used to describe these children as they became 'increasingly less visible as they progress through the system' (Ofsted, 2013: 4), suggesting a link between low income and academic achievement, stating that this gap has been around for over 20 years.

DOES GENDER MAKE A DIFFERENCE TO PUPIL ACHIEVEMENT?

In 2016 and 2017, the attainment gap between boys and girls at KS2 was a difference of eight percentage points, with a three percentage points difference at the higher standard. Girls outperformed boys in reading and writing. In maths there was not a gap at the expected standard, but boys outperformed girls by being more likely to achieve a high score (DfE, 2017). It is interesting to note that these differences in achievement are relatively small when compared with the gap in achievement between disadvantaged and all other children. A report commissioned by Ofsted in 2000 suggested that disadvantage has the most significant impact on a child's achievement and that this is 'one of the longest-established trends in British education' (Gillborn and Mirza, 2000: 18). As stated earlier, this gap still remains to be the most significant, even though we have been challenging stereotypes and exploring more gender-neutral pedagogies for decades.

APPROACHES IN DATA-LED ACCOUNTABILITY

The data used to hold schools to account is generated from two sources: teacher assessment and national Key Stage tests, sometimes referred to as statutory assessment tests (SATs).

Is there a relationship between teacher assessment and national Key Stage tests?

KEY STAGE 1

Teacher assessment (TA) accounts for the overall judgement of attainment at the end of Key Stage 1 (KS1) for English reading, English writing, mathematics and science. 'Teachers must use results of the KS1 tests in English reading and mathematics to support their TA judgement of how a pupil has performed throughout the key stage' (Standards and Testing Agency (STA), 2017c: 21). There is an optional English grammar, punctuation and spelling test for KS1. Teachers working within the school mark all tests at KS1, including the phonics screening check. STA has produced frameworks to support TA at KS1. For English reading, English writing and mathematics there are three standards which must be used: working towards the expected standard, working at the expected standard and working at greater depth within the expected standard. For science, there is one standard and it is reported as working at the expected standard or has not met the expected standard (STA, 2017c). This data is reported to DfE, via the local authority. It is not published in league tables but is used by Ofsted to hold schools to account. This data set is also used to measure progress from KS1 to KS2.

KEY STAGE 2

As with KS1, there are teacher assessment (TA) and national tests at KS2. TA judgements are made for English reading, English writing, mathematics and science, using the teacher assessment frameworks to decide what standard the child has met. At KS2 there are three standards for English writing which must be used: working towards the excepted standard, working at the expected standard and working at greater depth within the expected standard. For English reading, mathematics and science there is one standard, reported as working at the expected standard or has not met the expected standard (STA, 2017d). Unlike KS1, the KS2 tests do not form part of the TA at KS2. Test results at school level are published in performance tables.

Scaled scores are produced from the KS1 and KS2 test raw score. A scaled score of 100 represents the expected standard on each test. A child who has a scaled score of 100 or more has met the expected standard in the test, a scaled score of 99 or below has not met the expected standard in the test (STA, 2017a; 2017b).

TARGET SETTING

We teach in an era of targets. It is important, though, to be clear that there is a difference between a target and a prediction.

CRITICAL QUESTION

What is the difference between a target and a prediction?

In my experience, end of KS2 targets are based on a child's prior attainment and the expected progress each child should make. Potential barriers to each child's learning are considered, but the main criterion is often their KS1 data and the past performance of the school. It is expected that schools maintain or improve on the results of the previous year. This level of accountability is external to the context of the school and may not take into account the personal experiences of each child as they progress in KS2. Predictions are rooted in the child as an individual and are based on a deep understanding of the child as a learner and the quality of their learning experiences to date. The prediction is what a child would most likely achieve based on current assessments and the context of their learning, taking into account all that can influence a child's achievement. Predictions can change over time. It is important to note that targets and predictions should be ambitious; both are an expression of high levels of accountability. Although targets are no longer shared formally with LAs, schools are expected to set rigorous targets to demonstrate their efforts for improvement.

In 2014, the government introduced a new curriculum in England and with it removed levels as a tool for statutory assessment. New statutory assessments were introduced to be in line with the demands of the new curriculum. In response to these new statutory assessments, John McIntosh led a commission on assessment without levels and a report was published in 2015, detailing recommendations for schools. This report also made clear the various accountability processes in play. In the report it was made clear that Ofsted, publication of test data in performance tables, government floor standards, school governing bodies and peer reviews are all part of the national accountability framework (DfE, 2015). Three forms of assessment are discussed: day-to-day in-school formative assessment; in-school summative assessment; and nationally standardised summative assessment. Accountability, in the form of assurance for parents, school leaders and Ofsted, is clearly indicated for each assessment type. There is an expectation that data will be generated by schools to track progress, but that 'Ofsted will not expect any particular data outputs from school's assessment systems' (DfE, 2015: 37). However, they will build a picture of how robust assessment systems are through lesson observations, work scrutiny, conversations with children and staff, and by reviewing the school's records.

FLOOR STANDARDS

The government uses floor standards to hold schools to account. These are the minimum attainment and progress measures that the government expects schools to meet. They will be reviewed each year to take into account any changes in data sets. At the time of writing, the floor standards published by the DfE in 2018 stated:

> *In 2017, a school is above the floor if:*
>
> - *at least 65% of pupils meet the expected standard in English reading, English writing and mathematics; or*
> - *the school achieves sufficient progress scores in **all three** subjects. At least -5 in English reading, -5 in mathematics and -7 in English writing.*
>
> *To be above the floor, the school needs to meet either the attainment or all of the progress element.*
>
> (DfE, 2018)

Data produced by the DfE in 2017 stated that 511 (4 per cent) of the state-funded mainstream primary schools were below the primary floor standard. This was a decrease of 154 schools, or 1 percentage point. This would seem to indicate that either standards are improving or teachers are getting better at teaching to the current version of the national tests. I believe that it was the former, and was a result of teachers and children becoming familiar with the expectations of the curriculum that the national tests are assessing.

ACCOUNTABILITY AND THE TEACHERS' STANDARDS

The Teachers' Standards (DfE, 2011) are a set of competences that have applied to all teachers, including students, since September 2012. There are three sections: the Preamble, Part 1: Teaching and Part 2: Professional and Personal Conduct.

CRITICAL QUESTION

How can the Teachers' Standards be used to hold me to account?

Accountability is woven throughout. The Preamble refers to teachers' accountability to themselves for 'achieving the highest possible standards in work and conduct' (p. 6). The accountability to children is clearly expressed in the first clause of the first sentence, 'Teachers make the education of their pupils their first concern,' (p. 6). There are clear examples where data is used to hold teachers to account, e.g. 'be accountable for pupils' attainment, progress and outcomes' (p. 6) and 'use relevant data to monitor progress, set targets, and plan subsequent lesson' (p. 7). External and internal accountability to the groups discussed earlier (see Table 25.1) is clear and the use of data is one way that these groups hold teachers to account.

CRITICAL QUESTION

Can there be complications with data-led accountability?

CHALLENGES FOR DATA AND ACCOUNTABILITY

If, for whatever reason, a child does not have KS1 data, how can progress be measured? The short answer is that in terms of the government's progress measure, it can't. However, I do not believe that any teacher would accept this as the only answer. Progress can be measured in different ways. Many schools will track pupil progress against set criteria for each year. These criteria may be decided by the staff of the school or an external company, data is input and how a child is progressing towards a desired goal or target is monitored. The overall process was the same when levels existed. Instead of levels, we now use the age-related expectations (ARE) for each year group, two-year band or Key Stage. Additionally, staff use in-school summative assessment to make judgements about what a child has achieved and the next steps needed in their learning. In the days of levels, the vocabulary was As, Bs and Cs. We now talk about emerging, expected and exceeding, or developing, secure and above, or use the government's language of working towards the expected standard, working at the expected standard and working at greater depth within the expected standard. This does not seem to me to be a significant change in how we think about summative assessment.

Another possible challenge is when the KS1 and KS2 assessments are completed in two different schools. This could be as a result of the child moving schools or there is no KS1 in the school. The government's policy is that if there is a KS1 result for the child, it will be used to measure the child's progress and this data will be used to calculate the school progress measure. If the individual progress is as expected, or more than expected then this will be advantageous to the school. However, if the progress is below expected, i.e. a negative measure, in a small cohort this could have a significant impact on the school progress measure. Again, schools have become adept at tracking progress of these children and will often complete a form of baseline summative assessment soon after the child has entered the school. In my experience, this on entry baseline assessment is also applied when junior schools receive the new cohort of Year 3 and there is a perceived mismatch between end of KS1 attainment and Year 3 initial assessments. One way that schools aim to overcome this is by Year 2 and Year 3 staff working closely together during the handover from one school to the other. However, this cannot always be managed if schools are a considerable distance apart or not all Year 2 children transition to the same school.

MODERATION

CRITICAL QUESTION

How does subjectivity and objectivity influence moderation practice?

LAs are required to facilitate interschool moderation of teacher assessment at EYFS, KS1 and KS2. This practice is well established and can go some way to standardising the judgements made by teachers about the attainment of the work discussed. These moderation meetings can be highly charged and subjective. The criteria can be interpreted in different ways and can highlight inconsistencies between colleagues. These inconsistencies can be within a school as well as between schools. The TA frameworks (STA, 2017e, 2017f) have been designed to lessen these differences in assessment by providing clear guidance and exemplar materials. Even with these considerations, it is still possible to reach a difference of opinion.

KEEPING THE INDIVIDUAL CHILD IN MIND

With all this data being generated by teachers, it is easy to become overloaded and lose sight of what the data is telling you. The Independent Teacher Review Group (2016) provided guidance on how to reduce the bureaucracy of data collection and analysis. In their publication *Eliminating Unnecessary Workload Associated with Data Management*, several recommendations were made at a variety of levels. For schools and teachers, the key recommendations included were to use summative assessment to collect data no more than three times a year, make data accessible to all stakeholders and for teachers to record data accurately (Independent Teacher Review Group, 2016). If we keep these recommendations in mind, data can become one of a variety of evidence sources teachers can use to identify where improvement is needed and, in my opinion as equally important, to celebrate success.

Finally, it is essential to remember that at the centre of all this data, graphs and charts are the children. We must ensure that we do not reduce the child to purely a number. If we look at the performance of groups in isolation of other groups, it is easy to forget that a child can be part of more than one group and that their individual learning profile must always be considered. A good way to help to keep the child at the centre of a drive to raise standards is to discuss their strengths and needs in terms of them as a learner and not only an attainment or progress measure.

GOOD PRACTICE AND PUPIL PROGRESS REVIEWS

Pupil progress reviews (PPRs) are meetings, usually between the class teacher and a senior leader in a school. Some schools are able to include other members of staff such as support staff, Special Educational Needs Lead or Inclusion Lead. The financial implications of inviting several staff members needs to be considered. The purpose of the meeting is to review the progress of the pupils. Some reviews focus on significant groups, others on the whole class. The most important thing is that the children are discussed as individual learners, reasons for their progress to date are articulated and supported with evidence, which often includes tracking data, work samples and the teacher's professional judgement. Next steps in learning and teaching are agreed, which could be in the form of a whole-class strategy, small group work or specific intervention.

CASE STUDY

How one primary school used pupil progress reviews

The PPR took place in a quiet room, during designated time so that the staff present could focus on the children, with interruptions minimised as far as possible. A senior leader would meet with the class teacher to review the progress of the class. The Inclusion Lead would attend if possible. Teachers attended three PPRs per year in October, February and June. If possible, the final one was with the class teacher who would be teaching the class the following year.

The senior leader and class teacher discussed each child in the class in turn. The discussion was guided by the available data and the class teacher's professional knowledge about the child. Comments and any actions to be taken were recorded for each child. These actions could be a new strategy for the whole class, specific support from the class teacher, intervention provided by a teacher or member of support staff, assessment by the Inclusion Lead. For ease of reference, actions were highlighted in different colours so responsibility could be quickly identified. After the first meeting, the comments included the impact of the previously agreed action. The forms were shared with the head teacher and Leader of Inclusion. Any SEN or disability (SEN/D) or English as an Additional Language (EAL) needs were recorded. If a change in status had occurred since the previous PPR, the original status had a line crossed through it and the new status and date were recorded. A different colour was used for each meeting, e.g. black PPR1, red PPR2 and blue PPR3.

When these meetings were first introduced, some class teachers found them challenging. As the meetings became more embedded, the discussions became focused on the achievements of each child and how the class teacher and colleagues could support the children to improve further.

Data reviewed:

- Current ARE and progress
- End of year targets
- Intervention tracking
- Attendance

ACTION KEY

- Teacher
- Inclusion Lead
- Learning Mentor
- TA

Pupil Performance Review Meeting

Class: Date: Present:

PPR1
PPR2
PPR3

Child	Comments	Action

Figure 25.2

HOW CAN TEACHERS' DATA SCRUTINY IMPACT POSITIVELY ON PUPIL PROGRESS?

CRITICAL QUESTION

What is the relationship between a teacher's scrutiny of the data and pupil progress?

We need to ask ourselves if it is acceptable for senior leaders to complete the analysis of the data and present the findings to staff, or should class teachers be involved in interrogating the data sets for the children they teach? Through my experience as a class teacher and senior leader, I found that being presented with an analysis of my class's performance did not fully help me to understand the story behind the data and the implications for my future practice. In short, there was 'no buy in' on my part. While I was working as a class-based deputy head in a school Ofsted had judged to require special measures, the senior leaders worked closely with the representative of Her Majesty's Inspector (HMI) who was assigned to our school, to develop a tool for class teachers to scrutinise data in a meaningful way. We called it a class standards overview and agreed it should include the proportion and percentage of children at age-related expectation or greater depth, as a whole class as well as by significant groups. These groups could include SEN/D, gender or eligibility for Pupil Premium funding. By reviewing the data in this way, class teachers could identify what the key issues were in their class and decide possible actions that could be taken to improve standards.

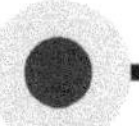

CASE STUDY

How one primary school used class standards overviews

Data was being produced at senior leadership level to inform the school development plan, but class teachers felt removed from the process. They felt as though the data did not belong to them and was not related to the work they did with the children in their class. Teachers felt accountable for the attainment of the children they taught, but were not using the data in a consistent way to inform their teaching. Class standards overviews were used to help teachers use data in a meaningful way, and to identify individual children and groups who would benefit from intervention.

Teachers completed the form three times a year, directly after the termly summative assessment had been input onto the school tracking system. Once the forms had been completed, the head teacher met with each member of staff to discuss the issues identified and possible actions to be taken. By focusing on the children's needs in this way, appropriate provision could be implemented.

Class standards overview

Academic year		Class	Completed by		Date	
Number of children in class		joined after 1st Sept.		Left after 1st Sept.		

Reading			Names of children not on track
proportion	%	Children at age-related expectation	
		Children with EAL at age-related expectation or greater depth	
		Children with SEN at age-related expectation or greater depth	
		Children eligible for Pupil Premium at age-related expectation or greater depth	
		Children identified as working at greater depth	
		Boys at age-related expectation or greater depth	
		Girls at age-related expectation or greater depth	
	Other significant groups at age-related expectation		

Issue 1: **Actions:**
Issue 2: **Actions:**

Figure 25.3

HOW CAN I DEMONSTRATE PUPIL PROGRESS AS A STUDENT TEACHER?

Many student teachers find it difficult to demonstrate that they have had a positive impact on pupil progress, especially at the beginning of their training. It can be difficult when you are working with small groups or teaching individual lessons to accurately demonstrate the progress that pupils have made. One way to support this would be the observation comments from your mentor. Another could be the annotated samples of work from the lessons you have taught. As you start to teach sequences of lessons, it becomes easier to evidence your impact. You can use samples of work from the initial and final lessons and through your annotations, draw conclusions about the impact you have had.

CASE STUDY

How Middlesex University has supported student teachers to evidence impact

Student teachers were required to write weekly reviews detailing their progress towards meeting targets set, analyse significant achievements and how they would improve their teaching in the coming week. These were a short document to support student reflection on the week as a whole rather than a recount of what had happened over the week. It was felt by the university staff involved with student support during school-based training that what was often missing was the impact the student was having on the children's learning.

A new approach to these reviews was introduced: impact reports. The purpose of the impact report was for the student to demonstrate the impact of their teaching on pupil progress across the curriculum, based on sequences of lessons taught by the student. The impact report drew on evidence from the student's planning, quality of their teaching and assessment of children's learning over time.

Over the course of the student's programme, several impact reports were completed for English, mathematics, science and foundation subjects.

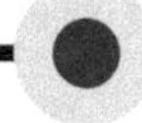

CHAPTER SUMMARY

- There are different approaches to accountability. This chapter has outlined systems of school accountability from other countries and made it clear that there is no one 'correct' approach.
- The chapter has considered the flow of data and accountability in schools; how data is used to hold teachers to account and the challenges that come with this.
- We have considered how accountability changes as your career develops.
- The chapter has outlined some differing approaches in data-led accountability and asked you to think more deeply about these.
- Possible complications and challenges with data-led accountability have been considered.
- The chapter has looked in detail at the system of PPR.
- We have explored how we can assess the impact of teachers' data scrutiny on pupil progress.

ASSIGNMENTS

If you are writing an ITE assignment on data-led accountability, it will be useful for you to think through the following:

- Is data the most effective way to hold teachers to account? Why do you think this? What other methods of accountability could be used?
- Should data be used to drive school improvement? If yes, is it the most important source of information? If no, what should school leaders use to inform school improvement?
- What can we learn from PISA (The Programme for International Student Assessment)? Are pedagogies that are successful in other countries applicable to England? Are there lessons we can learn from curriculum development from the past?

Useful texts to support an ITE assignment on data-led accountability

Harlen, W. (2014) *Assessment, Standards and Quality of Learning in Primary Education.* York: Cambridge Primary Review Trust.

Hutchinson, C. and Young, M. (2011) Assessment for learning in the accountability era: Empirical evidence from Scotland. *Studies in Educational Evaluation*, 37: 62–70.

West, A., Mattei, P. and Roberts, J. (2011) Accountability and sanctions in English schools. *British Journal of Educational Studies*, 59 (1): 41–62.

REFERENCES

Crooks, T.J. (2011) Assessment for learning in the accountability era: New Zealand. *Studies in Educational Evaluation,* 37: 71– 7.

DfE (Department for Education) (2011) *Teachers' Standards.* Crown copyright.

DfE (2015) *Final Report of the Commission on Assessment without Levels.* Crown copyright.

DfE (2016) *National Curriculum Assessments at Key Stage 2 in England, 2016 (revised).* Crown copyright.

DfE (2017) *National Curriculum Assessments at Key Stage 2 in England, 2017 (revised).* Crown copyright.

DfE (2018) *Primary School Accountability in 2017: A technical guide for primary maintained schools, academies and free schools.* Crown copyright.

Gillborn, D. and Mirza, H. (2000) *Educational Inequality: Mapping race, class and gender. A synthesis of research evidence.* Crown copyright.

Harlen, W. (2014) *Assessment, Standards and Quality of Learning in Primary Education.* York: Cambridge Primary Review Trust.

Hutchinson, C. and Young, M. (2011) Assessment for learning in the accountability era: Empirical evidence from Scotland. *Studies in Educational Evaluation,* 37: 62–70.

Independent Teacher Review Group (2016) *Eliminating Unnecessary Workload Associated with Data Management.* Crown copyright.

Ofsted (The Office for Standards in Education, Children's Services and Skills) (2013) *Unseen Children: Access and achievement 20 years on. Evidence Report.* Crown copyright.

Scottish Government (2016) *National Improvement Framework for Scottish Education. 2017 Evidence Report.* Crown copyright.

Smith, K. (2016) Assessment for Learning: A pedagogical tool, in Wyse, D., Hayward, L. and Pandya, J. (eds) *Curriculum, Pedagogy and Assessment.* London: SAGE, pp. 740–55.

STA (Standards and Testing Agency) (2017a) *How to Convert Key Stage 1 Raw Scores to Scaled Scores.* Crown copyright.

STA (2017b) *How to Convert Key Stage 2 Raw Scores to Scaled Scores.* Crown copyright.

STA (2017c) *Key Stage 1 2018 Assessment and Reporting Arrangements.* Crown copyright.

STA (2017d) *Key Stage 2 2018 Assessment and Reporting Arrangements.* Crown copyright.

STA (2017e) *Teacher Assessment Frameworks at the End of Key Stage 1.* Crown copyright.

STA (2017f) *Teacher Assessment Frameworks at the End of Key Stage 2.* Crown copyright.

West, A., Mattei, P. and Roberts, J. (2011) Accountability and sanctions in English schools. *British Journal of Educational Studies,* 59 (1): 41–62.

PART 4

TEACHING NOW

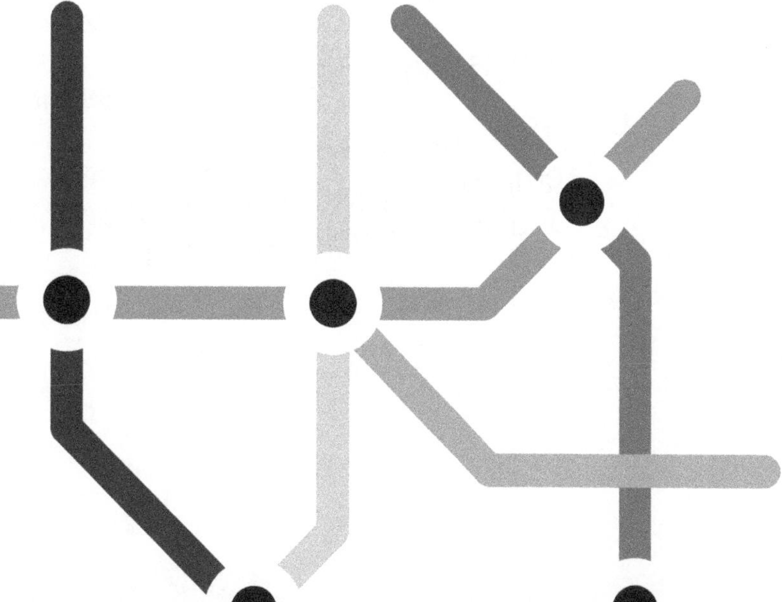

WHAT IS FEEDBACK?

- The vast majority of interactions between teachers and pupils involve feedback
- As we walk around the room we are providing individuals, groups and the class with feedback
- It's using strategies such as mini-plenaries
- It's all the questions that we ask
- It's asking pupils to self-assess their work against criteria
- It's modelling self and peer assessment strategies and empowering pupils to reflect on their progress and learning and identify their next steps

26

WHAT ARE THE ISSUES SURROUNDING TEACHER WORKLOAD?

Michael Green is the Head of Strategic Partnerships Education at the University of Greenwich. In December 2017 he was seconded to the Department for Education as an adviser focusing on teacher workload, specifically for trainee teachers and teachers in the early stages of their career.

In this chapter, Michael Green explores the evidence base surrounding teacher workload in England, including the issues and challenges that teachers face. He shines a light on the ways in which unnecessary burdens can be addressed.

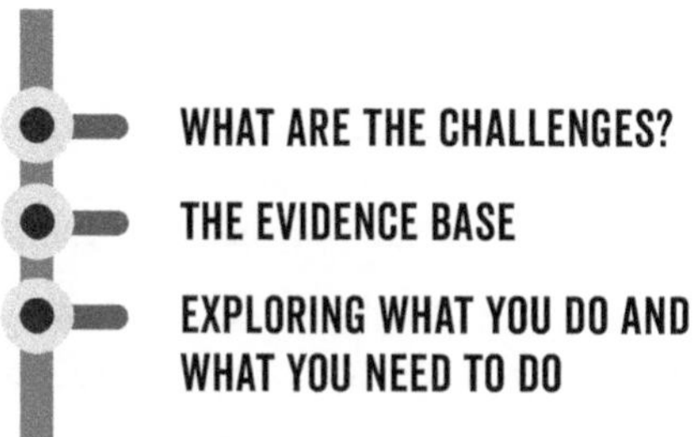

KEY WORDS

- Burdens
- Data management
- Marking
- Planning
- Prioritising
- Time management
- Workload

HOUSTON, WE HAVE A PROBLEM!

Teaching is, without question, a fantastic and rewarding job and should be a profession that many aspire to join. That buzz you get when you help pupils in your class fulfil their potential is unlike any other feeling. Despite these rewards, teaching is certainly not without its challenges. It almost seems impossible these days to discuss any topic relating to teaching without the topic of workload being raised. Too often we are seeing teachers being asked to do too much. The feeling of an endless list of jobs to get through; even after working all hours the list continues to be added to. It is when the list of jobs to perform becomes the driver of your life that the passion and enthusiasm for the job can ebb away. Is it any wonder that we currently have both a teacher recruitment and retention crisis? The House of Commons Education Committee's 2017 report on the recruitment and retention of teachers highlighted the pressure of teacher workload to be an important influencing factor.

TEACHER WORKLOAD: THE RECENT EVIDENCE BASE

CRITICAL QUESTION

What are the challenges relating to workload for teachers?

A number of recent surveys can help to inform the evidence base relating to teacher workload in England.

The 2013 Teaching and Learning International Survey (TALIS) survey by the Organisation for Economic Co-operation and Development (OECD, 2014) of lower secondary teachers across 34 countries suggested that teachers in England worked, on average, nine hours more than the median of all participating countries. Importantly, this additional time was not as a result of more hours spent teaching, but more time spent undertaking planning, marking, school management duties and carrying out administrative tasks.

KEY READING

The 2013 Teaching and Learning International Survey (TALIS) survey by the Organisation for Economic Co-operation and Development (OECD, 2014) can be found at:

www.oecd.org/education/talis/

Many of these tasks will resonate with primary teachers too. Importantly, the survey also found that those teachers who felt that their workload was unmanageable reported lower levels of job satisfaction.

In 2014, the DfE undertook the 'Workload Challenge' to understand more about teachers' experiences and also ways in which their workload could be reduced. There were just under 44,000 responses to the survey conducted.

CRITICAL QUESTION

Which of your working week tasks are of the most/least value to the pupils in your class?

A number of tasks were identified and while the majority acknowledged were important tasks undertaken as a teacher, the excessive level of detail required, the need to duplicate information in multiple places or over-bureaucratic systems made many of these tasks burdensome and impacted negatively on their workload. Some of the tasks that the respondents felt took up too much of their time included the following:

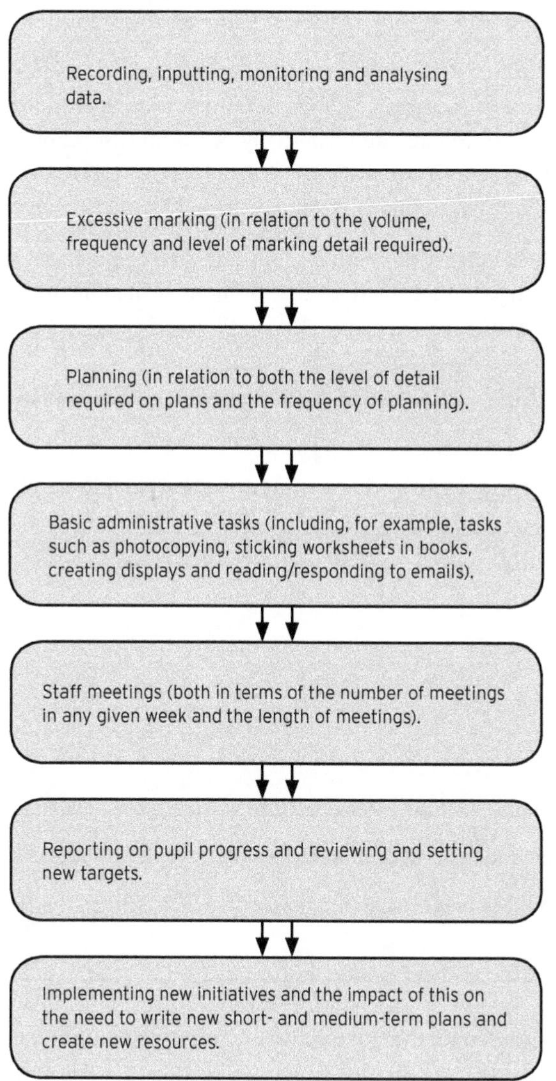

Many of the tasks listed above are ones undertaken in addition to teaching – a similar finding to the TALIS survey. With little time for teachers to undertake many of these tasks within the school day, many respondents commented that it is not uncommon for them to complete these in their own time in order to try to manage their workload.

CRITICAL QUESTION

Which tasks give you the most professional satisfaction?

Which tasks tend to cause you the most frustration or stress?

A key driver identified by teachers as adding a significant burden to their workload concerned the monitoring and accountability culture – both internally and externally. A fear of inspection and the resultant culture this created within schools through the need to always be 'Ofsted ready', collecting evidence, mock inspections, lesson observations and other forms of monitoring was keenly felt by many respondents.

Helpfully, the survey not only identified the burdens, but also sought potential solutions. Given the burdens identified, it will come as no surprise that many of the solutions related broadly to changes in accountability and the need for additional support.

KEY READING

The three independent reports to reduce unnecessary workload practice

In response to the 2014 Workload Challenge, the Department for Education launched three independent teacher workload review groups to develop principles, advice and guidance focusing on reducing unnecessary workload burdens relating to:

1. Marking
2. Planning and teaching resources
3. Data management

The reports of recommendations from the three groups can be accessed online at:

www.gov.uk/government/publications/reducing-teachers-workload/reducing-teachers-workload

It is certainly worth reading these and considering how, within your school, the recommendations have been acted upon.

As a result of the Workload Challenge, the government committed to undertake a large-scale survey every two years to track teacher workload; the first of which took place in 2016 and was completed by just over

3,000 teachers. A number of key findings relating to working hours, tasks undertaken by teachers and teachers' attitudes towards their workload are summarised below:

- The average, self-reported, working hours for all respondents was 54.4 hours during the week in question. Consistent with previous studies, primary teachers reported working longer hours – 55.5 hours. Of this, 17.5 hours were reported as hours worked out of school at evenings and weekends. Significantly, primary teachers in the early stages of their career reported even higher working hours – 59.5, of which 18.1 hours were worked out of school. Interestingly, of those 59.5 hours, teaching accounted for 23.9 hours. In other words, 60 per cent of time is spent on undertaking activities other than teaching.
- Given the responses to the early 2014 Workload Challenge, unsurprisingly, the three non-teaching activities that primary teachers felt they spent too much time on included planning and preparing for lessons (including resource preparation), general administrative tasks (which includes recording, inputting, monitoring and analysing data), and correcting and marking pupils' work.
- When asked about their perceptions of workload as an issue, the majority of all respondents (93 per cent) stated it was a problem. Furthermore, 97 per cent felt that they were unable to complete their workload within their contracted working hours. Given the two previous responses, it will come as no surprise that 85 per cent of teachers did not feel that they were able to achieve a good work–life balance.

Sadly, the rather depressing and bleak picture emerging from these recent surveys is not a new issue. Back in 2001, a study conducted for the government of the time by PriceWaterhouseCoopers found there to be an imbalance between teaching and administrative tasks, with many of the tasks undertaken not seen as positively supporting the learning of the pupils in their classrooms.

The 2001 study is generally regarded as the catalyst for a number of actions described as 'historic' by the government of the time. These actions included changes to teachers' contracts which identified 24 administrative tasks that teachers should not have to undertake, and the introduction in 2015 of guaranteed planning, preparation and assessment time.

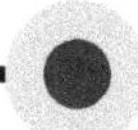

CRITICAL QUESTION

What steps can you take to ensure that you are focusing on the tasks that impact children's learning and spending less time on administrative tasks?

DISPELLING THE MYTHS ABOUT OFSTED

There exists, in some quarters of education, a misguided idea that certain activities must be 'carried out because Ofsted asks for them'. Much of this is pure myth. If you haven't already done so, it's worth reading the guidance by Ofsted on myths associated with inspections.

KEY READING

OFTED Inspection Myths can be accessed online at:

www.gov.uk/government/publications/school-inspection-handbook-from-september-2015/ofsted-inspections-mythbusting

Some key points to highlight include:

Ofsted are only interested in how marking and feedback promote pupil learning – the frequency and form that this takes is not within the remit of an inspection;

Ofsted do not wish to see written evidence of oral feedback being provided to pupils;

Ofsted are only interested in the effectiveness of planning – not the format that it is presented in nor the detail included;

Ofsted do not want teachers to undertake additional work purely if the reason is related to preparing for an inspection.

Implications for you:

Always reflect on why you are being asked to do something. If it's about promoting pupil learning – great, but if the reason you're being told is 'because of Ofsted' push back and refer them to the Ofsted myths guidance.

MARKING

Let's do the math . . .

INFO 26.1

If you teach, say, three lessons a day, which require marking, and there are 30 children in your class, that's 90 pieces of work to mark per day. Now, for the sake of argument, let's say that on average it takes three minutes per piece to mark – we're now at 270 minutes per day. Multiply that over a week – 1,350 minutes or 22½ hours. Is it no wonder that marking is seen as burdensome?

Now, don't get me wrong, I'm not advocating that marking should be scrapped, but marking has to be manageable and if teachers are left exhausted, then this goes against the grain of advice by the NCETM (National Centre for Excellence in Teaching Mathematics) that the most important activity for teachers is the teaching itself – supported by the design and preparation of lessons.

Over the years, the terms *marking* and *feedback* have come to be one and the same – but let's be clear – feedback and marking are not synonymous. As the accountability agenda within education has increased, so, in a significant number of schools, has the misguided thought that everything has to be evidenced. This practice has to stop.

Even though I have called this section marking, it's important to remember that marking is one type of feedback – of which there are many other types. Sadly, marking has become disproportionately valued within teaching.

CRITICAL QUESTION

Why has marking become disproportionately valued within teaching?

Worse still, the amount of feedback given has become confused with quality. The DfE's 2014 Workload Challenge consultation identified marking as the single biggest contributor to teacher workload being unsustainable. Is it any wonder we have cacophony within the profession?

Now, while it would be easy to simply blame the accountability agenda for this issue, teachers also have to burden some of the responsibility here. As a teacher, I can recall the guilt of feeling that I 'needed' to write something in the child's book. I would urge anyone thinking that they need to write a written comment in every child's book for each lesson to challenge both themselves and others to reject this 'false comfort' (DfE, 2016a: 8) that everything needs to be marked. Instead, consider the three principles outlined in the Independent Report on Eliminating Unnecessary Workload around marking, which states that feedback should be:

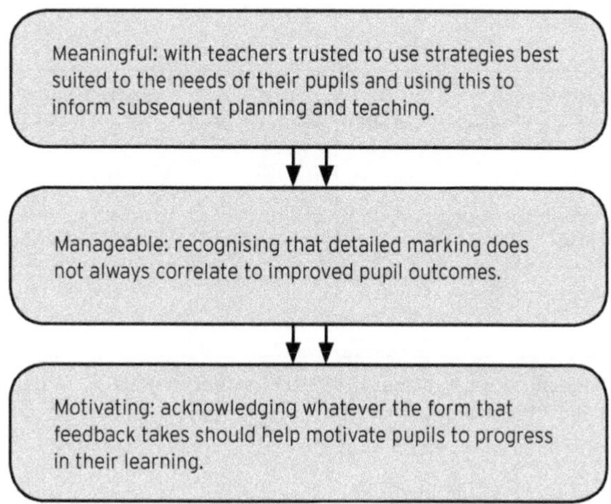

INFO 26.2

What is feedback?

- The vast majority of interactions between teachers and pupils involve feedback.
- As we walk around the room we are providing individuals, groups, the class with feedback.
- It's using strategies such as mini-plenaries.
- It's all the questions that we ask.
- It's asking pupils to self-assess their work against criteria.
- It's modelling self and peer assessment strategies and empowering pupils to reflect on their progress and learning and identify their next steps.

As you can see, none of the above even has to involve the use of a pen to provide a written comment. Let's now take a look at how one school has embedded the three principles above into their school policy.

CLASSROOM LINK

What does this mean for classroom practice?

Andrew Percival, Deputy Headteacher at Stanley Road Primary School in Oldham, shares the approach taken at his school to reduce workload and improve feedback:

At Stanley Road, we have introduced an approach to giving feedback to pupils that removes the need for written comments in pupils' books. We found that teachers were spending significant time marking work and were sceptical that this was an efficient use of teachers' time. We developed the following approach to reduce workload and, we believe, have also improved the quality of feedback given.

At the end of a lesson, teachers look through pupils' books and analyse the work carefully but, rather than write individual comments, they now make brief notes on the verbal feedback they will give in the next lesson. We use the following format to record these notes.

<table>
<tr><th>Work to Praise and Share</th><th>Need Further Support</th></tr>
<tr><td></td><td></td></tr>
<tr><th>Presentation</th><th>Basic Skills Errors</th></tr>
<tr><td></td><td></td></tr>
<tr><th colspan="2">Misconceptions and Next Lesson Notes</th></tr>
<tr><td colspan="2"></td></tr>
</table>

Teachers can now analyse a set of books quickly (often taking 15 to 20 minutes) and then use the time saved to plan the feedback they will give in the next lesson.

At the start of the next lesson, teachers use their notes to give feedback to the whole class to address common misconceptions. Good examples of work are shared under a visualiser to emphasise key teaching points and pupils may be given the chance to check their work for specific errors or given opportunities for further practice. These feedback sessions usually last between 5 and 10 minutes.

Teachers report that this approach has significantly reduced their workload. Not only do teachers no longer take books home to be marked but, we believe, that pupils are now taking much greater responsibility for responding to feedback and improving their own understanding.

PLANNING AND RESOURCES

Now don't get me wrong, planning is an essential task that teachers have to undertake. As Myatt (2016: 19) rightly asserts, it is 'fundamental in providing structure and architecture for pupils' learning'. Unfortunately, one of the issues surrounding planning is that it has become more about teachers filling in boxes on planning templates which is no more than a paper trail for accountability purposes. Jill Berry (2017), former head of Dame Alice Harpur School in Bedford, argues instead that the mind-set should shift from one of producing lengthy individual lesson plans to 'prove you're doing your job' to planning focusing on 'thinking, evaluating, adapting, improving'.

PLANNING MYTHS

Let's then debunk some of the myths associated with planning. The National Education Union (NEU) (2017) helpfully identified five important myths:

1. Sharing planning and resources, and using those of other people doesn't make anyone an ineffective teacher. The key is being able to use the time to adapt these to suit the needs of your class, rather than spending a disproportionate amount of time reinventing the wheel yourself.
2. Spending lots of time making a resource for yourself doesn't make you a better teacher. Look at resources that already exist. Shift your mind-set from making your own resources to evaluating the quality of existing resources and considering how they can be used to support your teaching.
3. Using high-quality textbooks doesn't make you a lazy teacher, nor does it replace your professional knowledge and skill. Clearly, this is dependent on stability within the curriculum – textbooks are a significant investment and, with a squeeze on school budgets and worries about texts becoming quickly out of date due to curriculum changes, it is no wonder that fewer than 10 per cent of teachers in the UK use textbooks in their lessons.
4. Ofsted does not require an individual lesson plan produced for a lesson observed during an inspection. Nor do they want to see a folder full of previous lesson plans from teachers.

5. A lesson plan, by itself, does not indicate good teaching. Looking at a lesson plan in isolation often bears little relation to what happens in the classroom. With this in mind, Myatt (2016) argues for an end to teachers having to produce compulsory lesson plans. She goes on to point out that impact on pupil learning cannot be judged by simply looking at someone's lesson plan.

Many of the above points chime with the findings of the Department for Education's Independent Review on Planning (2016b), which also identified that planning a sequence of lessons was far more important than teachers spending lots of time writing individual and often highly detailed lesson plans. In other words, teachers need to focus more on planning pupils' learning over a period of time rather than splitting it into individual lessons.

When considering planning in your context, it is often worth reflecting on Hattie's (2012: 37) advice and how this can be translated into practice for you:

> *Planning can be done in many ways, but the most powerful is when teachers work together to develop plans, develop common understandings of what is worth teaching, collaborate on understanding their beliefs of challenge and progress and work together to evaluate the impact of their planning on student outcome.*

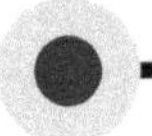

KEY READING

Why Textbooks Count – A policy paper by Tim Oates

It is worth reading Oates's policy paper where he puts forward a convincing argument behind the role that textbooks could play in supporting effective teaching while also reducing teacher workload. The paper challenges what Nick Gibb refers to as the 'ideological hostility' in primary schools to the use of textbooks. Available at:

www.cambridgeassessment.org.uk/Images/181744-why-textbooks-count-tim-oates.pdf

OTHER IMPORTANT STRATEGIES

CRITICAL QUESTION

What are some of the strategies that will help you to manage your workload?

Being an effective teacher requires you to develop habits and strategies so that you spend your time and energy on the things that help you become better as a teacher and also on those that have the most impact on the pupils in your class. It would be false for me to say that teaching doesn't have its highs and lows – what job doesn't? Yes, it can also be stressful at times and there will be pinch points in the academic year. There are, however, some important steps that you can take to help you.

MANAGING YOUR TIME

Managing your time is an important skill to master. A useful habit to develop is to set time limits to both your working day and also for specific tasks. It is really important that you are strict with this. Remember, there is no need or expectation for you to be the first one in school every morning and the last one to leave. This will soon take its toll on you, so start as you mean to go on. As you know, teaching is one of those professions where there is always something else to do, so it's important for you develop these habits and self-discipline to avoid work taking control of you. Also identify when you are at your most productive and try to maximise what you do during this time.

Managing your time also means ensuring that you build in 'me time'. Remember, you work really hard, so it's important that you factor in time for your hobbies and ring-fence this.

PRIORITISING TASKS

Stephen Covey (1999) popularised the concept of prioritising your workload with his self-help matrix.

	URGENT	NOT URGENT
IMPORTANT	Quadrant 1: Urgent & important	Quadrant 2: Not urgent & important
NOT IMPORTANT	Quadrant 3: Urgent & not important	Quadrant 4: Not urgent & not important

Covey's matrix is designed to help you organise your priorities so that you can manage your available time more effectively. The idea behind the matrix is to prioritise your tasks in relation to their importance and urgency; helping you to make decisions about whether you need to address a particular task immediately or if it can wait.

- **Urgent and important:** It's important to distinguish here between the two types of urgent and important – often they fall into two categories – unforeseen/unexpected and also the tasks that you have left until the last minute. Clearly, you can't foresee the unexpected but they will occur and it's therefore important that you factor in time when you may need to handle unforeseen events. When these occur you'll need to make use of your time management skills. For those tasks that you've left until the last minute – well – the obvious point here is to avoid these by planning ahead and utilising the strategies mentioned above about managing your time.
- **Important but not urgent:** An example of this could be marking some homework. Yes, it's important, but as you don't need to give it back to your pupils for a few days, you can plan in time to undertake this task. The important point here is to make sure that you plan in the time to do these tasks – and stick to it – to avoid them suddenly becoming urgent. Scheduling tasks into your working week will maximise your chances of using your time most effectively, avoiding unnecessary stress and not letting your workload take control of you.

- **Finally, the last two quadrants:** When considering those urgent but not important tasks, think about how you can streamline, reduce or delegate some of these. Sometimes for teachers it's really hard to identify not important tasks – aren't all the tasks that we do important? I'd suggest that they aren't. Sometimes these tasks may be important to others, but not for you in relation to the other priorities and deadlines you have. Remember – think to yourself – are these tasks positively impacting on the quality of my teaching and on the pupils in my class? If they aren't, why are you doing them? Now, for those not urgent and not important tasks. In teaching, these are sometimes what I like to refer to as the 'icing on the cake' tasks. While it may be lovely to laminate all the children's exercise books, ask yourself, could I be using my time more effectively?

CLASSROOM LINK

What does this mean for classroom practice?

- Consider all the typical activities you perform during the working week. Try to be specific.
- Which of these activities take up more time than they should?
- Are there ways that you could reduce this?
- Now begin to categorise the activities according to the quadrants. Look ahead to tasks and deadlines in the term/academic year.
- How can you build in time for these before they become urgent and important?

The trick, as Bubb (2014) rightly points out, is not to be a perfectionist – you have to think to yourself that 'good enough' will do. Prioritise the essential tasks and keep on top of these.

CHAPTER SUMMARY

Teaching, while hugely rewarding, does have its challenges. What profession, though, doesn't have challenges? Within this chapter we have explored some of the challenges concerning teacher workload, which, quite frankly, shouldn't be there.

I hope that in reading this you realise that teaching doesn't have to be a 24/7 profession. There are alternative ways that - importantly - positively impact on pupil learning and progress *and* reduce unnecessary workload burdens for teachers. Estelle Morris, a former Secretary of State for Education said in 2002: *A tired teacher is not an effective teacher. Nor is that teacher allowed to focus on what is most important - teaching.*

ASSIGNMENTS

If you are writing an ITE assignment on teacher workload, it will be useful for you to think through the following:

1. What are some of the internal and external factors that both positively and/or negatively impact on teacher workload?

2. What is the research and evidence base surrounding effective feedback, planning and resourcing? How can this support you with your workload?
3. What other strategies are there to support teachers to effectively manage their workload and work efficiently?
4. How have schools been addressing workload concerns?

REFERENCES

Berry, J. (2017) Tips to help schools reduce teacher workload, *The Guardian*. Available at: www.theguardian.com/teacher-network/2017/jul/19/tips-to-help-schools-reduce-teacher-workload (accessed 10/11/17).

Bubb, S. (2014) *Successful Induction for New Teachers: A guide for NQTs & induction tutors, coordinators and mentors*. London: SAGE.

Covey, S. (1999) *The 7 Habits of Highly Effective People*. London: Simon & Schuster.

Department for Education (DfE) (2016a) *Eliminating Unnecessary Workload Around Marking*. London: Department for Education.

Department for Education (DfE) (2016b) *Eliminating Unnecessary Workload Around Planning and Teaching Resources* London: Department for Education.

Gibson, S., Oliver, L. and Dennison, M. (2015) *Workload Challenge: Analysis of teacher consultation responses*. London: Department for Education.

Hattie, J. (2012) *Visible Learning for Teachers*. Abingdon: Routledge.

Higton, J., Leonardi, S., Richards, N., Choudhoury, A., Sofroniou, N. and Owen, D. (2017) *Teacher Workload Survey 2016: Research Report*. London: Department for Education.

House of Commons Education Committee (2017) *Recruitment and Retention of Teachers*. Available at: https://publications.parliament.uk/pa/cm201617/cmselect/cmeduc/199/199.pdf (accessed 01/03/17).

Myatt, M. (2016) The big picture on workload, in Ellis, N (ed.) (2016) *Managing Teacher Workload*. Woodbridge: John Catt Educational.

National Education Union NEU (2017) *Planning*. Available at: https://neu.org.uk/advice-and-resources/workload/planning (accessed 24/02/18).

Organisation for Economic Co-operation and Development (OECD) (2014) *Teaching and Learning International Survey: TALIS 2013 Technical Report*. Paris: OECD.

PriceWaterhouseCoopers (2001) *Teacher Workload Study Interim Report*. London: DfES.

ACKNOWLEDGEMENTS

With thanks to Andrew Percival at Stanley Road Primary School in Oldham for his help with the information on pp. 453-4.

27

WHY BOTHER WITH DIGITAL TECHNOLOGY?

Kelly Carabott is a lecturer in the Faculty of Education, Monash University, Australia. Previous to this life, she was a primary classroom teacher for 19 years. Her research interests include reading multimodal texts in the digital age, children's literature, educational digital technology integration and digital competence. Kelly also writes a blog in her spare time called Litology and more available at: https://ictintheclassroom.edublogs.org/

Amber McLeod is a lecturer in the Faculty of Education, Monash University, Australia. Amber was previously a microbiologist and then taught English as an additional language in Japan, Brunei and Australia. Her research focus is on increasing digital competence in the community, and as the Director of Pathway Programs at Monash, Amber is passionate about developing transferable skills in students.

In this chapter, Kelly Carabott and Amber McLeod explore the things that technology can help us to do in the classroom. Things that we were not able to do before. They consider the value that such experiences add to learning and ask - does the use of technology improve learning and teaching?

KEY WORDS

- Digital competence
- Digital learning
- Digital pedagogy
- Playfulness

STEPPING INTO A TRULY DIGITALLY ENABLED CLASSROOM

As you step into your classroom, you ensure that all of the VR headsets are ready to go. The students have been studying how children live in different cultures and you are excited to be able to offer them the experience of 'taking' them to several different countries as they are immersed in a 4D world. This experience will help to provide the context and stimulate questions for your Skype session with a class in Thailand next week. By talking to children in other cultures, you are hoping that the children's intercultural understanding will increase. That reminds you that you need to email the teacher and class you are connecting with; maybe this could be part of the writing block this morning. As the children put on their VR headsets, you remind them that they also need to be thinking about how they are going to use 'Scratch' to design a game that will teach other students about a different culture. These games will be shared via the class blog and also tweeted about through the class's Twitter feed.

CRITICAL QUESTION

Could you do this type of work without technology or is technology being used to design an experience that may not have been possible in the past?

What value does this experience add to learning?

Can't the students just read everything from a book and then design a paper poster?

Throughout this chapter we will explore such questions. If, by the end of the chapter, you are left with more questions than answers as you start to think seriously and critically about the use of digital technology in education, then this chapter has done its job!

WHY BOTHER TEACHING WITH DIGITAL TECHNOLOGY?

Children and adults are growing and living in a technologically saturated world. If you think about what you do in your day-to-day life, how much of what you do relies on technology? Think about the ways you use technology for work, for communication, for enjoyment. Do you use social media, use spreadsheets at work, use an ATM, play video games, or games on your phones? These are all examples of different ways that we use technologies to support our everyday lives. While students might be able to quickly use programs at a surface level to achieve their goals, many need a guide to expose them to the full potential of the programs.

Children of this generation have been called many things, from digital natives (Prensky, 2001) to the net generation (Oblinger *et al.*, 2005; Tapscott, 1998). However, we know that there is no such thing as a digital native; children are not born with an innate knowledge of technology, nor do all children enjoy using technology, and skills in digital technology use are not uniform. Enjoyment and competence in digital technology use is a result of exposure to technology, experimentation, persistence and direct instruction. For example, students may be amazing at using social media, but may not know how to use the review options in MS Word unless they are directed to them.

In addition to knowing how to use digital tools, there are many other facets of digital competence, which we, as educators, need to take into consideration when thinking about digital technology integration. Ferrari (2013: 4) outlines five key competencies:

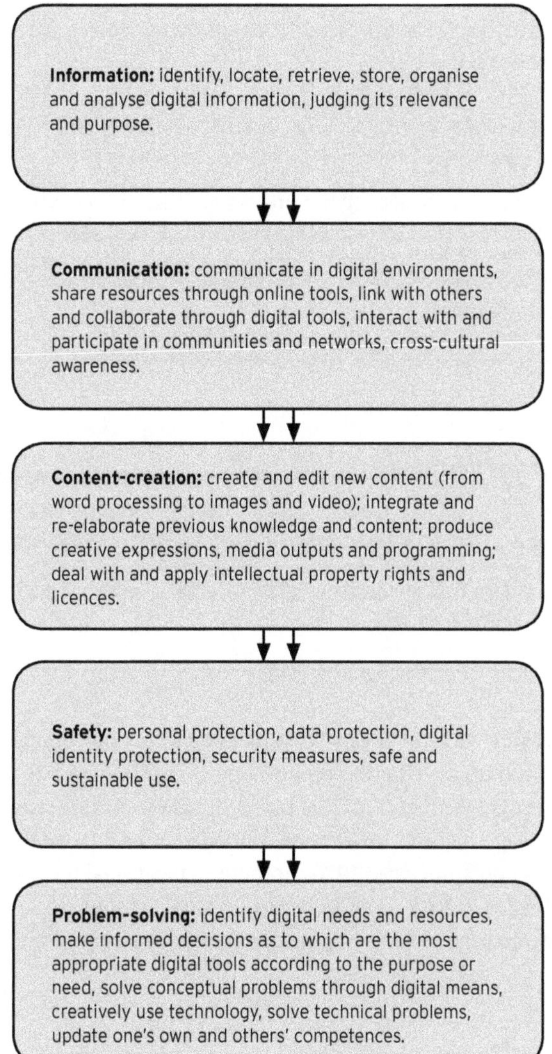

So, not only do students need to know how to use a spreadsheet, they must also be aware of privacy and copyright considerations when using the internet.

CLASSROOM LINK

What does this mean for classroom practice?

Have you ever been in a classroom and heard teachers say, 'For your enquiry project, you need to get onto the internet and do some research around your question'. The internet provides access to more information than we have ever been exposed to in the past and is certainly an important tool for learning in classrooms. But let's think about the skills that sit behind this task.

- The ability to apply critical digital literacy skills to internet searching (What types of keywords do I use? How will I know that this site is legitimate? How do I know that this is true?).
- The ability to use digital citizenship skills (What images and text are copyright? Do I have the rights to copy and then reuse this image? How do I stay safe online when I am searching?).
- The ability to use digital technology (How do I use a browser? What do I do if the device does not work? How can I troubleshoot any issues?).

CRITICAL QUESTION

If we just assume that all children we teach are digitally literate, what issues can you see arising from this?

Thinking about the underlying skills that children need to use, what aspects of digital technology do you need to be teaching in your everyday practice?

While most people are comfortable with the idea that students need to be competent with digital technology, there are many different perspectives on whether technology should be used as a pedagogical tool. It would appear that everybody (students, government, media) has an opinion on how and why technology should be used to support teaching and learning, and how much students should have access to. Even though educational technology has been in schools since the 1970s and 80s, educational technology is still a fairly new and highly contested space (Selwyn, 2016, 2017). You only have to look at some recent worldwide news headlines to gain an appreciation of how media and society view some aspects of technology.

KEY READING

France to ban mobile phones in schools from September

Available at: www.theguardian.com/world/2017/dec/11/france-to-ban-mobile-phones-in-schools-from-september

'Banning mobile phones in Swedish schools is as obvious as banning smoking'

Available at: www.thelocal.se/20180220/banning-mobile-phones-in-swedish-schools-is-as-obvious-as-banning-smoking

Putting More Technology in Schools May Not Make Kids Smarter: OECD Report

Available at: www.huffingtonpost.com.au/entry/technology-in-schools-oecd-report_us_55f32091e4b042295e362f19

Banning mobile phones will take education back in time experts say

Available at: www.abc.net.au/news/2018-02-05/debate-on-mobile-phones-in-the-classroom/9397898

Can Technology Change Education? Yes!: Raj Dhingra at TEDxBend

Available at: www.youtube.com/watch?v=lOs_M6xKxNc

Governments have advised how digital technology should be delivered in the curriculum. While some governments have embedded digital technology across all curriculum areas to be used for everyday teaching and learning, others have included it as a separate curriculum area, and others have a combination of both. Some countries have no mention of technology in curriculum documents. For some examples of how different countries have positioned digital technology in their curriculum, see Table 27.1.

Table 27.1 The position of digital technology in various curricula across the world

UK	National Curriculum 1. Computing as its own curriculum area
Australia	National Curriculum 1. Information and Communication Technology (ICT) embedded into all curriculum areas 2. Digital Technologies as its own curriculum area
Canada	Curriculum varies across provinces 1. ICT embedded into all curriculum areas
USA	Curriculum varies across states 1. ICT as a curriculum area 2. ICT embedded as its own curriculum area 3. A combination of embedded and separate curriculum areas
Netherlands	National Curriculum 1. Schools apply ICT in the curriculum as each individual school sees fit
Japan	National Curriculum 1. Not evident in the curriculum

Students in schools also have their own views on using technology for learning. Their preferences for content learning may be different to our own; sometimes rendering traditional classroom practices irrelevant to students' lived experiences (Pahl and Roswell, 2012; Pullen, 2015; Selwyn *et al.*, 2010). This could be an important conversation to have with students: what extra literacy practices do they need; what time-management skills are now relevant; what do they want their learning environment to look like?

What are your views on technology and learning? How should it be integrated into the curriculum?

This opens up spaces for meaningful technology integration and acknowledges the importance of student voice within their own learning. Isn't it time to move past the debates about which medium is better, paper or digital, and allow students and teachers to choose a variety of mediums suitable for the content? This is an illustration of Selwyn's observation that technology has become tied up in the big debates around 'what education is' and what education should be.

CRITICAL QUESTION

If the purpose of formal education is to enable students to navigate the world, how would banning mobile phones prepare students for the realities of the 21st century?

As a teacher, you need to take a critical stance on this debate, taking into account the diverse range of views. It is not helpful to position technology as either good or bad, rather it is important to recognise that the integration of technology in education is complex, with many shades of grey. There is no one size fits all approach. As educators, we cannot just introduce technology and then assume that because students are using it, they must be learning what was intended.

KEY READING

The following are great books that provide an overview of the key debates:

Selwyn, N. (2016) *Is Technology Good for Education?* Cambridge: Polity Press.

Selwyn, N. (2017) *Education and Technology: Key issues debates and debates*. London: Bloomsbury Academic.

DIGITAL TECHNOLOGY AND LEARNING: IS IT BENEFICIAL OR JUST DISTRACTING?

The research tells us that there are pockets of success where digital technology has enhanced understanding, but variables such as the students, the teachers, the task and the environment impact heavily on the success of digital technology integration for learning (Tamim *et al.*, 2011). The successful integration of technologies is complex, and there is certainly no one size fits all approach. When a digital activity is used as one of a number of tools to deliver content and chosen with all the variables in mind, it can be very effective. In addition, your own beliefs about how students learn and the role of technology within the space will impact on how, when and why you will use digital technology in your own teaching.

It has been proposed that using digital technology can enhance the learning environment in several ways. The Learning Environment Attributes Framework (Newhouse and Clarkson, 2008) was developed through a literature review of the main themes that were emerging within the research literature around technology and learning. The framework outlines ways that digital technology can contribute to the learning environment when it is used meaningfully. Some of these ways are outlined in Table 27.2.

Table 27.2 (adapted from Newhouse and Clarkson, 2008: 143)

Investigate Reality	Investigate the real world using tools to analyse, interpret and present information
Knowledge Building	Build a deeper knowledge base
Active Learning	Students are active participants in their learning, and they learn through applying and doing
Authentic Assessment	Assessment is based on real tasks (not set tests)
Engagement	Students are engaged with learning
High Level Thinking	Students are involved in the upper levels of Bloom's taxonomy (creative, analysis)
Learner Independence	Students have some ownership over their own learning, but they are still scaffolded by the teacher

To ensure that you are using technology in carefully considered ways that will enhance learning, what are some things to consider when deciding whether to include technology in your lessons?

1. **Are your students prepared?** Many teachers worry they will lose control of the class when technology is introduced in much the same way that a field trip might provide opportunities for students to 'misbehave'. You will need to have discussions with your class about the expectations surrounding the use of digital technology for learning. This discussion is not something that only happens once, rather it needs to be embedded into the everyday of teaching.

CRITICAL QUESTION

Students need to be taught to use technology in a safe and respectful way, and ground rules established before embarking on a task. How will you as the teacher monitor this?

2. **What is the task actually teaching the students?** If you have chosen a prepared task from the internet, how can you be sure it is valid? It is important to actually do the task yourself and determine whether it has the learning outcomes you intended. Is an online basketball game that changes the angle at which a ball is thrown into a hoop really enhancing students' understanding of angles, or is it just busy work? Rich tasks that are authentic and provide students with a real audience will help provide engagement.

3. **What are the pedagogical considerations?** Is technology being used meaningfully, and not just as an add-on? Is this technology going to be used to introduce, revise, or test knowledge? Are the students responding to the technology or creating their own? Will students work in groups or individually? Does the technology provide a space for students to make sense of new knowledge? Your understanding of effective pedagogical practices should be applied to digital technology in the same way they would be applied to paper and pen tasks. For example, from a behaviourist pedagogical perspective, the use of digital technology may result in direct instruction, and drill and practice software (e.g. a times-table game). A more constructive pedagogy may involve more open-ended tasks where students construct and create knowledge as they work through the task (e.g. the students use the app *Educreations* to explain how to work out times tables using the strategy of repeated addition).

KEY READING

Digital Technologies Hub

This website has some interesting case studies on how primary schools are using digital technology. This video in particular surrounds the pedagogical implications for choosing apps. Available at:

www.digitaltechnologieshub.edu.au/teachers/case-studies/primary/north-fitzroy-primary-school/choosing-the-right-apps-for-your-class

4. **What are the practical considerations?** What is the physical and virtual environment? What access to digital technology do you have? How does your school position and value the use of ICT? How much time do students have to complete the activity? Digital technology can often be seen as an optional extra to be tacked on at the end of a lesson if there is time. If the task is not worthy of proper planning, is it worth doing at all?

5. **Could this same task be done without technology?** Some digital tasks are replicas of pen and paper or face-to-face tasks.

CRITICAL QUESTION

Unless the technology is adding something, why bother using it?

Additions to traditional tasks range from links to extra information, online quizzes and games, to interactivity such as wearable devices or augmented or virtual reality. Think carefully about the value of a digital activity before choosing to use it in class.

CLASSROOM LINK

What does this mean for classroom practice?

Mr Jones is a Grade 3 teacher. The learning outcome he wants to focus on is 'for all students to develop communication and collaboration skills', through a task related to sustainability. Mr Jones notes that the local wetlands has begun work to protect some of the native species and comes up with a plan.

After searching on the internet, Mr Jones finds that there are many schools around the world who are working on local community sustainability projects. He contacts some of these schools and has an idea that will see his class start to collaborate with students around the world, looking at local sustainability through a global lens. He also contacts the local council and wildlife group; who have started the push.

The students' task is to come up with an advertising campaign to highlight the plight of the local species and the destruction of the natural habitat. They will work in small groups. They are to gain knowledge through virtual and real-life field trips, discussions both in person and virtually with experts locally and globally, and use of the internet to gain information. Their advertising will be online through the use of video-using apps such as puppet pals and imovie, and explain everything. At each point in this learning journey Mr Jones scaffolds students' understanding, and allows himself to become a learner along with the students.

Think about the following considerations in this scenario.

1. What is the teacher's role? How will he maintain control of the learning?
2. What is the task? Was the task planned to explicitly teach digital technology skills, or has the task allowed for learning through the use of digital technology?
3. How is the task authentic and how might this engage the students?
4. How has the environment been set up to facilitate learning?

MOVING FORWARD WITH DIGITAL TECHNOLOGY AND EDUCATION: WHERE TO NEXT?

Digital technology allows for the transformation of the learning environment where the outside world of the student can be brought into the classroom. Creatively harnessing the latest technological fads for learning allows students to showcase their knowledge, and increases engagement and highlights to the students the relevance of classroom learning.

KEY READING

Using pop culture and digital technology across curriculum areas

The link will take you to an article that discusses how *Pokemon Go* could be used across curriculum areas as a tool for teaching and learning. Although the hype surrounding *Pokemon Go* has declined, the ideas that underpin the creative use of innovative pop culture and digital technology can be applied to newer trends.

https://theconversation.com/gaming-in-the-classroom-what-we-can-learn-from-pokemon-go-technology-63766

As a teacher, you need to start to see yourself as a co-constructor of knowledge as digital technology changes at such a rapid speed that you will never be an expert – new programs and devices appear every day. Many teachers worry that they are not expert enough with technology to use it in class, but digital technology provides students and teachers with the opportunity to use their individual areas of expertise to co-construct knowledge. Imagine an activity where you and your class approach a brand new technology in order to create knowledge about map reading. While you are the map-reading expert (and certainly have at least some technological knowledge), asking the students to help you navigate the new technology gives them ownership of the activity and models risk-taking behaviour. As the whole class works together to solve problems with the technology, they are not only learning about map reading, but also to collaborate, communicate and manage failure. These transferable skills are highlighted as important educational outcomes by governments and private industry alike and as digital technology advances they are exactly the skills students will need in the future.

KEY READING

Predictions of new and emergent trends in digital technology

The Horizon Report created by the New Media Consortium is released every year. The report predicts the next five-year trends in educational technology.

The 2017 K-12 report predicts some new and emerging trends (www.nmc.org/nmc-horizon/)

1. Makerspaces
2. Robotics
3. Analytic technology
4. Virtual reality
5. Artificial intelligence
6. The internet of things

Some of the technologies that are appearing more often in schools include makerspaces, augmented and virtual reality and robotics. While teachers get creative with the possible ways these technologies could improve student learning, students have the opportunity to problem solve in a playful way and further develop their digital competence.

When we think about the fast-changing nature of digital technology, we can use a framework such as Gartner's hype cycle of technology (1995), which shows how many educational technologies come and go (van Wetering, 2016).

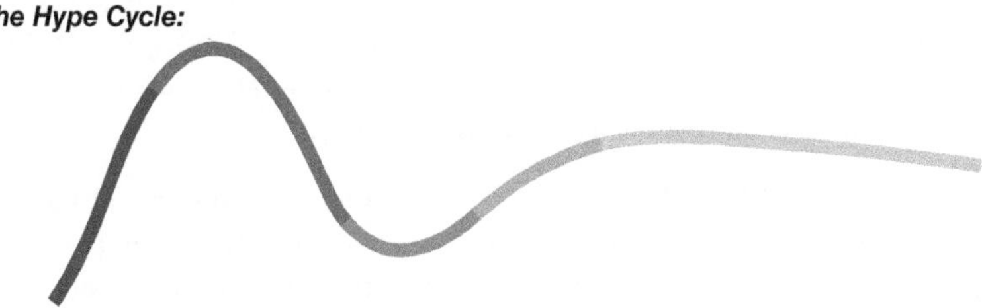

Figure 27.1 Gartner's hype cycle of technology image (from van Wetering, 2016: 5)

Gartner uses several terms to explore this journey.

- Peak of inflated expectations: the technology is hyped up; it will be the magic wand to fix or transform education.
- Trough of disillusionment: things start to go wrong.
- Plateau of productivity: a more realistic approach to technology integration.
- Cliff of obsolescence: the technology may disappear, often replaced with a newer form of technology.

While many new technologies may disappear, they nonetheless introduce new ideas and ways of creating knowledge that may be revisited in another form in the future. The electronic whiteboard, for example, introduced us to the idea of getting students to use their fingers to access technology – something that has reappeared in smartphones, tablets and laptops.

CRITICAL QUESTION

What's next for educational technology? How will classrooms look in 20 years' time?

Predictions for future educational technology development point to an increased presence of Artificial Intelligence (AI) which is able to analyse data on individual students and suggest activities in their zone of proximal development, provide a more knowledgeable other and let teachers know when students need individual help. Unfortunately, there is a tendency to wonder whether AI could just replace teachers altogether, but this view ignores the importance of relationships and social interaction which underpins learning. This view also ties into what Papert (1987) calls 'technocentric thinking', the belief that the technology will do all the teaching; however, we know that there is no clear link between learning and technology. A negative of AI is the extra time teachers spend preparing, collecting and reporting data, which can cause immense time pressures on already busy teaching lives. But what if all that data could be collected in another way?

The Internet of Things (IoT) refers to the network of physical devices, such as cars, phones, cameras and home appliances, that have sensors, electronics, software and the internet embedded in them. IoT devices can connect and exchange data, and are already being used in many homes and businesses. An IoT-enabled classroom could monitor student behaviour, and adjust light and temperature to achieve an optimum learning environment. It could even monitor each student's activities during the day.

As governments around the world consider the importance of digital technology in education, we can expect to see a gradual evening out of the digital competence of school graduates. Currently, while school graduates can be expected to have a certain level of literacy or numeracy, the same cannot be said for digital competence. Students who have attended a school where robotics and 3D printing are embraced might have much higher digital competence than those from a school where technologies are not available, banned or frowned upon. This can lead to inequalities in the workplace or higher education, and difficulties managing day-to-day technologies such as social media or government websites. Including technology in school curriculums will enable a minimum expectation of competence. However, the attitudes of teachers and the way that technologies are used in class will impact upon how students perceive technology – are they a necessary evil, or an opportunity to open up creative spaces?

CHAPTER SUMMARY

This chapter has posed more questions than answers. It has tried to develop your understanding of the complexity that exists when using digital technologies to scaffold learning in classrooms. Technology can enhance learning and increases understanding, but it needs to be in deeply meaningful ways, not just as an add-on to traditional pedagogy.

To finish, there are several key take-away messages:

1. You need to be a critical user of digital technology. Ask yourself questions such as, Why would I use this? How does it add value?
2. There is no one-size-fits-all approach. The way you use technology in your classroom will depend on your school, your access to technology, your learner needs, the task, and your own beliefs and values.
3. There is no good or bad technology, rather it is finding and allowing students and teachers to use the best medium for that purpose.

ASSIGNMENTS

If you are writing an ITE assignment on teaching and learning with digital technology, it will be useful for you to think through the following:

1. How is digital technology positioned within policy documents and curriculum, and how does this translate into everyday practice?
2. What does the inclusion of digital technology add to the learning experience?
3. What are the pedagogical implications when using digital technology? What things do you need to think about?

REFERENCES

Ferrari, A. (2013) DIGCOMP: A framework for developing and understanding digital competence in Europe. Available at: http://digcomp.org.pl/wp-content/uploads/2016/07/DIGCOMP-1.0-2013.pdf

Newhouse, C.P. and Clarkson, B.D. (2008) Using learning environment attributes to evaluate the impact of ICT on learning in schools. *Research and Practice in Technology Enhanced Learning*, 3(02): 139–58.

Oblinger, D., Oblinger, J.L. and Lippincott, J.K. (2005) *Educating the Net Generation*. Boulder, CO: EDUCAUSE.

Pahl, K. and Roswell, J. (2012) *Literacy and Education: Understanding the new literacy studies in the classroom* (2nd edn). London: SAGE.

Papert, S. (1987) Computer criticism verses technocentric thinking. *Educational Researcher*, 16(1): 22–30.

Pullen, D. (2015) The influence of the home learning environment on middle school students' use of ICT at school. *Australian Educational Computing*, 30(1).

Prensky, M. (2001) Digital natives, digital immigrants. *On the Horizon*, 9(5): 1–6.

Selwyn, N., Potter, John and Cranmer, Sue (2010) *Primary schools and ICT: Learning from pupil perspectives*. London; New York: Continuum International Publishing Group.

Selwyn, N. (2016) *Is Technology Good for Education?* Cambridge: Polity Press.

Selwyn, N. (2017) *Education and Technology: Key debates and debates*. London: Bloomsbury Academic.

The New Media Consortium (2017) *Horizon Report > 2017 K-12 Edition*. Available at: www.nmc.org/publication/nmccosn-horizon-report-2017-k-12-edition/ (accessed 12/07/18).

Tamim, R., Bernard, R., Borokhovski, E., Abrami, P.C. and Schmid, R. (2011) What forty years of research says about the impact of technology on learning: A second-order meta-analysis and validation study. *Review of Educational Research*, 81(1). Available at: www.jstor.org/stable/23014286 (accessed 12/07/18).

Tapscott, D. (1998) *Growing Up Digital: The rise of the net generation*. New York: McGraw Hill.

van Wetering, M.W. (2016) Technology compass for education: Kennisnet Trend Report 2016–2017. Available at: www.kennisnet.nl/fileadmin/kennisnet/corporate/algemeen/Kennisnet_Trendreport_2016_2017.pdf (accessed 12/07/18).

28

WHAT IS THE TRUE POWER OF READING?

Louise Johns-Shepherd, Chief Executive, Centre for Literacy in Primary Education. CLPE is a charity working to improve literacy in primary schools through creative, effective, evidence-based teaching that puts quality children's literature at the heart of all learning.

In this chapter, Louise Johns-Shepherd looks at how the teaching of reading has to be underpinned by secure knowledge of what reading is, how children develop as readers and what reading can do. She discusses the potential and the importance of text and reader identity in developing competent and confident readers.

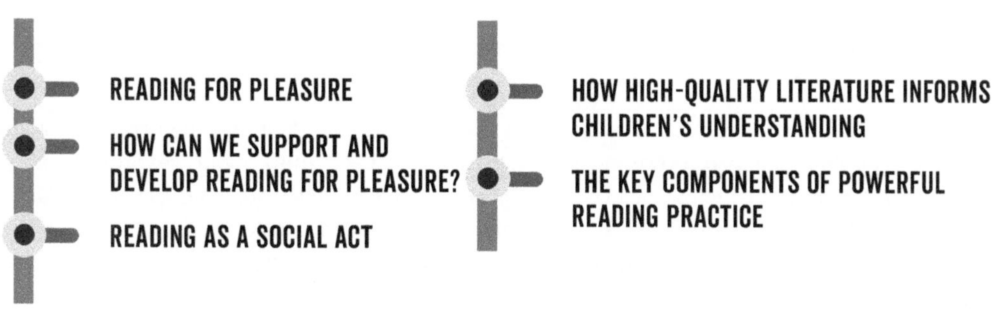

KEY WORDS

- Booktalk
- Books
- Communication
- Comprehension
- Curriculum
- Decoding
- Environment
- Fluency
- Literacy
- Literature
- Phonics
- Progress
- Read aloud
- Reading
- Reading for pleasure
- Text
- Vocabulary

READING FOR PLEASURE

The importance of reading for pleasure has become a universal truth. There is a large and growing body of research that tells us how reading for pleasure impacts on future life chances, on emotional well-being and on economic prosperity. If we want a wealthy, happy, intelligent population, then encouraging reading and developing readers is fundamental. Reading for pleasure is written into the National Curriculum, developing it is a statutory responsibility for our schools, and an overarching aim of the English Programme of Study is to develop a 'love of literature through widespread reading for enjoyment'. And yet we are working in times where this is an increasingly hard 'ask'. The numbers of publicly funded libraries and library provision in general is declining, the assessment framework for our schools focuses on the measurable and technical, effectively reducing curriculum time for reading, and school budgets are squeezed from all sides, reducing the ability of schools to spend on book stock and reading provision.

CRITICAL QUESTION

How can we stay focused on our responsibility to support children to 'develop a love of reading and books'?

Acknowledging both the importance and the difficulties of developing the skills and the habits of reading for pleasure are key steps along the road. However, as educators, we must also think about what reading for pleasure actually means. You can't just tell someone – 'enjoy this, it is pleasurable'. So, when we are working with children we need to think back to those times in our childhood or more recently, when we truly felt pleasure because of something we read. It is likely that the feeling of pleasure will be associated with the way a text or the experience of reading really moved us. Is it a memory of sharing a picture book over and over again with another person – until you know it so well the words and the phrasing stick in your head? Or is it the fact that a picture or a set of words stirred you, stayed with you, long beyond the reading of a book? Maybe it was the feeling of finding another person who loved a book as much as you, or the anticipation of receiving the next book in a series or by a favourite author. Perhaps it's that feeling you get when you are so immersed in a story that you just have to read one more page, one more chapter. It is this emotional response that we want children to feel, the connection, the achievement, the comfort, the addictive nature of something so pleasurable we want to do it again and again.

HOW CAN WE SUPPORT AND DEVELOP READING FOR PLEASURE?

CRITICAL QUESTION

What is the main thing we need to support our teaching of reading and develop reading for pleasure?

The answer is books of course. Books with stories, with poetry, with characters and with illustrations that will encourage engagement whoever you are and whatever your starting point. Texts that take you to new worlds and introduce you to new people – real and imagined – that help you to discover patterns and constructions in language, and bring you new ideas and understanding. Alongside books you need a range of experiences to help you discover and respond to those books in a variety of ways – privately or as a shared endeavour – and some skills that enable you to decode the text, make sense of the construction and allow you to respond to the experience. All of these things are what we need to provide in our classrooms to ensure that we are helping children to see reading as a pleasurable activity and understand the full power of the reading experience.

CRITICAL QUESTION

Do you know where all the children in your class sit on the reading continuum?

What do you need to do to find out about any children you're not sure about?

UNDERSTANDING PROGRESSION IN READING

Learning to read is a complex process and one that places great demands on children's cognitive abilities. Different children will have a varied range of experience and the route of their individual progress will very much depend on this prior experience. At CLPE, we worked with the other English subject associations to develop the Reading Scale – a free resource to support teachers planning for reading progress. This scale describes the progression through the complex process of learning to read. It offers teachers ways of looking at and analysing their observations of children's developing skills, knowledge and understanding of the reading process. The scale is based on extensive evidence and research about children as readers and will support teachers to understand and plan for individual progression in the journey towards reading independence.

KEY READING

The CLPE Reading and Writing Scales (2015) is a free resource which can be downloaded here:

www.clpe.org.uk/library-and-resources/reading-and-writing-scales

Because learning to read is such a multifaceted process and because not all children will necessarily take the same path, it is really important for teachers to understand all of the different observable behaviours that children may exhibit at each stage of their learning. Once they have thought about this, they will be able to think about the next set of observable behaviours they are likely to see if the child is progressing with reading. Every child will have a different reading journey. Their starting points and their rate and pattern of progression will depend on many factors including, their prior experience, their interests and the current experiences they are able to access.

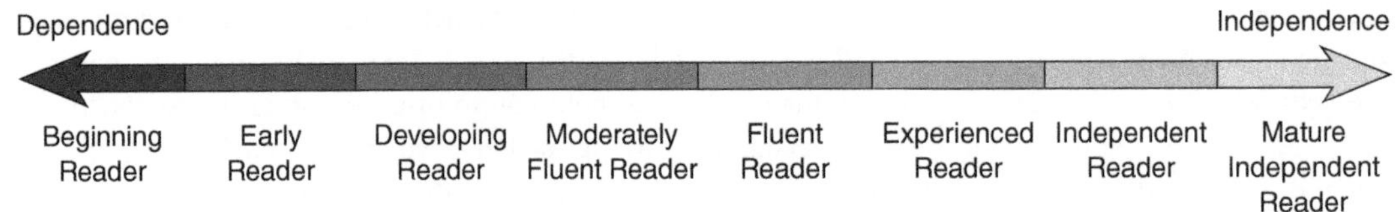

Figure 28.1 Illustration from CLPE Reading Scale (CLPE, 2015)

What enables 'good' readers to succeed?

If others haven't had these opportunities, how could you provide them in the classroom?

LAYING THE FOUNDATIONS FOR SUCCESS IN READING

Learning to read is a continuous development process that begins very early on in life. The first and most important resource that young readers have is a strong foundation in spoken language. This needs to be combined with activities that develop early phonological awareness through play with sounds, such as recognising sounds in their environment, using musical instruments, their bodies and voices to create sound. Simple nursery rhymes, poems, songs and rhyming texts should be an integral part of the curriculum at this stage, as will being able to listen to, share and join in with a familiar range of texts. Children also need to have experience of sharing reading for pleasure and purpose, and opportunities to play an increasingly participatory role in reading alongside adults. They need to have knowledge of the conventions of reading, and understanding of the large and small shapes in texts. Often, this will come from significant adults in their home or school lives modelling literate behaviour, pointing out how to handle books, how print works and the directionality of text.

Children will develop as readers if they experience personal involvement in reading. Reading for pleasure often begins as shared pleasures and emotional satisfaction arising from reading with an adult or experienced reader. Provision of a rich reading programme that enables shared experiences and the opportunity to encounter a wide variety of books will ensure the range of personal reading choice grows. Children will benefit from a repertoire of core texts that broadens as reading material becomes increasingly complex and wide ranging, and will be able to respond to texts with increasing inference, long before they can decode fluently. A diet of high-quality texts, rich in vocabulary with supportive features, strong shapes and tunes will enable children to learn how to co-ordinate the use of phonic, semantic and syntactic cues as they become increasingly mature, independent readers.

Children will need to talk about books in order to clarify ideas, relate reading to experience and reflect on what they have read. This is the real meaning of comprehension. They need to understand that readers can respond differently to the same book, and explore the idea that texts or illustrations might be biased, inaccurate or inadequate. If children are well read, they are better able to evaluate what is read and to make informed choices.

Reading aloud is probably the most important thing that teachers can do and needs to be a frequent and regular part of each school day – when children are beginning their journeys as readers and as they mature and develop. Reading aloud slows written language down and enables children to hear and take in tunes and patterns. It enables children to experience and enjoy stories that they might not otherwise meet. By reading well-chosen books aloud, teachers help classes to become communities of readers – ensuring that they can share in experiences of a wide repertoire of books they enjoy and get to know well.

As children mature as readers, they begin to engage with a greater selection of books and texts. In assessing children's progress and development as readers, it is really important to think about how we widen their reading horizons. The notion of range and variety plays an increasingly important part in interactions with texts alongside a growing ability to read silently, fluently and with ease.

CRITICAL QUESTION

How do you balance the teaching of decoding and comprehension skills across the school to ensure that all children become fluent readers?

WHAT ABOUT THE SKILLS?

If we want to support children to become readers, it is crucial that we develop their spoken vocabulary. The more words children know and understand because they have had opportunities for purposeful talk and reciprocal dialogue, the more words they are familiar with and can comprehend when they encounter them in their reading. Fluent readers are constantly cross-checking across a range of knowledge while they are reading. If children have a wide spoken vocabulary, they will be able to ensure that what they lift from the page with their reading makes sense from the start. This is another reason a regular read-aloud programme is so important. Through hearing stories read aloud regularly, children are often hearing new vocabulary in the correct context, as well as hearing and learning much about grammatical construction and punctuation.

Our Western print environment is extremely complex and demanding. Reading is not a natural or instinctive act, it does need to be taught. The research on learning to read shows that reading requires both decoding (the ability to translate written words on the page to the sounds of spoken language) and comprehension (an understanding of the words being read), but that these are not exclusive; children also need to be motivated to continue and build resilience and persistence.

Scarborough's 'Reading Rope' (see Figure 28.2) shows how the two aspects of reading – language comprehension and word recognition – are made up of separate skills that intertwine as the reader becomes more and more independent, eventually making one 'rope'.

Systematic phonic teaching where children are explicitly taught the letter-sound relationships and how to blend and segment individual phonemes has evidenced impact on early readers. It is, however, important that a phonics programme is seen as part of a rich reading curriculum where children can use and apply their knowledge in the context of a wide range of books, stories, poetry and songs. A diet of high-quality texts, rich in vocabulary with supportive features, strong shapes and tunes will enable children to learn how to co-ordinate the use of phonic, semantic and syntactic cues as they become increasingly mature, independent readers able to take on the reading demands of the curriculum.

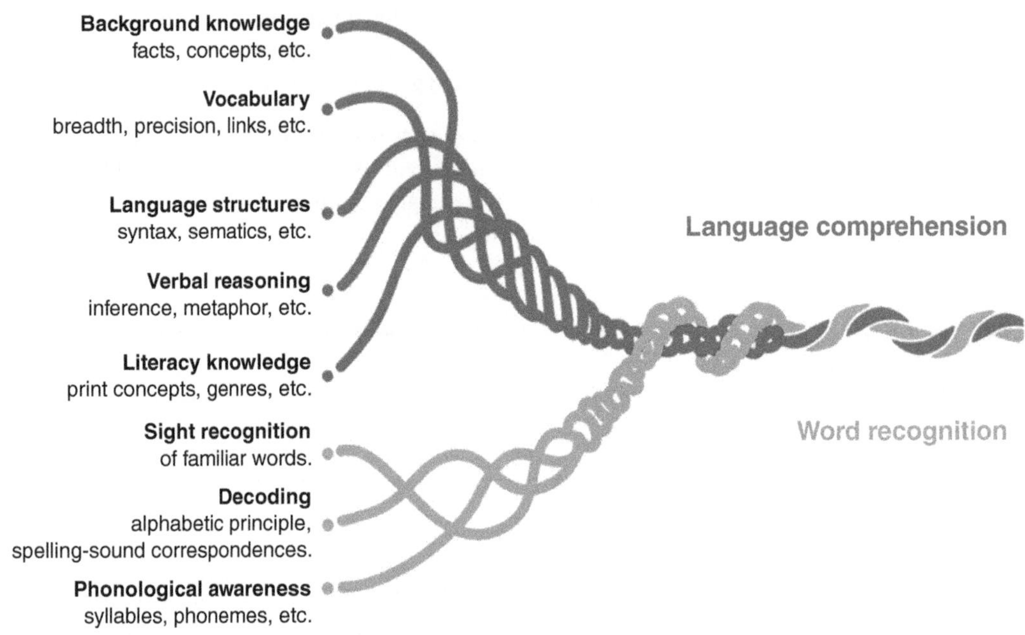

Figure 28.2 Scarborough's Reading Rope (EEF, 2017)

CRITICAL QUESTION

What opportunities are there in your classroom for reading dialogue and booktalk?

How do you use this as part of your assessment of reading?

READING AS A SOCIAL ACT

When we are looking at how we can support children's progress as readers, it is often more helpful to start from the point of what good readers do. Think about the part talk that plays in the lives of thoughtful readers who read for pleasure – maybe an adult book group. The people who are part of it are invested in the activity: they want to share, talk about (and sometimes disagree) on what they like and dislike; they share questions and make connections based on personal events, other texts they've read or seen, and delve deeper into why books made or didn't make an impact on them as a reader. It is really important that we recognise this 'transactional' relationship with texts when we are helping children to become readers, and understand that the process of making meaning from the words will always be dependent on them applying, reorganising or extending elements from their own experience – in life or as a reader.

Reading and writing are, of course, closely related processes. It is important to understand the role that reading plays in developing writers and the value of being immersed in high-quality literature for learning to write as well as to read. A well-chosen text provides rich language models and structures from which children can learn how writing works and the effect it can have on a reader. If you want confident young writers, read aloud and share high-quality texts across a range of genres, reflecting a range of writing styles. Choose texts that are rich in vocabulary and enable children to comprehend beyond their own reading fluency level. Create a rich reading environment that demonstrates the written word in all its forms, and shares how writing can be used for thinking, communication and as a means of expression. With a rich diet of quality texts and enriching experiences, children will be able to find their own reasons to write and develop a style that fits the purpose, audience and form intended.

CHAPTER SUMMARY

The key components of powerful reading practice

Being a reader brings with it access to whole new worlds, real and imagined. If you are a reader, you understand and empathise with those beyond your sphere, and can encounter thoughts, deeds and words that bring you new knowledge and understanding. Being a reader is a powerful experience; teaching someone to become a reader is a remarkable and wonderful thing to do, but it is also a complex, multi-layered process.

If we want children to move from beginner readers, to mature, independent readers we need a number of different things in place. It is really important to know what you want provision to look like in your classroom. You need to be clear about your pedagogical approach and willing to ensure that it is well evidenced and researched. You also need a thorough understanding of what progression looks like, what the observable features of progress are and how they might vary in different children.

You need texts in your classroom that will engage and support all the children in your class, whatever their starting point, and you need to ensure that you have a good knowledge of what is available. When you're thinking about teaching reading, you need to ensure that you teach the technical skills that will enable children to access texts and that you are doing this in a meaningful way where they can hear, see and explore examples of great writing, and understand the power and pleasure of a well-constructed text.

And all the time you need to be checking that you are providing the right environment, the most appropriate next steps, and literature that will inspire, engage and motivate children to go on their own reading journey, discovering the real power of reading.

ASSIGNMENTS

If you are completing an ITE assignment about supporting reading for pleasure in your classroom, it would be useful to consider the following aspects:

1. What are the key elements of practice that would help you to develop an ethos and an environment that excites, enthuses, inspires and values reading?

(Continued)

(Continued)

2. Why is reading aloud important and how can you make it a regular and integral part of your programme?
3. How can you plan for talking about books and stories, and what are the structures that support children to do this?

The following sources provide useful further reading:

Barrs, M. and Cork, V. (2001) *The Reader in the Writer*. London: Centre for Literacy in Primary Education.

Centre for Literacy in Primary Education (2014) *Reading For Pleasure, What We Know Works*. London: CLPE.

Centre for Literacy in Primary Education (2016) *Choosing and Using Quality Texts, What We Know Works*. London: CLPE.

Centre for Literacy in Primary Education (2017) *Writing, What We Know Works*. London: CLPE.

Clark, M. (2016) *Learning to be Literate: Insights from research for policy and practice*. Oxford: Routledge.

Clements, J. (2018) *Teaching English by the Book*. Oxford: Routledge.

Cremin, T. (2015) *Teaching English Creatively* Learning to Teach in the Primary School Series. 2nd Edn. Oxford: Routledge.

Dombey, H., with Bearne, E., Cremin, T. Ellis, S., Mottram M., O'Sullivan, *et al*. (2010) *Teaching Reading: What the evidence says*. Leicester: United Kingdom Literacy Association.

Goodwin, P. (2004) *Literacy through Creativity*. Oxford: David Fulton Publishers.

Holdaway, D. (1979) *The Foundations of Literacy*. Sydney: Ashton-Scholastic.

Krashen, S. (2004) *The Power of Reading: Insights from the research*. Westport, CT, Libraries Unlimited.

Meek, M. (1987) *How Texts Teach What Readers Learn*. London: Thimble Press.

The Reading Agency (2015) *Literature Review: The impact of reading for pleasure and empowerment*. London: BOP Consulting

Rosenblatt, L. (1988) *Writing and Reading: The Transactional Theory. Technical Report 416*, Center for the Study of Reading, University of Illinois.

Sullivan, A. and Brown, M. (2013) Social inequalities in cognitive scores at age 16: The role of reading. CLS Working paper 2013/10. London: Centre for Longitudinal Studies.

Tennent, W. (2015) *Understanding Reading Comprehension: Processes and practices*. London: Sage.

Tennent, W., Reedy, D., Hobsboum, A. and Gamble, N. (2016) Guiding Readers – Layers of Meaning: A guidebook for teaching reading comprehension to 7-11-year-old. UCL: 10E Press.

Wolfe, S. (2013) Talking policy into practice: probing the debates around the effective teaching of early reading. *Education 3-13*, 43(5): 498-513.

Wright, D. (2011), *Understanding Children's Books: A Guide for Educational Professionals* by Prue Goodwin (ed.). *Literacy*, 45: 51.

Wyse, D. (2017). *How Writing Works: From the invention of the alphabet to the rise of social media.* Cambridge: Cambridge University Press.

REFERENCES

Chambers, A. (2011) *Tell Me (Children, Reading & Talk) with the Reading Environment.* London: Thimble Press.

Centre for Literacy in Primary Education (CLPE) (2015) *The Reading and Writing Scales.* London: CLPE.

Cremin, T., Mottram, M. Collins, F.M., Powell, S. and Safford, K. (2014) *Building Communities of Engaged Readers.* Abingdon: Routledge.

Education Endowment Foundation (EEF) (2017) *Improving Literacy in Key Stage Two.* Available at: https://educationendowmentfoundation.org.uk/tools/guidance-reports/literacy-ks-two/ (accessed: 12/07/18).

29

WHAT IS THE POTENTIAL OF A PRIMARY STEM CURRICULUM?

Alan Cross is a Senior Fellow in Education at the Manchester Institute of Education, University of Manchester. His research interests lie in links between science and mathematics education in the primary years.

In this chapter, Alan Cross explores the potential of primary STEM curricula and looks at a range of influences and options. He draws a little on the recent history of STEM and the curriculum, and considers the pros and cons and options available to schools. He gives examples from schools and draws from discussions with teachers about STEM.

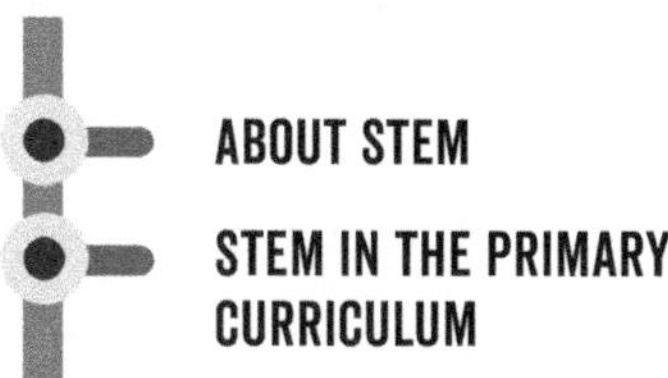

ABOUT STEM

STEM IN THE PRIMARY CURRICULUM

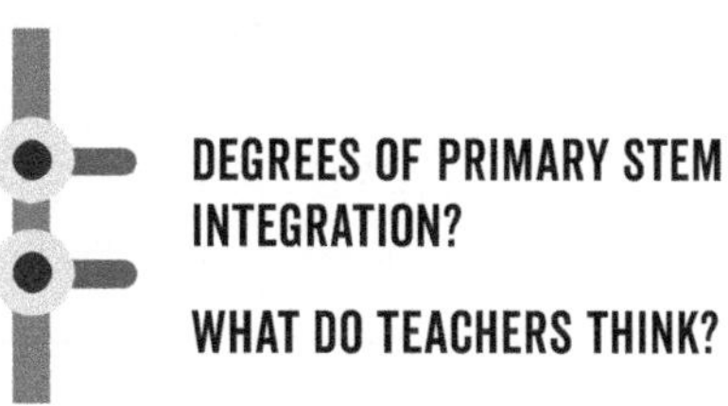

DEGREES OF PRIMARY STEM INTEGRATION?

WHAT DO TEACHERS THINK?

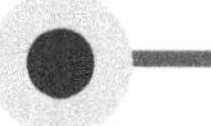

KEY WORDS

- Computing
- Design and technology
- Integration
- Mathematics
- Science

STEM

The acronym STEM (science, technology, engineering and mathematics) has been used around the world – for example, President Obama's 2016 *STEM for All* project announcement (Handelsman and Smith, 2016) – often in high schools, to recognise commonality and overlap between these four disciplines. Governments see these subjects as critical to economic development and seek to make study to a high level and associated careers attractive to young people. In this chapter I will refer, however, to primary STEM in the English context. Primary STEM is, of course, present in every primary school that teaches science, design and technology, computing and mathematics (DfE, 2014). This means that very many English primary schools have a STEM curriculum but may not realise or emphasise this.

The grouping or integration of primary STEM subjects – science, design and design and technology, computing and mathematics – brings together four National Curriculum subjects that all have a core interest in a human-made world of artefacts and systems invented and designed for a human purpose or perceived need. These subjects utilise numbers, values and relationships in organised and precise ways to systematically solve human problems or fulfil human perceived need. Of course, they do more than this, but these things are at their core and are commonly valued across the four subjects. Other subjects may do these things, but not with the same emphasis on purpose-focused artefacts and systems.

CRITICAL QUESTION

Do you see STEM in the world around you?

In your day-to-day life, do you notice how STEM subjects have shaped the made world you live in?

As you read this, be aware of artefacts around you, for example, the book or e-reader, electrical items, clothing, furnishings, and so on. Were these designed with a human purpose in mind? Was science required to inform the design? Perhaps the science of forces, materials, electricity? Were skills and approaches from design and technology utilised? Was computing (digital literacy, IT, computer science (Berry, 2013)) required? What about mathematics in measures, shape, pattern, proportionality? Clearly, these subjects come together in the world of design and manufacture of so many of the things we rely on in today's world. Making the most of the primary STEM subjects really ought to be on the agenda for primary schools.

STEM IN THE PRIMARY CURRICULUM

A primary STEM-focused curriculum offers primary learners the opportunity to link the curriculum subjects of science, design and technology, computing and mathematics (Cross *et al.*, 2016). Some primary schools embrace engineering, which is an often-undervalued sphere. However, for some primary teachers, the teaching of engineering might be seen presently as a step too far in terms of confidence and/or training.

Some teachers in English primary education have always sought to link subjects, most recently considered in the respective reports by Rose (2009) and Alexander *et al.* (2010). Different models were proposed, but both reports recognised the importance of school subjects taught in contexts that are meaningful to learners. That last sentence is worth considering. In the past, various integrated or cross-curricular approaches have been considered (Alexander *et al.*, 1992; Barnes, 2011) with advantages and disadvantages identified. Since its inception in 1998 (DES, 1998a, 1998b; DES, 1999; DfE, 2014), the English National Curriculum has been based on school subjects, including mathematics, science, design and technology, and computing (formerly ICT). There have been suggested links from subject to subject (non-statutory guidance) for those teachers wishing to make such links. Sadly, discussion about subject integration has often come down to so-called 'traditional' versus 'progressive' approaches. It is true that our current National Curriculum (DfE, 2014) is very traditional in tone with its numerous subjects and focus on content. What well thought-out integration of subjects offers is learning in meaningful contexts where links are made explicit to learners.

KEY READING

The ASPIRES project provides key reading related to STEM subjects and choices made by learners. Available at: www.ucl.ac.uk/ioe/departments-centres/departments/education-practice-and-society/aspires/summary-reports-books

Like high schools, English primary schools have operated in a context that is dominated by accountability procedures. Significantly in primary schools, pupil attainment in English and mathematics have been the key determinants as to 'how schools are judged by school inspectors in a punitive inspection regime. This has led to recognition by the schools' chief inspector that subjects other than English and mathematics have been "pushed to the margins" in many schools (Ofsted, 2016).

It appears to be felt that STEM-orientated school curricula have the potential to strengthen important parts of an economy. Evidence has shown that in England less and less students are opting to pursue STEM subjects in higher education and in careers (Archer *et al.*, 2013; ASPIRES Project; Brown *et al.*, 2008). The situation is even worse for girls (Archer *et al.*, 2013; Boaler, 2014). These concerns have led, in England, to national initiatives such as the establishment of a National STEM Centre (www.stem.org.uk), a network of regional STEM centres (Baker, 2006) and the STEM ambassadors scheme (http://msimanchester.org.uk/en/stem/ambassadors).

CRITICAL QUESTION

What challenges do you feel schools face in creating a strong STEM curriculum?

Some English high schools have adopted a so-called STEM approach which varies greatly from school to school; this can include degrees of interdisciplinary work, cross-curricular themes or simply a recognition that the school teaches sciences, design and technology, computing and mathematics. It is significant that there has been little research or evaluation to determine the success or otherwise of such approaches. The importance of subjects such as science and mathematics has been recognised by organisations such as the CBI (2015) and the Royal Society which published a report 'Vision for Science and Mathematics Education' (Royal Society, 2014) which suggested a number of recommendations aimed to strengthen teaching and learning of mathematics and science from ages five to eighteen. The document made numerous references to STEM education and the importance of being able to think both scientifically and mathematically.

Table 29.1 What it means to be scientifically and mathematically informed (Royal Society, 2014)

A scientifically informed individual:	**A mathematically informed individual:**
i) understands scientific theories and concepts and that these are subject to challenge and changes as new evidence arises;	i) understands mathematical concepts and recognises when they are present;
ii) can think and act scientifically (e.g. using hypotheses to test and solve problems while also using scientific knowledge) and uses essential reading, writing, mathematical and communication skills to analyse scientific information accurately;	ii) can think and act mathematically (e.g. applying knowledge and transforming methods to solve problems), uses mathematical skills and forms of communication to analyse situations within mathematics and elsewhere;
iii) makes informed interpretations and judgements (e.g. risk assessment) about scientific information and the world at large as well as engaging in debate on scientific issues;	iii) can make informed interpretations of information presented in a mathematical form and use it to engage constructively in debate on scientific and other issues;
iv) is able to apply scientific knowledge and understanding in everyday life; and	iv) is able to apply mathematical knowledge and understanding in everyday life; and
v) maintains curiosity about the natural and made worlds.	v) maintains curiosity in mathematical concepts, and in other phenomena understood from a mathematical perspective.

There has so far, beyond the provision of a National Curriculum (DfE, 2013), been little emphasis on primary STEM from the government. In primary education initiatives from government and other organisations there is often reference to primary (Royal Society, 2014) but rarely is this manifested in significant leadership, initiative or resourcing related explicitly to primary STEM. There are, of course, notable exceptions, e.g. The Astra Zeneca Teaching Trust.

Despite, and even in spite of, the accountability measures, which focus on mathematics and English, primary teachers value strongly opportunities to exploit meaningful contexts for learning. The idea of a meaningful context works well within a subject-based curriculum, but also in a curriculum that exploits a degree of subject integration. Fruitful links between primary STEM subjects have been recognised and more so it seems recently (Barnes, 2011; Markwick and Clark, 2016; Cross and Borthwick, 2016; Cross *et al.*, 2016).

DEGREES OF PRIMARY STEM INTEGRATION?

If we accept that the recognised disciplines or subjects are the most effective way humans have devised to organise knowledge (Alexander *et al.*, 2010), to deny learners the powerful approaches to knowledge and understanding offered by subjects would be to disempower them. What we, therefore, seek is a way to get around the shortcomings of a subject-based curriculum, a way to teach the subjects well in the context of the world, real life and all this has to offer. Primary teachers are well placed to do this as they:

A number of publications provide examples of primary STEM-related activities and curricula (Markwick and Clarke, 2016; Cross et al., 2016; Cross and Borthwick, 2016).

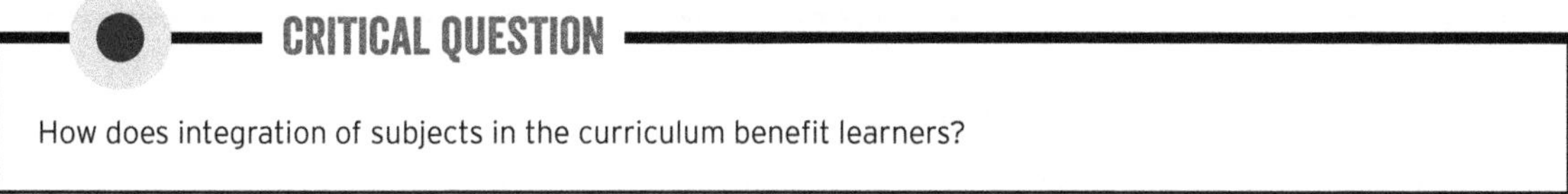

CRITICAL QUESTION

How does integration of subjects in the curriculum benefit learners?

Various approaches to interdisciplinary or integrated curricula exist including:

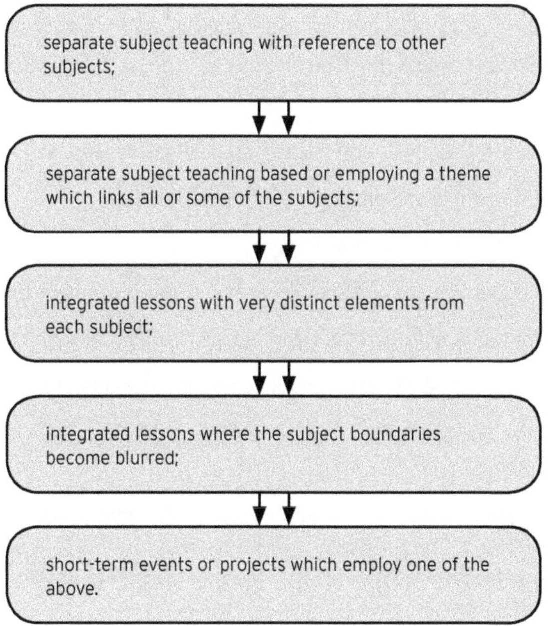

These can be exemplified and evaluated based on a number of criteria:

- Is the subject still present and being taught and learned?
- Does this integration add value in terms of:
  - coherence?
  - meaningfulness to learners?
  - use of time?
  - do the learners now appreciate subject links more than before?

It is important to consider the potential watering down of subjects considered by most authors (Alexander *et al.*, 2010; Cross and Borthwick, 2016) when integration is piecemeal or ill conceived. It is worth noting that almost all schools that integrate maintain separate English and mathematics lessons. Why is this? Are they more important? Too important to risk?

CLASSROOM LINK

What does this mean for classroom practice?

These examples demonstrate various approaches to interdisciplinary or integrated curricula.

'Workplaces' in an early years setting

An Early Years Foundation Stage (EYFS) setting established in each class base a STEM-related workplace, including a dentist's surgery, a garage, a builder's yard, an inventor's workshop and a garden centre. Classes and groups work on related tasks such as:

- in the outside play area, trikes, bikes and trolleys are taken in for repair;
- in the dentist's reception, texts and emails confirm appointment;
- in the workshop, toys and machines are invented;
- both indoors and outdoors, houses and shelters are built using various materials;
- prams and trolleys are improved with new elements such as canopies and tow ropes;
- visits are made to local examples of these workplaces, and workers are invited to school with artefacts and photographs.

A twilight code club

One primary teacher organised a twilight code club where Key Stage 2 pupils designed and made their own projects mainly based on DT and computing. One girl designed and made a control for her arcade game, another a bell and alarm for her bedroom door, and two boys designed a real-life Minecraft© world. These were showcased in school, at parents' evening and on Twitter©.

'What will our future hold?'

One school organised a whole-school theme called 'What will our future hold?' Part of this was a 'Children as Researchers Approach' (Kellett, 2005) (see the Open University Children's Research Centre at: www.open.ac.uk/researchprojects/childrens-research-centre/about-us). The theme looked at recent and future technological developments, environmental issues, and education and careers. This began with classes making visits to a local university, businesses, science museum and another school, alongside visits to school by specialists. After initial activities and the visits, classes selected themes to explore, some subdividing into subthemes, such as a mission to Mars, living in space, will children live in space?

KEY READING

Important sources of STEM information:

- National STEM Centre: www.stem.org.uk/
- Association of Science Education: www.ase.org.uk/home/
- Design and Technology Association: www.data.org.uk
- Computing at School: www.computingatschool.org.uk
- National Centre for Excellence in the Teaching of Mathematics: www.ncetm.org.uk
- ENRICH: https://nrich.maths.org

CLASSROOM LINK

What does this mean for classroom practice?

Figure 29.1 Bee-Bot© (www.tts-group.co.uk)

(Continued)

(Continued)

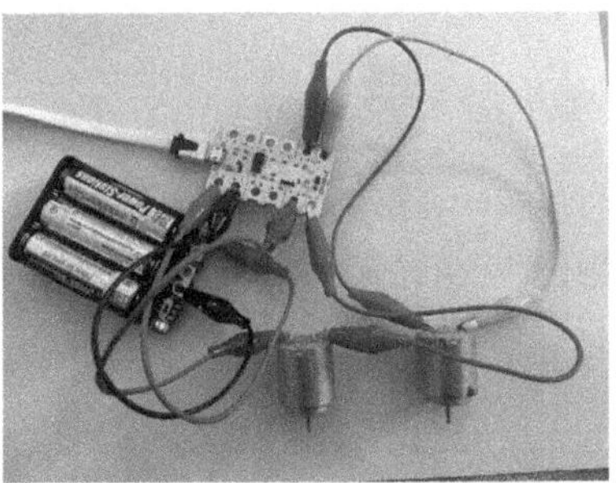

Figure 29.2 Crumble Controller (https://redfernelectronics.co.uk)

During one term, one school maintained subject teaching but established a link through a programmable toy BeeBot© (see Figure 29.1). Younger classes programmed the toy, designed and made hats, clothing, road systems and garages for the toy. Older children made look-alike and different two-wheeled and four-wheeled vehicles based on Beebot© and other toys and vehicles they examined. They programmed Beebot© and other vehicles via Scratch© (see Figure 29.3) and Crumble Controller© (see Figure 29.2). One class designed a range of trailers for Beebot©, another built a ride-on Beebot© constructed around an existing trike. During the term teachers planned distinct science, design and technology, and computing lessons and activities with links in some mathematics lessons, as well as explicit mathematics links made in all lessons.

```
program start
do 5 times
    motor 1 FORWARD at 75 %
    motor 2 FORWARD at 75 %
    set sparkle 0 to
    set sparkle 1 to
    wait 700 milliseconds
    motor 1 REVERSE at 75 %
    motor 2 REVERSE at 75 %
    set sparkle 0 to
    set sparkle 1 to
    wait 700 milliseconds
loop
motor 1 FORWARD at 75 %
wait 2 seconds
do 3 times
    set all sparkles to
    motor 1 REVERSE at 75 %
    motor 2 REVERSE at 75 %
    wait 600 milliseconds
    turn all sparkles off
    motor 1 STOP
    motor 2 STOP
    wait 600 milliseconds
loop
```

Figure 29.3 A section of code used to make two-wheeled buggy dance (Scratch available free from https://scratch.mit.edu)

In order to fully consider cases like these, we need ideally to see them occur and the learner outcomes in action. However, another useful question can be considered: given all we have learned about clarity, about the purpose of lessons to guide learners, ought we to maintain, in all lessons, subject-related lesson objectives? Would this be one way to maintain the valuable contribution of subjects while benefiting from degrees of integration?

WHAT DO TEACHERS THINK?

Recently, a number of primary teachers responded to a short questionnaire about their school's curriculum and their teaching of primary STEM subjects. Forty-eight teachers responded, including twelve teachers attending a primary STEM conference and similar numbers attending separate mathematics, science, and design and technology meetings for school subject leaders. Thus, the sample is by no means random, but is made up of primary teachers who teach all four subjects and lead one of them within their schools. All the teachers opted to complete the questionnaire and understood that they and their schools would be kept anonymous.

Asked about the proportion of time devoted to mathematics, science, computing and design and technology, they reported five lessons a week for mathematics, amounting to between 2 hours 40 minutes to around 3 hours per week. For science, it was more mixed at one or two lessons per week in most schools, but in a small number of cases less then this. Computing and design and technology were taught, but rarely a lesson per week throughout the year. In the case of design and technology it was often taught every other half term as a series of lessons or as a project taught over a series of days (often afternoons). Computing was the only subject that was at times taught by another teacher and usually was allocated less than one lesson per week for the year.

Integration or cross-curricular or interdisciplinary approaches were reported, on some occasions within an organised curriculum, but more often in ad hoc links made by teachers. About half of the teachers had heard of the term STEM and some could identify websites where they could find out more.

A high proportion of the teachers could identify links between the primary STEM subjects they taught. They referred in mathematics to data, measurement, problem solving and skills. Science links included bridge building, cross-curricular planning and links to design and technology were often cited.

CRITICAL QUESTION

What are the advantages of a STEM curriculum for children and for teachers?

The teachers were asked about the advantages of linking subjects together (see Info 29.1). This proved to be a rich area. Teachers talked about making lessons more meaningful with links – for example: 'apply maths skills more purposefully rather than "cold" calculations'.

INFO 29.1

Advantages of an Integrated STEM curriculum

What are the advantages of integration of STEM subjects?		
Primary maths leaders said	Primary science leaders said	Primary DT leaders said
Makes maths more purposeful/meaningful. Allows children to make links between their learning as skills/content used in different ways. Children see the learning as opposed to subjects. It makes the learning experiences richer for pupils. It means that children are doing maths/science in an enjoyable and meaningful way. They see connections/the whole view. It makes it more engaging/ exciting for children. Children can practise skills and connections. Time saving. Seeing practical relevance of learned skill. Children engagement. Revisiting of skills frequently. It's impossible not to integrate Increases fluency and maths subject time	Pupils can apply maths skills more purposefully rather than 'cold' calculations. Makes the curriculum more relevant by putting it into context. Children understand the meaning in the subjects; they see how they link. Ticks core subject boxes. Allows you to cover more. Makes subjects interesting by offering different angles of approach. Consolidates learning. Shows the children how different subjects overlap. Secure understanding. In a very full curriculum you can cover two lessons in one. Loss of coverage.	Cross-curricular links in learning and connections. Saves time. Children have greater understanding. Allows most topics to be placed in context and have real meaning. Children have opportunity to show strengths in own areas. Increased knowledge and skill. Teaching skills that are transferable in school so they have the knowledge that skills are used in real life. Creativity.

When reviewing the advantages and disadvantages identified by the teachers it is clear that they are able to see both sides of the situation. Advantages centre on the way that links and overlap is made explicit, on the opportunity to learn one subject in a more meaningful way, to make more use of skills which are being learned and to make learning more enjoyable. These are clearly seen to be advantages, but it is important to consider the shortcomings of any approach. Teachers expressed concern over links that might be contrived or forced, and that confusion might occur, particularly for some groups of children. There was concern about time available and about whether objectives might be missed or not covered thoroughly enough. The responses were fairly consistent across the subject leaders who are, of course, almost all teachers of all the STEM subjects.

These responses illustrate that this question is not perhaps as straightforward as one might imagine. There can be advantages, but care needs to be taken. Any notion that integration is in some way easy should be put aside. Those who integrate STEM curricula effectively talk of its advantages, but also that it requires considerable effort, certainly initially, to make it work well.

CHAPTER SUMMARY

A primary STEM curriculum offers much for learners. It can bring subjects such as mathematics and computing alive in the classrooms with practical meaningful activities. There is a range of options that a school and teachers might take. One great advantage here is that there is considerable flexibility and that a school can use a STEM focus to give their curriculum unique features, unique to their situation. In a world where companies and markets are global, individuals with relevant skills, including a capacity to recognise and exploit links, are more likely to thrive.

ASSIGNMENTS

If you are writing an ITE assignment about STEM in primary education, it would be useful for you to consider the following:

1. What does STEM mean in a primary context? Which parts of the curriculum will contribute to the T and E of STEM?
2. What are the advantages of links between these and other subjects for learners? Are there any potential shortcomings?
3. How will teachers cope with the demand on subject knowledge? Will they adapt pedagogy from one subject to another?

REFERENCES

Advisory Committee on Mathematics Education (ACME) (2011) *Mathematical Needs*. London: ACME.

Alexander, R. (ed.) (2010) *Children, their World, their Education: Final report and recommendations of the Cambridge Review*. London: Routledge.

Alexander, R., Rose, J. and Woodhead, C. (1992) *Curriculum Organisation and Classroom Practice in Primary Schools: A discussion paper*. London: DES.

Archer, L. *et al*. (2013) Young people's science career aspirations age 10–14. London: King's College.

Baker, Y. (2006) STEM support centres. *Education in Science*, September, ASE.

Barnes, J. (2011) *Cross-Curricular Learning*. London: SAGE.

Berry, M. (2013) *Computing in the National Curriculum: A guide for primary teachers*. Swindon: Computing at School/Naace. Available at: https://community.computingatschool.org.uk/resources/2618/single (accessed 29.3.18).

Boaler, J. (2014) *Changing the Conversation About Girls and STEM*. Washington, DC: The White House. Available at www.youcubed.org (accessed 12/07/18).

Boaler, J. (2016) *Mathematical Mindsets*. San Francisco, CA: Jossey-Bass.

Brown, M., Brown, P. and Bibby, T. (2008) 'I would rather die': Reasons given by 16-year-olds for not continuing their study of mathematics education. *Research in Mathematics Education*, 10 (1): 3–18.

Confederation of British Industry (CBI) (2015) *Tomorrow's World: Inspiring primary scientists*. London: CBI.

Cross, A. and Board, J. (2014) *Creative Ways to Teach Primary Science* (2nd edn). Maidenhead: Open University Press/McGraw Hill.

Cross, A. and Borthwick, A. (2016) *Connecting Primary Maths and Science*. Maidenhead: Open University Press/McGraw Hill.

Cross, A. *et al*. (2016) *Curious Learners in Primary Maths, Science, Computing and DT*. Maidenhead: Open University Press/McGraw Hill.

Department for Business Innovation and Skills (2015) *Policy Paper: 2010–15 government policy: public understanding of science and engineering*. Available at: www.gov.uk/government/publications/2010-to-2015-government-policy-public-understanding-of-science-and-engineering/2010-to-2015-government-policy-public-understanding-of-science-and-engineering (accessed 12/07/18).

Department for Education (DfE) (2012) *Development Matters in the Early Years Foundation Stage (EYFS)*. Available at: www.foundationyears.org.uk/files/2012/03/Development-Matters-FINAL-PRINT-AMENDED.pdf (accessed 12/07/18).

Department for Education (DfE) (2013) *The National Curriculum in England: Key Stage 1 and 2 framework document*. London: DfE.

Department for Education (DfE) (2014) *The National Curriculum in England: framework for key stages 1 to 4*. London: DfE.

Department for Education and Science and the Welsh Office (1998a) *Mathematics for Ages 5–16*. London: HMSO.

Department for Education and Science and the Welsh Office (1998b) *Science for Ages 5–16*. London: HMSO.

Department for Education and Science and the Welsh Office (1998) *DT for Ages 5–16*. London: HMSO.

Handelsman, J. and Smith, M. (2016) STEM for All. Presidential Announcement: White House blog. Available at: www.whitehouse.gov/blog/2016/02/11/stem-all (accessed 12/07/18).

Kellett, M. (2005) *How to Develop Children as Researchers*. London: SAGE.

Markwick, A. and Clarke, K. (2016) Science + Maths = a better understanding of science! *ASE: Primary Science*,145, November/December: 5–8.

Ofsted (2013) *Maintaining Curiosity: A survey into science education in schools*. Manchester: Office for Standards in Education, Children's Services and Skills.

Ofsted (2016) HMCI's monthly commentary: May. Available at: www.gov.uk/government/speeches/hmcis-monthly-commentary-may-2016 (accessed 12/07/18).

Rose, J. (2009) *Independent Review of the Primary Curriculum: Final Report*. DCSF: London.

The Royal Society (2014) Vision for science and mathematics education. London: The Royal Society. Available at: https://royalsociety.org/topics-policy/projects/vision/ (accessed 12/07/18).

The Royal Society (2012) Shut down or restart? The way forward for computing in UK schools. Available at: https://royalsociety.org/~/media/education/computing-in-schools/2012-01-12-computing-in-schools.pdf (accessed 12/07/18).

Skemp, R. (1976) Relational understanding and instrumental understanding, *Mathematical Teaching*, 77: 20–6.

WEBSITE

Collection of STEM publications. Available at: www.stem.org.uk/elibrary/collection/94077 (accessed 12/07/18).

30

WHAT EFFECT IS MASTERY HAVING ON THE TEACHING OF MATHEMATICS IN PRIMARY SCHOOLS?

Claire Morse is senior lecturer in primary mathematics at the University of Winchester, teaching across multiple routes into primary teaching. She also teaches on the Master's programme, developing a group of teachers who are interested in teaching primary mathematics for mastery. Prior to being a senior lecturer, Claire was an Adviser for Southampton Local Authority and a primary teacher, mathematics subject leader and leading mathematics teacher.

In this chapter, Claire Morse presents the background to teaching for mastery in England. She explores teacher subject knowledge around mastery and outlines the NCETM's four principles of mastery. The chapter considers a definition of 'a mastery curriculum' and asks what it means to master ideas in mathematics. Finally, examples of good practice in teaching for mastery in the classroom are included to help you link theory to practice.

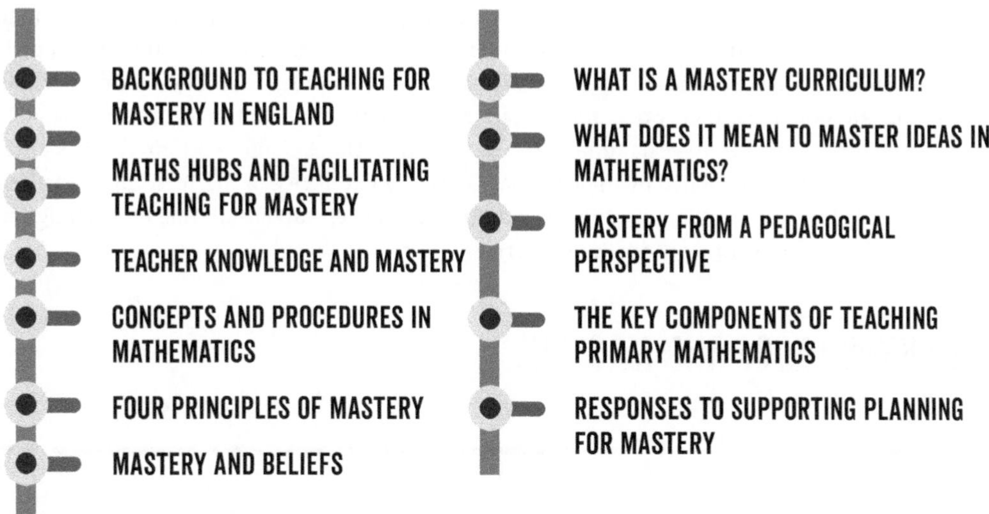

KEY WORDS

- Beliefs
- Concepts
- Connection
- Explanation
- Mastery
- Maths hubs
- Pedagogical knowledge
- Procedures
- Representation
- Shanghai

THE BACKGROUND TO TEACHING FOR MASTERY IN ENGLAND

Following concerns about the teaching of mathematics in England and how standards compared against other jurisdictions around the world, interest emerged in terms of what could be learnt from those educational systems that scored highly on the Programme for International Student Assessment (PISA) 2009 tests. Attention went to jurisdictions such as Shanghai and Singapore. Following a DfE-funded research trip in February 2014, the England-China Teacher Exchange was born, allowing teaching for mastery to be considered in England for the first time.

Three successive exchange visits have taken place since 2014, with Theresa May launching an extension of the exchange programme in January 2018 for a further two years to 2020, enabling around 200 English teachers to visit China. This commitment aims to take the total number of English schools benefiting from the teaching for mastery approach to 11,000 by 2023. The seriousness with which teaching for mastery is being taken is not only felt through the financial commitment of almost £75 million provided by the Department for Education, but also through a longitudinal evaluation of the England-China Teacher Exchange led by Sheffield Hallam University. The third interim evaluation suggests that 'the Mathematics Teacher Exchange (MTE) aims to foster a radical shift in primary mathematics teaching in England by learning from Shanghai mathematics education' (Boylan et al., 2017: 10).

MATHS HUBS AND FACILITATING TEACHING FOR MASTERY

There are currently 35 Hubs in England, with the DfE being the principal financial sponsor, devolving money for their work each year. These Hubs serve all regions of England and are led locally by an outstanding school or college. Each Hub is driven by partnership, with the lead school identifying strategic partners to support them in planning and evaluating their work, and operational partners who help to facilitate free or subsidised professional development from early years to post-16 mathematics. The 35 Hubs work together as a national network of expertise that is co-ordinated by the National Centre for Excellence in the Teaching of Mathematics (NCETM). The NCETM actively develops, promotes and deepens teachers' understanding of teaching for mastery, including the training of mastery specialist teachers.

TEACHER KNOWLEDGE AND MASTERY

CRITICAL QUESTION

How can we know what knowledge teachers need to enable them to 'teach' for mastery?

Teaching for mastery has ignited a renewed consideration of teacher knowledge and what knowledge is demanded of teachers in order to teach effectively. Lee Shulman, an American educational psychologist, was the first to explore how teacher knowledge in its broadest sense could be categorised, suggesting that this knowledge concerned what teachers know, do and understand. For Shulman (1987), the knowledge needed to teach any subject concerned three broad categories:

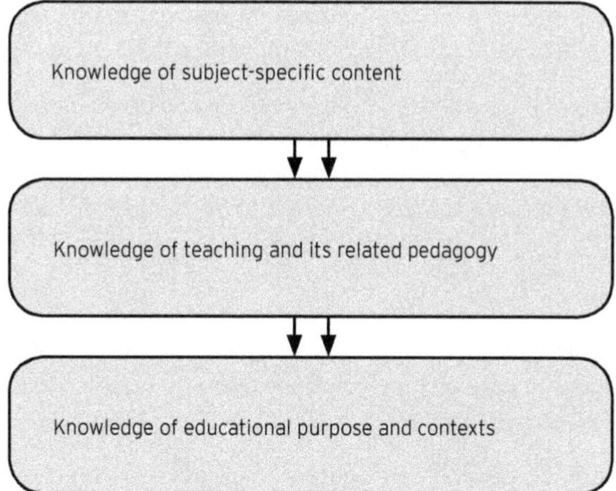

For Shulman (1987), knowledge of teaching was considered a dominant area of knowledge and this heightened view of pedagogy can be felt in schools as they explore teaching for mastery. In order for children to acquire and master new ideas in mathematics, teachers need to make a series of pedagogical decisions – for example, what language do I need to explain the exchange principle when adding a pair of 3-digit numbers. For Shulman, these pedagogical decisions involved 'the most useful forms of representation of those ideas, the most powerful analogies, illustrations, examples, explanations and demonstrations' (1987: 9) which will be considered later in this chapter.

Rowland *et al.* (2005) developed the Knowledge Quartet, capturing the knowledge needed to teach mathematics in four domains, as outlined in Figure 30.1. Like Ball *et al.* (2008), the 'in the moment' teaching of mathematics was emphasised, residing in two key pedagogical knowledge domains of transformation and connection, which emphasises pedagogical choices such as teacher demonstration, use of representations, choice of examples, forming connections and decisions about sequencing.

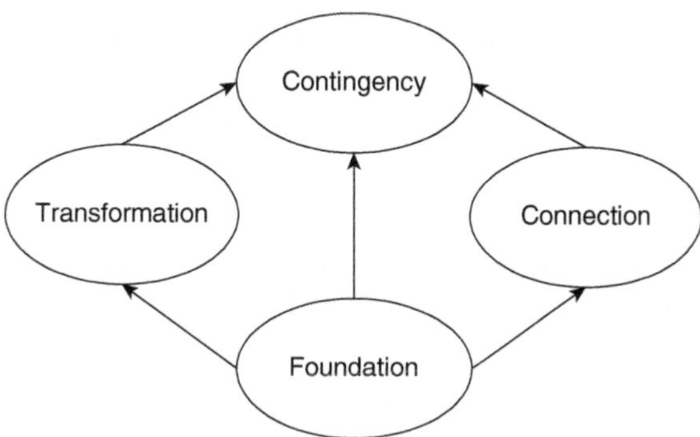

Figure 30.1 The Knowledge Quartet (Rowland et al., 2005)

KEY READING

Rowland, T., Huckstep, P. and Thwaites, A. (2005) Elementary teachers' mathematics subject knowledge: The Knowledge Quartet and the case of Naomi. *Journal of Mathematics Teacher Education*, 8: 255–81.

This paper draws on videotapes of mathematics lessons prepared and taught by pre-service elementary teachers towards the end of their initial training. The aim was to locate ways in which they drew on their knowledge of mathematics and mathematics pedagogy in their teaching. The research led to the creation of a 'knowledge quartet', with four broad dimensions of knowledge referred to as foundation, transformation, connection and contingency.

www.knowledgequartet.org

This website offers further exemplification of the 21 codes used in Rowland *et al.*'s original, Huckstep and Thwaites' original research above to develop the Knowledge Quartet. It offers support to those wishing to analyse the knowledge held by teachers to teach mathematics.

Ball, D.L., Thames, M.H. and Phelps, G. (2008) Content knowledge for teaching: What makes it special? *Journal of Teacher Education*, 59 (5): 389–407.

This article builds on Shulman's (1986) notion of pedagogical content knowledge. The purpose of the study was to investigate the nature of subject matter knowledge in mathematics by studying actual mathematics teaching.

The importance of transformation is recognised by Rowland *et al.* (2005), but they present the transformational tone as a dynamic one where knowledge emerges in action. Teaching actions are directed at learners, shaping a distinction between knowing an idea in mathematics for yourself and knowing how to enable others to learn that very same idea. For Ball *et al.* (2008) this transformational tone involves pedagogical characteristics that enable teachers to make visible to learners the ideas that they know, involving, for example, how to use representations effectively and be able to explain ideas. What emerges is the notion of instructional decision-making that will positively affect learners.

CRITICAL QUESTION

Based on the four categories of knowledge, what knowledge do you hold?

WHAT ARE CONCEPTS AND PROCEDURES IN MATHEMATICS?

Teaching for mastery has brought into sharp focus the difference between and the need for concepts and procedures. Concepts and procedures can be considered the visible and hidden side of mathematics. Although these two forms of knowledge cannot be easily separated at times, it is helpful to consider their different characteristics individually.

CRITICAL QUESTION

What is conceptual knowledge?

Conceptual knowledge is defined as knowledge that is rich in relationships and connections (Hiebert and Lefevre, 1986) – for example, finding that half of a quantity is equivalent to dividing by two, and one quarter is half of a half. Conceptual knowledge emphasises the more hidden side of mathematics in terms of personal comprehension and understanding. By contrast, procedural knowledge emphasises performance or knowing how to do something, or the visible side of mathematics, often characterised by the completion of calculations. Procedures are sequential in nature, a series of steps or actions undertaken to achieve a goal (Rittle-Johnson and Schneider, cited in R. Cohen Kadosh and Dowker, 2015). Procedural knowledge also has a second dimension, which is being familiar with our symbol system for communicating ideas in mathematics.

What is contested by writers in the field is whether, concepts or procedures develop first or whether in fact, they develop simultaneously with one informing the other.

CRITICAL QUESTION

Concepts and procedures are not an either/or element of mathematics. In order to be proficient, both need to be developed simultaneously. What is the balance of concepts and procedures in your mathematics lessons?

KEY READING

Rittle-Johnson, B. and Schneider, M. (2015) Developing conceptual and procedural knowledge in mathematics, in R. Cohen Kadosh and A. Dowker (eds) *Oxford Handbook of Numerical Cognition.* Oxford: Oxford University Press.

The chapter in this book presents a detailed consideration of the characteristics of conceptual and procedural understanding. The chapter reviews recent studies on the relations between conceptual and procedural knowledge in mathematics, and highlights examples of how this knowledge can be developed in the classroom and over time.

FOUR PRINCIPLES OF MASTERY

During a period of time when it feels like we are being buffeted by what is considered change and difference, Chap (2007) in his exploration of the characteristics of teaching in Shanghai, suggested that we should focus on the educational principles that are in our control and pay less attention to those that are beyond our control.

Table 30.1 Principles of education that are in and beyond our control

Within our control	Beyond our control
Teachers' depth of subject knowledge Teachers' depth of pedagogical content knowledge Teachers' beliefs and attitudes Learners' beliefs and attitudes	Curriculum demands External assessment Cultural context Expectations of society Parental demands

If we take into account the aspects that are in our control, we are in fact now faced with a shifting landscape of professional vocabulary. Words such as mastery, greater depth, conceptual understanding, variation, procedural fluency and coherence are not new terms in the world of mathematics education research, but they appear to be new to many primary teachers. If we are to move forwards as a professional body of primary mathematics teachers, we need to get a robust and shared understanding of these terms.

CRITICAL QUESTION

What does the term 'mastery' involve for you?

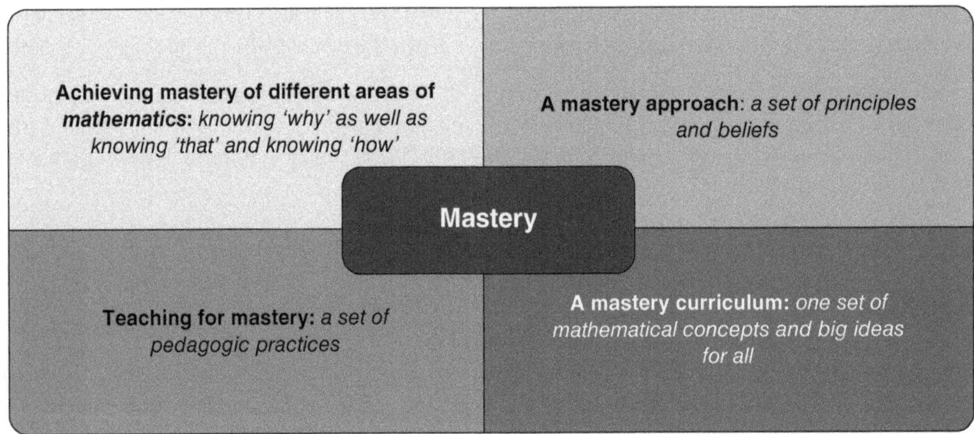

Figure 30.2 Four principles of mastery identified by the NCETM

The NCETM has outlined that mastery has four perspectives (see Figure 30.2). Interestingly, these perspectives are in our control, as suggested by Chap (2007). Within this shifting landscape of vocabulary that is being grappled with, multiple interpretations of the same single term are making conversations harder.

To have transformative and meaningful conversations we need to be referring to the same part of the mastery quadrant. Table 30.2 identifies a number of different interpretations of the term 'mastery'.

Table 30.2 Different perspectives on the term mastery

Interpretation	**Source**
Deep understanding by all children of age-related expectations.	(NCETM, 2014)
The expectation is that the majority of pupils will move through the programmes of study at broadly the same pace.	(DfE, 2013: 88)
We have developed a curriculum, where pupils spend more time on fewer topics. They explore concepts using objects, conversation and problem-solving to build confidence in their understanding.	www.mathematicsmastery.org
In simple terms it means spending enough time on a topic in order to comprehend it thoroughly. Teaching to mastery also means that children spend a consolidated amount of time on a topic to understand how it relates to concrete experiences.	www.mathsnoproblem.co.uk
Teaching mathematics that aims to raise attainment for all pupils and close the attainment gap between pupils from low-income families and their peers. The programme aims to deepen pupils' conceptual understanding of key mathematical concepts.	www.educationendowmentfoundation.org.uk
Competent learners are mathematically fluent and can reason and solve problems within mathematics. They develop mathematical fluency, conceptual understanding, select appropriate techniques, interpret and evaluate solutions.	(ACME, June 2014)

KEY READING

Drury, H. (2014) *Mastering Mathematics: Teaching to Transform Achievement*. Oxford: Oxford University Press.

This book explores the key principles of the mastery approach as developed by Mathematics Mastery. Content considers the notion of the term mastery and how the child is at its heart. A fundamental idea within this book is what it refers to as the Three Dimensions of Depth: multiple representations, language and communication, thinking mathematically.

NCETM (2014) Mastery approaches to mathematics and the new national curriculum. Available at:

www.ncetm.org.uk/.../Developing_mastery_in_mathematics_october_2014.pdf

This was the first summary report written by the NCETM on the principles underpinning teaching for mastery. The report outlined what teaching for mastery looked like in high-performing jurisdictions, changes to the current curriculum for mathematics and key features of the mastery approach.

MASTERY AND BELIEFS

What effect do beliefs have on our approach to teaching primary mathematics for mastery?

The NCETM has suggested that first and foremost, mastery concerns the belief that *all* pupils are capable of understanding and doing mathematics, given sufficient time. With effective, well-considered teaching and a 'can do' attitude, all children can achieve in and enjoy mathematics. This, however, puts demands on the mindset and belief systems of those working with children in mathematics.

Boaler (2016) has brought to our attention what she refers to as a path to equity where everyone can learn and enjoy mathematics. For her, mathematics is a beautiful subject with ideas and connections that can inspire all children, but all too often it is taught as a performance subject, which separates those who are considered to have the 'maths gene' from those without. Boaler (2016) offered a set of strategies designed to make mathematics lessons more equitable, but whether we see these strategies as valuable is likely to be connected to our views of our learners, and how we perceive the teaching and learning of mathematics.

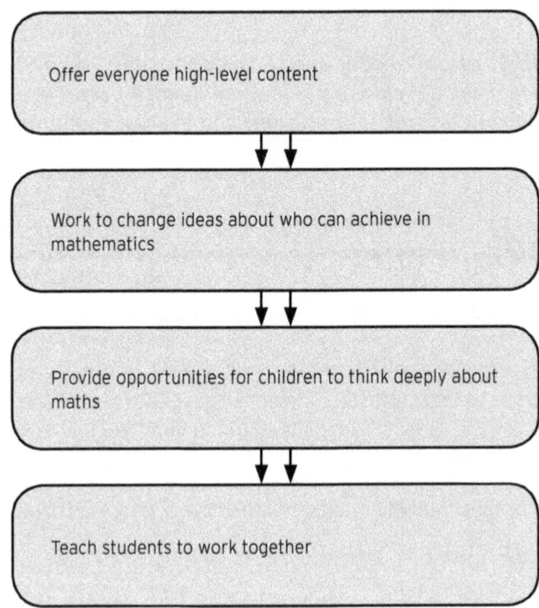

Wong (2002) has acknowledged the widely accepted influence that beliefs have on an enacted pedagogy and the children's lived experiences of mathematics lessons, with Frank Pajares stating much earlier in 1992 that beliefs are the best indicators of the decisions individuals make. Beliefs are said to be personally held assumptions that guide and direct individuals to make decisions and behave in the way they do (Liljedahl *et al.*, 2012). Belief systems have many characteristics. They are persistent and resistant to change. They are concretised and deep-seated, being more than fleeting notions or feelings. They are said to be unchanging and static. All of which could prove problematic for a period of change and flux when considering teaching and learning in mathematics.

Cai and Wang's (2010) report on an investigation into the beliefs held by Chinese mathematics teachers unsurprisingly found that teachers' views on how mathematics is best taught is inherently tied up with views on the nature of mathematics as a subject, which is exemplified in Table 30.3. Chinese teachers' value understanding in mathematics and this is facilitated by connecting ideas in mathematics. Memorisation is important, and contributes to conceptual understanding. Effective teaching that is coherently structured is driven by the teacher, and serves to develop mathematical thinking and the ability to manipulate numbers and symbols.

Table 30.3 The influence of belief on practice

PHILOSOPHICAL PERSPECTIVE	NATURE OF MATHEMATICS AS A DISCIPLINE	NATURE OF PEDAGOGY	HOW CHILDREN LEARN MATHEMATICS
INSTRUMENTALIST	An accumulation of facts, skills and rules within a body of unrelated topics	Emphasis on performance, drawing on a toolbox of rules and procedures	Mastering skills and a passive reception of knowledge
PLATONIST	A static and unified body of knowledge waiting to be discovered where connections are important	Emphasis on understanding and precision in language use	Active construction of understanding
PROBLEM SOLVING	About invention and process	About the learner	Autonomous exploration

KEY READING

Boaler, J. (2016) *Mathematical Mindsets*. San Francisco, CA: Jossey-Bass.

This is a comprehensive research-driven yet fully practical book that considers the principles underpinning effective teaching of mathematics. It takes a broad look at a range of ideas and principles that impact upon the teaching of mathematics: the brain in relation to learning mathematics, the power of mistakes and struggle, the importance of flexibility with numbers, the role of rich mathematical tasks and teaching for a growth mindset.

Beswick, K. (2012) Teachers' beliefs about school mathematics and the mathematicians' mathematics and their relationship to practice. *Educational Studies in Mathematics*, 79: 127–47.

It is widely accepted that mathematics teachers' beliefs about the nature of mathematics influence the ways in which they teach the subject. This paper presents case studies of two secondary mathematics teachers,

(Continued)

(Continued)

one experienced and the other relatively new to teaching, and considers their beliefs about the nature of mathematics as a discipline and as a school subject. The article starts by discussing the differences between mathematics at school and as a subject discipline before moving on to teacher beliefs about the nature of mathematics and their relationship to practice. It is suggested that beliefs about mathematics as a subject and how it is taught and learnt, can be considered in terms of a matrix that accommodates the possibility of differing views and beliefs.

Siemon, D., Beswick, K., Brady, K., Clark, J., Faragher, R. and Warren, E. (2015) *Teaching Mathematics Foundations to Middle Years* (2nd edition). South Melbourne, Victoria: Oxford University Press.

This comprehensive Australian book connects readers to the bigger picture of mathematics teaching and learning to subject-specific content spanning the Foundations to Year 9 curriculum. It offers big ideas and key terminology for each area of content and potential activities to use in class, while maintaining a rich vein of research and theoretical thinking.

WHAT IS A MASTERY CURRICULUM?

A mastery curriculum emphasises a set of mathematical concepts and big ideas for all children to achieve, with the expectation that all children will master their age-related content, while discouraging acceleration into content from subsequent years. This is reiterated by the National Curriculum when it says:

> *The expectation is that the majority of pupils will move through the programmes of study at broadly the same pace. However, decisions about when to progress should always be based on the security of pupils' understanding and their readiness to progress to the next stage. Pupils who grasp concepts rapidly should be challenged through being offered rich and sophisticated problems before any acceleration through new content. Those who are not sufficiently fluent with earlier material should consolidate their understanding, including through additional practice, before moving on.*
>
> (DfE, 2013: 3)

A shift from an embedded sense of 'levelness' to 'age-relatedness' appears to be the focus for some discussion. Since the arrival of the current National Curriculum, children's understanding in mathematics appears to be still characterised by gaps, making the achievement of age-related expectations a bigger task. Notions of readiness to move on bring further challenging discussions, as teachers grapple with the idea of what is sufficient understanding to move children onto the next idea. Equally, notions of challenge to develop a greater depth of understanding is proving an interesting idea, as deepening children's thinking and understanding is inherently connected to a teacher's subject knowledge.

WHAT DOES IT MEAN TO MASTER IDEAS IN MATHEMATICS?

This, I might suggest, is being grappled with by schools and teachers the most, as it is inherently connected to evidencing the progress and understanding being developed by learners. Making judgements of learners, whether they are working at age-related expectations or greater depth, requires a set of criteria. To some extent, this has been offered by the NCETM in their characteristics of mastery and mastery with greater depth as outlined in Table 30.4.

Table 30.4 Characteristics of mastery and mastery with greater depth

A pupil really understands a mathematical concept, idea or technique if he or she can:	Developing mastery with greater depth is characterised by pupils' ability to:
describe it in his or her own words represent it in a variety of ways (e.g. using concrete materials, pictures and symbols) explain it to someone else make up his or her own examples (and non-examples) see connections between it and other facts or ideas recognise it in new situations and contexts; make use of it in various ways, including in new situations	solve problems of greater complexity (i.e. where the approach is not immediately obvious), demonstrating creativity and imagination independently explore and investigate mathematical contexts and structures, communicate results clearly and systematically explain and generalise the mathematics

But demonstrating that you understand something in mathematics can involve so much more.

- Having a set of usable procedures and an understanding why they work.
- Having a reliable bank of known facts that can be used, recalled out of sequence and be used to derive other facts.
- Understanding how principles, such as the commutative law, can be applied.
- Drawing on relationships between ideas – for example, to divide by 4 you halve and halve again.
- Being able to use your understanding flexibly and appropriately.
- Grasping an aspect well enough to use it as a basis to move onto other aspects that depend on it.
- An ability to engage in rich and sophisticated problems; being able to explore and investigate.
- Understanding that could be considered sustained and sustainable.

CRITICAL QUESTION

What does it mean for you, for a child to understand something in mathematics?

WHAT DOES MASTERY LOOK LIKE FROM A PEDAGOGICAL PERSPECTIVE?

The NCETM has summarised the teaching for mastery approach first and foremost as the development of conceptual and procedural understanding, which leads to fluent and confident mathematicians. This interestingly is referring to the 'achievement' aspect of the mastery quadrant. This achievement dimension is achieved through the pedagogical dimension, suggesting a continuous shift between these two dimensions. Lessons are carefully constructed in order to build up understanding coherently and through small steps. The whole class is kept together, ensuring all master ideas, while some gain a greater depth of understanding. If a child fails to understand a concept or procedure, immediate intervention ensures the child is ready to move forwards with the whole class. The structure of mathematical ideas are exposed and deepened through precise use of visual representations and mathematical language, careful choices of examples and non-examples, teacher explanation and questioning. An emphasis is placed on practice and consolidation, and known facts are to be recalled to the point of automaticity.

KEY READING

NCETM (2016) The Essence of Maths Teaching for Mastery. Available at: www.ncetm.org.uk/resources/47230

This is the second summary of the principles of mastery by the NCETM. It is a helpful single-page document that identifies the most important characteristics of teaching for mastery. The ideas within this document are also considered further in the third longitudinal evaluation of the Mathematics Teacher Exchange undertaken by Sheffield Hallam University.

Unsurprisingly, Ma (1999) suggested that teachers needed to have a deep and far-reaching understanding of mathematics, but An *et al.* (2004) went on to suggest that this alone does not guarantee effective teaching and argued the case for profound pedagogical knowledge being the determining factor for effective mathematics teaching.

THE KEY COMPONENTS OF TEACHING PRIMARY MATHEMATICS

Leinhardt (1989) believed that lessons can be considered in terms of their discernible parts with the instructional element considered to be the one that must be the most carefully thought about. Through my work with qualified teachers, it was becoming increasingly observed that mathematics teaching appeared to be losing this instructional element. The mastery agenda has allowed teachers to reconsider those careful pedagogical decisions that enable others to learn or develop an idea in mathematics. Literature leads us to be able to conceptualise the pedagogy of teaching mathematics to three significant domains: explanation, representation and connection, all of which are reflected in the teacher-led instruction that is characteristic of teaching for mastery.

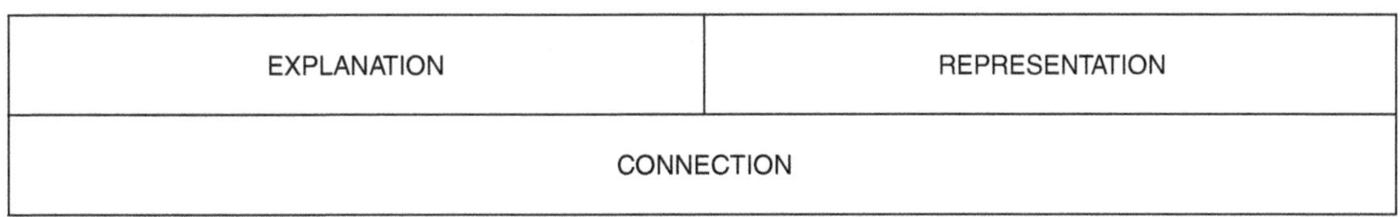

Figure 30.3 The three significant domains of mathematics teaching pedagogy

WHAT IS EXPLANATION?

Charalambous (2016) places explanation central to the work of mathematics teachers and, as such, can feature at different points in a mathematics lesson to help shape the understanding children form. For Wittwer and Renkl (2008: 60), explanation 'convey[s] the content of a domain to help learners develop a basic understanding and clarify concepts, ideas, and procedures to deepen their understandings further', thus supporting the development of more robust structures for their thinking. Effective explanation of ideas, for example, the steps needed to carry out the column addition of a pair of three-digit numbers has a number of characteristics:

- Accurate, fluent and precise terminology is used.
- Is free from error and ambiguity.
- Draws on justification and reasoning to help children understand 'why'.
- Engages children in dynamic verbal interactions to shape and transform their understanding.

Explanation must not be considered a singular pedagogical strategy (Wittwer and Renkl, 2008). Mathematical explanations are most powerful when used simultaneously with visual representations. Effective teachers seek out a more coherent and complete view for learners by mapping their explanation onto representation use (Leinhardt, 1989).

WHAT DOES IT MEAN TO VISUALLY REPRESENT IDEAS IN MATHEMATICS?

The NCETM has identified five aspects of teaching mathematics for mastery and suggest that visually representing ideas and mathematical structures is a significant pedagogical element (see Figure 30.4).

Visual representations offer children an increasingly robust and externalised view of important and difficult mathematical ideas (Cobb *et al.*, 1992; Pape and Tchoshanov, 2001). Visual representations illuminate mathematical ideas (Dreher and Kuntze, 2015). This illumination of ideas for the learner requires knowledge of what each representation offers to the learner, the salient points held by the representation. Visual representations need to be carefully selected and judiciously used to suit specific mathematical need (Mitchell *et al.*, 2014) so that they are mathematically helpful to the learner (Charalambous, 2016).

McNeil and Jarvin (2007) have suggested that teachers fail to use visual representations properly, seeking to use them to raise levels of interest rather than engaging learners with knowledge construction. Bills *et al.* (2006) refer to the notion of exemplification, where something specific is used to represent an idea in

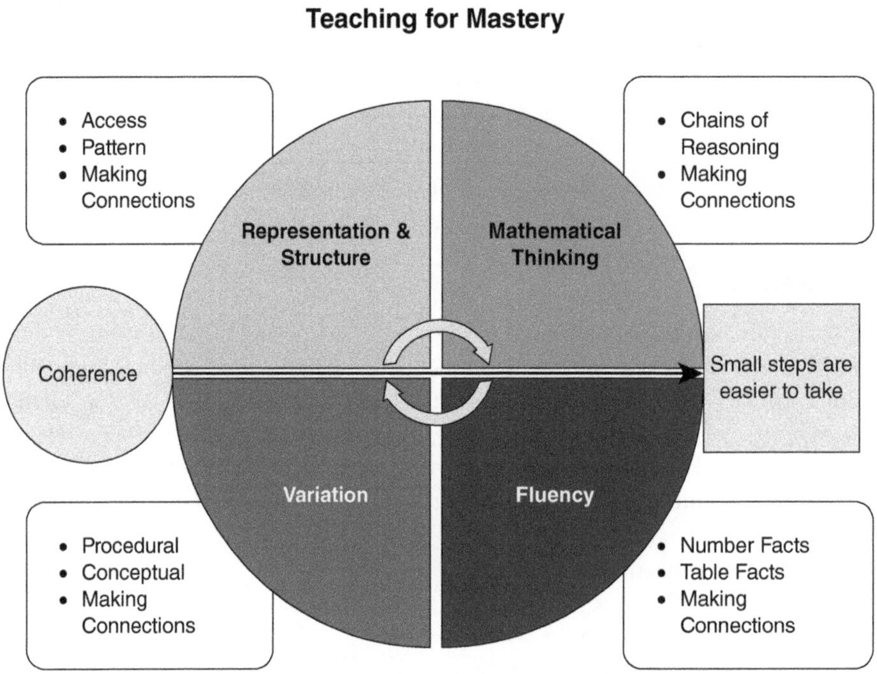

Teaching for Mastery

- Access
- Pattern
- Making Connections

- Chains of Reasoning
- Making Connections

Representation & Structure

Mathematical Thinking

Coherence

Small steps are easier to take

Variation

Fluency

- Procedural
- Conceptual
- Making Connections

- Number Facts
- Table Facts
- Making Connections

Figure 30.4 Five aspects of teaching for mastery identified by the NCETM

mathematics and to which the attention of others is drawn. Examples become the raw material of the teacher of mathematics, illustrating and communicating ideas and procedures or indicating relationships and principles. For Zaslavsky (2006), effective use of examples requires the drawing of attention to the deep structural ideas located within the representation, and also the difference between the essential and non-essential ideas.

Robust understanding in mathematics requires the careful interplay between five representational forms: oral language, manipulatives, pictures, real-world contexts and symbols (Lesh *et al.*, 1987). Each form is as important as another, but what is more important is the fluid movement between each representational form as this movement denotes how well something is understood. This does not mean that representational thinking ignores the power held by symbolic notation. Visually rich instruction, according to Ball *et al.* (2008), does involve the accurate use of conventional mathematical notation.

WHAT IS CONNECTION AND COHERENCE IN MATHEMATICS?

When you watch the Chinese teachers who have come to teach mathematics in England as part of an exchange programme, you are struck by their emphasis on developing children's ability to think mathematically through well thought-out lessons that are sequential in nature and build up understanding incrementally. This strong sense of coherence is a powerful element of their lessons, with an expectation that instruction supports children in keeping up and, therefore, reduces the need for any catch-up.

CLASSROOM LINK

What does this mean for classroom practice?

A lesson taught by a Chinese teacher as part of an exchange programme worked sequentially through a series of teaching points to support children in mastering the comparison of unit fractions.

- A series of carefully chosen images led to the initial idea that when comparing fractions you need to use the same size whole.
- A period of short independent practice using a fraction wall led the children to saying the complete sentence of, for example, the whole is divided into (4) equal parts; one coloured part is ($\frac{1}{4}$) of the whole; ($\frac{1}{4}$) is larger than ($\frac{1}{5}$).
- This same idea was then tested with circular images leading to the generalisation, the smaller the denominator the larger the fraction.
- This generalisation was taken further by comparing a set of fractions with varied denominators and numerators.
- $\frac{1}{33}$ and $\frac{3}{33}$ $\frac{1}{5}$ and $\frac{2}{5}$ $\frac{1}{3}$ and $\frac{1}{30}$ $\frac{1}{50}$ and $\frac{1}{5}$
- The importance of the unit fraction was reiterated through careful explanation.
- The lesson moved onto comparing three unit fractions in a more open-ended way.
- $\frac{1}{4} > \frac{1}{\ } > \frac{1}{10}$
- The lesson ended with three 'challenge' questions to take the generalisations and teaching points even further. An example of one of the questions can be seen below.

Challenge 2

David and Joe have the same cake.

David ate $\frac{1}{8}$ cake. Joe ate $\frac{1}{9}$ cake.

Who left more?

Because $\frac{1}{8} > \frac{1}{9}$

David ate more

So Joe left more $\frac{7}{8} < \frac{8}{9}$

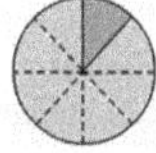

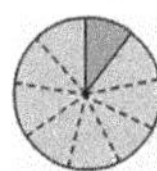

Amador and Lamberg (2013) suggest that effective teachers are goal-orientated, with Olson and Ihrig (2010) arguing that effective teachers 'carefully work with students' thinking, navigating them along a thoughtfully planned sequence that begins with their current thinking and ends with the desired conceptual understanding'

(cited in Land and Drake, 2014: 112). Land and Drake (2014) suggest that pedagogical knowledge needs to have a coherent and progressive forward-moving view of learning which ensures that a clear route to learning an idea in mathematics had been established, ensuring that ideas became more sophisticated. Networks of knowledge need to be created by connecting ideas and procedures, and connecting this to appropriate visual models. These pedagogical choices and decisions, therefore, help learners to develop more sophisticated ideas. Presenting an alternative phrase, Weber *et al.* (2015) see the term 'learning trajectory' as about learners in terms of understanding the need for them to have a coherent perspective of an idea in mathematics and the sequence of instruction that will enable this coherent view to emerge.

KEY READING

Dreher, A. and Kuntze, S. (2015) Teachers' professional knowledge and noticing: The case of multiple representations in the mathematics classroom. *Educational Studies in Mathematics*, 88: 89–114.

This article researches German student teachers' pedagogical understanding of the use of multiple representations to teach mathematics. The consideration of the literature around visual representations is particularly helpful. The article on the one hand acknowledges that visual representations are essential for mathematical understanding, but on the other hand they can also be an obstruction for learning.

Charalambous, C.Y., Hill, H.C. and Ball, D.L. (2011) Prospective teachers' learning to provide instructional explanations: How does it look and what might it take. *Journal of Mathematics Teacher Education*, 14: 441–63.

Several studies have documented the difficulties student teachers have in using instructional explanations as part of their teaching. This research considered the extent with which student teachers can learn to provide explanations during their teacher preparation. The article provides a helpful consideration of the literature around explanations as a pedagogical tool and a detailed presentation of the sample of student teachers in action in mathematics lessons.

Land, T.J. and Drake C. (2014) Enhancing and enacting curricular progressions in elementary mathematics. *Mathematical Thinking and Learning*, 16(2): 109–34.

This article provides a synthesis of the literature around learning progressions and trajectories in science and mathematics education. Videos of lessons were analysed alongside the researcher. For significant moments in the lesson, the video was stopped and each teacher was asked to state and explain her intended goal, provide details about how that element of the lesson was designed, and describe what was noticed about student learning.

CRITICAL QUESTION

The pedagogy of mathematics is characterised by three elements: explanation, representation and connection or coherence. These three elements ultimately work together to contribute to effective teacher-led instruction. How is your teaching of mathematics characterised by these three aspects?

RESPONSES TO SUPPORTING PLANNING FOR MASTERY

WHAT SOLUTIONS DO THE WHITE ROSE PLANNING MATERIALS OFFER TEACHERS?

In response to the challenge being felt by teachers when planning for mastery, while simultaneously developing the three aims of the mathematics curriculum, the White Rose Maths Hub created a suite of materials to support teachers at the planning stage. The White Rose materials offer the small steps in learning which are not identified by the National Curriculum, and supplementary notes and guidance on the important mathematical ideas that underpin these small steps. Carefully considered tasks driven by rich and varied practice seek to develop the three aims of the National Curriculum: fluency, problem solving and reasoning. Following feedback from teachers, questions to promote mathematical talk have subsequently been added.

Although termed a scheme of work, these materials still require considerable thought in terms of creating coherent lessons for children. These materials appear to have been well received and have found their way into many schools in England. Teachers who are drawing on these materials to support their planning value them in a number of ways:

- The breaking down of statutory curriculum content into small, coherent steps, which in turn gives confidence that the curriculum is being covered with the child's understanding in mind.
- The notes and guidance that are supportive of subject knowledge.
- The use of different visual representations that support children in developing understanding of structural ideas in mathematics and the development of concepts over process.
- Embedded opportunities for problem solving and reasoning.
- Written with the whole class in mind.
- Key questions which highlight the important idea for the block of work.

WHAT SOLUTIONS COULD THE NCETM MASTERY PROFESSIONAL DEVELOPMENT MATERIALS OFFER TEACHERS?

The NCETM has also presented teachers with their own response to planning for mastery, acknowledging that:

> *Successful teaching for mastery depends to a large degree on a teacher's subject knowledge, as well as their understanding of the learning steps required, and the order of those steps. Teaching based on knowledge of mathematical structures and relationships gives pupils the best chance of building deep and secure mathematical understanding.*

With this in mind, and also with the opportunity to develop teachers professionally, a suite of materials is currently being developed, starting with number, addition and subtraction. Drawing on expertise from the

Mastery Specialist Teachers developed through the Maths Hubs programmes, the material developed so far has populated the number, addition and subtraction 'spine' with Year 1 content broken down into 10 'segments'. Over time, the remaining 20 segments will build up this spine coherently to the end of Year 6.

The NCETM is equally clear to say that this material is not lesson plans, but what teachers now have access to is high-level subject knowledge and pedagogical guidance regarding carefully thought through visual representations. Each segment of learning has a teacher's guide that provides an overview of learning, detailed guidance regarding the mathematical knowledge inherent within that segment, including the most powerful and helpful visual representations, and also the aspects that children are likely to find challenging. Video guidance unpicking the mathematical knowledge is also offered, as is a PowerPoint providing the visual representations referred to.

CHAPTER SUMMARY

The mastery agenda in this country provides opportunity to re-evaluate and reflect upon how mathematics is best taught so that all children make progress, become proficient and achieve the age-related expectations set out in the National Curriculum. This opportunity is not without difficulty and challenge, as the term 'mastery' appears to be a multidimensional idea. Mastery is more nuanced than something we do and it remains common to hear teachers saying 'we are doing mastery'. How we approach mastery and the effect it can have is inherently connected to our own belief systems about mathematics and children. The first hurdle is to believe that the children we teach can achieve in mathematics and nothing is too hard for them. The second hurdle requires us to overcome the view that teaching for mastery is something new and different. The pedagogical essence of mastery remains rooted in seminal and long-standing research and literature about what characterises high-quality instruction. Primary teachers now have the chance to be part of changing the face of mathematics teaching in England, making it world-leading like the jurisdictions we have gone to as part of the England-China Teacher Exchange.

ASSIGNMENTS

If you are writing an ITE assignment on teaching primary mathematics for mastery, it will be useful to think through the following:

1. In what ways do your personal beliefs manifest themselves in the way you teach mathematics and believe children learn mathematical ideas?
2. How does the current curriculum for mathematics address concepts and procedures? To what extent is there any bias or emphasis? How are the three aims for mathematics of fluency, problem solving and reasoning reflected in the statutory content?
3. How are visual representations and a careful choice of examples used to transform children's understanding of mathematical ideas? What effect does your personal subject knowledge have on your effectiveness to use visual representations and a careful choice of examples?

The following sources provide useful further reading:

Beswick, K. (2012) Teachers' beliefs about school mathematics and the mathematicians' mathematics and their relationship to practice. *Educational Studies in Mathematics*, 79: 127-47.

Dreher, A. and Kuntze, S. (2015) Teachers' professional knowledge and noticing: The case of multiple representations in the mathematics classroom. *Educational Studies in Mathematics,* 88: 89-114.

Jerrim, J. and Vignoles, A. (2016) The link between East Asian 'mastery' teaching methods and English children's mathematics skills. *Economics of Education Review*, 50: 29-44.

Rittle-Johnson, B. and Schneider, M. (2015) Developing conceptual and procedural knowledge in mathematics, in R. Cohen Kadosh and A. Dowker (eds) *Oxford Handbook of Numerical Cognition.* Oxford: Oxford University Press.

REFERENCES

Amador, J. and Lamberg, T. (2013) Learning trajectories, lesson planning affordances, and constraints in the design and enactment of mathematics teaching. *Mathematical Thinking and Learning,* 15(2): 146–70.

An, S., Kulm, G. and Wu, Z. (2004) The pedagogical content knowledge of middle school mathematics teachers in China and the US. *Journal of Mathematics Teacher Education,* 7: 145–72.

Ball, D.L., Thames, M.H. and Phelps, G. (2008) Content knowledge for teaching: What makes it special? *Journal of Teacher Education,* 59(5): 389–407.

Beswick, K. (2012) Teachers' beliefs about school mathematics and the mathematicians' mathematics and their relationship to practice. *Educational Studies in Mathematics,* 79: 127–47.

Bills, L., Dreyfus, T., Mason, J., Tsamir, P., Watson, A. and Zaslavsky, O. (2006) *Exemplification in Mathematics Education: Proceedings of the 30th Conference of the International Group for the Psychology of Mathematics Education.* Prague, Czech Republic: PME.

Boaler, J. (2016) *Mathematical Mindsets.* San Francisco, CA: Jossey-Bass.

Boylan, M., Maxwell, B., Wolstenholme, C. and Jay, T. (2017) *Longitudinal Evaluation of the Mathematics Teacher Exchange: China–England third interim report.* Government Social Research. Reference: DFE-RR778. Available at: https://assets.publishing.service.gov.uk/government/uploads/system/uploads/attachment_data/file/666450/MTE_third_interim_report_121217.pdf (accessed 12/07/18).

Cai, J. and Wang, T. (2010) Conceptions of effective mathematics teaching within a cultural text: Perspectives of teachers from China and the United States. *Journal of Mathematics Teacher Education,* 13: 297–309.

Chap, S.L. (2007) Characteristics of mathematics teaching in Shanghai, China: Through the lens of a Malaysian. *Mathematics Education Research Journal,* 19(1): 77–89.

Charalambous, C.Y. (2016) Investigating the knowledge needed for teaching mathematics. *Journal of Teacher Education,* 63(3): 220–237.

Charalambous, C.Y., Hill, H.C. and Ball, D.L. (2011) Perspective teachers' learning to provide instructional explanations: How does it look and what might it take? *Journal of Mathematics Teacher Education,* 14: 441–63.

Cobb, P., Yackel, E. and Wood, T. (1992) A constructivist alternative to the representational view of mind in mathematics education. *Journal for Research in Mathematics Education,* 23(1): 2.

DfE (2013) *Mathematics Programmes of Study: Key Stages 1 and 2: National curriculum in England.* London: Crown copyright.

Dreher, A. and Kuntze, S. (2015) Teachers' professional knowledge and noticing: The case of multiple representations in the mathematics classroom. *Educational Studies in Mathematics,* 88: 89–114.

Hiebert, J. and Lefevre, P. (1986) Conceptual and procedural knowledge in mathematics: An introductory analysis, in Hiebert, J. (ed.) (1986) *Conceptual and Procedural Knowledge: The case of mathematics.* London: Lawrence Erlbaum.

Jerrim, J. and Vignoles, A. (2016) The link between East Asian 'mastery' teaching methods and English children's mathematics skills. *Economics of Education Review,* 50: 29–44.

Land, T.J. and Drake C. (2014) Enhancing and enacting curricular progressions in elementary mathematics. *Mathematical Thinking and Learning,* 16(2): 109–34.

Leinhardt, G. (1989) Maths lessons: A contrast of novice and expert competence. *Journal for Research in Mathematics Education,* 20(1): 52–75.

Lesh, R., Post, T. and Behr, M. (1987) Representations and translations among representations in mathematics learning and problem solving, in C. Janvier (ed.) *Problems of Representation in the Teaching and Learning of Mathematics.* Hillsdale: Lawrence Erlbaum Associates, pp. 33–40.

Liljedahl, P., Oesterle, S. and Berneche, C. (2012) Stability of beliefs in mathematics education: A critical analysis. *Nordic Studies in Mathematics Education,* 17 (3–4): 101–18.

Ma, L. (1999) *Knowing and Teaching Elementary Mathematics: Teachers' understanding of fundamental mathematics in China and the United States.* Mahwah, NJ: Lawrence Erlbaum Associates.

McNeil, N. and Jarvin, L. (2007) When theories don't add up: Disentangling the manipulatives debate. *Theory into Practice,* 46(4): 309–16.

Mitchell, R., and Hill, H. (2014) Examining the task and knowledge demands needed to teach with representations. *Journal of Mathematics Teacher Education,* 17(1): 1007, Charalambous, C.Y.

Olson, J. K. and Ihrig, L. M. (2010). The lethal mutation of content standards: Why inquiry and learning progressions are necessary but insufficient for student learning of central concepts in science. Paper presented at the annual meeting of the Association for Science Teacher Education, Minneapolis, MN.

Pajares, M. Frank (1992) Teachers' beliefs and educational research: Cleaning up a messy construct. *Review of Educational Research,* 62(3): 307–32.

Pape, S. J. and Tchoshanov, M.A. (2001) The role of representation(s) in developing mathematical understanding. *Theory into Practice,* 40(2): 118–27.

Rittle-Johnson, B. and Schneider, M. (2015) Developing conceptual and procedural knowledge in mathematics, in R. Cohen Kadosh and A. Dowker (eds) *Oxford Handbook of Numerical Cognition.* Oxford: Oxford University Press.

Rowland, T., Huckstep, P. and Thwaites, A. (2005) Elementary teachers' mathematics subject knowledge: The knowledge quartet and the case of Naomi. *Journal of Mathematics Teacher Education,* 8: 255–81.

Siemon, D., Beswick, K., Brady, K., Clark, J., Faragher, R. and Warren, E. (2015) *Teaching Mathematics Foundations to Middle Years* (2nd edn). Australia. OU Press.

Shulman, L.S. (1986) Those who understand: Knowledge growth in teaching. *Educational Researcher,* 15(2): 4–14.

Shulman, L.S. (1987) Knowledge and teaching: Foundations of the new reform. *Harvard Educational Review, 57:* 1–22.

Weber, E., Walkington, C., and McGalliard, W. (2015) Expanding notions of 'learning trajectories' in mathematics education. *Mathematical Thinking and Learning,* 17(4): 253–72.

Wittwer, J. and Renkl, A. (2008) Why instructional explanations often do not work: A framework for understanding the effectiveness of instructional explanations. *Educational Psychologist,* 43(1): 49–64.

Wong, N.Y. (2002) Conceptions of doing and learning mathematics among Chinese. *Journal of intercultural Studies,* 23(2): 211–29.

Zaslavsky, O. (2006) A teacher's treatment of examples as reflection on her knowledge base: Proceedings of the 30*th* Conference of the International Group for the Psychology of Mathematics Education. Prague: PME.

31

A BROAD AND BALANCED CURRICULUM?

Susan Ogier is Senior Lecturer in Primary Education, specialising in Art and Design. She works at Roehampton University, London, on both undergraduate and post-graduate courses. Her research interests include investigating the social, emotional and well-being aspects of teaching in art and design, and the role of developing an understanding of personal identities.

In this chapter, Susan explores the contribution that is made to children's development by ensuring a wide subject base within any primary curriculum, with a particular focus on the arts. It will discuss the importance of offering a well-rounded education and how this can be an influencing and motivating factor for children to learn across the curriculum. It will question why many schools are increasingly unable to provide this offer to their pupils and will further consider the potentially serious consequences for society in the future if today's children are, effectively, prevented from discovering their passion or talent. Furthermore, it will consider what teachers can do to redress the balance and to develop an inclusive and more holistic way of working with children in primary schools.

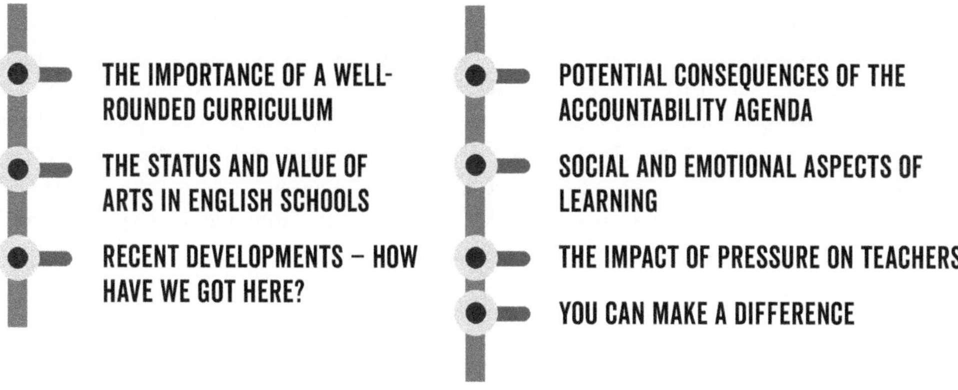

KEY WORDS

- Arts
- Broad and balanced
- Creative
- Cross-curricular
- Emotional health
- Individuality
- Mental health
- Motivation
- Skills for the future
- Well-being

> *Please, nothing without joy!*
>
> Loris Maloguzzi

THE IMPORTANCE OF A WELL-ROUNDED CURRICULUM

CRITICAL QUESTION

What has happened to the 'broad and balanced' curriculum?

If an alien dropped down to Earth and walked into a primary classroom, what do you think it would make of our curriculum? Assuming, of course, that it would be a highly intelligent and thoughtful alien. The alien might question why we are spending so much time teaching few, well – two to be precise – narrow subjects, where there are right and wrong answers, and endless tests to make sure that the knowledge has *really* gone in, when there are so many other wonderful and inspiring things we could be teaching children. They might question why we do not teach children enough about the key foundations of all there is to be excited about in learning and in life, and why we, well into the 21st century, comply with an outdated idea of what education is for (Claxton and Lucas, 2015). In 2015, Julian Thomas, Master of the prestigious independent school, Wellington College, stated in an article for *The Daily Telegraph* newspaper, that the exam system we have of constantly testing children will produce the wrong outcomes for future societies, and does not equip the young generation of today for their own futures. He points out that high-stakes testing limits children's abilities, and that it was designed for a pre-computer era, when white-collar workers needed the key skills of 'method and recall'. We do not need those skills in the same way today, nor will we in another 20 or 30 years' time, when the workplace will have changed beyond all current recognition.

KEY READING

What is the purpose of education?

Claxton and Lucas, in their 2015 book, *Educating Ruby*, are also critical of an education system that requires schools to teach facts to children with finite knowledge as an end goal, and to do this as fast as possible in order to move them on at a rapid rate. Some children respond well to this type of learning of course, but it is far from an inclusive system. Claxton and Lucas give examples of many children who have not responded well to this type of learning and have become at risk of slipping right through the proverbial net – if there is any net there at all. Their examples give demonstrations of children who have grown up to go on to great things despite having been told they were failures during their school years, including the likes of Jack Dee, Jo Malone, Tanya Byron and even Albert Einstein: school did not suit them, so one could argue that they have succeeded despite their education, not because of it. The question remains, however, about what we can do for the very many children who grow up without ever realising their full potential, and for those who continue to believe that they are failures well into their adult lives. It begs us to reflect upon what sort of education it is that teaches children what they can't do, rather than what they can.

Claxton, G. and Lucas, B. (2015) *Educating Ruby: What our Children Really Need to Know*. Carmarthen: Crown House. Available at: www.educatingruby.org/

THE STATUS AND VALUE OF ARTS IN ENGLISH SCHOOLS

CRITICAL QUESTION

Why is there a hierarchy of subjects?

In the last few years there has been a severe narrowing of the curriculum in many primary schools, making subjects that are not classed as core almost redundant. Indeed, the term *'core'* has now come to mean only mathematics and some aspects of English, such as learning reading through phonics, and writing through SPaG, so even these two subjects have been narrowed right down to their own core. Arts subjects in particular are suffering the most, and this is for a number of reasons which we shall look at later, but humanities subjects are also in serious decline. According to Barnes and Scoffham (2017), despite the fact that many headteachers are more than aware of the innate value that these subjects bring to a child's developing understanding of the world around them, and their belief in the necessity to provide a well-rounded education, there is intense pressure to comply with political will that dictates another view. A report for the National Union of Teachers in 2015, recognised that 'the accountability agenda in England has changed the nature of education in wide-ranging and harmful ways. It is not serving the interests of children and young people and is undermining their right to a balanced, creative and rewarding curriculum' (Hutchings, 2015). Hutchings states in this report that schools are being turned into 'exam factories' (ibid.), and that this approach has detrimental effects on children's emotional and mental health. Rather than centring upon the development of the whole child, which includes offering a well-balanced curriculum full of interesting and practical learning, social and emotional development, and learning *how to learn*, primary schools have become more and more solely academically and information focused, which would seem to have little to do with children's individual achievements, and much more to do with how schools, and the UK as a whole, might appear on both national and international league tables (Irwin, 2016).

This narrow focus has further negative effects by making schools a less inclusive environment for young children who have particular challenges or needs, who do not respond well to a relentless learning-by-rote system. In addition, children who have interests, talents and abilities in foundation subject areas, are being denied the chance to find out about their abilities, because these subjects are being side-lined, and even axed from the curriculum (Brown, 2015). This alarming scenario is also potentially divisive for us as a society, as it is often schools in socially and economically deprived areas where there is an enormous pressure to ensure that children achieve limited goals, rather than opening them up to a wider world of possibilities. This last point is now developing into a more serious debate about the creativity of the nation, as children grow up not really having had access to a full and broad curriculum that will allow them to discover their own talents, nor to develop those talents and interests into something that can gain them useful employment in the creative industries of the future (Hutchings, 2015). Given that Britain is currently so proud of the success of its creative industries (Harris, 2017; DfDCMS, 2016), it is even more surprising that the place of subjects, such as art and design and music, are suffering such an enormous decline in status within state education in England (Atkinson, 2016). Statistics show that in recent years arts subjects in English schools have been reduced and eroded, and in some state schools, arts subjects are just not part of the offer for children any more (NSEAD, 2016; Neelands *et al.*, 2015).

Despite the lowering of the status of arts and other foundation subjects, it is not to say that teaching and learning in these areas is no longer statutory, because it is. Arts subjects, such as art and design and music, remain on the list of subjects that *must* be taught, but schools find it very difficult to prioritise a broad and balanced curriculum when success in testing of the core subjects is the only thing they are really judged on. The impact of these changes is far-reaching, as evidenced by the 2016 survey report by NSEAD, where it was found that primary education arts subject provision is being seriously reduced, especially in the state sector on the lead-up to standardised tests (see Figure 31.1).

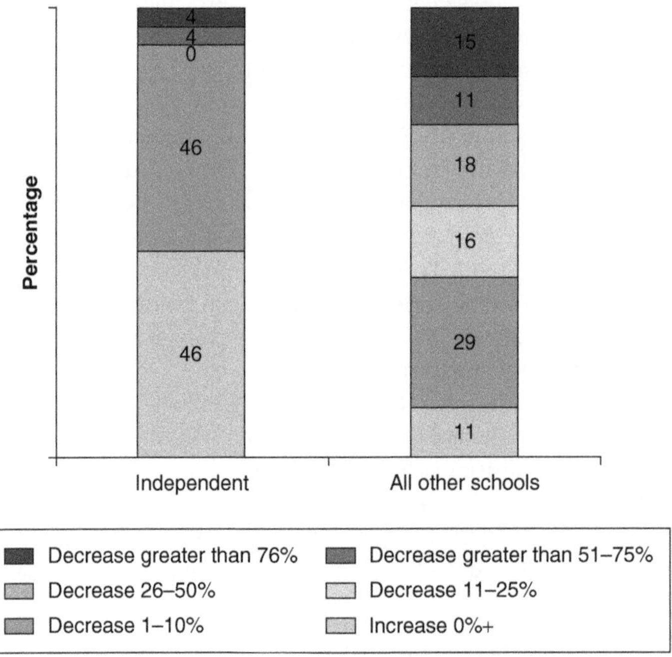

Figure 31.1 Key Stages 1 and 2: Sector differences in the reduction in time allocated for art and design in the two terms before National Curriculum tests in the last five years.

Source: NSEAD Survey Report, 2016 (p.13). Available at: www.nsead.org/downloads/survey.pdf

CLASSROOM LINK

What does this mean for classroom practice?

Sheryl is a Year 2 teacher in a suburban primary school. She is anxious that the children in her class are not exceeding the expected levels, and some might not reach the goals at all. She feels under great pressure to ensure that they pass their tests well and has informed the art and music specialist teachers, who are due to teach the class for one hour a week each, that all these lessons are cancelled during the spring term so that she has more time to prepare the children for their tests in the core subjects.

Do you recognise this scenario? Do you agree with Sheryl's decision? What effect do you think her decision has for the children, socially, emotionally and intellectually?

Standardised testing for Year 2 children is to be scrapped by 2023 and replaced with baseline tests for four -year-olds. Will this help us to reintroduce a wider curriculum in primary schools? It might do, and this is the intention of OFSTED, who are beginning to look more deeply at schools that do not provide breadth and balance in the curriculum (Hall, 2016). We must hope, however, that the new baseline tests do not pose a further conundrum, as four-year-olds develop at vastly different rates, and 'one-size-fits-all' is even less appropriate in the very early years of children's education. It is an English obsession with testing that seems to drive our education system and individuals are not really part of that equation. Perhaps we should look at other education systems for inspiration, such as Finland, Denmark or Norway, where young children learn in all subject areas through play until age six or seven. So, while we are merrily testing our four-year-olds, children in those countries have not even started school. Perhaps we should ask the following big questions:

CRITICAL QUESTION

What exactly are we testing for? Who decides what is important or not?

Why are we testing at all? Who benefits from this?

KEY READING

STEAM not STEM

In his TED talk of 2006, Ken Robinson asked the question whether schools kill creativity by advocating and promoting a hierarchy of subjects where the arts are at the bottom of the list underneath humanities, and *way* beneath the core areas of maths, English and science, which take top places in the league tables of subject importance. Although this talk was given over 10 years ago, and has had over 47 million views on

(Continued)

(Continued)

YouTube, the issues he raised have remained the same, and the situation is arguably in an even worse state for arts education in England right now. It is a complete myth that a world without arts education will enable pupils to focus more on core subjects. Talk to any author and they will describe the process of writing in the same way that a visual artist might describe their process of creating artworks. If it's true that the universe is an enormous mathematical organisation, then we use our artistic understanding to see those patterns; the sciences cannot exist without arts, as there are overlaps wherever you look. NESTA released a report in 2016, which demonstrates the success of companies where arts and sciences are fused, and they call for STEAM, not STEM subjects to be taught.

You can watch Ken Robinson's very entertaining talk by using this link: www.ted.com/talks/ken_robinson_says_schools_kill_creativity

You can read the NESTA report, *The Fusion Effect: The economic returns to combining arts and science skills* here: www.nesta.org.uk/publications/fusion-effect-economic-returns-combining-arts-and-science-skills

This article calls for a more creative and broad curriculum for children: www.nesta.org.uk/blog/fix-pipeline-steam-talent-creative-economy

RECENT DEVELOPMENTS

CRITICAL QUESTION

How have we got here?

The worlds of literacy, mathematics, science, technology and the arts cross over at many levels, and links should not be underestimated in relation to the status of each of the subjects. It is important to remember that science and art are finely attuned to one another, and should not be seen as separate entities, as they are often portrayed in educational terms. Nicola Morgan, Secretary of State for Education in England during the years, 2014–16, made it clear that she believed that the two areas of arts and sciences are far apart, and attempted to actively discourage young people from taking arts subjects, by claiming that pupils were 'held back' by focusing on arts instead of maths and science (Paton, 2014). For many contemporary artists, however, the way forward in art and design is to embrace and engage with the digital and scientific worlds. Technology and science are intrinsically intertwined with fundamental art and design principles, and this is nothing new – it has been evident for at least 500 years, as we can see by the work of the great Leonardo da Vinci. So, what is going on, that in the 21st century, we cast all of our history aside, and say to our young people that the arts do not matter?

POTENTIAL CONSEQUENCES OF THE 'ACCOUNTABILITY AGENDA'

It is becoming clear that the 'accountability agenda' comes at the expense of teachers being able to have concern for children as individuals. This makes it difficult for children to achieve well because their education is not situated within and for the benefit of their own learning (Weale, 2017). In 2013, the English government introduced a new curriculum and exam system for 16-year-olds in England, known as the *English Baccalaureate*, in which so-called academic subjects hold a central position and arts subjects do not feature at all. This system, however, while designed for 16-year-olds, has an impact upon primary schools.

Many young people who have come through the English Baccalaureate, have not had good experiences of arts subjects at school, and signs now show that some are developing a negative attitude towards the value of the subjects and their own abilities. Very often, pupils who are deemed to have good academic abilities are now actively prevented from taking an arts-based GCSE suite, as this would prevent them or, perhaps more pointedly, their schools, from achieving target EBacc results.

For the next generation of primary teachers, this is an extremely concerning position, as it is likely that they will pass their own negative attitudes on to the children they will teach. For many, the last time they would have engaged in arts learning would be when they were aged 13 or 14, and they will have since lost confidence and interest. Many teacher training institutions have very little or, in some cases, no arts learning for their students: some primary student teachers have as little as one two-hour session in the whole of their training, especially if they are on a school-based route, and the likelihood of them changing an already negative attitude within such a short timescale is almost negligible.

This is, however, not an altogether recent phenomenon: art and design, among other arts subjects, have been declining over a number of years, and while many teachers suggest that this is purely due to the high demands and pressures of core areas of the National Curriculum (DfE, 2013) and OFSTED expectations (Hutchings, 2017), some teachers also believe that the subject is too messy and inappropriate to teach in their classrooms (Clement and Page, 1992). This, however, perhaps indicates the pressure on time felt by a stressed workforce, and the implication that teachers are not able to cope with a subject that involves physicality, creativity or any kind of unnecessary classroom upheaval (Lekue, 2015; Watts, 2005). Worse than this, the impoverished diet that a very narrow curriculum offers to children not only has unfavourable consequences for those who miss a chance to reach their full potential, it can prevent them from developing a questioning and critical outlook. All this creates issues for child mental health and well-being, as children feel they have no voice in their own learning, which is becoming more and more apparent as time progresses (Mental Health Foundation, 2017).

SOCIAL AND EMOTIONAL ASPECTS OF LEARNING

CRITICAL QUESTION

What can we do about it? Why do arts matter?

So, what are children missing out on exactly? Arts education provides crucial subject-specific learning that encourages children to express their own ideas, develop their imagination and creativity, while also providing children with a feeling of self-worth, a 'can do' attitude and multiple ways to communicate (Hallam et al., 2014; Addison and Burgess, 2003). While it is essential that the nation's youngest generation is literate and numerate, there is a realisation that they also need to have other skills, that include social and emotional literacy and creative confidence, that will stand them in good stead for the future (Sharp, 2001). This means that children need to be able to think flexibly and broadly in order to solve the problems in the world that we are currently storing up for the generations ahead. It is very unhelpful to encourage children to think in narrow terms, so that they can only follow instructions, and are unable to think and question for themselves.

Increasingly, there is research that suggests that by engaging with arts activity children develop physically, socially, emotionally and intellectually. And now, more general health and well-being benefits are becoming apparent (APPGHW, 2017). Cutcher (2013) states that an education that is rich in arts experiences has benefits for learners of all ages, from young children all the way through to adulthood.

The value of an education in and through the arts is well documented (Deasy, 2002; Eisner, 2002; Hickman, 2010), and yet still we find ourselves having to justify the place of arts subjects within the educational curriculum. In terms of personal well-being, recent research by Stride and Cutcher (2015: 2) demonstrates that participating in arts activity affords the

> *ability to withstand or adapt positively to change (and this) is a necessary tool to navigate the world in which we live. Many constructs exist as a means of understanding the process of positive adaptability, such as emotional intelligence, intrapersonal intelligence and resilience.*

Stride and Cutcher (2015) suggest that while creativity is accepted as a key skill for the future, and that this has been well researched and validated (NACCCE, 1999), our linear and logical world continues to promote a marginalisation of the attributes that engagement in creative activity and enterprises facilitates. A research review of policy and practice by the College Board for the National Coalition for Core Arts Standards in America (2012) reveals that at every age phase the collaborative nature of *making* creates an enabling environment for social, emotional and relational developments to occur. It is suggested that through arts subjects, teachers are naturally particularly mindful to 'facilitate a learning environment in which the students know one another, support one another, and a have a sense of shared goals and values, as such environments are conducive to learning and creativity' (2012: 56).

THE IMPACT OF PRESSURE ON TEACHERS

Where is the joy of learning?

The level of pressure for schools and teachers to perform is now negatively impacting upon teachers themselves (Smith, 1991) and the number of teachers leaving, or wanting to leave the profession is at a dangerously high level (Savage, 2017). Ask almost any teacher why they came into the profession and they will say it was because they loved the variety, creativity and dynamism that being in the classroom entails, but for those working under intense pressure to perform and comply, it becomes harder to retain the magic of what starts to feel like an idealistic notion. The pedagogist and theorist, Loris Maloguzzi, founder of the Reggio Emilia pre-schools movement in Northern Italy, once said 'Please, nothing without joy!'. Maybe we should ask ourselves: where is joy within our own curriculum?

CLASSROOM LINK

What does this mean for classroom practice?

How can you make your classroom a joyful place to learn? Do you feel excited about your lessons? Are you offering children a broad and balanced curriculum?

Charlie taught a Year 4 class and wanted to enliven and broaden the usual curriculum to make it more palatable for the children. He was familiar with the Take One Picture programme at the National Gallery, London, which encourages cross-curricular learning using a work of art as a starting point. He planned to promote learning through and in the arts in some form every day, using a different artwork as a starting point on alternate weeks to see if this would make a difference to how the children responded. Charlie felt excited by his plan and developed a series of open-ended lessons that were interesting and practical, which stimulated the children's curiosity and creativity. The children were introduced to historical and cultural concepts as well as enabled to express their own thoughts and ideas, and to communicate these in a variety of ways. Charlie was able to build in all mathematics and English learning in a natural and meaningful way and was impressed to see that the children had not only made good progress, but often went beyond his expectations.

Let's explore why this works: If you show that you are enthused and motivated, the children will pick up on that too. The atmosphere of variety, positivity and creativity facilitates a joyful learning environment where children want to learn. To understand more about Take One Picture visit: www.nationalgallery.org.uk/learning/teachers-and-schools/take-one-picture

CHAPTER SUMMARY

You can make a difference

Reflect for a moment on the reasons you came into teaching. Does this match with how you feel today? Do you offer a rounded curriculum to your class? How might you change your timetable around to ensure children have positive and meaningful experiences in the arts and other foundation subjects?

If you are feeling positive, perhaps you might think about what you are doing, or what the school is doing, to help you maintain your positive attitude. Is there something you can build upon to develop breadth and balance even more in your daily curriculum? What impact does this methodology have on the children? Can you observe their engagement and interest in the topics you are covering? How does this affect your personal philosophy in relation to your commitment to the subjects?

If your feelings are more on the negative side, then try revisiting your initial reasons for joining the profession. This might help you to analyse what needs to change in your own practice. Make a conscious decision to give space on the timetable for the arts as discrete subjects, as well as bringing in elements through cross-curricular links. What difference does this make to you and your enjoyment of your role as a teacher? What difference does this make to the children and their attitudes to learning?

(Continued)

(Continued)

Reflective questions

- How have the issues raised in this chapter affected your thinking in relation to the curriculum offered to the children in your class/school?
- Reflect upon your own education: were you prevented from taking subjects that you enjoyed? What effect do you think this has had on you and your personal attitudes towards what you think is important?
- What simple actions can you take to redress the balance of your offer?
- Which skills and what subject knowledge do you need to develop to enhance your teaching practice?
- Can you take a long hard look at where and when you can introduce lively, practical and active learning opportunities, and bring arts into your classroom?
- Can you let go of some control, and enjoy learning with the children?

ASSIGNMENTS

If you are writing an ITE assignment on teaching and learning with the broad and balanced curriculum, it will be useful for you to think through the following:

1. Can you write a rationale that explains why a broad and balanced curriculum is so important in the primary school?
2. What research can you find to validate an argument for a curriculum that is well rounded and holistic?
3. Which learning theories would you advocate so that children would get the most out of learning through a broad and balanced curriculum?

The following sources provide useful further reading:

Many schools are interested in the concept of *Growth Mindset*. Psychologist Carol Dweck introduced this with her book, *Mindset: The new psychology of success* (New York: Random House) in 2006. Dweck reminds us that intelligence is incremental rather than a fixed entity, and that learning has much to do with motivation and resilience. This theory will help you to justify ensuring breadth and balance in the curriculum that you offer.

www.childstudysystem.org/uploads/6/1/9/1/6191025/mindset_book_study.pdf

This YouTube video explains the theory visually, through graphic recording: www.youtube.com/watch?v=KUWn_TJTrnU

If you are still not entirely convinced about how important the arts are to our lives and our futures, have a look at this 2015 report, *Cultural Times - The First Global Map of Cultural and Creative Industries* (published:

France, CISAC: Ernst & Young): www.worldcreative.org

These two schools are beating a creative path for all to follow:

Plymouth School of Creative Arts:

http://plymouthschoolofcreativearts.co.uk/

West Rise Junior School

www.westrisejunior.co.uk/

There are several blogs by passionate arts-inclusive teachers, both UK-based and from the USA, with good tips on how to integrate arts into your everyday teaching. Have a look at the examples on the following websites.

http://minds-in-bloom.com/art-integration-for-classroom-teachers/

www.teachingchannel.org/blog/2013/05/17/arts-integration/

www.teachhub.com/12-ways-bring-arts-your-classroom

www.britishcouncil.org/voices-magazine/eight-steps-becoming-more-creative-teacher

REFERENCES

Addison, N. and Burgess, L. (2003) *Issues in Art and Design Teaching.* Abingdon: Routledge.

Atkinson, M. (2016) The devastating decline of the arts in schools will hit the poorest children the hardest. *Times Educational Supplement.* Available at: www.tes.com/news/school-news/breaking-views/devastating-decline-arts-schools-will-hit-poorest-children-hardest (accessed 10/07/18).

American College Board, National Coalition for Core Arts Standards in America (2012) *Child Development and Arts Education: A review of recent research and best practices.* Available at: www.nationalartsstandards.org/sites/default/files/College%20Board%20Research%20-%20Child%20Development%20Report.pdf (accessed 10/07/18).

APPG for Arts Health and Wellbeing (APPGHW) (2017) *Creative Health: The arts for health and wellbeing, inquiry report.* Available at: www.artshealthandwellbeing.org.uk/appg-inquiry/ (accessed 16/08/17).

Barnes, J. and Scoffham, S. (2017) The humanities in English primary schools: Struggling to survive. *Education 3–13*, 45: 3.

Brown, M. (2015) Arts and culture being 'systematically removed from UK education system', *The Guardian.* Available at: www.theguardian.com/education/2015/feb/17/arts-and-culture-systematically-removed-from-uk-education-system (accessed 10/07/18).

Claxton, G. and Lucas, B. (2015) *Educating Ruby: What our children really need to know.* Carmarthen: Crown House.

Clement, R. and Page, S. (1992) *Principles and Practice in Art.* Essex: Oliver & Boyd.

Cutcher, A. (2013) Art spoken here: Reggio Emilia for the big kids. *International Journal of Art and Design Education,* 9(2): 318–30.

Deasy, R.J. (ed.) (2002). *Critical Links: Learning in the arts and student academic and social development*. Washington, DC: Arts Education Partnership.

DfDCMS (2016) Creative industries worth almost £10 million an hour to economy. Available at: www.ft.com/content/cd7fec10-9eb5-11e7-8b50-0b9f565a23e1

DfE (2013) *The National Curriculum in England: Key Stages 1 and 2 framework documents*. Available at: www.gov.uk/government/publications/national-curriculum-in-england-primary-curriculum (accessed 10/07/18).

Eisner, E.W. (2002) What can education learn from the arts about the practice of education? *The Encyclopaedia of Informal Education*. Available at: www.infed.org/biblio/eisner_arts_and_the_practice_of_education.htm (accessed 10/07/18).

Hall, J. (2016) *A Broad and Balanced Curriculum: Key findings from OFSTED*. Available at: www.insidegovernment.co.uk/uploads/2016/09/joannahall-1.pdf (accessed 10/07/18).

Hallam, J., Hewitt, D. and Buxton, S. (2014) *An Exploration of Children's Experiences of Art in the Classroom*. Available at: http://web.b.ebscohost.com/ehost/pdfviewer/pdfviewer?vid=9&sid=e32a3495-9ce9-40bd-ad6c-34b356ac9e69%40sessionmgr101 (accessed 10/07/18).

Harris, M. (2017) Creative industries are growing at twice the rate of the UK economy, new figures show. Available at: www.digitalartsonline.co.uk/news/creative-business/creative-industries-are-growing-at-twice-rate-of-uk-economy-new-figures-show/

Hickman. R. (2010) *Why We Make Art, and Why it is Taught*. Bristol: Intellect.

Hutchings, M. (2015) *Exam Factories: The impact of accountability measures on children and young people*. National Union of Teachers. Available at: www.teachers.org.uk/files/exam-factories.pdf (accessed 10/07/18).

Hutchings, M. (2017) Accountability measures: The factory farm version of education. *The Psychology of Education Review*, 41(3): 15.

Irwin, M.R. (2016) Arts shoved aside: Changing art practices in primary schools since the introduction of National Standards. *International Journal of Art and Design Education*. doi:10.1111/jade.12096

Lekue, P. (2015) Artistic understanding and motivational characteristics. *International Journal of Art & Design Education*, 34(1):44-59.

Mental Health Foundation (2017) *Surviving or Thriving*? Available at: www.mentalhealth.org.uk/publications/surviving-or-thriving-state-uks-mental-health (accessed 10/07/18).

Neelands, J., Eleonora Belfiore, Catriona Firth, Natalie Hart, Liese Perrin, Susan Brock, Dominic Holdaway, Jane Woddis and John Knell (2015) *Enriching Britain: Culture, creativity and growth*. University of Warwick: The Warwick Commission. Available at: www2.warwick.ac.uk/research/warwickcommission/futureculture/finalreport/ (accessed 10/07/18).

NSEAD (National Society for Education in Art and Design) (2016) *Survey Report 2015–16*. Available at: nsead.org/downloads/survey.pdf (accessed 11/10/16).

Paton, G. (2014) Nicky Morgan: Pupils 'held back' by overemphasis on arts. *The Telegraph*, 10 November. Available at: www.telegraph.co.uk/education/educationnews/11221081/Nicky-Morgan-pupils-held-back-by-overemphasis-on-arts.html (accessed 10/07/18).

Robinson, K. (2006) Do schools kill creativity?, TED. Available at: www.ted.com/talks/ken_robinson_says_schools_kill_creativity?language=en

Savage, M. (2017) Almost a quarter of teachers who have qualified since 2011 have left profession. *The Guardian*, 8 July. Available at: www.theguardian.com/education/2017/jul/08/almost-a-quarter-of-teachers-who-have-qualified-since-2011-have-left-profession (accessed 12/07/18).

Sharp, P. (2001) Nurturing emotional literacy: A practical guide for teachers, parents and those in the caring professions, *Health Education*, 101(6): 292–94.

Smith, M. (1991) Put to the Test: The Effects of External Testing on Teachers. *Educational Researcher*, 20(5): 8–11.

Stride, Y., and Cutcher, A. (2015) Manifesting resilience in the secondary school: An investigation of the relationship dynamic in Visual Arts classrooms. *International Journal of Education and the Arts*, 16(11). Available at: www.ijea.org/v16n11/ (accessed 10/07/18).

Thomas, J. (2015) Make do and mend approach in education is failing children. *The Telegraph*, 16 November. Available at: www.telegraph.co.uk/education/educationopinion/11995597/Julian-Thomas-Make-do-and-mend-approach-in-education-is-failing-children.html (accessed: 21/11/17).

Watts, R. (2005) Attitudes to making art in the primary school. *International Journal of Art & Design Education*, 24(3): 243–53.

Weale, S. (2017) More primary school children suffering stress from Sats, survey finds. *The Guardian*, 1 May. Available at: www.theguardian.com/education/2017/may/01/sats-primary-school-children-suffering-stress-exam-time (accessed 10/07/18).

- [ ] Have you noticed a change in a child's typical behaviour?
- [ ] How long has this change in behaviour occurred for?
- [ ] How are the behaviours impacting on the child's ability to participate fully in school (do consider academic and recreational aspects of school life)?

32

WHY DO TEACHERS NEED TO KNOW ABOUT CHILD MENTAL HEALTH?

Sarah Adams is a specialist in primary education, teacher training at the School of Education, University of Leicester.

Dr Michelle O'Reilly is a specialist in qualitative methods and childhood studies at the School of Media, Communication and Sociology and School of Psychology, University of Leicester, and Leicestershire Partnership NHS Trust.

Dr Khalid Karim is a Consultant Psychiatrist and specialist in working with schools for the University of Leicester School of Psychology and Leicestershire Partnership NHS Trust.

Today, organisations are recognising an increasing prevalence of mental health problems in school-aged children and consequently, governments are expressing greater commitment to tackling this issue. There is a greater emphasis now on promoting positive mental health, preventing the development of conditions and treating mental illness. Schools are at the forefront of addressing the issue. In this chapter, Sarah, Michelle and Khalid focus on some of the core issues related to child mental health, and introduce key concepts and ideas for the field. This introduction to mental health and illness in primary-aged school children provides a foundation information guide for teachers new to this issue.

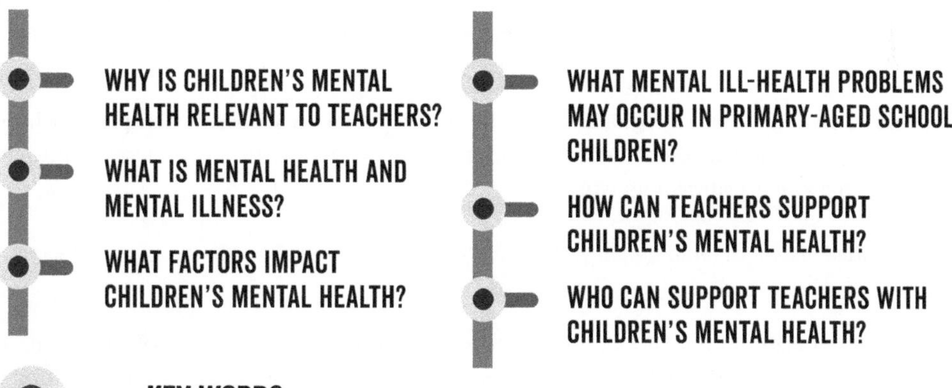

KEY WORDS

- Adults
- Children
- Diagnosis
- Difficulties
- Experiencing
- Health
- Mental health
- Mental illness
- Problem
- Professional
- Resilience
- School
- Support
- Teacher
- Well-being

WHY IS CHILDREN'S MENTAL HEALTH RELEVANT TO TEACHERS?

Children's mental health has attracted increasing attention from policy makers and the media worldwide. In the UK, it is generally accepted that 10% of children and young people, one in three in an average sized classroom, have a diagnosable mental health difficulty and that the likelihood of the onset of a mental health condition increases as the child gets older (Green *et al.*, 2005). An estimated 50% of adults with mental health difficulties reported that they first experienced these before the age of 15 years old (Kessler *et al*, 2005). Collaboration between the Department of Health and Social Care and the Department for Education (2017) recognises that preventive action and early intervention are important measures to reduce the number of children and subsequently adults from experiencing mental health difficulties.

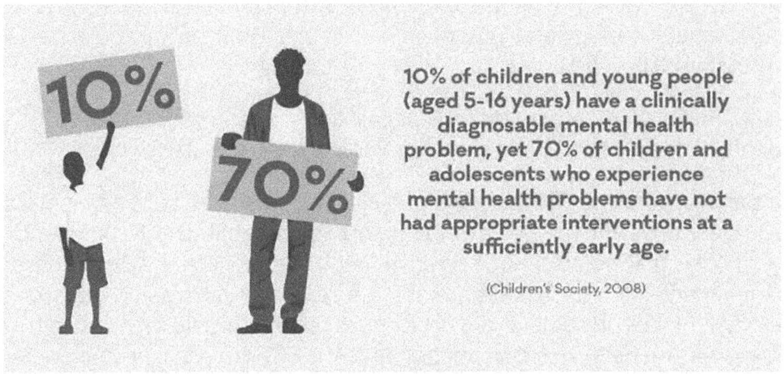

Figure 32.1 The prevalence of mental health issues in children and young people

(Source: Mental Health Foundation: www.mentalhealth.org.uk)

Children and young people spend a considerable amount of their time in school, which places schools in a strong position to support holistic development (Humphrey and Wigelsworth, 2016). One of the statutory roles of a teacher is to provide a curriculum which

> *promotes the spiritual, moral, cultural, mental and physical development of pupils at the school and of society*
>
> (DfE, 2014)

Internationally, and especially in the UK, schools are being positioned at the forefront of supporting mental health (Weare, 2010; DoH and DfE, 2017) which recognises that academic attainment can work in harmony with mental health development. Research has shown that children with good mental health achieve better outcomes in school, which ultimately promotes better life outcomes (Public Health England, 2014).

A recent DoH and DfE, 2017 Green Paper advocates that teachers have a responsibility to promote positive mental health while also having skills to identify signs of mental ill-health and know what to do to offer support. It is, therefore, important that teachers develop a knowledge and understanding of mental health in relation to children.

WHAT IS MENTAL HEALTH AND MENTAL ILLNESS?

CRITICAL QUESTION

How you would define the term 'mental health'? What words come to mind?

'Mental health' is a complex term and there are no universally agreed definitions. Typically, when the term is considered, people often conflate health and illness. For example, when asked to define mental health, often people describe mental ill health, for example, depression and anxiety, which may mean being mentally healthy is forgotten about (Pilgrim, 2017).

CRITICAL QUESTION

What does it mean to be in 'good mental health'?

This is especially true when asking children and young people to define mental health (Bone *et al.*, 2015), as they often use quite negative terminology (O'Reilly *et al.*, 2009; Rose *et al.*, 2007). However, the differentiation between being mentally healthy and mentally unwell is an important one.

The World Health Organisation (WHO) define mental health as:

> *Mental health is defined as a state of well-being in which every individual realizes his or her own potential, can cope with the normal stresses of life, can work productively and fruitfully, and is able to make a contribution to her or his community.*
>
> (WHO, 2014)

This stance promotes the positive aspects of having good mental health.

As a teacher, it is important to be able to find ways to promote positive mental health and recognise any ill aspects of mental health in the children in your care. Perhaps one of the challenges to this is being able to make a distinction between what emotions a child would be expected to experience as part of normal development and when it may raise some concern. Children, just like adults, feel a range of emotions, for example, happy, sad, angry and worried. Emotions can change throughout the day and more than one emotion can be felt at any one time. Emotions can also have different levels of intensities, for example, sad might be described as gloomy, down, blue or depressed. Depending on their developmental ability, children sometimes find it difficult to articulate their emotions to others.

The lay use of the concept 'depressed' is often muddled with the medical concept of clinical depression. Feeling depressed can mean you feel unhappy and are unable to enjoy activities. It is okay, and often natural to feel depressed sometimes, and would be a very normal response to certain life events, perhaps the death of a pet or a best friend moving school. Clinical depression is more profound however, and is a condition whereby an individual experiences the emotional state for a sustained period of time, sometimes with or without an obvious external cause, and is an emotional state that it is significantly impacting on their quality of life. The boundaries between typical and atypical mental health are not always clear-cut and to some extent are subjective, which makes it challenging to make a distinction between the two.

You may find it helpful to think of mental health as a continuum ranging from mental illness to positive mental health.

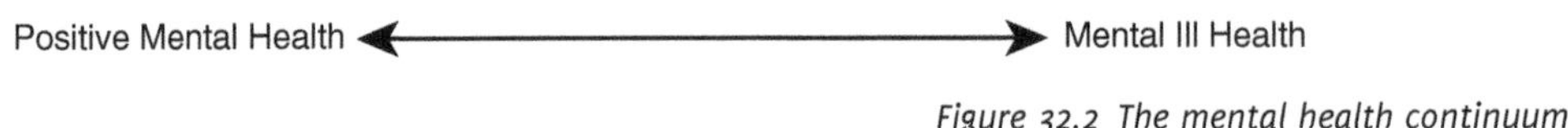

Figure 32.2 The mental health continuum

CRITICAL QUESTION

Think of children you have taught in your classrooms. Where might you place them on the continuum?

One of the challenges in considering children's mental health needs is they can often complain of somatic symptoms, e.g. headaches, tummy aches and feeling nauseous. Children may not have acquired the language to fully explain their emotions and cognition, which may mean they find it easier to explain the physical symptoms they are experiencing.

If a child has a positive mental health, they should have positive well-being, be thriving and be able to cope with their day-to-day demands both inside and outside of school. At the other end of the continuum a child displaying signs of mental ill-health will have low well-being, will not be thriving and struggle to cope with their daily lives. There will, of course, be children at different points on the continuum and this is changeable with many different factors affecting a child's mental health.

WHAT FACTORS IMPACT CHILDREN'S MENTAL HEALTH?

Mental health is complex and there are many factors that may impact on a child's mental health, either beneficially or detrimentally. It may be helpful to consider factors from the following perspectives:

Weerasekera (1996) proposed a useful framework for considering the mental health needs of children by taking into account four factors:

- Predisposing – factors more likely to make a child vulnerable to mental ill-health.
- Precipitating – factors that occur just before that may be a trigger to mental ill-health.

- Perpetuating – factors which increase the likelihood of mental ill-health reoccurring.
- Protective – factors which reduce the likelihood of the occurrence of mental ill-health.

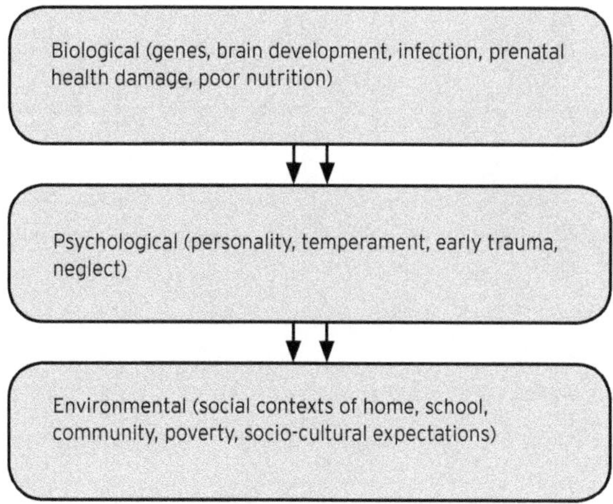

	Examples		
Factors	**Biological**	**Psychological**	**Environmental**
Predisposing	Genetics Medical condition	Learned helplessness Low self-esteem	Social deprivation Poor family relationships
Precipitating	Infection/illness	Low academic achievement	Conflicts with family/peers/ teachers Bullying Abuse and/or neglect
Perpetuating	Chronic illness Disability	Repeated sense of failure at school	Ongoing conflicts Ongoing poor relationships Unresolved bullying Ongoing abuse and/or neglect
Protective	Good health Genetics	Good coping strategies School satisfaction Positive self-esteem	Positive relationships

Weerasekera acknowledged that factors impacting on a child's mental health can be within and outside of the child. Brofenbrenner's (1979) ecological systems usefully explains that a child operates in relation to the different systems they interact with. A simplified version is demonstrated in Figure 32.3.

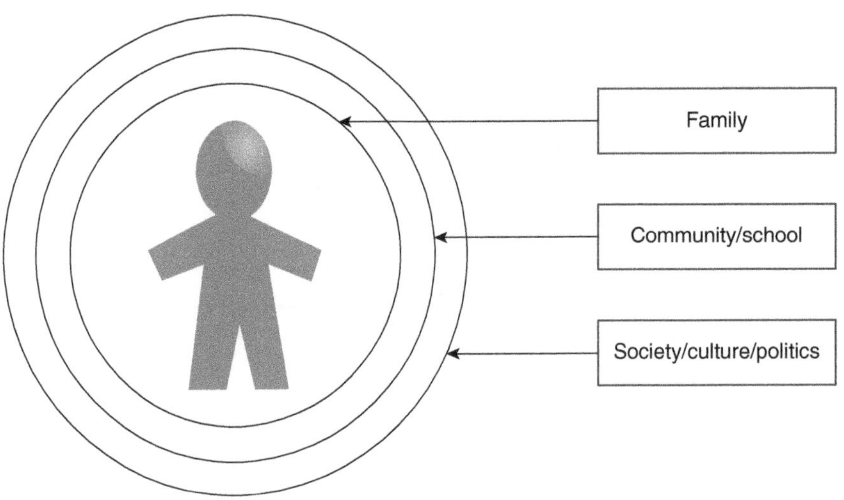

Figure 32.3 Systems of children's interaction

Factors within and outside the child reflect the elements of biopsychosocial influences and it is generally accepted that there is an interplay between biological, psychological and social factors (Wade and Halligan, 2017).

KEY READING

To further develop your understanding of the factors that can impact on a child's mental health, you can refer to DfE (2016) Mental Health and Behaviour in Schools document, which provides a useful table on the risk and protective factors for child mental health. Available at:

www.gov.uk/government/publications/mental-health-and-behaviour-in-schools--2

You should also note that not all children who have known risk factors that may predispose them to mental health difficulties will go on to experience these. A child's resiliency is also an important factor to consider (Rutter, 1985).

WHAT MENTAL ILL-HEALTH PROBLEMS MAY OCCUR IN PRIMARY-AGED SCHOOL CHILDREN?

Children may present with a wide range of mental health difficulties, some which occur in adults and some which are more specific to childhood. Common mental illnesses in children range from:

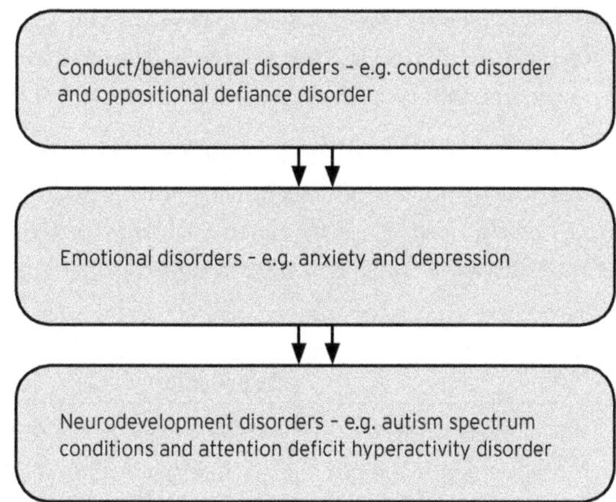

Children may present in more than one area and may have co-existing difficulties.

Other behaviours that may occur in younger children that affect mental health and reflect more emotional states, but which are not clinically recognised independently as mental illness are substance abuse, self-harm and suicidal thoughts and suicide.

In primary-aged children it has been noted that boys are more likely to experience mental illness than girls and that the likelihood of onset increases with age (Green *et al.*, 2005).

While we recognise that there are a broad range of conditions that primary-aged children can experience, there is not room to deal with them all in this chapter, and we would encourage you to do more reading in this area. However, to introduce you to some of the common difficulties experienced in this age group, we provide a brief introduction to some of the conditions or related issues that you may come across in your daily work and how to spot indicators of a mental illness.

CONDUCT DISORDER

Conduct disorders in children present as aggressive and destructive behaviours. While it is normal for children to act out, when these behaviours become persistent and are consistently breaking societal norms and harming others, it may highlight that the child has a conduct disorder. This is more prevalent in boys than girls. Conduct disorders are often viewed as especially problematic in the school classroom, as these children can be disruptive and challenging to teach.

EMOTIONAL DISORDERS

Common emotional disorders that may occur in children are anxiety and depression. The two disorders can also co-exist.

As discussed earlier, feeling depressed can be very normal; the same applies to anxiety. Feeling worried and anxious are normal feelings and can be considered a protective factor in some situations. For example, you may start to feel anxious if there is a perceived threat, which may mean you adapt your behaviour in order to keep safe. Children often have typical childhood anxieties such as fear of the dark, monsters under the bed, and animals such as dogs and horses, and will typically grow out of these without causing too much distress.

Anxiety and depression become problematic when the worrying and feelings of sadness become persistent and are excessively out of proportion to the context a child is within, and it is impacting on their ability to function in their daily life. Drawing from the National Health Service (NHS, 2017a and 2017b) guidelines, the following table has been created to help you spot the indicators of anxiety and depression.

	Anxiety	**Depression**
Signs to notice	• finding it hard to concentrate • not sleeping, or waking in the night with bad dreams • not eating properly • quickly getting angry or irritable, and being out of control during outbursts • constantly worrying or having negative thoughts • feeling tense and fidgety, or using the toilet often • always crying • being clingy • complaining of tummy aches and feeling unwell	• sadness, or a low mood that doesn't go away • being irritable or grumpy all the time • not being interested in things they used to enjoy • feeling tired and exhausted a lot of the time • having trouble sleeping or sleeping more than usual • not being able to concentrate • interacting less with friends and family • being indecisive • not having much confidence • eating less than usual or overeating • having big changes in weight • seeming unable to relax or being more lethargic than usual • talking about feeling guilty or worthless • feeling empty or unable to feel emotions (numb) • having thoughts about suicide or self-harming • actually self-harming, for example, cutting their skin or taking on overdose

NEURODEVELOPMENT DISORDERS

AUTISM SPECTRUM CONDITIONS

These are conceptualised as autism spectrum disorder in clinical manuals, but we favour the less negative notion of 'condition'. Historically, Autistic Spectrum Condition (ASC) was characterised by a triad of impairments, which were impairments in social interaction, in communication, and the presence of repetitive and restrictive behaviours, but recently these were integrated into two broad domains by DSM-5 (American Psychiatric Association, 2013) as:

- difficulties in social communication;
- restrictive and repetitive patterns of behaviour.

Children with an ASC may engage in ritualistic behaviours and have difficulties understanding and interpreting metaphorical language, e.g. 'it's raining cats and dogs'. Diagnosis of autism has steadily increased over the years, with ASC being the most common primary need for those children with a statement of special educational needs or an Educational Health Care Plan (EHCP) at 26.9 per cent (DfE, 2017a).

ATTENTION DEFICIT HYPERACTIVITY DISORDER (ADHD)

Similarly to ASC, diagnosis of ADHD in children has also been increasing. ADHD is characterised by:

- inattentiveness;
- impulsiveness and hyperactivity.

The NHS (2016) describes typical indicators of ADHD, which occur at both home and school as follows:

Inattentiveness	Impulsiveness and Hyperactivity
• having a short attention span and being easily distracted • making careless mistakes - for example, in schoolwork • appearing forgetful or losing things • being unable to stick at tasks that are tedious or time-consuming • appearing to be unable to listen to or carry out instructions • constantly changing activity or task • having difficulty organising tasks	• being unable to sit still, especially in calm or quiet surroundings • constantly fidgeting • being unable to concentrate on tasks • excessive physical movement • excessive talking • being unable to wait their turn • acting without thinking • interrupting conversations • little or no sense of danger

It is important to note that ASC and ADHD may also co-exist. Children with these diagnoses are also more likely to experience symptoms of anxiety and depression, but these can be missed due to their primary classification (NHS 2017b).

SELF-HARM

The National Institute Clinical Excellence (NICE, 2004: 16) defines self-harm as:

> *self-poisoning or self-injury, irrespective of the apparent purpose of the act.*

The DfE (2016: 49) suggests common examples of deliberate self-harm in school-age children:

> *include "overdosing" (self-poisoning), hitting, cutting or burning oneself, pulling hair or picking skin, or self-strangulation.*

Self-harm in primary age school has attracted media attention, with schools leaders reporting an increase in this type of behaviour in the primary school age range (Key, 2017). This is also reflected in admissions to A&E (Morgan *et al.*, 2017).

However, it would be more useful to consider these behaviours as 'in need of attention' with the aim of understanding what is triggering and driving the harmful behaviours, so that the appropriate support and help can be put in place.

DIAGNOSING MENTAL ILL-HEALTH

Remember, only those qualified to do so can diagnose a mental illness. Medical professions will need to consider other alternatives to mental illness to rule out any underlying medical illness, which may present similar symptoms. If you do have concerns about a child's mental health, it is important that these are raised with the appropriate members of staff in school and to work in partnership with the child's parents/carers to discuss further and gain greater insight, unless there are any safeguarding concerns, which should be reported to the Designated Senior Safeguarding Lead in your school.

HOW CAN TEACHERS SUPPORT CHILDREN'S MENTAL HEALTH?

The DfE (2017b: 6) research revealed that schools felt that they could support children's mental health by:

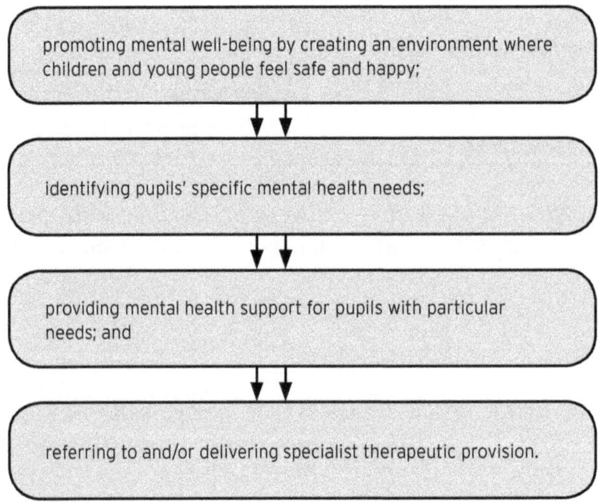

As a teacher, it is important you develop safe and trusting relationships with the children in your class to optimise their chances of thriving.

This includes providing opportunities to help develop children's social and emotional literacy.

IDENTIFYING CHILDREN'S MENTAL HEALTH NEEDS

Identifying children's mental health needs is an important aspect of classroom teaching. Fundamentally poor mental health can negatively impact on children's academic attainment and life chances (PHE, 2014).

INFO 32.1

As a teacher, you are in a prime position to notice changes to a child's behaviour and the impact that this is having at school, both academically and socially. As discussed earlier, there are indicators that may suggest that a child is experiencing mental ill health. Helpful questions to ask yourself are:

- Have you noticed a change in a child's typical behaviour? Are they acting out more or are they more withdrawn?
- How long has this change in behaviour occurred for?
- How are the behaviours impacting on the child's ability to participate fully in school (do consider academic and recreational aspects of school life)?

KEY READING

You may also consider completing a Strengths and Difficulties Questionnaire, which is free to access at: www.sdqinfo.com, to support you in identifying any difficulties.

PROVIDING MENTAL HEALTH SUPPORT FOR CHILDREN WITH PARTICULAR NEEDS

To meet the mental health needs of children, most educational systems adopt a graduated/tiered approach (Weare and Nind, 2011).

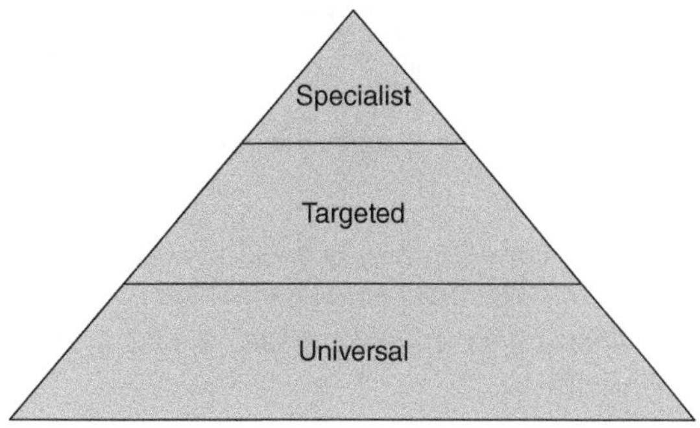

Figure 32.4 A graduated approach

Humphrey and Wigelsworth (2016) suggested the following:

UNIVERSAL LEVEL

The mental health provision is designed to reach all children to equip them with the intra- and inter-personal skills to aid resilience and prevent the likelihood of a mental illness occurring.

TARGETED LEVEL

The mental health provision targets those children who are at risk of developing a mental illness due to presenting symptoms.

SPECIALIST LEVEL

The mental health provision is designed to support children with identified mental illnesses and will usually be designed in collaboration with the advice of more specialists services.

A recent review of universal approaches to promoting mental health in schools demonstrated that involving a

CRITICAL QUESTION

Consider what the universal offer might be in your school. Is there a whole-school approach?

range of people in mental health is very important, including families, communities, layers of school personnel and, most importantly, the child (O'Reilly *et al.*, 2018).

One useful strategy for schools is to dedicate set time through the delivery of PSHE. The PSHE association is a useful resource for curriculum guidance and resources. Additionally, the Anna Freud National Centre for Children and Families has also produced a toolkit for primary school teaching on how to talk about mental health in schools.

Schools may also adopt particular approaches, for example:

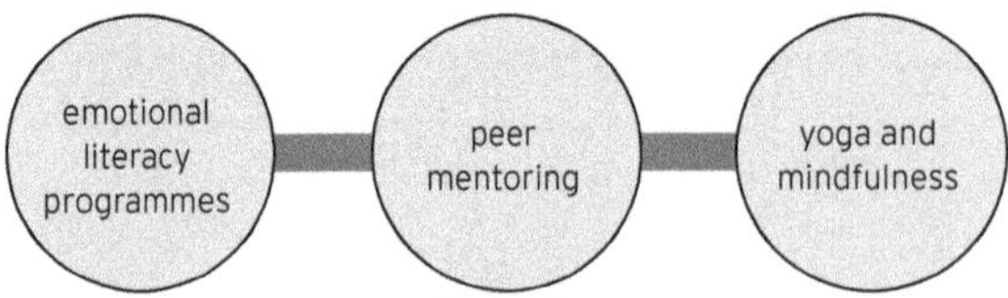

We (the authors of this chapter) are undertaking research suggesting that social media might be more positively harnessed in conjunction with schools.

For an overview of the types of interventions that may be used in schools, you may find it useful to refer to DfE (2017c) *to SEN support: A rapid evidence assessment research report (DfE, 2017c: 50–9).* Clarke *et al.* (2015) have also provided a review of evidenced-based interventions used in UK schools to enhance social and emotional development in children and adolescents.

At the specialist level whereby children have diagnosed disorders, or you feel you need a diagnosis, schools should refer for extra support from multi-agencies.

WHO CAN SUPPORT TEACHERS IN SCHOOLS WITH CHILDREN'S MENTAL HEALTH?

There are different professionals with responsibility for supporting children's mental health needs, which range from school nurses, GPs, counsellors, clinical or educational psychologists and child psychiatrists. The government is currently investing in training mental health champions within the education environment, with the aim for all schools to have a champion by 2023 (DoH and DfE, 2017).

Schools, with agreement with the child's parents/carers, can refer to services available in their area for additional support. Referrals should clearly state the concerns about the child and how it is impacting, and evidence of support that the school has provided and what impact this has had. We offer a reflection from one of the authors of this chapter in his capacity as a child and adolescent psychiatrist in the box below on how schools can help children.

CLASSROOM LINK

What does this mean for classroom practice?

Reflection from a child psychiatrist about how schools can support children's mental health

Dr Khalid Karim, Child and Adolescent Psychiatrist

In my experience, schools play an essential role in supporting children in both primary and secondary school. It is freely accepted that there are many factors that have a considerable effect on children, including poverty, the challenges of having a parent with their own mental health problem or substance abuse problem: and how this affects the child's stability and ability to develop emotionally and behaviourally. Schools therefore have the potential to provide an alternative environment where children can be safe and nurtured, which is especially important when the child spends so much time there. Due to this close relationship, a teacher can develop a unique understanding about a child, which is hard to replicate by other professionals, and this provides opportunities to identify problems early, especially mental health problems. I have seen excellent examples of this in schools, but I am also aware that teachers are concerned about the growing numbers of children in primary school with mental health difficulties, especially anxiety. Teachers have told me that they often feel uncomfortable in dealing with mental health problems as they worry they will make it worse or are not sure how to progress, particularly if a parental difficulty underpins the issue, and this is entirely understandable. Schools as organisations need to take this area seriously in order to support the children and staff.

I have always valued the perspective of the teacher on a child and generally we agree on a way forward, but even if there are difference the child remains upmost in the consideration of all involved. As a child psychiatrist, I wish I could work closer with schools and teacher and there is clearly much we can teach each other about children - but the most important element that is common to all good outcomes for children has been good communication between the professionals. This is from your first description of your concerns right through to understanding how everyone should be working with a particular child.

KEY READING

What about a teacher's mental health?

While the aim of this chapter was to explore child mental health, we acknowledge that maintaining teachers' positive mental health and well-being is of equal importance. It is well recognised that teaching can in some ways be a stressful role, and therefore inevitably has some impact on teachers. Arguably, to provide the best possible educational outcomes for children, this is best delivered by teachers who are mentally healthy.

For those of you who are interested, the Mental Health Foundation has a brief and enlightening survey for you to 'Find out your good mental health score'. Of course, this is just a short snapshot survey, but the questions prompt you to consider areas of your own mental health and can be a good starting point for thinking about good mental health. It is available at: www.mentalhealth.org.uk/your-mental-health/good-mental-health-survey

We recognise that most teachers cope well in the profession and find ways to cope with the demands and stresses of the job. However, life events, coupled with job stress, or other adverse circumstances, may for some, mean that managing can be difficult. If you are concerned about your own mental health, we would advise seeking support from your GP. Your own school or training provider should also have guidance about the support available to you as an employee/student.

CHAPTER SUMMARY

Child mental health is a complex and multifaceted issue. In this chapter we have aimed to provide you with a brief introduction of key concepts and policies related to child mental health, how mental illness may present in primary-aged children and how schools may support children's mental health. We would encourage you to extend your knowledge and understanding by reading the key readings mentioned throughout the chapter and critically reflect on our own experiences and how you, as a teacher going forward, would like to support children's mental health. Do also remember that while teachers have been positioned at the forefront of promoting children's positive mental health and reducing ill mental health, where children's needs are complex, a multi-agency approach is required.

ASSIGNMENTS

If you are writing an ITE assignment on children's mental health in schools, it will be useful for you to think through the following:

1. Is mental health in children on the increase? Why do you think this?
2. What mental health problems occur in primary-aged children? What might be the impact on classroom practice?
3. To what extent can teachers support children's mental health in schools?

Useful resources

Anna Freud Talking Mental Health Animation and Toolkit:

www.annafreud.org/what-we-do/schools-in-mind/youre-never-too-young-to-talk-mental-health/talking-mental-health-animation-teacher-toolkit/

Minded – free e-learning modules for educational professionals: www.minded.org.uk/

PSHE Association: www.pshe-association.org.uk/

REFERENCES

American Psychiatric Association (2013) *Diagnostic and Statistical Manual of Mental Disorders* (5th edn) (*DSM-5*). Washington, DC.

Bone, C., Dugard, P., Vostanis, P. and Dogra, N. (2015) Students' understandings of mental health and their preferred learning platforms. *Journal of Public Mental Health,* 14(4): 185–95.

Bronfenbrenner, U. (1979).*The Ecology of Human Development: Experiments by nature and design.* Cambridge, MA: Harvard University Press.

Clarke, A., Morreale, S., Field, C., Hussein, Y. and Barry, M. (2015) *What works in enhancing social and emotional skills development during childhood and adolescence? A review of the evidence on the effectiveness of school-based and out-of-school programmes in the UK.* A report produced by the World Health Organization Collaborating Centre for Health Promotion Research, National University of Ireland Galway.

Department for Education (DfE) (2014) *The National Curriculum in England: Framework document.* Available at: www.gov.uk/government/uploads/system/uploads/attachment_data/file/381344/Master_final_national_curriculum_28_Nov.pdf (accessed: 12/07/18).

Department for Education (DfE) (2016) *Mental Health and Behaviour in Schools: Departmental advice for school staff.* Available at: www.gov.uk/government/uploads/system/uploads/attachment_data/file/508847/Mental_Health_and_Behaviour_-_advice_for_Schools_160316.pdf (accessed: 12/07/18).

Department for Education (2017a) Special education needs in England: January. Available at: www.gov.uk/government/statistics/special-educational-needs-in-england-january-2017 (accessed: 12/07/18).

Department for Education (2017b) Supporting mental health in schools and colleges summary report. NatCen Social Research & the National Children's Bureau Research and Policy Team. Available at: https://assets.publishing.service.gov.uk/government/uploads/system/uploads/attachment_data/file/634725/Supporting_Mental-Health_synthesis_report.pdf (accessed: 12/07/18).

Department for Education (2017c) SEN support: A rapid evidence assessment: Research report. Available at: https://assets.publishing.service.gov.uk/government/uploads/system/uploads/attachment_data/file/628630/DfE_SEN_Support_REA_Report.pdf (accessed: 12/07/18).

Department of Health & Department for Education (2017) *Transforming Children and Young People's Mental Health Provision: A Green Paper*. Available at: www.gov.uk/government/uploads/system/uploads/attachment_data/file/664855/Transforming_children_and_young_people_s_mental_health_provision.pdf (accessed: 12/07/18).

Green, H., McGinnity, A., Meltzer, H., Ford, T. and Goodman, R (2005) *Mental Health of Children and Young People in Great Britain, 2004*. Basingstoke: Palgrave Macmillan.

Humphrey, N. and Wigelsworth, M. (2016) Making the case for the universal mental health screening. *Emotional and Behavioural Difficulties*, 21(1): 22–42.

Kessler, R., Berglund, O., Demler, R., Jin, R. and Walters, E. (2005) Lifetime prevalence and age-of-onset distributions of DSM-IV disorders in the National Comorbidity Survey Replication. *Archives of General Psychiatry*, 62: 593–602.

The Key (2017) *State of Education Survey Report 2017: Rising to the challenge: Examining the pressures of schools and how they are responding*. Available at: https://view.joomag.com/state-of-education-report-2017/0676372001494577623 (accessed: 12/07/18).

Morgan, C., Webb, R., Kontopantelis, E., Green, J., Chew-Graham, C., Kapur, N. and Ashcroft, D. (2017) Incidence, clinical management, and mortality risk following self-harm among children and adolescents: Cohort in primary care. *British Medical Journal*, 359: 4351

National Institute for Health and Care Excellence (2004) *Self-harm: The short-term physical and psychological management and secondary prevention of self-harm in primary and secondary care*. London: British Psychological Society.

National Health Service (2016) *Attention Deficient Hyperactive Disorder*. Available at: www.nhs.uk/conditions/attention-deficit-hyperactivity-disorder-adhd/symptoms/ (accessed: 12/07/18).

National Health Service (2017a) *Anxiety Disorders in Children*. Available at: www.nhs.uk/conditions/anxiety-disorders-in-children/#symptoms-of-anxiety-in-children (accessed: 12/07/18).

National Health Service (2017b) *Depression in Children and Teenagers*. Available at: www.nhs.uk/conditions/stress-anxiety-depression/children-depressed-signs/ (accessed: 12/07/18).

O'Reilly, M., Svirydzenka, N., Adams, S. and Dogra, N. (2018) Review of mental health promotion in schools. *Social Psychiatry and Psychiatric Epidemiology*.

O'Reilly, M., Taylor, H. and Vostanis, P. (2009) 'Nuts, schiz, psycho': An exploration of young homeless people's perceptions and dilemmas of defining mental health. *Social Science and Medicine*, 68: 1737–44.

Pilgrim, D. (2017) *Key Concepts in Mental Health* (4*th* edn). London: Sage

Public Health England (PHE) (2014) *The Link between Pupil Health and Well-being and Attainment: A briefing for head teachers, governors and staff in education settings*. London: Public Health England.

Rose, D., Thornicroft, G., Pinfold, V. and Kassam, A. (2007) 250 labels used to stigmatise people with mental illness. *BMC Health Services Research*, 7: 97–104.

Rutter, M. (1985) Resilience in the face of adversity. Protective factors and resistance to psychiatric disorder. *British Journal of Psychiatry*, 147: 598–611.

Wade, D. and Halligan, P. (2017) The biopsychosocial model of illness: A model whose time has come. *Clinical Rehabilitation*, 31(8): 995–1004

Weare, K. (2010) Mental health and social and emotional learning: Evidence, principles, tensions, balances, advances. *School Mental Health Promotion*, 3(1): 5–17.

Weare, K. and Nind, M. (2011) Mental health promotion and prevention in schools: What does the evidence say? *Health Promotion International*, 26(1): i29–69.

Weerasekera, P. (1996) *Multiperspective Case Formulation: A step towards treatment inegratation.* Malabar: Krieger Publishing Company.

World Health Organization (2014) *Mental Health: A state of well-being.* Available at: www.who.int/features/factfiles/mental_health/en/ (accessed: 12/07/18).

PART 5

BUILDING A CAREER

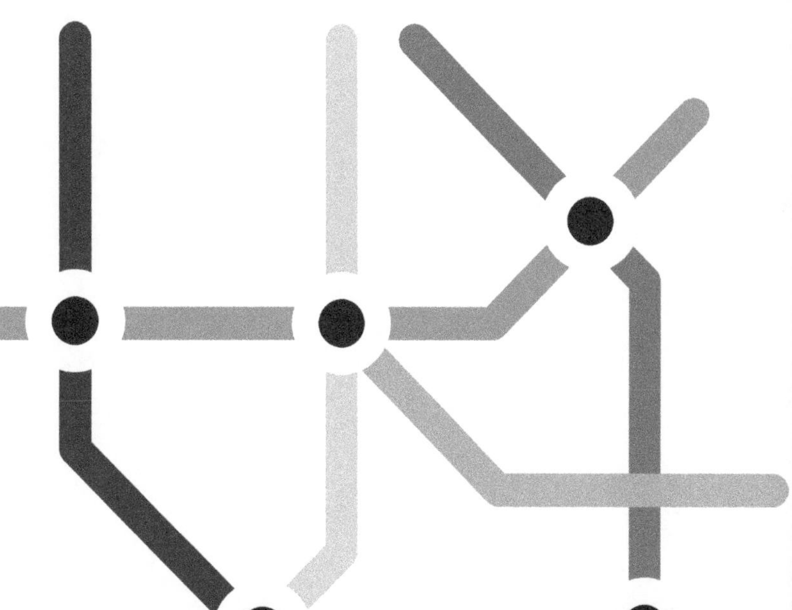

33

WHAT NEXT? BEGINNING TEACHING AND MOVING FORWARD

Lucy Barker is senior lecturer and NQT lead at Northumbria University. Her research interests are SEND and inclusive practice; trainee teachers and teaching assistants; continuous professional development (CPD).

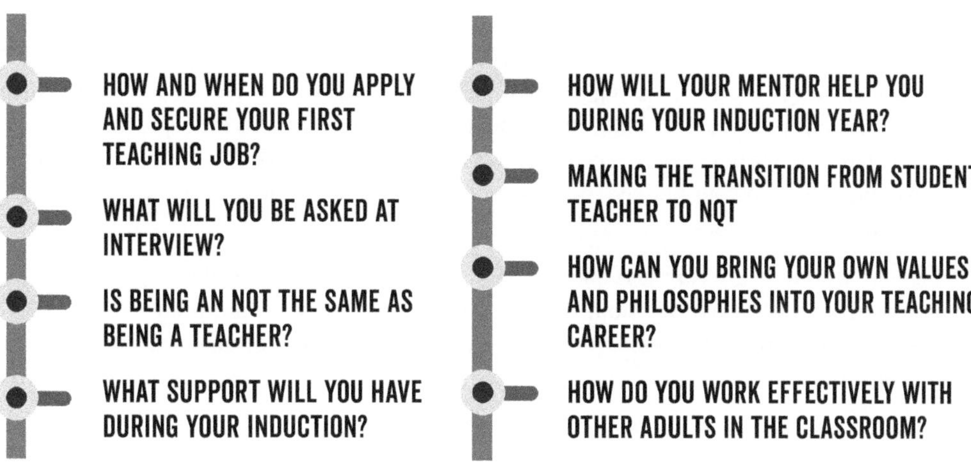

KEY WORDS

- Application
- Identity
- Interview
- Job
- Mentor
- NQT
- Professionalism
- Reflective practice
- Teaching assistants

INTRODUCTION

This chapter explores life after your training. It begins with your future steps and asks how you apply for a job. It then goes on to cover your induction year and the support you should receive from your mentor. The chapter continues by looking at how to develop your teacher identity, and how collaboration and working with other adults in the classroom is achieved. By the end of the chapter you will have a good understanding of what the NQT induction year is about and you will be ready to start your first job.

HOW AND WHEN DO YOU APPLY AND SECURE YOUR FIRST TEACHING JOB?

Should you take the first job that is offered? Or be more discerning in your first choice of teaching position?

Securing your first teaching job and becoming a newly qualified teacher (NQT) is an exciting but perhaps formidable task. Think about your first job while still studying. Many appointments for September NQT jobs are posted as early as January. Speak to your placements schools (if you had a good experience). Sign up to job websites and get email alerts to your phone. Think about moving further afield, as many parts of the country have teacher recruitment shortages.

Many teaching jobs are temporary contracts and the NQT year is sometimes akin to a long interview process. New teachers have to contribute usefully from the start and make an impression quickly (Newton, 2015). To some extent, an NQT is untried. Head teachers and governors have to look for qualities, highlighted in the application process.

Research the school via its website and consider what kind of school it is and whether you will fit in.

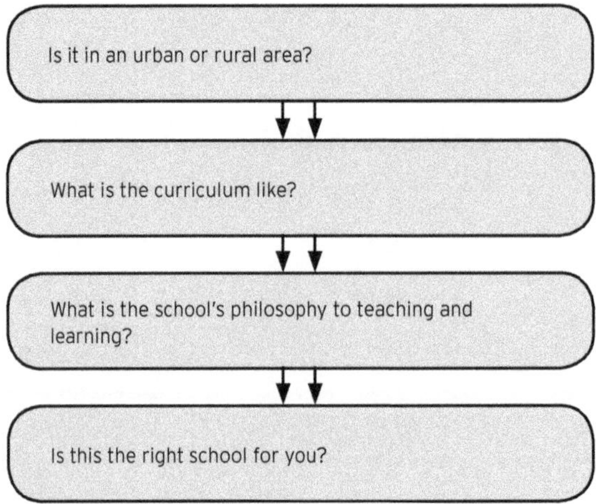

If the school does a lot of outdoor learning and you don't own a pair of wellies, you may consider applying elsewhere! Make an appointment to visit the school and have a guided tour. Ask questions while you are there to get a feel for the school ethos.

YOUR ONLINE FOOTPRINT

Before applying, consider your online profile and check your digital footprint. Are your Facebook and Twitter pages private? Delete any photos on your social media sites that you would not want a future employer to see and ask your friends to seek your permission before tagging you in any of their photos.

YOUR APPLICATION

Tailor your application to the school. Look carefully at the job description and write about how you meet the criteria. Your application will be discarded if there are errors, so have someone proofread it for you. Newton (2015) carried out research, regarding the views on what counts when selecting a new teacher. The head teachers and student teachers in the study had similar ideas. Both groups felt that enthusiasm was the most important quality to have, closely followed by a variety of communication skills (interpersonal, oral, listening, and writing). 'Most of these qualities are probably more readily considered at interview, although enthusiasm may be evident in an applicant's letter of application – as, of course, should be their writing skills' (Newton, 2015: 11).

WHAT WILL YOU BE ASKED AT INTERVIEW?

CRITICAL QUESTION

Can you talk about your own philosophies of teaching and learning? Will you be ready to answer a question on this at interview?

Dress for success; wear smart clothes that you feel comfortable in. If you are asked to do a lesson as part of the interview, keep it simple and use a learning objective. Have a 'plan B' in place in case the technology doesn't work, and try and 'hook' the pupils immediately into learning with either a picture or an artefact or some active learning. Use some of the names of the children to show that you can build relationships and engage effectively with pupils.

The panel interviewing you will be made up of the head teacher and some of the governors. It is likely that you will be asked about your strengths and weaknesses, what an outstanding lesson entails, and your own philosophy of learning and how it fits with the school. Tell them about your subject strengths and offer your support to extra-curricular clubs.

They will also ask you about safeguarding the pupils.

KEY READING

You can find out more about safeguarding in schools via the following websites:

Keeping Children Safe in Education:

www.gov.uk/government/publications/keeping-children-safe-in-education--2

NSPCC:

www.nspcc.org.uk/preventing-abuse/safeguarding/

Prepare your answers to interview questions by reviewing material from your training and your assignments, but also speak from the heart. Show your passion and commitment to teaching. Give examples from your placement experiences. At the end of the interview they may ask if you have any questions. This is the opportunity to ask about the support you will receive from a mentor in school and possible professional development opportunities as an NQT.

You may also be questioned by the children in the school council. They will be assessing your friendliness, so smile and answer their questions in child-friendly language.

IS BEING AN NQT THE SAME AS BEING A TEACHER?

CRITICAL QUESTION

How much more learning is there to do?

For NQTs, the induction period of support is an important phase which has the potential to deepen learning that has already taken place in initial teacher education (ITE) as well as preparing the NQT for future learning. A particularly crucial time in the induction process is the first term of teaching, when NQTs are likely to be facing a 'reality shock' in relation to their new responsibilities (Haggarty and Postlethwaite, 2012).

'Statutory induction is the bridge between initial teacher training and a career in teaching' (DfE, 2018: 6). You can only begin your induction period once you have successfully gained Qualified Teacher Status (QTS). The purpose of the NQT induction year is to help you become a successful teacher. Your head teacher should offer you support and guidance from a mentor through your first year. It has also been argued that new teachers are reluctant to ask more experienced colleagues for advice in order to avoid being regarded as incompetent

(Dinham, 1992; Rust, 1994). However, if you are to learn and move forward in your teaching, you will need to continue to ask questions and take on feedback from more experienced colleagues.

WHAT SUPPORT WILL YOU HAVE DURING YOUR INDUCTION?

You will hopefully have access to a programme of professional development (this may be through the local authority). You should also receive:

- a 10 per cent reduction in your teaching timetable in order for you to develop your skills out of the classroom. This is in addition to your 10 per cent planning, preparation and assessment (PPA) time. Use this time wisely. Visit other classrooms or even other schools. Observe outstanding teachers in a variety of subjects;
- support from your induction tutor/mentor;
- reviews on your progress, together with formal meetings each term with your head teacher and/or induction tutor.

Your induction will be assessed over an academic year, with an assessment at the end of each full term. You can complete your induction on either a full-time or part-time basis. There can also be gaps between terms once the induction period has started.

When you are reaching the end of a term, you should meet with your head teacher or induction mentor for formal assessment. This is to enable you to monitor your progress towards Teacher Standards consistently over your practice.

Following the first two meetings, your head teacher will provide a report to the appropriate body (Local Authority or Teaching School) detailing your progress towards the Teachers' Standards (DfE, 2011). After your assessment at the end of the third term, your head teacher will make a recommendation to the appropriate body as to whether your progress towards the standards has been satisfactory.

The Local Authority or Teaching School will then decide whether you have successfully met the requirements to complete your induction period and will write to your head teacher and the NCTL (National College for Teaching and Leadership) to inform them of their decision. You will then be contacted directly by the NCTL in writing to confirm whether you have successfully completed your induction period.

KEY READING

For further information, refer to the government's statutory guidance on NQT induction:

www.gov.uk/government/publications/induction-for-newly-qualified-teachers-nqts

HOW WILL YOUR MENTOR HELP YOU DURING THE INDUCTION YEAR?

Figure 33.1

Statutory requirements for induction set out the responsibilities of induction mentors. The induction mentor has day-to-day responsibility for the monitoring, support and assessment of the NQT.

The induction mentor needs to be fully aware of the requirements of the induction period and to have the skills, expertise and knowledge they need to work effectively in the role. They should be able to provide or co-ordinate guidance and support, and to make rigorous and fair judgements about the new teacher's performance in relation to the Induction Standards.

Your first year is tough. Try to get as much support as you can from your colleagues and try not to do too much at once. Ensure that you get enough sleep during the week and give yourself the time to socialise or pursue sports and activities you enjoy at the weekend. If you are struggling to keep up with the expectations of the workload, including planning, marking and meetings, speak to your mentor. Join a union. Unions such as the National Education Union (NEU) have good advice for NQTs on their websites and on social media such as Twitter.

HOW DO YOU MAKE THE TRANSITION FROM STUDENT TEACHER TO NQT?

Use the following journal starter to reflect on the answers to the questions posed before and during your first term as an NQT.

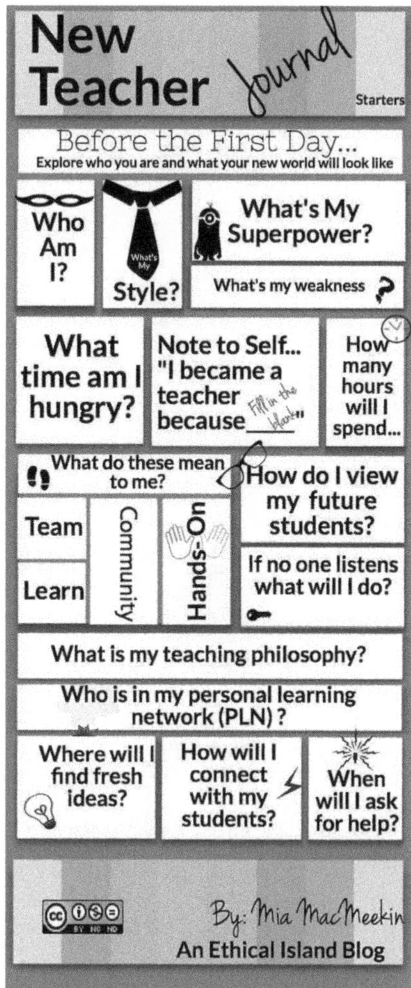

Figure 33.2

ets.publishing.service.gov.uk/government/uploads/system/upload

HOW CAN YOU BRING YOUR OWN VALUES AND PHILOSOPHIES INTO YOUR TEACHING CAREER?

The process of learning to teach is not only very complex but also very personal (Olsen, 2010). When beginning teachers enter the teaching profession, they bring with them their own conceptions of teaching and learning based on their prior experiences as students, their biographies, personal characteristics, norms and values. At the same time, the contexts in which they (are going to) work expose them to a great number of expectations from, for instance, students, parents, colleagues, school leaders and the community (Pillen *et al.*, 2013).

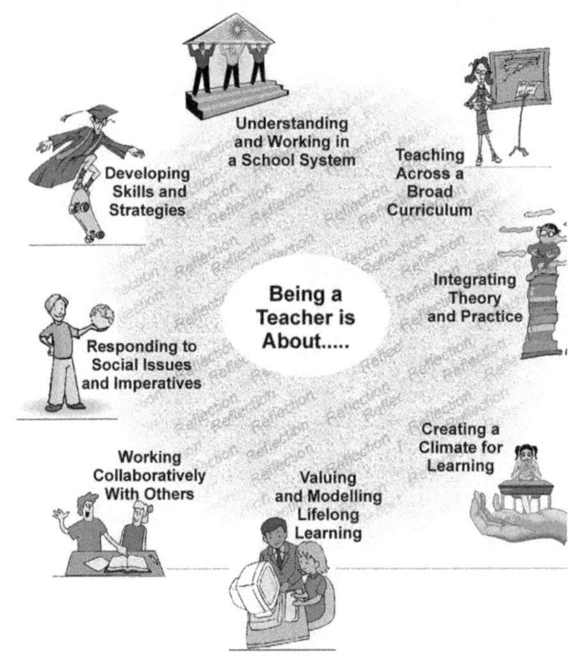

Figure 33.3 Graham and Phelps (2003) discuss the notion of 'being a teacher'.

Reflecting critically on the implications of 'being a newly qualified teacher' means the following:

ACKNOWLEDGING THE SOCIAL, POLITICAL AND CULTURAL CONTEXTS OF THE PROFESSION IN WHICH YOU ARE (AND WILL) BE WORKING

Working in a school system means being responsible to and communicating with stakeholders: governors, parents, colleagues. Ensure that you go to the staffroom in breaks and talk with colleagues about your teaching and learning. Build relationships with parents quickly and try and communicate with them regularly. Share good news with parents and governors by celebrating the learning in your classroom. Keep up to date with education news stories and examples of others' outstanding practice. Reflect on the impact it may have on your own practice.

EVALUATING EFFECTIVE TEACHING AND LEARNING THROUGH STRUCTURED OBSERVATION AND EXPERIENCE

Your head teacher or mentor will be observing you each term and giving you feedback. Don't dwell on the parts of the lesson that could have gone better; use the feedback to move forward positively. Use your

10 per cent NQT time in school effectively, by observing exemplary teaching across a broad curriculum. You will be planning and teaching all subjects in a primary school so get as much opportunity during your placements to practice teaching *all* of the subjects.

REFLECTING ON YOUR PRACTICE

Now is the time to put all the theory and practice from assignments, reading and lectures into action. Reflect on your own lessons in terms of what the children learned and what *you* learned in terms of your teaching. As a teacher, you have to be flexible and resilient.

EVALUATING AND CHALLENGING TAKEN-FOR-GRANTED ASSUMPTIONS ABOUT TEACHING AND LEARNING

You will be creating a climate for learning based on your philosophy of education. The learning environment is often described as the 'other' teacher. Reflect on the practice you have seen while on placement and question whether the practice is in line with your philosophy of teaching and learning. You should continue to develop critical approaches to teaching and learning through professional development, NQT meetings and professional networks. You will also develop your teaching skills and strategies by observing and talking with colleagues.

CULTIVATING COLLABORATIVE APPROACHES TO LEARNING AND TEACHING

You can demonstrate learning at any age to the children by co-construction of learning. Ask the children at the start of a new topic what they already know and what they want to find out. This will help you to engage the learners and co-construct their learning. As the teacher, you might visibly learn a new skill, e.g. a musical instrument such as the ukulele with the children or a new language. You can also model collaborative approaches to learning by working effectively with your teaching assistant (TA) and other adults in the classroom (see section on working with your TA on pp. 565–7).

'Reflective practice is more than just thoughtful practice, it is the process of turning thoughtful practice into a potential learning situation' (Jarvis, 1992: 176). Jarvis also claims that reflective practice is a key tool used by professionals as they face new and different situations and challenges. In the following case study, two undergraduate education students acknowledged the value they perceived reflective practice to be for their future work as teachers.

CASE STUDY

Anna and Erin - reflections from final placement to NQT year

Anna: 'For my final placement I am in a small rural first school. There are only 90 children in the whole school. I quite like the ethos of the school as it is very friendly. The staff make the trainee teacher feel like a fully qualified teacher already as they include you in everything.

(Continued)

(Continued)

I see this final placement as important in preparing for the NQT year. I will be looking at everything differently, for example, asking for assessment and data about the children, because I know this is something important I will need to do next year with my own class.

I am nervous talking to parents, so I am hoping to observe a parent/teacher meeting during this placement. I feel that I could contribute to the meeting by speaking positively to a parent about their child after using the observations and assessment data I have gathered about them.

I reflect on my practice by talking with the class teacher before planning. Once I have carried out a lesson, I reflect on it and ask the class teacher anything I have been unsure of if it didn't go exactly to plan. In my NQT year I will still ask my mentor questions, but I feel that it should be expected that I know the answer to most things by the end of my training.'

Erin: 'I am on placement in a one-form entry school. There is a nurturing, holistic approach in the school, as the whole staff place as much emphasis on the children's well-being as the academic side. This is really important to me as I feel that teaching personal, social and health education (PSHE) is a key aspect of my emerging philosophy of learning.

I feel determined to succeed, as after three years of training at university, I have been building up to this final placement. It is really important to enjoy the experience, but it does depend on the school you are placed in; fitting in makes all the difference. If the teachers are supportive, then it means you can go into the NQT year confidently.

It is important that you have good relationships with the staff in the school. If you feel nervous, you wouldn't be able to talk honestly about the errors you may have made. I think teachers will talk to you more if you are open with them. I am excited at the prospect of going into the NQT year because I can use all of the teaching approaches that I have learned across all placements, and develop and alter them to suit my own class.

I get a lot from observations with the teacher. When they sit down and give you feedback, it is really useful as you can amend things straight away for the next lesson. You can also reflect on the lesson in your own head, but often it is easier to focus on the negatives rather than the positives! To realise my goals, I just need to keep applying myself, stay motivated, be a self-directed learner, reflect, manage my time, listen, observe, discuss and remember "I can do this!"'

Both student teachers are anticipating their transition to NQT during their final placement experience. They both understand the importance of building relationships with staff, children and parents. Erin understands the need to still ask questions as an NQT and Anna feels that she is expected to know it all by the time she starts her first year of teaching.

Remember, you are not a finished product when you finish your training! You will be reflecting on your practice, while learning and developing, all the way through your teaching career.

HOW DO YOU WORK EFFECTIVELY WITH OTHER ADULTS IN THE CLASSROOM?

CRITICAL QUESTION

Is the Teaching Assistant (TA) there to support the teacher or the children?

Within Standard 8 of the Teachers' Standards (DfE, 2011) there is a requirement for teachers to 'Deploy other adults effectively'. You will inevitably work with a TA during your career. This is a key partnership and could have an effect on the learning outcomes for the children, as well as an impact on inclusive practice in your classroom. Working in a school, you may also meet other professionals, parent helpers, office staff, governors, administrators, faith leaders, advisers from the local authority, and many more. This next section focuses on the research in this area, and how working collaboratively and as a team with other adults will produce the best outcomes.

RESEARCH FOCUS

The Deployment and Impact of Support Staff (DISS) project (Blatchford *et al*., 2009) was the largest, most in-depth study ever to be carried out in this field, and it aimed to provide an accurate, systematic and representative description of the types of support staff and their characteristics and deployment in schools and the impact of support staff on teachers, teaching and pupil learning, behaviour and academic progress (Russell *et al*., 2013).

The research team found quite alarming results. Pupils who received the most TA support made less progress than similar pupils who received little or no TA support - even after controlling for factors like prior attainment and SEN status.

As a developing practitioner, you may have observed in classrooms on placement, a TA predominantly working with the lowest attaining children either in or outside the classroom. One of the key factors to emerge from the DISS and EDTA projects is the way that change is required in the teacher's role. As a newly qualified teacher, you may have to challenge the status quo and learn 'to work through a more inclusive pedagogical strategy, which deals with the learning of all pupils, and not delegate the day-to-day responsibility for the learning and care of pupils with SEN and lower attaining pupils to teaching assistants' (Russell *et al*., 2013: 4).

These key recommendations from Russell *et al.* (2013: 65) may help you to define the pedagogical role of TAs:

- Watch for the signs of ineffective deployment, such as evidence of pupil dependency on TAs (known as 'the Velcro model' of TA support where pupils with SEN are always with a TA).
- Consider the ways in which you deploy *yourself* in lessons, in terms of the groups you tend to support.
- Ensure that lower-attaining pupils and those with special educational needs are not routinely and unnecessarily separated from you and the classroom. Consider rotating the groups you and the TA work with across the week.
- Consider additional classroom organisation strategies that do not require adult support, for example peer-led group work.

WHY IS IT IMPORTANT TO WORK AS A TEAM WITH YOUR TA?

Team members' interactions should be co-operative and not competitive, and a team's goals are agreed together rather than set by individual members (Vincett *et al.*, 2005). Teamwork in an educational setting might involve tasks such as setting goals, identifying problems, assessing pupils' needs and skills, exchanging information, brainstorming (e.g. ideas for the role-play area), problem-solving, and making, implementing and evaluating plans.

Table 33.1 The Teacher/TA lesson planning tool

When?	What?
Before the lesson	• Conversation about lesson plans, learning objective and success criteria • TA and teacher to discuss any issues regarding pupils • Share the TA/teacher lesson planning tool • Check that learning objectives are in books
During the lesson introduction	• Refocus students • Ensure that they have the correct equipment needed, e.g. whiteboard and pen, fidget toy, etc. • Use mini-whiteboards, key vocabulary prompts, visual prompts for ____________ • Scribe for the teacher (point of reference for pupils in the lesson)
During whole-class work	• Act as a talk partner for ____________ and ______________ so that they can rehearse their ideas and thinking aloud • Encourage responses from _________ • Emphasise key vocabulary: _______ ______ ___________ _________ • Record words in book for __________ • Model for the pupils or role-play activities with the pupils • Rephrase information

When?	What?
	• Scan the room and notice when students need rather than ask for help • Access arrangements: scribe for __________ and read for __________ • Use questioning to ensure that students have understood instructions as to what they are to do, what they will learn and what outcome is expected • Check they are using success criteria • Correct spellings/errors in green pen
In group work	• Use open questioning to ensure that students have understood instructions as to what they are to do, what they will learn and what outcome is expected of them by the end of the group session • Explain roles, prompt and give time checks • Allow thinking time before helping or giving the pupil the answer • Note issues, mistakes, misconceptions and difficulties on post-it notes, so that the teacher can address these in the plenary or in future lessons • Rehearse reflection on learning so that the students can present their ideas in plenary sessions
In plenary sessions	• Prompt and help students explain strategies and reasoning to reflect on their learning • Monitor responses of ________________; note any difficulties/misconceptions
At the end of the lesson	• Clarify with students what the next steps in their learning will be • Ensure that students have homework and are clear about any follow-up required
After the lesson	• Provide assessment feedback to the teacher as required

Questions for reflection:

- Can you find some time to share the weekly or daily lesson plans with the TA?
- Does the TA know which pupils they will be working with and the learning objectives?
- During whole-class work when the teacher is modelling, can the TA scribe pupils' suggestions on the board?
- Could the TA support low-attaining pupils in the whole-class start of the lesson by scribing for them on mini-whiteboards or showing pupils pre-made key words and/or picture cues?
- During discussions with pupils, could you give the TA specific questions to ask specific groups; for example, high-attaining (HA) or low-attaining (LA)?
- Could the TA plan a plenary with the higher-attaining pupils or draw up a list of success criteria with them?
- Can the TA give you some assessment feedback about the pupils they worked with during the lesson?
- Can you both find time after the lesson to be reflective and discuss what went well during the lesson and what we could improve?

CHAPTER SUMMARY

This chapter explored getting your first teaching job, your NQT year and working with other adults in the classroom. It has included practical advice on finding and applying for jobs, and succeeding in interviews. The importance of learning and reflection in your NQT year has been highlighted, and the NQT mentor's role has been outlined to help you understand the kind of support you should be offered. We have reflected on the thoughts of two new teachers and have begun to think about reflecting on your own training and development.

It is important for you to understand the role of the TA in the classroom and the chapter has explored this. After reading this chapter, you should be prepared for 'what comes next'.

ASSIGNMENTS

If you are writing an ITE assignment on working collaboratively with others, it will be useful for you to think through the following:

1. What is your understanding of collaboration and teamwork? Why do you think teamwork is important? Is this view shared by others?
2. How central is working with other adults effectively key to pupil learning? To what extent does it impact inclusive outcomes for children? Can you find any evidence that collaboration and teamwork among adults supports learning?
3. What can we learn from looking at other countries' practice? Can you find examples that can support your argument?

Suggested reading

Blatchford, P., Webster, R. and Russell, A. (2012) Challenging the Role and Deployment of Teaching Assistants in Mainstream Schools: The Impact on Schools. Final Report on the Effective Deployment of Teaching Assistants (EDTA) project. Online. Available at: www.schoolsupportstaff.net/edtareport.pdf

Chapter 12 'Working with Teaching Assistants' by Emma Clarke, in *Building Skills for Effective Primary Teaching*, Rachael Paige, Sue Lambert and Rebecca Geeson (2017). London: Learning Matters/SAGE.

Wenger, E. (1998) *Communities of Practice*. Cambridge: Cambridge University Press.

REFERENCES

Blatchford, P., Bassett, P., Brown, P., Koutsoubou, M., Martin, C., Russell, A., and Webster, R. with Rubie-Davies, C. (2009) *The Impact of Support Staff in Schools: Results from the deployment and impact of support staff project. (Strand 2 Wave 2) (DCSF-RR 148).* London: DfES.

Department for Education (DfE) (2011) *Teachers' Standards in England from September 2012.* London: DfE.

Department for Education (DfE) (2018) *Statutory Guidance: Induction for newly qualified teachers (NQTs) Statutory guidance on NQT inductions for headteachers, school staff and governing bodies.* Available at: www.gov.uk/government/publications/induction-for-newly-qualified-teachers-nqts (accessed: 13/07/18).

Dinham, S. (1992) Teacher induction: Implications of resent research for educational administrators. Paper presented at the Annual Meeting of the Australian Council for Educational Administration, July, in Darwin, Australia.

Graham, A. and Phelps, R. (2003) Being a teacher: Developing teacher identity and enhancing practice through metacognitive and reflective learning processes. *Australian Journal of Teacher Education,* 27(2): 2.

Haggarty, L. and Postlethwaite, K. (2012) An exploration of changes in thinking in the transition from student teacher to newly qualified teacher. *Research Papers in Education,* 27(2): 241–62

Jarvis, P. (1992) Reflective practice and nursing. *Nurse Education Today,* 12: 174–81.

Newton, L.D. (2015) Professional development: Selecting and appraising the newly qualified teacher in the primary school, *MiE,* 15(2).

Olsen, B. (2010) *Teaching for Success: Developing your teacher identity in today's classroom.* Boulder, CO/London: Paradigm Publishers.

Pillen. M.T., Den Brok, P.J. and Beijaard, D. (2013) Profiles and change in beginning teachers' professional identity tensions. *Teaching and Teacher Education.* 34: 86–97.

Pillen, M., Beijaard, D. and Brok, P. (2013) Tensions in beginning teachers' professional identity development, accompanying feelings and coping strategies, *European Journal of Teacher Education,* 36(3): 240-260.

Russell, A., Webster, R. and Blatchford, P. (2013) *Maximising the Impact of Teaching Assistants: Guidance for school leaders and teachers.* Abingdon: Routledge.

Rust, F. (1994) The first year of teaching: It's not what they expected. *Teaching and Teacher Education,* 10(2): 205–17.

Vincett, K., Cremin, H. and Thomas, G. (2005) *Teachers and Assistants Working Together.* Berkshire: Open University Press.

INSET COURSES

- ☑ FOCUSSED STAFF MEETINGS
- ☑ REFLECTIVE DIARY/CRITICAL REFLECTION
- ☐ TEACHER (ACTION) RESEARCH
- ☐ COLLABORATION WITH COLLEAGUES
- ☑ LESSON STUDY
- ☐ COACHING/MENTORING
- ☐ FURTHER STUDY (EG MA) ?
- ☑ LEADERSHIP TRAINING
- ☐ SELF-DIRECTED, SUCH AS READING, SOURCING VIDEOS, ETC. ?

34

CONTINUING PROFESSIONAL DEVELOPMENT: WHAT DOES IT REALLY MEAN, AND HOW CAN TEACHERS BEST ENGAGE WITH IT?

Mary McAteer is Director of Professional Learning Programmes, Edge Hill University, Ormskirk. Her research interests include teacher professional learning, and action research/participatory and emancipatory research.

Conor McAteer is a Newly Qualified Teacher.

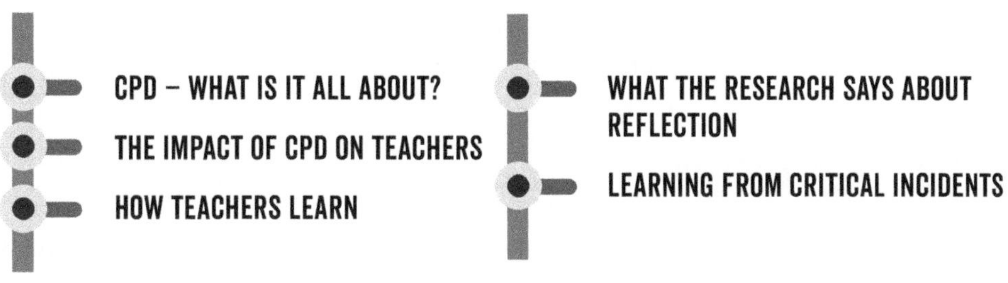

KEY WORDS

- Continuing
- Professional
- Development
- Career
- Critical
- Incident
- Impact
- Learning
- Research
- Reflection
- Opportunity
- Journey
- Skills
- Knowledge
- Standards

INTRODUCTION

The sense of achievement on qualifying as a teacher is well earned, but may be short-lived. I remember well, and have often seen, the challenges faced by NQTs, as they begin to develop their own professional identity and skill. It becomes evident to most teachers early on in their new career that there is still much to learn. Indeed, to embark on a career in teaching is to also embark on a journey of life-long learning. Throughout this learning journey, teachers' needs change as their practical knowledge grows and develops. The first year in practice brings with it many challenges as well as opportunities. Many of the challenges are recognised in the support mechanisms provided for new teachers. Strategies such as mentoring, peer-support and in-service professional development are of particular importance during this early career stage.

This chapter explores the professional needs of teachers as they embark on this journey of life-long learning. It will outline some of the opportunities that teachers can both take, and make, in their professional learning journey. As authors of this chapter, we bring a unique and authentic dynamic to it. One author is an experienced teacher, researcher and lecturer in Higher Education, having spent 40 years working as a teacher, the past 18 of which were on teacher professional learning programmes. The other author is an NQT who, at the time of writing, is just over halfway through his induction year. Together, we bring differing perspectives on professional learning in theory and practice, and authentic voices from our experiences.

We start by exploring the nature and purposes of Continuing Professional Development (CPD), exploring its relevance to beginning teachers and those with more experience. This brings us to a consideration of both the intended and unintended ways in which CPD impacts on teachers. Finally, we look at tools that teachers can employ in their everyday practice, to bring systematicity and rigour to their reflections, turning them into rich and deep learning experiences with the opportunity to transform practice.

CPD: WHAT IS IT ALL ABOUT?

There is an expectation that, after qualifying, teachers will continue to update and upgrade their professional skills and knowledge throughout their career. This CPD takes place in many ways and serves a variety of purposes. In some cases, it happens through formally organised activities and courses, which, for a beginning teacher, may be compulsory as part of their induction. There is an explicit recognition that beginning teachers should have access to high-quality professional development opportunities. During the initial phase of a teacher's career in the United Kingdom, there is an entitlement to an Induction Programme, which supports the new teacher in achieving full Qualified Teacher status. For many newly qualified teachers, this may happen through their engagement with the various CPD/INSET activities that are scheduled within their school and/or local area. It is often the case that the completion of these activities serves as part of the induction assessment; identifying and measuring their progress against Teachers' Standards (DfE, 2013; GTC, 2012; GTCNI, 2007). Successful completion of the induction year (including participation in relevant CPD events) leads to full recognition as a qualified teacher.

More experienced teachers also undertake CPD as part of their continued professional updating. Changes in the curriculum, for example, mean that teachers may require either updated content knowledge, or pedagogical skills, or both. The move towards Mastery Teaching in Mathematics in England is one such example, where there is a large-scale offer of professional development activities to address subject knowledge and pedagogy 'gaps' in practising teachers. Other systemic change, such as different record-keeping requirements, new assessment practices, child welfare and safeguarding, for example, may all be the focus of INSET activities for teachers. Also, as teachers progress in their career, it is often the case that they take on middle and senior leadership roles, requiring a whole new set of skills and knowledge. Again, this is often gained through planned and formal CPD activities.

The case of the beginning teacher is a good example of the ways in which formal CPD serves a range of core purposes such as the following:

- Complementing and building on Initial Teacher Education, through additional training in skills such as Behaviour Management, Lesson Planning, Pedagogy and Assessment (some of which will be subject specific), Support and Challenge for Learners, Inclusion, and so forth. These are normally provided through one-day training sessions provided in local networks.
- Providing evidence for an Induction portfolio, which forms part of the assessment of progress towards relevant standards or competencies. This is the evidence a teacher uses in order to satisfactorily complete the statutory induction period.

However, as any teacher will attest to, much CPD happens in unplanned and informal ways. Some of this is demonstrated in the Learning Conversation below:

LEARNING CONVERSATION 1

Mary: *It's interesting to hear you talk about your early days in teaching, and the way in which you began to develop your practice as an independent teacher, with full responsibility for your class.*

Conor: *One of the main things I had to develop early on was how to keep the day running in a fluid way. Transitions between lessons were an important area to work on, but this seems to be gained from experience and by the discipline needed to decide that a lesson needs to be continued later rather than have it overrun.*

Mary: *So trial and error, and a conscious disciplined approach to your practice?*

Conor: *That's right. And of course, the very simple step of effective timetabling helped enormously.*

Mary: *I guess that felt very different when you had your own class?*

Conor: *Yes – and also to add to this, the experience you have going into your first teaching job is very limited. You find you are almost constantly in new territory with your teaching – you are teaching the vast majority of curricular areas for the very first time. So, on top of basic scheduling, there's a lot of curriculum to learn.*

Mary: *I guess that's particularly true in a primary setting where you have to cover all subject areas, and may have a year group different to the ones you experienced while training. It must have been a real challenge to get to grips with it all.*

Conor: *Well, I was very lucky. I had a senior member of staff who was generous with her time and support. I also talked a lot to other, more experienced staff, asking about what was expected, how best to approach new topics, for example, or when to move to something new. What really helped me here was that I felt trusted and the atmosphere was supportive. I also attended some courses, which helped, though some were less help than I'd hoped they would be. In some cases, the link with the curriculum wasn't made clear, or delivery was not very engaging, which was disappointing. That said, I did find that often there can be unintended learning from all courses. It is only later that some of the learning becomes obvious, that you can make an explicit connection with your teaching.*

Mary: *Ah yes – a supportive atmosphere and trust must be great at this stage in your career.*

Conor: *What was really important to me was that my mentor also recognised my strengths, and helped me build on them, while at the same time helping me identify where and how I needed to improve. I knew I could talk about my development needs without feeling judged. For example, I was recommended a really good book on behaviour management that helped me enormously with this aspect of my work.*

CRITICAL QUESTION

Do NQTs benefit more from formal or informal CPD opportunities?

While it is beyond the scope of this chapter to discuss all the ways in which teachers learn about and improve their practice, it quickly becomes evident that the list is large and varied.

INFO 34.1

INSET courses

focused staff meetings

Reflective diary/critical reflection

Teacher (action) research

Collaboration with colleagues

Lesson study

Coaching/mentoring

Further study (e.g. MA)

Leadership training

Self-directed, such as reading, sourcing videos, etc.

THE IMPACT OF CPD ON TEACHERS

Reviewing Conor's conversation, we see evidence of his attendance at formal CPD events, his deliberate engagement with informal support and, also, the unintended learning that occurred after he had taken part in a formal, planned CPD event. You may also have now realised that CPD takes place in many ways and, therefore, its impact is often hard to predict. This illustrates the complexity of the ways in which professionals learn about practice, and the learning journeys they undertake, particularly during the induction year. It also raises questions about the nature of professional development and learning, the role of the individual within that, and the role of the school context. Much of the early learning may be at an operational level; what to do and when to do it are key drivers in getting through the school day for an early career teacher. In primary schools, where teachers tend to have a little more flexibility in scheduling of the school day, ineffective timetabling can have serious ramifications for pupils and teachers alike. It is clear also that much of the early learning in practice that occurs for beginning teachers, complements, supplements and extends the knowledge gained during the training period. The importance of an encouraging learning environment, where strengths are amplified and learning needs effectively, but supportively addressed, would seem to be significant here in supporting the early stages of a teacher's career. In this way, both formal and informal CPD can support the development of subject and pedagogical skills, and the building of general classroom craft.

WHAT DOES THE RESEARCH SAY?

There is a range of research in relation to the 'effectiveness' of teacher CPD. We will explore two examples below, one that reflects the impact of subject-specific CPD, and the other that explores the 'pedagogical' structures of CPD.

First of all, there is evidence that well-targeted CPD, and in particular, that directed towards subject knowledge is particularly valued by teachers, and may aid teacher retention.

A study conducted for the Wellcome Trust in 2017 suggests that 'science teachers who participate in CPD courses through STEM Learning (www.stem.org.uk/) are much more likely to remain in teaching'.

At a time when there is a retention crisis in teaching, this is important. Daniel Muijs, head of research at OfSTED, suggests that this is true for subject-specific CPD in general, not just STEM subjects. Speaking at a recent DfE conference in London, he added, 'We know from research that professional development that is subject-embedded is more effective than generic CPD' (Ward, 2018). It is also the case that high-quality, subject-specific CPD has the potential to 'lead to more engaging and effective teaching' for young people (Wellcome Trust, 2017: 5).

KEY READING

You can read the report from the Wellcome Trust here: *Improving Science Teacher Retention: Do National STEM Learning Network professional development courses keep science teachers in the classroom?* Dr Rebecca Allen and Sam Sims. Education Datalab, 2017. Available at:

wellcome.ac.uk/sites/default/files/science-teacher-retention.pdf

In relation to the 'pedagogical' structures of CPD, the work of Aileen Kennedy (2005) is significant in this respect. She suggests a nine-part typology of professional development activity, which belongs to three categories, as follows:

Model of CPD	Purpose of model	
• training model • award-bearing model • deficit model • cascade model	Transmission	↓ Increasing capacity for professional autonomy
• standards-based model • coaching/mentoring model • community of practice model	Transitional	
• action research model • transformative model	Transformative	

Source: Kennedy, 2005: 248

'Transformative' aligns with the capacity for professional autonomy and changed practice. Of particular significance here is her definition of professional autonomy, suggesting that the activity requires 'teachers to be able to articulate their own conceptions of teaching and be able to select and justify appropriate modes of practice' (p. 236). She uses the term 'transformative' as an overview one, recognising that transformative activities have a range of features, but will normally have an enquiry focus, an awareness of issues of power, and a consciously proactive approach.

Other analyses of the 'effectiveness' of CPD have similar findings.

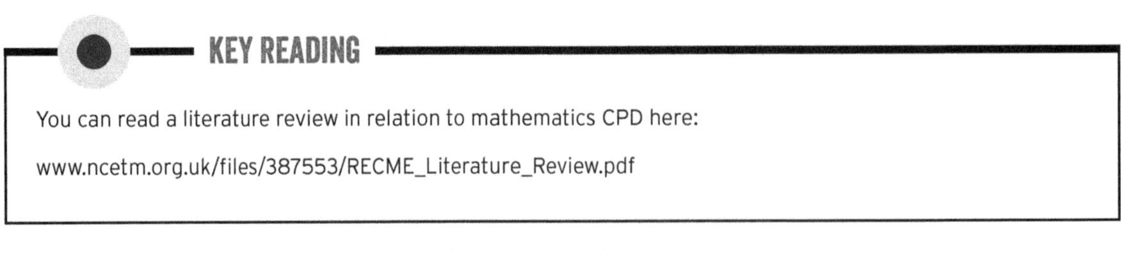
KEY READING

You can read a literature review in relation to mathematics CPD here:

www.ncetm.org.uk/files/387553/RECME_Literature_Review.pdf

CRITICAL QUESTION

Is 'transformative' CPD the best kind?

REFERENCES

Allen, R. and Sims, S. (2017) *Improving Science Teacher Retention: Do National STEM Learning Network professional development courses keep science teachers in the classroom?* Available at: https://wellcome.ac.uk/sites/default/files/science-teacher-retention.pdf (accessed: 13/07/18).

Angelides, P. (2001) The development of an efficient technique for collecting and analyzing qualitative data: The analysis of critical incidents. *Qualitative Studies in Education*, 14(3): 429–42.

Bolton, G. (2005) *Reflective Practice: Writing and professional development.* London: SAGE.

Department for Education (DfE) (2013) *Induction for newly qualified teachers (NQTs).* Available at: www.gov.uk/government/publications/induction-for-newly-qualified-teachers-nqts (accessed: 13/07/18).

Ghaye, A. and Ghaye, K. (1998) *Teaching and Learning Through Critical Reflective Practice.* London: David Fulton Publishers.

General Teaching Council for Northern Ireland (GTCNI) (2007), *Teaching: The Reflective Profession*, Belfast: GTCNI.

GTC (2012) *The Education (Induction Arrangements for School Teachers) (England) (Amendment) Regulations 2012.* Available at: www.legislation.gov.uk/uksi/2012/513/made (accessed: 13/07/18).

Joubert, M. and Sutherland, R. (n.d.) A perspective on the literature: CPD for teachers of mathematics. NCETM. Available at: www.ncetm.org.uk/files/387553/RECME_Literature_Review.pdf (accessed: 13/07/18).

Kennedy, A. (2005) Models of continuing professional development: A framework for analysis. *Journal of In-service Education*, 31(2): 235–50.

McAteer, M. (2013) *Action Research in Education.* London: SAGE/BERA.

McAteer, M. and Dewhurst, J. (2010) 'Just thinking about stuff'. Reflective learning: Jane's story. *Journal of Reflective Practice*, 11(1): 31–41.

Mason, J. (2002) *Researching Your Own Practice: The Discipline of Noticing.* London: RoutledgeFalmer.

Moon, J. (2006) *Learning Journals: A handbook for reflective practice and professional development.* Oxford: Routledge.

OECD (2007) *Quality and Equity of Schooling in Scotland.* Available at www.oecd.org/education/school/40328315.pdf (Accessed 10/09/18)

Tripp, D. (1993) *Critical Incidents in Teaching: Developing professional judgement.* London: Routledge.

Ward, H. (2018) *Times Educational Supplement*, March. Available at: www.tes.com/news/school-news/breaking-news/dfe-says-rekindling-teachers-passion-their-subjects-could-help (accessed: 13/07/18).

Woods, P. (1993) *Critical Events in Teaching and Learning.* London: Falmer

TEACHING STANDARDS WEBSITES

https://assets.publishing.service.gov.uk/government/uploads/system/uploads/attachment_data/file/665520/Teachers__Standards.pdf

www.educationscotland.gov.uk/professionallearning/prd/proflearning.asp

www.education-ni.gov.uk/sites/default/files/publications/de/strategy-document-english.pdf

Blogs are personalised websites where you can share what you're doing with the world. They form a series of posts, like diary entries, and people can leave comments, reblog and connect with you through what you post and share. You can learn through reading other people's blogs and sharing their posts through social media, and through creating your own posts to share. Blogging is a really good way to encourage reflection and ensure you're always iterating on lessons and ideas – even if they're a success.

The easiest way to find relevant blog posts to read is through links that are shared on Twitter, Facebook groups or Google+ communities. Here, you already have a shared interest with the author as you either follow them on Twitter or are part of their group/community, so the blogpost is more likely to be relevant to you.

KEY READING

Teacher Toolkit (www.teachertoolkit.co.uk/) 1 minute CPD (1minutecpd.wordpress.com) and Teaching is Messy (www.learningismessy.com/) are all good places to start reading!

There is also a lot of power in creating your own blog to share your practice. The easiest way to get started is to use a blogging platform such as Wordpress (www.wordpress.com), Blogger (www.blogger.com) and Edublogs (www.edublogs.org) – sign up and get started! While you probably think that you don't do anything interesting, or that you're new to teaching so others will know better, everyone has their own unique story to tell! Anything from 'our favourite picture books in Year 4' to 'Today we used whiteboard pens on the table'. It doesn't have to be groundbreaking, but it allows you to share and reflect on what you're doing and get feedback from educators all over the world. Don't forget to share your posts on social media!

TEACHMEETS

CRITICAL QUESTION

Why should we make time for informal learning? What can these settings offer that sometimes formal CPD doesn't?

Teachmeets are (generally) in-person CPD events organised, run and attended by currently practising teachers. They're (usually) free to attend and are an opportunity to learn from other teachers who are still doing the job that you do every week. Often, presentations are kept short (between 2 and 7 minutes – always under 10!) to encourage everyone to share. As well as ensuring the presentations are diverse enough to cater to everyone's needs, sometimes teachmeets will specialise; for example, 'primary' or 'maths'.

To look for a teachmeet in your area, either look on the Teachmeet website (http://teachmeet.pbworks.com) or search Eventbrite (www.eventbrite.co.uk) with the word Teachmeet. You can attend as an 'enthusiastic lurker' or a presenter, so there are no worries about having to present your first time. Come away with some great ideas and take them back to class straight away.

MOOCS

CRITICAL QUESTION

How can you evaluate other people's ideas? Will everything you learn be appropriate for your setting?

MOOC stands for Massive Open Online Course. These courses are often written in collaboration with universities and are a great source of CPD. They offer you the chance to continue learning and frequently have online community spaces for participants (usually in their hundreds) to share what they've learned and to support each other. These spaces can also be a great place to expand your PLN. Some MOOCs run on specific dates, with participants all taking part in weekly activities and many outline the time commitment you need to have before you undertake it (frequently between 2 and 5 hours a week), but others are available all the time. Many MOOCs are free, although some providers are now moving towards a model of it being free to take part, but you have to pay for a certificate. In all honesty, I include any MOOC courses on my CV without a certificate – as long as you can talk about what you learned and did as a consequence of it, the certificates often aren't necessary.

KEY READING

Common places to find MOOCs are: Coursera (www.coursera.org/), edX (www.edx.org/), FutureLearn (www.futurelearn.com/); however, many other universities and organisations offer them sporadically such as Google's Computational Thinking MOOC (computationalthinkingcourse.withgoogle.com/). By developing your PLN you will hear about many more opportunities as they become available.

Each platform has a slightly different format and layout, so it's worth having a look around before trying one out to see which suits your learning style. To make the most of these opportunities, visit their website and browse through what's on offer. As there are so many to choose from, use the filters or search to view education-related MOOCs. It's also worth following the platforms on Twitter as they frequently announce new courses there which might catch your interest.

PROFESSIONAL COMMUNITIES

CRITICAL QUESTION

How can I hear about tried and tested initiatives supported by valid research?

Alongside your informal PLN you may wish to join a professional community, many of which share the aim to 'connect, inform and inspire' educators.

THE CHARTERED COLLEGE OF TEACHING

The Chartered College of Teaching is a recently formed organisation uniting teachers to make use of research to enhance their practice and make them better teachers. It empowers teachers to make the most of their profession and provides resources to support personal growth such as a quarterly magazine of current research-based initiatives. It also holds many face-to-face events and these are a great way to build your local PLN.

Student teachers get free membership for the first year and NQTs get a reduced rate, so it's worth exploring straightaway!

THE COUNCIL FOR SUBJECT ASSOCIATIONS

As you progress through your career, you will be given subjects to lead within your school. These are invaluable opportunities to begin developing your leadership skills early on in your career and can widen the possibilities for career progression if you wish to impact on education beyond your own classroom. The Council for Subject Associations co-ordinates specialised professional communities focusing on improving and developing a specific subject area.

Each subject association has its own aims, requirements and joining information, but if you're passionate about a subject, it's worth exploring the PLNs you can develop here.

LIFELONG LEARNER

CRITICAL QUESTION

How can you continue to learn while managing the teaching workload?

By developing your PLN, you will likely be joining at least one, but perhaps several, 'communities of practice' (Ozturk and Ozcinar, 2013). A 'community of practice' is a model of learning where social interaction facilitates the adoption of new skills, knowledge and understanding (Wenger, 1998). This is different to just having a learning network which you can connect with (your PLN) as it involves a specific shared goal, e.g. a year group/phase, a school subject, etc. that you want to get better at by interacting with others regularly. This could be something you've decided formally, by asking people in your PLN to join a sub-group of people focused on a topic, or informally, by joining a group that already has an aim specified (Wenger-Trayner and Wenger-Trayner, 2015). As a teacher, this is a brilliant opportunity to continue your professional development.

The Department for Education (2011: 1) states in section 8 of the Teachers' Standards:

> *develop effective professional relationships with colleagues, knowing how and when to draw on advice and specialist support.*

This is exemplified within these communities of practice, as you will take on a role such as 'newcomer' or 'explorer' to begin with. When your familiarity with the group grows, you might transition from 'newcomer' to 'recruiter' or from 'explorer' to 'guide' (Caldwell and Cox, 2018). This is the power of participating in groups with networks of colleagues as you draw on specialist support and advice throughout. By taking on these varied roles, Pellegrino *et al.* (2017: 1) described the impact of a community of practice on a group of music teachers:

> *(a) feeling empowered through a sense of community and support;*
>
> *(b) coming to new understandings of ourselves as music teacher educators;*
>
> *(c) experiencing benefits and challenges of our collaborative research process; and*
>
> *(d) still learning/becoming.*

Communities of practice offer an opportunity for you to learn from your colleagues, while also connecting you with specialists around the country and potentially even the world. You are simultaneously learning and gathering resources and ideas for your next topic/lesson plan.

WEBINARS

Webinars are a popular option for teachers who want to learn new skills outside of school hours. A 'webinar' is a 'web seminar' which involves a group of teachers meeting online to discuss and learn about a topic. Participants usually gather at a predefined time and may communicate to each other through a microphone or through text-chat. The host leads and guides the content, but each person may contribute to discussions and share their own experiences.

The content of webinars varies greatly depending on who is hosting it, but they're usually no longer than an hour and contain practical ideas you can use straight away in your classroom. Although webinars are designed as interactive sessions, most are also recorded and shared online after the event so that you can refer back to them. Webinars may run in series, but there is not usually a commitment to attend more than the one you've signed up to, so they can be useful to 'dip in and out' around your teaching schedule.

Many companies use webinars as a way to teach teachers about the tools their products offer, such as Seesaw's 'Professional Development in your PJs' webinar series. As well as this, professional organisations, such as the British Council and the Society for Education and Training, produce webinars around related topics. A simple way to hear about upcoming webinars is through your PLN who will often share webinars on topics that are of interest to you.

MASTERS

CRITICAL QUESTION

How can furthering my own academic ambitions help me be a better teacher?

Whether you already gained some Master's credits through a PGCE that you wish to utilise, or you want to experience the challenge of an academic environment again, there are a plethora of routes to gaining a Master's level qualification in education. Working at this level can hone your abilities to critically reflect on your practice and can facilitate opportunities to effectively measure the impact you are having in your own classroom through action research. It also gives you an opportunity to widen your PLN to include an academic group of educators who can challenge and inspire you in different ways.

As with any university study, every course is different and so it's important to read around what they entail. Some require intense, full-time study, where you'd need a career break, whereas others can be completed alongside a full-time work schedule. Some are distance-learning courses, utilising social media and web technologies, whereas others are face-to-face. It's also worth talking to your school, as some will fund or part-fund your Master's if you pursue an area which the school is developing.

Completing a Master's isn't required for a teaching job; however, by utilising the PLN you will gain, making the most of access to research to inform your practice and measuring the impact of your own classroom initiatives – there are many advantages to gaining one.

CERTIFICATIONS

As you become more experienced as a classroom practitioner, you may start looking towards other means of accreditation to recognise everything you do and also to extend your PLN and the communities of practice that you're already a part of. There are many popular ways of doing this, such as:

- Specialist Leader in Education
- Google Certified Innovator
- Apple Distinguished Educator
- Raspberry Pi Certified Educator
- Microsoft Innovative Educator

These certifications will often expose you to a different group of educators and are definitely worth pursuing as a target to measure your personal development successes, but there is little evidence to support the impact that gaining these achievements will have directly on the students within your classroom. Having them isn't enough, you must use the status to build on your PLN and communities of practice to ensure you keep growing as a lifelong learner.

There are many different ways in which you can form your own Personal Learning Network of colleagues who will support and challenge you. It takes work to maintain and build, but by utilising your connections you will be both reducing your workload and meeting teaching standards such as 'take responsibility for improving teaching through appropriate professional development, responding to advice and feedback from colleagues' (Department for Education, 2011: 1). Social media and the internet allows us to connect in new and innovative ways, but don't try and do everything at once. Start with a platform you're familiar and comfortable with and work towards others as and when you're ready for the next step. Remember, engagement is key: passively viewing content is not the end, it's the starting point in a much larger journey.

CRITICAL QUESTION

Where will your PLN journey begin?

CHAPTER SUMMARY

- A PLN is a Personalised Learning Network: a group of colleagues who you regularly communicate with to share classroom experiences, reflect on successes and encourage you to develop professionally.
- Social media such as Twitter, Facebook and Google+ can be used professionally to communicate and connect with educators around the country and the world.
- Blogging, Teachmeets and MOOCs are ways that you can grow your PLN, learn new things and share them with a group of like-minded individuals.
- Utilising a PLN to become a community of practice ensures you're developing professionally and utilising the networks that you are part of. You establish this by having shared aims and ensuring that you're sharing as well as consuming.
- Certifications are useful when you use them to direct your own professional development, but the badge alone isn't enough. Utilising the PLN you unlock through these titles is the key to ensuring they have classroom impact.

FURTHER READING

The Importance of Developing Your PLN: http://inservice.ascd.org/the-importance-of-developing-your-pln/ – this article discusses first hand the power and the importance of developing your PLN.

Teachers on Twitter: why you should join and how to get started: www.theguardian.com/teacher-network/2017/apr/20/teachers-on-twitter-why-join-get-started-social-media – this article contains a first-hand account as to the benefits of joining Twitter as an educator.

20 Social Media Tips for Teachers: www.teachertoolkit.co.uk/2015/07/02/20-social-media-tips-for-teachers-by-teachertoolkit/ – this blogpost covers everything from blogging to Twitter with top tips to get started.

Introduction to communities of practice: http://wenger-trayner.com/introduction-to-communities-of-practice/ – this website looks in more detail at what a community of practice is and the structures that need to be in place for its success.

REFERENCES

Caldwell, H. and Cox, A. (2018) *Technology-enabled learning communities: How technology can facilitate high quality social learning in online and blended environments within teacher education.* Google Slides – MESH Guide (unpublished). Available at: https://docs.google.com/presentation/d/1cAGOwe1l3BBxC02c08im3Vb47mWuq-Ve33LSmNmPL3o/edit#slide=id.g1e285aa4ea_0_80 (accessed 13/04/18).

Department for Education (2011) *Teachers' Standards.* Available at: www.gov.uk/government/publications/teachers-standards (accessed 13/04/18).

Ozturk, H.T. and Ozcinar, H. (2013) Learning in multiple communities from the perspective of knowledge capital. *The International Review of Research in Open and Distributed Learning,* 14(1): 204–21.

Pellegrino, K., Kastner, J., Reese, J. and Russell, H. (2017) Examining the long-term impact of participating in a professional development community of music teacher educators in the USA: An anchor through turbulent transitions. *International Journal of Music Education,* 0(0): 5–6. Available at: http://journals.sagepub.com/doi/full/10.1177/0255761417704214 (accessed 13/04/18).

Wenger, E. 1998. *Communities of Practice: Learning, meaning, and identity.* Cambridge: Cambridge University Press.

Wenger-Trayner, E. and Wenger-Trayner, B. (2015) *Introduction to Communities of Practice.* Available at: http://wenger-trayner.com/introduction-to-communities-of-practice/ (accessed 13/04/18).

36

IS ENGAGING WITH AND IN RESEARCH A WORTHWHILE INVESTMENT FOR TEACHERS?

Cat Scutt is Director of Education and Research at the Chartered College of Teaching and Ph.D. student, at the UCL Institute of Education, London. Cat is interested in using research to inform decision-making at a classroom, school and system level.

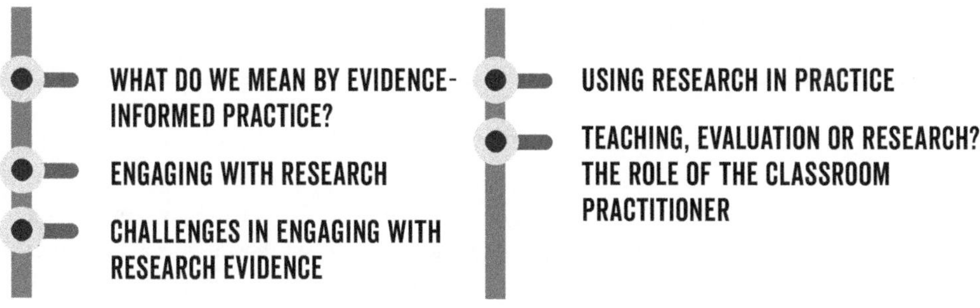

KEY WORDS

- CPD
- Enquiry
- Evidence
- Evidence-informed practice
- Pedagogy
- Professional judgement
- Professional learning
- Research

INTRODUCTION

Over the past decade, interest in the concept of 'evidence-informed practice' in the teaching profession has increased substantially, both in the UK and internationally. While the premise that decisions made by teachers to support student learning should be informed by the best available evidence seems straightforward, the idea is not without contention, and nor is it without challenges. In this chapter, the definition and rationale for evidence-informed practice in education are explored, and the potential benefits and pitfalls of engaging *with* and *in* research are discussed. The chapter ends with a summary of implications for practice and consideration for the opportunities for career development in this area.

WHAT DO WE MEAN BY EVIDENCE-INFORMED PRACTICE?

CRITICAL QUESTION

What sources of evidence can help to inform our practice as teacher?

There has been growing interest in the use of research and evidence to inform teaching practice over a number of years. This is demonstrated by the popularity of John Hattie's work to synthesise research findings (Hattie, 2009). The establishment of the Education Endowment Foundation and the emergence of grass-roots movements such as ResearchEd, aiming to help teachers to understand 'what works' in education, are part of this. Likewise, the focus placed on supporting teachers to be more research informed by the newly launched professional body for teachers, the Chartered College of Teaching, shows a growing interest in research from within the teaching profession.

At the heart of any discussion about the use of research, evidence and the notion of evidence-informed practice must be a clear understanding of what is meant by those terms in this context.

Research is considered here as a structured, rigorous programme of investigation, which might encompass both qualitative and quantitative approaches.

Evidence, meanwhile, can be conceptualised more broadly as including evidence from external research, a range of different types of data (for example, school or pupil data), and the outcomes of research and evaluation activity (Stoll, 2017).

A move towards evidence-informed practice took place somewhat earlier in medicine than in education; indeed, calls for education to catch up in this regard have been one of the drivers for the current movements in education. Two prominent examples of this are a speech given at the Teacher Training Agency by David Hargreaves (1996) and a paper written for the Department for Education by Ben Goldacre of 'Bad Science' fame (Goldacre, 2013).

KEY THEORY

Ben Goldacre's paper *Building Evidence into Education* can be downloaded here:

www.gov.uk/government/news/building-evidence-into-education

The paper explores how Goldacre believes that teachers themselves can work to transform teaching into an evidence-based profession.

In coming to a definition of evidence-informed practice in education it is useful, therefore, to start with a definition from the medical profession. Sackett *et al.* describe evidence-based medicine as:

> *the conscientious, explicit, and judicious use of current best evidence in making decisions about the care of individual patients... integrating individual clinical expertise with the best available external clinical evidence from systematic research.*
>
> (Sackett et al., 1996: 71)

In a similar vein, then, evidence-informed practice in education might be described as the critical use of the current best available evidence from research alongside teachers' experience, expertise and professional judgement, to inform approaches to the teaching of individual students and groups of students in context.

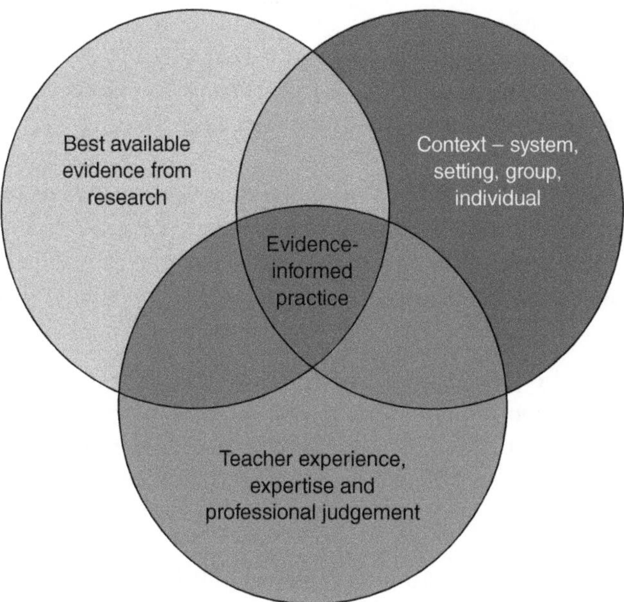

Figure 36.1 Evidence-informed practice

This integration of teachers' professional expertise here to make judgements in their own specific context addresses two common criticisms of the notion of evidence-based practice: First, that it devalues or disregards teacher expertise, and second, that it does not take account of the variety inherent in different teaching contexts and approaches to implementation – or, as Dylan Wiliam succinctly puts it, that 'everything works somewhere and nothing works everywhere' (Wiliam, 2015).

A RATIONALE FOR ENGAGING WITH RESEARCH

At the simplest level, the underlying premise for the use of evidence to inform practice in education is that in making decisions by drawing on rigorous research evidence of 'what works' in education rather than simply on 'hunches' or long-established practices, teachers' practice may be improved and, in turn, students' outcomes will be improved.

CRITICAL QUESTION

Can engaging with research help teachers to improve pupil outcomes?

This is not without contention; the notion of 'what works' is problematic both because of the context-specific nature of education, discussed above, and because there is not profession-wide consensus on what we should measure to know if something works. Academic outcomes, measured through test performance, are perhaps the most widely used measure, but some challenge this as not recognising the myriad other things which are also perceived as important; for example, student well-being, passion for learning, and so-called 'soft skills'.

However, even if we accept that there may be many and varied goals in education and that some of these will be harder to measure than others, the underlying idea that the purpose of evidence-informed practice is to lead to improvement in student outcomes remains. The types of change in practice that may take place to bring about this improvement can be broadly categorised into two groups:

1. **The identification and introduction of new, effective approaches to teaching, learning and assessment**. An example of this is the growing popularity of approaches drawn from cognitive science, for example the use of 'retrieval practice', to help students retain learning; similarly, a range of teaching and learning approaches building on ideas from psychology can be found in *Psychology in the Classroom* (Smith and Firth, 2018).
2. **The identification and rejection of existing, ineffective practices**. An example of this would be the recognition that differentiating activities to cater to students' so-called 'learning styles' has no evidence of effectiveness, and is therefore a poor use of teachers' time; this and other common practices which are not supported by evidence are critiqued in books like *Urban Myths about Learning and Education* (De Bruckyere *et al.*, 2015).

The latter of these is important in highlighting that evidence-informed practice should not always lead to the introduction of new initiatives, and should instead often involve changing, refining or stopping existing practices. Many different approaches and interventions may have some limited effect on student outcomes, but it is important that the extent of this effect is considered alongside the *efficiency* of these approaches in terms of both cost and workload to ensure they are worthwhile.

While the premise that engaging in evidence-informed practice should lead to improved student outcomes is simple, there is as yet limited evidence of research-engagement initiatives that have actually demonstrated impact on outcomes in the form of academic results. Chris Brown and Toby Greany (2017) assert that there are 'nascent and emerging benefits associated with practitioners using research evidence, to enhance their practice', but that as yet these largely only identify correlation, rather than causation. Recent evaluation reports from the Education Endowment Foundation of projects looking at 'light touch' approaches to engaging teachers in using research found no evidence of impact on student outcomes (Rose *et al.*, 2017; Lord *et al.*, 2017).

There are number of possible reasons for this. 'Evidence-informed practice' does not merely consist of teachers being given access to research and evidence (although that is, of course, a prerequisite); it will rarely be sufficient on its own to change teacher practice, and therefore to have any impact on student outcomes. Instead, teachers need support in the various steps that come between access to research and evidence and potential improved outcomes for students (see Figure 36.2).

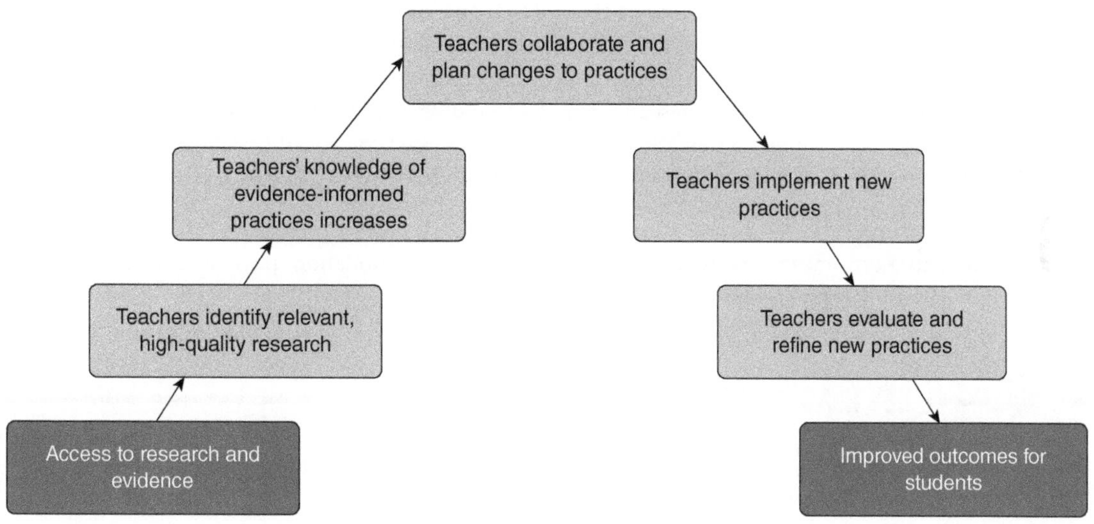

Figure 36.2 The steps involved in changing practice based on research

There is, however, some evidence that engaging with and in research can enhance teachers' self-reflection and discussion about their practice, and imbue a renewed sense of themselves as professional learners (Stoll and Temperley, 2016; Brown and Greany, 2017; Rose et al., 2017; DeLuca et al., 2017). Case Study 1 in this chapter provides an example of how research-engagement has influenced the professional learning culture in one school.

CHALLENGES IN ENGAGING WITH RESEARCH EVIDENCE

There are significant challenges across many of the steps involved in changing practice based on research (illustrated in Figure 36.2). Even where teachers have access to a wide range of research (for example, through a university or through a research database such as that provided by the Chartered College of Teaching), filtering this in order to locate research that is relevant to their context and needs is time-consuming, as is reading often-lengthy research papers.

CRITICAL QUESTION

How can teachers know what research is worth reading?

There also still exists a question about the nature of the body of knowledge held about what makes effective teaching and learning, which Hargreaves (1996) pointed out is not yet comparable to the equivalent body of knowledge in the medical profession.

Another challenge lies in assessing the quality of the research and the claims made, and in ensuring that the findings and implications are fully understood; this requires what is often termed 'research literacy': expertise in interpreting and critiquing research. An understanding of different approaches to research design is critical in judging the implications a piece of research may have and what conclusions it might be reasonable to draw from its findings. For example, systematic reviews and randomised controlled trials tend to be positioned towards the top of 'evidence hierarchies', with findings from these being seen as being more valid and generalisable than from some other approaches.

A number of organisations, most notably the Education Endowment Foundation, have developed approaches to rating and synthesising research findings.

KEY RESOURCE FOR PRACTICE

The Education Endowment Foundation's 'Teaching and Learning Toolkit' is an internet-based resource that offers 'an accessible summary of the international evidence on teaching 5-16 year-olds'. Available at:

https://educationendowmentfoundation.org.uk/evidence-summaries/teaching-learning-toolkit

The toolkit scores the evidence on 'cost' and 'evidence strength'. This is a useful tool to help you begin to engage with research evidence for teaching.

While the Education Endowment Foundation and many others have started to produce a range of resources, such as research, summaries and curated lists of research to help address some of these challenges, other organisations, for example the Chartered College of Teaching, have developed resources to help teachers to develop their research literacy, and it is also increasingly a focus in teacher training programmes. A list of useful sources of research articles, summaries and resources is included below.

INFO 36.1

Useful sources of research evidence

The Education Endowment Foundation (**https://educationendowmentfoundation.org.uk/**) provide a toolkit of research evidence, guidance reports and guides on implementation and evaluation; they also carry out and report on large-scale randomised controlled trials.

The Best Evidence in Brief newsletter (www.beib.org.uk) is a fortnightly newsletter which includes summaries of new research that may be of particular interest to teachers.

The Chartered College of Teaching (https://chartered.college) is the professional body for teachers, offering a termly research journal, a research database, research summaries and syntheses, and a Chartered Teacher certification programme.

Research Schools (https://researchschool.org.uk) have a particular role in helping schools and teachers to become more research-informed through training, support, events and communications.

ResearchEd (https://researched.org.uk) is a grass-roots organisation offering events and publications helping teachers to engage with research.

BERA (www.bera.ac.uk), the British Education Research Association, is a membership association committed to promoting high-quality educational research. They offer a range of journals, events and special interest groups, as well as guidance on research ethics.

CASE STUDY

Engaging with research as a driver for professional reflection and discourse

Graham Chisnell, Primary Headteacher

As a primary school headteacher, life is busy and at times chaotic. Finding space to engage in research can be a challenge. Research, however, provides an opportunity for me to still the noise of everyday life in school, and take time to ask challenging questions and engage in deep observations that allow me to reflect on what does and does not work in my school. For this reason, I encourage a culture of research in all staff across my school.

We support our staff through mentoring and coaching, enabling an ongoing conversation about their practice and their use of research to inform it. They are also given time and funds to support them in engaging with research; some teachers use this to join a professional organisation such as the Chartered College of Teaching to access research journals, while others travel to compare practice beyond their setting, or join local and national events. Many staff engage in Journal Club sessions where teachers meet and discuss education

(Continued)

(Continued)

journal articles and relate these to their own practice, and they are also linked with local universities to develop their skills in interpreting and using research further.

Engagement with research and evidence provides a platform for professional dialogue across the school and beyond. Staff have also grown their leadership skills as they share their experiences of engaging with research and trialling new approaches with colleagues within the school and beyond through TeachMeets or at staff meetings. Critically, though, evidence-informed practice has created a passion for teaching and learning across the school that ensures that learning is irresistible for all; enabling us to stop for a moment, look around and breathe before selecting the path ahead.

USING RESEARCH IN PRACTICE: THE IMPORTANCE OF IMPLEMENTATION AND EVALUATION

CRITICAL QUESTION

How can we know whether something has worked in our own context?

Even after research has been located, digested, critiqued and understood, there is a substantial challenge for teachers in translating this knowledge of evidence-informed practices into changes in their own classrooms. The difficulty of changing habits and established practices, and the importance of approaches to professional development that are sustained, and include collaboration and expert challenge, are well documented (see, for example, Timperley *et al.*, 2007 and Higgins *et al.*, 2015), and this requires investment from school leadership to ensure that appropriate time, resources and culture are in place to enable change to take place in classrooms and at a whole-school level.

KEY RESOURCE FOR PRACTICE

How can schools embed evidence-based change?

The Education Endowment Foundation's *Putting Evidence to Work: A School's Guide to Implementation - Recommendations Summary* gives schools and teachers some guidance around the implementation of new approaches. This is designed to support teachers to embed evidence-based change in schools (Sharples *et al.*, 2018).

Here is a summary of the guidance - based on six steps:

1. Treat implementation as a process, not an event; plan and execute it in stages.

2. Create a leadership environment and school climate that is conducive to good implementation.
3. Explore - Define the problem you want to solve and identify appropriate programmes or practices to implement.
4. Prepare - Create a clear implementation plan, judge the readiness of the school to deliver that plan, then prepare staff and resources.
5. Deliver - Support staff, monitor progress, solve problems, and adapt strategies as the approach is used for the first time.
6. Sustain - Plan for sustaining and scaling an intervention from the outset and continually acknowledge and nurture its use.

The guidance summary in full can be found here:

https://educationendowmentfoundation.org.uk/public/files/Publications/Campaigns/Implementation/5665_EEF_-_Implementation_Guidance_

A critical step in the introduction of any new approach is the evaluation of these changes; research evidence rarely provides a 'silver bullet' and so the introduction of any new intervention, regardless of how well supported by research evidence, should involve evaluation of the impact of the intervention in context. Coe (2017) highlights the importance of evaluation and suggests that effective evaluation involves being clear on the answer to three questions:

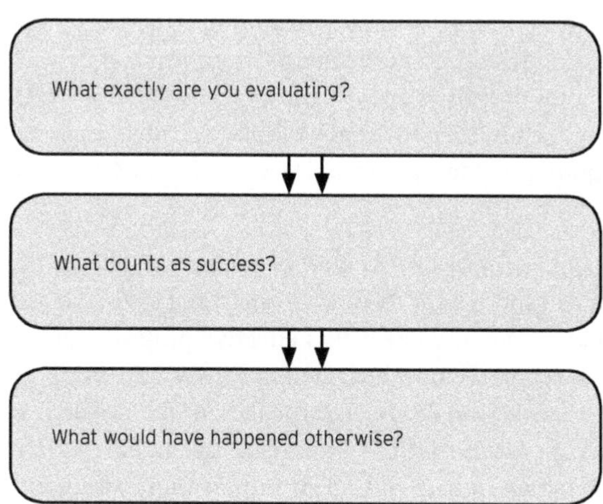

Without robust evaluation, we are at risk of introducing new approaches, which either have no effect on learning, or worse, have a negative effect.

TEACHING, EVALUATION OR RESEARCH? THE ROLE OF THE CLASSROOM PRACTITIONER

As well as a growing interest in reading and engaging with research to inform classroom practice, there has been a growth in interest in teachers carrying out their own small-scale research, typically termed 'action research' or 'practitioner research'. The idea of teachers carrying out research in their classrooms raises a number of challenges and tends to divide opinion. On a practical level, the workload involved in carrying out research is substantial. There are also issues about ensuring that ethical guidelines are followed, as well as a question of whether teachers have the skills and resources to carry out and evaluate research with sufficient rigour for the findings to be valid and meaningful.

CRITICAL QUESTION

Should teachers also be researchers?

While these challenges are important to consider, it is also worth reflecting on what is actually meant by research in this context. A typical cycle of practitioner research might involve the steps shown in Figure 36.3 on the next page; it is worth noting that these are very similar to the steps that would be carried out in the evaluation of a new intervention. It is possible to see reflective practice, evaluation of interventions and practitioner research being different points on a continuum, with each step involving increased rigour in how a teacher reviews existing research and evidence to inform the new approaches trialled; identifies goals and baselines, and evaluates outcomes against these; and collates and disseminates findings within a research community within or beyond their school. Approaches such as Research Learning Communities, Lesson Study or Spirals of Inquiry provide support for teachers in undertaking this kind of research in their schools.

It is also useful to be clear about the goal of this kind of research. Findings from practitioner research will not be comparable to large-scale randomised controlled trials, but nevertheless may provide useful insight. Reflecting again on what we know about what makes effective professional development (Timperley *et al.*, 2007; Higgins *et al.*, 2015), it is easy to see how engaging in a cycle of research or enquiry can support professional learning. Approaches such as Lesson Study or participation in a Research Learning Community provide a collaborative, practice-based approach that is by necessity sustained over a period of time. With that in mind, for some schools and some teachers, involvement in practitioner research – with appropriate time and support – has the potential to support improved practice and form a valuable part of teachers' ongoing professional development, as can be seen in the case study below.

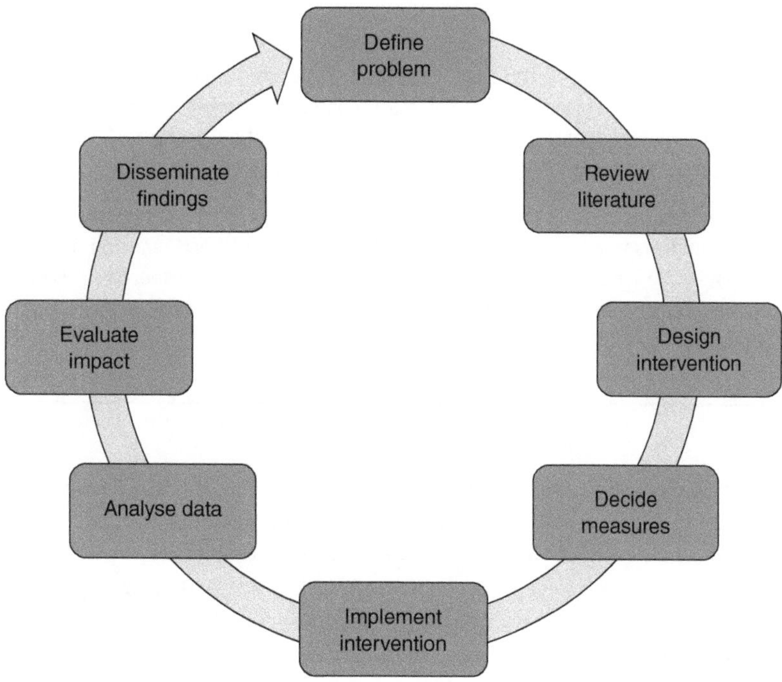

Figure 36.3 A cycle of practitioner research

CASE STUDY

Engaging in a Research Learning Community to improve student outcomes

Jane Flood, Early Years teacher and Research Lead

Improving children's learning and achievement has always been a fundamental reason for joining the teaching profession. It was in this context that I became involved as a Research Lead in a two-year project as part of a Research Learning Community (RLC) with Professor Chris Brown. Our federation of three small infant schools undertook a cycle of enquiry aimed at reducing the gap in attainment for summer-born children in writing.

Building on research-informed strategies, we adopted different pedagogical models for the youngest children, alongside a series of family workshops (where parents came in for six one-hour sessions to work alongside their child and teacher and learn how to best support their child at home). Visits to other schools, regular learning conversations with colleagues and academic seminars added rigour and challenge.

The federation's leadership team were fundamental in providing the resources and structures required.

(Continued)

(Continued)

Changes to PPA organisation provided time to undertake research activities, recognising the competing priorities on teachers' time. A research library for staff was set up and a research blog is used to share research outcomes and readings. Many staff are active members of the Chartered College of Teaching, and attend events like ResearchED and TeachMeets; two teachers are working on Ph.D.s.

The project culminated in an increase in the number of summer-born children achieving end-of-year expectations in 2015 and 2016, but also had a wider impact. It has changed teachers' learning and behaviour, giving power to class teachers by encouraging innovation based on high-quality research findings. A culture has developed that teachers learn from, and build upon existing academic knowledge to develop new and effective teaching strategies to improve pupil outcomes in their classrooms.

As the importance placed on engaging with and in research has increased, so too have opportunities to develop a career around engagement with research. The specialist knowledge and skills required to find, interpret and implement change based on research, as well as to carry out cycles of evaluation or practitioner research, mean that schools are increasingly creating roles such as 'Research Lead' with particular responsibility for this area, and for practitioners who do not aspire to traditional leadership roles, these may be very appealing. Achieving Chartered Teacher Status also requires candidates to demonstrate engagement with research throughout all of the assessments, and most Master's programmes will require students to carry out a piece of research. Engaging with evidence, therefore, can be a fruitful endeavour both in its own right and in terms of the opportunities it may provide.

CHAPTER SUMMARY

- Interest in the use of research and evidence to inform practice in education is growing.
- Evidence-informed practice involves the integration of research evidence with teacher expertise in context.
- There is widespread belief that in using evidence to inform practice, teachers can make better decisions based on knowledge of 'what works'.
- There is limited evidence of the impact of research engagement projects on pupil outcomes, but it does appear to have an effect on teachers' professional learning and reflective practice.
- Engaging with research is not a simple process and involves a number of steps.
- Challenges include accessing research, interpreting it and translating it into practice.
- There are a number of organisations that aim to support teachers in engaging with research.
- Careful implementation of research-informed practices and evaluation of their impact is important.
- Practitioner research involves teachers carrying out small-scale research or enquiry in their own setting.

- The idea of teachers as researchers is controversial, with questions about whether they have the required time, knowledge or skills to carry out rigorous research.
- Carrying out practitioner research can, however, be an effective form of professional development.
- There are, increasingly, opportunities to develop a career pathway centred on engaging with research, and supporting other teachers to do so.

ASSIGNMENTS

If you are writing an ITE assignment looking at evidence-informed practice, it will be useful for you to think through the following:

1. Why is there so much interest in the idea of evidence-informed practice?
2. What are the challenges in engaging with research? How might these be addressed?
3. To what extent do you believe research can provide the answer to 'what works' in education? Why?

Useful texts

Evidence-informed teaching: An evaluation of progress in England - Coldwell *et al.* (2017): This recent study explored progress towards evidence-informed practice in the education system in England.

Teaching as a Research-engaged Profession: Problems and possibilities - McAleavy (2016): This report provides a comprehensive picture of the challenges and opportunities in engaging with and in research.

Evidence-informed practice in education: meanings and applications - Nelson and Campbell (2017): This journal editorial provides a useful overview of evidence-informed practice, and introduces a range of other articles in a special journal issue focused on the topic.

REFERENCES

Brown, C. and Greany, T. (2017) The evidence-informed school system in England: Where should school leaders be focusing their efforts? *Leadership and Policy in Schools.*

Coe, R. (2017) Evaluation: Why, what and how. *Impact: Journal of the Chartered College of Teaching* (Interim Issue).

Coldwell, M., Greany, T., Higgins, S., Brown, C., Maxwell, B., Stiell, B., Stoll, B., Willis, B. and Burns, H. (2017) *Evidence-informed Teaching: An evaluation of progress in England Research Report.* Department for Education.

De Bruckyere, P.A., Kirschner, P. and Hulshof, C.D. (2015) *Urban Myths about Learning and Education.* Cambridge, MA: Academic Press.

DeLuca, C., Bolden, B. and Chan, J. (2017) Systemic professional learning through collaborative inquiry: Examining teachers' perspectives. *Teaching and Teacher Education*, 67.

Goldacre, B. (2013) Building evidence into education. Available at: www.gov.uk/government/news/building-evidence-into-education (accessed: 13/07/18).

Hargreaves, D.H. (1996) *Teaching as a Research Based Profession: Possibilities and prospects*. London: Teacher Training Agency.

Hattie, J. (2009) *Visible Learning*. London: Routledge.

Higgins, S., Cordingley, P., Greany, T. and Coe, R. (2015) *Developing Great Teaching*. London: Teacher Development Trust.

Lord, P., Rabiasz, A., Roy, P., Harland, J., Styles, B. and Fowler, K. (2017). *Evidence-based Literacy Support: The 'Literacy Octopus' trial*. London: Education Endowment Foundation.

McAleavy, T. (2016) *Teaching as a Research-engaged Profession: Problems and possibilities*. Reading: Education Development Trust.

Nelson, J. and Campbell, C. (2017) Evidence-informed practice in education: Meanings and applications. *Educational Research*, 59(2): 127–35.

Rose, J., Thomas, S., Zhang, L., Edwards, A., Augero, A. and Roney, P. (2017) *Research Learning Communities Evaluation*. London: Education Endowment Foundation.

Sackett, D.L., Rosenberg, W.M., Gray, J.A., Haynes, R.B. and Richardson, W.S. (1996) Evidence based medicine: What it is and what it isn't. *British Medical Journal*, 312 (7023): 71–2.

Sharples, J., Albers, B. and Fraser, S. (2018) *Putting Evidence to Work: A school's guide to implementation*. London: Education Endowment Foundation.

Smith, M. and Firth, L. (2018) *Psychology in the Classroom: A teacher's guide to what works*. Abingdon: Routledge.

Stoll, L. (2017) Five challenges in moving towards evidence-informed practice. *Impact, Journal of the Chartered College of Teaching* (interim issue).

Stoll, L. and Temperley, J. (2015) *Narrowing the Gap with Spirals of Enquiry*. London: Whole Education.

Timperley, H.S., Wilson, A., Barrar, H. and Fung, I. (2007) *Teacher Professional Learning and Development: Best evidence synthesis iteration*. New Zealand Ministry of Education.

Wiliam, D. (2015) The research delusion. *TES*, 10 April.

IN YOUR ACADEMIC ASSIGNMENTS FOR INITIAL TEACHER EDUCATION YOUR TUTORS ARE NOT LOOKING FOR:

Your personal, unsubstantiated opinion

A patchwork of other people's ideas and words

A description of your experiences in school

THEY ARE LOOKING FOR:

Your reasoned, justified position or argument in relation to the assignment focus

Your understanding of what you have read, expressed in your own words

Carefully chosen examples of your practice, which relate directly to the points you are making

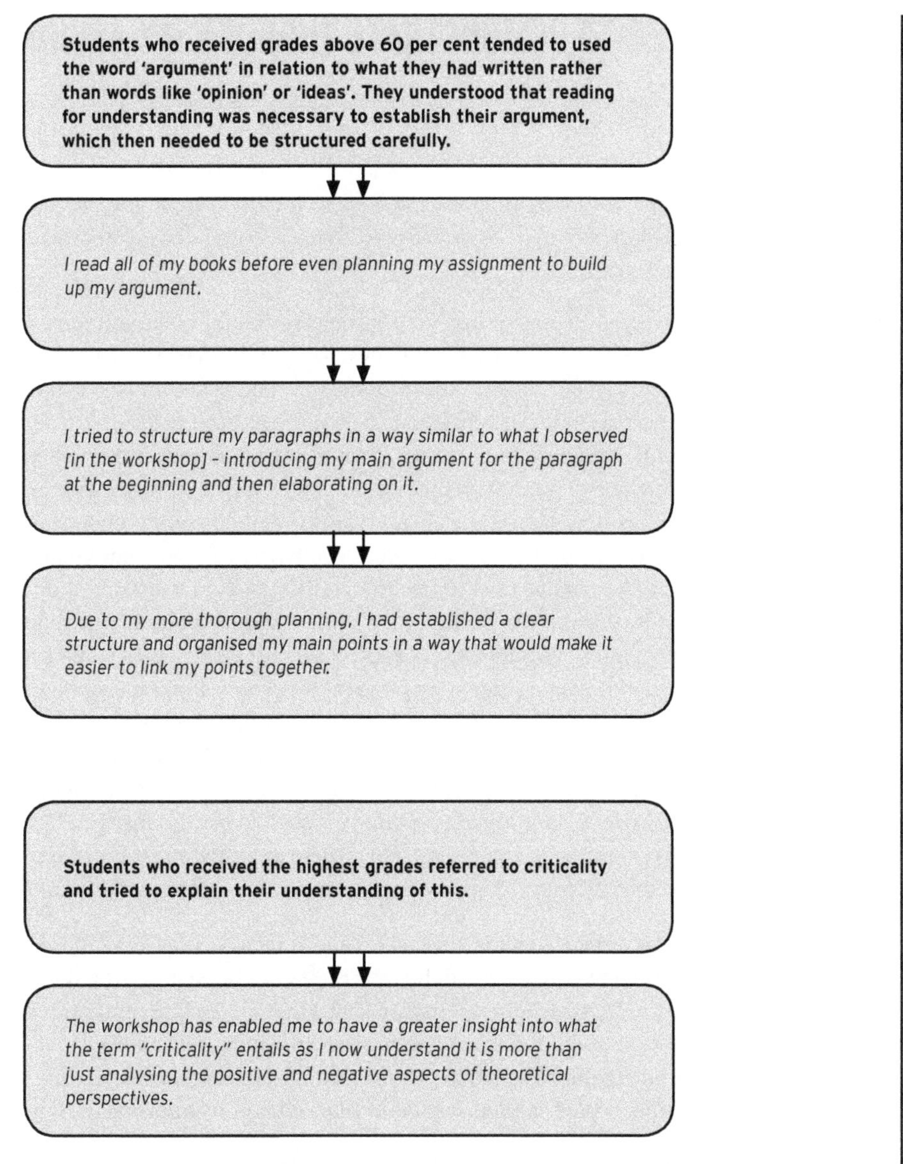

Most universities have marking criteria – often in the form of a grid or rubric – that will be divided into sections that outline generic criteria in relation to the assignments. These will vary from university to university, but will be a valuable guide to the expectations for different grade boundaries. It is sometimes worth having these grids in front of you, along with the assignment title, as you work. It can keep you focused on the elements that your marker will be looking for.

SO WHAT DO I NEED TO DEMONSTRATE THROUGH MY ASSIGNMENTS?

Your assignments are an opportunity for you to demonstrate/evidence/show your skills and knowledge. Your tutors are looking for:

Knowledge: Have you read the right books/texts? Have you understood the focus/scope of the assignment and engaged in the reading you need to understand the key issues? Have you articulated the key areas that relate to the assignment focus?

Understanding: Have you demonstrated your understanding of what you have read? Have you understood what the key issues are – why they are issues? Do you understand what is contested (where there is disagreement)? What is given? Have you expressed *your* understanding? If you have extensively drawn on quotations or near paraphrases or repetitions of what you have read, then your reader will not know whether *you* understand. When you are taking a driving test your examiner will want to know that you are using your rear-view mirror – many people demonstrate this by turning their whole head towards the mirror rather than just taking a sideways glance. In a way, demonstrating understanding in assignments is rather like this – you may well understand the quote you have just used – but you need to show the marker you understand – so add a sentence to reinforce the point the quote is making. I once had a student say to me that she thought it was patronising to her tutors if she explained points that seemed obvious to her and that she knew her tutors already understood. I appreciated her dilemma to some extent, but an important thing to remember is that it really is immaterial what tutors know and understand – you are demonstrating what *you* know. There are no hard-and-fast rules and as you develop a written style you might find ways to demonstrate understanding that move beyond 'This means ...' – for example, using an instance from your practice to illustrate a point. Keeping focused on the title of the assignment might also help; if the assignment is about behaviourism in the classroom, you need to be sure that you have demonstrated a solid understanding of behaviourism. So you might say: 'There are different ways of responding to children in the classroom, such as the behaviourist approach of using extrinsic rewards for good behaviour.'

Criticality: A frequent error assignment writers make is mistaking criticality for criticising. You are *not* being subjectively critical, but objectively so. It is the difference between saying that homework is awful and damages children, and a more measured response that looks at the different kinds of homework provided by schools, its different purposes and the different ways in which it is enforced – all linked to reading. You can then substantiate an argument which might say that most homework at primary school does not have a significant impact, but that there are nuances about the reality of its implementation.

Analysis: This is where you offer a 'so what?' stance – often linked to a critical perspective. So where you have understood what is meant by learning styles and the suggestions that there are some limitations to the ways in which they are adopted by some schools, you might go on to demonstrate that you understand the implications of this.

Argument: This is the heart of it – this is the whole point of your assignment! In your argument you take an informed position and put your case to your reader. This is not the 'unsubstantiated personal opinion' that often makes students fearful of using 'I' in their writing, nor is it a 'balanced view' that merely describes alternative points of view. This is where your understanding, criticality and analysis meets your considered opinion. You believe that children in Key Stage 2 should read picture books – not because it seems like a good idea, but because you have read, understood, analysed and evaluated the arguments around the issue and re-created them in your own, personalised assignment.

Structure/organisation: As you construct your argument you will need to be sure that you have presented it in such a way that your train of thought is evident to your reader. You will start with the premises you wish to explore and build up a series of points through to an overall conclusion. Each point will link to the one before and each point will have its own paragraph (or two) which ensures that it is clearly articulated before moving to the next. Your plan (if you are a planner!) will consist of the main argument, broken down into points you wish to make. The ways in which you then support your points, with reference to the reading you have examined, will be crucial in underlining the robustness of the arguments you make.

Referencing: Referencing is not a hoop to jump through. It is fundamental to the ways in which you can demonstrate that you have engaged with the scholarly community and that you understand that who said what, when they said it and why they said it are highly significant. You are demonstrating that you understand that you are joining this community by acknowledging that you are standing on the shoulders of others who have been there and already thought about the things you are now engaging with. So referencing the work of others is vital – but referencing them correctly and accurately is also important. Your reader needs to be able to know where your ideas have come from and who has influenced your thinking.

Sometimes it might be that the reading you have done has contributed broadly to the way you think about something – so reading Vygotsky has made you consider the importance of the social aspect of learning. Where this is the case you might just put the author's/authors' names in brackets after a discussion about group work. In fact, you might list two or three or even more. What you are acknowledging is that this is not a new idea and that you have learnt about it in general terms from those you are referencing. You will need to reference the name of the author and the date that they were writing to help contextualise the ideas that you are referring to.

If the idea is very specific and identified in a particular place in one text or if you are using a direct quote then you should ensure that you include the page number too – so that this can be easily found by your reader.

Each university will subscribe to a particular form of referencing and they will provide guides as to the specific ways in which your references and reference list should be presented. There will also be guides within your university library and librarians are an excellent source of information too.

Style: There are two different elements operating here – your personal written/spoken style and the academic style to which you are being asked to conform. It might help to think of academic writing as a genre, with particular features which you are required to use. It helps if you are aware of those stylistic features. Just as when you teach children to write traditional tales, you outline the unique features of traditional tales that they will need to include and the kind of language and structures they might draw on. Voice is what comes through when you read one of those stories and immediately recognise which child has written it.

Voice: When you write, you want something of you to come through. The voice in your writing is the way in which you inject yourself into the words and the argument. As above with children writing stories, can a tutor recognise you from your writing? When you are writing academically it is tempting to try to project a neutral, unrecognisable voice, but this is not necessary. You can still be you! Where one student might write, 'I have always passionately believed that children's rights should be at the forefront of their education', another might write, 'I think that children's rights deserve due consideration when planning curricula' – do you get a different sense of what these two students might be like? That is voice.

FREQUENT ERRORS IN INITIAL TEACHER EDUCATION ASSIGNMENTS

The following errors frequently occur:

Stating the obvious: 'Children need to be taught well in order to learn effectively' – Well, yes. But what you are demonstrating in an assignment is that you know what effective teaching and learning looks like and why it is effective. It would be like saying: 'You have to write a good assignment in order to get a high grade'!

Overuse of the thesaurus: While the built-in thesaurus in Word can be extremely helpful it does not identify for you the nuanced differences in meaning of the different synonyms. Synonyms do not mean *exactly* the same thing and you need to be sure that the word you have chosen as a substitute for your first choice does what you want it to do in the context of the sentence. 'Effective teaching and learning' is *not* the same as 'Operative instruction and erudition'!

Over-complicating the language as a substitute for expressing complexity: As a general rule in assignments, express your understanding as simply and clearly as possible. Many students' understanding is obscured by unnecessarily convoluted or complicated sentences. If your reader cannot understand what you are trying to express, they cannot possibly know what you yourself understand. I have a clear memory of a student beginning her assignment with the words: 'Notwithstanding absolute advocacy …' – I spent some time trying to work out what it was she was trying to say and in the end had to resort to the kind of comment that most markers try hard to avoid: 'I don't understand what you mean by this.'

Muddling connectives: Therefore, nevertheless, so, whereas, and so on all mean very different things and will have an effect on your argument and how you present it. Make sure you have used the right word for the right meaning. There are several helpful online resources that list conjunctions and their function.

Cohesion: Using conjunctions carefully is one way to ensure that you are writing cohesively – in a way that holds together. Issues with cohesion can also appear in other ways. There are often times where students engage in a long discussion about a particular issue. The word 'this' will then appear: 'This shows that …'. It is often the case that in the course of a longer argument, it is not clear what 'this' refers to.

Rhetorical questions: As you are writing and exploring an issue it is good that questions arise for you – it shows you are thinking about things in some depth. As you address those questions you will develop your understanding and can use it in your developing argument. What you should avoid, however, is simply stating the questions and not answering them. Rather than saying: 'Why is it, then, that so many schools continue to use stickers to encourage good behaviour?' You might write: 'Stickers are used to encourage good behaviour in many schools – this might be simply because it is familiar, embedded practice'.

Letting quotes speak for themselves: If you use a quotation from literature, either use it to introduce a point that you then go on to develop, or use it to support the point/argument you have already made.

Simply throwing a quote into an assignment without further discussion or development shows only that the author of the quote knows what he/she means.

STUDY SKILLS

Study skills is rather a broad umbrella term. It is likely that there is some support with study skills such as assignment writing, built into your course. This might be more obvious in degree programmes than postgraduate courses – because if you already have a degree it is likely that you require less support than undergraduates. Universities also provide support for study skills built into their package of student support – if you feel this is what you need, don't hesitate to take up what is on offer. Study support at university is not just for those who feel they are particularly weak at writing, either – students who want to improve their grades also seek support from the university.

GETTING FEEDBACK

Providing feedback on your assignments and awarding grades are aspects of our work that all tutors take very seriously. We understand how important it is to you: how hard you have worked on your assignments; how difficult it can be if you don't get as high a grade as you had hoped for; and that you want feedback that enables you to know how to improve your work for each assignment.

You should expect that the feedback that you get on your assignment provides what you need to know in order to understand why your assignment has been awarded the grade it has been given and how you can move forward.

There is likely some variation in the style in which tutors provide the written feedback – the way they phrase their comments, what they do and don't comment on and whether they write more in the general comment box or as individual comments on the script. All marking tutors' comments, however, will provide you with:

- an understanding of why you have the numerical grade you have been awarded (where relevant);
- an understanding of specific aspects of the assignment where you have done well;
- an understanding of what you can do to improve;
- an indication of where you have made errors in spelling, punctuation and grammar (however, tutors will not necessarily point out every error);
- an indication that special considerations have been applied where appropriate;
- comment about the content of your writing in relation to the title and learning outcomes;
- comment about the range of reading you have undertaken and its relevance to the assignment;
- comment about the way in which you have positioned yourself in relation to what you have read and how this informs your argument;

- comment about how well you demonstrate your knowledge and understanding of key concepts and issues;
- comment about your specific subject knowledge where appropriate;
- recognition of your engagement with the assignment focus, including how you relate this appropriately to your experiences of learning and teaching.

DEALING WITH A FAILED ASSIGNMENT

If you find yourself in the position of having failed an assignment, always take advantage of whatever help is offered to you by your university in the process of resubmission. Take time to read and digest the comments that the marker has provided, and be proactive in how you go about ensuring that you know exactly where you went wrong and what you need to do to put it right.

REFERENCES

Austin, R. (ed.) (2016) *Researching Primary Education.* London: Sage.

Bell, J. (2014) *Doing Your Research Project: A guide for first-time researchers.* London: McGraw-Hill Education.

Brookfield, S. (2017) *Becoming a Critically Reflective Teacher.* Oxford: John Wiley & Sons.

Durrant, J. (2016) What is evidence-based practice and why does it matter? In R. Austin (ed.) *Researching Primary Education.* London: Sage.

Lysaker, J. and Sedberry, T. (2015) Reading difference: Picture book retellings as contexts for exploring personal meanings of race and culture. *Literacy* 49(2), pp. 105–11.

Stenhouse, L. (1975) *An Introduction to Curriculum Research and Development.* London: Heinemann.

Wilson, V. (2016) Academic Writing: How do I write it up? and The Literature Review: What is already out there? In R. Austin (ed.) *Researching Primary Education* London: Sage.

Wingate, U. (2012) 'Argument!' helping students understand what essay writing is about. *Journal of English for Academic Purposes,* 11(2): 145–54.

APPENDIX 2

THE TEACHERS' STANDARDS FOR ENGLAND

INTRODUCTION

The Teachers' Standards were introduced in September 2012. They replaced the existing (QTS) standards and the Code of Practice for Registered Teachers in England (from the General Teaching Council).

The Teachers' Standards are statutory and outline the minimum requirements for all teachers and student teachers' professional practice and conduct. Teachers and student teachers must demonstrate that they have met the Teachers' Standards.

School leaders use the Teachers' Standards to assess teachers' performance in schools. They do not detail a complete a list of the elements of good teaching. Instead, they provide a clear framework within which judgements on the quality of teaching can be made.

The Teachers' Standards are an important part of Initial Teacher Training. Trainees' ability to evidence their performance against the standards is essential and all student teachers make reference to the standards throughout their training.

FURTHER GUIDANCE ON THE TEACHERS' STANDARDS

The Learning Matters text *The Teachers' Standards in the Classroom* by Roy Blatchford provides full and detailed information on how and why the standards were developed. The text explores each of the eight standards and gives guidance on:

- How each standards relates to and impacts on classroom practice.
- How performance against each standard can be evidenced.
- Some examples of good practice in classrooms.

Also included are reflective questions to help beginning teachers to explore the impact of their teaching and detailed observations of good teaching and learning.

THE TEACHERS' STANDARDS

PREAMBLE

Teachers make the education of their pupils their first concern, and are accountable for achieving the highest possible standards in work and conduct. Teachers act with honesty and integrity; have strong subject knowledge, keep their knowledge and skills as teachers up-to-date and are self-critical; forge positive professional relationships; and work with parents in the best interests of their pupils.

PART ONE: TEACHING

A teacher must:

1. **Set high expectations which inspire, motivate and challenge pupils**
   - establish a safe and stimulating environment for pupils, rooted in mutual respect
   - set goals that stretch and challenge pupils of all backgrounds, abilities and dispositions
   - demonstrate consistently the positive attitudes, values and behaviour which are expected of pupils.

2. **Promote good progress and outcomes by pupils**
   - be accountable for pupils' attainment, progress and outcomes
   - be aware of pupils' capabilities and their prior knowledge, and plan teaching to build on these
   - guide pupils to reflect on the progress they have made and their emerging needs
   - demonstrate knowledge and understanding of how pupils learn and how this impacts on teaching
   - encourage pupils to take a responsible and conscientious attitude to their own work and study.

3. **Demonstrate good subject and curriculum knowledge**
   - have a secure knowledge of the relevant subject(s) and curriculum areas, foster and maintain pupils' interest in the subject, and address misunderstandings
   - demonstrate a critical understanding of developments in the subject and curriculum areas, and promote the value of scholarship
   - demonstrate an understanding of and take responsibility for promoting high standards of literacy, articulacy and the correct use of standard English, whatever the teacher's specialist subject
   - if teaching early reading, demonstrate a clear understanding of systematic synthetic phonics
   - if teaching early mathematics, demonstrate a clear understanding of appropriate teaching strategies.

4. Plan and teach well-structured lessons

- impart knowledge and develop understanding through effective use of lesson time
- promote a love of learning and children's intellectual curiosity
- set homework and plan other out-of-class activities to consolidate and extend the knowledge and understanding pupils have acquired
- reflect systematically on the effectiveness of lessons and approaches to teaching
- contribute to the design and provision of an engaging curriculum within the relevant subject area(s).

5. Adapt teaching to respond to the strengths and needs of all pupils

- know when and how to differentiate appropriately, using approaches which enable pupils to be taught effectively
- have a secure understanding of how a range of factors can inhibit pupils' ability to learn, and how best to overcome these
- demonstrate an awareness of the physical, social and intellectual development of children, and know how to adapt teaching to support pupils' education at different stages of development
- have a clear understanding of the needs of all pupils, including those with special educational needs; those of high ability; those with English as an additional language; those with disabilities; and be able to use and evaluate distinctive teaching approaches to engage and support them.

6. Make accurate and productive use of assessment

- know and understand how to assess the relevant subject and curriculum areas, including statutory assessment requirements
- make use of formative and summative assessment to secure pupils' progress
- use relevant data to monitor progress, set targets, and plan subsequent lessons
- give pupils regular feedback, both orally and through accurate marking, and encourage pupils to respond to the feedback.

7. Manage behaviour effectively to ensure a good and safe learning environment

- have clear rules and routines for behaviour in classrooms, and take responsibility for promoting good and courteous behaviour both in classrooms and around the school, in accordance with the school's behaviour policy
- have high expectations of behaviour, and establish a framework for discipline with a range of strategies, using praise, sanctions and rewards consistently and fairly
- manage classes effectively, using approaches which are appropriate to pupils' needs in order to involve and motivate them

- maintain good relationships with pupils, exercise appropriate authority, and act decisively when necessary.

8. **Fulfil wider professional responsibilities**
    - make a positive contribution to the wider life and ethos of the school
    - develop effective professional relationships with colleagues, knowing how and when to draw on advice and specialist support
    - deploy support staff effectively
    - take responsibility for improving teaching through appropriate professional development, responding to advice and feedback from colleagues
    - communicate effectively with parents with regard to pupils' achievements and well-being.

PART TWO: PERSONAL AND PROFESSIONAL CONDUCT

A teacher is expected to demonstrate consistently high standards of personal and professional conduct. The following statements define the behaviour and attitudes which set the required standard for conduct throughout a teacher's career.

- Teachers uphold public trust in the profession and maintain high standards of ethics and behaviour, within and outside school, by:
    - treating pupils with dignity, building relationships rooted in mutual respect, and at all times observing proper boundaries appropriate to a teacher's professional position
    - having regard for the need to safeguard pupils' well-being, in accordance with statutory provisions
    - showing tolerance of and respect for the rights of others
    - not undermining fundamental British values, including democracy, the rule of law, individual liberty and mutual respect, and tolerance of those with different faiths and beliefs
    - ensuring that personal beliefs are not expressed in ways which exploit pupils' vulnerability or might lead them to break the law.
- Teachers must have proper and professional regard for the ethos, policies and practices of the school in which they teach, and maintain high standards in their own attendance and punctuality.
- Teachers must have an understanding of, and always act within, the statutory frameworks which set out their professional duties and responsibilities.

APPENDIX 3

THE NORTHERN IRELAND TEACHER COMPETENCES

INTRODUCTION: OVERVIEW OF THE TEACHER COMPETENCES

The General Teaching Council Northern Ireland, in its deliberations on the competences, has rejected any attempt to adopt a reductionist approach to teacher education. It is imperative that this publication be read in its entirety and that it is used within the context of the Council's core philosophy which seeks to celebrate the complexity of teaching and, as importantly, the reality that it is concerned with values and professional identity as much as knowledge and competences.

The full publication can be found here: www.gtcni.org.uk/userfiles/file/The_Reflective_Profession_3rd-edition.pdf

THE PROFESSIONAL COMPETENCES

The competence statements have been set out under three broad headings:

PROFESSIONAL VALUES AND PRACTICE

Teachers should demonstrate that they:

1. understand and uphold the core values and commitments enshrined in the Council's Code of Values and Professional Practice.

PROFESSIONAL KNOWLEDGE AND UNDERSTANDING

Teachers will have developed:

2. a knowledge and understanding of contemporary debates about the nature and purposes of education and the social and policy contexts in which the aims of education are defined and implemented.

3. (i) a knowledge and understanding of the learning area/subject(s) they teach, including the centrality of strategies and initiatives to improve literacy, numeracy and thinking skills, keeping curricular, subject and pedagogical knowledge up-to-date through reflection, self-study and collaboration with colleagues; and

   (ii) in Irish medium and other bilingual contexts, sufficient linguistic and pedagogical knowledge to teach the curriculum.

4. a knowledge and understanding of how the learning area/subject(s) they teach contribute to the Northern Ireland Curriculum and be aware of curriculum requirements in preceding and subsequent key stages.

5. a knowledge and understanding of curriculum development processes, including planning, implementation and evaluation.

6. a knowledge and understanding of the factors that promote and hinder effective learning, and be aware of the need to provide for the holistic development of the child.

7. a knowledge and understanding of a range of strategies to promote and maintain positive behaviour, including an acknowledgement of pupil voice, to establish an effective learning environment.

8. a knowledge and understanding of the need to take account of the significant features of pupils' cultures, languages and faiths and to address the implications for learning arising from these.

9. a knowledge and understanding of their responsibilities under the Special Educational Needs Code of Practice and know the features of the most common special needs and appropriate strategies to address these.

10. a knowledge and understanding of strategies for communicating effectively with pupils, parents, colleagues and personnel from relevant child and school support agencies.

11. a knowledge and understanding of how to use technology effectively, both to aid pupil learning and to support their professional role, and how this competence embeds across all of the competences.

12. a knowledge and understanding of the interrelationship between schools and the communities they serve, and the potential for mutual development and well-being.

13. a knowledge and understanding of the statutory framework pertaining to education and schooling and their specific responsibilities emanating from it.

PROFESSIONAL SKILLS AND APPLICATION

PLANNING AND LEADING

Teachers will:

14. set appropriate learning objectives/outcomes/intentions, taking account of what pupils know, understand and can do, and the demands of the Northern Ireland Curriculum in terms of knowledge, skills acquisition and progression.

15. plan and evaluate lessons that enable all pupils, including those with special educational needs, to meet learning objectives/outcomes/intentions, showing high expectations and an awareness of potential areas of difficulty.

16. deploy, organise and guide the work of other adults to support pupils' learning, when appropriate.

17. plan for out-of-school learning, including school visits and field work, where appropriate.

18. manage their time and workload effectively and efficiently and maintain a work/life balance.

Teaching and Learning

Teachers will:

19. create and maintain a safe, interactive and challenging learning environment, with appropriate clarity of purpose for activities.

20. use a range of teaching strategies and resources, including eLearning where appropriate, that enable learning to take place and which maintain pace within lessons and over time.

21. employ strategies that motivate and meet the needs of all pupils, including those with special and additional educational needs and for those not learning in their first language.

22. secure and promote a standard of behaviour that enables all pupils to learn, pre-empting and dealing with inappropriate behaviour in the context of school policies and what is known about best practice.

23. contribute to the life and development of the school, collaborating with teaching and support staff, parents and external agencies.

ASSESSMENT

Teachers will:

24. focus on assessment for learning by monitoring pupils' progress, giving constructive feedback to help pupils reflect on and improve their learning.

25. select from a range of assessment strategies to evaluate pupils' learning, and use this information in their planning to help make their teaching more effective.

26. assess the levels of pupils' attainment against relevant benchmarking data and understand the relationship between pupil assessment and target setting.

27. liaise orally and in written reports in an effective manner with parents or carers on their child's progress and achievements

DIMENSIONS OF DEVELOPMENT

As teachers progress in their careers they will encounter different challenges and expectations; they grow in confidence, share in the knowledge of colleagues and learn from experience. It can also be anticipated that their practice will become progressively more sophisticated and nuanced. This will be evidenced by:

- greater complexity in teaching, for example, in handling mixed-ability classes, or reluctant learners, or classes marked by significant diversity, or inter-disciplinary work;
- the deployment of a wider range of teaching strategies;
- basing teaching on a wider range of evidence, reading and research;
- extending one's impact beyond the classroom and fuller participation in the life of the school;
- the capacity to exercise autonomy, to innovate and to improvise;
- and a pronounced capacity for self-criticism and self-improvement; the ability to impact on colleagues through mentoring and coaching, modelling good practice, contributing to the literature on teaching and learning and the public discussion of professional issues, leading staff development, all based on the capacity to theorise about policy and practice.

THE COMPETENCE STATEMENTS AND PHASE EXEMPLARS

For the full document including all phase exemplars, see the full document online at:

www.gtcni.org.uk/userfiles/file/The_Reflective_Profession_3rd-edition.pdf

In presenting the competences along with the phase exemplars, the Council has sought to emphasise that the acquisition of competence is very much related to context and phase, whether this be initial teacher education, induction, early professional development or beyond into career-long continuing professional development.

It can be said that the phase exemplars attempt to articulate the necessary widening and deepening of experience related to classroom and the whole-school context in which teachers work. However, they also emphasise the growing collective responsibilities inherent in the development of professional communities of practice, within which the individual's growing professional competence is situated. The Council takes the view that it is within these wider professional communities that school improvement is promoted and sustained. It is also important that the exemplars are not viewed as a teacher education curriculum, or as prescriptive benchmarks to be applied irrespective of the specific context within which teachers work or the challenges and development opportunities afforded them; rather, they are the basis for reflection and dialogue, and a vehicle for needs analysis and forward planning.

THE COMPETENCE STATEMENTS

1. Teachers should demonstrate that they understand and uphold the core values and commitments enshrined in the Council's Code of Values and Professional Practice.

2. Teachers will have developed a knowledge and understanding of contemporary debates about the nature and purposes of education and the social and policy contexts in which the aims of education are defined and implemented.

3. (i) Teachers will have developed a knowledge and understanding of the learning area/subject(s) they teach, including the centrality of strategies and initiatives to improve, literacy, numeracy and thinking skills, keeping curricular, subject and pedagogical knowledge up-to-date through reflection, self-study and collaboration with colleagues.

   (ii) Teachers will have developed, in Irish medium and other bilingual contexts, sufficient linguistic and pedagogical knowledge to teach the curriculum.

4. Teachers will have developed a knowledge and understanding of how the learning area/subject(s) they teach contribute to the Northern Ireland Curriculum and be aware of curriculum requirements in preceding and subsequent key stages.

5. Teachers will have developed a knowledge and understanding of curriculum development processes, including planning, implementation and evaluation.

6. Teachers will have developed a knowledge and understanding of the factors that promote and hinder effective learning, and be aware of the need to provide for the holistic development of the child.

7. Teachers will have developed a knowledge and understanding of a range of strategies to promote and maintain positive behaviour, including an acknowledgement of pupil voice, to establish an effective learning environment.

8. Teachers will have developed a knowledge and understanding of the need to take account of the significant features of pupils' cultures, languages and faiths and to address the implications for learning arising from these.

9. Teachers will have developed a knowledge and understanding of their responsibilities under the Special Educational Needs Code of Practice and know the features of the most common special needs and appropriate strategies to address these.

10. Teachers will have developed a knowledge and understanding of strategies for communicating effectively with pupils, parents, colleagues and personnel from relevant child and school support agencies.

11. Teachers will have developed a knowledge and understanding of how to use technology effectively, both to aid pupil learning and to support their professional role, and how this competence embeds across all of the competences.

12. Teachers will have developed a knowledge and understanding of the interrelationship between schools and the communities they serve, and the potential for mutual development and well-being.

13. Teachers will have developed a knowledge and understanding of the statutory framework pertaining to education and schooling and their specific responsibilities emanating from it.

14. Teachers will set appropriate learning objectives/outcomes/intentions, taking account of what pupils know, understand and can do, and the demands of the Northern Ireland Curriculum* in terms of knowledge, skills acquisition and progression.

15. Teachers will plan and evaluate lessons that enable all pupils, including those with special educational needs, to meet learning objectives/outcomes/intentions, showing high expectations and an awareness of potential areas of difficulty.

16. Teachers will deploy, organise and guide the work of other adults to support pupils' learning, when appropriate.

17. Teachers will plan for out-of-school learning, including school visits and field work, where appropriate.

18. Teachers will manage their time and workload effectively and efficiently and maintain a work/life balance.

19. Teachers will create and maintain a safe, interactive and challenging learning environment, with appropriate clarity of purpose for activities.

20. Teachers will use a range of teaching strategies and resources, including eLearning where appropriate, that enable learning to take place and which maintain pace within lessons and over time.

21. Teachers will employ strategies that motivate and meet the needs of all pupils, including those with special and additional educational needs and for those not learning in their first language.

22. Teachers will secure and promote a standard of behaviour that enables all pupils to learn, preempting and dealing with inappropriate behaviour in the context of school policies and what is known about best practice.

23. Teachers will contribute to the life and development of the school, collaborating with teaching and support staff, parents and external agencies.

24. Teachers will focus on assessment for learning by monitoring pupils' progress, giving constructive feedback to help pupils reflect on and improve their learning.

25. Teachers will select from a range of assessment strategies to evaluate pupils' learning, and use this information in their planning to help make their teaching more effective.

26. Teachers will assess the levels of pupils' attainment against relevant benchmarking data and understand the relationship between pupil assessment and target setting.

27. Teachers will liaise orally and in written reports in an effective manner with parents or carers on their child's progress and achievements.

CODE OF VALUES AND PROFESSIONAL PRACTICE

FOREWORD

One of the hallmarks of any profession is the commitment of its members to a code of ethics which sets out professional values and responsibilities. In establishing our Code of Values and Professional Practice we are affirming our commitment to these values and setting out our aspirations. The achievement of these lofty goals will require diligence and energy allied to a clear sense of purpose and an understanding of the significance, for both pupils and society at large, of our endeavours. The importance to society of the process of schooling and the work of teachers should not be underestimated. Indeed, education lies at the heart of both social and economic progress. It empowers and celebrates; it shapes society and effectively secures future well-being. It is appropriate that those who are entrusted with this role should publicly affirm their commitment to excellence. The codification of the underlying values, responsibilities and aspirations of the profession is eloquent testimony to the profession's commitment to excellence in and for all.

INTRODUCTION

Teachers as a group have always understood the professional nature of their task. They have always been conscious of the special purpose behind their endeavours and how, in essence, they shape the future of society through their work with those young people entrusted to their care. That duty of care, allied to a sense of professional responsibility, is the hallmark of true professionals. In discharging this responsibility, teachers have been guided by a set of values that, to date, have been implicit rather than explicit. Values are often seen as aspirations or driving forces, often not openly articulated, which effectively shape people's lives and determine where they will direct their energies and what they will hold to be of importance. Many within our community have both understood and benefited from the profession's implicit values, and the commitment and professionalism that were an inevitable outcome of these. There is, however, merit in articulating those values if only to celebrate the high ethical standards that underpin the work of teachers in Northern Ireland. This Code provides our teachers, for the first time, with an explicit and public statement of values and professional practice. The values enshrined within the Code are also those that underpin the work of the General Teaching Council for Northern Ireland and will inform its deliberations in regard to internal policy development and external policy initiatives.

The Code seeks to:

- set out clearly the core values underpinning professional practice;
- encourage attitudes and conduct commensurate with the core values of the profession;
- provide a framework for evaluating both policies and practice; and
- enhance the status of the profession in the eyes of the public.

CORE VALUES

The core values of the profession are as follows:

- Trust
- Honesty
- Commitment
- Respect
- Fairness
- Equality
- Integrity
- Tolerance
- Service

A commitment to serve lies at the heart of professional behaviour. In addition, members of the profession will exemplify the values listed above in their work and in their relationships with others; recognising, in particular, the unique and privileged relationship that exists between teachers and their pupils. In keeping with the spirit of professional service and commitment, teachers will at all times be conscious of their responsibilities to others: learners, colleagues and indeed the profession itself. Many of the commitments outlined below are also underpinned by legislation and the profession will always seek, as a minimum, to comply with both the spirit and detail of relevant legislative requirements.

COMMITMENT TO LEARNERS

Teachers will:

- maintain professional relationships with those pupils/learners entrusted to their care which respect the pupil/learner as a person and encourage growth and development;
- acknowledge and respect the uniqueness, individuality and specific needs of each pupil and thus provide appropriate learning experiences; and
- aim to motivate and inspire pupils with a view to helping each realise their potential.

COMMITMENT TO COLLEAGUES AND OTHERS

Teachers will:

- work with colleagues and others to create a professional community that supports the social, intellectual, spiritual/moral, emotional and physical development of pupils;
- promote collegiality among colleagues by respecting their professional standing and opinions and, in that spirit, be prepared to offer advice and share professional practice with colleagues;
- cooperate, where appropriate, with professionals from other agencies in the interests of pupils;
- ensure that relationships with the parents, guardians or carers of pupils, in their capacity as partners in the educational process, are characterised by respect and trust; and
- respect confidential information relating to pupils or colleagues gained in the course of professional practice, unless the well-being of an individual or legal imperative requires disclosure.

COMMITMENT TO THE PROFESSION

Teachers will:

- as reflective practitioners, contribute to the review and revision of policies and practices with a view to optimising the opportunities for pupils or addressing identified individual or institutional needs; and
- in keeping with the concept of professional integrity assume responsibility for their ongoing professional development needs as an essential expression of their professionalism.

APPENDIX 4

THE STANDARDS FOR REGISTRATION: MANDATORY REQUIREMENTS FOR REGISTRATION WITH THE GENERAL TEACHING COUNCIL FOR SCOTLAND

GTC Scotland, December 2012. www.gtcs.org.uk

INTRODUCTION

The Standard for Provisional Registration (SPR) and The Standard for Full Registration (SFR) are part of the suite of GTC Scotland's Professional Standards which also includes The Standard for Career-Long Professional Learning and The Standards for Leadership and Management. These standards are underpinned by the themes of values, sustainability and leadership. Professional values are at the core of the Standards for Registration. They are integral to, and demonstrated through, all our professional relationships and practices.

The Standard for Provisional Registration specifies what is expected of a student teacher at the end of Initial Teacher Education who is seeking provisional registration with GTC Scotland. (It also acts as one of the set of subject benchmark statements for professional qualifications in Scotland developed by the Quality Assurance Agency for Higher Education.) Having gained the SPR, all provisionally registered teachers continue their professional learning journey by moving towards the attainment of the Standard for Full Registration. The SFR is the gateway to the profession and the benchmark of teacher competence for all teachers. It must therefore constitute standards of capability in relation to teaching (with such reasonable adjustments as may be required under Equalities Legislation) in which learners, parents, the profession itself and the wider community can have confidence.

1. PROFESSIONAL VALUES AND PERSONAL COMMITMENT

The Professional Values and Personal Commitment should be read in conjunction with the GTC Scotland Student Teacher Code and Code of Professionalism and Conduct (COPAC).

The Professional Values and Personal Commitment core to being a teacher are:

SOCIAL JUSTICE

- Embracing locally and globally the educational and social values of sustainability, equality and justice and recognising the rights and responsibilities of future as well as current generations.
- Committing to the principles of democracy and social justice through fair, transparent, inclusive and sustainable policies and practices in relation to: age, disability, gender and gender identity, race, ethnicity, religion and belief and sexual orientation.
- Valuing as well as respecting social, cultural and ecological diversity and promoting the principles and practices of local and global citizenship for all learners.
- Demonstrating a commitment to engaging learners in real world issues to enhance learning experiences and outcomes, and to encourage learning our way to a better future.
- Respecting the rights of all learners as outlined in the United Nations Convention on the Rights of the Child (UNCRC) and their entitlement to be included in decisions regarding their learning experiences and have all aspects of their well-being developed and supported.

INTEGRITY

- Demonstrating openness, honesty, courage and wisdom.
- Critically examining personal and professional attitudes and beliefs and challenging assumptions and professional practice.
- Critically examining the connections between personal and professional attitudes and beliefs, values and practices to effect improvement and, when appropriate, bring about transformative change in practice.

TRUST AND RESPECT

- Acting and behaving in ways that develop a culture of trust and respect through, for example, being trusting and respectful of others within the school, and with all those involved in influencing the lives of learners in and beyond the learning community.
- Providing and ensuring a safe and secure environment for all learners within a caring and compassionate ethos and with an understanding of wellbeing.
- Demonstrating a commitment to motivating and inspiring learners, acknowledging their social and economic context, individuality and specific learning needs and taking into consideration barriers to learning.

PROFESSIONAL COMMITMENT

- Engaging with all aspects of professional practice and working collegiately with all members of our educational communities with enthusiasm, adaptability and constructive criticality.

- Committing to lifelong enquiry, learning, professional development and leadership as core aspects of professionalism and collaborative practice.

2. PROFESSIONAL KNOWLEDGE AND UNDERSTANDING

2.1 CURRICULUM

The Standard for Provisional Registration	**The Standard for Full Registration**
2.1.1 Have knowledge and understanding of the nature of the curriculum and its development	
Professional Actions Student teachers: • develop an understanding of the principles of curriculum design and the contexts for learning; • know about and understand the processes of change and development in the curriculum; • develop an awareness of connections with other curricular areas, stages and sectors.	Professional Actions Registered teachers: • have secure and detailed understanding of the principles of curriculum design and can apply them in any setting where learning takes place; • have secure working knowledge and detailed understanding of the processes of change and development in the curriculum; • know how to identify and highlight connections with other curricular areas, stages or sectors, promoting learning beyond subject boundaries.
2.1.2 Have knowledge and understanding of the relevant area(s) of pre-school, primary or secondary curriculum	
Professional Actions Student teachers: • acquire knowledge and understanding of theory and practical skills in curricular areas, referring to local and national guidance; • understand how to match the level of curricular areas to the needs of all learners; • understand the importance of using and designing materials for teaching and learning to stimulate, support and challenge all learners; • know how to develop realistic and coherent interdisciplinary contexts for learning, particularly in relation to sustainability.	Professional Actions Registered teachers: • have detailed knowledge and understanding of the theory and practical skills required in curricular areas, referring to local and national guidance; • know how to match and apply the level of the curricular areas to the needs of all learners; • know how to use, design and adapt materials for teaching and learning which stimulate, support and challenge all learners; • know how to work collaboratively with colleagues to facilitate interdisciplinary learning; • know how to work with the local and global community to develop realistic and coherent interdisciplinary.

(Continued)

(Continued)

<table>
<tr><td colspan="2">2.1.3 Have knowledge and understanding of planning coherent and progressive teaching programmes</td></tr>
<tr><td>Professional Actions
Student teachers:

• know how to plan for effective teaching and learning across different contexts and experiences;
• know and understand how to justify what is taught within curricular areas in relation to the curriculum and the relevance to the needs of all learners.</td><td>Professional Actions
Registered teachers:

• know how to plan systematically for effective teaching and learning across different contexts and experiences;
• have a secure working knowledge and detailed understanding to justify what is taught within the curricular areas, in relation to the curriculum and the relevance to the needs of all learners;
• understand their role as leaders of curriculum development.</td></tr>
<tr><td colspan="2">2.1.4 Have knowledge and understanding of contexts for learning to fulfil their responsibilities in literacy, numeracy, health and wellbeing and interdisciplinary learning</td></tr>
<tr><td>Professional Actions
Student teachers:

• know how to promote and support the cognitive, emotional, social and physical wellbeing of all learners in their care, and show commitment to raising these learners' expectations of themselves;
• know how to apply knowledge and understanding of areas of the curriculum which contribute to personal and social development and health and wellbeing;
• have knowledge and understanding of current guidance on the use of digital technologies in schools and know how to use digital technologies to enhance teaching and learning;
• know and understand the content of the curriculum in relation to literacy, numeracy and health and wellbeing as set out in national guidance;
• know and understand the methods and underlying theories for effective teaching of literacy, numeracy and health and wellbeing; and select the most appropriate methods to meet all learners' needs;
• have knowledge and understanding of current educational priorities such as learning for sustainability.</td><td>Professional Actions
Registered teachers:

• know how to promote and support the cognitive, emotional, social and physical wellbeing of all learners, and demonstrate a commitment to raising all learners' expectations of themselves;
• have knowledge and understanding of areas of the curriculum which contribute to personal and social development and health and wellbeing;
• have secure knowledge and understanding of current guidance on the use of digital technologies in schools and know how to use digital technologies competently to enhance teaching and learning;
• have appropriate and increasing knowledge and understanding of the content of the curriculum in relation to literacy, numeracy and health and wellbeing as set out in national guidance;
• have secure knowledge and understanding of the methods and underlying theories for effective teaching of literacy, numeracy and health and wellbeing; and effectively select the most appropriate methods to meet all learners' needs;
• have secure knowledge of current educational priorities such as learning for sustainability.</td></tr>
</table>

2.3.2 Have knowledge and understanding of the importance of research and engagement in professional enquiry	
Professional Actions Student teachers: • know how to access and apply relevant findings from educational research; • know how to engage appropriately in the systematic investigation of practice.	Professional Actions Registered teachers: • know how to access and apply relevant findings from educational research; • know how to engage critically in enquiry, research and evaluation individually or collaboratively, and apply this in order to improve teaching and learning.

3. PROFESSIONAL SKILLS AND ABILITIES

3.1 TEACHING AND LEARNING

The Standard for Provisional Registration	**The Standard for Full Registration**
3.1.1 Plan coherent, progressive and stimulating teaching programmes which match learners' needs and abilities	
Professional Actions Student teachers: • plan appropriately for effective teaching and in order to meet the needs of all learners, including learning in literacy, numeracy, health and wellbeing and skills for learning, life and work.	Professional Actions Registered teachers: • plan appropriately, in different contexts and over differing timescales, for effective teaching and learning in order to meet the needs of all learners, including learning in literacy, numeracy, health and wellbeing and skills for learning, life and work.
3.1.2 Communicate effectively and interact productively with learners, individually and collectively	
Professional Actions Student teachers: • model appropriate levels of literacy and numeracy in their own professional practice; ϖ use communication methods, including a variety of media, to promote and develop positive relationships and to motivate and sustain the interest of all learners; • communicate appropriately with all learners, and promote competence and confidence in literacy;	Professional Actions Registered teachers: • model appropriate levels of literacy and numeracy in their own professional practice; • use a range of communication methods, including a variety of media, to promote and develop positive relationships to motivate and sustain the interest and participation of all learners;

(Continued)

(Continued)

• demonstrate effective questioning strategies; • communicate the purpose of the learning and give explanations at the appropriate level(s) for all learners; • stimulate learner participation in debate and decision-making about issues which are open-ended, complex, controversial or emotional; • reflect on the impact of their personal method of communication on learners and others in the classroom.	• communicate appropriately with all learners, and promote competence and confidence in literacy; • demonstrate effective questioning strategies varied to meet the needs of all learners, in order to enhance teaching and learning; • communicate the purpose of the learning and give effective explanations at the appropriate level(s) for all learners; • create opportunities to stimulate learner participation in debate and decision-making about issues which are open-ended, complex, controversial or emotional; • reflect on the impact of their personal method of communication on learners and others in the learning community.
3.1.3 Employ a range of teaching strategies and resources to meet the needs and abilities of learners	
Professional Actions Student teachers: • demonstrate that they can select creative and imaginative strategies for teaching and learning appropriate to learners as individuals, groups or classes; ϖ demonstrate that they can select and use a wide variety of resources and teaching approaches, including digital technologies and outdoor learning opportunities; • demonstrate the ability to justify and evaluate professional practice, and take action to improve the impact on all learners.	Professional Actions Registered teachers: • consistently select creative and imaginative strategies for teaching and learning appropriate to the interests and needs of all learners, as individuals, groups or classes; • skilfully deploy a wide variety of innovative resources and teaching approaches, including digital technologies and, where appropriate, actively seeking outdoor learning opportunities; • justify consistently and evaluate competently professional practice, and take action to improve the impact on all learners; • create opportunities for learning to be transformative in terms of challenging assumptions and expanding world views.
3.1.4 Have high expectations of all learners	
Professional Actions Student teachers: • develop tasks and set pace of work to meet the needs of learners, providing effective support and challenge, seeking advice appropriately; • demonstrate an awareness of barriers to learning, recognising when to seek further advice in relation to all learners' needs.	Professional Actions Registered teachers: • ensure learning tasks are varied, differentiated and devised to build confidence and promote progress of all learners, providing effective support and challenge; • identify effectively barriers to learning and respond appropriately, seeking advice in relation to all learners' needs as required; ϖ show commitment to raising learners' expectations of themselves and others and their level of care for themselves, for others and for the natural world.

3.1.5 Work effectively in partnership in order to promote learning and wellbeing	
Professional Actions Student teachers: • ensure learners contribute to planning and enhancement of their own learning programmes; • demonstrate an ability to work co-operatively in the classroom and the wider learning community with staff, parents and partner agencies to promote learning and wellbeing.	Professional Actions Registered teachers: • establish a culture where learners meaningfully participate in decisions related to their learning and their school; • create and sustain appropriate working relationships with all staff, parents and partner agencies to support learning and wellbeing, taking a lead role when appropriate.

3.2 CLASSROOM ORGANISATION AND MANAGEMENT

3.2.1 Create a safe, caring and purposeful learning environment	
Professional Actions Student teachers: plan and provide a safe, well organised learning environment, including effective use of display; • make appropriate use of available space to accommodate whole class lessons, group and individual work and promote independent learning; • use outdoor learning opportunities, including direct experiences of nature and other learning within and beyond the school boundary; • organise and manage classroom resources and digital technologies to support teaching and learning; • know about and be able to apply health and safety regulations as appropriate to their role.	Professional Actions Registered teachers: • ensure their classroom or work area is safe, well-organised, wellmanaged and stimulating, with effective use of display regularly updated; • plan and organise effectively available space to facilitate whole-class lessons, group and individual work and promote independent learning; • use outdoor learning opportunities, including direct experiences of nature and other learning within and beyond the school boundary; • enable learners to make full use of well-chosen resources, including digital technologies to support teaching and learning; • know about and apply appropriately health and safety regulations as an integral part of professional practice.
3.2.2 Develop positive relationships and positive behaviour strategies	
Professional Actions Student teachers: • demonstrate care and commitment to working with all learners; • demonstrate knowledge and understanding of wellbeing indicators;	Professional Actions Registered teachers: • demonstrate care and commitment to working with all learners; • demonstrate a secure knowledge and understanding of the wellbeing indicators;

(Continued)

(Continued)

• show awareness of educational research and local and national advice, and demonstrate the ability to use a variety of strategies to build relationships with learners, promote positive behaviour and celebrate success; • apply the school's positive behaviour policy, including strategies for understanding and preventing bullying; • know how and when to seek the advice of colleagues in managing behaviour; • demonstrate the ability to justify the approach taken in managing behaviour.	• show in-depth awareness of educational research and local and national advice, and use in a consistent way, a variety of strategies to build relationships with learners, promote positive behaviour and celebrate success; • implement consistently the school's positive behaviour policy including strategies for understanding and preventing bullying, and manage pupil behaviour in and around the school, in a fair, sensitive and informed manner; • seek and use advice from colleagues and promoted staff, as appropriate, in managing behaviour; • evaluate and justify their approaches to managing behaviour and, when necessary, be open to new approaches to adapt them; ϖrecognise when a learner's behaviour may signify distress requiring the need for further support, and take appropriate action.

3.3 PUPIL ASSESSMENT

3.3.1 Use assessment, recording and reporting as an integral part of the teaching process to support and enhance learning	
Professional Actions Student teachers:	Professional Actions Registered teachers:
• use a range of approaches for formative and summative assessment purposes, appropriate to the needs of all learners and the requirements of the curriculum and awarding and accrediting bodies; • enable all learners to engage in self-evaluation and peer assessment to benefit learning; • record assessment information to enhance teaching and learning; • use the results of assessment to identify strengths and development needs which lead to further learning opportunities.	• systematically develop and use an extensive range of strategies, approaches and associated materials for formative and summative assessment purposes, appropriate to the needs of all learners and the requirements of the curriculum and awarding and accrediting bodies; ϖ enable all learners to engage in self evaluation and peer assessment to benefit learning; • record assessment information in a systematic and meaningful way in order to enhance teaching and learning and fulfil the requirements of the curriculum and awarding bodies; • use the results of assessment to identify development needs at class, group and individual level and as a basis for dialogue with learners about their progress and targets; • produce clear and informed reports for parents and other agencies which discuss learners' progress and matters related to personal, social and emotional development in a sensitive and constructive way.

3.4 PROFESSIONAL REFLECTION AND COMMUNICATION

<table>
<tr><th colspan="2">3.4.1 Read and critically engage with professional literature, educational research and policy</th></tr>
<tr><td>Professional Actions
Student teachers:

• read and analyse a range of appropriate educational and research literature;
• use what they have learned from reading and research to challenge and inform practice.</td><td>Professional Actions
Registered teachers:

• read, analyse and critically evaluate a range of appropriate educational and research literature;
• systematically engage with research and literature to challenge and inform professional practice.</td></tr>
<tr><td colspan="2">3.4.2 Engage in reflective practice to develop and advance career-long professional learning and expertise</td></tr>
<tr><td>Professional Actions
Student teachers:

• reflect and engage in self evaluation using the relevant professional standard;
• adopt an enquiring approach to their professional practice and engage in professional enquiry and professional dialogue;
• evaluate their classroom practice, taking account of feedback from others, in order to enhance teaching and learning;
• engage where possible in the processes of curriculum development, improvement planning and professional review and development;
• work collaboratively to share their professional learning and development with colleagues;
• maintain a record of their own professional learning and development, culminating in an Initial Professional Development Action Plan.</td><td>Professional Actions
Registered teachers:

• reflect and engage in self evaluation using the relevant professional standard;
• demonstrate an enquiring and critical approach to their professional practice and development and engage in systematic professional dialogue;
• evaluate, and adapt their classroom practice rigorously and systematically, taking account of feedback from others, to enhance teaching and learning;
• demonstrate constructive participation and engagement with curriculum development, improvement planning and professional review and development;
• work collaboratively to contribute to the professional learning and development of colleagues, including students, through offering support and constructive advice and through disseminating experience and expertise, seeking opportunities to lead learning;
• maintain an effective record and portfolio of their own professional learning and development and a professional development action plan, including analysis of impact on learners and on own professional practices.</td></tr>
</table>

APPENDIX 5

THE PROFESSIONAL STANDARDS FOR TEACHING AND LEADERSHIP FOR WALES

INTRODUCTION

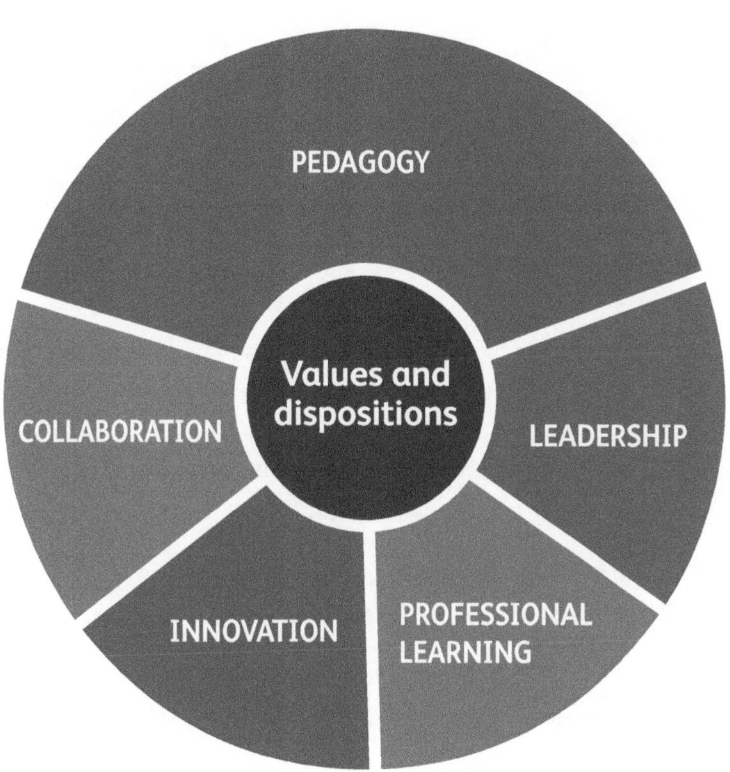

WHAT ARE THE PROFESSIONAL STANDARDS FOR TEACHING AND LEADERSHIP?

Professional standards describe the skills, knowledge and behaviours that characterise excellent practice and support professional growth. The five professional standards for teaching and leadership concentrate on the five essential elements of every teacher's work.

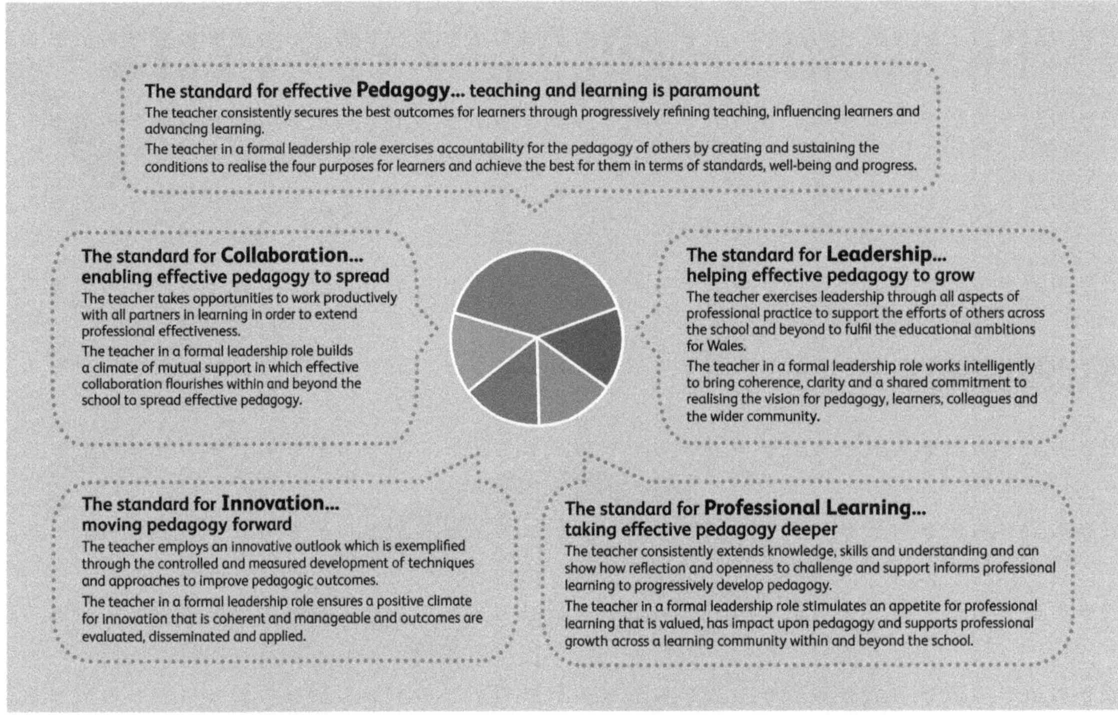

Download the interactive PDF to explore the professional standards in more detail at www.learning.gov.wales/professionalstandards

Each of the five standards contains different elements. The element descriptors for each standard are:

PEDAGOGY

- Accepting accountability for outcomes and learner wellbeing
- Ensuring and protecting learner entitlement
- Monitoring and evaluating impact
- Reporting on effectiveness

‘WELCOME TO THE BEST, MOST CHALLENGING, REWARDING AND IMPORTANT PROFESSION IN THE WORLD.

YOU HAVE ALREADY MADE TWO EXCELLENT CHOICES. YOU HAVE CHOSEN TO BECOME A TEACHER AND YOU HAVE CHOSEN TO PICK UP THIS BOOK.

THIS BOOK IS A REALLY RICH SOURCE OF RESEARCH, IDEAS AND ADVICE TO GET YOU STARTED. IT WILL HOPEFULLY GET YOU EXCITED BY SOME OF THE BIG IDEAS THAT WILL BRING EDUCATION TO LIFE FOR YOU AND YOUR CHILDREN. IT IS ALSO PRAGMATIC AND ‘GROUNDED’ IN THE REALITY OF PRIMARY SCHOOLS TODAY.’

SAMANTHA TWISELTON, OBE

www.uk.sagepub.com/learningmatters

ISBN 978-1-5264-3644-3

9 781526 436443

Cover design by Wendy Scott